STUDIES IN MATTHEW

STUDIES IN MATTHEW

Ulrich Luz

translated by Rosemary Selle

WILLIAM B. EERDMANS PUBLISHING COMPANY
GRAND RAPIDS, MICHIGAN / CAMBRIDGE, U.K.

Wm. B. Eerdmans Publishing Co.
255 Jefferson Ave. S.E., Grand Rapids, Michigan 49503 /
P.O. Box 163, Cambridge CB3 9PU U.K.

Printed in the United States of America

09 08 07 06 05   7 6 5 4 3 2 1

ISBN 0-8028-3964-9

www.eerdmans.com

Contents

Preface

Matthew has accompanied me for more than half my life. My main preoccupation has been with the commentary, which is now complete. An American translation of the first volume appeared early in the Continental Commentaries series. The succeeding volumes and a new translation of the revised Volume One have been published in the Hermeneia series or are being prepared for publication. My concern in the commentary is twofold: I seek to interpret the biblical text in the light of its reception history, and at the same time to reflect on the position of the interpreter in the light of this reception history.

This volume is far less ambitious. It contains a number of my essays on Matthew dating from 1971 to 2003. Only a few of them are known in Britain and North America. The essays originated during my work on the commentary, some in an attempt to develop basic hypotheses or overall perspectives on difficult questions before formulating the commentary, others as retrospective summaries of my work on the biblical texts. The final essays, chapters 13-18, contain hermeneutical perspectives. I did not want to rework them; therefore they document the state of discussion at the time of their original publication. Two chapters are published here for the first time. I hope to publish the hermeneutical fruits of my work in the near future in the form of a textbook.

The essays are not intended to be revolutionary. Rather, they are pieces of solid exegesis which document my exegetical journey with Matthew. Each has a place in academic history which I have not attempted to "modernize." For this reason, some readers may find some of the work outdated. But I readily admit to not numbering myself with those who think exegesis needs to be reinvented every ten or twenty years.

The academic and personal links between "old" Europe and North

America are important and precious to me. At a time when our political paths are increasingly divergent and we raise our eyebrows at each other on both sides of the Atlantic, these links are all the more important. So this volume also wants to tell my American friends how important and precious they are for me.

Finally, I should like to express my heartfelt thanks. I thank especially my translator Rosemary Selle (Durham/Heidelberg), who has translated my sometimes difficult texts with precision and clarity. When something sounds convoluted or complicated, it is probably my responsibility! Ms. Selle translated all but chapters 6 and 7. I also thank cordially Peter Ben Smit (Berne), who meticulously corrected and formally standardized the texts, and Simon Hofstetter (Berne) who prepared the indexes. My thanks are due to Sheffield University Press and T. and T. Clark for permission to reprint chapters 6 and 7. Lastly, I thank my publisher Wm. B. Eerdmans and his staff, especially Dr. John Simpson, who have given this volume exemplary attention.

Berne, October 2003   ULRICH LUZ

Biblical quotations are from the New Revised Standard Version Bible (Nashville: Nelson, 1989), sometimes adapted by Ulrich Luz for exegetical purposes.

Abbreviations

AAWG.PH	Abhandlungen der Akademie der Wissenschaften in Göttingen — Philologisch-historische Klasse
AKathKR	Archiv für katholisches Kirchenrecht
AKG	Arbeiten zur Kirchengeschichte
ANF	Ante-Nicene Fathers
ANRW	*Aufstieg und Niedergang der römischen Welt*
AThD	Acta theologica danica
BEThL	Bibliotheca Ephemeridum theologicarum Lovaniensium
BEvTh	Beiträge zur evangelischen Theologie
BGLRK	Beiträge zur Geschichte und Lehre der reformierten Kirche
Bib	*Biblica*
Billerbeck	*Kommentar zum Neuen Testament aus Talmud und Midrasch,* ed. Strack and Billerbeck
BoA	*Luthers Werke in Auswahl,* ed. Otto Clemen
BSLK	Bekenntnisschriften der evangelisch-lutherischen Kirche
BThSt	Biblisch-theologisch Studien
BU	Biblische Untersuchungen
BZ.NF	*Biblische Zeitschrift,* n.s.
BZNW	Beihefte zur *Zeitschrift für die neutestamentliche Wissenschaft*
CBQ	*Catholic Biblical Quarterly*
CChr.SL	Corpus Christianorum — Series Latina
CCSL	Corpus Christianorum — Series Latina
CNT	Coniectanea neotestamentica
CR	Corpus Reformatorum
CSEL	Corpus Scriptorum ecclesiasticorum Latinorum
DiKi	Dialog der Kirchen
DS	*Enchiridion symbolorum,* ed. Denzinger and Schönmetzer

EHS	Einleitung in die Heilige Schrift
EK	Evanglische Kommentare
EKK	Evangelisch-katholischer Kommentar zum Neuen Testament
ÉtB	Études Bibliques
EthL	Ephemerides theologicae Lovanienses
EThS	Erfurter theologische Schriften
EThSt	Erfurter theologische Studien
EvTh	*Evangelische Theologie*
FRLANT	Forschungen zur Religion und Literatur des Alten und Neuen Testaments
FS	Festschrift
FZB	Forschung zur Bibel
GCS	Die griechischen christlichen Schriftsteller der ersten drei Jahrhunderte
HNT	Handbuch zum Neuen Testament
HThK	Herders theologischer Kommentar zum Neuen Testament
IBS	*Irish Biblical Studies*
ICC	International Critical Commentary
JBL	*Journal of Biblical Literature*
JSHRZ	Jüdische Schriften aus hellenistisch-römischer Zeit
JSNT	*Journal for the Study of the New Testament*
JSNTSup	*Journal for the Study of the New Testament* Supplement Series
KBANT	Kommentare und Beiträge zum Alten und Neuen Testament
KEK	Kritisch-exegetischer Kommentar über das Neue Testament
KNT	Kommentar zum Neuen Testament
LCL	Loeb Classical Library
LD	Lectio divina
LiLi	Living Light
LM	*Lutherische Monatshefte*
LThK	*Lexikon für Theologie und Kirche*
MSSNTS	Monograph Series. Society for New Testament Studies
MThSt.	Marburger theologische Studien
NCEB	New Century Bible
Neotest	*Neotestamentica*
NHC	*Nag Hammadi Codices*
NovT	*Novum Testamentum*
NPNF	Nicene and Post-Nicene Fathers
NTA	Neutestamentliche Abhandlungen
NTA.NF	Neutestamentliche Abhandlungen, n.s.
NTD	Das Neue Testament Deutsch

NTD Erg.	Das Neue Testament Deutsch Ergänsungsschrift
NTLi	New Testament Library
NTOA	Novum Testamentum et Orbis Antiquus
NTS	*New Testament Studies*
NTSup	*Novum Testamentum* Supplement Series
OBO	Orbis biblicus et orientalis
PG	Patrologia cursus completus, series Graeca (ed. Migne)
PL	Patrologia cursus completus, series Latina (ed. Migne)
PuP	Päpste und Papsttum
QD	Quaestiones disputatae
RGG[3]	*Religion in Geschichte und Gegenwart*
SBLMS	Society of Biblical Literature Monograph Series
SBS	Stuttgarter Bibelstudien
SHAW.PH	Sitzungsberichte der Heidelberger Akademie der Wissenschaften — Philosophisch-historische Klasse
SIG[3]	Sylloge inscriptionum Graecarum
SNT	Schriften des Neuen Testaments
SNTSMon	Society for New Testment Studies Monograph Series
SNTU	Studien zum Neuen Testament und Seiner Umwelt
SPAW.PH	Sitzungberichte der Preußischen Akademie der Wissenschaften — Philosophisch-historische Klasse
StANT	Studien zum Alten und Neuen Testament
StPB	Studia Post-biblica
StTh	*Studia Theologica*
StUNT	*Studien zur Umwelt des Neuen Testaments*
SVTP	Studia in veteris testamenti pseudepigrapha
TDNT	*Theological Dictionary of the New Testament*
ThHK	Theologischer Handkommentar zum Neuen Testament
ThLZ	*Theologische Literaturzeitung*
ThÖ	Theologie der Ökumene
ThPr	*Theologia Practica*
ThWNT	*Theologisches Wörterbuch zum Neuen Testament*
TLZ	*Theologische Literaturzeitung*
TRE	*Theologische Realenzyklopädie*
TTZ	*Trierer theologische Zeitschrift*
TU	Texte und Untersuchungen zur Geschichte der altchristlichen Literatur
UB	Urban-(Taschen-) Bücher
UTB	Uni-Taschenbücher
VT	*Vetus Testamentum*

WA	Martin Luther, *Werke,* Weimar edition
WA DB	Martin Luther, *Werke,* Weimar edition, Deutsche Bibel
WdF	Wege der Forschung
WMANT	Wissenschaftliche Monographien zum Alten und Neuen Testament
WStBeih	Wiener Studien — Beiheft
WuD	*Wort und Dienst*
WUNT	Wissenschaftliche Untersuchungen zum Neuen Testament
ZAC	*Zeitschrift für antikes Christentum*
ZNW	*Zeitschrift für die neutestamentliche Wissenschaft*
ZThK	*Zeitschrift für Theologie und Kirche*

MATTHEW'S STORY

1 Matthew the Evangelist:
A Jewish Christian at the Crossroads

In this essay I take up the narrative thread of Matthew's Gospel, reading it not only as an autonomous textual world but also as a "text in the world." My concern is to understand Matthew's Jesus story in its historical situation, beginning with observations on composition technique (1). I then outline the historical situation (2) and finally attempt to paraphrase the whole of the Matthean Jesus story (3). The opening hypotheses of each section are argued in the text which follows.

1. Composition

> *1.1. The Gospel of Matthew is a book intended to be read as a whole and not in parts or pericopes. It is intended to be read not just once but several times.*

Matthew's Gospel is not a lectionary or a collection of material for instruction. It is written to be read aloud. It makes considerable demands on its readers. My premise is that the evangelist expresses himself in a manner that is intelligible to his imagined readership.

My argument is based on a large number of formal and compositional elements observable in the Gospel. For example, Matthew makes use of *keywords*. In the Sermon on the Mount he repeats the word δικαιοσύνη (righ-

---

A slightly different version of this essay was published in French under the title "L'évangéliste Matthieu: Un judéochrétien à la croisée des chemins. Réflexions sur le plan narratif du premier Evangile" in: Daniel Marguerat/Jean Zumstein (eds.), *La mémoire et le temps,* Le Monde de la Bible 23 (FS P. Bonnard, Geneva: Labor et Fides, 1991), pp. 77-92. The translation presented here is based on the unpublished German original.

teousness) five times and the word πατήρ (father) fifteen times. Taken together, these two keywords express the theology of the Sermon on the Mount. In Matt. 8–9 the keyword ἀκολουθέω (to follow) occurs nine times, and in chapters 11–12 there are eleven instances of the keyword κρίσις (judgment). In each case the keywords are central to the theme of the passage. Only a reader following the text in full could recognize this.

The same is true of the *repetitions*. Matthew has not only adopted doublets from his sources, such as the two feedings of the crowds or the two demands for signs. He himself has created repetitions, such as the passage on the tree and its fruits (7:15-20; 12:33-35), the healing of two blind people (9:27-31; 20:29-34), or the summary of Jesus' healing and preaching activity among the people of Israel (4:23; 9:35). Since he creates such doublets through his own redaction, we are ill advised to reproach Matthew with clumsiness when he adopts doublets from his sources. He repeats what is important to him, and once again this can be recognized only by reading the whole text continuously.

The same is true of the *inclusions*. Smaller and larger parts of Matthew's Gospel are framed by *inclusio,* a well-known one being the name "Immanuel" for Jesus (1:23) and the promise "I am with you always" (28:20), which frames the whole Gospel. The main section of the Sermon on the Mount is framed by "the law and the prophets" (5:7; 7:12). This too is apparent only when the Gospel is read as a continuous text.

Then there are the *"signals"* in Matthew's Gospel, distinctive features in the narrative which point beyond their immediate context and whose meaning is not readily apparent to readers.[1] The prologue is full of such signals. "son of Abraham" (1:1), "Galilee of the Gentiles" (4:15), the mountain on which Jesus refuses the devil's offer of the kingdoms of the world (4:8-10) or the bizarre episode of 2:3-4 in which all Jerusalem, all the chief priests and scribes of the people, and the hated half-Jewish Herod are united in fright when three Gentiles ask where the Messiah has been born: all these are "signals" pointing to what Matthew will later narrate concerning Jesus' rejection by all Jerusalem and the coming mission to the Gentiles. Only readers familiar with the whole Gospel will recognize the signals.

The same is true of the *key pericopes* which are closely linked with the Gospel as a whole. Peter's confession in Caesarea Philippi in 16:13-20 for example takes up the central passage 11:25-27 in which the Father reveals the Son to infants, as well as the blessing of the disciples in 13:16-17 and the disciples'

---

1. For further detail on the term "signals" see Ulrich Luz, *Matthew 1–7: A Commentary* (Minneapolis: Augsburg, 1989), p. 41; idem, *Das Evangelium nach Matthäus (Matt. 1–7),* EKK I.1 (Neukirchen/Düsseldorf: Neukirchener Verlag/Patmos, ⁵2002), pp. 31-32.

recognition of Jesus as Son of God in 14:33. The confession by Peter is itself taken up in 18:18 and 23:13 as well as in the interrogation scene before the high priest in 26:59-66. This last scene is as it were the negative equivalent of Peter's confession. The high priest's question on the Messiah and the Son of God obliges Jesus to reveal himself, and the high priest responds by tearing his clothes and saying "He has blasphemed." That the interrogation scene is a counterpart to 16:13-20 can be recognized only by reading the whole Gospel, possibly more than once.

1.2. Matthew is a highly tradition-oriented author. On the other hand parts of his Jesus story are deliberately fictitious. He wants to write a real story of Jesus, knowing at least in part that it is fiction.

The first part of my hypothesis is more familiar and I shall argue it only in outline. Matthew is a tradition-oriented author. With the exception of four pericopes, he takes over the whole of Mark's Gospel, not altering its order from ch. 12 onward. He recasts the discourses himself, but apart from the Sermon on the Mount he appends them to existing Markan discourses. His own redactional language is traditional. Often it is words and topoi from his tradition which are given considerable weight in his own language or theology, for example ἀκολουθέω from Mark's Gospel or the title Son of David for the healing Messiah (cf. Mark 10:46-52), the expression "fulfillment of the scripture" originating in Mark 14:49, which becomes crucial to the "fulfillment formula" of Matthean citations from Scripture, or the Son of God title which opens Mark's Gospel. Matthew takes from the Sayings source Q the expressions "the law and the prophets" (cf. Luke 16:16) and "weeping and gnashing of teeth" (cf. Luke 13:28), the important theological topos "you of little faith" (cf. Luke 12:28) and Jesus' words "truly I say to you." His favorite word πραΰς (humble, cf. 5:5) comes from Q-Matt., and the repeated ὑποκριτής (hypocrite, cf. 6:2, 5, 16) of the woes discourse in ch. 23 probably comes from a special tradition. Matthew's preferred language often follows that of his sources, and I suggest his theology also owes a great deal to them.

On the other hand, Matthew is extraordinarily bold. A good example of this can be found in chapters 8–9 on the Messiah's miracles in Israel. Taken together, these chapters create the impression of a continuous story with one event succeeding another. On the short journey from the mountain to Peter's house, Matthew places two miracles (8:1-13), and at the house of the tax collector (9:10) two controversy discourses and the encounter with the leader of the synagogue (9:11-18). Hardly has Jesus crossed the lake when the demoniacs approach him (8:28). Everything happens in quick succession. Yet in terms of composition history the section is remarkable. Matthew has assembled two separate sections of Mark (1:29–2:22 and 4:35–5:43), two miracles from Q and a further Q text to create a completely new narrative thread. For this purpose he has destroyed the connected narrative he received from Mark, so we may assume that Matthew was aware that the connected Jesus story he was telling was fictitious. This is confirmed by Matthew's doubling of two of the miracles. He tells the story of the healing of blind Bartimaeus from Mark 10:46-52 twice (9:27-31; 20:29-34). The same is true of the healing of mute demoniacs, taken from Q 11:14-15 (= Matt. 9:32-33; 12:22-24). An author does not do this inadvertently. Pursuing this a little further, we find that Matthew generally shapes his discourses by appending appropriate material to a smaller or larger Markan complex. This creates a connected discourse by Jesus on a particular theme. Matthew must have known that Jesus did not deliver these discourses; rather, he, Matthew, has written them himself. In the parables discourse a narrative insert interrupts the flow. In 13:36 Jesus leaves the lakeshore and the listening crowds, goes into the house and addresses the remaining discourse to the disciples alone. In 24:1-3 Jesus leaves the temple, as in Mark, and goes with his disciples to the Mount of Olives, where he speaks only to them. He does what has been predicted in 23:38, leaving the house desolate. In the passion narrative it is Matthew who inserts the episodes of Pilate washing his hands (27:24-25), the guard on the tomb and the deception by the Jewish leaders (27:62-66; 28:11-15) on the basis of oral traditions or — in the first case particularly — as pure fiction. By these means Matthew intensifies and changes the course of the narrative.

I now turn to a final example. Matthew inserts into chapter 11 material from Q. In chapter 12 he appends a long section from Q to three Markan texts, ending the chapter with the pericope on true kindred from Mark 3:31-35. However, chapter 11 is far from being a mere collection of remnants and chapter 12 is more than a combination of two sources. The two chapters are similarly structured. In each, a passage referring to Jesus' miracles (11:2-6; 12:1-21) is followed by rebukes of Israel or the Pharisees (11:7-19; 12:22-37). Each chapter has a double ending. In chapter 11 the pronouncement of judgment against the Galilean cities which have failed to recognize Jesus' miracles is set against Jesus' thanks for God's revelation to infants (11:20-24, 25-30), and in chapter 12 the prophecy to the Pharisees of the sign of Jonah, with its subsequent pronouncement of judgment on Israel (12:38-45), is set against the pericope on the true kindred of Jesus (12:46-50). Bringing the sources together in this way creates a new and compact narrative unit and, at the same time, gives chapters 11 and 12 a similar structure. They are ingenious in the best sense of the word, and I am certain that Matthew was fully aware of this.

So Matthew the traditionalist is also a bold composer, bringing traditions together to form completely new and unified compositions. He creates sequences of the Jesus story and of Jesus' preaching which are fictional in character, and he knows this. Matthew is both tradition-oriented *and* innovative. How do these go together? Are we dealing with the formal sophistication of a skilled author steeped in tradition? There is more to it, I think.

I suggest that the fictitious elements in Matthew's story can be understood only from the perspective of the transparency of his Jesus story for the situation of the post-Easter Matthean community. In order to argue this I shall now leave the world of Matthew's text and turn to the external world of the story of Matthew's community. This brings me to the second part of my essay, which is concerned with the historical place of Matthew's Gospel in the story of Jewish Christianity.

2. History

> *2.1. Historically, the Matthean community is part of the post-history of the Sayings source Q. It is a Jewish Christian community originating in the activity of the Jesus messengers who were among the bearers of the Q tradition. Later, after the failure of the mission to Israel and the Jewish War, the community settled in Syria, where it received significant theological inspiration from the Gospel of Mark.*

The starting point for my reflections is the assumption that historical developments lie behind Matthew's compilation of sources and traditions, e.g. the bringing together of Mark and Q, as well as behind the adoption of special material. The Evangelists were not, as I see it, simply compilers who sat at their desks cutting and pasting together various sources. Rather, we must examine whether certain Christian groups are behind the various sources and traditions, and to what extent the history of the sources reflects that of the groups. Odil Hannes Steck once proposed the following hypothesis for the Gospel of Matthew: Jewish Christians forced out of Palestine by the Jewish War, whose own traditions were collected in the Sayings source, joined the Gentile Christian communities in Syria, whose book was the Gospel of Mark.[2] This would mean the Gospel of Matthew represents a fusion of communities such as we find for the apocalyptic prophet John and his circle in the

---

2. Odil Hannes Steck, *Israel und das gewaltsame Geschick der Propheten*, WMANT 23 (Neukirchen: Neukirchener, 1967), pp. 310f.

Pauline communities of Asia Minor. This would make the Gospel of Matthew an ecumenical Gospel. I shall take up Steck's hypothesis and modify it.

It can be shown, I think, that the Matthean community is relatively close to the environment of Q in sociological terms. It is virtually certain that the Sayings Source is strongly influenced by early Christian itinerant radicalism. Itinerant prophets of the ascended Lord founded settled communities, returned to visit them, wrote down Jesus traditions, collected them in a kind of notebook[3] and transmitted them to the communities. The Matthean community hosts these itinerant radicals (Matt. 10:40-42; cf. 25:31-46), and Matthew's Gospel also refers elsewhere (Matt. 5:12 [redacted from Q]; 10:41; cf. 7:22; 21:11) to prophets associated with the Sayings Source (Q 11:49). The scribes and teachers who are important for the Matthean community may also have been in the Sayings Source (13:52; 23:8, 34; cf. 8:19; 16:19; 18:18; cf. Q 6:40; 11:49 [σοφοί, the wise]). The idea of doing without possessions as an element of Christian perfection is central to the life of the itinerant radicals, and it is unexpectedly influential too in the Matthean community (cf. 6:19-33; 13:12, 44-46; 16:24-26; 19:16-22). The Jesus messengers responsible for the Sayings Source have undertaken mission to Israel and have to an extent failed. As I see it, there is no mission to the Gentiles in Q. Various traditions record the resistance and persecution faced by the community in its preaching to Israel (e.g. Q 6:22-23; 11:49-51; 13:34-35).

This is in keeping with Matthew's treatment of Mark's Gospel. The Matthean Jesus is not a missionary to the Gentiles (cf. Mark 5:1-20) and does not travel extensively in Gentile areas (Mark 7:24–8:13). He has only sporadic contact with Gentiles and ventures only once — and without particular emphasis — into the region of Tyre and Sidon, which actually comprised large areas of formerly Israelite Galilee. For Matthew the stories of the Capernaum centurion and the Canaanite woman are exceptions to the rule. He relates each of these stories to Jesus' mission to Israel, giving a "signal" of what is to change when the risen Lord commands it. Elsewhere Matthew restricts Jesus' mission to his own people (4:23; 9:35; 15:24) and treats the disciples' mission similarly (10:5-6).

I also find it significant that Matthew does not adopt Mark's freedom from the ritual law. The Matthean community does observe the Sabbath (24:20) and emphasizes that justice, mercy and faith are more important than tithing (23:23). In 15:1-9 the community resists the Pharisees' attempt to insist on their ritual washing of hands before meals for all Israel, such as we

3. Migaku Sato, *Q und Prophetie*, WUNT II.29 (Tübingen: Mohr Siebeck, 1988), pp. 62-65.

must assume for the second half of the first century in particular. Matthew has great difficulty with the freedom from purity laws clearly propagated in Mark 7:15-23. In 15:11, 17-20 he appears to be trying to restrict the consequences of the Markan tradition without being able or willing to negate it completely. Finally, the Matthean community affirmed the temple cult before the destruction of Jerusalem but insisted with reference to Jesus that the temple tax should be voluntary. This tax had probably been made obligatory for all Israel by the Pharisees in the first century (17:24-27). All this is in keeping with the Sayings Source traditions, which do not appear to abrogate parts of Torah.

The Matthean community, then, appears strongly influenced in its sociological structure and its legal practice by the bearers of the Q traditions. This does not exclude the possibility of Matthew receiving significant *theological* impulses from the Gospel of Mark, which is a Roman Gospel and not a Syrian one.[4] These impulses include the Son of God christology, the miracles, the overall narrative design, the perspective of mission to the Gentiles and the judgment on Israel. I think it significant that while Mark's Gospel has shaped Matthew's theology, the continuity with the Sayings Source has influenced the life and structure of the community. My assumption is that Mark's Gospel was an external influence on a community shaped by the traditions and Jewish Christian piety of the Sayings Source.

2.2. *The Gospel of Matthew originated in a Jewish Christian community which was becoming more open to the Gentile Christian Church in the period after A.D. 70. It retained however its particular Jewish Christian identity, so that Matthew's Gospel had a particular impact in Jewish Christianity.*

The period after A.D. 70, i.e. after the destruction of Jerusalem, was one of fundamental decision-making for Jewish Christianity. Judaism at that time was isolating itself and looking inwards for consolidation. It saw the Jewish Christians as "dissenters," the "minim" who could no longer pray the Eighteen Benedictions with the curse on minim and who had now left the synagogue. Jewish Christians could be integrated in the Gentile-influenced church only if they were prepared to accept both mission to the Gentiles and Gentile freedom from the law. In so doing they would risk their own adher-

---

4. Cf. Martin Hengel, "Entstehungszeit und Situation des Markusevangeliums," in: Hubert Cancik (ed.), *Markus-Philologie*, WUNT I.33 (Tübingen: Mohr Siebeck, 1984), pp. 1-45, here: pp. 43-45.

ence to the law becoming an adiaphoron. This implied the risk that in a Gentile environment they would eventually, as a new generation grew up, lose their own identity. The alternatives for Jewish Christians were either integration into the church, with gradual though not yet visible loss of identity, or a separate existence as a distinct group between the church and the pharisaic synagogue. This latter was probably an option for them only in Palestine, Syria or possibly Egypt, where there were sizeable self-contained Jewish settlements.

An early example of a special Jewish Christian group which may even be directly significant for the later history of Matthew's Gospel can be found in the Jewish Christians of Antioch. Ignatius has them in mind above all in *Magnesians* 8–9. Apparently there were some who lived κατὰ Ἰουδαϊσμόν (in a Jewish manner), including observance of the Sabbath and other παλαιὰ πράγματα (old customs), but probably not circumcision.[5] Unlike Justin after him, Ignatius rejects this, saying that even the Old Testament prophets lived κατὰ Χριστὸν Ἰησοῦν (according to Christ Jesus) and were persecuted for that very reason. In the preceding ch. 7, Ignatius exhorts the Magnesians to be part of the one church represented by the bishop and presbyters, and immediately afterwards he calls to mind the "one teacher" Jesus Christ, with reference to Matt. 8. The rest is speculative, of course, but is it not possible that these Jewish Christians were early descendants of a Matthean type of Jewish Christianity? The Gospel of Matthew was known in Antioch, probably not only to Ignatius. It is conceivable that Matthean Christians with their communal understanding of church did not think much of Ignatius's attempt to create a unified church under his leadership in the big city of Antioch with its numerous synagogues and — probably — house churches. But at this point my speculations will end.

An example of Jewish Christians taking a different path and becoming part of the church not living under the law can be found in the Epistle of James. Although its Jewish wisdom traditions blend easily with Christian ethics, the "perfect law of liberty" (1:25) appears to refer only to moral law.

The reception history of the Gospel of Matthew[6] gives rise to a number of statements concerning its historical location. On the one hand, it can be shown to have been received very early by the church. It was known (though not necessarily preferred) by Ignatius of Antioch; it is τὸ εὐαγγέλιον (*the* Gospel) in the *Didache,* which has a similar environment to Matthew in terms of

5. Cf. Ignatius, *Philadelphians* 6.1.
6. Cf. particularly Wolf-Dietrich Köhler, *Die Rezeption des Matthäusevangeliums in der Zeit vor Irenäus,* WUNT II.24 (Tübingen: Mohr Siebeck, 1987).

church sociology. It is known to Polycarp and to Melito of Sardis as well as in 5 Ezra, the *Gospel of Peter,* and possibly in *1 Clement* and 1 Peter,[7] and of course to Justin. Moreover, reception of Matthew's Gospel is especially known in Syrian Jewish Christianity. The most significant text here is the *Gospel of the Nazarenes,* which was probably simply an edition of Matthew's Gospel.[8] Then there is the *Gospel of the Ebionites,* which, although it probably presupposes all the Synoptic Gospels, is especially close to Matthew and may well be intended as a Gospel according to Matthew.[9] Matthew's Gospel also has a highly significant role in the pseudo-Clementine letters, the *Didaskalia,* and the Jewish Christian Gnostic *Apocalypse of Peter* from Nag Hammadi.[10] All this reaffirms the fact that Matthew's Gospel originates among Jewish Christians loyal to the Law. Unlike the later *Gospel of the Nazarenes,* however, it was accepted in the church and even took pride of place there among the Gospels, perhaps because of its well-structured discourses and later because of its apostolic origin. As I see it, the Matthean community took this path, opening up to mission to the Gentiles, gradually giving up circumcision and other requirements of the law and being absorbed by the church.[11]

> 2.3. *The Gospel of Matthew has a very concrete intention in the period after* A.D. 70. *It seeks to provide a new perspective for the Jewish Christian communities in Syria in the name of the exalted Lord, calling them to mission to the Gentiles now that their mission to Israel has failed.*

Further detail can be sought in Matthew's Gospel itself. What does it have to say about mission to the Gentiles? The most striking finding is the sharp contrast between 10:5-6 and 28:19-20. In 10:5-6 the earthly Jesus tells the twelve disciples: "Go nowhere among the Gentiles (ἔθνη) and enter no town of the Samaritans, but go rather (πορεύεσθε) to the lost sheep of the house of Israel." Its position at the beginning of the mission discourse gives this sen-

---

7. So Rainer Metzner, *Die Rezeption des Matthäusevangeliums im 1. Petrusbrief,* WUNT II.74 (Tübingen: Mohr Siebeck, 1995).

8. Cf. Wilhelm Schneemelcher, *New Testament Apocrypha* I (Louisville: Westminster/ John Knox, ²1991), pp. 154-160. On the influence of Matthew cf. Köhler, pp. 290-294 (see note 6). That the *Gospel of the Nazarenes* was read as a Gospel of Matthew is shown by fragment 10 = Schneemelcher, p. 160.

9. According to Epiphanius, *Haereses* 30.3.7 (= Schneemelcher, p. 140) it is a Gospel of Matthew that the Ebionites themselves call *Gospel according to the Hebrews.* According to fragment 4 (Schneemelcher, p. 170) it claims Matthew as its author. On the influence of Matt. cf. Köhler (see note 6), pp. 272-284.

10. Cf. Graham Stanton, *A Gospel for a New People* (Edinburgh: Clark, 1992), pp. 272-277.

11. Cf. Ulrich Luz, *Matthew 1–7,* pp. 84-87.

tence crucial significance. It is taken up again in Matthew's redaction of the story of the Canaanite woman in 15:24. Jesus' final words on the mountain in Gentile Galilee in 28:19 appear to allude to it directly: "Go therefore (πορεύεσθε) and make disciples of all nations (πάντα τὰ ἔθνη)." The programmatic wording in each case suggests that a real shift has taken place and that an earlier commandment by Jesus is being replaced by a new one. Even if πάντα τὰ ἔθνη is to be translated as "all nations" following 24:9, 14, and even if the mission command of 28:19 need not fully exclude any further mission to Israel, I do not think it is merely a matter here of extending the mission to include the Gentiles. The clear juxtaposition of 28:19 and 10:5-6 as well as passages like 22:8-10 indicate that the commandment given to his disciples by the risen Lord in Galilee is a *new* one, which replaces the earlier one. The Gospel ends with the withdrawal of one of Jesus' commands and a change of direction by Jesus. It is the only one in a Gospel in which the missionaries are told to teach the nations "to obey everything I have commanded you" (28:20).

Looking back to earlier parts of the Gospel, we find this anticipated in many ways. The whole Gospel is full of prophecies and signals alerting the reader to the shift that will take place. Examples include the four Gentile women in Jesus' genealogy (1:3-6), the arrival of the Gentile astrologers in Jerusalem and Bethlehem (2:1-12), the flight of the infant Jesus to Gentile Egypt (2:13-15), his making his home in "Galilee of the Gentiles" (4:13-15), the centurion of Capernaum (8:5-13) and the Canaanite woman (15:21-28), the universalist ecclesiology of e.g. 5:13-16 ("light of the world") and 13:38 ("the field is the world"), Jesus' prophecies in the eschatological discourse (24:9-14). There is a concealed allusion in 10:18, and there is the pronouncement of judgment on Galilean cities which uses Tyre and Sidon for contrast (11:22), and of course the declaration by the Gentile centurion at the death of Jesus (27:54). All this is juxtaposed with increasingly sharp polemic against Israel's leaders and finally against the whole people led by the scribes and Pharisees (23:34-39), culminating in the prophecy of Jerusalem's destruction. This enumeration shows that mission to the Gentiles is a dominant theme in the Gospel, and that Matthew makes careful literary preparation for the shift taking place in 28:19. Even though the shift marks a real and important turn in salvation history, Jesus is not presented as being contradictory either to himself or to God's plan of salvation foretold in Scripture.

This shift corresponds to the significant step in salvation history now to be taken by the Jewish Christian Matthean communities which have separated from Israel. Living in dispersion in Syria following the destruction of the temple, they are to undertake mission to the Gentiles in the way that other communities have long since done. We may assume on the basis of 13:37-43 and 24:9-14 that some groups in the Matthean communities had already taken this step. But it is possible that mission to the Gentiles was controversial among the Matthean communities and that after the separation from mother Israel, fundamental reconsideration of their place and work in salvation history was needed.[12] Matthew the Evangelist offers them this reorientation with his story of Jesus.

Acceptance of the mission to the Gentiles makes Matthew a late successor to Paul, who was probably unknown to him. We may well have direct testimony in the pseudo-Clementine *Recognitions* 1.64[13] to such communities turning to mission to the Gentiles after the year 70. I shall leave open the question of loyalty to the law among the Matthean communities which now undertook this mission. There is no reference to circumcision in the Gospel, but keeping every stroke and letter of the law is referred to, as is Jesus' coming to fulfill and not to abolish it (5:17-19). Matthew's theology of the law, unlike his treatment of mission to the Gentiles, is not Pauline. We should not exclude the possibility that the Matthean community embarked on a mission to the Gentiles which included converting them to the law which Jesus fulfilled. Many Jewish Christians before and after Matthew did this, from the Judaists in Galatia and in Philippi and the Jewish Christians noted by Justin, *Dialogue* 47, but not recognized by him as brethren because they sought to lead the Gentiles to the law, to the Ebionites of whom Irenaeus says that they observe circumcision, temple and other laws, reject Paul and accept only the Gospel according to Matthew.[14] The evidence is even more substantial if we include the Jewish Christians who required the keeping of part of the law, such as those who used the pseudo-Clementines, the Elkesaites and possibly the Cerinthians as well.[15]

It is far from certain however that the Matthean communities combined mission to the Gentiles with the demand for loyalty to the Law, and if so, for how long they did this. The unproblematic reception of Matthew's Gospel in the church speaks against this, while the lack of reflection on freedom from the law supports it. In the former case the Judaizers of the Epistle to the Galatians would be most closely related to Matthew's Gospel in the New Testament, in the latter case to the Epistle to James. In my opinion Mat-

---

12. Cf. U. Luz, *Matthew 1–7*, pp. 84f.

13. The time of sacrifices will be at an end, the desolating sacrilege will be standing in the holy place, "et tunc gentibus evangelium praedicabitur." Ed. Bernd W. Rehm, GCS 51, 44, 21-24. Matt. 24:4-14 seems to presuppose this very chronology.

14. Irenaeus, *Haereses* 1.26.2.

15. According to Epiphanius *Haereses* 28.5 Cerinthus made use of Matthew, rejected Paul, and retained circumcision.

thew himself wanted to retain the law, but his community's mission to the Gentiles gradually changed its attitude to the law, a change which is not yet visible in the Gospel. Certainly we should not assume that with the Apostolic Council the question of freedom from the law for the whole church was resolved once and for all. This would mean unquestioning acceptance of the Lukan and Pauline view of history which presents the Council as *the* crucial event in the earliest days of the church.

3. The Narrative

Matthew's Gospel is a Jesus story with double meaning. It tells the story in a manner which makes it transparent for the community's own story. In this way Matthew's Gospel works through the history of the community and prepares it for reorientation.

Matthew's Jesus story begins with the *prologue,* which I take to be 1:1–4:22. The prologue tells the beginning of Jesus' story, narrating his infancy and the start of his activity. At the same time it anticipates the whole of Matthew's story. It narrates the story of Immanuel (1:23) the son of Abraham, the father of the proselytes (1:1), the son of David, i.e. of Israel's Messiah (1:1, 18-25), and above all the Son of God (1:18-25; 2:15) who is obedient to his Father (3:13–4:11), providing the model for the disciples' way of obedience. The infant Jesus goes his way. Matthew has introduced a large number of fulfilment quotations in the prologue, four of them indicating the way Jesus is to take: from Bethlehem the city of David (2:6), to Gentile Egypt (2:15) and on to Nazareth (2:23) in the Galilee of the Gentiles (4:15-16). That is where light will dawn and Jesus will call his disciples (4:18-22). In this way the whole story of Jesus is anticipated in the prologue. The arrival of the Gentile wise men, the fear in Jerusalem (2:3) and the lament of Rachel over her children who are no more (2:18) are the clearest signals of the end of the story.

In 4:23 the gospel narrative proper begins. Jesus is active among his people, the holy people of Israel. He preaches the gospel of the kingdom and heals every disease and every sickness (4:23). The preaching unfolds in the Sermon on the Mount, the healing in the miracle chapters 8 and 9. What is meant by "every" disease and sickness is shown by 11:5: "the blind receive their sight, the lame walk, the lepers are cleansed, the deaf hear, the dead are raised." Matthew structures chapters 8–9 as a compact and continuous sequence of events leading up to the climax in 11:5. The Messiah does good things for his people throughout. Matthew also portrays the people's reaction in the calling of the first disciples, the first embarking in the boat (8:18-27), the first resistance among the leaders of the people (9:1-17). At the end of the section the narrative is no longer at its starting point. The Pharisees show a negative reaction when Jesus casts out demons "in the name of the ruler of demons." The people's reaction is cautiously positive. "Never has anything like this been seen in Israel." The rift between them is becoming apparent (9:33). The position of the disciples has changed too. They are no longer hearers of Jesus' preaching as in the Sermon on the Mount, but are becoming preachers themselves. Chapter 10 can be seen as the first ecclesiological extension of Jesus' activity to his people Israel and to them alone. The disciples receive their authority and their commission from Jesus, and his fate will be theirs too.

Chapters 11 and 12 continue the narration of Israel's beginning crisis. The two chapters actually are concerned with the keyword κρίσις (crisis, judgment) in Israel, and their structure can be followed with this in mind. The rift in Israel is deepening, and Israel and the disciple community are confronted at the end of each chapter as two groups. The rift worsens in the section 13:53–16:20. Three times Jesus and his disciples withdraw from the people and their hostile leaders, twice — as in 12:15 — with the keyword ἀναχωρέω (to withdraw, 14:13; 15:21; cf. 16:4). Two of these parallel narrative strands end with a confession of Jesus as Son of God, by the disciples in 14:33 and by Peter as their representative in 16:16. Midway between the two sections 11-12 and 14-16 is the parable discourse of chapter 13. In the middle of it Jesus again withdraws from the crowds and goes into the house to teach only his disciples there (13:36). Before this he has spoken of the people's failure to understand (13:10-16, 34-35). In the house the disciples are to be led to understanding through Jesus' teaching (13:51). This is repeated in the chapters which follow. Matthew shows how, as the hostility of Israel's leaders increases, Jesus withdraws with his disciples. The church comes into being in Israel. It is no coincidence that the word ἐκκλησία (church) occurs for the first time at the end of this section, in 16:18.

The section 16:21–20:34 which follows is the ecclesiological part of Matthew's Gospel. The conflicts with Israel's leaders and the people itself are in the background now. The focus is on the life of the community, its suffering (16:21–17:22) and its new practice (19:1–20:34). In the center of this section is the community discourse of chapter 18 with its two main themes of love and forgiveness.

Chapters 21–25 are set in the holy city of Jerusalem. The conflict with Israel's leaders is coming to a climax, and Jesus speaks to them in three salvation history parables (21:28–22:14). He tells them that tax collectors and prostitutes have understood his message better than they have (21:32), that the kingdom of God will be taken away from them like the vineyard from the tenants (21:43), and that the city of these villains will be destroyed (22:7). The Matthean community has already experienced this divine judgment. After a major confrontation with the various Jewish groups (22:15-46) Jesus pronounces his sevenfold prophetic woes against the Pharisees and scribes, not only warning of judgment but fully declaring it. The woes discourse ends with two pericopes pronouncing judgment on the leaders and on the whole people (23:34-36, 37-39). Jesus and his disciples then leave the temple which is to be destroyed (24:1-2). Finally, in his last great discourse, the eschatological discourse, Jesus sets out the consequences for the community. They must not think themselves safe as inheritors of God's chosen people Israel but must realize that Israel's fate might become theirs also (24:3–25:46).

The Passion narrative follows. It shows how Jesus who is judged by Israel is in reality Israel's judge. The high priests and elders are foregrounded as doers of evil. Some scenes are almost Johannine in their ambiguity. With their cry "His blood be on us and on our children!" (27:25) the whole people take on themselves what Jesus prophesied in 23:35. Jesus' final self-revelation before the Sanhedrin, which closely parallels Peter's confession at Caesarea Philippi, is answered by the high priest with the words: "He has blasphemed." Jesus' own prophecy that he will rise again after three days (12:40) results in the high priests and Pharisees asking Pilate for a guard on the tomb. On the resurrection morning the guard fall to the ground as if dead (27:62-66; 28:4). The resurrection, the source of life, becomes the source of death for Israel. The Gospel ends with a double outlook on the present. The rumor of the stolen body is still told "among Jews to this day" (28:15). This is the first and only time that Matthew uses the word "Jews" rather than Israel or λαός (people). The disciples on the other hand are sent by the risen Lord, on the mountain in Galilee — not in Jerusalem as in Luke — to make disciples of all nations. Again there is an outlook on the present with the promise that the Lord will stay with the disciples "always, to the end of the age" (28:20).

A Jewish Christian at the crossroads, then. Jesus' disciples, who knew it was their calling through God's Son to gather God's people Israel, and who saw themselves as the core of all Israel, experienced rejection and persecution in Israel. Overall their mission was a failure and they were not at Israel's center but found themselves excluded from the synagogue. This must have been a traumatic experience. Matthew's two-level story of Jesus seeks to work through the trauma and to give the community a new perspective based on Jesus. It is a perspective for a church which is now separated from Israel. This church knows that the risen Lord is with it at all times, including the difficult period of reorientation. The two levels of Matthew's Gospel, which tells the past story of Jesus and includes in it the story of the community's experience in and with Israel, is also an expression of the presence of the Lord with his community. The past story of the one who is present with his community as living Lord can never be only a story of the past.

We are left pensive. I have not of course dealt with all aspects of Matthew's Gospel here, and I have concentrated on its darkest side. We can be certain that Matthew and his community had to work through traumatic experiences and that these are taken up in his story of Jesus. We have said that his Jesus story is at least in part fictitious. The core of its content is how Jesus, rejected and executed in Israel, pronounces judgment on Israel's leaders and the people itself and becomes the salvation of the Gentiles. In the name of Jesus who loved his enemies, we feel moved to protest against Matthew's portrayal of Christ, especially since we ourselves as Gentile Christians are according to Matthew the fruit of the rejection of Israel (21:43; 22:8-10). But our protests are also problematic. After all, Matthew works through his sufferings in Israel with the help of the story of Jesus Son of God. In this way Matthew has — albeit unintentionally — presented us later generations of Gentile Christians with theological problems which we shall have to solve if we want to remain true both to Jesus and the Bible, and remain honest at the same time.

2 The Gospel of Matthew:
A New Story of Jesus, or
a Rewritten One?

Matthew's Gospel stands at the inception of a transmission process similar to that of Israel's basic story in earlier centuries. In the course of that process, the story of Jesus was retold several times, like the foundational story of Israel in the Biblical and Jewish traditions. However, there are differences between the two transmission processes. The four main differences are as follows:

1. The transmission process in early Christianity took place far more rapidly, essentially over a period of a hundred years.
2. The process of canonization was also rapid. As a result, what gained acceptance was not a New Testament equivalent of today's Pentateuch, i.e. the Diatessaron, but the individual stories of Jesus.
3. Rapid canonization had crucial consequences for later Jesus narratives. Of all the Jesus stories written after the four which were canonized, not one has come down to us complete.[1]
4. The most important difference however is a change in the basic story. With the Gospel of Matthew it is no longer the fundamental tradition of Israel, concerning the Patriarchs, the Exodus and the entry into the land of Israel that is retold, but a new story, the story of Jesus according to the Gospel of Mark.

---

1. This includes, for example, the *Gospel of Peter,* the *Gospel of the Nazarenes* and the *Gospel of the Hebrews,* the *Secret Gospel of Mark,* and the Egerton Papyrus.

The German original of this chapter was "Das Matthäusevangelium — eine neue oder eine neu redigierte Jesusgeschichte?" in: Stephen Chapman/Christine Helmer/Christof Landmesser (eds.), *Biblischer Text und theologische Theoriebildung,* BThSt 44 (Neukirchen: Neukirchener, 2001), pp. 53-76.

This leads to the question expressed by my title, "Is the Gospel of Matthew a new Jesus story or a rewritten one?" In the first section of my article I shall deal with the question of the extent to which Matthew is to be seen as a loyal transmitter or a bold rewriter. My second section, which for its lack of systematic unity I have simply called "Afterthoughts," presents some basic conclusions to be drawn from what I have to say in the first section.

1. Matthew as Transmitter and Innovator

Matthew is not easy to grasp. The overall picture presented by his story is one of very great loyalty to his sources and traditions. At some points, however, we unexpectedly come across *very* bold innovations which I shall now exemplify.

1.1 The Title

Matthew gives his book a new title. He does not make use of Mark's title, probably because he has understood εὐαγγέλιον (gospel, good news) differently and more precisely than Mark.[2] This is an early indication of the innovative element in his Jesus story. I have been convinced by William D. Davies, Dale C. Allison and by Moises Mayordomo[3] that there are no great problems involved in extending Matthew's title to the whole of his book. Βίβλος (book) does indeed draw the reader's attention to the whole book, whereas γένεσις in 1:18 seems to recall only the nativity stories and perhaps the genealogy. But with reference to Gen. 2:4 and 5:1 and in accordance with the language usage of the time, γένεσις also calls to mind the first book of the Greek Bible. This provides, on the one hand, a point of connection. Βίβλος γενέσεως (book of generations) reminds readers of the book of Genesis, preparing them for the constant programmatic references to the Bible in Matthew's story of Jesus. Like the book of Genesis, Matthew's book is to be a basic story of faith. On the other hand, the genitive Ἰησοῦ Χριστοῦ (Jesus Christ) provides a counterpoint. This "genesis" tells of Jesus Christ the Son of David and Son of Abraham. It is a new basic story, the story of Jesus Christ. With his new title, Matthew sets a new frame of reference for the story of Jesus, different from that of Mark.

2. Εὐαγγέλιον means, as εὐαγγέλιον τῆς βασιλείας, the proclamation of Jesus, or rather in 24:14 probably already the story of Jesus.

3. William D. Davies and Dale C. Allison, *The Gospel according to St Matthew*, I, ICC (Edinburgh: Clark, 1988), pp. 150-54; Moises Mayordomo-Marín, *Den Anfang hören*, FRLANT 180 (Göttingen: Vandenhoeck und Ruprecht, 1998), pp. 208-213.

1.2 Matthew 1–11

The first part of Matthew's Jesus story (chs. 1–11) has little to do with Mark's story of Jesus. Only in 3:1–4:22 does Matthew follow the Markan order. Otherwise, he has received Mark's materials and supplemented them with material from Q, but in doing so he has created a completely new story. His boldest innovations vis-à-vis Mark are to be found in ch. 8–9. Here Matthew assembles miracle stories and controversy discourses from Mark 1:40–2:22, Mark 4:35–5:43 and from the Sayings Source to form an entirely new narrative fabric which is chronologically and geographically unified.[4] More precisely, Matthew does not simply assemble a block of miracle stories but creates a new and unified chronological and geographical course of events. In doing so, he tells a new *story:* Jesus, the Messiah of his people, servant of God and Son of David, constantly heals the sick among the people of Israel. He travels to the other side of the lake and then returns to his own town. Here the first conflicts with his future opponents, the scribes and the Pharisees, take place. At the end of this story of Jesus' activity in Israel a rift occurs, with the crowds reacting positively to Jesus and the Pharisees rejecting him as an agent of the devil (9:32-34). Chapter 11 is only at first sight a supplement consisting of leftover Q material. In fact, the "supplement" turns out to be a call for repentance directed against "this generation" and the cities of Galilee (11:16-24), contrasted by the Evangelist with Jesus' thanksgiving to the Father for choosing the νήπιοι (simple). In this case too a lengthy narrative sequence ends with a rift or separation in Israel. In *conclusion* we can say that Matthew creates, from entirely given materials, an entirely new story.

After this impressive new opening section it is surprising to find the Evangelist using a quite different procedure from chapter 12 onwards. He now reproduces the narrative thread of Mark's Gospel, without any rearranging and almost without omissions. It is as if, following a major innovative effort, Matthew suddenly found his creative energy flagging.

1.3 The Prologue (1:2–4:22)

The infancy narrative of Matthew 1–2, the story of the annunciation, persecution and escape of Jesus the royal child is not, as I see it, a new story, but one already familiar to the community. It is a story inspired by biblical and other

---

4. Cf. in this volume "The Miracle Stories of Matthew 8–9," pp. 221-240.

motifs, put into writing for the first time by Matthew.[5] Yet at the same time the Matthean prologue is something completely new. The beginning of Matthew's story of Jesus may remind readers of the biographies of other men of God, not least of Moses, and yet they are disappointed in their expectation of reading a biography. The education and development of a hero are important in biographies, but Matthew's story has nothing to say on this. Although there was some discussion of prologues and book beginnings in antiquity,[6] Matthew does not seem to abide by any literary convention. All he has in common with other writers of narrative proems is the formal concern to prepare his readers for the story and give pointers to their own construction of meaning.

Readers of Matt. 1–4 will linger over the numerous formula quotations which function as stopping points in the narrative, inviting them to reflect on its meaning. Their content is concerned, as has often been noted since Stendahl,[7] with the "Quis?" and the "Unde?" i.e. with christology and the way of Jesus. In answer to the question "Who?" Matthew gives two pointers which provide orientation: "Immanuel" (1:23) and "my Son" (2:15). While the stories of Jesus' baptism and temptation (3:13–4:11) give readers a first idea of what is important to the narrator about Jesus' divine sonship, the "Immanuel" motif of 1:23 stands alone at first. Only the Matthean story in its entirety will make "Immanuel" audible as a basic motif in the music which accompanies the Jesus story. As far as Jesus' way is concerned, its beginning and above all its destination are significant.[8] From the perspective of the end of the Gospel, "Galilee of the Gentiles" (4:15) is not only the starting point of Jesus' story but also its destination. Matthew's Jesus story tells how Israel's Messiah comes from Bethlehem, the city of David, and goes via Galilee to Jerusalem and finally to the "Galilee of the Gentiles." I think that the prologue anticipates the whole

---

5. This is evidenced by various indicators such as the formula quotations. In most cases these Old Testament texts were not first discovered by Matthew but were part of Christian scribal tradition. He has inserted them in his narrative, altering their wording slightly in places. In the majority of cases the quotations are meaningful only in association with the narratives they accompany in Matthew's Gospel.

6. Cf. Francis M. Dunn and Thomas Cole (eds.), *Beginnings in Classical Literature*, Yale Classical Studies (Cambridge: Yale University, 1992). Dennis E. Smith, "Narrative Beginnings in Ancient Literature and Theory," *Semeia* 52 (1990), pp. 1-9, distinguishes in terms of form criticism between the "preface" (προοίμιον), the dramatic prologue, and the "incipit." Matt 1:1 can be regarded as an "incipit," but his prologue does not fit any of the three categories.

7. Krister Stendahl, "Quis et unde? An Analysis of Mt 1–2," in: Walther Eltester (ed.), *Judentum — Urchristentum — Kirche*, BZNW 26 (FS Joachim Jeremias; Berlin: de Gruyter, 1964), pp. 94-105.

8. Taking account of the whole Matthean story of Jesus, one should speak not so much of "Quis et unde" as of "quis et quo."

Jesus story and that Matthew seeks to prepare his readers for what his *whole* story is about. This double function of the Matthean prologue, being both "beginning" and "prolepsis" of the whole is, as far as I can see, without analogy. It is a stroke of genius on Matthew's part.

Conclusion: Matthew has shaped his prologue using traditional materials, i.e. a traditional cycle of stories on the early childhood of Jesus the royal child, the beginning of the Markan story and the beginning of the Sayings Source. Almost everything he uses is traditional, and yet the whole — not only a couple of supplemented parts — he creates is new.

1.4 The Discourses

The impact of Matthew's Gospel owes a great deal to his inspired idea of assembling in five thematic discourses the sections of Jesus' preaching which were relevant for the present. Explicit references in Matt. 5:1 and 8:1 to the Sinai narrative indicate that Matthew himself was inspired by the Pentateuch. Even though we cannot establish any clear correspondence between the individual books of the Pentateuch and individual passages of Matthew's Gospel, we can say that his basic literary model, i.e. the story of God's activity interspersed with discourses that address the current readers directly, corresponds to that of the Pentateuch. Matthew's text succeeds also in terms of literary quality, as a comparison with Luke's far more chaotic and less organized Gospel will show.

The particular character of the five discourses becomes apparent if they are contrasted with the "shorter" discourses by Jesus which are not distinguished by the use of a similar concluding formula (that is, 11:7-25; 12:25-37+38-45; 21:28–22:14 and 23:1-39). These discourses are concerned, in the main, with judgment against Israel or interpretation of God's dealings with Israel. They are closely associated with the Matthean story of Jesus' conflict with Israel, interpreting it and moving it forward. The function of these texts as direct address to the readers is, overall, only secondary.

This is most in evidence in the great woes discourse against the scribes and Pharisees in Matt. 23. Matthew has made it the close and climax of Jesus' extended conflict with his opponents in the temple.[9] It is, primarily, a direct pronouncement of judgment, directed first against Israel's hostile leaders and then at the end, in vv. 34-39, against

---

9. It is not to be seen, then, as part of the final "great discourse," the judgment discourse, which encompasses only chs. 24-25. Cf. Ulrich Luz, *Das Evangelium nach Matthäus III (Matt. 18–25)*, EKK I.3 (Neukirchen/Düsseldorf: Neukirchener Verlag/Benziger, 1997), pp. 172f.

the whole people. Its narrative function is to bring Jesus' numerous conflicts with his opponents to an end and to prepare for him to leave the temple together with his disciples (24:1-2). Only a few exceptional passages (particularly 23:8-12) have direct parenetic meaning for the community. Thus the discourse is not a counterpart to the Sermon on the Mount.[10] Rather, its intention is to help Christian readers who see themselves as followers of Jesus intra muros to find a clear identity. The sevenfold woe addressed to the scribes and Pharisees by Jesus, who will come to judge the world, is intended to make it impossible for its readers to sit inside the fence any longer. They are to leave Israel's temple with Jesus and his disciples.

Thus Jesus' "short" discourses in Matthew's Gospel generally have an important function within the Matthean story of Jesus and his people Israel. This is quite different when it comes to the five "big" discourses. They have their distinctive place within the Jesus story, but they do not — or hardly — move the story forward. In them Jesus speaks "out of the window" of the past story into the present situation of the readers. This is most apparent in ch. 10, when the disciples sent out by Jesus do not go out or come back. Similarly in ch. 13, where Jesus speaks of the people's lack of response and then withdraws into the house with his disciples. Afterwards he continues his activity among the people, without any consequences from the discourse of ch. 13. The five discourses contain the proclamation of Jesus, his gospel of the kingdom (εὐαγγέλιον τῆς βασιλείας).

The five great discourses contain the "gospel" of Jesus as it is valid for Matthew's own present. He has composed them himself. Yet at the same time the discourses are indebted to tradition. They contain hardly any purely redactional sayings of Jesus.[11] To the reading or listening community, the sayings of Jesus used in the discourses were not new or "secret sayings" whose meaning had to be discovered. Rather, they were the long familiar words of Jesus their one teacher (23:8), spoken to them in their own situation. In this sense, tradition takes precedence over interpretation in Matthew. Interpretation does not engulf and transform what has been handed down, but lets it stand. This is immediately apparent from Matthew's organization of the discourses. He does not high-handedly decide where to position them in his book, but takes up and expands shorter or longer Jesus discourses from Mark's Gospel or — in the case of the Sermon on the Mount — from Q. In almost every case he combines the basic Markan text with parallel words from

---

10. Here I disagree with Hubert Frankemölle, "Pharisäismus in Judentum und Kirche. Zur Tradition und Redaktion in Mt 23," in: Frankemölle, *Biblische Handlungsanweisungen* (Mainz: Grünewald, 1983), pp. 168-183.

11. The explanation of the parable of the darnel (Matt. 13:37-43) is a great exception.

Q and/or supplements this with further Jesus sayings from Q. Sometimes these are complete blocks as found in Q, sometimes appropriate sayings excerpted from various passages of Q.

For Matthew the Sayings Source is evidently of lesser status than Mark's Gospel. The latter is the basic story of Jesus, which he is rewriting, whereas the former is a collection of material which he uses and excerpts.[12] In the discourses he gives precedence to Markan material over Q material. Moreover, Matthew has a tendency to place Q materials in the discourses before special material, at least when the latter was transmitted only orally. One is tempted to say that Matthew has constructed his discourses quite externally, according to the dignity of his sources. Yet their construction is both coherent and meaningful. The Sermon on the Mount with its magnificent structure bears this out most impressively, as does the three-part outline of the eschatological discourse of chs. 24–25 with its parenetic central section.[13] In both these cases, as with the other discourses, the elaborate structure also makes a significant theological statement.

Conclusion: In the discourses too Matthew succeeds in creating new designs while handing down the tradition virtually untouched. This is a significant artistic achievement, and I consider Matthew a highly gifted writer.

1.5 Omissions and Radical Changes

Overall, Matthew omits hardly anything of Mark's Gospel. He has transmitted it more completely than has Luke, unless one adopts the thesis that Mark 6:45–8:26 was not included in the copy used by Luke. The episodes from Jesus' life as narrated by Mark are precious to Matthew. It is similar with the Sayings Source, which he may have compressed in a few places but has hardly, as far as we can tell, omitted from.[14] Thus it is all the more striking when Matthew boldly innovates. For example, he omits the story of the widow's offering (Mark 12:41-44), good and appropriate though it is to his understanding of Jesus, because in its Markan position it is in the way. After Jesus has pronounced judgment on Israel and Jerusalem (23:34-39), he and his disciples are to leave the temple immediately, never to return (24:1-2). Clearly Matthew has sacrificed the episode with the widow to the close texture of his Jesus story.

---

12. Cf. in this volume "Matthew and Q," pp. 39-53.

13. Cf. Ulrich Luz, *Matthew 1–7. A Commentary* (Minneapolis: Augsburg, 1989), pp. 211-213; cf. *Matthäus III* (see note 9), pp. 407f.

14. Cf. pp. 42-43 in this volume.

Matthew shows even greater boldness with other details. There is for example the story of the healing of blind Bartimaeus from Mark 10:46-52. Matthew tells the story twice, as two separate healings of, in each case, two blind men. He has deliberately created a doublet, for obvious reasons. For Matthew healings of the blind are the most significant of all Jesus' acts of healing, whereas the scribes and Pharisees are "blind." Jesus gives the blind their sight, and not only those who are physically blind. Similarly, there are two accounts of the episode of the mute demoniac from Q 12:22-24, and once again Matthew's overall structure reveals why. After the healing, the people are divided. Matthew introduces further detail into the Q text in the form of separation between the acclaiming crowds and their leaders who are hostile to Jesus. Because this episode is so important to his narrative thread, Matthew recounts it twice. Such repetition is a useful narrative device for emphasizing significant material, and it is particularly effective within a continuous reading.

Conclusion: Although he is a highly tradition-conscious Evangelist, Matthew acts with great boldness in some cases, usually in the interests of the overall design of his Jesus story.

1.6 The Ending of the Jesus Story

In general it is the beginning and ending of a narrative which reveal the narrator's intention most clearly. The ending of the Gospel, from about 27:62 onward, is almost completely Matthew's own creation. The narration is similar to that of ch. 2, alternating episodes in which Jesus' opponents are at work with accounts of God's activity (27:62-66; 28:4, 11-15, and 28:1-3, 5-10, 16-20). As a result, the Matthean story of Jesus has a double ending. There is on the one hand the entanglement of the scribes and the high priests in their own untruthfulness and the lack of faith in Jesus' resurrection among many Jews "to this day" (28:15). There is on the other hand the commandment of the risen Lord to the eleven disciples to go to all nations and the promise, deliberately exceeding the "to this day," that he will be with his community "to the end of the age" (28:20). The double ending is accompanied by a geographical separation. The disciples are directed by Jesus to leave the holy city of Israel on which he has pronounced harsh judgment, and to withdraw to Galilee, the "Galilee of the Gentiles" of 4:15. Here Jesus gives them a new commission, extending the exclusive mission to Israel (10:5) to the nations and thus canceling its exclusivity. The disciples' way to the future begins in Galilee and not in Jerusalem.

In this "double ending" the amount of Matthew's editorial shaping is, as

I see it, greater than anywhere else in his Gospel.[15] The episode with the tomb guard (27:62-66; 28:11-15) is so closely interwoven with the macrotext of the Gospel and contains such deep, sophisticated and malicious irony, visible only within the macrotext, that I tend to attribute the main shaping to Matthew. The difficult discussions on the relation between the Gospel of Matthew and the tomb guard and resurrection stories of the Gospel of Peter seem to me to indicate clearly that the Gospel of Peter is a later development of the tomb guard tradition and cannot possibly be a source for Matthew. Matthew may have known an older tomb guard tradition, but the story he tells is most certainly *his*. And once the tomb guard has made its appearance, Matt. 28:2-4 is not so difficult to understand. In biblical colors, Matthew has described the appearance of the angel presupposed in Mark, and has withheld from the tomb guard what he had to withhold from them, namely that they should hear the angel's words. And so they shake and become like dead men. As I see it, then, Matt. 28:2-4 is a piece of narrated haggada which presupposes the Markan text, the tomb guard and the Bible, in particular Dan. 10:5-6.

In Matt. 28:16-20 the Evangelist's own contribution is also very considerable. I assume that there was a pre-Matthean tradition of Jesus appearing to the eleven on a mountain (in Galilee?), but I cannot say what it was like. Apart from the commandment to baptize, the compact text we now have has been conceived and formulated by Matthew. I can only interpret the text Matt. 28:16-20 as we have it as the ending of Matthew's story. It has the Risen Lord command his disciples, in accordance with the authority over the whole cosmos which he has been given, to go and make disciples of all nations. The Evangelist is a Jewish disciple of Jesus himself and he represents a Jewish Jesus community, and so I cannot imagine that he means to say that any mission to Israel is now in principle excluded. What is cancelled in 28:19 is the exclusive nature of the mission to Israel. I do think however that for Matthew, whose community probably lived in Syria, i.e., outside Eretz Israel, the mission commandment means a re-orientation, or the confirmation of a re-orientation already undertaken in the new homeland after the traumatic experiences of the Jewish War and the parting of the ways with Israel.

Thus the ending of Matthew's Gospel points once again to the newness of the Matthean story of Jesus. The small proportion of traditional material in this section has to do, of course, with the fact that the copy of Mark's Gospel available to Matthew breaks off at 16:8. I can no longer say with certainty

---

15. The reasoning behind this is provided in my analyses of Matt. 27:62–28:20 in Ulrich Luz, *Das Evangelium nach Matthäus IV (Matt. 26–28)*, EKK I.4 (Neukirchen-Vluyn/Düsseldorf: Neukirchener/Benziger, 2002), pp. 389-391, 397-400, 417, 420-421, 430-432.

whether the Gospel of Mark actually does end at this point. At any rate, Matthew *had to* shape his own material, and he also *wanted to* do so. His story of Jesus reflects the story of his own community in Israel, including the conflicts and hostility they probably experienced. It reflects the destruction of Jerusalem and their own separation from the Pharisee-dominated synagogues in the region. As well as his beginning, it was especially important to Matthew to reshape his ending, when the story of Jesus touches his own world.

1.7 Conclusion

I shall now attempt a *conclusion* to this first section. Is Matthew telling a new Jesus story or merely editing Mark's story? It is difficult to answer this in terms of either/or. Matthew writes a *new* Jesus story, as his beginning and ending make clear. It is new because its narrator is living in a new situation which his Jesus story reflects. It is new because Jesus has to give answers to the questions of Matthew's present time and cannot simply remain in the past as a figure of the past. This is why Matthew tells his Jesus story as the story of Jesus' fate in Israel and as the story of the separation in Israel because of Jesus. The story ends with those in Israel who believe in Jesus becoming part of a new community made up of all nations, which takes on Israel's inheritance. Read at this level, the Matthean story is surprisingly coherent.

At the same time, Matthew's story is surprisingly tradition-oriented. We may compare it with the Gospel of John, in which the earthly Jesus is frequently in danger of being engulfed by the deep insights of the Paraclete. Both of these Gospels reflect the experiences of the present, and in both cases these are similar experiences (Israel's rejection of Jesus and the separation from the synagogues). This makes the differences between Matthew and John all the more striking. The Gospel of Matthew is a highly tradition-related story of Jesus, whose author deals cautiously and carefully with the sources he has received. The story of Jesus is to remain a *Jesus* story. Unlike John, Matthew does not select freely from the rich tradition material but is loyal to the tradition *as a whole*. His εὐαγγέλιον τῆς βασιλείας (gospel of the kingdom) is the proclamation of *Jesus,* and so the story he tells must be the complete and unabbreviated story of Jesus.

What does this mean? That Matthew is attempting a balancing act? That he is limping on two feet? That he has not quite the courage of his innovative convictions? As I see it, Matthew's way of proceeding is part of his relation to tradition. Part of the legacy he inherited from the tradition was that the Jesus traditions and the whole of the Jesus story had to be *re*told time and again. A common feature of Matthew's and Mark's Jesus stories is that they are transparent for their own present time, functioning as a "two-level drama," as Louis Martyn convincingly puts it with reference to the Gospel of John.[16] The Matthean story of Jesus' conflicts in Israel and its progress towards the mission to all nations takes up *one* of the main lines in Mark's story of Jesus — possibly the second most important, since Mark seems more concerned with Jesus' relationship with his uncomprehending disciples than with the problem of "Israel and the nations."[17] At any rate, Matthew unfolds in his new Jesus story something already contained, partly implicitly and partly explicitly, in Mark's Gospel, and in this respect he actually owes his *new* story of Jesus to his most important source.

I consider it even more crucial to point to the christological reason why Matthew's story is transparent for the present. It is fundamental to his story that the Jesus of *then* is at the same time Immanuel, that is, the form of God's presence *now*. Immanuel is none other than Jesus and will be none other to the end of the age, and this is why not only the sayings of Jesus but also his story is so important to Matthew. For this reason he cannot completely reshape Jesus' sayings from the perspective of his own faith, any more than he can reduce Jesus' story to a few selected episodes. Or to put it differently, Matt. 28:20 says "*I* am with you always, to the end of the age," and not the Spirit or the Paraclete as in John 14:16. This obliged Matthew to follow the Markan story of Jesus, the given text which enabled him to develop his own story. I think this takes him very close to Mark, whose concern throughout his book is to safeguard the ἀρχή (beginning, basis) which is both the *beginning* and the lasting *foundation* of his church's proclamation.

2. Afterthoughts

2.1 Novelty and Truth

The novelty of Matthew's Jesus story confronts us with the question of its truth. Does it contain any pointers to how the Evangelist himself reflected on the truth of his Jesus story? There is no direct access to this question in the

16. J. Louis Martyn, *History and Theology in the Fourth Gospel* (Nashville: Abingdon, ²1979), pp. 129-148.

17. Cf. Zenji Kato, *Die Völkermission im Markusevangelium*, EHS 23.252 (Bern: Peter Lang, 1986).

text. The word ἀλήθεια (truth), whose usage in John and — to some extent at least — in Paul has inspired our current theological debates on "truth," does not occur in Matthew. Merely en passant and as a symbolic comment, I draw attention to the fact that of the three occurrences of the adverb ἀληθῶς (truly) in Matthew, two are to be found in the central confession of faith: ἀληθῶς θεοῦ υἱὸς εἶ (you are truly a son of God; 14:33, cf. 27:54). This may be indicative of a Matthean christological "preference criterion."[18] Beyond this, however, Matthew's Gospel leaves us in the dark when it comes to reflection on its underlying understanding of truth. Certainly truth is more for Matthew than correspondence between report and what is reported. Truth is "given" in the story of Jesus. How does this relate to the liberty Matthew allows himself in changing the Jesus story, for instance in chs. 8–9? He does not do what ancient biographers do when they assemble a number of similar deeds of their hero to exemplify his virtues. For Matthew, the chronological sequence is crucial. What is the meaning of this? In Matthew's words, it is intended to show that "throughout Galilee" Jesus "cured every disease and every sickness among the people" of Israel (4:23). This then is how the activity of the Son of David in Israel began, characterized by care for Israel. So I do not think it was Matthew's intention to create a "more correct" order of events vis-à-vis the Markan order ("more correct" in the sense of "how it actually happened"). Rather, he chose a different sequence because he accented the story of Jesus differently from Mark. In other words, his new *perspective* on the story of Jesus changes the story itself. History is always interpreted history, and this was quite clear to the author Matthew when he changed the story.

My second example is Matthew's well-known additional episode of the people's — conditional — self-cursing in 27:25. Matthew must have been aware that he was supplementing Mark's text here. Probably he would not have understood the modern question whether this was really what happened, since "the people as a whole" could hardly have gathered in the small space outside the praetorium.[19] He would have pointed out that in his own time the people of Israel as a whole — which does not of course mean each individual Israelite — led astray by its false leaders, had rejected Jesus. In this sense the large or small crowd of people present at that time represents in retrospect "the people as a whole." And in answer to the modern question of what gave him the right to create this terrible scene of the people's self-

---

18. Christof Landmesser, *Wahrheit als Grundbegriff neutestamentlicher Wissenschaft*, WUNT I.113 (Tübingen: Mohr Siebeck, 1999), pp. 459-479.

19. Pinchas Lapide, *Wer war schuld an Jesu Tod?* (Gütersloh: Gütersloher, 1987), p. 88.

cursing, he would probably have replied as a Jew that the destruction of the temple obliged him to reflect on the people's guilt,[20] since the destruction of the temple and the Holy City must be God's punishment for the sin of the people. For Matthew this sin was the deliberate rejection of Jesus. Thus Matt. 27:25 haggadically illustrates God's activity in history, making it the climax of Matthew's depiction of the trial before Pilate.[21] In short, the *interpretation* of Jesus' story, fed by the experience of Matthew and his community with that story, determines his narrative to the extent that *the story itself changes.* "History" for Matthew is always narrated, interpreted and therefore significant history and not simply "fact."

2.2. The Gospel of Matthew Is a Book of the Type "Rewritten Bible," but with a New Basic Text

In terms of genre, I find Matthew's Gospel closely related to Jewish books which retell the biblical story with the intention of updating it. Geza Vermes has designated this type "rewritten Bible," while Addison G. Wright terms it "narrative midrash." Qumran research speaks of "para-biblical literature."[22] Close relatives of Matthew's Gospel are, for example, *Jubilees,* the Genesis Apocryphon, or Pseudo-Philo's *Liber Antiquitatum.* Constitutive elements they have in common are, first, their reference to a basic text;[23] second, their focus on one or more leading points; and third, their general attention to the requirements of the present.[24] In *Jubilees,* for instance, the basic text is Gene-

20. In the prophetic tradition, the destruction of the Holy City was always interpreted as God's punishment for Israel's sin, e.g., in Josephus as the punishment for the sin of the Zealots. Rabbinic references in Luz, *Matthäus III* (see note 9), p. 242 note 57.

21. The verse is not however a "dogmatic theologoumenon" (in the words of Wolfgang Trilling, *Das wahre Israel. Studien zur Theologie des Matthäusevangeliums,* EThS 7 [Leipzig: St. Benno, ³1975], p. 72). We are dealing here with a narration of past history which interprets the present, and not with salvation-historical theories on the end of Israel as God's chosen people or something similar.

22. Geza Vermes, *Scripture and Tradition in Judaism,* StPB 4 (Leiden: Brill, ²1983), pp. 67-126; Florentino García Martínez, *The Dead Sea Scrolls Translated* (Leiden: Brill, 1994), pp. 217-99.

23. In the works mentioned the basic biblical text is sometimes quoted verbatim, sometimes summarized, sometimes omitted and sometimes expanded. The Gospel of Matthew and similar Jewish texts differ from works of history such as, e.g., Josephus' *Antiquities* in that the actualizing, present-oriented interpretation is a dominant feature of the account. The same is true if we compare Matthew's Gospel with some of the Pentateuch paraphrases found in Qumran, or with the Targums.

24. Here the re-interpretation of the old story in the re-written Bible comes close to the intention of the derash, described by Addison G. Wright, "The Literary Genre Midrash," *CBQ*

sis 1 to Exodus 12, and the leading points are the idea of revealed history centering on the law, and in particular the centrality of the Sabbath and the solar calendar. The general reference to the given situation can be found in anti-Hellenist conservatism and, as it may be assumed, in opposition to the ruling lunar calendar. A comparison of the Gospel of Matthew with *Jubilees* reveals specific features they have in common, such as the indissoluble unity of metatext and pretext, the frequency of passages created by the author at the beginning and end of the text, the anonymity of the author and. above all, the creative approach to history.[25] We have to place Matthew's Gospel in *this* tradition, rather than in the Hellenistic tradition of biography or history. But there are also distinctive features which cannot be overemphasized.

The first and most important is that Matthew actualizes *a new basic story* which is no longer the biblical story. He does write a Genesis, but it is a γένεσις Ἰησοῦ Χριστοῦ (Genesis of Jesus Christ). His basic text is not the Bible but the Gospel of Mark. The fact that *Mark's Gospel* becomes the basic text of a midrash-type book entitled "Genesis" indicates its huge significance for the writer. Matthew is writing a *new* Genesis!

The second distinctive feature is to be found in the five Matthean discourses. Like the biblical Moses in the Book of the Covenant, in Deuteronomy and later in *Jubilees, Jesus* now speaks from the mountain directly into the present. The instruction he gives is valid for the present. It is not the Torah, but the εὐαγγέλιον τῆς βασιλείας (gospel of the kingdom) which incorporates the Torah. With the five discourses, the "proclamation of the kingdom" corresponds to the fivefold Torah. Jesus' discourses unfold a new proclamation of the valid will of God, given by one who is greater than Moses, that is, the Immanuel himself.

A third distinctive feature of Matthew's Gospel in comparison with related Jewish parabiblical texts may be found, I think, in Matthew's treatment of the Jesus story he receives from Mark. He has taken it so seriously that he has omitted hardly any of it. Here Matthew differs considerably from Pseudo-

---

28 (1966), pp. 105-138, 417-457, here: p. 134, as "edifying" and meant to be "religiously relevant"; and by Günter Stemberger, *Midrasch* (Munich: C. H. Beck, 1989), pp. 25f., as "actualization." In spite of this proximity, I would not refer to the Gospel of Matthew as a "midrash." As a form-critical term, this should be reserved for the actualizing Jewish interpretations based on the fixed biblical text as a hypotext, and not used to refer, as Addison G. Wright does, to new versions of the biblical texts.

25. "Midrash is chiefly concerned with the creation of meaning — not with exegesis" (Ithamar Gruenwald, "Midrash and the 'Midrashic Condition': Preliminary Considerations," in: Michael A. Fishbane [ed.], *The Midrashic Imagination* [Albany: State University of New York, 1993], pp. 6-22, here: p. 9).

Philo, for instance, but also from the writer of the Genesis Apocryphon or the book of *Jubilees*. This is a further indication of just how important this new basic text was to Matthew.

2.3. The Bible Is No Longer the Basic Text

The Bible is no longer the basis of Matthew's Gospel but only the most important interpretative text of its new basic text.[26] It has unique significance as an aid to interpretation of the basic text, and nothing can replace it in this role. But the fact remains that it is not the basic text. Undeniably, in the development of the Jesus story some of its elements have been assembled from biblical texts, though I regard these as details rather than basic statements. I would not deny either that a group of γραμματεῖς (scribes) in the Matthean community reflected on and deepened the Jesus traditions, including the Gospel of Mark, in the light of the Bible.[27] In my judgment the formula quotations show that some special materials, for example in Matt. 2 and in Matt. 27:3-10, had already been reflected on and deepened by scholars before Matthew.

The starting point of this reflection is in most cases not the biblical text but the story of Jesus. This is evidenced, firstly, by the fact that the biblical reference material always occurs in a strangely fragmented and multi-layered form. Unlike Dale Allison, for instance, I do not assume a unified Moses christology in or behind the Gospel of Matthew.[28] The infant Jesus does have a fate in Matthew 2 which is typologically anticipated in the fate of the infant Moses, and in particular there is close correspondence between Herod and Pharaoh. At the same time, there is antithesis here. While Moses flees *from* Egypt and leads the people to the land of Israel, Jesus flees from the land of Israel *into* Egypt. Secondly, many texts have several overlying strata of various biblical traditions which aid interpretation. In Matt. 2 there is maybe, as well

---

26. This new role of the Bible is strongly emphasized by Augustin del Agua, "Die 'Erzählung' des Evangeliums im Lichte der Derasch-Methode," *Judaica* 47 (1991), pp. 140-154, here: p. 147. Del Agua finds much evidence of the derash way of thinking in the Gospels, without referring to them as "midrashim." He is chiefly concerned however with the derash-type actualization of Scripture in the Gospels, and not with the actualization of the basic story of Jesus by the later Evangelists. This is why he places *all* the Gospels in a Jewish derash context, whereas I see only the Gospel of Matthew as analogous to the Jewish "re-written Bibles." It is not the case with the Gospels of Mark and John, neither of which depends on a given hypotext, and only partially so with the Gospel of Luke, a Hellenistic-influenced historical monograph.

27. Cf. the pre-Matthean scribal versions of Jesus material, e.g., in Matt. 12:9-14; 21:1-9 and 27:46.

28. Dale C. Allison, *The New Moses: A Matthean Typology* (Edinburgh: Clark, 1993).

as the Moses tradition, the Balaam oracle from Num. 24:17; Matt. 27:51-53 does not only presuppose Ezek. 37:12-13, but also Zech. 14:4-5. The back-reference to Hos. 11:1 (= Matt. 2:15) calls to mind an Israel typology rather than a Moses typology. Thirdly, the same biblical verse or passage is sometimes interpreted in very different ways. The best example of this is Dan. 7:13-14. As was common in primitive Christianity, Matthew takes this passage to refer to Jesus' parousia (24:30; 26:64). Then he uses the same passage to refer (in 28:18), not to his everlasting kingship but to the Lord's authority here and now, limited in time by the end of the age.

All these examples make clear that it is not the biblical tradition which provides the frame of reference for the Jesus story, but vice versa. Biblical tradition is used specifically and selectively, sometimes as explicit prophecy, either typically or antitypically, and sometimes merely to render the language more colorful. This manner of using the Bible is clearly evident in the formula quotations, where Matthew draws selectively on prophecies, giving examples of how they have been fulfilled in the life of Jesus. With the Jesus story unquestionably being his frame of reference, Matthew feels free to alter the wording of the quotations. Even though he uses the Scriptures only selectively, Matthew's claim that in Jesus the law and the prophets have been "fulfilled" (cf. 5:17) leaves no room for those in Israel who do not believe in Jesus to actualize the biblical texts themselves. He denies their claim to find fulfillment of the Scriptures anywhere but in Jesus. From the perspective of the Jewish derash, which understands a new sense of the text as part of its fullness of meaning and for this reason does not privilege any one sense of the text exclusively against others,[29] what Matthew does is highly problematic. For this very reason, his claim must be accounted for differently, that is, from his perspective of the Jesus story. This also forms the Archimedean point for his hermeneutical treatment of the Bible, which has become only a secondary reference text for him. Thus the Gospel of Matthew, as well as rewriting a new basic text, also adopts a new approach to the Bible.

It follows from this that I would not find it possible, in dealing with the Jewish Christian Gospel of Matthew, to speak of the "essential unity of Old and New Testament, the *one* biblical process of tradition,"[30] unless we define the radical newness as *the* distinctive feature of this tradition process. But then we would do justice neither to the biblical and Jewish tradition process of the Tanach and its continuation in early Judaism, in which Israel's basic

---

29. Cf. Stemberger (see note 24), p. 23.

30. As does Hartmut Gese, "Erwägungen zur Einheit der biblischen Theologie," in: Gese, *Vom Sinai zum Zion*, BEvTh 64 (Munich: Kaiser, 1974), pp. 11-30, here: p. 17.

story remains the constitutive reference text, nor to the New Testament Christian tradition process, in which the same is true of the story of Jesus. *Between the two, however, a change of basic story has taken place.* It is a revolutionary change, even if the new basic story is re-narrated and developed *in the same way* or similarly to the old one and *with the help of the old one.* The change of basic story itself is a unique and revolutionary shift, and I can well understand that the majority in Israel could not accept it.

2.4. Holistic Understanding in the Present

By means of a Jewish midrash, the present meaning of the basic biblical text is drawn out and applied to life. How can the present meaning of Mark's story of Jesus as found in Matthew be described? It is not only, and not even primarily, noetic and propositional. Matthew is not concerned with a better *insight* into the basic story of Jesus, neither in the sense of the ἀσφάλεια (certainty) of the historian nor in the sense of theological doctrine or a christological confession. Rather, the meaning for the present is to be found primarily on the existential and practical level. For this reason, the combination of semantic with emotive and pragmatic linguistic elements is important for interpretation of the Gospel of Matthew. Attention must also be given to intended and actual *effects* of the text on its readers, and the inclusion of reader theory, rhetorical and psychological considerations.

Two dimensions are significant for the meaning of Matthew's Jesus story:

1. It is concerned with reassurance of identity. The relation of the Matthean community with Israel is called into question. As followers of Jesus, they saw themselves as part of God's people Israel, yet by Matthew's time they were probably already "contre coeur" and separated from "their" synagogues.[31] This was hugely unsettling for them. They lived in the tension between the Israel they were part of and the increasingly Gentile Christian Church in dispersion which had largely detached itself from Israel. To this too they belonged, since it had adopted their identifying rituals of baptism (and not circumcision!) and the Lord's Supper (which was probably observed outside the framework of the annual Passover in Matthew's community). This situation of double belonging could no longer be sustained, and so Matthew attempts in his

---

31. See Luz, *Matthäus III* (see note 9), pp. 392-396.

Jesus story to clarify and strengthen their identity. In its demarcation of the malicious Jewish leaders and the "whole people" led astray by them, Matthew's Jesus story is quite problematic. But in terms of social psychology such demarcation vis-à-vis outside groups is an important element in identity reinforcement and preservation.[32]

2. From an ethical perspective, Matthew is concerned to activate his community on the "path of justice." He seeks to ensure that its members will not flag in their obedience, their love, their striving for "perfection" and their fellowship. This is his main concern in the five Matthean discourses in which Jesus, Immanuel, who is with them to the end of the age, addresses them directly and points to the judgment which they too will face.

Thus "understanding" in Matthew's Jesus story takes place in the present, as in the Jewish midrashim, and is embedded in an act of life. Understanding who Jesus is, in the story told by Matthew, means confessing, and confessing is bound up with risk and with one's own religious experience. Peter and the disciples experienced this on the lake (14:31-33). Confessing leads to suffering, as the disciples were taught not long afterwards (16:13-24). Matthew distinguishes in vocabulary between "hearing" and "doing," but only when hearing leads to doing can a solid house be built (7:24-29). As a concept, "understanding" is not identical with "bearing fruit," but only where the word bears fruit has it been fully understood (13:19, 23).

Such "understanding" in the present is a theological risk. And if the basis of such understanding is a new Jesus story written with the present in mind, the risk is even greater. As the author of a "rewritten Markan Gospel," Matthew narrates his Jesus story directly for the present, his own narrative fusing with the story he has received.

Matthew has however shown respect for the basic story of Jesus he updated and for the words of Jesus he received, which were to him the "gospel of the kingdom." He has left them largely untouched and has written a markedly conservative new story. In this way he makes clear that his story renarrates a *given* story. There are no indications in Matthew's Gospel (as has been suggested for Luke) that he intended his new story to replace the Markan Gospel with which, as evidenced here and there, he assumed at least some of his readers to be familiar.

This is probably the reason why the communities soon began to use the

32. See in this volume "Anti-Judaism in the Gospel of Matthew as a Historical and Theological Problem: An Outline," pp. 243-261.

Gospels in parallel. As I see it, Matthew himself would have approved of this. For him, the gospel is the proclamation of *Jesus,* and the One who is with his community always, to the end of the age, is not some kind of spirit or paraclete but Jesus himself. It seems to me that this theological wisdom guided the church when it handed down to us four Gospels and not just one. All of them without exception tell the story of Jesus, naming the foundation on which their actualizations rest.

MATTHEW AND HIS TRADITION

3 Matthew and Q

For Paul Hoffmann
on the occasion of his 65th birthday

The Sayings Source Q runs like a theme tune through Paul Hoffmann's academic work. He encountered it early in his career[1] and it has accompanied him ever since. As co-editor of the *Evangelisch-Katholischer Kommentar* I can only hope that he will continue what he has begun.[2] And so I greet Paul Hoffmann, the energetic companion and critic of my own work on Matthew's Gospel,[3] with a short piece that focuses on his own academic origins and on what I hope will be his future. This chapter presupposes the findings of my analyses in the four volumes of my commentary on Matthew[4] and for this reason the literary references are kept deliberately brief.

1. Cf. Paul Hoffmann, *Studien zur Theologie der Logienquelle*, NTA 8 (Münster: Aschendorff, 1972).

2. Cf. Paul Hoffmann, "QR und der Menschensohn," in: Frans van Segbroeck (ed.), *The Four Gospels 1992* I, BEThL 100 (FS Frans Neirynck; Leuven: Peeters, 1992), pp. 421-456. Hoffmann is the European partner in the International Q Project, Claremont, California. He has promised a commentary on Q for the *Evangelisch-Katholischer Kommentar* (EKK).

3. The EKK uses the σύζυγοι (companions) system. A Catholic partner reads and criticizes the manuscript of a Protestant author working on a similar biblical book, and vice versa. Paul Hoffmann is the ideal σύζυγος for me. I owe a great deal to his close readings of my commentary and his often spirited marginalia!

4. Ulrich Luz, *Matthew 1–7: A Commentary* (Minneapolis: Augsburg, 1989); *Matthew 8–20*, Hermeneia (Minneapolis: Fortress, 2001); *Das Evangelium nach Matthäus (Matt. 18–25)*, EKK I.3 (Neukirchen/Düsseldorf: Neukirchener/Benziger 1, 1997); *Das Evangelium nach Matthäus (Matt. 26–28)*, EKK I.4 (Neukirchen/Düsseldorf: Neukirchener/Benziger ²2002). Abbreviated in the following as Luz, *Matt. 1–7*; Luz, *Matt. 8–20*; Luz, *Matt. 18–25*; Luz, *Matt. 26–28*.

German original: "Matthäus und Q," in: Rudolf Hoppe/Ulrich Busse (eds.), *Von Jesus zum Christus. Christologische Studien*, BZNW 93 (FS Paul Hoffmann; Berlin: de Gruyter, 1998), pp. 201-215.

1. The Extent of Q

The extent of Q is a matter of dispute. It is possible simply to designate all the double traditions found in Matthew and Luke as "Q," which is what Siegfried Schulz did for example.[5] It is equally possible however that, on the one hand, certain double traditions were not part of Q, and that on the other hand both Evangelists have omitted texts they found in their version of Q. If this is so, we need further criteria for attributing a text to Q. Such criteria are all circular, since they presuppose a certain hypothesis concerning the form of the source and retrospectively reinforce this hypothesis. The circularity is inevitable, but we must at least state our assumptions. If we assume, as I do, a written form for the Sayings Source, it follows that

1. *for Q texts we can expect a verbal agreement that exceeds the minimal agreement necessary by reason of the common material, such minimal agreement also being expected in tradition variants transmitted orally.*

If moreover we assume, as I do, that the written Sayings Source had for the greater part a recognizable structure, that is, an arrangement of Jesus sayings in thematic blocks of text, then it follows that

2. *when assigning an individual text to Q one can at least hope that the Q order of texts largely preserved in Luke can be confirmed in Matthew on the basis of certain indicators.*[6]

A further major difficulty is presented by the fact that these two criteria cannot always be combined. The logion on serving Mammon for instance (Luke 16:13/Matt. 6:24) shows maximum verbal agreement, but its place in Q is a mystery. Conversely, the order of the Sermon on the Plain in Q 6:20-49 is largely confirmed in Matthew's newly composed Sermon on the Mount, yet the number of verbal deviations not clearly attributable to the Evangelist's editing is in this case particularly large.[7] The case of the woes discourse in Q

5. Siegfried Schulz, *Die Spruchquelle der Evangelisten* (Zürich: Theologischer, 1972).

6. Fundamental research is provided by Vincent Taylor, "The Original Order of Q," in: Angus J. B. Higgins (ed.), *New Testament Essays* (FS Thomas Walter Manson; Manchester: Manchester University Press, 1959), pp. 246-269.

7. Thomas Bergemann, *Q auf dem Prüfstand*, FRLANT 158 (Göttingen: Vandenhoeck und Ruprecht, 1993), p. 230, calculates common verbal material amounting to some 30 per cent. An earlier analysis of the Sermon on the Mount/Sermon on the Plain by Hans T. Wrege, *Die Überlieferungsgeschichte der Bergpredigt*, WUNT I.9 (Tübingen: Mohr Siebeck, 1968) found that

11:39-52 is even more difficult. The verbal deviations which cannot be explained as editing are considerable, but at the same time a common order of the individual woes in Q can scarcely be reconstructed. Only the assignation of Q 11:39-52 to the large block Q 11:2–12:59 offers encouragement to those who support the Q hypothesis.[8] These two textual complexes are usually reckoned to belong to Q, and in the case of the woes discourse in particular it is remarkable that virtually no one has questioned this so far. If this assumption is correct, there must be a third criterion for assigning a text to Q, namely that

> 3. *it must be possible to place the text within the macrotext of Q, i.e. in a sizeable Q block.*

In the case of the woes discourse this appears to be the reason why all researchers who assume a written Sayings Source assign this text to Q, since it belongs to the larger Q block Q 11:2–12:59. This is also decisive for the Sermon on the Plain: the placement of the Sermon on the Mount in Matthew's Gospel corresponds to that of the Sermon on the Plain, between the temptation narrative in Q 4:1-13 and the narrative of the centurion from Capernaum in Q 7:1-10. The excellently transmitted Mammon saying Q 16:13 still presents a difficulty, however, since the macrotext of Q 16:13-18 is fragmentary and uncertain.[9]

Thus the assigning of individual texts to Q is especially problematic when these texts are outside the text blocks in Luke's Gospel which consist largely of Q texts, i.e. outside Luke 3:1-17; 4:1-13; 6:20–7:35; 9:57–10:16; 11:2–12:59; 13:18-35; 17:1-6, 20-37. These problematic texts include Luke 14:15-27, 34-35; 15:3-7; 16:13-18; 19:12-27; 22:28-30. Most researchers use their own judgment to decide on these texts, without reference to clear criteria. They always decide, however, according to the ideas they have of Q. One has the impression that in cases of doubt most of them boldly opt for inclusion, since they support the hypothesis of a written Q source. There is of course a theoretical problem in such discretionary decisions, but it is one I cannot solve.

Now follows a survey of my deviations from the principle "double traditions = Q."

---

the common tradition was an oral and not a written source. This corresponds to the basic thesis of Joachim Jeremias, who rejected the idea of a written form of Q. The weakness in Wrege's analysis is that it proceeds one-sidedly from the problem of the verbal agreements and neglects the order of the individual texts.

8. On this issue see Luz, *Matthew 18–25* (see note 4 above), pp. 318f.

9. Cf. (a) below.

(a) I am very uncertain about the logia transmitted in Luke in the small block 16:13-18, i.e. in Q(?) 16:13, 16, 17, 18. That these sayings do not belong to Q is suggested by the fact that the small, isolated Q section 16:13, 16-18 lacks a clear theme of its own and is not thematically associated with the Q blocks that precede and follow it. Moreover, although all three sayings deal with the law, they do so in very different ways. The Matthean arrangement of the sayings (criterion 2) would support the assigning to Q in the case of Q 16:17 and 18 (= Matt. 5:18, 32)[10] and probably in the case of the nearby saying Q 16:13 = Matt. 6:24. From the perspective of verbal agreement (criterion 1) only Q 16:13 = Matt. 6:24 is a clear case. With the other sayings the verbal agreement is too insignificant to support the argument for Q.[11] My conclusion is thus an (albeit rather skeptical) *non liquet*.

(b) In my opinion the following texts do not belong to Q: Luke 15:3-7 = Matt. 18:12-13;[12] Luke 22:28-30 = Matt. 19:28; Luke 14:16-24 = Matt. 22:1-10;[13] Luke 19:11-27 = Matt. 25:14-30. These passages meet none of the three criteria. I thus assume Q 17:37 to be the end of the Sayings Source.

The question of *which words of Q may have been omitted by Matthew* is of course especially difficult. We cannot exclude the possibility of such omissions, though we need to proceed very carefully here since Matthew has left out very little of his Markan source. With a few Q passages it seems evident that Matthew tended to compress and shorten.[14] But we can suggest that he deliberately omitted a Jesus saying found in the Sayings Source only if:

10. That v. 32 belongs to Q is also supported by the Matthean redaction process in Matt. 5:21-48. He supplements his "primary" antitheses drawn from a written antithesis source with Q material in the form of individual sayings and complete antitheses.

11. In the case of Q(?) 16:16 = Matt. 11:12-13 the question of wording is particularly difficult. The usual reconstruction of the Q saying as a combination of Luke 16:16a with Matt. 11:12 (see, e.g., Athanasius Polag, *Fragmenta Q* [Neukirchen-Vluyn: Neukirchener, 1979, p. 74]) appears arbitrary to me, since Luke 16:16a corresponds exactly to Luke's understanding of the law!

12. The verbal agreements are relatively few, and only some of the deviations can be identified as redaction. Cf. Luz, *Matt. 8–20* (see note 4), pp. 438f.

13. Or should we assume a Q block made up of Luke 14:16-24, 26-27 + Luke 17:33 + Luke 14:34? As I see it, the agreement between the parables in Matt. 22:1-10 and Luke 14:16-24 is so slight that I prefer to assume a Q block consisting only of sayings, which might be designated "supplement" or "scattered sayings." It could have comprehended Luke 14:26 + Luke 17:33 + Luke 14:34-35 [16:13, 16-18]; 17:1-6. These sayings do not have a common theme, however, and in spite of Hans Klein's redaction history considerations ("Botschaft für viele — Nachfolge von wenigen? Überlegungen zu Lk 14:15-35," *EvTh* 57 [1997], pp. 427-437) I question why Luke should have taken the Q block apart in this manner. It would be the only instance of his doing so!

14. This is true of Q 6:27-36, where Matthew divides the Q sequence into two antitheses, apparently applying a certain principle of symmetry between the antitheses. Cf. Luz, *Matthew 1–7* (see note 4), pp. 245, 292.

1. the saying is found in a complete Q context in Luke's Gospel, and if
2. it is a saying in tension with the basic theological ideas of Matthew's Gospel.

It is sometimes scarcely possible to distinguish between a saying from Q omitted from Matthew's Gospel and a Jesus saying added to Luke or Q-Luke. Possibly the following were omitted by Matthew: Q 10:4b,[15] Q 12:49-50,[16] Q 12:54-56(?),[17] Q 17:20-21, 28-31(?).[18]

2. The Version of Q-Matt.

I take Q-Matt. to be the written version of Q used by Matthew. When dealing with ancient minor religious texts and "sub-literature," the assumption of two different versions of a text is by no means exceptional. From the perspective of source criticism it is nonetheless the result of a problem, an uncertainty which Thomas Bergemann formulates clearly as follows: "There is no explanation for why the tradents took over part of the tradition almost unchanged and modified other parts very considerably."[19] The difficulties are

15. The contradiction to Matt. 5:46-47 is self-evident!

16. Matthew has fully integrated the Q block Q 12:39-46 in his eschatological discourse and excerpted or omitted the following Q texts. As well as Q 12:49-50 he appears to have omitted Q 12:54-56, cf. note 17. His omission of Q 12:50 is supported by the fact that Matthew also omits Mark 10:38b. His omission of Q 12:49 is supported by the fact that nowhere else (pace Matt. 3:10) does Matthew associate hell fire with Jesus' present ministry.

17. The relations between Luke 12:54-56 and Matt. 16:2-3 are very difficult to assess. In terms of textual criticism, Matthew's short text 16:1-4 appears more original to me; cf. Luz, *Matthew 8–20* (see note 4), p. 443, contra Claus Peter März, *"Lasst eure Lampen brennen!"*, EThS 20 (Leipzig: St. Benno, 1991), pp. 32-43. Deletions by Matthew are suggested by the fact that apart from the sign of Jonah (12:38-40) and the sign that is the Son of Man himself (24:30) Matthew does not include signs. The Son of Man comes like lightning (24:27). But we cannot be certain in our judgment here!

18. Matthew has combined Q 17:31 with Mark 13:15-16 and included this in 24:17-18. It seems that Q 17:30 inspired Matt. 24:39b. The example of Lot is taken by many to be a secondary extension. This is contradicted however by Matthew's frequent abbreviation of eschatological sayings in Q which could not be harnessed parenetically: see Q 12:35-38(?); 12:49-50, 54-56(?); 17:20-21(?). Further reasons for these omissions by Matthew are given by David Catchpole, *The Quest for Q* (Edinburgh: Clark, 1993), pp. 248f.

19. Q (see note 7), p. 233. There are indeed considerable differences between individual Q sections. The variation between Q-Matt. and Q-Luke appears very great for the Sermon on the Plain and the woes discourse, but only slight for the temptation narrative and a number of other individual texts such as Q 12:39-40, 42-46; 13:34-35; 16:13.

not insurmountable however, as in my opinion the existence of pre-redaction variants of the text cannot be completely excluded for any of the larger Q texts. Moreover, Bergemann has given himself an easy task by taking the Sermon on the Plain, a text with a particularly large number of pre-redaction differences in wording, as his "test case" and not the whole Sayings Source.[20] If one rejects the hypothesis of various versions of Q, strongly suggested by the Sermon on the Plain (and elsewhere), and seeks an alternative explanation for the pre-redaction textual differences, the special solutions one is obliged to posit for individual blocks of text lead automatically to the dissolution of an overall hypothesis of a written Sayings Source. In other words, the assumption of various different versions of Q is a difficulty which has to be faced by those who, for other reasons, are convinced that a written Sayings Source exists. They will not be able to verify their thesis. It may be some consolation to them that in the case of text blocks which we can assume were especially important for the communities and often in use, such as the Sermon on the Plain, pre-redaction textual variants are particularly numerous and to be expected. To this extent I too support the idea of a special Q-Matt. version. It is, however, a conjectural hypothesis born out of uncertainty.

I list here the texts which were probably in Matthew's copy of Q but not in Luke's copy. This is possible particularly with texts which in Matthew are fully integrated in a text block taken from Q but are lacking altogether in Luke. I assume this possibility (with varying probability)[21] with the following texts:

Matt. 5:5, 7-9; Matt. 5:19(?); Matt. 5:41; Matt. 6:34; Matt. 7:6(?);[22] Matt.

---

20. Bergemann assumes a special "basic text" for Q 6:20-49. Wrege's (see note 7) analysis is also restricted to the Sermon on the Mount/Sermon on the Plain. Hans Dieter Betz, *The Sermon on the Mount,* Hermeneia (Minneapolis: Fortress, 1995), suggests a special solution of a different kind. He assumes that the Sermon on the Mount and the Sermon on the Plain each have a separate special source, closely related to their present form in Matthew and Luke, with no more than a "common pattern of composition" (p. 70) between them. Thus Q dissolves into a "pattern," whereas only the special sources (corresponding to Q-Matt. and Q-Luke) are written texts. Such theses are not helpful in the quest for Q as long as they do not falsify the existence of a Sayings Source completely but concern themselves only with individual and particularly suitable blocks of text! On this basis one would in principle have to search for a special solution for every individual part of the double traditions, and it would be impossible to integrate the considerable indications that Matthew knew the order of all the double traditions as found in Luke (cf. section 3 below).

21. Very uncertain passages are marked (?).

22. This thesis amounts to conjecture. Matthew's insertion of the logion would still be inexplicable (cf. Luz, *Matthew 1–7* [see note 4], p. 419). But this is precisely why 7:6 as an extension of Q in Q-Matt. can hardly be explained. In the context of the Q Sermon on the Plain the logion would remain an isolated fragment. Was this why Luke deleted it from his Q source?

10:5-6(?); Matt. 10:16b; Matt. 10:23(?); Matt. 10:41(?); Matt. 18:15b-17, 18;[23] Matt. 23:15(?).

In most cases it is less probable that Luke, who inserts Q in large blocks, would have omitted these texts.[24]

Conclusion: Overall, this list shows that Q-Matt. did not differ substantially from the main body of the Q source. The pre-redaction extensions in Q-Matt. are brief and their forms all correspond to the Q blocks into which they have been inserted. In different ways they are all Jewish Christian in character and offer insight into the tradition environment from which Matthew has taken his Q source. In Luke's Gospel the compositional confusion between Q and special traditions, particularly in the big journey narrative, cannot as I see it be explained successfully by redaction criticism and may point to the fact that Luke had access to Q in a much extended form which also included other genres. Matthew's Gospel, on the other hand, appears to be relatively close to the original literary form of Q and also to the Q community.[25]

3. How Has Matthew Incorporated Q in His Gospel?

The most striking contrast with Luke is that Matthew treated his two main sources Mark and Q in quite different ways. He has taken over Mark's Gospel from 2:23 = Matt. 12:1 onwards, without changing its order, so that his Gospel can be read as a new edition of Mark's. But he has "gutted" the Sayings Source and destroyed its structure in the process.

4QMMT (= 4 Q 396, 9f.) and the further halachic passages given by William D. Davies/Dale Allison, *The Gospel according to St Matthew* I, ICC (Edinburgh: Clark, 1988), p. 675, make clear that the imagery in the first part of the logion has a Jewish cultic background. But the second half of the saying shows that the cultic aspect has become a mere metaphor. The logion still cannot be interpreted.

23. The observations of Dieter Lührmann, *Die Redaktion der Logienquelle*, WMANT 33 (Neukirchen-Vluyn: Neukirchener, 1969), pp. 110-117, on these two passages and on Matt. 5:19 are of lasting significance.

24. A Lukan deletion is improbable where Q-Luke has another pre-redactional "substitute text," as in Q-Matt. 5:5, 7-9; 6:34, or where the text of Q-Matt. is evidently an inserted extension, as in Q-Matt. 10:16b; 10:41 and 18:15b-18. There would be no satisfying reasons for a Lukan deletion of Q-Matt. 5:41 and 23:15. Q-Matt. 7:6 and 10:5-6, 23 remain highly problematic.

25. This is supported too by Hoffmann (see note 2), p. 454, following a thesis by Odil Hannes Steck.

Summarizing Survey of Incorporations of Q in Matthew

	Mark	Q = Luke	Matt.
Preaching of John the Baptist	1:2-8	3:7-9, 16-17	B 3:1-12
Temptation of Jesus	1:12-13	4:1-13	B 4:1-11
Programmatic preaching	[1:21-22]	6:20-49	B 5-7
Centurion of Capernaum		7:1-10	B 8:5-13
John the Baptist		7:18-35	B* 11:2-19
Discipleship and Commission	(6:7-13)	9:57–10:24	E 8:19-22 B 9:37; 10:5, 16, 40 B* 11:20-27 E 13:16-17
Prayer		11:2-13	E+ 6:9-13; 7:7-11
Beelzebub debate, Jonah sign	3:22-30	11:14-32	B 12:22-35
Words of light		11:33-36	E+ 5:15; 6:22-23
Woes	(12:38-40)	11:39-52	B 23
On Confessing		12:2-12	B* 10:26-33
On Possessions		12:22-34	B* 6:19-33
Preparedness for Judgment		12:35-59	B* 24:39-46 E 10:34-36; 5:25-26
Parables	4	13:18-21	B 13: [30-33]
Eschatological warnings		13:22-35	E+ 7:13-14, 22-23, 8:11-12; 23:37-39
Various sayings	8:34	14:25-27, 34-35; 16:13, 16-18	E 10:37-38; 5:13 E(+) 6:24; 5:18; 11:12-13; 5:32
	9:42	17:1-6	E(+) 18:6-7, 15-22; 17:19-20
Eschatological sayings	13	17:20-37	E(+) 24:17-18, 23, 27 B 24:37-41

Key:
Underlining: The order of Q blocks and Markan parallels or starting points is identical.
B Block technique. Matthew takes over a complete Q block, occasionally with minor internal repositioning
* The order of the block differs from that of Q
E Excerpt technique: Matthew excerpts from Q blocks and places the individual logia at various points in his Gospel
+ Matthew largely retains the order of the Q logia

A brief review of this table indicates the following:

1. Matthew has two fundamentally different techniques for incorporating Q. Either he takes over Q blocks wholesale (= B, block technique), or he excerpts Q blocks, incorporating the individual logia in contexts of their own (= E, excerpt technique).
2. When employing the B technique, Matthew tends not to preserve the order of blocks as found in the Sayings Source. Rather, he reorders the blocks (= *). Thus Matthew has no independent interest in the order of the Jesus traditions in Q.
3. Where Matthew has retained the order of some large blocks of material from the Sayings Source, the reason is that it corresponds to the order of related blocks of material in Mark's Gospel.
4. Where Matthew has excerpted he has quite frequently, though not always, excerpted the Q blocks consecutively, keeping entirely or largely to their Q order (= +).
5. All these observations can best be explained by assuming that Matthew had Q palaeographically at his disposal in the form of a notebook.[26]

A few further observations can be added:

When Matthew composes his discourses, he generally starts with a passage from Mark's Gospel which then dominates the beginning of the discourse. This is true of the *Mission Discourse* (Matthew 10), which begins with the introduction from Mark 6:7. Matthew then inserts the list of the apostles from Mark 3:16-19 and includes in its first part a parallel to Mark 6:8-11 extended according to the Q parallel Q 10:2-12. Only when the Markan text is "exhausted" does Matthew use largely Q text. A further Markan passage is taken up in Matt. 10:17-22 = Mark 13:9-13, with the Q parallel Q 12:11-12 incorporated. The order of the Q sayings may be altered (cf. Q 10:2-3). In the second half of the discourse (Matt. 10:24-39) Matthew excerpts Q materials consecutively from other parts of the Sayings Source, retaining their Q order (Q 6:40; 12:2-9; 12:51-53; 14:26-27 [+ Luke 17:33]) before returning to the original ending of the Q Mission discourse (Q 10:16).

A similar pattern can be found in other discourses. The *Parables Discourse* (Matt. 13) begins with Markan material (Matt. 13:1-23, 31-32 = Mark 4:1-20, 30-32) and the Matthean counter-parable to the omitted parable of the growing seed (Mark 4:26-29), that of the darnel in the field of wheat (Matt.

---

26. This corresponds to the hypothesis of Migaku Sato, *Q and Prophetie*, WUNT II.29 (Tübingen: Mohr Siebeck, 1988), pp. 62-68, based on different tradition-history considerations.

13:24-30).[27] The only additional parable in Matthew, that of the leavened bread (13:33), is inserted in the most appropriate position within Mark's structure. The *Community Discourse* (Matt. 18) opens with Markan material in the position given in Mark's Gospel (Mark 9:36-37, 42-48 = Matt. 18:2-9) and incorporates parallel Q material in the Markan sequence (Q 17:1-2). In the second part of the discourse special material dominates. Probably only a single piece of Q, i.e. Q 17:3, which directly follows on the passage 17:1-2 has been incorporated in Matthew's composition, probably in the extended form of Q-Matt. The same applies to the *Eschatological Discourse,* Matt. 24–25. Its framework is a description of the last things, made up of Mark 13:3-32 (= Matt. 24:3-36) and the special material Matt. 25:31-46. Individual Q sayings are inserted or taken account of in appropriate positions in the first text sequence, taken mainly from Mark (Q 17:31, 23-24, 37).[28] For the following section Matt. 24:37–25:30 Matthew excerpts two Q sequences, abbreviating both (Q 17:26-27, 30, 34-35 = Matt. 24:37-41, and Q 12:39-46 = Matt. 24:43-51) and retaining here too the order found in Q.

The rest of the Matthean texts present a partially similar picture. The *Woes Discourse* in Chapter 23 is very difficult to assess because of the uncertainty of the Q text. Its starting point is the Markan Woes Discourse (Mark 12:38-40) which Matthew has used to open his own discourse, combining it with a woe from Q (Q 11:43). The main body of the Woes Discourse from Q 11:39-52 follows, somewhat augmented (Matt. 23:13-36). It is difficult to say which Evangelist has preserved the Q order better. Matthew ends with another Q logion excerpted from elsewhere (Q 13:34-35 = Matt. 23:37-39). In the *polemic* of Matt. 12:22-45, the passage Mark 3:22-30, whose turn it is following Matt. 12:1-21, has been harmoniously combined with Q 11:14-23. At the end of this section Matthew has once again inserted additional material from other sections of Q (Matt. 12:31-37). The position of the demand for signs that follows is, exceptionally, not determined by Mark. Rather, Matthew uses texts which in Q are within the context of the Beelzebub debate, though he does not retain the order found in Q (Matt. 12:38-45 = Q 11:16, 29-32, 24-26). The reason Matthew does this is that the demand for signs is so important to him that he includes it twice.[29] Thus the section Matt. 12:22-45 can be read as a passage whose position is determined by the Markan source but which Matthew has as usual expanded using additional Q materials.

27. Cf. Luz, *Matthew 8–20* (see note 4), p. 253.

28. The Q order is preserved.

29. Matt. 12:38-40; 16:1-4. Repetition in Matthew is a pedagogic device; cf. Janice C. Anderson, *Matthew's Narrative Web. Over, and Over, and Over Again,* JSNTSup 94 (Sheffield: Sheffield Academic, 1994).

The *polemical* chapter, Matthew 11, is easily understood in terms of composition. It has no starting point in Mark. Matthew has combined the deliberately deferred second John the Baptist sequence Q 7:18-35 and the Q sayings Q 10:13-15, 21-22 which he had not used in the mission discourse to form an impressive discourse of Jesus. The words show the increasing tension between Jesus and Israel and at the same time they contrast the γενεά (generation) that rejects Jesus with the community of his βασιλεία (kingdom). Matthew supplements this composition, owed largely to Q, by two texts, the "taking by force" of 11:12-13 which in its Matthean version takes John the Baptist into the time of the βασιλεία, and the Savior's summons to rest 11:28-30 which emphasizes the parenetic dimension of the revelation to the νήπιοι (simple ones).

The *Sermon on the Mount* (Matthew 5–7) does not quite fit the general pattern. There is a point of connection with Mark (Mark 1:21) but there is no Markan source text. Hence, *faute de mieux,* the Sermon on the Plain in Q 6:20-49 provides the frame that Matthew works with. But this statement has to be qualified immediately, since wherever Matthew had other written texts at his disposal he has given them priority and only inserted or appended the Q texts. This appears to be the case for the (probably) written antithesis source available to him (Matt. 5:21-22, 27-28 [33-37]), into which he has inserted and appended Q materials from the Sermon on the Plain and elsewhere (Q 12:57-59 = Matt. 5:25-26; [Matt. 5:29-30 Q?]; Q 16:18 = Matt. 5:32; Q 6:27-30, 32-36 = Matt. 5:39-42, 44-48). The same is true of the (probably) written rules of true piety Matt. 6:2-18, in which Q 11:2-4 has been inserted. In the second part of the Sermon on the Mount, Matthew expands Q 6:37-49 with excerpts from several other parts of Q (Q 12:22-34; 11:34-36; 16:13; 11:9-13; 13:23-27). In at least one case a "consecutive excerpting" can be found (Q 13:23-24, 25-27, 28-29 = Matt. 7:13-14, 22-23; 8:11-12). Thus we can state here too that Q serves in part as "excerpt material," though the basic text in which these excerpts are incorporated is also taken from Q.

What conclusions can be drawn from all this? *First,* it is apparent that Matthew's incorporation procedure for the Sayings Source is remarkably homogenous. He proceeds in similar fashion with almost all the larger sections determined by Q. This is, *post factum,* an argument in favor of the actual existence of such a source.

Second, it is apparent that Matthew was extremely familiar with the Q source. Not only has he excerpted it several times consecutively, and integrated several large Q blocks in new contexts.[30] In addition, he has deliber-

---

30. For example, Q 12:22-34; 11:2-13, 39-52; 12:2-9; 13:22-30.

ately taken individual sayings from quite different Q contexts and inserted them, sometimes in key positions, in his own composition. Examples are 5:13 (= Q 14:34-35); 5:14-15 (= Q 11:33); 5:25-26 (= Q 12:57-59); 6:22-23 (= Q 11:34-36); 6:24 (= Q 16:13); 10:24-25 (= Q 6:40); 12:31-32 (= Q 12:10); 23:37-39 (= Q 13:34-35). Matthew evidently has an excellent overview of the Sayings Source, unlike Luke, who stacks his sources quite mechanically one after the other. One can thus assume that where Matthew has found duplicates in Q and Mark and retained them,[31] he has done so just as deliberately as where he has created duplicates himself.[32]

Third, it is apparent that for Matthew the Q source was of a different character than Mark's Gospel. For him, Q was not a complete book like Mark's Gospel. Although the Sayings Source shows, particularly in its later tradition layers, substantial beginnings of a narrative form, Matthew did not regard it as a second Jesus narrative comparable to the Gospel of Mark. Rather, he saw it as a collection of material with sayings of the Lord. He respected its dignity by retaining its wording — often more closely than Luke — and by excerpting it very thoroughly. Its order and composition were not important to him, however. He gave priority to Mark even in incorporating his discourses, and respected the order of Q almost only when this was suggested by the Markan source and when it naturally resulted from his "consecutive" excerpting. Thus Matthew read the Sayings Source much as the Gospels were often read in the second century, as "memoirs" which were significant because they preserved the living words of the κύριος (Lord). But for him it was important that the κύριος was not to be had or heard without the "basis" of his story.[33] And this he found in Mark's Gospel.

4. The Theological Significance of Q for Matthew

For Matthew the εὐαγγέλιον τῆς βασιλείας (gospel of the kingdom) (4:23; 9:35) is Jesus' own preaching.[34] Matthew is concerned that the church's preaching should take its orientation from Jesus' own. All Jesus' commands form the content of the mission preaching (28:20). Mark's Gospel was not a

31. For example, 12:39-40 and 16:1-4.

32. For example, 7:16-20//12:33-37, cf. also 9:32-33//12:22-23.

33. Cf. Eduard Schweizer, "Aufnahme und Gestaltung von Q bei Matthäus," in: Lorenz Oberlinner/Peter Fiedler (eds.), *Salz der Erde — Licht der Welt* (FS Anton Vögtle, Stuttgart: Katholisches Bibelwerk, 1991), pp. 112-130. "The content of Q can be transmitted and understood only within the context of the proclamation of the whole of Jesus' ministry" (p. 129).

34. Luz, *Matthew 1–7* (see note 4), pp. 207f.

book of preaching but as ἀρχὴ τοῦ εὐαγγελίου (the basis of the "good news," i.e.: the story of Jesus) it was the beginning and the foundation of gospel (Mark 1:1). Thus Matthew has supplemented the "foundation" by the gospel itself.[35] He does not use Q as a second Jesus narrative but as a collection of material from which he adds the "gospel of the kingdom" to the Markan narrative which transmits it in only rudimentary form. This supplementation is found primarily in Matthew's five discourses. The first, programmatic discourse, the Sermon on the Mount, follows the outline of Q's Sermon on the Plain and is explicitly understood by the Evangelist as Jesus' "gospel of the kingdom" (Matt. 4:23). Like the editor of Q (7:22), Matthew looks back on it in the expression πτωχοὶ εὐαγγελίζονται (the poor are evangelized) in 11:5. This is in keeping with the fact that Matthew's discourses, in which the bulk of the Q materials is collected, are directed "out of the window." That is, they are not primarily part of the Jesus story but are addressed directly to the readers of Matthew's Gospel in the situation of that time. Hence in his βίβλος (book) Matthew binds the proclamation of his community, which is none other than the proclamation of Jesus himself, to its ἀρχή (foundation) told by the Gospel of Mark. Only as part of a Jesus story can the Matthean "gospel of the kingdom" be Jesus' own gospel; the gospel of the kingdom must of necessity be embedded in the Jesus story. This embedding is Matthew's theological achievement, and it reveals the main theological significance of Q for Matthew: Q contains what the church is commissioned to proclaim. As a mere ἀρχή Mark's Gospel was inadequate for Matthew at this point, and the "unbiographical" Sayings Source had to be interpreted. Thus Matthew's concern could not be to reproduce the Jesus proclamation of Q in the order and arrangement found in the source. Rather, he was concerned to incorporate the proclamation in his Jesus narrative in such a way that the Jesus story and the gospel of the kingdom should illuminate and interpret each other. In this way, they could become "gospel" in a more comprehensive sense.

Apart from the incorporation of Q materials in the five major discourses, three other independent sections of the Gospel which Matthew has

---

35. James M. Robinson, "The Sayings Gospel Q," in: Van Segbroeck, *Gospels* (see note 2), pp. 361-388, offers stimulating speculations on what the wording of the lost Q "incipit" may have been. Not only οἱ λόγοι (Q 6:47) is relevant and important here but also the keyword εὐαγγελίζομαι with which Q 7:22 refers back to the Sermon on the Plain. Robinson (p. 388): "The reference to οἱ λόγοι of Jesus at the conclusion of the Inaugural Sermon (Q 6:47-49/Matt. 7:26) . . . , the succinct clause πτωχοὶ εὐαγγελίζονται in referring back to the Sermon (Q 7:22), and then the expression τὸ εὐαγγέλιον τῆς βασιλείας, in Matthew's references to the Sermon (Matt. 4:23; 9:35) do present the trajectory somewhere in the middle of which the *incipit* of Q (. . .) may reasonably be expected to lie."

composed largely from Q materials are particularly remarkable. These are the sections 11:2-27; 12:22-45 and the Woes Discourse of ch. 23. In formal terms it is notable that towards the end of each section there are words against "this generation" (11:16; 12:39-45; 23:36). In terms of content, each of these sections is an increasingly sharp pronouncement of judgment on Israel. Chapters 11 and 12 end with "this generation," the disobedient Israel of Jesus' time (11:16-24; 12:38-45) being contrasted with the disciple community from Israel (11:25-30; 12:46-50). It is a stark contrast indeed. The rhetorical strategy of the Woes Discourse aims to separate the readers definitively from Israel's evil leaders, the scribes and Pharisees.[36] The prediction of judgment at the end extends the judgment to the whole people (23:34-39). Afterwards — and here Matthew resumes the thread of Mark's narrative — Jesus leaves the temple with his disciples and never speaks to the people of Israel again (24:1-2). So for Matthew the Sayings Source was crucial as a document containing Jesus' intensifying pronouncement of judgment against Israel. This corresponds to Matthew's use of individual sayings from Q, several of which he inserts in other contexts to sharpen their impact against Israel.[37]

Paul Hoffmann — with whom I agree on this — sees the historical site of the Sayings Source at the end of the mission to Israel, at the time when the Q community turns away from Israel.[38] "The redactional rearrangement of the wisdom saying Matt. 23:34 'Therefore I send you prophets, sages and scribes' could be read as the stenogram of the history of the Palestinian Jewish Christian prophet movement and its development into the Matthean community with its scribes (cf. 13:52; 23:8-11)."[39] Matthew has directed only part of Jesus' pronouncement of judgment against Israel, as transmitted in the Sayings Source, "inwards," that is, towards Jesus' own community (in particular, 24:37-51). As for the rest, he has taken Jesus' pronouncement of judgment

---

36. Cf. Luz, *Matthew 18–25* (see note 4), pp. 221f.

37. Schweizer, *Aufnahme* (see note 33) points out (p. 133) that it is no coincidence that Matthew places the Q episode Q 11:14-15 at the end of the miracles cycle of chs. 8-9 (9:32-34), sharpening the ending to focus on Jesus' rejection by the Pharisees. Matthew has excerpted from Q 13 the words of 13:28-29, critical of Israel, and his insertion in 8:11-12 points the whole of his miracles section in chs. 8–9 towards the aim of his story, the judgment with which Israel is threatened. Matthew has kept the sharp Q saying about the blind leading the blind (Q 6:39-40 = 15:14) for his polemical section 15:1-20 and thus connected this section with the Woes Discourse (cf. 23:16-26).

38. "QR" (see note 2), p. 455: "Thus in the history of Palestinian Jewish Christianity QR marks the decisive turning point at which the groups of Jewish Christian followers of Jesus took leave of what had until then been their natural religious association with the Jewish people, and constituted a separate religious group."

39. "QR" (see note 2), p. 454.

against Israel from the Sayings Source and, corresponding to its intention there, has directed it against Israel's leaders and against the people in three sections (11:2-24; 12:22-45; 23:1–24:2) of increasing sharpness.

So is Q a collection of Jesus traditions for the Jesus groups at a time when the mission to Israel had finally failed? Paul Hoffmann offers many good reasons for this situating of the source.[40] And his proposal is confirmed in Matthew's Gospel by Matthew's telling of the Jesus story from the same perspective. He narrates how Jesus and his disciples preached the gospel of the kingdom and healed in Israel; how Jesus' conflict with Israel's leaders intensified; how he withdrew from Israel with his disciples and gathered them in an "assembly" (16:18) in Israel according to the Father's will; and how finally, in Jerusalem, he denounced the leaders and the disobedient people and was put to death in Israel as Son of Man, that is, as the future judge of the world.[41] Matthew tells his Jesus story as an inclusive story, i.e. as the basic story for what his own community has experienced. Matthew's plot is exactly the situation and dilemma of the tradents of the Sayings Source. Following the failure of the mission to Israel and the separation from the synagogues, Matthew is attempting by means of his Gospel to give fresh orientation and a new perspective to his communities living in gentile Syria: the perspective of mission to gentiles. Thus Matthew and Q are probably temporally close; the tradents of Q and Matthew's communities are in historical continuity.[42] This corresponds to the fact that Matthew's version Q-Matt. is relatively close to the basic material of the source and is Jewish Christian in character, as are both Q itself and Matthew's Gospel. This in turn supports Hoffmann's relatively late dating of Q.[43]

---

40. "QR" (see note 2), pp. 450-456.

41. Cf. Ulrich Luz, *The Theology of the Gospel of Matthew,* New Testament Theology (Cambridge: Cambridge University, 1995).

42. Cf. Luz, *Matthew 1–7* (see note 4), pp. 74-76, 83f.

43. "QR" (see note 2), pp. 451-453. Many questions on which we disagree may remain open. For example, I cannot speak as confidently as Hoffmann of a "redaction" of the source, since I do not think Q ever achieved a final shape — and this, in Gospel research, is what would be termed "redaction." We also differ on the question of the relation between Q and Son of Man christology. The fact that the Son of Man sayings in the individual thematic blocks of the source are in key positions and sometimes form the culmination of the arrangement in terms of composition does not in my opinion necessarily imply that Jesus' identification with the Son of Man took place relatively late. It may well be very old and even date back to Jesus himself. This would explain all the urgency of the missionary activity of his disciples in Israel which ended in failure. But we need not discuss that in detail here!

4 Fictionality and Loyalty to Tradition in Matthew's Gospel in the Light of Greek Literature

A belated birthday greeting for Frans Neirynck

1. Introduction

I am concerned here with the narrative fictions in Matthew's Gospel, which contrast strangely with his overall marked loyalty to tradition. I reflect on them in the light of approaches to a theory of fictionality in ancient literature. My aim is to introduce some thoughts on Matthew's understanding of reality and of truth.

1.1. Definition

Fictions may be defined in many different ways. They can be distinguished by text type: a poetic fiction is not the same as a dramatic fiction or a narrative fiction. They can be semantically determined, based on the relation between the signifier and the signified. "A feature of the concept of fictional speech is that it is defined as laying no claim to referentiality."[1] Fictions can be pragmatically determined in communication theory, stating that in the "fictional communication situation (. . .) it is not a given field of reference which is informatively enlarged, but a new field of reference which is itself constituted by the text."[2]

1. Gottfried Gabriel, *Fiktion und Wahrheit. Eine semantische Theorie der Literatur,* Problemata 51 (Stuttgart-Bad Cannstatt: Frommann Holzboog, 1975), p. 20.
2. Aleida Assmann, *Die Legitimität der Fiktion,* Theorie und Geschichte der Literatur und der schönen Künste 55 (Munich: Wilhelm Fink, 1980), p. 11. I find this definition problematic

German original: "Fiktivität und Traditionstreue im Matthäusevangelium im Lichte griechischer Literatur," *ZNW* 84 (1993), pp. 153-177.

An additional problem is that in some periods of cultural history there appears to have been no awareness of fiction. Such awareness seems to depend on a certain awareness of criticism.[3]

1.2. Application to Matthew's Gospel

Our initial starting point is what *we* feel to be "fictional" in Matthew's Gospel today, without assuming that Matthew and his first readers could even have understood our feelings. I shall base my analysis on a definition of narrative fiction[4] as a way of speaking which is non-referential. This facilitates the approach both to the Gospel of Matthew and to the ancient debate on truth, fictions and lies. Matthew writes a story of Jesus, which initially suggests his reference. But we cannot simply describe the parts of his Gospel that are unhistorical in our modern sense as "fiction." Matthew's understanding of reality was not that of a modern historian, and he knew the Jesus story only as it came to him from his sources, primarily the Gospel of Mark and the Sayings Source.[5]

The "non-referential" nature of fiction in Matthew should therefore be understood diachronically. In what ways has he consciously changed what he received in his sources as a report of actual events? I understand "narrative fiction" as an individual story or episode newly created by Matthew beyond his sources or oral community tradition. At the macrotextual level a narrative fiction is a re-arrangement of source materials resulting in a new order of events in Jesus' life. In contrast to novels or dramas, with the Jesus story there is always a basic claim to referentiality. Not a single feature in any of Mat-

---

however, since a new field of reference may also be constituted in the listener by a non-fictional text, for example one which contains completely new information. For this reason I consider it more practicable to take non-referentiality as the starting point for defining the concept of fiction.

3. Cf. below section 3.1.

4. I am not concerned here with "fictionality" in the discourses. This would require a separate analysis.

5. Matthew's structuring of the Jesus story benefits from the considerable agreement between the sequence of events in the Sayings Source and Mark: baptism, temptations, programmatic proclamation (Mark 1:21-22!), healings (Q 7:1-10), Beelzebub dispute, parables (Q 13:18-21), stumbling-block warning (Mark 9:42; Q 17:1-2), Eschatological Discourse. Of the double traditions, only the Mission Discourse is placed quite differently. This time Matthew follows the Sayings Source and places the discourse earlier (cf. Mark 6:6-13). Evidently Matthew does not find it difficult to insert Q in the chronological scheme of the Markan Jesus story. In this respect he sees Q as a "quasi gospel" which can be harmonized with Mark's.

thew's fictional texts suggests that this or that episode has no reference to the story of Jesus. This raises the problem of the truth of such fictions for us. But did this problem already exist for Matthew?

2. Findings in Matthew

2.1. The Starting Point: Matthew as an Author Committed to Tradition

Matthew takes over Mark's Gospel almost in its entirety (without Mark 1:23-28; 4:26-29; 9:49-50; 12:41-44; 14:51-52) He does not change its order from ch. 12:1 onwards. His attachment to Markan phraseology is also striking. What appear to be redactional passages may be composed almost entirely of set phrases of Markan tradition.[6] A considerable proportion of Matthew's redaction vocabulary is inspired by Mark (or also by Q).[7] Matthew does omit many Markan passages from their Markan contexts, but he conspicuously returns to them later in his text.[8] As far as we can judge, he omits little of what he finds in the Sayings Source. Matthew's positioning and construction of the discourses is conservative. Four of the five discourses which he introduces follow a corresponding Markan discourse.[9] For the Sermon on the Mount one can point to Mark 1:21-22 (cf. 3:13). While scarcely altering the sequence of the Sermon on the Plain in Q, Matthew succeeds in combining it with the written antithesis source[10] he has received as well as with some additional material to form a new and splendidly composed whole. Where he inserts the Q blocks as a whole rather than excerpting them, he virtually always retains the order of the Sayings Source (see Q 3:2-17; 4:1-12; 6:20-49; 7:1-10; 9:57–10:16; 11:14-32; 11:39-52; 17:23-37). Matthew's procedure is similarly conservative when he "excerpts" consecutively the Q blocks he has not made use of. This is well exemplified in the Mission Discourse[11] as well as in the Sermon on the Mount and in the Es-

---

6. Cf. e.g. 4:23-25 = Mark 1:21, 28, 32, 34; 3:7-8; 14:34-36 = Mark 6:53-56 + 1:28.

7. Cf. Ulrich Luz, *Matthew 1–7. A Commentary* (Minneapolis: Augsburg Fortress 1989), pp. 73-75. Among the examples inspired by Mark are ἀναχωρέω, πάντα τὰ ἔθνη, μικροί, πληρόω of the Scriptures.

8. Cf. e.g. Ulrich Luz, *Matthew 8–20*, Hermeneia (Minneapolis: Fortress, 2001), pp. 5, 46.

9. The Mission Discourse follows Mark 6:7-13, the Parable Discourse Mark 4:1-34, the Community Discourse Mark 9:33-50, and the two discourses of Matt. 23, 24–25 follow Mark 12:38-40; Mark 13:1-37.

10. Cf. Luz, *Matthew 1–7* (see note 7), p. 214.

11. Q 10:2-12; 12:2-9, 51-53; 14:26-27 appear in the same sequence in Matthew 10.

chatological Discourse.[12] Yet despite all this, Matthew has given new shape to the Jesus story at many points, i.e. he has fictionalized it.

2.2. Doubling of Individual Pericopes

Matthew has doubled two stories from his sources, i.e. Mark 10:46-52 = Matt. 9:27-31; 20:29-34; and Q 11:14-15 = Matt. 9:32-34; 12:22-24.[13] In doing so he must have been aware that he was narrating one single story as two different ones. Because of the Jesus saying in 11:5 he had first to narrate healings of the blind and dumb.[14] It is theologically important to Matthew that what Isaiah prophesied and Jesus quoted has been fulfilled in Jesus' life and is visible also to John's disciples. But for reasons of composition and theology Matthew cannot remove these episodes from their original placements (12:22-24; 20:29-34). In both cases the doubling is part of his new, fictional beginning of the Jesus story in chs. 8–9. Here Matthew takes considerable liberties with tradition.

One may wonder how conscious Matthew was of the doublings he undertook in agreement with his sources. Some texts, such as those concerning carrying one's cross or gaining one's life, or the rejection of signs are doubled by Matthew because he found them both in Mark and in Q. Normally he worked such Q/Mark doublings into a single text, and hence I assume that where he has proceeded differently he has done so deliberately. Clearly these texts are of particular significance for Matthew. Not avoiding a Q/Mark doubling does not indicate bad editing or a poor memory but is evidence of a skilled accentuating technique.

2.3. Newly Created Narratives

Matthew has often created written versions of orally transmitted texts, formulating them in his own language. It is not always easy to differentiate between what is tradition and what Matthew has invented. Generally speaking, we can assume redaction in cases where a story does not stand independently but supplements one handed down in the sources. A further indication of redaction is the close interlocking of a text with the macrotext. As I see it, the

---

12. Q 11:33; 12:57-59; 16:18 occur in Matt. 5; Q 11:9-13; 13:23-24, 25-27 in Matt. 7 and Q 12:39-40, 42-46; 17:23-24 and 26-35 in Matt. 24 in the same order.

13. Examples of redactional doubling in discourses are Q 6:43-45 = Matt. 7:16-18; 12:33-35; Mark 13:9-13 = Matt. 10:17-21; 24:9-14; Q 3:9b = Matt. 3:10b; 7:19.

14. Cf. Luz, *Matthew 8–20* (see note 8), p. 134.

instances in Matt. 1–26 of Matthew inventing stories with no reference to the tradition are relatively few. I assume one of them to be 2:22-23, i.e., the strange "second stage" of the infant Jesus, moving from the "land of Israel" to the "district of Galilee,"[15] and others to be Peter's walking on the water (14:28-31)[16] and the healings summary of 21:14-16. The summary, well anchored in the macrotext, presents for the last time the "other" Israel contrasted with that of the scribes and Pharisees.

The two final chapters of the Gospel appear to have a larger number of additional redaction texts. In the case of Judas' death (27:3-10) I assume the adoption of a legend from oral tradition (cf. Acts 1:15-20). With the second and third witnesses to Jesus' innocence, Pilate's wife (27:19) and Pilate himself washing his hands (27:24-25), there is good reason to regard them as entirely redactional fiction.[17] In terms of composition this last episode forms the climax of Jesus' trial. Matthew has expressed it in biblical language and anchored it firmly within the macrotext. This would mean it is Matthew who has created the scene of Pilate washing his hands and declaring his innocence in biblical words, so that "the whole people" can answer "His blood be on us and on our children!" As a Jewish Christian, Matthew must have realized the absurdity of Pilate the Gentile behaving like a devout Jew. Historically the scene is grotesque, as is the possibly redactional detail of 2:3-4 which has all Jerusalem and its priests and scribes, together with the half-Jewish Herod, frightened at the news of the Messiah's birth. In both these cases the fiction adheres only in a very external sense to what is "possible." The grotesque element is a stylistic device drawing the readers' attention to the end of the Matthean Jesus story, an "impossible" ending in terms of God's salvation history.

The narratives of the guard at the tomb and the bribing of the guard (27:62-66; 28:11-15) are particularly problematic. Matthew has received the widely known rumor that Jesus' body was stolen from the tomb (cf. Justin,

15. It may be assumed that Matthew had access to the cycle of infancy narratives as oral tradition.

16. John 21:7 may indicate that Matt. does have some reference to tradition here. But if so, he has deliberately reworked a tradition that was part of the Easter narrative.

17. Here I disagree with earlier attempts to identify an independent oral tradition behind Matt. 27:24-25 (cf. Martin Dibelius, *Die Formgeschichte des Evangeliums* [Tübingen: J. C. B. Mohr, ³1959], pp. 113f.), as well as with more recent attempts in source criticism to reconstruct an independent Gospel tradition based on the Matthean special traditions with the help of the Gospel of Peter (John Dominic Crossan, *The Cross That Spoke* [San Francisco: HarperCollins, 1988], esp. pp. 95-101, cf. pp. 249-280 on the tomb guard episodes). The most straightforward hypothesis for me is that the Gospel of Peter is of later date than the Synoptic Gospels and presupposes their existence. The productive force of the Old Testament, which Crossan stresses, is to be assumed in all phases of tradition, including the 2nd century.

Dialogue 108) and, in my judgment, the fact that a Roman guard was placed on the tomb.[18] I suggest that Matthew could have been familiar with a community tradition which attempted to refute the rumor of the hoax by reference to the Roman guard. In the *Gospel of Peter* this tradition is expanded considerably. There the guards themselves, led by Petronius, are the actual witnesses of the Resurrection, and the Jewish tradition of the stolen body is no longer a problem. But the role of the Jewish leaders does appear to be Matthean and cannot have been formulated without 12:38, 40, 45.[19] The passage Matt. 28:11-15 also interlocks closely with its context. There are the Jewish leaders influencing the action for their own ends; the second incidence of bribery with ἀργύρια (silver pieces, following 26:15) which runs like a thread through the Matthean Passion narrative; the first naming of Ἰουδαῖοι (Jews) in v. 15, forming a contrast with the πάντα τὰ ἔθνη (all the nations) of v. 19; and the outlook on the present, corresponding to that of v. 20. The part played by the high priests is historically grotesque. They "stage-manage" the (Roman!) guard at the tomb; they seal the stone; the guard reports to them; and once again they reduce Pilate's role to that of a supernumerary not even capable of punishing a sleeping guard. Both passages contain a number of ironic devices unfavorable to the Jewish leaders. They address Pilate, the despised Roman governor, as κύριος (Lord), and he tells them meaningfully to secure the grave ὡς οἴδατε (as you know how)! Their "testimony to the resurrection" relies on witnesses who are to admit they were asleep at the time. And the bribed witnesses behave as they are directed by their "teachers."[20] By means of ironic commentary and close literary interlocking with the macrotext, Matthew the author has strengthened the decisive role of the Jewish leaders. This must be narrative fiction on his part, possibly within an apologetic tradition of the tomb guard, which he has received.[21] As in 27:19, 24-25, Matthew employs fictional devices to present his readers with the de-

---

18. The guard episode in Matt. is clumsily inserted in the Markan narrative. Ἔχετε κουστωδίαν (27:65) takes no account of the fact that Roman soldiers were already present at the crucifixion (Matt. uses the root τηρε-) in 27:36 and 28:8, whereas the Roman Pilate uses the Latinism κουστωδία. The insertion of the guards in 28:4 is similarly awkward. Their fear is referred to, but in v. 5 the angel is concerned only with the *women's* fear, unmentioned up to this point.

19. The Pharisees appear in both. The Son of Man resurrection prophecy of 12:40 is Matthean, as is the reference to the saying on the return of evil spirits to Israel (cf. 12:45). The mention of Gentile witnesses against Israel in vv. 41-42 corresponds to the mission to the Gentiles on which the Matthean community is now embarking.

20. Cf. 1:24; 21:6; 26:19.

21. There is similar irony in 28:4. On the morning of the resurrection the guards fall over ὡς νεκροί. For the Jewish leaders' guards, the day of resurrection brings a sign of death.

finitive separation of the community from the Jews. In this way the narrative is subservient to the theological message.

These are not the only fictions in Matthew's last chapter. To some extent I also include Matt. 28:9-10. The appearance to Mary Magdalene in John 20:14-18 could be a parallel (cf. 20:17 ἀδελφοί μου [my brothers]!), but in this case Matthew has not adopted the content of a traditional apparition narrative. He has constructed the episode as a doubling of his own apparition of the angels in 28:5-8. I regard the appearance to the Twelve on the mountain in Galilee (Matt. 28:16-20) as an entirely Matthean fiction. He has received only the triadic baptismal formula, I suggest, as well as the words of Daniel 7:13-14 LXX already familiar to him and the knowledge attested in Mark 16:7 of an appearance to the disciples in Galilee. The passage 28:16-20 is fully Matthean in its language and embraces numerous motifs and narrative strands of Matthew's Gospel. It forms, as it were, the terminal in which all the lines of the narrative finally come together. If this is so, it means that the decisive legacy of the risen Jesus to the Matthean community, and the decisive command to go to the Gentiles now that the Jews have been revealed as entangled in their unbelief, are in fact Matthean fiction.

True though he is to his tradition, Matthew the Evangelist does not hesitate to introduce new narratives into his Jesus story at decisive points. This occurs mainly at the end, where the aim of God's activity in Jesus becomes apparent. Israel is hopelessly entangled in guilt and unbelief, and God's offer of salvation is to be extended to the Gentiles.

2.4. Observations on the Narrative Thread

From ch. 12 to ch. 28 Matthew basically follows the Markan narrative. He has given new shape to the introductory chapters 1:1–4:22 and to the first main section 4:23–11:30. The reshaping of ch. 8–9 is particularly remarkable. Here Matthew has interwoven miracles from two sections of Mark's Gospel (1:29–2:22; 4:35–5:43), and inserted a miracle found in Q (7:1-10) as well as two variations of his own on other episodes from Mark and Q (Mark 10:46-52; Q 11:14-15). It is incorrect to describe these chapters simply as a "collection" of miracles, placed together because they are all miracles. This overlooks the fact that 9:33-34 clearly formulates a "result" of this first phase in Jesus' story, i.e. the first separation in Israel because of Jesus. It also ignores the significance of the passages which are not miracle narratives, i.e. 8:18-27 and 9:9-17. These passages describe the emergence of the community of disciples in Israel and the first separations, laying the foundations for what is then narrated in chs.

12–16. Matt. 8–9 does not merely bring together a collection of miracle narratives but describes a compact chronological series of events following directly one after another.[22] The episodes occur in quick succession, Matt. 8–9 covering a period of just a few days. The inevitable conclusion to be drawn is that Matthew has destroyed the narrative thread of his Markan source and created a new *chronological* narrative thread, fully aware that it does not agree with the older chronology of Mark's Gospel. What reason did he have for doing this? Did he think he was offering a historically more "correct" chronology? There is no evidence for this, and in fact it is clear from some of the detail in his Gospel that Matthew was not particularly concerned with the external historical course of Jesus' life.[23] Most of the ancient biographies known to us do not narrate the deeds and experiences of their heroes from birth to death in chronological order but provide collections of episodes illustrating various virtues and weaknesses, periods of time etc. Matthew's narrative however creates the perfect illusion of a chronological course of events.

It can thus be said that Matthew, like Mark, has not written a biography but a fictional narrative. They accentuate differently, however. Mark concentrates mainly on the disciples and tells the story of their relationship with Jesus, characterized by experiences of miracles, misunderstanding, confession, misunderstood suffering, flight and reacceptance. For Matthew the relationship between Jesus and Israel is decisive. He tells the story of the healing work of Jesus, son of David and Messiah of his people, in Israel. He tells of how the circle of disciples comes together, of early tensions and conflicts, of the withdrawal of the disciples from Israel, of Jesus' final reckoning with Israel and its leaders in Jerusalem, ending with the final decision in the Passion and Easter narratives which prepares the way of the disciples to the Gentiles. This narrative reflects the story of the Jewish Christian Matthean community after Jesus' death. Unsuccessful in proclaiming Jesus' message to Israel in Palestine, they later (after the Jewish War, and now separated from the synagogues) engaged in mission to the Gentiles in Syria.[24] Matthew is not simply telling a historical Jesus story. He is telling the story of *Jesus* as *foundational* for the history of his own community. He begins this in the opening sections 4:23-25;

---

22. Cf. 8:1a, 5a, 14a, 16a, 18a, 28a; 9:1, 9a, 14 (at dinner!), 18a, 27a, 32a.

23. Matt. fails to notice in 9:2 for instance that he has not yet mentioned the πίστις of the bearers. 12:46 assumes a house that is not introduced until 13:1. In 14:13 Matt. follows the beheading of John the Baptist with the feeding of the five thousand, forgetting that he had introduced John's death in the form of a retrospective (14:1-3). 21:7 fulfils the Scriptures literally, by having Jesus ride on both donkey and colt.

24. Cf. in this volume "Matthew the Evangelist: A Jewish Christian at the Crossroads," pp. 3-17.

8:1–9:35 in which the healing work of Jesus the Messiah among his people is narrated. This, however, is also the point at which the separation from Israel begins.

The separation becomes more marked and overt in chs. 11 and 12. Once again Matthew has "assembled" the course of events in these chapters from various sources. Ch. 11 presents a compact chronological narrative[25] which does not however make much sense as an account of events. After John's disciples have left, Jesus launches into unmotivated scolding of the crowds around him and then proceeds to curse Galilean cities which have never previously been marked out for reproach. Next, there is an abrupt transition to Jesus thanking his heavenly Father for the understanding he has experienced among the νήπιοι (the simple). Readers of vv. 25-30 can at least surmise that they themselves are meant. Once again the historical course of events is found to be implausible and fragmented on the surface of the narrative. We cannot simply say however that in ch. 11 Matthew has loosely coupled the (not yet used) section from Q on John the Baptist with (not yet used) material from the Mission Discourse to form a new sequence of events. That would make ch. 11 something like a supplement. It is much more than that, however. On the macrotextual level, ch. 11 prepares the overall objective of Matthew's Gospel: It summarizes the healing activity of the Messiah in Israel narrated in chs. 8–9 (vv. 2-6) and has Jesus react to Israel's divided reaction as anticipated in ch. 8–9. Jesus addresses himself in a prophetic reproach to the majority in Israel, seeking to rouse them (vv. 7-24). He contrasts them with the minority of the νήπιοι (the simple), i.e. the community (vv. 25-30). The same sequence is repeated in ch. 12. Once again Matthew creates a compact chronology[26] which is fragmented on the narrative surface. The Pharisees come and go as required (vv. 14, 24); the scribes suddenly appear from nowhere (v. 38). These two groups are the villains of the piece, and yet the whole of Israel finds itself suddenly and undeservedly the addressee of Jesus' prophetic reproaches: ἡ γενεὰ αὕτη (this generation, vv. 41-42, 45). Jesus withdraws from his enemies (v. 15a) but is then surrounded by crowds and among his enemies. Once again the scene is not set with care. Although Matthew has created a new chronological sequence from various disparate sources, his interest does not lie in the external clarity of the account. The structure is similar to that of ch. 11. The description of Jesus' healing activity among his people (12:9-21) is followed by polemical reproaches addressed to the Pharisees and scribes (12:22-45). Matthew's main concern is especially apparent at the end. Once again, as

25. 11:2a, 7a, 20 (τότε), 25a (ἐν ἐκείνῳ τῷ καιρῷ).
26. Vv. 9a, 15a, 22 (τότε), 38 (τότε), 46a (ἔτι αὐτοῦ λαλοῦντος).

in ch. 11, the generation heading for destruction (12:38-45; cf. 11:20-24) is contrasted with the community, that is, the true kindred of Jesus, doing the will of the Father (12:46-50; cf. 11:25-30). Both ch. 11 and ch. 12 form a prelude to the separation between Israel and the community with which Matthew then ends his Gospel (28:11-15, 16-20). Jesus' threatening words are addressed to the Israel that seals its own fate by rejecting him. Once again the narrative fiction Matthew has created by means of the sequence of events in ch. 12 can be understood only within the macrotext of the Gospel.

2.5. Summary

Matthew is a tradition-oriented author who resorts to bold fictions when it suits his purpose. These are not mythical fictions but operate on the level of real history. Matthew was well aware of them. He must have realized too that in some cases he verges on the historically grotesque. Many of his fictions serve the plot of his Jesus narrative. I would describe it as the story of Jesus' conflict with Israel, transparent for the post-Easter history of the community. The story ends with Jesus' pronouncement of judgment against Israel and the disciples' turning to the Gentiles.

3. Comparison of Matthean Fictions with Greek Literary Theory[27]

3.1. The Beginnings of Awareness of Fictionality

"Neither in ancient nor in medieval literature does the distinction we so naturally make between fiction and reality exist from the beginning. It is attested relatively late."[28] Wolfgang Rösler has made an interesting study of the discovery of fictionality in Greek literature.[29] He identifies three stages in the discovery of fictionality in Greek culture up to the fifth century. (1) Poets of the early period saw themselves as divinely inspired and thus claimed fundamental truth for their works.[30] The poet is "responsible bearer" and "guaran-

---

27. I am indebted to Philipp Wälchli for his assistance in this section.

28. Hans Robert Jauss, "Zur historischen Genese der Scheidung von Fiktion und Realität," in: Dieter Henrich/Wolfgang Iser, *Funktionen des Fiktiven*, Poetik und Hermeneutik 10 (Munich: Fink, 1983), pp. 423-432, here: p. 423. Translation here: Selle.

29. Wolfgang Rösler, "Die Entdeckung der Fiktionalität in der Antike," *Poetica* 12 (1980), pp. 283-319.

30. Cf. Homer, *Iliad* 1.1; 2.484-487; *Odyssey* 1.1; Hesiod, *Theogony* 36-38; *Erga* 10.

tor of the collective memory,"[31] a "master of truth."[32] (2) Early criticism, such as that of Heraclitus, Xenophanes or Solon, does not in principle call the poets' claim to truth into question, but does so in certain cases. A distinction is to be made between true reverence for the gods and the πλάσματα τῶν προτέρων (fictions of the earlier generations), for example the battles of Titans and giants.[33] The same is true of the early historians, Hecataeus or Herodotus, and even later of Thucydides. In principle they accept Homer as a historical source, even if he is inaccurate in places. At this second stage the poets' claim to truth is still recognized in principle though it may in practice be restricted.[34] (3) The third stage is reached with Aristotle, the first to distinguish in his *Poetics* between various literary genres. In critical contrast to his mentor Plato, Aristotle accords to poetry a truth *sui generis.* Only at this stage is there a critical appreciation of poetic fictionality. This presupposes, according to Rösler's study, that culture has meanwhile become literary. The chiefly oral traditional knowledge of a closed society, in which the poet or speaker is the guarantor for the truth of what is said, has given way to the world of written texts whose reception is in the "private acts of reading"[35] of individual readers. Only now can a real awareness of fictionality develop.

Rösler's comment on the significance of literacy and the related individual act of reading for the development of awareness of fictionality is crucial. The emergence of a literate culture whose texts can be received by individuals and whose truth can no longer be secured by the transmitters of tradition is the precondition, e.g., for Heraclitus contrasting his own knowledge with that of Hesiod, the "teacher of most."[36] The distinction between truth and lie in ancient poetry as we find it in the pre-Socratic critics assumes the existence of written texts open to various interpretations. A literate culture is the precondition for the decline of a closed tradition and interpretative community whose 'mémoire collective' was the poetic texts.

Individual reception of written texts means reception from certain reading perspectives and with various interests. The *historian's* reception is different from that of the poet, the philosopher or the literary critic. The his-

---

31. Rösler, "Entdeckung" (see note 29), 291.

32. Marcel Detienne, *Les Maîtres de vérité dans la Grèce archaïque* (Paris: Maspero, 1967).

33. Xenophanes, Fr B 1 line 22 (Diels/Kranz).

34. According to Rösler, "Entdeckung" (see note 29), 300. However, I find Thucydides 1.21-22 more skeptical toward the ancient poets: they and their exaggerations are sources faute de mieux. For this very reason the scholarly historian Thucydides concerns himself with contemporary history and not with the distant past.

35. Rösler, "Entdeckung" (see note 29), 314.

36. Heraclitus, fragment B57 (Diels/Kranz).

torian doubts the truth of poetry from the perspective of historical reliability, granting the poetic "myth" the ability to "please" but no longer the ability to be σαφής (certain) and to teach ὠφέλιμα (useful things).[37] The *philosopher* criticizes the poet for example from a moral perspective: "Homer and Hesiod have ascribed to the gods all that is worst in humanity: stealing, adultery and betrayal."[38] Since this is inappropriate to truth, Xenophanes reads the poetic texts as "ascriptions" of their human authors Homer or Hesiod. Plato is far more dogmatic, going beyond any moral considerations to criticize the poetic texts ontologically. He sees them, as well as the work of painters and sculptors, as tertiary imitations of secondary human imitations and thus far removed a priori from the truth of ideas.[39] The scholar and *literary theorist* Aristotle however, who regards poetic texts as μίμησις (imitation) of human πράξεις (deeds), no longer has to judge every text in principally the same way. He can differentiate between them, and thus focus on the various forms and functions of fictional texts in society. This is what made Aristotle the father of rhetoric.[40]

This brings to our attention a further factor, beyond the mere existence of literal culture, contributing to the development of an awareness of fiction. It is the awareness of literary genres and thus of various forms and shapes of truth and lies.

We shall now study the understanding of fiction in various genres of Greek literature related to Matthew's Gospel.

3.2. The Understanding of Truth in Historiography

I refer to the "strict," purist type of historian as represented by Thucydides, Polybius and Lucian in his work Πῶς δεῖ ἱστορίαν συγγράφειν (How to write history).[41] This means that many other historians are excluded, such as the novelistic historiographer Ktesias or Xenophon (in the *Cyropaedia*), the dramatic historiography of Phylarch or Duris[42] or the strongly person-oriented historiography of Isocrates' disciple Theopompus, who according to Strabo

37. Thucydides 1.22.
38. Xenophanes, fragment B11 (Diels).
39. Cf. below section 3.3.
40. Cf. below section 3.4.
41. Cf. particularly Gert Avenarius, *Lukians Schrift zur Geschichtsschreibung* (Meisenheim: Hain, 1956).
42. On Ktesias's understanding of truth see Klaus Meister, *Die griechische Geschichtsschreibung* (Stuttgart: Kohlhammer, 1990), p. 64; on Duris, *op. cit.*, pp. 95-99.

(*Geographica* 1.2.35) deliberately wove myths into history. But not all the texts of these historians have been preserved, and not all of them comment clearly on their methodology and their understanding of truth.

For the "strict" historians, above all Thucydides, the antithesis of ἀλήθεια (truth) and μῦθος (myth) is crucial. Even if τὸ μὴ μυθῶδες ἀτερπέστερον φανεῖται (the absence of the fabulous will be less pleasing, Thucydides 1.22.4, trans. Charles Foster Smith, LCL, 1962), the historian must keep to the truth, understood as τῶν δὲ γενομένων τὸ σαφές (the things that have certainly happened, ibid.). The historian does not aim to entertain but to benefit the reader. The benefit arises from the fact that similar events will occur in the future, so that statesmen in particular can learn from history. Polybius sees truth as the proper canon of history, having the function of the eyes for the body. Where truth is lacking, books can no longer be ἱστορία (history, cf. Polybius 12.12.7). He distinguishes between unintentional and intentional distortion of historical truth and is unequivocal in condemning the latter. This condemnation would apply to Matthew and his fictions if he intended to be read as a historian. Polybius' position even leads him to reject the generally accepted principle that a historian may freely create speeches (12.25b). Lucian's position too is a widely held one. He makes a basic distinction between the κανόνες (rules) and ὑποσχέσεις (undertakings) of poetry and those of history.[43] Poetry has the license of μῦθος (myth) and ἐγκώμιον (eulogy) and the accompanying ὑπερβολαί (exaggeration), whereas history is committed to truth alone as its τέλος (goal, cf. Lucian, *Quomodo* 8-9). Lucian compares combining the two genres with the absurd notion of an athlete in female clothing, adorned with jewelry, or with Hercules engaged in women's work at Queen Omphale's court. Τέρπειν (to entertain) cannot and must not be the aim of historiography; Lucian accepts it only as a subsidiary effect. An athlete may be good-looking as well as strong and agile, but this cannot be a requirement.

Truth then, for the historian, is exact agreement between what is reported and what happened. The historian is to pay homage to truth alone (Lucian, *Quomodo* 40). Fictions are to be rejected on principle: either they are μῦθοι, absurdities, "poetry," suitable only as amusement, or they are exaggerations, more suitable as eulogy than as historiography (op. cit., 7). Lucian qualifies everything written by poets, writers and philosophers as τεράστια καὶ

---

43. Cf. also Diodorus, *Bibliotheca* 1.2.7 (poetry is more pleasing than useful; history is useful in providing good examples); Cicero, *De Legibus* 1.5 *(in illa [sc. historia] ad veritatem quaeque referantur, in hoc [sc. poemate] ad delectationem pleraque)*; Polybius, *Histories* 2.56.11 (tragedy and history have opposite aims; decisive for tragedy is τὸ πιθανόν, κἂν ᾖ ψεῦδος, διὰ τὴν ἀπάτην [illusion] τῶν θεωμένων, ἐν δὲ τούτοις [sc. of historiography], τἀληθὲς διὰ τὴν ὠφέλειαν τῶν φιλομαθούντων).

μυθώδη (monstrosities and legends), as ψεύσματα (lies). In his Ἀληθῆ διηγήματα (True accounts) he presents for the purpose of amusement and reflection πιθανῶς τε καὶ ἐναλήθως (plausible and in accordance with the truth! cf. *Verae Historiae*).

3.3. The Myths of the Ancient Poets

A negative assessment of mythical poetic fictions can be traced as far back as the 5th century. The reasons for it are various. In Xenophanes' criticism of Homer, ethical reasons are paramount: Homer's gods cannot be models.[44] Gorgias the sophist has ethical objections to the tragedians, arguing that by means of μῦθοι and πάθη (passions) tragedies lead to illusion (ἀπάτη).[45] In the second sophistic Lucian's polemical tract Φιλοψευδὴς ἢ ἀπιστῶν *(The Lover of Lies or The Unbeliever)* is a particularly radical example of sophistic enlightenment. The enlightened Tychiades — and Lucian himself — can allow the "Lovers of Lies" and their literary ancestors Homer, Herodotus and Ktesias only the right of opportunism or literary interests.[46] Within Hellenism, only allegorical interpretation rescued Homer from damnation and made him *the* classical author read at school.

In the tenth book of his *Republic,* Plato bans the poets for ontological reasons. The works of poets and artists are "imitations of imitations, the third and lowest level of truth" (*Republic* 10 = 597e, 598e-599a). Their works weaken reason and strengthen the emotions (op. cit., 605ab). Οὐκοῦν τιθῶμεν ἀπὸ Ὁμήρου ἀρξαμένους πάντας τοὺς ποιητικοὺς μιμητὰς εἰδώλων ἀρετῆς εἶναι καὶ τῶν ἄλλων περὶ ὧν ποιοῦσιν, τῆς δὲ ἀληθείας οὐχ ἅπτεσθαι (shall we then lay it down that all the poetic tribe, beginning with Homer, are imitators of images of excellence and of the other things that they create and do not lay hold to truth).[47] Here poetry as μίμησις is already "fiction" and thus removed from truth.

Plutarch's small piece Πῶς δεῖ τὸν νέον ποιημάτων ἀκούειν (How a young man has to listen to poetry) is in the Platonic tradition. Only with great reservations can Plutarch accept the inevitable use of the poets in education (Homer was after all *the* school author of the time!). He does not reject poetry as radically as Plato, but he sees it as imperfect philosophy. Poetry re-

---

44. Cf. note 33.

45. Plutarch, *Moralia* 348C.

46. Patriotic benefits, for example, or touristic interest such as that of the Cretes who show Zeus' grave (Lucian, *Philopseudes* 3), or literary interest in τερπνόν (op. cit., 4).

47. Plato, *Republic* 10.600e, tr. Paul Shorey (LCL, 1956).

ceives its λόγοι (words, contents) from philosophy but mixes it with myths. This makes it easy and pleasant to read, but mingled with untrue and immoral matter (*Moralia* 2.15F). Μυθοποίημα (the narration of fables) καὶ πλάσμα (fiction) occur πρὸς ἡδονὴν ἢ ἔκπληξιν (for the pleasure or astonishment) of the listeners but are lower forms of truth (op. cit., 17A). At best, poetry can be a pleasant propaedeutic to philosophy. It has didactic worth, gives enjoyment and is even suitable for women (op. cit., 16F). On the other hand, the poetic fictions mean that poetry always contains an element of ἀπάτη,[48] detracting from philosophical truth.

Our main interest here is in the position of those who defend the truth of myths. In Lucian there is a clear religious interest behind the position of these criticized and caricatured "philosophers" (*Philopseudes* 10). Σύ μοι δοκεῖς, says the "devout" Stoic Deinomachos, οὐδὲ θεοὺς εἶναι πιστεύειν εἴ γε μὴ οἴει τὰς ἰάσεις οἷόν τε εἶναι ὑπὸ ἱερῶν ὀνομάτων γίγνεσθαι ("it seems to me, that when you talk like that you do not believe in the gods, since you do not think that cures can be effected through holy names," trans. Austin Morris Harmon, LCL, 1960). Tychiades is an "unbeliever" whose opponents defend the truth of their "myths" partly through eye-witness evidence, partly with reference to witnesses. The "superstitious" Pythagorean Arignotos, on whom Tychiades first sets his hopes, is both famous for his wisdom and regarded as ἱερός (holy, sacred). He narrates his own experience in order to authenticate his "lies." This reveals the "post-enlightenment" character of a religiosity which can no longer expect society to accept its claim to truth without question but must adopt apologetic devices. These devices are borrowed from the discipline whose claim to "truth" was undisputed at that time, i.e. historiography.[49] The πίστις (faith) required by the devout for their myths is not blind belief but the belief that what happened is what everyone can attest to (op. cit., 30). The enlightened Tychiades protests that if he had seen it himself, καὶ ἐπίστευον ἂν δηλαδὴ ὥσπερ ὑμεῖς (I would believe in them, just as you do, loc. cit.)

There are other similar cases. Philostratus uses witnesses such as Damis to prove — against Moiragenes — that his hero Apollonius is not a sorcerer and that his deeds are based on actual events. This is reminiscent of the

---

48. 15CD, following Gorgias, see note 45.

49. In Polybius' view a good historian is one who does not rely on secondary literature but on eyewitnesses (should he not be one himself) (*Histories* 12.28a). Seeing for himself is said to be the most difficult and significant task for the historian, whereas assembling secondary literature is the least difficult and least significant. According to op. cit. 12.25e, the scholar who merely studies the literature is a fool. This would even apply then to Luke and certainly to Matthew, since working with sources does not make them historians.

"Lovers of Lies." Ancient novel writers such as Chariton construct their own "credibility" by introducing historical characters or literary devices borrowed from historiography. The examples given indicate the degree to which historiography determined the understanding of truth in the Hellenistic period. There is an obvious analogy with many current polemical debates on the truth of biblical texts defined as the question of the factuality of what is recounted in them.

3.4. The Discovery of the Difference between μῦθος (Fable) and πλάσμα (Fiction)

There is a reassessment of poetic fiction and the relation between poetry and history in Aristotle's *Poetics*. Unlike history, poetry is not concerned with what has actually happened but with what might happen according to the rules of probability and necessity (οὐ οἷα τὰ γενόμενα . . . ἀλλ᾽ οἷα ἂν γένοιτο, καὶ τὰ δυνατὰ κατὰ τὸ εἰκὸς ἢ τὸ ἀναγκαῖον). In order to be credible, the fable (μῦθος) of a drama, tragedy, or comedy must be probable. Only what is probable is also credible. It is precisely because poetry is concerned with what might happen that Aristotle finds it more philosophical than history, which treats of particular facts (τὰ καθ᾽ ἕκαστον). Poetry on the other hand can be applied by listeners or readers to their own lives and is thus universal. Aristotle saw in the transference of the tragic fable to the life of the listener a cleansing from the παθήματα (emotions), ἔλεος (compassion), and φόβος (fear, cf. *Poetica* 6 = 1449b). He introduces not only a new assessment of poetry vis-à-vis Plato but also a new perspective on fiction.

Following Aristotle, the *rhetorical tradition* now recognized two distinct types of fiction, the probable or possible (πλάσμα) and the impossible (μῦθος). Cicero (*De Inventione* 1.27) appears to me to be the first to make this distinction. He differentiates three types of *narratio: fabula* (= τὸ μυθικόν, τὸ ψευδές), *argumentum* (= τὸ πλασματικόν, τὸ δραματικόν, τὸ ὡς ἀληθές) and *historia* (= τὸ ἱστορικόν, τὸ ἀληθές). "History" is a narration of what has actually happened in the past. An *argumentum est ficta res, quae tamen fieri potuit*. Like others,[50] Cicero points to comedy[51] as an example. The real "fa-

---

50. Sextus Empiricus, *Against Dogmatists* 252 (after Richard Reitzenstein, *Hellenistische Wundererzählungen* [Darmstadt: Wissenschaftliche Buchgesellschaft, ²1963], p. 90); *Against Mathematicians* 1.252f. or 263; Quintilian, *Institutio Oratoria* 2.4.2; *Auctor ad Herennium* 1.12f.

51. This is a secondary classification of comedy, of course. Aristophanes' "Frogs" or "Peace" with their journeys into the underworld or the heavens indicate that comedies may well include "mythical" elements.

ble" is that *in qua nec verae, nec verisimiles res continentur.* This is the domain of the poets. Tragedy may be classified as mythical or possible.[52]

Although the rhetorical texts do not of course evaluate the different types of narrative — true, probable and fictional — they classify them as different literary genres. Thus awareness of fictionality and differentiation of types of fiction are connected with the knowledge that there are various distinct literary genres.[53]

3.5. Fictionality in the Novels

Ancient literary theorists and rhetoricians are concerned with historiography, tragedy, comedy and poetry. They have little to say about the genres most closely related to the Gospels, which are biography and novel. Unfortunately, this leaves us high and dry in the very environment of the Gospels.

There is of course a basic difference between the novels and the Gospels. The novels are entirely fictional *sui generis,* while Matthew's Gospel contains fictions alongside and within historical traditions. Historical reminiscences in the novels, including historical characters, are part of the fiction. The canonical Gospels and the contemporaneous novels appear to have very little in common, so that in terms of literary history it is rather the apocryphal stories of the apostles which first suggest a comparison.

I should like to draw attention however to a complex and highly controversial issue in novel research, and that is the religious interpretation of the novels. We have established that many of Matthew's fictions operate on a second level, that of the present experiences of his readers. The reality here lies in the separation from the Jews, mission to the Gentiles or the "Galilee of the Gentiles." We have seen that Matthew's story is transparent for the story of the post-Easter Matthean community.[54] A possible interpretation of the ancient novels is to read them similarly as ambiguous, symbolic stories. This

---

52. The *Auctor ad Herennium* 1.12f. and Quintilian, *Institutio Oratoria* 2.4.2 classify tragedy as poetry. By contrast Aristotle in *Poetics* 9 = 1451b classifies tragedy with comedy as a story of the probable, similar to Hermogenes, *Progymnasmata* 2 (17) [= Rabe 4].

53. Unlike comedy, tragedy and mime (Sextus Empiricus, *Against Dogmatists* 252 = Reitzenstein 90), neither biography nor novel is considered by the rhetoricians. Carl Werner Müller ("Chariton von Aphrodisias und die Theorie des Romans in der Antike," *Antike und Abendland* 22 (1976), pp. 115-136) rightly points out that the classification of the novel as δρᾶμα, which was significant in earlier novel theory (Rohde, Reitzenstein, Kerényi), goes back only to Byzantine authors.

54. Cf. pp. 5-7, 14-17 above.

religious interpretation has been undertaken by Kerényi and by Merkel-bach,[55] who see the majority of ancient novels as encoded mystery *logoi* on human suffering and experiences leading to final mystical unification with the deity. The most significant deity for the novels is Isis,[56] but Helios, Mithras and Dionysus also play their part.[57] This reading of the novels sees their fictions as largely determined by the everyday and cultic experiences of the mystics, just as some stories in the Gospels reflect everyday and liturgical experiences of the community.[58] Naturally this thesis cannot be extended to all novelists in the same fashion. Merkelbach takes Chariton of Aphrodisias to be the main exception.

This interpretation of the novels has not gained much acceptance.[59] Current research tends to see the novel as an original child of the epic, born out of the circumstances of a depoliticized cosmopolitan and bourgeois Hellenistic world.[60] The novel is interpreted predominantly in terms of social history and psychology. It is read as a "fictional ideal world," a kind of "dream factory"[61] for educated urban citizens in a depoliticized, cosmopolitan Greco-Roman world.[62] But for me the question remains whether this fictional ideal world may not be religious in character. The advance of oriental

---

55. Karl Kerényi, *Die griechisch-orientalische Romanliteratur in religionsgeschichtlicher Beleuchtung* (repr.: Darmstadt: Wissenschaftliche Buchgesellschaft, 1973, original: 1927); Reinhold Merkelbach, *Roman und Mysterium in der Antike* (Munich: Beck, 1962); Merkelbach, *Die Hirten des Dionysos. Die Dionysos-Mysterien der römischen Kaiserzeit und der bukolische Roman des Longos* (Stuttgart: Teubner, 1988).

56. In Apuleius, Aristides, Xenophon of Ephesus, Achilleus Tatius.

57. Helios: in Heliodorus; Mithras: in Iamblichus; Dionysos: in Longos.

58. Classic examples of this are the stilling of the storm (experience of Christ's presence and help in the storms of life) and the feeding of the five thousand (Lord's Supper!).

59. Ben Edwin Perry, *The Ancient Romances* (Berkeley/Los Angeles: University of California, 1967), p. 336, declares tersely: "This is all nonsense to me." Cf. also Isolde Stark, "Religiöse Elemente im antiken Roman," in: Heinrich Kuch (ed.), *Der antike Roman* (Berlin: Akademie-verlag, 1989), pp. 135-149; Graham Anderson, *Ancient Fiction* (London: Croom Helm, 1984), pp. 75-87; Tomas Hägg, *The Novel in Antiquity* (Oxford: Basil Blackwell, 1983), pp. 101-104.

60. Cf. partic. the important essay by Carl Werner Müller, "Chariton" (see note 53). Müller draws particular attention to the influence of the (frequently cited) *Odyssey* on Chariton (126ff.).

61. Niklas Holzberg, *The Ancient Novel. An Introduction* (London: Routledge, 1994), pp. 42, 30.

62. On social history aspects of the ancient novel cf. Heinrich Kuch, "Die Herausbildung des Romans als Literaturgattung," in: Kuch, *Roman* (see note 59), pp. 32-34; Klaus Berger, "Hellenistische Gattungen im Neuen Testament," in: *ANRW* II.25.2 (Berlin: De Gruyter, 1984), pp. 1031-1432, esp. p. 1266, and above all Kurt Treu, "Der antike Roman und sein Publikum," in: Kuch, *Roman*, pp. 178-197.

religions such as the Isis cult as well as Christianity in the late Hellenistic period, and the increasingly defensive position in which science and sophistic
enlightenment found themselves give rise to this question. Without wanting
to interpret the Hellenistic novel entirely in religious terms, I suggest that
Kerényi and Merkelbach have made two important points:

First, they draw attention to the literary myths and symbolic stories
open to religious readings. An example for me is Apuleius's novella of Amor
and Psyche, inserted in the middle of his novel (4.28–6.25). This is not a min-
iature novel, as I see it, but a literary myth. In the terminology of rhetoric it is
a μῦθος and not a πλάσμα. The name of the protagonist, Ψυχή (Soul), calls for
a symbolic interpretation. The hero is a god, and the wedding chamber is in
paradise.[63] Similarly symbolic narratives, mythical in parts, are that of *Joseph
and Aseneth*,[64] *Vita Adae* 1-17, and the "Hymn of the Pearl" in the *Acts of
Thomas*. In all three cases the story is transparent for the destiny of an individual. Although we cannot establish direct analogies with Matthew's
redactional fictions, these examples demonstrate that a symbolic reading of
stories such as the temptations of Jesus, the stilling of the storm or the healing
of the blind would have suggested itself to readers of the time.

Second, some of the ancient novels, in my judgment those of the later
period especially, are religious in their overall character. I can read Apuleius's
Metamorphoses, for example, only as a propaganda novel for Isis. Otherwise
his 11th book with its initiation into the mysteries of the cult could only be read
as an appendix and not as the culmination of and possibly the key to the whole
work. So I like to see the entertaining novel frame, with Lucius as a donkey, as a
symbolic representation of the fetters in which those not initiated in the Isis
religion are forced to live. I consider Longos's *Daphnis and Chloe* to have a religious background too. This novel, rich in oracles and dreams, is set on the Di-
onysian island of Lesbos and focuses on the mythical shepherd Daphnis,[65] son
of Dionysophanes (!).[66] There is also, as Merkelbach demonstrates, an undeniable religious element in the story of Chariklea. Chariklea is descended from

63. I wonder however whether Merkelbach's interpretation in terms of Isis is a correct
one (*Roman*, see note 55, pp. 8-53). Venus, whom he identifies as Isis, is a hostile goddess in the
novella. However, his particular thesis is not even required for a symbolic interpretation. The
reference to the Platonic myth about the souls (*Phaidros* 24-29) alone indicates that such a reading suggested itself.

64. The usual designation of Joseph and Aseneth as a "novel" (cf. Christoph Burchard,
Joseph und Aseneth, JSHRZ II.4 [Berlin: De Gruyter, 1983], esp. p. 591) is used only for lack of a
better expression.

65. On the traditional link between Daphnis and Dionysos cf. Virgil, *Eclogue* 5.

66. Cf. Merkelbach, *Hirten* (see note 55).

Helios, finds herself in Greece[67] and then makes a circuitous journey from Delphi (!) back to her home in Ethiopia. The narrator of the novel is Heliodorus, descendant of Helios, and he comes from Emesa in Syria, the city of the sun-god. I suggest that both these novels have a basic religious dimension, though I do not see them as religious mystery stories dressed up as novels. It is quite possible however that readers of a later period, familiar with mystery religions and allegorical interpretations of Homer, did in fact interpret novels in general in symbolic and religious terms.[68]

But this does not help to make Matthew's fictions comprehensible overall. On the contrary. His fictions are not concerned to interpret a superficial story psychologically or spiritually in terms of a religious experience. Apuleius's novel may be understood as a story of the liberation of humanity from its earthly fetters by means of encounter with the deity. Not so the Matthean story. Rather, the analogies we have considered provide evidence of the religious environment in which the Gospel of Matthew was received.

3.6. Fictions in Biographies

We still do not know to what extent and in what way biography was defined as a genre. Alfred Dihle bases his genre categorization on Plutarch and sees biography primarily as an ethical genre in the Aristotelian sense. Thus its task is the δήλωσις ἀρετῆς ἢ κακίας (the manifestation of virtue or vice, trans. Bernadette Perrin, LCL, 1958) of a hero.[69] I find it more helpful to start from Polybius' observations on his biography of Philopoimen. In 10.21 he speaks of a work in three books that he had written earlier.[70] He had treated in it the person of Philopoimen, his parents, his education and a selection of his greatest deeds. The work served as a eulogy to Philopoimen and thus restricted itself to recounting his most significant deeds as well as affirming and celebrat-

---

67. According to Merkelbach, *Roman* (see note 55), p. 293, Greece symbolizes the earthly world, as does Egypt in the Hymn of the Pearl.

68. Cf. Hägg, *Novel* (see note 59), p. 103.

69. Cf. Albrecht Dihle, *Studien zur griechischen Biographie,* AAWG.PH III.37 (Göttingen: Vandenhoeck und Ruprecht, 1970), partic. pp. 57-88. The quotation is from Plutarch, *Alexander* 1. Plutarch, writing relatively late, does not seem to me a typical ancient biographer. His biographies, aiming at the synkrisis of a Greek and a Roman, required distance and neutrality and the avoidance of one-sided eulogy. His tendency towards neutrality in apportioning praise and blame connects Plutarch with historiography, while his choice of material distinguishes him from it.

70. The keyword βίος is not used in 10.21, however. Polybius speaks only of λόγος and σύνταξις.

ing him (μετ' αὐξήσεως τῶν πράξεων ἀπολογισμόν, a somewhat exaggerated defense of his achievements, trans. William Roger Paton, LCL, 1960). History on the other hand must, according to Polybius, keep to the truth and be just in its apportioning of praise and blame. As well as Polybius' there are numerous other biographies with encomiastic tendencies. Varied examples are Philo's Περὶ τοῦ βίου Μωϋσέως *(The life of Moses)*, Philostratus's Τὰ ἐς τὸν Τυανέα Ἀπολλώνιον *(Apollonios of Tyana)*, Lucian's Δημωνάκτος βίος *(The Life of Demonax)* and Nicholas of Damascus's Βίος Καίσαρος *(The Life of Caesar)*. A comparison with Quintilian's description of the *encomium* of a human being[71] shows clear parallels. The encomium too is divided into periods and begins with origins and parentage and possibly oracles and omens. The deeds of the hero *may* be presented chronologically, first indicating the talents and learning process, then the whole series of deeds and speeches. Alternatively, the deeds may be presented systematically, with the praise accorded *in species virtutum* (3.7.15).[72] Thus I find the roots of the biographical genre in encomiastic writings. Later, in Plutarch's comparative biography and especially in the Roman environment (with Cornelius Nepos and Suetonius) it developed in the direction of historiography.[73] On the basis of Quintilian we could define a biography as a eulogy on a deceased person which includes the end of the person's life.

This perspective suggests a certain external resemblance between biography and the Gospels.[74] The biographies of philosophers in particular resemble the Gospels in that they are especially important for the schools of philosophy they give rise to.[75] In some of these biographies there are external

71. *Institutio Oratoria* 3.7, 10-18.

72. This is also true of encomiastic biographies. Apollonius of Tyana follows a chronological outline; Philo's *Vita Mosis* has a chronological outline in the first book, followed by a *species virtutum* sequence in the second. Each book ends with the death of Moses. Lucian's *Demonax* includes description of the hero's descent and education, some basic characteristics and the end of his life. No structural principle is apparent.

73. Cf. Albrecht Dihle, *Die Entstehung der historischen Biographie*, SHAW.PG (Heidelberg: Winter, 1987).

74. Philip L. Schuler, *A Genre for the Gospels* (Philadelphia: Fortress, 1982), has undertaken this for the Gospel of Matthew. Albrecht Dihle ("Die Evangelien und die griechische Biographie," in: Peter Stuhlmacher [ed.], *Das Evangelium und die Evangelien*, WUNT I.28 [Tübingen: J. C. B. Mohr, 1983], pp. 383-411), relying primarily on Plutarch's understanding of biography, sees the distance between the Gospels and Greek biography as relatively great.

75. Cf. e.g. Porphyrius' biography of Plotinus or the biographies of Diogenes Laertios. On the sociological location of biographies of philosophers as propaganda writings and "founding legends" cf. also C. H. Talbert, "Biographies of Philosophers and Rulers as Instruments of Religious Propaganda in Mediterranean Antiquity," in: *ANRW* II.16.2 (Berlin: De Gruyter, 1978), pp. 1625-1647. There was not however, as the subtitle of a superficial book by Mo-

analogies to the fictions we have found in Matthew's Gospel. Comparison is complicated however by the fact that our knowledge of their sources is far more limited than with Matthew.

In the case of Philostratus our assessment of the *chronological fictions* depends of course on the unresolved issue of the account of Damis. Evidently Philostratus intends to present a basically chronological biography of Apollonius, but in parts the positioning of anecdotal material in a geographical and chronological frame is far less stringent than in Matthew (see, e.g., 4.1-46; 6.35-43). Bearing in mind that the genesis of the Apollonius biography was probably similar to that of the Gospels, it is striking that Philostratus does not appear to share Matthew's concern for a *continuous* chronological and geographical course. The first book of Philo's life of Moses adheres overall to the sequence of events presented in the biblical source. For systematic reasons[76] Philo reorders the plagues in Egypt and creates a new chronological sequence (1.96-146). One can also see the jump from Exodus 17 to Numbers 13 (between 219 and 220) as a chronological fiction created in the interest of systematic presentation. The main material omitted here — Moses' activity as law-giver, priest and prophet — is presented in book two from a systematic perspective. Deliberate or inadvertent chronological errors and fictions arising from the systematic presentation are found elsewhere too in biographies, for example in Suetonius[77] and Plutarch.[78]

Within the framework of ancient biography technique, Matthew's treatment of the chronologies he has received from his sources is, then, by no means exceptional. His motives are however unusual. In reordering the chronology he is not concerned to subordinate the course of events to a higher

---

ses Hadas/Morton Smith suggests, a particular type of "spiritual biography" (*Heroes and Gods. Spiritual Biographies in Antiquity* [London: Routledge, 1965]). Elsewhere the authors refer to this type as "aretalogy." Much mischief has been caused by the use of "aretalogy" as a genre designation, and I can only refer readers to Klaus Berger's commendable and considered treatment of this in "Hellenistische Gattungen" (see note 62), partic. p. 1228.

76. He describes first the plagues caused by Aaron, then those caused by Moses, then those caused by both, ending with plagues occurring without human intervention.

77. Cf. Helmut Gugel, *Studien zur biographischen Technik Suetons*, WStBeih 7 (Vienna: Böhlau, 1977); Dieter Flach, *Einführung in die römische Geschichtsschreibung* (Darmstadt: Wissenschaftliche Buchgesellschaft, 1985), pp. 180-184. Inaccurate chronologies may occur as a result of systematic interests, or be due to ignorance or poor research. With Tiberius for instance the purpose is to ascribe the deeds of the emperor clearly to his good early period or his bad later one.

78. On the chronological fictions in Plutarch's *Pericles*, cf. Adolf von Weizsäcker, *Untersuchungen über Plutarchs biographische Technik*, Problemata 2 (Berlin: Weidmann, 1931), partic. pp. 11-18, 32, 46f., 57.

systematic perspective. His concern is to create a new historical course of events, corresponding to the historical experiences of his own community. In this respect Matthew's Gospel is not a biography but a "work of history" of a very distinctive nature.

Even less can be said of the fictional accounts of individual episodes. From its very beginnings in Socratic tradition and in Xenophon,[79] biography has been free to use fiction. While with Philostratus anything seems possible, as it were, Philo is overall more cautious. The wealth of material for comparison with Matthew in this matter renders a comparison very difficult.

At this point I attempt a *conclusion*. Matthean fictions and fictions in biographies do indeed have points in common. But the purpose of Matthew's fictions is different from that of fictions in the ancient biographies. And there is no indication in Matthew — unlike in Philo — that he was familiar with the forms and rules of the biographical genre or well-read in ancient biographies.[80] So if we speak of Matthew's Gospel as a biography we are giving him a cap that does not fit, even though it would have been the most appropriate one in the eyes of many readers at that time.[81]

4. Consequences for Matthew

4.1. Although we find deliberate use of fiction in Matthew, he evidently has *no awareness of the problem of fictionality*. Why is this? In view of the development of awareness of fictions in the Greek history of ideas, one could speculate that as a book Matthew's Gospel is the "identity-forming work of the collective memory" of a particular social group, i.e. the Matthean com-

---

79. Cf. Arnaldo Momigliano, *The Development of Greek Biography* (Cambridge, MA: Harvard University, 1971), pp. 52-56, on the origins of biography in Xenophon. Momigliano says of Xenophon's *Memorabilia* and the *Cyropaedia:* "True biography was preceded or at least inspiringly accompanied by fiction" (p. 56).

80. This contrasts with well-read Philostratus, whose figure of Apollonius is intended, as Graham Anderson aptly puts it in *Philostratus, Biography and Belles Lettres in the Third Century* A.D. (London: Croom Helm, 1986), p. 235, to outdo the best ancient θεῖοι: "Apollonius performs the labours of Hercules, the voyages of Odysseus, the conquests of Alexander, the trial of Socrates and the transmigrations of Pythagoras, all in one."

81. The distance between Matthew's Gospel and biography is most evident where its greatest proximity has often been suggested, that is, in the prologue. The βίβλος γενέσεως and the biographical material on descent and parentage appear to belong together, yet Matthew does not include elements important to a biography. There is no mention of education and teachers presenting the characteristics and abilities of the hero: Reports on Jesus' formative years are what interest biographers most, yet Matthew provides none (cf. Luke 2:41-52!).

munity.[82] It is embedded in the living oral tradition of the community. It is not part of a literary culture in which it is read by individuals, and its author probably does not have readers from elsewhere in mind. Given this situation, we can certainly expect changes in the tradition and hence some fictions, but we cannot expect a self-critical awareness of fictionality on the part of the author or a corresponding critical awareness on the part of readers. Evidently a living, community-bearing tradition to which one owes loyalty but which can for this very reason "go with the times" is still natural for Matthew.

In this respect Luke is more advanced. The threat to the community through teachers who distort the truth is reality for him (Acts 20:29-30), as is the fact that educated readers of his work will make literary comparisons. This is why he has conscious recourse to forms of historiography which help him to secure and defend his traditions. It is difficult to say however whether this means that Luke had an awareness of fictionality, and if so, what the nature of his awareness was.

4.2. Matthew has *no developed awareness of genre distinctions.* He knows Mark's history of Jesus but is unlikely to have perceived it as representing a genre. Whereas Luke displays his familiarity with Hellenistic literature for instance in his prologues,[83] Matthew gives no evidence of knowing Hellenistic historiography, tragedies, biographies or novels.[84] Our survey of Greek literature has indicated that awareness of fictionality is closely linked with awareness of genre distinctions, so this too would lead us to expect such lack of awareness in Matthew.

4.2.1. Within the context of serious ancient historiography, Matthew's fictions are inexplicable and unacceptable. Given that person-oriented history is increasingly significant in Hellenism after Theopompus and Kallisthenes, Luke's work does approach to ancient historic monography. Matthew's Gospel is miles away from it. This is especially visible in an area Matthew shares, in formal terms, with the historiographers: that of the discourses. The five great discourses of Matthew's Gospel are not formulated by the Evangelist "according to his own judgment to serve the given pur-

---

82. Rösler, "Entdeckung" (see note 29), p. 291.

83. Luke is unfamiliar however with the distinction in Aristotle and the rhetoricians between μῦθος, πλάσμα and ἱστορία. It is not found anywhere in the NT. Philo is familiar with the opposition between μῦθος and truth but makes parallel use of μῦθος and πλάσμα//πλάσσω (Gustav Stählin, "μῦθος," *ThWNT*, 1942, pp. 769-803, here: p. 792 note 139).

84. Matthew's prologue (Matt. 1–2) does develop Mark's story in the direction of a heroic vita; cf. Berger, "Hellenistische Gattungen" (see note 62), p. 1245. It does not give the impression however that Matthew is consciously adopting a literary model.

pose,"[85] as was in principle permitted to historians. His discourses are compilations of tradition, that is, collections of Jesus sayings arranged according to theme. Matthew's fictional activity focuses on the arrangement of the material. The Matthean fictions fail to meet a further requirement of ancient historians' discourses. They do not relate to the situation of the time, explaining its possibilities and behavior. Matthew's fictions are addressed "out of the window" to his readers in the present, leaving the past behind.

In this respect the discourses resemble those of Moses in Deuteronomy[86] and not those of Thucydides. This accords with the fact that Matthew's only allusions to literary models point to the Old Testament. The title βίβλος γενέσεως Ἰησοῦ Χριστοῦ . . . υἱοῦ Ἀβραάμ κτλ. ("The book of the generation of Jesus Christ, son of Abraham," etc.), which the Evangelist is presumed in 1:1 to have given to his book, is reminiscent of Gen. 2:4; 5:1, suggesting that Matthew intends his story of Jesus to be read as an analogy to the foundational biblical history of Israel. The opening genealogy is reminiscent of Chronicles. His basic conception of Jesus as "Immanuel," the specific form of what is narrated in the Old Testament as the presence of God "with us" (cf. 1:23), indicates that Matthew is seeking both to repeat and surpass Old Testament history of God.

4.3. Correspondingly, Matthew does not appear to have an *explicated understanding of truth*. When is his Jesus tradition true? Matthew gives no indication of his thinking on this. We can be certain that he does not regard his Jesus tradition as true only in the sense of the Greek historians, i.e. if the account is in agreement with the facts and refrains from any poetic exaggeration and fantasies. Matthew is far removed from the Greek distinctions between "history," "fiction" and "myth." For him, all these are indistinguishably part of the living Jesus tradition. As I see it, the truth of both mythical and non-mythical fictions in Matthew lies in their incorporating and interpreting the experiences of his implied readers with Christ. This is my modern attempt at interpretation, however, and is not offered by Matthew himself. We can certainly establish that the truth of Jesus traditions does not depend on them containing no "mythical" elements in the sophistic sense.[87] Although Matthew himself creates hardly any "mythical" fictions, they are part of his Jesus story, the story of "*God* with us." The Evangelist has no need to defend himself in this respect. He shows no interest in increasing the credibility of

---

85. Thucydides, *History* 1.22 (tr. here: Selle).

86. See the significant considerations of this by Hubert Frankemölle, *Jahwebund und Kirche*, NTA.NF 10 (Münster: Aschendorff, 1973), pp. 339-342.

87. 1:25–2:23; 3:13-17; 4:1-11; 14:22-33; 17:1-8; 27:52-53; 28:1-10, 16-20 would be mythical in ancient understanding.

disputable and possibly "fabricated" traditions — in particular the miracles — by means of devices such as reference to witnesses.[88] Matthew does create "fictions" in the Greek sense of the term, but he does not reflect on their problematic aspects. The purpose of his fictions is to identify his Jesus story with the present situation of the community now separated from Israel, to serve the "collective memory." There is neither a conscious reflection on the understanding of truth in his Gospel, nor any awareness of fictionality. Thus we cannot speak of "split understanding of truth" in Matthew. This is only the case from an external perspective such as that of the conception of truth in Greek historiography or Greek myth criticism.

4.4. Following our survey of Greek literature, we may well ask whether there are other texts which could throw more light on the Matthean fictions. I think there are. The closest analogy to Matthew's Gospel is the Gospel of Mark. Mark too assembled a wide variety of materials and text collections to form a chronologically and geographically coherent story. This chronological fiction was probably created consciously. Matthew continued and "restructured" it. Mark too created a Jesus story which is transparent for the community. In the interests of the present reference of his story, he too introduced fictional details such as the Gentile centurion (15:39) and the disciples' lack of understanding. Mark too doubled some pericopes such as the predictions of suffering. Matthew walks in Mark's footsteps, and in answer to the "genre" question we can say that his concern is to write a new Gospel of Mark for his community, supplemented by Jesus' teaching.[89]

Looking beyond the Christian community, I recommend some attention to Jewish literature. There we find similar transparency for the community to that of Matthew's Gospel, for instance in Deuteronomy, where Moses gives the people in the desert a law that is valid for Josiah's time, or in *Jubilees,* when the patriarchs keep laws valid for the time the book was written. One should also look out for fictions comparable with Matthew's in the Jewish area, but this would go beyond the task we have set ourselves here.

---

88. The only important point for Matthew is that Jesus' miracles are not the result of "devilish" magic, cf. 12:22-30. Those who consider Jesus a γόης (sorcerer), as do the Pharisees and scribes, expose their own unbelief and place themselves outside the community for whom the Gospel of Matthew is identity-forming.

89. Cf. Luz, *Matthew 1–7* (see note 7), p. 46: From the Matthean perspective, the early church was fully justified in entitling the Matthean story "εὐαγγέλιον" and not "βίος."

CHRISTOLOGY

5 Matthean Christology Outlined in Theses

Dedicated to Ferdinand Hahn for His 65th Birthday

Thirty years ago, Ferdinand Hahn gave us a New Testament christology which takes as its orientation the honorific titles accorded to Christ. As was to be expected, it was a work of tradition history.[1] The Evangelists, not dealt with by Hahn, make the honorific titles secondary to their Jesus narrative. By doing so they transform the traditional semantic field of such titles and define them within a new context. I should like to demonstrate this in the following outline with reference to Matthew, restricting myself to the three most important christological titles he uses, υἱὸς Δαυίδ (son of David), υἱὸς τοῦ ἀνθρώπου (Son of Man) and υἱὸς τοῦ θεοῦ (Son of God) (II-IV). I open with a number of summary theses on Matthew's narrative (I).[2]

1. Narrative Christology

1.1. The Gospel of Matthew is *a story that needs to be read from beginning to end.* It discloses itself only when read — several times if possible[3] — in its entirety.

1. Ferdinand Hahn, *Christologische Hoheitstitel. Ihre Geschichte im frühen Christentum*, FRLANT 83 (Göttingen: Vandenhoeck & Ruprecht, 1963).
2. The brevity of this sketch, restricting itself to theses, unfortunately does not allow for full discussion of differing opinions in Matthew research. Thus the function of the sparse annotations is primarily to draw attention to expositions (my own and others') which support my theses in greater detail.
3. Cf. in this volume "Matthew the Evangelist: A Jewish Christian at the Crossroads," pp. 3–17.

German original: "Eine thetische Skizze der matthäischen Christologie," in: Cilliers Breytenbach/Henning Paulsen (eds.), *Anfänge der Christologie* (FS Ferdinand Hahn, Göttingen: Vandenhoeck und Ruprecht, 1991), pp. 221-235.

1.2. Matthew's story of Jesus is kerygmatic in character. In other words, *the story of "Jesus then" is at the same time the founding story of readers with "Jesus now."* It is the constitutive experience for its readers and is transparent for them. The transparency[4] of the Matthean story of Jesus is twofold:

1.2.1. It tells the story of Jesus as the story of Israel's healing Messiah who causes a division in his people (8:1–11:30). It tells how Israel's leaders reject Jesus and how he withdraws from Israel into the special circle of his disciples (12:1–16:20; 16:21–20:34). When the Messiah passes judgment in Jerusalem (21:1–24:2), it is the judgment on Israel's leaders by the one who is himself to be judged and condemned. Matthew's Passion narrative is paradoxical in an almost Johannine style. It tells how the Jewish leaders (together with the whole people) make their own condemnation definitive by condemning Jesus. The end of the Matthean story relates how Israel becomes the non-believing "Jews" and how the disciples are sent by the exalted Lord to the Gentiles (28:11-15, 16-20). This story becomes *indirectly transparent* for the history of the Matthean church, whose roots were probably in the Palestinian Jesus movement, whose mission to Israel was a failure,[5] whose members were expelled from Palestine to Syria (possibly during the Jewish War of A.D. 66-70) and now find a new task, given them by the Lord, in the mission to the Gentiles.

1.2.2. The individual pericopes of Matthew's Jesus narrative directly reflect the fundamental experience of the Matthean community of Christians with their Lord *(direct transparency)*. They see themselves as Jesus' disciples,[6] obeying his commands and experiencing with Jesus the healing, forgiveness, "coming to see," etc. of the miracle stories. At the same time they experience the persecution and suffering which Jesus prophesied and exemplified in his own life and suffering.

1.3. The Matthean Jesus story tells of the community's experiences on their journey with Jesus, and thus "with God." It is the story of *Jesus "Immanuel"*[7] (1:23; cf. 28:20), telling how in Jesus "God (is) with us," accompanying his church in its obedience, its faith and its suffering.

1.3.1. The Immanuel formula, a characteristic expression for God's pres-

---

4. Cf. in this volume "The Miracle Stories of Matthew 8–9," pp. 221-240.

5. I take this stage in the history of the Matthean community to be represented by the Sayings Source Q, whose composition is shaped by the pronouncement of judgement against Israel.

6. Cf. in this volume "The Disciples in the Gospel according to Matthew," pp. 115-42.

7. A basic book is Hubert Frankemölle's *Jahwebund und Kirche Christi*, NTA.NF 10 (Münster: Aschendorf, 1972), pp. 7-83. The author draws attention to the fundamental inclusiveness of Matt. 1:23–28:20, determining Matthew's narrative christology.

ence in the biblical story of his people Israel, shows how Matthew seeks to shape his entire christology according to Old Testament ways of thinking, in particular Old Testament history.

1.3.2. The Immanuel formula shows the *christo*logical concentration of Old Testament *theo*logy in Matthew's Gospel, and *vice versa* the *theo*logical dimension of Matthean *christo*logy. God's presence with his people in the Bible is represented in Matthew's Gospel by Jesus. He is the new and definitive form in which *God* is present with his people.

1.4. The Immanuel christology which frames Matthew's story shows that *Matthew's christology as a whole is narrative in character*. The Matthean Jesus story is the new story of God's presence with his people. Originally the christological titles functioned predicatively, stating who Jesus is. In Matthew the reverse is true: the Matthean story of Jesus functions predicatively and redefines the content of the traditional honorific titles. It "liquefies," so to speak, the "solid" meaning of the traditional titles.

1.5. For this reason, the following theses must above all take the *synchronic aspect* into account, i.e. what happens to the christological honorific titles in the course of Matthew's Jesus story and how their meaning changes.

1.5.1. The theses also seek, within the author-reader relationship, to take account of where Matthew meets his readers in their traditional christology and then proceeds to change it by means of his story. The diachronic aspect is thus also addressed.

2. The Son of David

Matthew narrates the meaning of the title "son of David" in his story. Jesus is Israel's expected Messiah, but for many in Israel he does not act among his people as expected. After all, Israel's Messiah is to be the Lord of all the world.

2.1. *Tradition history* is not the key to understanding the meaning of "son of David" in Matthew's Gospel. However, tradition history considerations can indicate the starting point at which Matthew meets and engages his Jewish Christian readers.

2.1.1. The expectation of Davidic Messianic king is widespread in Judaism,[8] although the technical designation דוד בן is relatively late (*Pss. Sol.* 17:21; frequent in early rabbinic texts).[9]

---

8. Christoph Burger, *Jesus als Davidssohn*, FRLANT 98 (Göttingen: Vandenhoeck und Ruprecht, 1970), pp. 16-23.

9. Eduard Lohse, "υἱὸς Δαυίδ," in: *TDNT* VIII, pp. 478-488, partic. p. 481.

2.1.1.1. The frequency of the expression υἱὸς Δαυίδ (son of David) in Matthew could, as for example with βασιλεία τῶν οὐρανῶν (kingdom of heaven), reflect some proximity in Matthew to early rabbinic use of language.[10]

2.1.2. Matthew did not see the healing son of David as the eschatological antitype to the first son of David, Solomon, who was known only in parts of Judaism (the *Testament of Solomon*) and only late as an exorcist but not as a miracle healer.[11]

2.1.3. The miracles expected in the messianic era could be a tradition history bridge which Matthew needed in order to interpret Jesus' miracles as messianic (see 2.3.3). Jewish tradition does not speak of the Messiah's miracles in a specific way, however.[12]

2.1.4. The only tradition from which Matthew's image of Jesus as the healing son of David can be derived is a Christian one. Mark 10:46-52 appears to be the basic text which inspired Matthew to develop this idea. As he so often does, Matthew develops and accentuates basic ideas that he encounters in his sources.[13]

2.2. *The prologue.* The concept of "son of David" is introduced in the book's title and in the genealogy (Matt. 1:2-17). By divine intervention, Jesus is the descendent of the royal dynasty of David, in other words the Messiah according to Israel's expectations. Matt. 1:18-25 tells how the virgin's Son became the son of David by being recognized by Joseph, the righteous Davidian, as his son. The genealogy helps in identifying God's Son Jesus with Israel's traditional messianic hopes and expectations and also with the earlier expectations and hopes of the Jewish Christian readers of the Gospel.

2.2.1. By naming the son of David as Jesus and Immanuel (1:18-25), Matthew paves the way for the story of the healing and merciful son of David in the main body of his Gospel.

2.3. In *the main part of the Gospel*, set in Galilee *(chs. 8–20)*, Matthew narrates how Jesus the son of David heals Israel's sick. The title υἱὸς Δαυίδ (son of David) is associated exclusively with miracles, especially with healing

10. I am sceptical towards Reinhart Hummel's speculation (*Die Auseinandersetzung zwischen Kirche und Judentum im Matthäusevangelium*, BEvTh 33 [Munich: Kaiser Verlag, 1963], p. 120) that particularly the Pharisees opposed by Matthew were the bearers of the Son of David expectation. Evidence from the Qumran texts and from Jewish prayer texts indicates that the expectation of a Messiah of David's lineage was general and widespread in Judaism.

11. Contrary to Klaus Berger, "Die königlichen Messiastraditionen des Neuen Testaments," *NTS* 20 (1973/74), pp. 1-44, here: pp. 3-9.

12. Cf. Brian M. Nolan, *The Royal Son of God*, OBO 23 (Freiburg: Universitätsverlag, 1979), pp. 165f.

13. Cf. Ulrich Luz, *Matthew 1–7* (Minneapolis: Augsburg, 1989), pp. 73-76.

of the blind (9:27; 12:23; 20:30-31, cf. 21:14-16).[14] Jesus the Messiah acts in and for his chosen people Israel (4:23). Prompted by Mark 10:46-52, Matthew as narrator changes Israel's traditional messianic expectations by means of his Jesus narrative.

2.3.1. It is important to note that Matthew *narrates* how Jesus heals in Israel (8:1–9:26) before the title υἱὸς Δαυίδ (son of David) occurs for the first time in the concluding section of chs. 8–9 (9:27).

2.3.2. The title son of David is often associated with healing of the blind. Metaphorically, Jesus the Messiah heals Israel's blindness, while the scribes and Pharisees remain blind (cf. 23:16-26). Matthew's perspective on blindness in the macrotext of his Gospel approaches John 9.

2.3.3. The grace of the healing Jesus helps the ordinary people of Israel (νήπιοι, 21:16) to identify Jesus as the son of David, i.e. the Messiah (12:23; 21:9, 15). Thus Matthew sees Jesus' healing activity not only as a change but also as a positive link with the messianic hopes of ordinary people.

2.3.4. For Israel's Jewish leaders, Jesus' healings do not confirm messianic hopes at all. On the contrary, they often reject the healings categorically (9:34; 12:24-32, 38-42; cf. 16:1-4 [following 15:29-39]; 21:15). Is this a historical reflection of later rabbinic rejection of Jesus as a magician? Matthew does not give reasons why they reject Jesus' miracles; it is incomprehensible and hence culpable. Matthew ignores the fact that his own understanding of Jesus' Davidic messiahship means a shift of Jewish hopes from the "political" to the "human" level. It is this shift which makes the frequent Jewish rejection of Jesus as son of David understandable in historical terms.

2.4. Matt. 22:41-46 suggests to Matthew's Christian readers that Israel's Messiah, the son of David, is more than this, namely κύριος (Lord) of the world. This pericope points to the end of Matthew's Jesus story (cf. 28:16-20), and has a dual function in the narrative. It takes up, on the one hand, what the sick had anticipated when they addressed the son of David as "Lord" (9:28; cf. 21:9; 15:22, 25) and followed him. This helps Christian readers to view the story of Jesus son of David from a broader, more universal perspective. On the other hand, the passage leads the Pharisees into an impasse. Their rejection of Jesus means they cannot understand why in Psalm 110 the son of David is called "Lord." They can no longer understand their own Scriptures. Thus Matt. 22:41-46 affirms Christian readers in their separation from Israel and in their claim to Israel's biblical heritage.

2.5. The title "son of David" is absent from the christological climactic

---

14. This is emphasized above all by James M. Gibbs, "Purpose and Pattern in Matthew's Use of the Title 'Son of David'," *NTS* 10 (1963/64), pp. 446-464.

pericopes in the final part of the Gospel, for example 26:59-66; 27:41-54 and 28:16-20. Its scope is limited in the Matthean story, where its function is to characterize Jesus' coming as the fulfilment and transformation of Israel's messianic hopes and to help soften the blow of division between Christian community and synagogue.

3. Son of Man

Matthew unfolds the meaning of the expression ὁ υἱὸς τοῦ ἀνθρώπου (the Son of Man) through the various stages of his Jesus story, from homelessness and persecution to passion, death, resurrection and exaltation, culminating in his parousia as eschatological judge. *At every stage, "Son of Man" reminds the readers of the Jesus story of the journey as a whole.*

3.1. The *positioning of the Son of Man sayings in the Gospel* is not arbitrary but shows clear tendencies even at the surface level of the text:

3.1.1. Before 8:20, and especially in the Sermon on the Mount, Son of Man sayings are absent.

3.1.2. In 16:13–17:22 and 24:27–26:64 the Son of Man sayings have high frequency (6 and 12 logia).

3.1.3. Up to 16:13 most Son of Man sayings are addressed to the people; after 16:13 Jesus speaks of the Son of Man solely to the disciples (20 logia). 26:64 is the only exception.

3.1.4. The Matthean Jesus does not speak to the people about the coming Son of Man (exception: 26:64) or about the suffering and rising Son of Man (exception: 12:40), but only to his disciples. The majority of sayings concerning the "present" Son of Man are public sayings, most of them in the early part of the Gospel.[15]

3.2. In his *syntax* Matthew follows the language of his sources and uses "the Son of Man" coherently:

3.2.1. The expression occurs only in sayings of Jesus and never in the narrative text itself. Jesus comments in the Son of Man sayings on his own history.

---

15. It is misleading to suggest, as Jack D. Kingsbury does ("The Title 'Son of Man' in Matthew's Gospel," *CBQ* 37 [1975], pp. 193-202, here: pp. 193, 201), that the Son of Man title is "public." Kingsbury means that the efficacy of Jesus the Son of Man extends to the people of Israel, his opponents and the whole world. But the expression "public" conceals both the special knowledge of the disciples about Jesus' history and future and the fact that Matthew employs the Son of Man title largely and consciously in teaching of the disciples.

3.2.2. "Son of Man" never occurs in the vocative case; Jesus is nowhere addressed or confessed as Son of Man.

3.2.3. Apart from the allegorical interpretation of 13:37, "Son of Man" never occurs predicatively. It is not used to state who Jesus is but to narrate what he does or suffers.

3.3. Matthew adopts all the Son of Man sayings he finds in his *sources.* Only in a very few cases does he replace the expression "Son of Man" by "I."

3.3.1. With regard to the redactional occurrences of Son of Man in Matthew it is interesting to note the following:

3.3.1.1. Quite a large number of the new sayings are concerned with the coming of the Son of Man (13:41; 16:28; 19:28?; 24:30a; 25:31).

3.3.1.2. Two sayings cannot readily be assigned to a specific group of Son of Man sayings. They appear to be general sayings about Jesus (13:37; 16:13).

3.3.1.3. Contrary to the tradition, Matthew speaks also about the Son of Man exalted in the present (26:64a ἀπ' ἄρτι [from now on]; cf. 13:37-41; 28:18-19).

3.4. For Matthew's readers the expression "Son of Man" is not, like "son of David," primarily an expression of Jewish hope. Rather, it is *part of the "Christ language."* The readers know from their Christian tradition that Jesus the "Son of Man" is homeless and rejected, that he will suffer and die and rise again, and that he will return as the eschatological judge. Thus for them the expression "Son of Man" is not primarily Jewish and apocalyptic.[16]

3.4.1. This is supported by:

3.4.1.1. The fixed and scarcely Jewish use of language,[17] employing the definite article throughout the synoptic tradition.

3.4.1.2. The relatively stable semantic field of many Son of Man sayings with their Christian stamp, in particular the sayings concerned with the suffering, dying and rising Son of Man and the coming Son of Man. This points to a fixed use of language within the community.[18]

3.4.1.3. General considerations. The Matthean community is probably descended from the mission of itinerant Christian missionaries who knew and valued the traditions collected in Q.

16. Daniel Marguerat, *Le jugement dans l'Evangile de Matthieu* (Geneva: Labor et Fides, 1981), p. 71, takes the emphasis on Jesus' future activity as judge and the Jewish-apocalyptic dimension of the title to be the crucial aspect of Matthew's understanding of the Son of Man. This conclusion suggests itself if one relies primarily on Matthew's editorial additions (cf. 3.1.1.1 above) without taking sufficient account of the function of these additions within the narrative as a whole.

17. Probably the only exception is the similitudes of 1 Enoch. On this see Ulrich Luz, *Matthew 8–20*, Hermeneia (Minneapolis: Fortress, 2001), p. 389, note 79.

18. Luz, *Matthew 8–20*, p. 390 notes 80f.

3.4.2. Matthew (together with his readers) knows Daniel 7 and occasionally reinforces the allusions to it (24:30; 26:64; cf. 28:18-19; 25:31). At the same time it is apparent that Dan. 7:13-14 does not determine the basic structure of the sayings about the coming of the Son of Man[19] but only serves Matthew as a means of introducing biblical color to some genuinely Christian Son of Man sayings.

3.4.3. Apart from Dan. 7 Matthew does not appear familiar with Jewish traditions on the coming Son of Man.[20]

3.4.4. The expression ὁ υἱὸς τοῦ ἀνθρώπου (the son of the man) is meaningless and puzzling for Greek-speaking readers at the level of everyday language. It is remarkable for bilingual Syrian readers because its double determination (ὁ υἱὸς τοῦ ἀνθρώπου = the Son of the man) does not correspond to the Aramaic בר אנש ("one," "a man," "I as a man"), which is usually completely undetermined. For these readers too it is a puzzling expression at the level of everyday language.

3.5. It is crucial to Matthew's use of sayings concerning Jesus the Son of Man that his Christian readers already know the story of Jesus the Son of Man and Jesus' own "commentary" on the story and on his future. Hence when Jesus uses Son of Man sayings publicly they understand more than did the people or Jesus' Jewish opponents. *Matthew uses the expression Son of Man in his Gospel to distinguish between the understanding disciples and the ignorant and malevolent opponents* on whom, quite unprepared, the judgment of Jesus the Son of Man will some day break in.

3.5.1. In the Sermon on the Mount, addressed to the disciples and the people, the title is not used in 5:11 and does not occur in the saying concerning the future eschatological judge (7:21-23). The title Son of Man is absent from the Sermon on the Mount because Matthew never has Jesus speak publicly of the coming Son of Man–eschatological judge.

3.5.2. The majority of the public Son of Man sayings in chs. 8–12 are polemical (9:6; 11:19; 12:8, 32, 40). In 11:19 and 12:32 "this generation" speaks against the Son of Man. Had the Jewish leaders understood what it meant to blaspheme the one who is to come as Son of Man, they would not have done so. Their resolution to destroy him in 12:14 is the response to his Son of Man saying in 12:8. The Jewish leaders do not understand who Jesus really is. The

---

19. In terms of tradition history Matthew connects here with early Christian development, in which the influence of Dan. 7:13 is consistently secondarily reinforced in the Son of Man sayings. I owe this insight to Mogens Müller, "Der Ausdruck Menschensohn in den Evangelien," AThD 17 (Leiden: Brill, 1984), pp. 89-154.

20. Johannes Theison, *Der auserwählte Richter,* StUNT 12 (Göttingen: Vandenhoeck und Ruprecht, 1975), pp. 158-200, assumes a literary influence of the similitudes on some of Matthew's editing. In my opinion one can speak only of a congruence of motifs.

words concerning his death and resurrection after three days (12:40) are rendered by them as the words of "that imposter" (27:63-64). 8:19 also points to the great division: only the disciples who get into the boat and take on the homelessness of the Son of Man have really understood who he is.

3.5.3. Jesus ceases to speak of the Son of Man to the enemies who do not understand who he is. He "withdraws" from them in the face of hostility towards him from Israel (12:15; 14:13; 15:21).

3.5.4. Only in the crucial final scene before the Sanhedrin, in 26:64, does Jesus speak publicly to his judges about the judgment of the Son of Man. But his judges do not grasp that it is they who are to be judged! The high priest tears his clothes, but because Jesus (!) has blasphemed! The scene takes on a Johannine irony.

3.5.5. In Matthew's Gospel there is a "Son of Man secret" which separates the disciples from the Jews. It is formed in and by the course of the narrative and is only occasionally secured by a (traditional) commandment of secrecy (16:20; 17:9).

3.6. For the disciples the expression "the Son of Man" is *an expression with a horizontal dimension, encompassing the entire story of Jesus, his life, his death, his resurrection and exaltation and his coming again to judge the world.* In contrast to the traditional categorization of the Son of Man sayings in three separate groups, it is important for the readers of Matthew's Gospel that the three groups are connected. The expression "Son of Man" forms the link between the various stages of Jesus' story in which it occurs (see also 3.3.1.2 and 3.3.1.3). The readers of Matthew's Gospel cannot understand a Son of Man saying without the expression "the Son of Man" reminding them of the whole Jesus story and of his present *and* future role. They understand what the "goats" on the left (25:32-33) cannot, namely that Jesus the homeless person whose story is told by Matthew is none other than the eschatological judge before whom they will one day stand.

3.6.1. Unlike Jesus' Jewish opponents, the readers of Matthew's Gospel — and the disciples instructed by Jesus in 10:23 and elsewhere — know that the man Jesus, who has no home (8:20) and who is blasphemed (cf. 12:40) for alleged use of divine privilege (9:6), who is regarded as a glutton and a drunkard (11:19) and who is accused of humanitarian interpretation of the Sabbath (12:1-14) is none other than the risen and coming eschatological judge. The readers and disciples find hidden depths in the public Son of Man sayings and understand the non-comprehension of the Jews (13:10-16). It is they who already have understanding and are given further understanding through Jesus' instructions (13:12). From those who have no understanding and who reject Jesus, even the promised kingdom will be taken away (13:12; 21:43).

3.6.2. Jesus will also be the judge of the readers of Matthew's Gospel (and the disciples in the Gospel). But they will not be unprepared: Jesus instructs them again and again concerning his coming as eschatological judge (13:37-43; 16:27; 24:30-31, 37-44).

3.6.3. The judgment of Jesus Son of Man will not lead them into a hopeless situation, because they have the opportunity to make the way of the Son of Man, the way of homelessness, obedience, persecution and suffering, their own way and to follow him on his path to resurrection and exaltation.

3.6.4. Thus the "horizontal" expression "Son of Man" helps to integrate the individual stages of Jesus' story. His death is counterpointed by his resurrection, his present persecution and homelessness are counterpointed by his enthronement, his present condemnation by his future judgement.

3.6.5. Unlike the title "son of David," "Son of Man" has a universal and future perspective.[21] The Son of Man *will* judge the *world,* and only then will his way be at its end. The way of his disciples will end only when they have gone to the Gentiles and stand before the judge of the whole world in the place of judgment.

3.7. Matthew's "horizontal" idea of the Son of Man, formed by the Jesus story, creates a bridge between the Jewish apocalyptic expectation of a heavenly judge and the later christology of the two natures, which used the expression "Son of Man" to refer to Jesus' history-bound humanity.

3.7.1. Matthew's most important predecessor is Mark's Gospel. In transforming the apocalyptic concept "Son of Man" into a horizontal "title" which circumscribes Jesus' way through history, Matthew follows Mark especially in the second part of the Gospel (Mark 8:31–14:62). He deepens and strengthens Mark's horizontal concept of the Son of Man by means of the paradoxical use of the expression in Q (e.g., Q 9:58, where the homeless Jesus is eschatological judge).

3.7.2. Matthew's most important "successor" in horizontal Son of Man christology is Ignatius, who lived in his sphere of influence. In Ignatius, *Ephesians* 20:2 the expression ὁ υἱὸς τοῦ ἀνθρώπου ("the Son of Man") is used for the first time to designate Jesus' humanity, in characteristic contrast to non-Christian Gnosis, where "Son of Man" refers to the son of the *god* Anthropos.[22]

---

21. This is emphasised by Heinz Geist, *Menschensohn und Gemeinde,* FZB 57 (Würzburg: Echter, 1986), esp. pp. 420-426.

22. Carsten Colpe, "ὁ υἱὸς τοῦ ἀνθρώπου," in: *TDNT* VIII, pp. 400-477, here pp. 474-475. Justin, *Dialogue with Trypho* 100.3, and Irenaeus, however, associate the title with the virgin birth.

4. Son of God

Unlike "Son of Man," the title "Son of God" has a vertical dimension already in the Markan tradition. It denotes Jesus' special and unique relation to God and his unique God-given status. Matthew has adopted this dimension and, like Mark, uses "Son of God" as a confession title.[23] The most significant Matthean feature is that God's Son proves himself by walking the way of obedience to the Father. In this way *Matthew adds a horizontal, ethical dimension to the vertical dimension of the Son of God title* in his Jesus story. Apart from some inspiration from Mark (discipleship in suffering) and Q (the temptation narrative) Matthew draws above all on a Jewish model familiar to him, that of the suffering of the righteous (Wis. 2:5; cf. 4.3.6 below).

4.1. In the *prologue* (1:1–4:22), ὁ υἱὸς τοῦ θεοῦ ("the Son of God") occurs frequently. The prologue is a summarizing prelude to the Matthean Jesus story, and its function is to anticipate significant aspects of Matthean Son of God christology.

4.1.1. One such accent found in the prologue is that God alone reveals Jesus as his Son, either directly (1:22-23; 2:15; 3:17)[24] or through an angel (1:21-23); cf. 11:25-27; 16:17; 17:5.

4.1.2. It is even more significant that the Son revealed by the Father "fulfils all righteousness" (3:15) and obeys the will of the Father as revealed in the Scriptures (4:1-11). As the *inclusio* of 3:15–4:11 with 27:43-54 shows, the obedience of the Son of God is highly significant for the Gospel. The antitypical reference to 4:8-10 in 28:16-18 suggests that the obedient Son of God will one day be the true ruler of the world.

4.2. Matthew places some Son of God texts prominently in the main part of his Gospel. 11:25-30 comes at the end of the first main section 4:23–11:30, and 16:16 at the end of a further main section (12:1–16:20). 28:16-20 is the grand finale, a text that binds the whole of Matthew's Gospel together. 27:43, 54 are emphasized by means of the *inclusio* with 3:15–4:11.

4.3. Almost all the significant Son of God references in Matthew *combine the vertical moment*, i.e., the revelation of God the Son by God the Father, *with the horizontal moment*, i.e., Jesus' proving his divine sonship by his obedience, and the model character of his life for the disciples. Matthew's Jesus story overall develops this horizontal dimension. The function of the Son of

---

23. Kingsbury, "Title" (see note 15), p. 193.

24. Only the two Son-of-God citations 1:22-23 and 2:15 have κύριος (Lord) in their introductory formulae. Cf. Rudolf Pesch, "Der Gottessohn im matthäischen Evangelienprolog (Mt 1–2)," *Bib* 48 (1967), pp. 395-420, here pp. 397, 411-413.

God references placed prominently in Matthew's narrative is to illuminate the christological significance of Jesus' way of obedience and to supplement it by the "perspective from above."

4.3.1. 11:25-30 is a key text for Matthean christology. Much of it resonates with other fundamental parts of the Gospel. The Father revealing the secret of the Son (v. 25fin.) recalls 1:21-23; 2:15; 3:17 and anticipates 16:16-17; 17:5. The secret of the Son being given to infants and hidden from the wise is shown in 21:15-16; 26:63-64; 27:43. Πάντα μοι παρεδόθη (all is given to me) is exceeded in 28:18, where not only revelation but also all authority is given to the Son. Moreover, vv. 25-26 recall the Christian prayer per se, the Lord's Prayer.

4.3.1.1. 11:27 is a post-Easter commentary saying of the community on v. 25, giving substance to the secret of the Son as the content of the revelation to the νήπιοι (infants, simple). At the same time it is made clear that the secret can be revealed to the νήπιοι only through the Son's mediation. On the basis of the relation between v. 27 and v. 25, παρεδόθη refers to the "tradition" of divine revelation and not to the handing over of authority.

4.3.1.2. In the Matthean context, the absolute ὁ υἱός (the son) means none other than Jesus the Son of God. Probably this is already the case for the traditional commentary saying, since the formulation with an absolute ὁ υἱός is necessitated rhetorically by the rhetorical opposition to ὁ πατήρ (the father) and not in terms of tradition history by a particular christology (Wisdom or Son of Man christology) underlying the text.

4.3.1.3. What v. 27 emphasizes, in the tradition and in Matthew, is not the choosing of the Son by the Father[25] nor the recognition of the Father by the Son,[26] but their mutual mystic "knowledge." This remains restricted to the Father and the Son, whose relationship is unique. The "knowledge" is not extended to the νήπιοι (the simple ones), who do not "know" (ἐπιγινώσκειν) the Father and the Son but receive revelation through the Son.

4.3.1.4. 11:27 shows, together with 1:22-23; 2:15; 3:17 and 17:5 and the Immanuel statements, that Matthew who is so concerned with Jesus in history ("horizontal christology") and the model character of Jesus' life can also combine this interest with elements of "high christology" "from above."

4.3.1.5. The (Matthean!) addition of the wisdom words of vv. 28-30 and particularly the (redactional!) addition of v. 29b demonstrate the Evangelist's concern for the Son of God's obedience. The Son reveals himself as the meek and humble Son (= πραΰς, ταπεινός) who will act on behalf of humankind

25. Why should only the Father choose the Son?
26. The double use of the verb ἐπιγινώσκειν (to know) suggests that the relation between the Father and the Son is a reciprocal and symmetrical one.

accordingly (cf. 12:1-14). It is his presence and the model he provides which make his yoke easy.[27]

4.3.2. The central fulfilment quotation 12:18-21 does not speak of the servant of God but, in the biblical language of Isaiah, of the child of God,[28] i.e. the Son who is familiar to readers from 3:17. Placed in the center of Matthew's Gospel, the words from Isaiah 42:1-4 give readers the opportunity to view the whole story of Jesus the beloved, chosen, peace-loving Son of God who will judge the world and be the hope of the heathen. There is no specifically Matthean servant of God christology in Matt. 12:18-21.

4.3.3. In 16:16-17 Jesus the Son of Man is revealed by the Father himself to be the Son of God and confessed as such by Peter. His confession, corresponding to that of all the disciples in 14:33, makes Peter, the typical disciple, the first apostle and the rock on which the church will be built. 16:16 belongs to the first part of the "diptych"[29] of 16:13-28. The second part speaks in 16:21 of the suffering Jesus will undergo,[30] the model for the life of his disciples. The diptych shows, moreover, that the Son of God goes his way, which is from now on the way to his Passion, in obedience to the Father. Peter's verbal confession of the Son of God ("vertical christology") needs to be supplemented by a "living confession" of obedience, self-denial, suffering and martyrdom.

4.3.4. The revelation of Jesus' divine sonship in 17:5, the scene on the mountain at the beginning of the journey to Jerusalem, recalls 3:17 and — antithetically — 4:8-10. The most significant interpretative element in Matthew is vv. 6-8: the disciples cannot bear the revelation of the Son's divinity and fall to the ground. It is "Jesus alone" who touches them, speaks with them, helps them up and instructs them concerning his way to suffering and theirs (vv. 6-13). Once again the sonship of Jesus is interpreted by means of the way that Jesus and the disciples are to go.

4.3.5. The interrogation scene before the Sanhedrin counterpoints 16:13-20. In 26:63 the High Priest asks in the name of the living God whether Jesus is God's Son (this is not revealed to him by the Father!). In 26:65 he acts as judge towards one who has publicly revealed himself to be the Son of Man and judge of the world.

4.3.5.1. 27:40.43 takes up 26:59-66 antithetically, making clear that Jesus shows himself to be the Son of God not by performing the miracle of destroy-

---

27. In contrast to that of the Pharisees in 23:4-7.

28. Cf. Ulrich Luz, *Matthew 8–20* (see note 17), p. 193.

29. Jan Lambrecht, "'Du bist Petrus,'" *SNTU* 11 (1986), pp. 5-32; here: p. 6.

30. Here it is not the suffering of the Son of Man. The absence of the title here and the fact that it is brought forward to 16:13 make the connection between the two parts of the diptych clear.

ing and rebuilding the temple in three days but by obeying and trusting God. The fundamental concept in Matthew is that of the suffering Righteous (Psalm 22; Wis. 2:18). 27:54 forms the positive contrast, in that the death of the righteous Jesus inspires the heathen centurion to confess that Jesus (living and dying in obedience!) "was" the Son of God.

4.3.6. In 28:16-20 there is no title for Christ apart from the triadic baptism formula. There is however considerable resonance with motifs of earlier key christological texts (cf. 1.2.1; 2.4; 3.4.2; 4.1.2; 4.3.1 above). These verses, the finale to Matthew's narrative, demonstrate how his narrative christology goes beyond the christology of the titles. Matthew's christology is more than a semantic field structured by titles which define various aspects of the field. Rather, it is the story of a human being in whom God is and was "with us."

5. Conclusion

5.1. Of the three most important christological titles in Matthew, "son of David" is most limited in scope. The expression "Son of Man" goes further, encompassing the story of Jesus in the present and future as well as the past. "Son of God" is the most fundamental title for Christ in that it has both a horizontal dimension, that of Jesus' lived obedience, and a vertical dimension, that of Jesus' unique relationship with the Father.

5.2. One cannot however declare a single christological title to be the "main" one. Each of the titles encompasses particular aspects vis-à-vis the others; each denotes only aspects of Matthean christology.[31] From the perspective of Matthew's Jesus story it is true to say: "Christology is in the whole story."[32]

5.3. The connection of horizontal and vertical aspects in Matthew's christology, particularly in his understanding of Jesus as Son of God and his connecting of Son of God and Son of Man statements, anticipates remarkably closely the doctrine of two natures in the later church.

---

31. Critical of Jack D. Kingsbury, *Matthew. Structure, Christology, Kingdom* (Philadelphia: Fortress, 1975), pp. 82f.

32. Dale C. Allison, "The Son of God as Israel. A Note on Matthean Christology," *IBS* 9 (1987), pp. 74-81, here: p. 75.

6 The Son of Man in Matthew:
Heavenly Judge or Human Christ?

The Son of Man problem is still a riddle. Angus J. B. Higgins, many years ago, wrote an article with the nice title "Is the Son of Man Problem Insoluble?"[1] I do not know the answer. What I do know is that it has not yet been solved. We still have the alternatives of an apocalyptic concept of a heavenly Son of Man figure coming with the clouds of heaven, and several forms of non-apocalyptic Sons of Man, of which Thomas Walter Manson's idea that the Son of Man is a late conceptual embodiment of the Old Testament remnant idea is an important one.[2] I do not share his opinion, but what I want to do is to pay homage to this great Mancunian scholar by taking up one of his leading questions again. My problem is not the question of the origin of the Son of Man. I only want to mention as background to this paper that I think that the earliest Christians, and even Jesus himself, shared the conviction of some Jewish apocalyptic circles that a messianic heavenly judge called "the son of the man"[3] would appear and that they believed that Jesus was that Son of the Man. My problem is a different and much more specialized one. At the beginning of the second century Ignatius speaks about the twofold nature of Jesus,

1. In E. Earle Ellis and Max Wilcox (eds.), *Neotestamentica et Semitica: Studies in Honour of Matthew Black* (Edinburgh: Clark, 1969), pp. 70-87.
2. Thomas Walter Manson, *The Teaching of Jesus* (Cambridge: Cambridge University Press, 1963), p. 227.
3. The definite article is colloquial and probably identifies the general "son of the man" with the special Danielic tradition (Thomas Walter Manson, *Studies in the Gospels and Epistles* [Manchester: Manchester University Press, 1962], pp. 130-31). In the Ethiopic Enoch the normal form of the expression has a demonstrative pronoun, which might have the same function; cf. Matthew Black, *The Book of Enoch or 1 Enoch*, SVTP 7 (Leiden: Brill, 1985), pp. 206f.

The Manson Memorial Lecture, delivered in the University of Manchester, November 1990. Original publication in English in: *JSNT* 48 (1992), pp. 3-21.

who is at the same time υἱὸς ἀνθρώπου (Son of Man) and υἱὸς θεοῦ (Son of God; cf. Ignatius, *Ephesians* 20.2). This is the first example of how "Son of Man" became part of the nascent christology of two natures. The next proof texts are Barnabas 12.10 and the Valentinian epistle to Rheginos, where we read: "The son of god . . . was son of man, and encompassed both, because he had human and divine nature" (*Nag Hammadi Codices [NHC]* 1.44.21-26). In the second century the appearances of "Son of Man" are comparatively rare. Linguistically and semantically there is a considerable discontinuity between the usage of the expression in the Gospels and in the texts of the second century. The expression is no longer used in words of Jesus and, as far as we can tell from the mostly non-Greek texts, the double definite article ὁ υἱὸς τοῦ ἀνθρώπου (the Son of the Man) which is so characteristic of the NT usage, tends to disappear. Semantically "Son of Man" means now "son of a human being" and could be combined with incarnation (Irenaeus, *Adversus Haereses* 3.18.6; 3.19.3; 3.22.1; 5.17.3; *Testimony of Truth, NHC* 9.30.18ff.), with the virgin birth (Justin, *Dialogue* 100.3; 3.16.5 and passim; Tertullian, *Adversus Marcionem* 4.10.7-8 — here the "man" is Mary!), or with the Gnostic conviction that the Savior is male and not female (*Treatise of Seth, NHC* 7.65.18ff.). One has the impression that most of these texts have no idea of an apocalyptic background of the expression and make no use of the Gospel usage, but try to interpret a difficult and mysterious expression in their own new context. There seems to be a striking discontinuity between first- and the second-century usage.

This is the point of departure of my paper. I would like to ask, is there a bridge between the earliest Christian and the second-century usage of the expression "Son of Man"? And concerning the Gospels I would like to ask, could they function as this bridge? I want to examine the usage of "the Son of the Man" in the Gospel of Matthew as a test case.[4]

1. Preliminary Observations

1.1. Survey. Son of the Man sayings are missing in the prologue and in the Sermon on the Mount. This is astonishing, because other leading christological titles like "Son of God" or "Son of David" are carefully introduced in the pro-

---

4. Cf. the similar question in Douglas R. A. Hare, *The Son of Man Tradition* (Minneapolis: Fortress, 1990), pp. 113-114. Hare rightly states that Matthew is the most difficult Evangelist for a possible "bridge" to the second century, because his way of using "the Son of the Man" seems closer to apocalyptic traditions than in any other Gospel.

logue. In the main section of the Gospel narrative they start to appear occasionally from 8:20. The expression is never introduced or explained in the Gospel. There is a high density of Son of the Man sayings in two sections, namely between 16:13 and 17:22 (6 sayings) and between 24:27 and 26:64 (12 sayings). In the Gospel 18 out of 30 occurrences appear in these two passages. Most of the sayings about the coming Son of the Man are found in the latter section (chs. 24–26). Unlike the title "Son of God," one cannot say that Matthew places his Son of the Man logia at crucial points in his narrative. Neither the beginning nor the end of the Gospel, nor texts opening or closing a main section of the Gospel, are normally "marked" by the title "Son of the Man." In this respect, Matthew seems to be different from the source Q, where at least sometimes Son of the Man sayings occupy an important position. With regard to the customary three different groups of Son of the Man sayings, most of the sayings about the coming Son of the Man, and all except one about his suffering and resurrection, occur after 16:13. There are only two sayings about the coming Son of the Man in the first part of the Gospel, both in special teaching to the disciples (10:23; 13:37), and only one about his suffering and rising (12:40). On the other hand, most of the words about the earthly Son of the Man are publicly spoken and are therefore concentrated in the first part of the Gospel.

1.2. The Addressees of the Son of the Man Sayings. After 16:13 Jesus speaks only to the disciples about himself as Son of the Man (20x). The only exception is the last occurrence (26:64), the self-revelation of Jesus before the Sanhedrin, which is public. Therefore almost all sayings about the coming and all sayings about the suffering and rising Son of the Man are private instructions to the disciples. The nine Son of Man sayings before 16:13 have mixed addressees. Only three times are the disciples the addressees (10:23; 13:37, 41). Four times Jesus' Jewish adversaries are the addressees (9:6; 12:8, 32, 40), twice the people (8:20; 11:19).

1.3. Syntactically "Son of the Man" never appears as an address to Jesus or as the content of a confession. Only once is "Son of the Man" a predicate, namely 13:37. In many of the other references it appears as the grammatical or logical subject. This means that "Son of the Man" is never used to say who Jesus is, but very often occurs in sayings which tell what Jesus the Son of the Man does or suffers.[5] "Son of the Man" is not a title in the normal sense of the word.[6]

5. Jack D. Kingsbury, "The Figure of Jesus in Matthew's Story: A Literary-Critical Probe," *JSNT* 21 (1984), pp. 22-27.

6. Cf. Mogens Müller, *Der Ausdruck 'Menschensohn' in den Evangelien* (AThD 17, Leiden:

1.4. Almost all of the public sayings about the earthly Son of the Man are in a polemical context. The only exception is 8:20. This saying is indirectly polemical; its context is the first separation between the disciples who embark with Jesus towards the other shore of the lake and the people remaining on the shore.

1.5. Source-critically Matthew is a conservative author, particularly in connection with the sayings of Jesus. He does not omit a single one of the Son of the Man sayings of his sources.[7] In only three instances does he replace a "Son of the Man" by "I" (5:11; 10:32; 16:21). Seven or eight times new Son of the Man sayings are created by the Evangelist.[8] Matthew must have had a special interest in this expression. Most of the additions (four or five) speak about the coming Son of the Man and the judgment (13:41; 16:28; 24:30a; 25:31 and, if it is redactional, 19:28). Matt. 26:2 is a variant of other traditional sayings about the handing over of the Son of the Man into the hands of his murderers. The other two redactional sayings, 13:37 and 16:13, cannot easily be attributed to a specific group. Summing up, two things can be said: (1) Matthew has an interest in the Son of the Man since he has increased the number of sayings considerably, and (2) he seems to have a special interest in the future of Jesus, the Son of the Man, as judge.

2. The Meaning of the Expression "Son of the Man"

2.1. "Son of the Man" is a strange and even mysterious expression without an obvious meaning for the average person in Syria, where Matthew was written. It does not exist in Greek. The most likely meaning for Greek-speaking readers would be genealogical: this was the way in which the second-century Gnostics spoke about the son of the primary God Ἄνθρωπος and in which Christians spoke about Jesus as son of a human being, namely Mary.[9] For those who un-

---

Brill, 1984), pp. 190-191, 198; Helmut Merklein, "Die Auferweckung Jesu und die Anfänge der Christologie," *ZNW* 72 (1981), pp. 1-26, here: p. 24; Heinz Geist, *Menschensohn und Gemeinde* (FZB 57, Würzburg: Echter, 1986), p. 69, and especially Hare (see note 4), pp. 115-182.

7. Matt. 16:21 is not a "true" omission, because Matthew does not simply omit "Son of the Man" but moves it to 16:13. The replacement in 10:32 meant a formal clarification and improvement of the logion and removes the traditional, and somewhat awkward, juxtaposition of the "I" and "Son of the Man." In any case, after 10:23 the disciples and readers of the Gospel will associate Jesus' judgment with his coming as the "Son of the Man."

8. Already this makes it difficult to assume with Hare (see note 4), p. 181 that "Son of the Man" in Matthew is nothing but a denotation of Jesus.

9. Cf. above p. 98.

derstood or spoke Aramaic or Syriac — and this is a real possibility both for the author of the Gospel and for his readers — there existed the colloquial expression בר אנש (literally: son of man) with the meaning "one," "somebody," sometimes also in connection with a first person singular verb with the meaning "I as a human," "a human being therefore I also."[10] But this expression was not normally determinate at all. Therefore bilingual readers of Matthew are not likely to have associated the Greek expression ὁ υἱὸς τοῦ ἀνθρώπου (Son of the Man) with this Aramaic usage.[11] Rather, they would have interpreted it in a generic sense ("the species man"). And then they would have been all the more puzzled about Jesus' use of this expression in sayings which interpreted or predicted Jesus' particular history, not that of everybody.[12] In short, at the level of the colloquial language the expression "Son of the Man" was for everybody a very strange, even mysterious expression.

2.2. Matthew did not draw on a Jewish apocalyptic expectation of a messianic figure called *"Son of the Man,"* which might have been familiar in certain Jewish circles, but not everywhere in Judaism. He never presupposes or hints at such an expectation. He knows Dan. 7:13-14, because he assimilates his Markan texts to Dan. 7:13-14 in 24:30 and 26:64. Matt. 28:18 is also, I think, a conscious allusion to Dan. 7:13-14. But this does not mean that he was familiar with the Danielic or Jewish apocalyptic concept of a Son of Man, because naturally he as a Christian did not read anything else in Dan. 7:13-14 but that Jesus would sit on the clouds of heaven and that to him all power would be given. Did he know other traditions, for instance the *Similitudes of Enoch,* as is assumed by Theisohn?[13] I do not think so, because the expression "the throne of glory," which is Theisohn's main argument, is a rather common biblical expression for the throne of God[14] and part of Matthew's "biblical" language. Using this expression he wants to say in 19:28 and 25:31 that Jesus the Son of the Man sits on the throne of God. There is no indication whatsoever that Matthew presupposed an apocalyptic meaning of "Son of the Man"

10. Carsten Colpe, "ὁ υἱὸς τοῦ ἀνθρώπου," in: *TDNT,* VIII, pp. 403-481, here: pp. 405-406; cf. also Joseph A. Fitzmyer, "The New Testament Title 'Son of the Man,'" in his *A Wandering Aramean,* SBLMS 25 (Missoula, MT: Scholars, 1979), pp. 152-153.

11. Similarly Hare, *The Son of Man Tradition* (see note 4), p. 123.

12. Cf., e.g., 10:23 (indirect opposition: the persecuted disciples); 11:19 (direct opposition: John the Baptist); 12:32 (indirect opposition: the people, through whom the Spirit works); 16:13 (the question is, what people think about Jesus only); 25:31 (only Jesus will sit on the throne); 26:64 (only Jesus will be exalted ἀπ᾽ ἄρτι); all the sayings about the dying and rising Christ etc.

13. Johannes Theisohn, *Der Auserwählte Richter,* StUNT 12 (Göttingen: Vandenhoeck und Ruprecht, 1974), pp. 158-200, tries to show that Matthew depended directly upon the similitudes of Enoch. I do not think that the few points of contact are decisive.

14. 1 Sam. 2:8; Isa. 22:23; Jer. 14:21; 17:12; Dan. 3:54; cf. Sir. 47:11; Wis. 9:10; 1 En. 14:18-20.

among his readers, because there is no indication whatsoever that he himself was conscious of such a meaning besides his own Christian traditions about Jesus the Son of the Man.

2.3. What then did give "meaning" to the strange and uncolloquial expression "Son of the Man" for Matthew and his readers? My thesis is that it is the Christian tradition, the words of Jesus, which are decisive for Matthew and his readers.[15] Matthew, probably a leading representative of Christian communities, wrote for Christian readers who were familiar with most of the Jesus tradition. His implied readers knew already most of what he was going to tell them and Matthew reckons with this. It is a widely shared assumption that the churches of Matthew belong somehow to the post-history of the Sayings Source Q. There is no christological expression of comparable weight in Q to ὁ υἱὸς τοῦ ἀνθρώπου (the Son of the Man). This expression was thus part of Matthew's church's own tradition. As for the Gospel of Mark it is much more difficult to decide if Matthew presupposed that his readers were familiar with it. I would like to say two things only: (1) since the Gospel of Mark must have been available at the bookshelf of his church, he must have presupposed that at least some of his readers could have known it; (2) even for those of his readers who had not read the Gospel of Mark, it is likely that they were familiar with some of the traditions contained in it. Therefore it is sound to assume that Matthew writes for an audience familiar with many or most of his Son of the Man sayings.

At this point I want to recall an observation of Paul Hoffmann concerning the meaning of the expression "Son of the Man" in the source Q, which seems to me important for my own thesis. Hoffmann says correctly that one must neither exclude the memory of the earthly Jesus from the so-called future sayings nor the associations of the future judge of the world in the sayings about the present Son of the Man.[16] In Q Jesus is identified with "the Son of the Man," and all the different Son of the Man sayings speak about the

15. Similarly Geist (see note 6), p. 415. But Geist tries to define the meaning of the "title" in theological, not narrative categories. This is the point where I depart from the conclusion of the valuable book of Hare. His main thesis is (cf. *The Son of Man Tradition*, pp. 181f.) that ὁ υἱὸς τοῦ ἀνθρώπου has no connotation (particularly no apocalyptic connotation), but is an expression denoting Jesus. As such it is more than a simple nickname; rather it is an "elevated term, pointing to the mystery of Jesus' destiny, without 'containing' that destiny as its connotation" (ibid. p. 181). Yes! But Hare neglects the fact that the Christian readers did know many things about the fate and future of this Jesus, denoted by himself by means of ὁ υἱὸς τοῦ ἀνθρώπου, and that the occurrence of this denotation reminds Matthew's Christian readers of all that Jesus had said about himself as Son of the Man.

16. Paul Hoffmann, *Studien zur Theologie des Logienquelle*, NTA 8 (Münster: Aschendorff, 1972), pp. 147-158.

same person. "Son of the Man" therefore functions in Q as a kind of common denominator to remind readers that Jesus is not just a homeless or persecuted person and not just the coming judge of the world, but both. It is important that the one who will play an important role in the future judgment has now no place of dwelling (Q 9:58) and that none other than the future judge of the world is called a glutton and a winebibber (Q 7:34). The preaching of Jesus is of the utmost importance in the final judgment because it is the preaching of the earthly Jesus, the coming Son of Man (Q 12:8-9; 11:30).[17] In this Q is an important forerunner of Matthew, as we shall see.

Let me *summarize* this section. We have seen (1) that for non-Christians in the environment of Matthew "Son of the Man" was a strange expression, which Jesus used from time to time when he interpreted or predicted his history. Therefore it should not be translated colloquially "this man," but rather uncolloquially, like "this somebody." (2) There is very little basis for assuming that the expression "Son of the Man" was to a large extent part of a common Christian-Jewish apocalyptic horizon of expectation in the Matthean church. For Matthew and his readers it did not serve to locate Jesus within a Jewish messianic expectation, even if historically its roots were there. Therefore it is not without problems to translate it as a title with "the [well known from Daniel] Son of Man." (3) For Matthew's readers the expression "the Son of the Man" was part of their own Christian insider language. They only, not the outsiders, knew about the Son of the Man, his destiny and his future, and Matthew knew that they knew. My assumption is that Matthew used this special knowledge of his readers in his narrative.

3. Son of the Man in the Matthean Narrative

In this section I want to analyze how the Son of the Man sayings function in the Matthean narrative. In doing this, I am interested in the Matthean narrative, not simply as a text, but as a piece of communication between the author, Matthew, and his readers.

---

17. Luke 12:8-9 and 11:29-30 are very close in content, in spite of the fact that in one the Son of Man is "future," in the other "present." Cf. the (correct) interpretation of Luke 11:29-30 in the commentary words of Luke 11:31-32.

3.1. A General Remark about Matthew's Gospel

I think that the Gospel is an "inclusive story" which reflects the experiences and the history of the post-Easter church. Matthew is what J. Louis Martyn called, in his analysis of the Fourth Gospel, a "two-level drama."[18] Matthew tells the story of Jesus, the messiah of Israel, who heals the sick and suffering among his people (ch. 8–9). At that time he and his disciples are active in Israel only (cf. 10:5-6). But he meets with growing opposition and strong enmity in Israel. He has to retire from Israel[19] together with his disciples (12:1–16:20) into a separate community in Israel, the church (16:21–20:34). In Jerusalem the conflict reaches its peak (chs. 21–25). Jesus announces solemnly the coming judgment of Israel and retires from the temple (24:2). After his passion and resurrection he gives to his disciples a new orientation towards the gentiles, and towards the gentiles only (28:16-20). This story of Jesus is at the same time the story of Matthew's church, a Jewish-Christian group originating from Palestine. Its initial mission to Israel has come to an end; it had to leave Palestine and lives now in Syria where Matthew's Gospel gives them a new orientation towards the gentiles or strengthens the universalist tendencies already existing in the church. What kind of role does the expression "the Son of the Man" play in this two-level narrative?

3.2. The Prologue

The Matthean prologue (1:1–4:22) is not only the beginning of the story of Jesus from his infancy on, but at the same time an anticipation of his whole way, namely from the city of David to Galilee, the land of the Gentiles, and it is a christological summary about Jesus Immanuel, Son of God and son of David. The "Son of the Man" is absent here. My tentative explanation is that ὁ υἱὸς τοῦ ἀνθρώπου is missing because this expression does not say who Jesus is.[20] On the contrary, the Matthean narrative, or rather, Jesus, through his own comments about his way and future, tells who the "Son of the Man" is. "Son of the Man" is much more closely connected with the narrative than

18. J. Louis Martyn, *History and Theology in the Fourth Gospel* (Nashville: Abingdon, ²1979), pp. 129-51; for Matthew as an "inclusive story" cf. David B. Howell, *Matthew's Inclusive Story*, JSNTSup 42 (Sheffield: JSOT, 1990).

19. Three times ἀναχωρέω: 12:15; 14:13; 15:21; cf. 16:4.

20. If it is correct that one main purpose of the prologue is to "present" Jesus (as Immanuel, Son of God and son of David), then the prologue, with the absence of any mention of "the Son of the Man," makes it clear that our expression is no title.

"Son of God." That is the reason why Matthew uses the expression only in the main part of the narrative, which begins at 4:23.

3.3. Matthew 4:23–16:20

This part of the Gospel is characterized by the beginning and growing split in Israel. In 8:23, just after the first Son of the Man saying, the disciples separate for the first time from the people. In 9:3, just before the second saying, the first hostile reactions of the Jewish leaders are narrated. From ch. 10 on the disciples have a new position vis-à-vis the people: they are no more, as in ch. 5–7, together with the people listening to the proclamation of Jesus; rather, they are on the side of Jesus, collaborators (ἐργάται), having a share in Jesus' mission towards the people (cf. 9:38; 10:1-23). Here the first private instruction of Jesus about his coming as Son of the Man takes place. In chs. 11 and 12 the split between Jesus and his opponents deepens. Both chapters contain a lengthy speech of Jesus concerning the hostility which he faces addressed to the people and to his opponents (11:7-19; 12:23-45). Both these speeches contain a reference to "the Son of the Man" towards their end (11:19; 12:40). Most of the public Son of the Man sayings of this section occur in a polemical context. The disciples hear them too, but beyond that Jesus begins with his special instruction to them about his future as Son of the Man.

The key to Matthew's use of "the Son of the Man" in this section is the observation that the understanding held by the disciples and by the hostile Jews is not the same.[21] Its final pericope opens with a question of Jesus to the disciples, what do the people say about "me, the Son of the Man" (16:13)? The redundant μὲ τὸν υἱὸν τοῦ ἀνθρώπου,[22] represented by most of the important witnesses, explains all the different variants and is the most difficult reading. Τὸν υἱὸν τοῦ ἀνθρώπου must add something to the mere μὲ. What is this sur-

---

21. This observation marks my objection against Kingsbury's hypothesis (in "The Title 'Son of Man' in Matthew's Gospel," *CBQ* 37 [1975], pp. 193-202, here: pp. 201f.; idem, "The Figure of Jesus in Matthew's Story: A Literary-Critical Probe," *JSNT* 21 [1984], pp. 3-36, here: pp. 28-29), that ὁ υἱὸς τοῦ ἀνθρώπου in Matthew functions as a "public" title: (1) Kingsbury neglects the addressees of the sayings; (2) it is natural that the "Son of the Man" sayings, telling and commenting on the history of Jesus, have something to do with the outside world. But they also have something to do with the disciples' world: the Son of the Man is a model of Christian discipleship (8:20), he is the origin of their own power and freedom (9:6; 12:8), the model of their own suffering and martyrdom (16:13, 21, 24-26; 20:18-28) and also the Lord of the judgment over his disciples (24:37-44) as a warning to the church.

22. For the text-critical problem, cf. Ulrich Luz, *Matthew 8–20*, Hermeneia (Minneapolis: Fortress, 2001), p. 354 note 1.

plus of meaning? It wants to remind the disciples — and the readers — of all that they know already about the Son of the Man Jesus, of everything that Jesus has told them already about the Son of the Man in the previous chapters (for example in 10:23; 12:40 and 13:37-43). Jesus asks: what do people say about me, the Son of the Man, as you remember, because I have told you? The disciples have more knowledge about Jesus than do the people. This special knowledge, shared also by the readers, is the reason that the answers of the people are insufficient for them. Matthew starts to build up a special knowledge about the fate of Jesus the Son of the Man in this section of the Gospel.

But it is not only because the disciples have heard more Son of the Man sayings that they know more about Jesus the Son of the Man. The outsiders and hostile Jewish leaders understood only the surface of Jesus' Son of the Man sayings, but not the real depth of them. Their misunderstanding has a semantic level. Ὁ υἱὸς τοῦ ἀνθρώπου (the Son of the Man) is, as we have seen, a strange expression. That Matthew plays with this semantic strangeness becomes evident in 11:19. Here he uses its strangeness as a literary tool in the wordplay between ὁ υἱὸς τοῦ ἀνθρώπου (the Son of the Man/human being) and ἄνθρωπος (human being); the outsiders take Jesus merely as "a man." But their misunderstanding has also an existential level. In Matt. 8:23-27 nobody but the disciples join the Son of the Man's homelessness and enter the boats; the "other boats" of Mark 4:36 are omitted. The hostile Jews blaspheme the Son of the Man (11:19; 12:32). They reject his authority to forgive sins (9:6) and his authority to use the Sabbath commandment for the benefit of human beings (12:8). They even want to kill him for that (12:14). The most impressive example of this existential misunderstanding is 12:40, Jesus' explanation of the sign of Jonah. The enemies hear that Jesus the Son of the Man will be in the heart of the earth for three days. What kind of consequences they draw from this saying is shown by Matthew in a masterful scene at the end of his Gospel (27:62-66) where he takes up the logion again: the Pharisees — Matthew introduces them into his passion narrative here in order to remind his readers of 12:38-45 — ask for guards for the sepulcher, because they remember that this "seducer" (πλάνος) — Jesus the Son of the Man! — had announced that he would rise up again from the dead after three days. On the morning of the resurrection, the guards fall down "like dead men" (28:4). At the end the high priests have no other choice but to conceal God's salvific action by means of a fraud (28:12-13), like Judas! This is the reason why the rumor about the theft of Jesus' body continues among Jews until Matthew's own day. Here Matthew shows with great literary skill where the misunderstanding of Jesus the Son of the Man leads.

Let us look now at the reaction of the disciples towards Jesus' Son of the

Man sayings. The expression "the Son of the Man" is never introduced or explained to the disciples, but it is, so to speak, filled with narrative materials, that is, information about the present and future fate and actions of Jesus. In many of the sayings about the present fate or power of the Son of the Man Jesus, the disciples realize an inclusive dimension: they follow the homeless Son of the Man in the boat (8:18-27). Matt. 10:5-23 predicts the disciples' own homelessness (cf. 8:20). Matt. 9:6, together with 9:8, again makes clear that they share the power of the Son of the Man to forgive sins. In 12:8 not only is Jesus the Lord of the Sabbath but also his disciples participate in his interpretation of the Law for the benefit of the needy and therefore they are attacked by the Pharisees together with their Lord. The actions, the life style and the power of Jesus have an inclusive dimension (but not the expression "Son of the Man").[23]

Matt. 12:40 is for the disciples the beginning of Jesus' special instructions about his coming death and resurrection; later Jesus will explain openly and in more detail to them what this saying means and what its existential implications are. Our section contains also the first special instructions to the disciples about the future coming of the Son of the Man. The disciples hear from Jesus that he will come soon (10:23). They get further explanation of this "cryptic" saying in 13:40-43 and a full explanation in ch. 24 and 25. When Jesus asks them in 16:13 what people think about him, the Son of the Man, they, and they alone, know what kind of future awaits Jesus. It is not by chance that this main section of the Gospel ends with one of the very few silencing commands of the Gospel (16:20; cf. 17:9). It is possible, I think, to speak about a "Son of the Man secrecy" in the first Gospel which corresponds to the "Son of the Man misunderstanding" of the outsiders. It consists in the fact that the disciples know the whole of the way of Jesus.

The disciples are identification figures for the Christian readers. There is only one difference between the disciples and the readers: the disciples gradually learn through the private instruction of Jesus what the readers know already through their Jesus tradition, but learn again through reading or hearing the Gospel. The readers know already about Jesus' future. Hoffmann's obser-

---

23. Against Margaret Pamment, "The Son of Man in the First Gospel," *NTS* 29 (1983), pp. 116-29. For her the Son of the Man is "every righteous man" (p. 119). Do the disciples grasp such an inclusive dimension of the expression "Son of the Man," which was frequently postulated particularly in British scholarship after Thomas Walter Manson? Many Son of the Man sayings, particularly those about his resurrection and his second coming, exclude a model-character for every man, for example 10:23 (Pamment, pp. 121-22: "cryptic"); 11:19 (only John and Jesus are blasphemed in this way); 12:40 (only Jesus will die and rise in three days); 13:41; 24:27; 26:64 and so on.

vation, that in Q the expression "Son of the Man" does not have a different meaning in each of the classic three groups of logia, is important also for the readers of the Gospel. For them also the expression "Son of the Man" functions as a common denominator, which reminds them of the other stages of the history of Jesus, commented on or predicted in the Son of the Man sayings. When Jesus speaks, for example, in 8:20 about the homelessness of the Son of the Man, the expression reminds the readers of his future as risen, exalted and coming judge of the world. Through this the saying gets its pointed and paradoxical character: he who will come to judge the world, who will sit on the divine throne of glory, has less in this world than do animals! Or when the Christian readers hear in 11:19 that Jesus the Son of the Man is a glutton and winebibber, they know that it is about God's future judge of the world that this evil generation is speaking like that! They have a presentiment of the real depth of Israel's error. Or when they read about the future judgment of Jesus the Son of the Man (13:40-43), they remember that this judge shared their life, suffered and died like them and instructed them in advance about his judgment; and all this is a source of comfort for them.[24] "Son of the Man" helps the readers to read all the individual sayings of Jesus in the perspective of his whole history.

3.4. Matthew 16:21–25:46

Now, as the split between the disciples and the people has become apparent, Jesus continues and intensifies his instruction of the disciples. His suffering, his death, and (not in all the sayings) his rising as the Son of the Man are one focus of his instructions (17:12, 22; 20:18; 26:2, 24, 45, cf. 17:9; 20:28). These sayings function in the narrative as preparation for the disciples of what is going to happen. The instructions are rather stereotyped and repetitive: six times the Matthean Jesus repeats the παραδίδοσθαι (to be handed over) of the Son of the Man, three times he repeats χεῖρες (hands), ἄνθρωποι (men), ἐγείρεσθαι (to be raised). The other main focus of Jesus' private instructions to the disciples in the Son of the Man sayings concerns his future coming as judge of the world (16:27-28; 19:28; 24:27, 30-31, 37, 39, 44; 25:31). Again we observe the repetitive character of three instructions (16:27-28//24:30; 19:28//25:31; 24:37//24:39). It is Matthew's conviction that through continuous and

---

24. Maybe this is another reason why Matthew has omitted "Son of the Man" in 10:32: because in this traditional saying both the earthly Jesus ("I") and his coming ("the Son of the Man") are mentioned, there was no "common denominator" of the different stages of the history of Jesus necessary to remind the readers of the other stages of Jesus' history.

repeated instructions the understanding of the disciples will grow.[25] Many of the sayings in this section have a purely narrative character (16:27; 19:28; 24:30-31; 25:31). The Son of the Man sayings do not so much interpret, but pre-tell the history of Jesus. Particularly important is the fact that Matthew is the only Evangelist who really narrates how the judgment of Jesus the Son of the Man will take place, albeit in a rather metaphorical form (25:31-46). Jesus had started the private instruction of the disciples about his death and resurrection (12:40) and about his future coming (10:23; 13:41) already in the previous section of the Gospel, and now he enlarges and deepens the disciples' knowledge. In Matthew's own words, "The man who has will be given more, until he has abundance" (13:12). After Jesus' private instructions the disciples (and the readers) are fully aware of the goal of the Jesus story, at the very moment when in Matthew's story the future judge is going to be condemned and the one who will rise from the dead is going to be killed.

3.5. The Son of the Man in Chapters 26–28

Matt. 26:63-65 is a crucial scene in Matthew's Gospel. As several common catchwords[26] indicate, it is a reversion of 16:13-20: In contrast to that passage Peter is watching only from a distance, while the high priest, his direct opposite, takes over his role as interlocutor with Jesus. But he is evil. This is indicated from the beginning: he looks for a ψευδομαρτυρία (a false witness); he wants to kill him (26:59); he swears an oath (26:63; cf. 5:33-37). That Jesus is the Christ, the Son of God, is not revealed to the high priest by the Father, but he demands a revelation in a malign way. Jesus' answer is a summary of the next two stages of history ἀπ' ἄρτι (from now on); the Son of the Man will be exalted and sit on the right hand side of the divine Power and he will come with the clouds of heaven for the final judgment (26:64). At this last public revelation, the high priest tears his clothes, not because he is shocked about his own behavior, but because Jesus blasphemes! The scene is very concentrated: Jesus' own revelation is his "guilt," for which he is liable to a death penalty! Jesus' revelation was formulated with the words of Scripture; Matthew used, as Mark, the two classic references for the exaltation of Jesus and for his coming as Son of the Man, Ps. 110:1 and Dan. 7:13. He is consciously reinforcing the affinity to the biblical texts.[27] Matthew wants to indicate that the Jew-

---

25. Cf. 13:51; 15:10; 16:12; 17:13 (συνιέναι!). Matthew is a real school teacher!

26. Θεὸς ζῶν, χριστός, υἱὸς θεοῦ, ὁ υἱὸς τοῦ ἀνθρώπου.

27. Cf. Müller (see note 6), pp. 106-107, 121, 123; Joachim Gnilka, *Das Matthäusevangelium* (HThK 1.2, Freiburg: Herder, 1988), pp. 429, 508.

ish high priest does not understand or take seriously his own Scripture, an idea also expressed elsewhere in the Gospel (cf. 22:41-46). The scene is paradoxical and full of almost Johannine irony: the high priest, unknowingly, judges the judge.

This is the last place where Jesus uses the expression "the Son of the Man" in Matthew's Gospel. He need not speak any more about his future history of death, resurrection, exaltation and final judgment, because now this history happens. The catastrophe of Judaism has begun. In the final text, 28:16-20, the Evangelist does not mention the Son of the Man, although this text contains, as I think, an allusion to Dan. 7.13.[28] This is consistent, because the Son of the Man in Matthew's Gospel is not a title which expresses what Jesus is, his status or dignity, but a narrative expression of Jesus' special language, which Jesus uses in order to comment on and pre-tell his whole history from his humility until his final exaltation and vindication.

4. Conclusions

4.1. Matthew's Jesus speaks about "the Son of the Man" when he speaks about his history and his way. As "the Son of the Man" Jesus is the one who is homeless, rejected, blasphemed, the one with power over sins, the one who is handed over, killed, risen and who comes for judgment. He is also the exalted one — in 26:64 Matthew makes clear, by inserting ἀπ' ἄρτι (from now on), that Jesus is the Son of the Man also in his present status before the parousia (cf. 28:18). Thus, there is no stage in the history of Jesus which is not commented upon by a Son of the Man saying. The "Son of the Man" therefore is a christological expression with a horizontal dimension, by means of which Jesus describes his way through history.[29] In this it is different from the title "Son of God,"[30] which has a vertical dimension: God reveals Jesus as his Son (1:22-23; 2:15; 3:17; 11:27; 16:17; 17:5), and men confess him as Son of God (14:33; 16:16; 27:54). Closely connected with this horizontal dimension is its universal dimension.[31] The story of Jesus the Son of the Man tells of his way from earthly life in Palestine until the point where he appears as judge over the whole gentile world (24:30-31; 25:31-46). In this it is different from the title

---

28. Ἐδόθη αὐτῷ ἐξουσία πάντα τὰ ἔθνη.

29. Similarly Geist (see note 6), p. 425: "Mt (fasst) die drei zeitlichen Ebenen des Handelns Jesu nebeneinander unter eine christologische Forme."

30. For Matthew's use of "Son of God" and "son of David" see pp. 85-88 and 93-96 above.

31. Cf. Geist (see note 6), p. 368.

"son of David," which takes into account only one very limited dimension of Jesus' history, namely his relation to the people of Israel.

4.2. It is not possible to interpret ὁ υἱὸς τοῦ ἀνθρώπου as a christological title because it never says who Jesus is. It is not its traditional, probably apocalyptic, meaning which determines the content of Matthew's Son of the Man sayings. It is, unlike other christological titles, a typical expression of the Jesus language, and its content is entirely filled by the history of Jesus. It is not the title "Son of the Man" which makes clear who Jesus is; rather the history of Jesus makes clear who Jesus the Son of the Man is. It is not the title "Son of the Man" which adds to Matthew's christology an apocalyptic dimension, but because Jesus the Son of the Man will exact the future judgment, the expression "Son of the Man" has also an apocalyptic dimension.[32] The history of Jesus, narrated by Matthew, determines the significance of the expression "Son of the Man" entirely anew.

4.3. I would agree with Jack D. Kingsbury that the Matthean narrative is decisive for the meaning of "Son of the Man" in Matthew, but I do not think he has exploited this sufficiently in his own direction, when he interprets "Son of the Man" as a "public title."[33] He does not consider the interaction which takes place between the narrator and his readers, an interaction clearly intended and provoked by the narrator. He overlooks the fact that Matthew has interwoven the expression "Son of the Man" into his story of the split in Israel and of the way of God's βασιλεία (kingdom) from Israel to the Gentiles. He has overlooked the fact that Matthew used the "public" meaninglessness and strangeness of the expression "Son of the Man" and its insider character as a token of "Christ language" in order to build up his story and to narrate the split in Israel and the final disaster into which the Jews, led by the Pharisees, were falling. I do not want to conceal that this narrative, and also Matthew's use of the expression "Son of the Man" poses serious theological problems to me: by means of Jesus' Son of Man sayings, Matthew has interpreted the split between Israel and the church eschatologically as a final split. He has thus cemented this split and prepared the way for its disastrous effects in the future history of Jewish-Christian relations. Because Israel has rejected Jesus, who the Christians knew would come again as Son of the Man and disown those who have disowned him on earth (10:33), the condemnation of Israel becomes final in Matthew's eyes. Matthew's story of Jesus the Son of the Man

32. Contra Heinz Eduard Tödt, *Der Menschensohn in der synoptischen Überlieferung* (Gütersloh: Gütersloher, 1959), p. 86; Daniel Marguerat, *Le jugement dans l'évangile de Matthieu* (Geneva: Labor et Fides, 1981), p. 71.

33. Cf. n. 21 above.

thus sets a limit to the limitless love which Jesus himself was proclaiming as the arrival of the kingdom of God.

4.4. We asked in the beginning if there is a bridge between the understanding of "Son of the Man" in the Gospel of Matthew and the second-century usage of the expression from Ignatius on. The answer is: both yes and no. There is a great distance between Matthew and Ignatius, at this point and elsewhere. Matthew's basic concept, that "Son of the Man" is a kind of "common denominator" which recalls the whole of the history of Jesus, has not been taken over by Ignatius, nor by anybody else in the second century. The fate of the Synoptic Son of the Man tradition in the second century is for me another example of the striking fact that the history of Jesus as a whole, as it is narrated in the Gospels, seems to be almost totally without effect in the next centuries. It is only the individual traditions, particularly the words of the Lord, which were influential. What the authors of the Gospels added to their traditions when they fitted them into the framework of a Gospel narrative itself, which is more than the sum of its single pericopes and traditions, seems to have passed more or less unnoticed by contemporary and later readers. This is a great problem for me, one lacking a full explanation, and the reception history of "the Son of the Man" is part of it. Only in a very limited sense can we interpret the Matthean concept as a preparation for future Son of the Man christologies. First, since the expression "Son of the Man" has a horizontal and not a vertical dimension in Matthew, this naturally is somehow related to the usage of the expression to denote the human nature of Christ from the second century on. Secondly, the freedom in using the tradition was similar in the Gospel tradition and in the second century. Just as Matthew's use of "Son of the Man" was entirely determined by his story of Jesus (and that means also by his christology), and not by the apocalyptic tradition, in the same way in the second century the expression again was entirely determined by their new christologies and not by the Gospels. The main bridge is the newness of the concepts, the way in which the traditional expression "Son of the Man" was filled with new christologies. On the whole I think the second century is a new beginning in the field of Son of the Man christology. It was not the Jesus tradition which guided the understanding of people in the second century, as it did in Matthew's Gospel, but rather they made new guesses in the context of new christological concepts as to what the meaning of this strange and mysterious expression "son of a (the) human" could be.

ECCLESIOLOGY

7 The Disciples in the Gospel according to Matthew

In recent years several monographs using redaction criticism have brought more clarity to the theology of Matthew's Gospel. Above all, Bornkamm, Barth and Held (1963), Trilling (1959), Strecker (1963), and Hummel (1963)[1] have helped to clarify several features of Matthew's theology, even though in the interpretation of this Gospel we are still a long way short of a generally accepted overall view.[2] One of the points which still seems to be unclear is Matthew's understanding of the disciples. There are two tendencies evident in the interpretation of this. One can be characterized by the term "transparency." This is stressed by Reinhart Hummel: the title "disciple" remains the exhaustive ecclesiological term.[3] Gerhard Barth speaks of an "equating of the time of the church with the time of the life of Jesus."[4] The other tendency is best described by the word "historicizing." That Matthew's understanding of the dis-

---

1. Günter Bornkamm/Gerhard Barth/Heinz Joachim Held, *Tradition and Interpretation in Matthew* (trans. Percy Scott, Philadelphia: Westminster, 1963); Wolfgang Trilling, *Das wahre Israel,* EThS 7 (Leipzig: St. Benno, 1959); Georg Strecker, *Der Weg der Gerechtigkeit,* FRLANT 82 (Göttingen: Vandenhoeck und Ruprecht, 1963); Reinhart Hummel, *Die Auseinandersetzung zwischen Kirche und Judentum im Matthäusevangelium,* BEvTh 33 (Munich: Kaiser, 1963).

2. Cf. Kenzo Tagawa, "People and Community in the Gospel of Matthew," *NTS* 16 (1969-70), pp. 149-62.

3. Hummel, p. 154.

4. Gerhard Barth, "Matthew's Understanding of the Law," in: Bornkamm et al., pp. 58-164, here: p. 111. Cf. Douglas R. A. Hare, *The Theme of Jewish Persecution in the Gospel according to S. Matthew,* SNTSMon 6 (Cambridge: Cambridge University, 1967), esp. pp. 81ff.

German original: "Die Jünger im Matthäusevangelium," *ZNW* 62 (1971), pp. 141-171. English translation by Robert Morgan in: Graham Stanton (ed.), *The Interpretation of Matthew* (Philadelphia/London: Fortress/SPCK), pp. 98-128; new edition: (Edinburgh: Clark, 1995), pp. 115-148.

ciples has a historicizing thrust is stressed above all by Georg Strecker: "The disciples, like Jesus himself, are set in a unrepeatable holy past."[5] Other interpreters find both elements present in Matthew: "Matthew has consistently painted the situation of the post-Easter community back into historical discipleship to Jesus without thereby dissolving the group of disciples in the salvation-historical past into the eschatological self-understanding of his own day."[6] "On the one hand it is clear that we have before us here the preaching of the community in Matthew's time. On the other, these proclamations now have their etiology in the story of Jesus which substantiates them."[7] One notices a certain inconsistency in some authors. Neither historicizing nor transparency seems total. Strecker can say that the historical Peter is "transparent of the contradictions involved in being a Christian."[8] Conversely Hummel, who understands μαθητής (disciple) as an ecclesiological concept, not a salvation-historical concept, sees Peter as "guarantor for the authority of legal and disciplinary regulations,"[9] that is, guarantor of the halakah in Matthew's tradition. This complex situation justifies a fresh treatment of the discipleship theme in Matthew. Special attention will be paid to historicizing and transparency in Matthew's picture of the disciples.

1

We begin by testing Strecker's theses. Can one really see a historicizing tendency in Matthew's understanding of the disciples, and if so, what is its meaning?

The first argument listed by Strecker goes as follows: Matthew identifies the disciples with the Twelve.[10] The Evangelist can on occasion fill out Mark's frequent δώδεκα (twelve) with μαθηταί (disciples) (10:1; perhaps 20:17; 26:20). He can speak redactionally of the twelve disciples (11:1), and he can replace Mark's δώδεκα with μαθηταί (13:10; cf. 18:1). But precisely this last possibility warns us to be careful: if Matthew can omit Mark's δώδεκα and replace it with μαθηταί, this shows not that the number of the disciples was important to him but that he took the number for granted. Above all, he never replaces

5. Strecker (see note 1), p. 194.

6. Siegfried Schulz, *Die Stunde der Botschaft* (Hamburg: Furche, 1967), p. 217.

7. Willi Marxsen, *The Evangelist Mark* (trans. James Boyce et al., Oxford: Blackwell, 1969), p. 141.

8. Strecker (see note 1), p. 206.

9. Hummel (see note 1), p. 60.

10. Strecker (see note 1), p. 191.

μαθηταί in his tradition with δώδεκα μαθηταί ("twelve disciples"). The result is that he speaks of the Twelve less often than Mark does.[11] A tendency to identify the circle of disciples with the Twelve is already present in the pre-Matthean tradition, above all in Mark.[12] So we gain the impression, contrary to Strecker, not that Matthew consciously equates the Twelve with the disciples, but rather that this had by his day already become established and that Matthew is laying no particular stress on it. The analysis of the individual passages does not contradict this. Matthew does not speak of the Twelve at all until 10:1. This tells against his consciously historicizing the disciples with the help of a consistent identification of disciples and the Twelve. It cannot be proved at any point before 10:1 that Matthew had any other disciples than the Twelve in mind either.[13] But the fact that Matthew, unlike Mark, never establishes the group of twelve but presupposes it without comment at 10:1, shows how unimportant it is to him.[14] In short, a conscious historicizing by identifying the disciples with the Twelve cannot be shown. Matthew is here simply following the tradition.

Another point at which Matthew might be thought to be historicizing the picture of the disciples is in their participation in Jesus' mission. Strecker[15]

---

11. Eight times in Matthew against 11 in Mark.

12. Cf. Rudolf Bultmann, *The History of the Synoptic Tradition* (trans. John Marsh, Oxford: Blackwell, 1963), p. 345; a different view is found in Anselm Schulz, *Nachfolgen und Nachahmen*, StANT (Munich: Kösel, 1962), pp. 51ff. Schulz considers the identification of the disciples with the Twelve to be pre-Marcan.

13. The same is true of Matt. 8:21. The parallel between εἷς γραμματεύς (one scribe) and ἕτερος τῶν μαθητῶν (another of the disciples) does not mean that the γραμματεύς is made one of the disciples. The following agree with this interpretation: Pierre Benoit, *L'évangile selon Saint Matthieu*, La Sainte Bible (Paris: Cerf, ³1961), p. 70; Pierre E. Bonnard, *L'évangile selon Saint Matthieu*, CNT 1 (Neuchâtel: Delachaux et Niestlé, ²1970), p. 118; Erich Klostermann, *Das Matthäusevangelium* HNT 4 (Tübingen: J. C. B. Mohr, ²1927), p. 77; Strecker, p. 191. For the contrary view, see Alan Hugh McNeile, *The Gospel according to St Matthew* (London: Macmillan, 1915), p. 109; Walter Grundmann, *Das Evangelium nach Matthäus*, ThHK, 1 (Berlin: Evangelische, 1968), p. 258. "῞Ετερος (another) is a careless addition" (Klostermann) and does not imply that the person thus referred to belongs to the same species as the first named; cf. Luke 23:32 and the evidence given by Bauer under 1bB of his dictionary (ed. Arndt and Gingrich). Matt. 17:6 is the only passage where μαθηταί clearly does not mean the Twelve but the three named at 17:1.

14. If anything can be inferred from Matt. 10:1 it is this: that Matthew inserts μαθηταί into Mark. Is he concerned to show that the authority which is there given to the Twelve to heal and to exorcise is given to the disciples, i.e., to the whole community? But 10:2ff. inserts the names of the Twelve and this can refer only to the historical Twelve. However, the Twelve are there called not μαθηταί but ἀπόστολοι. Is this a coincidence?

15. Strecker (see note 1), pp. 99-122.

and Walker[16] especially have shown that in Matthew's understanding of salvation history the earthly Jesus is sent only to Israel. This is particularly clear in the mission discourse in ch. 10, so we shall take this as an example to clarify the problem. The disciples are sent to Israel (10:5-6) just as Jesus himself is sent only to the lost sheep of the house of Israel (15:24). The mission discourse is interesting for our concerns because Matthew has in his redaction consciously related the mission of the disciples to the mission of Jesus. As Jesus preaches only to Israel (cf. 9:35), so the disciples are sent only to Israel (10:5-6; cf. vv. 17, 23). As Jesus has power to heal all diseases (4:24; 9:35), so have the disciples (10:1; cf. v. 8). One reason that Matthew enriches the two miracle chapters (8 and 9) with miracle stories not found in the parallel chapters in Mark (1–3) is certainly that he wants to relate the authority to perform miracles, even their very details, to the authority of the master.[17]

But it is clear that the historicizing in ch. 10 is not consistent. First, on observation of its external shape: the disciples are indeed sent out in Matthew, but they do not come back — certainly in contrast to Mark and presumably also to the Q tradition. Instead, the mission discourse ends at 11:1 as follows: "And it came to pass, when Jesus had made an end of commanding his twelve disciples . . . ." There is no mention of the disciples going or later coming back. By contrast, both Mark and Luke (Q?) expressly mention the absence of the disciples. So we may say that in Matthew the disciples are evidently not sent out during the lifetime of Jesus: they have only got their instructions. So when are they sent out? This question does not seem to bother Matthew because he is concerned only with Jesus' instructions. Jesus wants to bring salvation to Israel, and this naturally plays a large part in the Evangelist's construction of the discourse, as does the prophecy of persecutions the disciples will experience from Israel itself (10:17, 23). But it is clear, especially in the second part of the chapter, that Jesus' instructions will be fulfilled in the post-Easter period. The post-Easter situation of Jewish Christians persecuted by Israel shines through (10:17-18). Gentile mission and Jewish mission

16. Rolf Walker, *Die Heilsgeschichte im ersten Evangelium*, FRLANT 91 (Göttingen: Vandenhoeck und Ruprecht, 1967), esp. pp. 114ff.

17. There are different, not mutually exclusive, motifs which may explain the position of chapters 8 and 9 in Matthew's outline. (a) The miracle stories come after the Sermon on the Mount because Jesus is being shown primarily as teacher and only then as healing son of David and servant of God healer. But cf. below, n. 102. (b) The Marcan material is perhaps being enriched by new material in Matt. 8–9 for three reasons: (i) to tighten up the composition, and bring together related miracle stories and material interpreted in similar terms; (ii) the fulfilment of the Isa. 61:1 quotation in Matt. 11:5-6 is to be demonstrated in the biography of Jesus; (iii) the authority given to the disciples at 10:1, 8 is to be based on the authority of Jesus.

seem to take place simultaneously (10:18).[18] In a whole series of sayings the Evangelist's wording itself makes it clear that it is intended to be understood as commands that are valid for the present (e.g. vv. 26, 30-31). Elsewhere this is clear from the content.[19] Even the authority given to the disciples to perform miracles (vv. 1 and 8) is probably an authority given to the Matthean community, as we shall see.[20] Finally, in this chapter the word μαθητής is clearly used in a sense which goes beyond the historical situation. Even though v. 24 can be understood as a general principle, this is no longer possible in v. 42. Μαθητής there must plainly be understood from the perspective of the Matthean community. That is, it is transparent.[21] So we conclude that in the mission discourse there is no consistent historicizing of the understanding of the disciples.[22] That can at best be claimed more or less convincingly for 10:1-16. At the latest, in vv. 17-18 the transparent character of the discourse is clear. But there is no formal break between vv. 16 and 17. The commands of Jesus are in principle valid for all time.[23]

The expression μαθητής is fitted into the discourse's transparency for the present. It is, of course, true to say that Matthew intends to stress the mission of the earthly Jesus to Israel. But this aim has not led to a consistent

---

18. The passage 24:9-14 is certainly not a mere "resumé" (Klostermann, p. 193), or "repetition" (Floyd Vivian Filson, *A Commentary on the Gospel according to St. Matthew* [London: Black, 1960], p. 253), or "summary" (Krister Stendahl, "Matthew," in: Matthew Black/Harold Henry Rowley [eds.], *Peake's Commentary on the Bible* [London: Nelson, 1962], p. 793), of Matt. 10:17ff. It is far too long to be that. Rather it is of fundamental significance for the Evangelist.

19. Cf. Eduard Schweizer, *Church Order in the New Testament* (London: SCM, 1961), p. 52 on 10:32, 42.

20. On this, see below, section 2.

21. Strecker's interpretation of εἰς ὄνομα μαθητοῦ ("into name of a disciple") as "on appeal to the name" of a member of the Twelve (cf. Strecker [see note 1], pp. 191f.) seems strained. Linguistically one would then expect ἐν ὀνόματι (in the name) instead of εἰς ὄνομα (into a name). The parallel in v. 42 also supports taking μικροί (little ones) and μαθηταί as synonymous. The difference in wording is because εἰς ὄνομα μικροῦ (into the name of a little one) would have been difficult. Μικροί, however, is plainly to be related to the community, as is clear from 18:6, 10, 14.

22. Béda Rigaux, *Témoignage de l'évangile de Matthieu* (Bruges: Desclée de Brouwer, 1967), pp. 205f., rightly speaks of a *glissement* ("oscillation") in the discipleship discourse between history and "type."

23. Cf. Matt. 28:20. That, of course, clashes with the statements which emphasize the mission of Jesus to Israel alone, and leads to a peculiar mixing of historical statements and those which are valid for the present day. In the light of Matthew's understanding of miracle I would include vv. 10:1, 7-8 among the latter. 10:9-15 is more difficult to interpret. But I see no compelling reason why this verse should not have contained a mission instruction which was still obligatory for Matthew.

periodizing of salvation history.[24] The antithetical scheme "mission of the earthly Jesus to Israel — mission of the apostles only to the Gentiles" seems one-sided, at least in its second part, as is shown by 22:3-6 and 23:34-36 as well as ch. 10. The rejection by Israel of its Messiah means God's judgment, but this does not exclude a mission of the church to Israel. On the contrary, the fiasco of this mission demonstrates the rejection of Israel; Israel's guilt and God's judgment are confirmed by this.[25]

A third argument which needs discussing is Matthew's so-called idealization of the disciples.[26] For Strecker this is the result of "the distance of the redactor from his subject, . . . a sign of the comprehensive historicizing of the gospel tradition: the disciples are . . . set in an unrepeatable holy past."[27] Is this so? Matthew occasionally seems to improve the image of the disciples. That is clearest at 20:20ff. (= Mark 10:35ff.) where Zebedee's wife makes the request instead of Zebedee's sons.[28] In a few passages where Matthew seems to have a more favorable picture of the disciples, the tendency to tighten up the composition is probably at least partly responsible. That is true of Matt. 19:23 (Mark 10:23-24);[29] Matt. 20:17 (Mark 10:32);[30] and Matt. 18:1 (Mark 9:33-35).[31] Abbre-

24. See also Ferdinand Hahn, *Das Verständnis der Mission im Neuen Testament,* WMANT 13 (Neukirchen: Neukirchener, 1965), pp. 124f.

25. The difficulty with any theory of a consistent periodizing of salvation history in Matthew becomes again very clear if we ask when the replacement of Israel by the church, i.e. by the Gentiles, is thought of as completed. In Jesus' death and resurrection? Matt. 28:11-20 would support that, but at least within Walker's scheme the mission to the Jews, which also takes place after the death of Jesus, is clearly presupposed by Matthew and tells against it. Or in the destruction of Jerusalem in A.D. 70? This is emphasized by Walker (see note 16) throughout. Cf. esp. p. 115.

26. Cf. the material in Willoughby C. Allen, *A Critical and Exegetical Commentary on the Gospel according to St Matthew,* ICC (Edinburgh: Clark, 1912), pp. xxxiiif., and in Strecker (see note 1), pp. 193f.

27. Strecker (see note 1), p. 194.

28. The alteration in Matt. 20:20-21 is presumably redactional and does not derive from an alternative tradition. The insertion of προσκυνέω (to worship) supports this assumption. On the βασιλεία (kingdom) of Jesus, cf. 13:36ff.; 16:28.

29. The disciples' θαμβεῖσθαι (to wonder) is missing in Matthew. It is difficult to unravel the composition of Mark 10:23-25. Both Luke and Matthew have smoothed it out by the obvious expedient of omitting Mark 10:24.

30. The disciples' fear and the crowd's astonishment are lacking, as they are however also in the Lucan parallel. Mark 10:32 belongs to the Marcan redaction which, as is well known, is treated quite freely by the authors of the larger Gospels. One reason for omitting Mark 10:32 may also have been that in Matthew's redaction fear is consistently understood as the expression of human unbelief and little faith, not as the expression of the disciples' failure to understand, as it is at Mark 9:32; 10:32; 16:8.

31. Here, too, Matthew like Luke has tightened up his composition of a complicated

viation without change of content is found at Matt. 26:9 (Mark 14:5).[32] It is no use arguing in this connection that Matthew occasionally speaks emphatically about the disciples following Jesus, because he can speak equally emphatically about the crowd following Jesus.[33] In a few passages Matthew changes the wording: in various places he reproaches the disciples for their little faith (8:26; 14:31; 16:8; 17:20); but he can also speak of the disciples' lack of faith (21:21) or their doubt (14:31; 28:17). Since these are not all passages in which a Markan motif is reinterpreted but include some in which the motif first emerges, we cannot interpret them as a weakening of Mark's reproaching their unbelief. In a few places Matthew has erased the motif of the disciples' fear, especially where it was connected with Mark's motif of the disciples' lack of understanding (Mark 9:32;[34] 10:32; 16:8), but in some places he has introduced or considerably strengthened it (Matt. 14:30; 17:6-7; 28:4ff.). The worship of Jesus by the disciples, which is mentioned from time to time, is not meant to describe the believing attitude characteristic of the disciples during his lifetime, but the appropriate attitude toward Jesus in general. That is plain from the fact that not only disciples but also other people fall on the ground before Jesus (8:2; 9:18; 15:25).[35] There is also to be mentioned that Peter's image is considerably worsened in comparison with Mark.[36]

In short, the only point at which Matthew has quite consistently "improved" the picture of the disciples is in his elimination of the Markan motif

---

Marcan pericope. There is probably no intention of improving the disciples' image. On the contrary, since Mark 10:15 is inserted in the Matthean pericope and is formulated in the second person plural, the disciples themselves are challenged to conversion, otherwise they will not enter the kingdom of heaven (v. 3). That is quite strong, but corresponds to Matthew's conception of the community as a corpus mixtum ("mixed body"). The concept of disciple is thus to be understood here as a "type," not in a historicizing way.

32. It is true that in contrast to Mark, Jesus' blame is missing here. But the indignation which occasions it is found in v. 8. And in Matthew, unlike Mark, it is expressly the disciples who are indignant. If anything their image is worse here.

33. Redactional: 4:25; 8:1; 14:13; 19:2; 20:29. Contrary to Strecker (see note 1), p. 193 note 10.

34. One cannot say that the image of the disciples is improved by the parallel formulation in Matthew, "'. . . on the third day will he be raised'; and they were greatly distressed." The great grief of the disciples follows directly after the prediction of the resurrection.

35. The argument of Strecker (see note 1), p. 193 note 15, that on the basis of 24:3; 26:8 the disciples are the "only people who accompany Jesus" in the passion is curious. The anointing at Bethany is admittedly not yet the passion; in Mark too, the disciples are self-evidently present up to the arrest, as in Matthew.

36. Cf. the material in Barth (see note 4), p. 119. It can be shown in some passages that the redactional blackening of Peter's character serves his function as a "type." Cf. Strecker (see note 1), pp. 198ff.

of their failure to understand. In Matthew the disciples do understand. And at this point Matthew is as consistent as he seems everywhere else to be inconsistent.[37] But if that is so, it is methodologically unsound to explain on the one hand his consistent and on the other his thoroughly inconsistent procedure by the same catch-phrase "comprehensive historicizing." Instead we must ask why Matthew treats the knowledge of the disciples differently from their other qualities.

The evidence for Matthew's removal of the Markan motif of the disciples' lack of understanding has been exhaustively presented by Gerhard Barth;[38] we can therefore refer to him. There is only one point at which we would differ from him. He thinks that understanding is given to disciples whereas the people are hardened.[39] But the disciples would then have had no need to ask about the meaning of the parables at Matt. 13:10. Mark 4:34 ("but privately to his own disciples he expounded all things") is also absent from Matthew. On this last point it can be said that the Evangelist is heading consistently for his formula quotation at Matt. 13:35. Mark 4:34 is not absent but is brought up later at Matt. 13:36, where the disciples expressly ask for an explanation of the parable of the tares among the wheat. But at Matt. 13:10 the Evangelist simply adapts the disciples' question to the explanation which follows. Since Matthew has a longer passage between the disciples' question at 13:10 and the explanation of the parable of the sower at 13:18ff., the formal incongruence of question and answer is considerably worse than in Mark.

But above all, the disciples receive far more frequent special instructions in Matthew than in any other Gospel, and this contradicts the thesis of Barth.[40] It means that the disciples often fail to understand, but that they come to understand through Jesus' explanation (13:51). For Matthew it is important that the disciples do finally — after Jesus' instruction — understand. That fits 15:16 and 16:9, too, where it is expressly said that the disciples do not *yet* understand. In each case this is followed by instruction of the disciples intended to remove their lack of understanding. It is then expressly stated at 16:12 and 17:13 that the disciples now understand after this exhaustive instruction by Jesus. So Jesus is shown here as a good teacher who successfully gives the disciples full instructions about everything. They do not understand of

37. So too, Strecker (see note 1), p. 194.
38. Barth (see note 4), pp. 106ff.
39. Barth (see note 4), pp. 107f.
40. Matt. 9:37 to 11:1 (in Luke spoken to the seventy); 13:10-23 (Mark is expanded); 13:36-52; 15:12ff. (Mark expanded); 16:5ff. (Mark); 16:24ff.; 17:10ff. (Mark); 17:19ff. (Mark expanded); 18; 19:23–20:19, cf. 20:17 (Mark expanded); 21:21ff. (Mark); 24:1-2, 3ff.

their own accord. They come to understand through Jesus' instruction. The purpose of this common and consistently applied motif in Matthew is probably not to idealize the picture of the disciples. It is concerned with something else. When the eleven disciples are commissioned to teach all nations what Jesus has commanded them (28:20), the inescapable presupposition for this is that they themselves have understood. A teacher who does not understand what he himself teaches is a blind man leading the blind.[41]

Strecker himself has shown very well how the understanding spoken of by Matthew has a practical side too.[42] Corresponding to that, Jesus' teaching is also very practical; it is a teaching about the better righteousness. So Jesus is the teacher who leads his disciples to understanding. Understanding is related to the teaching of Jesus. Faith and understanding are separated in Matthew. The disciples are men of little faith, but they do understand. Faith is directed to the person of Jesus; understanding is related to his teaching. In Mark the disciples' lack of understanding is conceived with reference to christology. It applies to the person and later particularly to the suffering of the Son of God. In Matthew, by contrast, the disciples' understanding is directed to something different, namely Jesus' *teaching*. It is no coincidence that understanding usually has an object here.[43] Where there could be no object, Matthew deletes Mark's lack of understanding motif, but does not himself speak of the disciples' understanding (cf. 14:32-33). So it is not only that in comparison with Mark the disciples have gained in understanding; the horizon of understanding has shifted too. Full understanding is for Matthew not the expression but the presupposition of Christian existence, and this consists in loyalty to the message of the earthly Jesus. For Matthew understanding is the presupposition of both Christian life and Christian teaching.

On the other side, Matthew's concept of faith has been detached from understanding and it has probably also been narrowed.[44] It is no coincidence that Matthew has taken up and reflected theologically, above all, on the usage of "faith" in the miracle stories, even though the more general use of the word was not unfamiliar to him. Gerhard Barth put it like this: "The intellectual element . . . is excluded from Matthew's concept of faith."[45] Πίστις (faith) becomes mainly trust. With the one exception of 16:8-9, understanding is not

41. Cf. the contrast between Pharisees and disciples, Matt. 15:14, 15.

42. Strecker (see note 1), pp. 228ff.

43. The parables (chapter 13 passim); that Jesus used pictorial speech (16:12) or that he spoke about John the Baptist (17:13).

44. On Matthew's conception of faith, see below section 2.

45. Barth (see note 4), p. 113.

the presupposition of faith[46] but is separated from it. Faith is directed at the miraculous power of the Lord which is still at work in the community; understanding relates to the teaching of Jesus. In terms of form criticism "faith" is found largely in the miracle stories, "understanding" in the catechetical material. Theologically speaking, "faith" seems to be mainly linked to the exalted, and "understanding" to the earthly, Jesus. For Matthew faith is largely[47] the human attitude corresponding to the divine Power of salvation, whereas understanding is the presupposition for loyalty to the earthly Jesus, that is, for Christian ethics. Faith seems to be mainly correlated with the indicative of salvation, understanding more with ethics. And this lack of any close relation between faith and understanding which we seem to find in Matthew seems to present us with a fundamental problem about his theology.

A further observation corresponds to the disciples' understanding. In the First Gospel the disciples are basically designated as hearers of Jesus' message. That does not exclude the crowd hearing Jesus' message too. They, too, are hearers of Jesus' parable discourse. But the disciples' eyes and ears are called blessed because they do not only hear and see but also understand it (13:16). Something similar is found in ch. 15. There, too, the crowd is present at the controversy dialogue with the Pharisees (15:10), but only to disappear while Jesus explains the "parable" to the disciples (15:12, 15). Because the crowds to whom Jesus preaches in parables do not understand (13:13), they are a foil to the disciples who hear and understand all Jesus' instructions.

In line with this, the disciples are always hearers of Jesus. They are never absent, not even after they have been sent out. It is not always self-evident that the disciples should be especially mentioned as hearers of Jesus. For example, it is not self-evident in the discourse in ch. 23, which apart from vv. 1-12 is directed at Israel. But there, too, the disciples are expressly named in v. 1 as among Jesus' hearers. In ch. 24, too, it is not only a chosen few but all the disciples who are hearers of Jesus (24:3). Whether the Sermon on the Plain in Q was addressed to the disciples or to the people can no longer be ascertained since both the Matthean and the Lukan introductions and conclusions come from the Evangelists themselves,[48] but it is notable that in 5:1, Matthew particularly mentions that it is disciples who hear the Sermon on the Mount because this does not naturally follow from his redactional composition of 4:25–5:2. In 16:24, too, it is the disciples who are named as the hearers of Jesus'

46. Contrary to Barth (see note 4), p. 113.

47. Substantially, because Matthew's conception of faith is not finally systematized; cf. below, part 2.

48. Contrary to Jacques Dupont, *Les Béatitudes. Le Problème litteraire. Le message doctrinal* (Bruges: Abbaye de Saint-André, 1954), pp. 30f.

message. The crowds are deleted here. We have already mentioned that Matthew has a particularly large number of instructions to the disciples. In short, for Luke the apostles, who are witnesses of all that Jesus did in the land of the Jews and in Jerusalem (Acts 10:39), and especially witnesses of the resurrection (Acts 1:22), are primarily eyewitnesses. But in Matthew the disciples are men who have heard and understood all that Jesus taught in his lifetime. That is, they are ear-witnesses.

To *summarize,* we have not found a thoroughgoing historicizing in the understanding of the disciples in Matthew's Gospel. At only one point is Matthew consistent: discipleship is always related to the teaching of the earthly Jesus. The disciples are hearers of that teaching and understand it. This is the presupposition for the definition of discipleship at Matt. 12:50 as doing the will of God.[49] The difference between Matthew and Luke seems to be that in Matthew the (limited) "historicizing" of the disciples is not connected with any idea of succession. That is clear, for example, in Matthew's picture of Peter, who is not to be interpreted as guarantor of the halakah but as the model or "type" of discipleship, as Strecker has shown, in my opinion, convincingly.[50] This means that alongside the historicizing there is typification which frames it, and alone makes it truly meaningful. It is as pupils of the earthly Jesus that the disciples become transparent and are models of what it means to be a Christian. That will be clarified in what follows, first by reference to the miracle stories.

2

The miracle stories in Matthew have been thoroughly investigated by Heinz Joachim Held, and we here latch on to the results of his work.[51] He has shown that in both Matthew's feeding miracles the echoes of the Eucharist already present in Mark become much clearer through Matthew's abbreviations of these narratives.[52] These echoes made it possible for the Christian hearer to

---

49. On the analysis of the text cf. Trilling (see note 1), pp. 15f. Mark 3:31-35 is tightened up by Matthew. In v. 49 Jesus now stretches out his hand over the disciples and designates them as brothers, sisters and mother because they do God's will. Is that stretching out of his hand to be understood symbolically as an indication of the authority of Jesus which protects the community?

50. Cf. above, n. 36.

51. Heinz Joachim Held, "Matthew as Interpreter of the Miracle Stories," in: Bornkamm et al. (see note 1), pp. 165-300.

52. Held (see note 51), p. 187.

understand his own experiences in the Eucharist in the light of the miracle reported in the story. Both the people who are filled, and especially the disciples who share out the loaves and fishes, become transparent in the light of the eucharistic experiences of Christians.[53] However, neither story is simply made into a Eucharist story. The presence of the fishes, which are retained despite Matthew's abbreviation of Mark and which do not fit the eucharistic practice of the Matthean community,[54] precludes that. The fishes and also the mention of the precise number of the baskets with the pieces of food left over, plus the giving of the numbers fed,[55] show that Matthew, too, sees the feedings as a matter of events which happened once in the historical past by Lake Gennesareth (where there are fish!). We must, therefore, say that it is precisely as past historical events that these two miracle stories become transparent for the present life of the community.

The two stories of stilling the storms in Matt. 8:23-27 and 14:23-33 have been analyzed by Bornkamm.[56] He has clearly shown their character of transparency for the present life of the church. It is plain that in the disciples following Jesus into the boat, in the swamping by the σεισμός (storm),[57] in the request κύριε σῶσον ("Lord, save"), in the anxiety of the disciples or their little faith, experiences of the community are reflected. It is clear that the Evangelist is interested not simply in the miracle that happened in the past, but in

53. In the history of the tradition the eucharistic experience of the community presumably played, even in the early period, a big part in the formation and handing on of the feeding stories. Nevertheless the narrative of the feeding is fully historicized as early as the pre-Marcan tradition, as is shown by its inclusion in the old pre-Marcan narrative sequence, feeding — crossing the lake — controversy dialogues — miracle (on this cf. Eduard Schweizer, *The Good News According to Mark* [trans. Donald H. Madvig, London: SPCK, 1970], pp. 136f.). Mark has not destroyed this historicizing by his kerygmatic outline; the kerygma presupposes the history. In Matthew the experience which contributed to the original shaping of the pericope is even clearer, without the pericope losing its character of reporting history.

54. Matt. 15:36 shows that despite his abbreviating the story the Evangelist did not want to omit the fish. He has put them in here out of the omitted verse Mark 8:7. Matt. 14:19 also shows that the fish are important to the Evangelist. For the sake of mentioning them he is prepared to imply the awkward phrase "breaking fish."

55. In contrast to Mark, Matthew has both times given the number more precisely and probably heightened the miraculous character of the story. That shows that he did not understand the pericope simply as a presentation of the experience of the community, but also as a miracle which really happened in the life of Jesus.

56. Cf. Bornkamm (see note 1), pp. 52ff.

57. Illustrations of σεισμός (storm), accoding to which Bornkamm designates apocalyptic horrors, might be present at 5:11-12; 23:32ff. The connection between persecution and eschaton is found in 10:22; 24:9. Cf. also how 24:7 (σεισμός = earthquake) occurs near to persecution and execution for the sake of faith in 24:9.

the community's experience of the still ever-helping presence of the Lord. But Bornkamm rightly observes, "In Matthew this characteristic of the story [i.e. as a real miracle] . . . is not completely abandoned."[58] There remains a historical residue which the Evangelist could easily have omitted: mention of the fourth watch of the night (14:25) and the comment, which is even more exact than in Mark, that the boat was several furlongs away from the land (14:24). The "choral ending" in Matt. 8:27 also seems to be more appropriate in a miracle story than in a purely symbolic story. The stories of stilling of the storms were evidently proclaimed by the Matthean community as miracles of Jesus. And from its own experiences of the power of the Lord Jesus the community knew that this power was still at work in their midst. So again it is precisely the past event which is transparent for the present.

The position is similar with the healing miracles. Redaction criticism has shown that the Matthean interpretation is found on different levels. Again the past historical fact as such is itself important. Matthew interprets Jesus' miracles as the fulfillment of Old Testament prophecies (8:17; 11:5-6; 12:18-21). His filling out of the Markan miracle collection for the sake of a complete fulfillment of the Isa. 61:1 quotation at 11:5-6[59] shows that the Evangelist was at least partly interested in the factuality of the individual miracle stories. The frequent use of the title "Son of David" in the miracle stories (9:27; 12:23; 15:22; 20:30-31) also indicates that Matthew interprets these as fulfilling the specific mission of Jesus, which was meant for the people of Israel and which did not continue in this way in the post-Easter community.[60] But alongside that, the healing miracles were themselves transparent for the present. This transparency becomes clear at different points. I give only two of them.

First, the Matthean understanding of faith: Matthew gives every indication of being familiar with the πίστις (faith) concept of Hellenistic Christianity, which used the word to paraphrase Christian existence as such: "John came . . . and you did not believe him; but the tax-gatherers and the harlots believed him; . . . you however did not repent and believe him" (21:32). In this redactional verse πιστεύω (to believe) is an all-encompassing term for relationship to John the Baptist. The expression is, of course, taken from the believers' relationship to Christ and applied to John. The verse from the tradition, 18:6, also shows that Matthew, i.e. his readers and hearers, clearly understand the term as describing Christian existence. So when Mat-

---

58. Bornkamm (see note 1), p. 54.

59. Held (see note 51), p. 248.

60. Cf. Strecker (see note 1), pp. 118ff.; Hummel (see note 1), pp. 116ff.; Christoph Burger, *Jesus als Davidssohn*, FRLANT 98 (Göttingen: Vandenhoeck und Ruprecht, 1970), pp. 72ff.

thew repeatedly orients the healings to the theme of "faith,"[61] he is certainly speaking to the community about their faith, or their need of it. One might even wonder whether the frequent reference to "little faith" in Matthew's miracle stories (8:26; 14:31; cf. 16:8; 17:20) is perhaps aimed at a contemporary situation in the community; namely, that although it is a community of believers, miracles are sometimes absent. This experience would obviously be quite likely toward the end of the first century, as experiences of the spirit generally receded.[62] Matt. 17:19ff. would offer the clearest support for this interpretation. It would make good sense of Matthew's distinction between unbelief (e.g. that of the people at Nazareth, 13:58, or the Jews at 21:32) and little faith, which always refers to the disciples. The Christians, here represented by the disciples, are on the one hand believers — in that faith is the obvious characteristic of everyone who believes in the Lord and is the mark which distinguishes them from non-Christians, who are ἄπιστοι (unbelievers) — and, on the other hand, themselves unbelieving in the sense that they often lack that special faith which moves mountains and experiences miracles. In terms of the history of the tradition, Matthew's concept of ὀλιγοπιστία (little faith) would then represent an attempt to reconcile by means of terminology two quite different understandings of faith current in Hellenistic Christianity.[63] Existentially, the experience of, and reflection on, the cessation of the Spirit played a role. Be that as it may, Matthew seems to understand faith in the light of his present situation without giving it very clear conceptual expression.[64]

Second, the transfer of Jesus' authority to the community.[65] This trait is particularly clear in Matthew and again helps us to be more precise about the nature of faith in this Gospel. Matt. 7:22 presupposes in the community charismatic activity, of which the Evangelist is evidently critical. But he is himself — at least so far as his basically positive attitude to miracles is concerned — not

---

61. Cf. Held (see note 51), pp. 178ff., 193ff.

62. Cf. Bonnard (see note 13), pp. 259, 261.

63. We find both types of understanding of faith in pre-Pauline Christianity too. Cf. miracle faith in 1 Cor. 13:2, and for the other meaning the "general" understanding of faith found in the pre-Pauline connection of faith and the so-called faith formula or in the technical term ἄπιστος (unbelieving) already in use (1 Cor. 6:6; 7:12ff.; 10:27; 14:22ff.; etc.).

64. At 21:32 the preceding parable of the two sons, and the interpretative phrase "he came . . . in a way of righteousness," seem to imply that faith means something like accepting the demand for righteousness which John (and Jesus) present. In the miracle stories where most of the occurrences of the stem πιστευ- (believe) are found, it means trusting in the unlimited power of Jesus. The two different nuances have different roots in the history of the tradition prior to Matthew. They cannot be completely harmonized.

65. Cf. on that Held (see note 51), pp. 270ff.

all that far from the charismatics he is attacking.[66] One might, indeed, understand the authority to perform miracles, which in 10:1 and 10:8[67] is given to the disciples with explicit reference to Jesus' miracles, as limited to the mission of the disciples during Jesus' own lifetime. But we have already seen that despite all its connection with the particular mission of Jesus to Israel the mission discourse nevertheless consciously goes beyond that historical situation. This is confirmed by other passages. In 14:28-31, Peter, whose own doubt and little faith here make him a model of Christians, participates in Jesus' authority to walk on the water. In 17:19ff., where the tradition's instruction of the disciples about doing miracles is considerably developed and made a matter of principle, it is assumed that miracles happen, or ought to happen, in Matthew's community. Eduard Schweizer[68] draws attention to Matt. 10:24-25, where the disciples are "explicitly equated with their master who after the healing of the dumb man . . . is called Beelzebul (cf. 9:34)." Particularly clear, however, is the transference to the whole community of the authority to forgive sins that Jesus exercises at the healing of the lame man (9:8). That Matthew's community practiced forgiveness of sins and considered this important is clear not only from the community discourse in chapter 18, but also from the Matthean addition to the Last Supper liturgy at 26:28: "for the forgiveness of sins." This makes it probable that the Evangelist Matthew did, in fact, understand the authority to bind and loose promised to Peter (16:19) as applying to the whole community. Here, too, Peter for him is the "type" of a Christian;[69] the authority which is given to him is exercised by the whole community (18:15ff.).[70]

Outside the miracle stories, there is so much material showing the transparency of the concept of discipleship that we can select only a few observations to round off the picture. First, Matthew avoids the word ἀπόστολος (apostle). He has it only in the heading given to the list of apostles in 10:2. It is applied there to the Twelve, which shows that the idea of the twelve apostles, which Luke developed into a theological concept, was evidently some kind of

66. Cf. also Eduard Schweizer, "Observance of the Law and Charismatic Activity in Matthew," *NTS* 16 (1969/70), pp. 216ff.

67. Cf. 10:1 with 9:35.

68. Schweizer (see note 66), p. 220.

69. Strecker (see note 1), pp. 201ff.

70. Against Schweizer (see note 19), p. 59, Matthew would not say that the whole community is the successor of Peter. For Matthew there was probably never a special period in which Peter had a special authority which the whole community then inherited. That would mean that the other disciples did not possess this authority during Peter's lifetime, which 18:18 makes impossible. If the Matthean community understands itself as the group of Jesus' disciples, then Peter, in the eyes of the Evangelist, exercises no other authority than that given to the disciples as such.

trend at this time.[71] In Acts, Luke clearly differentiates between the twelve apostles, who have a once for all historical function as witnesses of the life of Jesus and the resurrection, and the μαθηταί, who in Acts represent the totality of believers (cf. for example, 6:2; 9:1, 10, 26; 11:26; 16:1, etc.). This linguistic usage affects his Gospel as well (Luke 6:13, 17, 20; 19:37, 39; 24:9). In contrast Matthew consistently avoids the title apostle, even where he is speaking of the mission of the Twelve.[72] Why? The reason may be as follows: the members of his community could identify with the μαθηταί but not with the ἀπόστολοι, who had already become by that time figures of the past. Conversely, the word μαθητής is very well suited for teaching people to understand the essence of being a Christian as a relationship to the earthly Jesus. Ἀπόστολος is more strongly colored by the post-Easter function of the apostles.

Second, the transparency of μαθητής is clear in Matthew's use of the verb μαθητεύω ("to disciple"). It occurs three times in this Gospel, all probably redactional: 13:52; 27:57; and 28:19. At 27:57, Matthew replaces Mark's προσδεχόμενος τὴν βασιλείαν (awaiting the kingdom) with ἐμαθητεύθη τῷ Ἰησοῦ (he was discipled to Jesus). We may take that as an interpretation of his source, Mark, not as a correction. Discipleship for Matthew consists in acceptance of the βασιλεία (kingdom), i.e. of the good news from Jesus. In the same way the difficult passage in 13:52 relates μαθητεύειν (to disciple) to the βασιλεία τῶν οὐρανῶν ("kingdom of heaven"), i.e. to Jesus' teaching. 28:19 should also be understand in a similar way. Μαθητεύω (to disciple) is here interpreted by "teaching them to observe what I have commanded you,"[73] i.e. again by a reference to the teaching of the earthly Jesus.[74] That corresponds to the way in

---

71. Cf. Günter Klein, *Die Zwölf Apostel. Ursprung und Gehalt einer Idee,* FRLANT 77 (Göttingen: Vandenhoeck und Ruprecht, 1961), pp. 202ff. But against Klein, cf. also Mark 6:7 where the idea of the twelve apostles is probably also presupposed in the verb ἀποστέλλω (to send), and also Rev. 21:14 where again the idea of the twelve apostles as founders and representatives of the new people of God, the church, is probably present.

72. Cf. the alteration of Mark 6:7 at Matt. 10:1 and the omission of Mark 6:30.

73. The baptismal command which at once follows is probably traditional, as Strecker (see note 1), p. 209, has rightly shown. Matthew's placing the traditional baptismal command before the command which is to him far more important, to teach the nations to keep all that Jesus has commanded the disciples, is probably not conditioned by any strong emphasis on baptism in Matthew. The reason for it is rather that baptism stands at the beginning of Christian existence, whereas teaching and keeping the commands determine the whole of a Christian's life following his baptism.

74. The aorist ἐνετειλάμην there emphasizes that it is a matter of the commands of the earthly Jesus. Cf. Günther Bornkamm, "The Risen Lord and the Earthly Jesus: Matthew 28:16-20," in: James M. Robinson, *The Future of Our Religious Past* (FS Rudolf Bultmann, London: SPCK, 1971), pp. 203-229, here: pp. 223f.

which Matthew profiles discipleship in his Gospel. Disciples are those who hear and understand the commands and teachings of Jesus,[75] and do God's will (12:50). At the same time, however, they are according to 28:20 those with whom the Lord with his authority is present always, even to the end of the world. What that might mean is explicated by Matthew in his miracle stories. In short, it is highly unlikely in the light of these three passages that Matthew uses the verb μαθητεύω in a quite different sense from the substantive μαθητής, as Strecker argues.[76] Rather, the verb μαθητεύω functions as transparency to make discipleship in the Gospel illuminate the Evangelist's own day.

Third, the transparency of the disciple concept in this Gospel is also secured by other parallel concepts, for example ἀδελφός (brother). In most cases the word is taken over by Matthew from his tradition and is only relatively seldom used by him redactionally (18:21, 35; 28:10?). Since it was current as a self-designation by Christians, the passages in which the word occurs gain a certain transparency automatically. At 12:46ff. and 23:8 it is synonymous with μαθητής. Another parallel concept is the early term for disciples, μικρός (little one),[77] which crops up in Matthew's tradition and is also probably understood by the Evangelist as synonymous with μαθητής.[78]

3

We shall now pause for a moment and try to summarize what has emerged from our survey concerning the way the disciples are understood in the first Gospel.

1. The disciples of Jesus are transparent for the present situation. Behind them stands Matthew's community. Μαθητής is an ecclesiological term.[79]

The question of whether the disciples represent the leaders or the mem-

75. Cf. above, section 1.

76. Strecker (see note 1), pp. 192f. He points out that μαθητεύειν is never said of a member of the Twelve. Since there are only three occurrences of the word, however, that might be coincidence. Strecker himself establishes that μαθητεύειν and μαθητής agree in content. Against him Günther Baumbach, "Die Mission im Matthäusevangelium," *ThLZ* 92 (1967), pp. 889-893, here: p. 891, formulates the matter correctly: μαθητεύω alludes not to some particular missionary practice of the community but to its own life. Hahn (see note 24), p. 121 note 5, understands μαθητεύω in a similar way, as does Schweizer (see note 66), p. 218.

77. Cf. Otto Michel, "Diese Kleinen — eine Jüngerbezeichnung," *Theologische Studien und Kritiken* 108 (1937-8), pp. 401-415.

78. Cf. above n. 21, and on Matthew's redaction also Barth (see note 4), pp. 121ff.

79. Similarly Bornkamm (see note 74), p. 221; Barth (see note 4), p. 111; Hummel (see note 1), p. 154; Bonnard (see note 13), p. 416.

bers of the community has considerable significance, for example, for the interpretation of Matt. 18, but cannot be decided with certainty. In both feeding stories they seem to represent the leaders, but this restriction cannot be maintained in the stillings of the storms or the miracle story at 17:14ff. But that in itself shows that this distinction between leaders and community is, in fact, relatively unimportant for Matthew's understanding of discipleship. The parallel between μικρός and μαθητής at 10:42[80] provides further support for interpreting chapter 18 in the same way and making no distinction between μικροί (members of the community) and μαθηταί addressed at 18:1. That means that community members who fulfill a leadership function are disciples in the same way as all other members. This would count against the common interpretation of Matt. 18 as instructions for appointed leaders.[81] Institutional problems seem to be not yet very significant for Matthew's community.[82]

Other problems arising from Matthew's discipleship transparency technique can here remain open — for example, the often discussed question of whether we may conclude from the instructions to the disciples in Matthew that the Matthean community saw itself as still part of the Jewish synagogues.[83] Another question that has recently been raised is whether the frequent redactional use of πορεύομαι (to go) implies that in Matthew's church itinerant missionaries and prophets played a special role.[84] The answer to this

---

80. Cf. above, n. 21.

81. Contrary to Joachim Jeremias, *The Parables of Jesus* (trans. Samuel Henry Hooke, London: SCM, 1963), p. 40; and idem, "Κλείς," in *TDNT* III, p. 752; Georg Dunbar Kilpatrick, *The Origins of the Gospel according to St. Matthew* (Oxford: Clarendon, 1946), p. 127; Rudolf Schnackenburg, *The Church in the New Testament* (London: Burns and Oates, 1965), pp. 69ff.; Trilling, p. 100 (admittedly with reservations); Rigaux (n. 22), p. 210.

82. Against Georg Strecker, "Das Geschichtsverständnis bei Matthäus," *EvTh* 26 (1966), pp. 57-74. Strecker says correctly that the church in Matthew is "representative of the ethical demand in history." That is right, in that the disciples have learnt from being with the earthly Jesus and represent his interpretation of the law in their own day. But that has nothing to do with institutionalizing. Strecker is thinking here too much in Lucan categories.

83. So Ernst Lohmeyer/Werner Schmauch, *Das Evangelium des Matthäus*, KEK Sonderband (Göttingen: Vandenhoeck und Ruprecht, 1958), pp. 335, 341; Bonnard (see note 13), p. 333. Bornkamm, "End-expectation and Church in Matthew," in: Bornkamm (see note 1), p. 43; Hummel, op. cit. (see note 1), pp. 31f.; Georg Kretschmar, "Ein Beitrag zur Frage nach dem Ursprung frühchristlicher Askese," *ZThK* 61 (1964), pp. 27-67, here: p. 60. Ernst Haenchen, "Matthäus 23," *ZThK* 48 (1951), pp. 38-63, here: pp. 51f., 59; Trilling (see note 1), pp. 94f.; cf. 13f., 70ff.; and Hare (see note 4), pp. 104f. have rejected this hypothesis, in my view rightly, pointing out that most of the passages which support it belong to the tradition, or more exactly to a particular layer of tradition standing behind the Gospel.

84. This hypothesis is now supported by Schweizer (see note 66), pp. 221ff., 229, taking up Kretzschmar (see note 83), p. 61, and Baumbach (see note 76), p. 890.

question makes no difference to Matthew's basic conception and can here be left out of the discussion.

2. In the miracle stories we ascertained in each case a historical residue. They are understood as historical events and the Lord Jesus is clearly understood as a figure in the past who fulfilled a unique mission in the history of salvation. But at the same time in the earthly Jesus the risen Lord is present.[85] So transparency in the disciple means becoming contemporary with a figure of the past. The temporal distance is bridged, but evidently not in a way that simply dissolves the earthly Jesus in the community's experiences of the Spirit. Rather, Matthew makes it clear that it is the power of the earthly Jesus that is efficacious in the community and calls for faith. The same result emerged from an investigation of Strecker's arguments for Matthew's historicizing of the disciple concept.[86] All that is essential is hearing, understanding and doing the words of the earthly Jesus. And precisely that is the essence of true discipleship in every age. Thus, characteristic for Matthew's concept of discipleship is the tendency to make the past — which Matthew emphasizes — transparent for the present.

Both aspects, the past and the transparency, seem to be correlated in Matthew in a quite different way with christology. The transparency of the disciple concept seems to be particularly important for the promise of salvation, i.e. for the indicative. Salvation in Matthew is essentially the continuing authority of the Lord in the community; it is receiving the efficacious forgiveness of sins which Jesus committed to the community's charge. Salvation is both the continuation in the community of miracles done in Jesus' name, which guarantee the nearness of the kingdom of God, and also the experience in discipleship of the power of Jesus which overcomes all doubt and all cowardice. In Matthew the miracle stories themselves have a central function in announcing salvation. Without miracles, proclamation of the gospel of the kingdom of God is impossible. That is why Matthew has so consistently placed Jesus' miracles and his teaching alongside one another and emphasized both as equally important.[87] In my view it is impossible to speak of a devaluation of the miraculous in Matthew. Negatively, that means that it is not the kerygma of Jesus' death and resurrection which spells salvation. Positively, salvation is the abiding presence of Jesus in the

---

85. Held (see note 51), pp. 262f., rightly points to the κύριος title, the worship, the way human traits recede in Matthew's picture of Jesus, and the verbs σῴζω and ἐλεέω.

86. Cf. above, section 1.

87. Cf. Matt. 4:23; 9:35; 10:7-8; 19:2, and in addition 14:14 in comparison with Mark 6:34; also the way chapters 5–7 and 8–9 are placed alongside each other, and 21:13-14.

community.[88] To express that, the transparency use of the disciple concept is necessary.

On the other hand, connecting being a disciple with the person of the earthly Jesus seems to be fundamental above all for the ethics of this Gospel, i.e. for the imperative. It has often been rightly emphasized that the Evangelist has to defend himself, at least in part, against Hellenistic Christian enthusiasts, as is apparent, for example, at the end of the Sermon on the Mount.[89] Against these he points to the commands of Jesus which the disciples heard; obedience to these constitutes the nature of true discipleship. Only by keeping his commands can true Christians be distinguished from false ones. Matthew has no institutional criterion for distinguishing them, such as is at least on the way in Luke. It corresponds to this lack of any such criterion that the separation can take place only at the last judgment. The relationship of discipleship to the earthly Jesus is decisive for this basic conception. For Matthew, historicizing is itself the presupposition for genuine transparency. For him true discipleship is at all times only possible as recourse to the earthly Jesus.[90]

The result corresponds exactly with the report of a resurrection appearance which is transmitted only in Matt. 28:16-20. Since this pericope has recently been discussed at length, especially by Günther Bornkamm and Anton Vögtle,[91] we can be brief. It lacks important form-critical characteristics of an appearance story:[92] an exact description of the appearance of Jesus and the motif of recognition by the disciples are both absent. It is striking that the text ends not with Jesus' disappearance, but with a reference to his abiding presence. The motif of doubt does correspond to what is normally found in an appearance story, but there is no reference here to it being overcome. Since the combination of doubt and worship is also found at 14:31-33, it is probably the work of the Evangelist. The disciples' doubt, is thus, not overcome by Je-

---

88. It is then, of course, correspondingly tragic for such a theology when miracles are absent, as was supposedly the case at Matt. 17:19ff.

89. Cf. Barth (see note 4), pp. 159ff.; Bornkamm (see note 74), p. 216; Schweizer (see note 66), pp. 216ff., 225ff.

90. After all this I cannot help being rather doubtful about the occasionally argued view that Matthew is a Catholic Gospel within the New Testament. In my opinion the theologically closest relatives to Matthew in the history of the church are the so-called "side movements" of the Reformation (Anabaptists etc.) in their tendency towards a loyal fulfilling of Jesus' law, and simultaneous emphasis upon the presence of the Lord's power in the community. A history of the interpretation of Matthew in these churches would be a worthwhile and much needed task.

91. Bornkamm (see note 74), pp. 203ff.; Anton Vögtle, "Das christologische und ekklesiologische Anliegen von Mt 28:18-20," in: Vögtle, *Studia Evangelica II*, TU 87 (Berlin: Akademie, 1964), pp. 266-294.

92. Cf. Bornkamm (see note 74), pp. 203ff.; Vögtle (see note 91), pp. 279ff.

sus' appearance, which is not itself important here. That reflects, as Otto Michel was probably right in seeing, the problem of the Matthean community which could not settle its doubts by looking at the Easter experiences of their predecessors.[93] Rather, the disciples' doubt remains, as it were, unresolved in this pericope — in fact, it is still found in the present (cf. 14:28ff.). It is confronted by the power of the exalted Lord and by his word which is identical with the word of the earthly Jesus. And that alone is evidently what matters for Matthew about being a Christian: the power of the exalted one and the word of the earthly one.

These two elements are both stressed in this pericope. On the one hand, Matthew speaks of the continuing presence of Jesus in the community. G. Bornkamm has pointed out that unlike the pericope John 20:19-23, which is in many ways similar, there is here no talk of the Spirit.[94] That is true, though the formulation "I am with you" probably means in effect the same as what is said with the word "Spirit." Matthew has made it clear in his miracle stories what he understands by the presence of the Lord. And it is notable that there are quite similar parallels of form in the Johannine Paraclete sayings (John 14:16, 17, 18, 23). Matthew himself at one point seizes hold of the same idea[95] of the presence of Jesus in his community back at 18:20, there in connection with the authority given to the community to exercise church discipline and to pray with the assurance of being answered. The closest theological parallel to Matt. 18:15-20 is presumably 1 Cor. 5:4-5. When the Hellenistic community in Corinth is assembled with the power (!) of the Lord Jesus, church discipline should be exercised. The theological parallels thus point us to Hellenistic Christianity, as on the whole do the miracle stories which Matthew tells in his Gospel as illustrations. It is, however, significant that this text speaks of the presence of Jesus, rather than the presence of the Spirit.[96] In this way the Evangelist again takes up everything that he has said in his Gospel about Jesus' power to perform miracles, and makes it transparent for the present and explains that it is valid now as it was then. Vögtle also has shown by another

93. Otto Michel, "Der Abschluss des Matthäus-Evangeliums," *EvTh* 10 (1950/51), pp. 16ff.; cf. Barth (see note 4), p. 132.

94. Bornkamm (see note 74), p. 216.

95. It is the same idea, contrary to the view of Trilling (see note 1), pp. 27f., which I would like to interpret at 18:20 as the "static presence" of Jesus (comparable to Jahweh's name dwelling in the Temple), in contrast to his "dynamic presence" at 28:20 (comparable to Jahweh's presence in history). But the linguistic indications are probably too weak to support this thesis.

96. Contrary to Strecker (see note 1), p. 209, I am of the opinion that a pre-Matthean formulation cannot be demonstrated in 28:20. But that the idea is pre-Matthean is plain from 18:20.

route that by referring to Jesus' authority in v. 18 the Evangelist intends to fasten primarily on to the authority given to the earthly Jesus because this remains effective after his exaltation.[97] Finally, Matthew intends with v. 20 to make the link with the one who was Immanuel for Israel (1:23) and rescues his people from their sins (1:21; cf. 9:8; 26:28). The one who is active in the community's experience of the Spirit is thus identical with the earthly Jesus.

On the other hand, Matthew speaks of keeping Jesus' commands and sees in that the essence of discipleship. Close parallels in respect of form with both the verb τηρέω (to keep) and the root ἐντελλ- (command) occur astonishingly again in John (14:15; cf. 14:16ff., 21; 15:10; 1 John 3:22). There, however, in magnificent and one-sided concentration, the commandment of Jesus refers only to the command to love the brethren. In contrast to that, Matthew specifies and details πάντα, ὅσα (all things whatsoever).[98] It is a matter of the individual commands, not one of which shall pass away, until all things come to pass (5:18).[99] The aorist ἐνετειλάμην (I commanded) interprets the commands quite unambiguously as those of the earthly Jesus. Jesus is the only teacher of the community.[100] The proclamation of the disciples is identical with the commands of the earthly Jesus. That is probably part of the reason why the Risen One meets the disciples in Galilee (28:16), because that is the place of his earthly activity, as the Evangelist particularly emphasizes.[101]

Both in Matthew's understanding of the disciples and in his christology we thus have an indicative and an imperative together. Jesus is the one to whom all power is given, the exalted one who is with his disciples even to the end of the world. To this corresponds discipleship, understood as participation in this authority and as being secure under the protection of the exalted Lord. And Jesus is the earthly one, the great teacher of God's law. To this there corresponds discipleship as understanding and obeying the commands of the earthly Jesus. Both components stand together.[102] Their relationship

97. Vögtle (see note 91), pp. 281ff. Cf. also Matt. 11:27.

98. Cf. however, John 14:26: "And he will bring to your remembrance all that (πάντα) I have said to you." It is striking throughout how the corresponding motifs in Matt. 28:18-20 pile up in John 14:14-26. The common background of the two texts is clear, even if it is scarcely possible to reconstruct an underlying tradition common to them. Cf. also Matt 18:19 with John 14:14.

99. On the interpretation, see Schweizer (see note 66), pp. 214f.

100. Baumbach (see note 76), p. 891. Cf. also Bornkamm (see note 74), pp. 223ff.; Strecker (see note 1), p. 212.

101. 4:13 (probably not an early tradition!); 4:23; 21:11, etc. Cf. also Bonnard (see note 13), p. 417.

102. In Matt. 28:18-20, however, the indicative (vv. 18b and 20b) seems to frame the imperative (vv. 19 and 20a). Did Matthew thus at least within the christology intend a clear distri-

does not seem to be clearly defined, either in the concept of the disciples, or in Matthew's conception of faith, or in Matthew's understanding of following. At any rate the relationship of the imperative to the indicative of salvation as something given is not made very clear in Matthew's conception of the church. That is apparent, for example, in that the eschatologically colored ecclesiological terminology, which expresses the priority of God's action for his people, is largely absent from Matthew. Expressions such as "true Israel" or ἅγιοι (saints) are absent. The ecclesiologically pregnant use of κλητός (called) and ἐκλεκτός (elected) is missing.[103] Λαός (people) is consistently applied to Israel[104] and ἐκκλησία (church) occurs only twice in Matthew's tradition.[105] To this corresponds a basic feature of his christology: the indicative of the salvation and the imperative of salvation as to make clear how in Matthew's theology the demand and the gift belong together. As the exalted one who is active in the community Jesus is giver; as the earthly teacher he makes demands. It is largely true to say that indicative and imperative are connected in the person of Jesus because he himself is both giver and author of the demand.

---

bution of weight so that the indicative preceded the imperative? Or is he here bound by an earlier tradition (cf. Strecker [see note 1], p. 210)? Or did this tradition correspond to his own intention? Of course in his debate with the Hellenistic charismatics Matthew stresses above all Jesus' teaching, i.e. his interpretation of the law. Of course, he places chapters 5–7 before 8–9, and a certain tendency to make the parable material serve a moral purpose is unmistakable. But on the other hand it seems to me to be no coincidence that even before the Sermon on the Mount there is the summary of healings at 4:23-25, and that is not sufficiently considered.

103. Cf. Strecker (see note 1), p. 219 note 1; κλητοί (those who are called) and ἐκλεκτοί (those who are chosen) are differentiated in Matt. 22:14, the saying that many are called, few chosen. 22:14 shows clearly how these concepts which are normally used synonymously can be made to serve Matthew's conception of the church as a mixed body. There are many κλητοί, but then the word, which does not occur elsewhere in Matthew or the Gospels, loses its eschatological dimension. There are few ἐκλεκτοί, but then this word, which otherwise in Matthew is bound only in the eschatological context of chapter 24, loses its reference to present historical reality.

104. Matthew's clear terminological distinction between λαός (people) and ἔθνος (nation) is consistently carried through. Cf. 21:43. It is particularly striking how often in Matthew λαός (mostly linked with the elders or high priests) occurs in the passion narrative to show the unity of the people with its leaders, and so the guilt of the whole people over the passion of Jesus. Cf. also Hummel (see note 1), pp. 145f.

105. In 18:17 the word is clearly defined by the context. It refers to the assembly of an individual community. What in 16:18 the word meant for the Evangelist can no longer be said with any certainty. Bornkamm (see note 74), pp. 219ff., points to the connections between ἐκκλησία and Hellenistic Jewish Christianity which might be significant for determining Matthew's position.

4

This final section contains a few more tradition-historical considerations which arise from Matthew's understanding of discipleship and which help us to place Matthew in the development of early Christian theology. All that is possible here is a provisional sketch and a few very fragmentary and hypothetical pointers.

We have already indicated that the transparency of Matthew's concept of the disciples is in principle already present in the tradition.[106] He himself has deepened this transparency and emphasized that it is in the disciples of the earthly Jesus that the nature of the church, including the church of his own day, is visible. Of course, the unity of the historical and the exalted Jesus which is fundamental for his conception, is also inherited from the tradition, even though Matthew has reflected more consciously on it than have some of his predecessors. This is the christological basis of Christians being designated μαθηταί. So we can expect that Christians designated themselves as disciples of Jesus in churches where his words and teaching were handed on as applicable also for the present. We can expect the label μαθηταί where Christian communities recognized in the miracles of Jesus their own experiences with the Spirit and where they understood the words spoken to them by Christian prophets as a confrontation with Jesus, and consequently historicized them.[107] We cannot expect this designation in those communities where no great value was placed upon the life and teaching of Jesus.

However, it is striking that we do not seem to find the transparent use of μαθητής in the texts of the Q source.[108] That is striking because the believers' understanding of themselves as "disciples" would fit well in the theology of Q, and the related application of the word ἀκολουθέω (to follow) is found there.[109] But the lack of the μαθητής designation may be a coincidence, un-

106. Cf. above, especially, n. 53.

107. The expression "historicizing" here does, of course, invite misunderstanding. The community can depict its own experiences as miracles of Jesus only because it thereby depicts not a past thing which as past is isolated. It can understand words spoken to it by Christian prophets as words of Jesus only because Jesus is not seen as simply a figure who lived in the past. So it can "historicize" only because it does not see Jesus as the "historical Jesus" in the modern sense of the word.

108. Matt. 10:24-25 and parallels do not allow us to affirm with any certainty an ecclesiological background for Q. There is certainly no ecclesiological reference in the present text of Matthew on account of its context in the mission discourse, but Luke uses the saying at 6:40 in a παραβολή (parable) context, i.e. as a pure aphorism. In Luke 14:26, 27, I do not dare decide whether μαθητής is original against Matthew's ἄξιος.

109. Thus certainly at Matt. 10:38 and parallel. Cf. Dieter Lührmann, *Die Redaktion der*

derstandable because Q consists mainly in sayings and apophthegms; miracle stories are relatively rare.

We do, however, probably find evidence in the pre-Markan community. In Mark's controversy dialogues, which with Bultmann I would consider in their present form as largely community constructions,[110] Jesus often defends the behavior of the disciples against the Pharisees (Mark 2:18, 23; 7:2; cf. 2:16). Behind these controversy dialogues one supposes there were communities in which the law was wholly or partly abolished on the basis of appeal to Jesus' authority. It is with this authority that the community defends its own freedom, i.e., in the text, the behavior of the disciples.[111] These communities will have spoken Greek; there are hardly indications of an Aramaic original in these controversy dialogues.[112] The Pharisees are here depicted from a certain distance. The narrator is not disturbed by the improbability of Pharisees being present at a tax-collectors' party (Mark 2:15ff.), or going for a walk in the cornfields on the Sabbath (Mark 2:23ff.). So there is good reason to place these controversy dialogues in Hellenistic Jewish Christianity at no great distance from central Jewish territory. Also from the pre-Markan communities come the two feeding stories where again experiences of the community are probably included.[113] The words and reports about following are also presumably transparent, insofar as the communities did at least use them in their own proclamation to strengthen and give basis for their own call to discipleship. Other texts should be mentioned too: Mark 9:28-29 seems to presuppose that the disciples do miracles in the name of Jesus. Mark 6:7-13, which the pre-Markan communities probably used in mission instruction, shows the role played by miracles in these communities' missionary work. One gets a similar picture from the mission legends in Acts where, as we shall see, the designation μαθηταί for Christians also possibly occurs. At any rate the transparent use of the disciple concept is at the root of pre-Markan mission in-

---

Logienquelle, WMANT 33 (Neukirchen: Neukirchener, 1969), and already Adolf von Harnack, *The Sayings of Jesus* (trans. John Richard Wilkinson, London: Williams and Norgate, 1908), p. 153.

110. Bultmann (see note 12), pp. 47f., who speaks, however, of the Palestinian primitive community (whatever that may be).

111. Cf. Bultmann (see note 12), pp. 48f.

112. Of course, individual elements of the controversy dialogues could go back to the Aramaic-speaking communities or to Jesus, especially the sayings, but in my view not the controversy dialogues as such. Evidence for this includes the Hellenistic-colored proverb in Mark 2:17a, and Mark 2:21-22, which fairly certainly contains a Greek linguistic feature that cannot be expressed literally in a Semitic language (cf. Klaus Beyer, *Semitische Syntax im Neuen Testament* 1 [Göttingen: Vandenhoeck und Ruprecht, ²1968], pp. 100, 303), and Mark 2:25-26, where, however, the LXX is probably presupposed.

113. Cf. above, n. 53.

struction. Mark 9:38-41 contains debate with the other Christian miracle-workers who do not belong to the circle of disciples, i.e. the community. Mark 10:28-31 also probably mirrors the situation of the community. At any rate the Christians of the pre-Markan communities understood themselves to be disciples of Jesus. This suggestion is strengthened in that no other kind of ecclesiological conceptions are visible in these strata of the tradition.

The evidence of Acts perhaps fits in with this. The designation "disciple" is commonly used there to refer to the post-Easter communities. It corresponds to Luke's linguistic usage,[114] and a clear linguistic separation between tradition and redaction in Acts is probably not possible either with the word μαθητής or anywhere else.[115] It is, however, striking that the first time Christians are called μαθηταί occurs in the tradition about Hellenists at Jerusalem (Acts 6:1, 2, 7). It then occurs repeatedly in the tradition of Paul's conversion in Acts 9 and again in the Peter traditions from Joppa (Acts 9:36, 38), in the Antioch tradition (Acts 11:26) and twice in the "we" passages (21:4, 16). That gives all the passages where the word is possibly preredactional. Prior to 6:1 the Christians are called πιστεύσαντες (those who have come to believe). Now so far as this evidence can be assessed at all, it supports the view that "disciples of Jesus" was a Christian self-designation above all in Hellenistic Jewish Christianity outside Jerusalem. The Christians of Galilee and Syria might accordingly have emphasized more strongly the link with the life and teaching of the earthly Jesus and therefore have continued to apply the label μαθηταί, i.e. Jesus' school or group, to themselves. That they were first called Christians, i.e. adherents of Christ, in Antioch would be more intelligible if it was these Hellenistic Jewish Christians who stressed the connection with Jesus. All this of course is no more than a proposal to be discussed, at best on arguable hypothesis. It can, however, be supplemented by the conclusion reached by Heinz-Wolfgang Kuhn from another direction, that it is above all in Greek-speaking communities that one finds a piety based on continuity with the proclamation of the earthly Jesus.[116]

The linguistic evidence does not contradict this. A widely held hypothesis sees the discipleship ideas as coming into rabbinic Judaism from Hellenism.[117] The idea also crops up in the Hellenistic θεῖοι ἄνδρες (divine men)

114. Cf. above, section 2, pp. 129-30.

115. Hans Conzelmann, *Die Apostelgeschichte*, HNT 7 (Tübingen: J. C. B. Mohr, 1963), on Acts 6:1.

116. Heinz-Wolfgang Kuhn, "Der irdische Jesus bei Paulus als traditionsgeschichtliches und theologisches Problem," *ZThK* 67 (1971), pp. 295-320, esp. 310.

117. Karl Heinrich Rengstorf's article on μανθάνω (to learn), etc., *TDNT* IV, pp. 392-465, here: p. 438; A. Schulz (see note 12), pp. 115ff.

sphere, there too in the sense of following beyond the death of the master[118] or in the sense of following great teachers of the past. In contrast to this, rabbinic Judaism stressed the direct teacher-pupil relation. For the rabbinic principle of tradition it is important that a pupil really has heard the tradition direct from the rabbi. There are references to pupils in an indirect sense, but these occur relatively seldom.[119] This does not, of course, mean that the idea of discipleship to Jesus can be derived from the Hellenistic background. It is quite clear that Judaism provided the model for it. But it is possible that the retention of the disciple label after Easter and among Christians who did not know Jesus himself makes particularly good sense on the basis of Hellenistic linguistic tradition.

It is interesting to compare the Matthean conception with John. Even in the pre-Johannine tradition the disciple concept is at least partly transparent. This is apparent in John 13 where it could be possible that a foot-washing rite practiced by the Johannine community provides the background.[120] It is apparent, too, in that the feeding of the 5,000 occurs also in the pre-Johannine tradition. For John himself μαθητής (disciple) and ἀκολουθεῖν (to follow) are important.[121] In John 1:35-51 the traditional stories about following are assimilated to the present situation when the disciples are won by the testimony of other disciples, not by Jesus' call, and where the christological definition of Christ's person plays such an extraordinarily large role (1:36, 41, 45, 49). But particularly interesting is the definition of the nature of discipleship in 13:35 and 15:8. When discipleship is defined here as bearing fruit and loving one's neighbor, John comes into very close theological proximity with Matthew who describes the disciple as the one who does God's will (12:46-50). For him, too, the love command is the content of God's will; and for him, too, the tradition's motif of bearing fruit is important for distinguishing between genuine and counterfeit Christianity (7:15ff.; cf. 21:43; and John 15:2ff.). There is no real likelihood of literary dependence; more likely is a theological continuation by John and Matthew of related traditions. The differences between them are clear enough against the background of what they have in common. In John being a disciple is ultimately to be defined as being in Christ or connected to him (15:2-4). That, of course, allows him to express the indicative of

118. Cf. Rengstorf, p. 421; Hans Dieter Betz, *Lukian von Samosata und das Neue Testament* (Berlin: Akademie, 1961), pp. 108ff., esp. 109.

119. Evidence in Rengstorf (see note 117), pp. 436f.

120. It need not be considered here whether this rite was nothing other than Christian baptism (so Hans von Campenhausen, "Zur Auslegung von Joh. 13:6-10," in *Aus der Frühzeit des Christentums* [Tübingen: J. C. B. Mohr, 1963], pp. 109ff.), or some special rite.

121. Cf. Bornkamm (see note 74), p. 225.

salvation clearly. Only by being in Christ is there any fruit at all. The danger here is of this Christ becoming an ultimately unrestrained spiritual reality. Matthew is different. Precisely because he is faced with some kind of Christian spiritual enthusiasts, he has built in a form of control. For him, to be a disciple means to be a disciple of the earthly Jesus. Having recourse to history here operates as a protection against unrestrained enthusiasm. Nevertheless, the common basis of Johannine and Matthean theology, both of which probably have the roots of their ecclesiology in Hellenistic Jewish Christianity, is clear. This is the more striking in that neither Evangelist lays much weight on offices in their church.

It is also significant that Ignatius of Antioch seems to have known both Gospels.[122] He is also one of the few[123] who is still familiar with the transparent use of the word μαθητής. Since for Ignatius only the martyr is Jesus' disciple in the full sense of the word, we may take it that where μαθητής designates the ordinary Christian this reflects a linguistic feature of the tradition.[124] Apart from Ignatius, none of the Apostolic Fathers knows the word μαθητής as a designation for Christians. Only in Justin does it occur again.[125] By then Matthew's specific aim in using the word μαθητής, namely to assert the connection with the earthly Jesus that being a Christian in every generation implies, was already overtaken by the way Christianity was developing. Guaranteeing the tradition by the ecclesiastical office had shown itself to be far more effective.

122. This seems to me to be shown for Matthew above all by 3:15 and *Smyrnaeans* 1:1, despite the attempt of Joop Smit Sibinga, "Ignatius and Matthew," *NovT* 8 (1966), 263-283, to argue that Ignatius is dependent on a pre-Matthean source, but Smyrnaeans 1:1 is dependent on the Matthean redaction. Admittedly Helmut Köster, *Synoptische Überlieferung bei den apostolischen Vätern* (Berlin: Akademie, 1957), p. 59, assumes that the contact with the Matthean redaction occurs within kerygmatic formula. But this turns out to be linguistically heavily mixed up with Ignatius' own explanatory comment. So the supposition of literary dependence still seems to be more probable. For John and Ignatius, the strong contact in terminology and background is clear enough; literary relationships are possible. Cf. Werner Georg Kümmel, *Introduction to the New Testament* (trans. Howard Clark Kee, London: SCM, 1975), p. 246.

123. Besides this there is also some sparse gnostic evidence. Cf. for example Gospel of Philip 119:14; 129:1-3; or Gospel of Thomas, logion 21. But generally μαθητής is used of the disciples of the earthly Jesus in Christian gnostic writings too.

124. Cf. for example *Magnesians* 10:1; Polycarp 2:1. For μαθητεύω, cf. *Ephesians* 10:1.

125. Neither, so far as I know, does the substantive occur without closer definition in Justin. Μαθητής is mostly used for disciples of the earthly Jesus. It is related to the present at *Trypho* 35:2, though with the addition διδασκαλίας (of teaching). The verb μαθητεύω is more frequent: *Trypho* 39:2, 5; *First Apology* 15:6; *Second Apology* 3(4):3.

8 Discipleship: A Matthean Manifesto for a Dynamic Ecclesiology

Matthew's account of the mission discourse in chapter 10 has always been eclipsed in the history of interpretation by the Sermon on the Mount. While the latter has aroused enormous interest as the "sermon of sermons," hardly any ecclesiastical texts are concerned exclusively with the mission discourse. There is virtually nothing on the history of its interpretation[1] and very little specialized exegetical literature.[2] Why has the interest been so slight?

A number of factors may be relevant. It is not insignificant, certainly for today, that unlike the Sermon on the Mount the mission discourse in Matt. 10 appears markedly concerned with the inner circle in the community. Jesus' audience here is not the disciples together with a huge crowd as in the Sermon on the Mount (5:1-2; 7:28-29), but only the disciples, or more precisely, the Twelve. Again unlike the Sermon on the Mount, the mission discourse is not concerned with an ethos both intended to be lived out by the disciples

---

1. Cf. only Hiltrud Stadtland-Neumann, *Evangelische Radikalismen in der Sicht Calvins. Sein Verständnis der Bergpredigt und der Aussendungsrede (Mt 10)*, BGLRK 24 (Neukirchen: Neukirchener Verlag, 1966), pp. 42-49.

2. The following are important: Francis W. Beare, "The Mission of the Disciples and the Mission Charge: Mt 10 and Parallels," *JBL* 89 (1970), pp. 1-13; Hans J. Bernardus Combrink, "Structural Analysis of Mt 9:35–11:1," *Neotest* 11 (1977), pp. 98-114; Schuyler Brown, "The Mission to Israel in Matthew's Central Section," *ZNW* 69 (1978), pp. 73-90; David Dungan, *The Sayings of Jesus in the Churches of Paul* (Philadelphia: Fortress, 1971), pp. 41-75; Christopher M. Tuckett, "Paul and the Synoptic Mission Discourse," *EthL* 60 (1984), pp. 376-381; Gottfried Schille, *Frei zu neuen Aufgaben* (Berlin: Evangelische, 1986), pp. 61-66.

German original: "Die Jüngerrede des Matthäus als Anfrage an die Ekklesiologie oder: Exegetische Prolegomena zu einer dynamischen Ekklesiologie," in: Karl Kertelge/Traugott Holtz/Claus-Peter März (eds.), *Christus Bezeugen* (FS Wolfgang Trilling, Leipzig: St. Benno, 1989), pp. 84-101. Originally delivered as a guest lecture in Prague and Greifswald, January 1986.

and applicable at the same time as God's will for the whole *world*. It is concerned with something far more specific, the conduct of the *disciples* and their destiny as bearers of the message. So the church should have every reason to show a particular interest in the mission discourse, yet it has received scant attention in interpretation history. The main reason may be that there is so much in the discourse that has contradicted and still contradicts church reality that the church exegetes have always had difficulty finding their own church addressed in it.

1. The Essential Validity of the Mission Discourse

Matthew emphasizes from the outset that Jesus sent out the "twelve disciples" (10:1, 5a). This clearly ties the whole mission discourse back into the past situation at the time when Jesus was alive and there were the twelve disciples.[3] After this, Matthew first selects that well-known logion from his special material which forbids the disciples to go to the Gentiles or to a Samaritan town (10:5-6). Their mission is meant only for the lost sheep of the house of Israel. This too clearly evokes the situation during Jesus' lifetime, already superseded by the mission charge of Matt. 28:16-20. Matt. 10:17-22 can lead to similar considerations. Here, Matthew has brought forward a section of the Synoptic Apocalypse, Mark 13:9-13, to which he returns more generally in ch. 24. Why this doubling? Is it because Matthew wants to distinguish the disciples' earlier mission to Israel from the later fate of the church in its mission to the Gentiles? If so, Matt. 10 would be about the former and Matt. 24 about the latter.

The validity of the mission discourse was thus limited to the early days of Christianity. The church has repeatedly made use of this approach in order to cope with the fact that the discourse contains so much material that is alien to its own situation. The approach suggests that the discourse is concerned *only* with the commissioning of the apostles in Jesus' lifetime.[4] This made it possi-

---

3. Cf. in this volume "The Disciples in the Gospel according to Matthew," pp. 115-42.

4. This interpretation has a long history. Tertullian, Fuga 6.1 = CCSL 2, 1142 restricts the text to the apostles. Hieronymus, *Commentariorum in Matthaeum libri IV*, CChr. SL 77, p. 65 distinguishes the time before and after the resurrection. This is widely supported today, see e.g. Georg Strecker, *Der Weg der Gerechtigkeit. Untersuchungen zur Theologie des Matthäus*, FRLANT 82 (Göttingen: Vandenhoeck und Ruprecht, 1962), p. 196; Günther Bornkamm, "The Risen Lord and the Earthly Jesus: Matthew 28. 16-20," in: James M. Robinson (ed.), *The Future of Our Religious Past. Essays in Honour of Rudolf Bultmann* (London: SCM, 1971), pp. 203-229, here: p. 205; Anton Vögtle, "Das christologische und ekklesiologische Anliegen von Mt 28,18-20," in: Vögtle, *Das Evangelium und die Evangelien*, KBANT (Düsseldorf: Patmos, 1971), p. 266.

ble to deal, first, with the restriction of the mission to Israel alone (Matt. 10:5-6),[5] and second, with the fact that although Jesus' command to perform miracles and heal the sick has the greatest prominence in this section (10:8), miracles became far less prominent in the later church or even disappeared completely. It was said that miracles had been necessary only at the beginning, not once faith had become accepted.[6] It was said further that the apostles had a special need for the gift of miracles because they were uneducated people lacking in eloquence;[7] their successors were no longer so dependent on miracles. In other words, good theological training, particularly in homiletics, had rendered the healing of the sick to some extent superfluous! The approach treats similarly the requirement that the apostles were to travel without money, security or provisions. Particularly in the time of the Reformation, early Christian itinerant radicalism was viewed with great suspicion. It was important to be distinguishable from the Anabaptists. Calvin above all stressed that this passage was not concerned with a timeless law to which all preachers of the word must submit.[8] He sees the "equipping" in Matt. 10:9 as a particular instruction given by Jesus because he expected the disciples' mission to preach in Israel to be brief, their journey taking them to the whole of Judea within a few days. For this reason they were to avoid unnecessary baggage. This reading also avoids the stumbling block that Jesus' messengers are to possess nothing and to go unprotected.[9] If all this were true, the mission discourse would have little or no application to the church, and this would vindicate the relatively limited attention it has received in the history of interpretation.

Three observations counter this interpretation. *First,* only very few of Jesus' words in ch. 10 apply exclusively to the situation of the first commissioning of the disciples. Much of what Jesus says is of a general nature and appears to be valid for the church of all time. This is evident, for example, in 10:24-25 where the servant can expect no better lot than the master, and in

5. This interpretation could easily be combined with a salvation history substitution thesis proposing that the mission of the disciples to the Gentiles replaces the mission of the apostles to Israel; cf. Ulrich Luz, *Matthew 8–20*, Hermeneia (Minneapolis: Fortress, 2001), pp. 74f. note 35. This may indeed have been Matthew's intention.

6. Thomas Aquinas, *Super Evangelium S. Matthaei Lectura* (Turin-Rome: Marietti, [5]1951), No. 818.

7. Jerome, *Commentariorum* (see note 4), p. 65.

8. Jean Calvin, *In Harmoniam ex Matthaeo, Marco et Luca Compositam Commentarii I*, ed. August Tholuck (Berlin: Thome, 1838), p. 235. English translation: *A Harmony of the Gospels — Matthew, Mark and Luke* (Carlisle: Paternoster, 1995).

9. Ibid., pp. 295f. "They might well possess bags, shoes and further tunics, but so that they might be better equipped for the road, he orders to them to leave behind anything that could be a burden."

10:38-39 where Jesus talks of carrying one's cross and losing one's life. Some teachings seem directed specifically to the post-Easter community, for example the prophecies of legal prosecutions and clashes in 10:17-22 or of family feuds in 10:34-37. As early as 10:18 the limitation of the disciples' mission to Israel alone is explicitly lifted when the mission to the Gentiles is alluded to: "as a testimony to them," i.e. governors and kings, "and the Gentiles." The events foreseen in 10:17-22 for the mission to Israel are basically the same as those the disciples can expect in their mission to the Gentiles (24:9-14). The account of how the disciples were to be equipped (10:9-10) and the instructions for entering a house or a town (10:11-14) do not give the impression that Matthew intended to limit their validity to the unique time of Jesus. The equipping in particular is demonstrably adjusted in all four Gospels to the changing circumstances. This will be undertaken only if a text is valid for one's own time. So the mission discourse is remarkable for its strange lack of concern about the time to which it applies. The time levels are never clearly distinguished. Where such distinction is hinted at, as in the prophecy of persecution in the mission to Israel in 10:17-22, the limitation is immediately countered. Nowhere — not even in 10:5-6 — is it suggested that there is a time limit on the validity of the mission discourse commands.[10] This contradicts the thesis that Matthew did not intend the discourse to apply to his own time. If that were so, the mission discourse would be unique in his Gospel in this respect.

This brings us to a *second observation.* What Matthew receives from Mark's Gospel is a *report* of the commissioning. In Mark the disciples actually are sent out and later return (6:30). Luke constructs the commissioning similarly as a report on the seventy disciples. Whether his report on the return of the seventy, Luke 10:17-20, had already appeared in Q is uncertain, as is the attributing of Luke 10:1 to Q. We can only say that the placing of the verses 10:17-20 (between two sections of Q) and its archaic style make this a possibility.[11] Be that as it may, the important point is that Matthew expressly did not construct the commission as a report of a singular event in the past. We could overstate this by saying that Jesus instructs his disciples but does not actually send them out. After the discourse, which goes far beyond an immediate commissioning to deal with the destiny of the disciples in proclamation, Jesus resumes his usual activity in Israel: "Now when Jesus had finished instructing

10. The disciples' mission to Israel corresponds to Jesus' own mission to Israel as narrated in chs. 8–9 and re-emphasized in Matthew's redaction of 15:24. There is no νῦν (now) with which Matthew could have placed a time limit on the validity of the commandment.

11. This is supported above all by the placing of vv. 17-20 between v. 16 (Q) and 21-22 (Q). As reminiscences are absent from Matthew and Lukan redaction may be assumed in vv. 17, 21, considerable uncertainty remains.

his twelve disciples, *he* (!) went on from there to teach and proclaim his message in their cities" (11:1). The mission discourse is, then, like all other discourses in Matthew, addressed "out of the window" and has no immediate consequences in the report of what happened at the time. This suggests that it speaks to the present.

A *third* important *observation* concerns the way in which the mission discourse has been made part of the overall composition of Matthew's Gospel. It is generally recognized that it deliberately connects with the miracle cycle of chs. 8–9. Matt. 10:1 records that Jesus gave the twelve disciples authority over unclean spirits and to cure every disease and every sickness. This takes up word for word the identical verses Matt. 4:23 and 9:35 which frame the Sermon on the Mount and the miracle cycle. Taking up three important miracles from chs. 8–9, Matt. 10:8 commissions the disciples to "cure the sick" and goes on to give specific examples: "raise the dead, cleanse the lepers, cast out demons!" Thus Jesus hands on his own authority to the disciples and commands them to do what he himself has done among his people. The same applies to Jesus' proclamation as summarized in 4:17: "Repent, for the kingdom of heaven has come near." This is repeated in 10:7. The Sermon on the Mount and the mission discourse are indeed very closely related. A number of themes from the Sermon are taken up in the mission discourse and made concrete for the disciples. Persecution of disciples had been spoken of in 5:10-12 and is now treated in detail from 10:16 onwards. Defenselessness of disciples had been spoken of in the fifth antithesis and is now made concrete in going without a staff (10:10), in being sheep among wolves (10:16) and above all in the words about carrying one's cross and losing one's life (10:38-39). Poverty for disciples had been spoken of in 6:19-34, now it is taken up in the rules for equipping and the commandments that follow (10:9-14). The exhortation not to worry (6:25) is made concrete in the court situation of 10:19, and the assurance of God's care for people, who are of so much more value than birds and lilies (6:26-29), is varied in 10:28-30. Thus Matthew refers deliberately to the Sermon on the Mount in his mission discourse. The disciples should, and will, act out the commandments of the Sermon on the Mount in their proclamation.

In my opinion, there are only two logia whose validity is limited to a time in the past, namely vv. 5-6 and the related v. 23. These two statements of Jesus are explicitly retracted or corrected in the Great Commission of 28:16-20. It is not the coming of the Son of Man that has ended the flight through the towns of Israel but his command to go to the Gentiles. As I see it, these two logia can be understood within the course of Matthew's narrative. Matthew's Gospel is a Jesus story with a deeper dimension, a double meaning so to speak. Matthew tells the Jesus story in such a way that the salvation history experience of his community in their own story is made transparent in it. In his prologue he had anticipated the story of the child who is born in Bethlehem, the city of David; who is pursued by all Jerusalem, its scribes and its king; who flees to the heathen country of Egypt and who, finally, will live in "Galilee of the Gentiles" (4:15) in the city of Nazareth, from which the Syrian Christians for whom Matthew is writing derive their name, "Nazorean" (2:23).[12] In this same way Matthew then unfolds the whole story of Jesus as one with a deeper dimension. He begins by portraying the activity of the Son of David among his people, the holy people of Israel, his preaching and healing in the towns of Israel. Already in chs. 8–9 there are signs of a division. Jesus' followers accompany him in a boat to the other side of the lake (8:18ff.).[13] In chs. 11–16 the division in Israel caused by Jesus' works becomes even more evident. After numerous conflicts with Israel's leaders, the real family of Jesus, made up of those who do the will of God, comes into being (12:46-50). The parable discourse also portrays how the community comes into being: Jesus withdraws from the crowds by the lake by going into the house with his disciples (13:36). The following chapters 13:54–16:20 are characterized by several "withdrawals" by Jesus into the company of the disciples.[14] In the midst of confrontation in and about Israel emerges the circle of the disciples — the church. The church, its internal structure and its life are then the subject of the community section 16:24–20:34. Chapters 21–25 portray the final confrontations with Israel and God's coming judgment of his people. This "second level" of Matthew's Gospel enables us to understand the function of the two verses 10:5-6 and 10:23. In ch. 10 Matthew is concerned with Jesus' mission to Israel. Just as Israel's Messiah proclaims in Israel's towns and heals among the holy people of Israel (ch. 5–9), his disciples are also sent to Israel. The moment at which the church emerges from Israel has not yet arrived, and certainly not the moment when this church, faced with Israel's rejection of its message, will turn to the Gentiles. These two logia seem to me, then, to be a literary device serving to fit the mission discourse into the whole narrative, as also with the withdrawal into the house in 13:36 and the departure from the temple in the middle of the final discourse in 24:1-3.

Matthew's composition makes clear that the disciples are given Jesus' own authority and have the same commission as their master. If this commission were seen as part of the past and subject to time limitation, the same would apply to Jesus' own commission. The disciples continue Jesus' own

12. Cf. Ulrich Luz, *Matthew 1–7. A Commentary* (Minneapolis: Augsburg, 1989), pp. 148-150.

13. Cf. in this volume "The Miracle Stories of Matthew 8–9," pp. 221-240.

14. Cf. Luz, *Matthew 1–7* (see note 12), p. 43.

proclamation. The behavior that Jesus requires of them makes concrete the commands of the Sermon on the Mount. As that sermon deals with fundamental teaching by Jesus that is to be preached to all the peoples of the world, it seems unlikely that the mission discourse is intended to refer to a unique commission of the past. Rather, it is concerned with fundamental instructions given by Jesus to those who proclaim.

We draw the following *conclusion:* The Matthean mission discourse is the first ecclesiological realization of what has been said in the Gospel so far. With this in mind, we do well to read it as Matthew's basic manifesto for his view of the church. It goes far beyond instructions for a specific commissioning. For this reason we shall no longer refer to it as the "mission discourse" but as the "disciple discourse." True, the theme of mission is focused on at the beginning,[15] but the overall theme of the discourse is a broader one. One could say that its theme is the church's commission and the church's relation to the world. I call it the "disciple discourse" because "disciple" is the most fundamental ecclesiological expression in Matthew's Gospel. Jesus' disciples become transparent for the Matthean community, whose members saw themselves as disciples of the earthly Jesus, following in his way.[16] In my opinion it makes no difference that the opening of the discourse speaks of the commissioning of twelve apostles: ἀπόστολος (apostle) and μαθητής (disciple) are used without distinction.[17] In the commissioning of the twelve apostles, Matthew is expressly not concerned with a special commission to individuals. In saying this, though, we have already reached the point of interpretation of the discourse itself.

2. Fundamental Characteristics of the Church according to Matthew 10

I am speaking here of "characteristics" of the church in the sense of the classical "notae ecclesiae" ("marks" of the church) of the Reformation era. As we know, this concept originated in Reformation ecclesiology and means what makes the visible church recognizable in the ambiguity of the world.[18] Clearly

---

15. Vv. 5, 16 (inclusion!).

16. Cf. pp. 116-125, 129-130 above.

17. Cf. 9:37; 10:2, 24-25; 11:1 with 10:2, 5.

18. According to the Augsburg Confession VII "consentire de doctrina evangelii et de administratione sacramentorum" (to agree about the doctrine of the gospel and the administration of the sacraments) is all that is required for the unity of the church. The Apology interprets this as "externae notae" (external characteristics) (BSLK⁴ 234f.). Calvin, *Inst.* 4, I, 8, 10 speaks of "symbols" which make the invisible church recognisable.

this cannot be applied to Matthew's Gospel, which could never speak of an invisible church. What I mean by it is simply "fundamental marks of the church" in Matthew's Gospel. I speak nonetheless of "notae" in order to invoke the tradition of the Reformation. My concern is to confront and compare Matthew's Gospel with Reformation tradition.

2.1. Church for Matthew is Missionizing, Proclaiming Church

The disciple discourse opens with the commissioning, the authorization of the disciples and the instruction to proclaim and to heal. So the first fundamental mark of the church is that it has a mission to the world. This is made clear in vv. 7-8 and also at the beginning of the second section of the discourse in v. 26.[19] Here Matthew reformulates the old prophecy that all will be uncovered at the last day as an instruction to the disciples to reveal everything in proclamation. I should like to highlight three particularly significant features:

1. As the twelve disciples represent the community, the instruction is addressed to the whole community and not just to special preachers. In agreement with almost the entire New Testament, Matthew's Gospel presents proclamation as the task of the whole community and not that of a particular office in the community.

2. If we take seriously the fact that Matthew sees proclamation and mission as part of discipleship and not as being restricted to a particular ministry, it is striking how little the disciple discourse has to say about the content of proclamation. The disciples are to proclaim that the kingdom of heaven has come near (10:7). This corresponds exactly to Jesus' own proclamation in 4:17 as well as that of John the Baptist in 3:2. But beyond that the entire discourse is concerned with the behavior and the destiny of the disciples. It is a discourse on their way of life and their way of suffering. This is striking and calls for theological interpretation.

3. The third notable feature is the weight given to the healings in Jesus' commissioning (10:8). The instruction to heal is developed in fourfold variation. For Matthew it is constitutive and of equal importance to the instruction to proclaim the good news. The significance of this is that Matthew consistently gives Jesus' preaching ethical emphasis and sees it in 28:20 as the proclamation of Jesus' commandments. But for Matthew the proclamation is not

---

19. Κηρύσσω ("proclaim") stands at the beginning of the introduction (9:35), of the first (10:7) and of the second main section (10:27) of the discourse.

simply an ethical imperative. It includes the concrete experience of healings. For this reason it is not just the commission of the disciples but their ἐξουσία (power) which is central for him (10:1), and for this reason the miracles are placed alongside the task of proclamation and given equal weight. This was later to become an exegetical problem in a church which scarcely experienced healings any longer. We have already spoken of the attempt to regard the miracles as a particular mark of the earliest church only.[20] There is also a widespread tendency to spiritualize the miracles: For John Chrysostom, for instance, the greatest miracle was liberation from sin;[21] according to Faber Stapulensis the disciples were to concern themselves above all with the spiritually sick and dead.[22] But the most frequent and the easiest option with v. 8 in the history of interpretation was to silence it altogether. In Matthew's proclamation, then, the proclamation itself is ethically accentuated, in other words it makes concrete demands of the community. But it is embedded in *experience* of salvation which is not least a concrete experience of *healing*. What is proclaimed in our churches today is often a very general, verbal assurance of salvation, as in the absolution, which is not experienced in a concrete way. The demands made of us do not often constitute part of the proclamation and have lost much of their binding character. Concrete experience of healing and salvation seems to go with binding demands in Matthew, just as what is now "abstract" assurance of salvation goes with non-binding ethics for us.

2.2. For Matthew the Community Consists of Potential Itinerant Radicals

Gerd Theissen has greatly increased our knowledge of the history of primitive Christianity by his rediscovery of early Christian itinerant radicalism.[23] Georg Kretzschmar has fitted this into the history of the Syrian church.[24]

---

20. Cf. p. 145.

21. John Chrysostom, *Commentarius in sanctum Matthaeum Evangelistam* 32, 7, PG 57, p. 387.

22. Faber Stapulensis, *Commentarii initiatiorii in quattuor Evangelia* (Basel: A. Cratandri, 1523), p. 44Bf.

23. Gerd Theissen, "The Wandering Radicals. Light Shed by the Sociology of Literature on the Early Transmissions of Jesus Sayings, Social Policy and the Early Christians," in: Theissen, *Theology, Ethics and the World of the New Testament* (Minneapolis: Fortress, 1992), pp. 33-59; Theissen, *Sociology of Early Palestinian Christianity* (Philadelphia: Fortress, 1978).

24. Georg Kretzschmar, "Ein Beitrag zur Frage nach dem Ursprung frühchristlicher Askese," in: *ZThK* 61 (1964), partic. pp. 32-62.

Eduard Schweizer saw the Matthean community as quite close to the itinerant radicals.[25] This assumption seems basically sound to me. The Matthean community lives in the tradition of the itinerant radicalism of the Sayings Source and was probably founded by wandering prophets such as appear in the Sayings Source.[26] The Gospel of Matthew speaks not only of wandering prophets but also of wandering scribes, teachers, righteous people and ordinary Christians (10:40-42; 23:34). On the other hand, it is clear that the Gospel emerged from a settled community for which it was written. This is paralleled by the situation in the *Didache,* in which we encounter a settled community faced with the issue of receiving wandering prophets, apostles and teachers (Did. 11-13). The *Didache* is visibly shaped by Matthew, which was the Gospel used in its community.[27]

How are we to determine the relationship between the Matthean community and itinerant radicalism? The question is of historical and theological interest. At the beginning of the disciple discourse, Jesus sends the twelve disciples out traveling. If we take the idea of the transparency of the disciple concept, all the members of the Matthean community should have been itinerant radicals. The whole discourse is strangely volatile, however. Up to about v. 23 we have repeated glimpses of the disciples traveling. The second half of the discourse, from about v. 24 onwards, seems to be neutral about the question of traveling. The words we find here could equally be addressed to itinerant or to settled Christians. The final section vv. 40-42 is particularly important. It begins with a promise to the travelers: Whoever welcomes you welcomes me, and whoever welcomes me welcomes the one who sent me (v. 40). Then the perspective appears to shift: in v. 41 it is no longer the travelers who are addressed but those who are at home and receive travelers. It is about receiving prophets, righteous people[28] and "these little ones." Evidently there were also quite ordinary community members on the road, i.e. "these little ones." In v. 41 those who stay at home are addressed, without any indication of the shift of perspective. In ch. 18 on the other hand "these little ones" refers to the community, without any apparent relation to itinerant radicalism. How is this to be understood?

25. Eduard Schweizer, "Die Kirche des Matthäus," in: Schweizer, *Matthäus und seine Gemeinde,* SBS 71 (Stuttgart: Katholisches Bibelwerk, 1974), pp. 163-167.

26. Cf. Luz, *Matthew 1–7* (see note 12), p. 83.

27. Cf. Wolf Dietrich Köhler, *Die Rezeption des Matthäusevangeliums in der Zeit vor Irenäus,* WUNT II.24 (Tübingen: Mohr Siebeck, 1987), pp. 55f.

28. Possibly a special group of Christian ascetics; this is supported by the special "reward of the righteous"; David Hill, *The Gospel of Matthew,* NCEB (London: Oliphants, 1972), p. 196, suggests the teachers.

In my opinion, only one solution is possible. We must abandon Theissen's schematic distinction between itinerant radicals and settled Christians. As I see it, the primitive church did not consist of two groups of people who differed fundamentally in lifestyle and ethos, i.e. the itinerant radicals and the settled communities. Rather, there was fluid interchange between them. Community members set out on mission and returned to their communities. Only this model corresponds to the fragments of historical evidence that we have.[29] Only on this basis can we understand why "discipleship" in primitive Christianity does not merely designate the way of life of a special group of Christians but, accentuated in Mark as discipleship of suffering, came to mean the Christian way of life in general. Only then can we understand why primitive Christianity did not in principle distinguish between commands applying to itinerant radicals and general commands, creating a two-tier ethic.

In Matthew all this is embraced in the idea of the way to perfection. All are to follow this way and all are to do what they can and as much as they can (cf. *Didache* 6:2). Matthew 19:21 makes clear that the perfection which proceeds from literally following Jesus is bound up with renunciation of property. Matt. 19:23ff. clarifies however that this demand applies to all disciples. Matt. 6:25-33, the text about anxiety, was certainly originally addressed to the itinerant radicals who like the birds of the air neither sow nor reap, i.e. do not do traditional men's work, and like the lilies of the field neither toil nor spin, i.e. do not do traditional women's work. But Matthew applies this text, in what it promises and what it requires, to all hearers of the Sermon on the Mount.[30] Nowhere does he say that all disciples *must* become itinerant radicals, but he does make it clear that traveling in the course of proclamation is a way of life to which all are basically called. The same is true of Matt. 10. If this really is a discourse on discipleship and not on a special form of discipleship, then the whole community is addressed as a group of potentially itinerant radicals. Those who are unable to carry the full yoke of the Lord — in the sense of Did. 6:2 — are to do what they can, such as receiving travelers in their homes and bearing witness to the Son of Man in their own locality.

29. Cf., e.g., Acts 13:2-3, or the reports on Philip, Peter, Barnabas, Aquila and Priscilla etc., indicating various forms of temporary settledness.

30. Cf. Luz, *Matthew 1–7* (see note 12), p. 408.

2.3. For Matthew, Poverty for the Sake of the Kingdom of God Is a Constitutive Mark of Discipleship

Let me begin with an exposition of the "rules for equipping" in Matt. 10:8-10: "You received without payment; give without payment. Acquire no gold, or silver, or copper in your belts, no bag for your journey, or two tunics, or sandals, or a staff; for laborers deserve their food."

It is probable that Matthew has replaced the μισθός (pay) of the text he received by τροφή (food, 10b). He has prefaced the text with the saying of 8b, indicating that his main concern here is the ban on making a living out of missionary work, in particular out of healing. Secular and Christian evidence of religious begging[31] shows what a great problem this was. So v. 10b states that Christian workers should receive *only* food from the community. This seems to be the context of what is a new word in Matthew, κτάομαι: to acquire, procure for yourself (instead of αἴρω, to carry). Hence v. 9 means "Do not acquire any gold or silver or copper," i.e. do not take payment! What then follows is strange, however. Why should one "acquire" a bag, a second tunic or a staff? It is clear that Matthew is still thinking of the equipping of the missionaries and what they should not take with them or procure on the way. The very general verb κτάομαι takes on two meanings here, two things being important to Matthew. On the one hand, missionary work is not to be a source of earning money — this is Matthew's own new emphasis — and on the other hand those who proclaim the kingdom of God cannot do so in good shoes, with a bag full of provisions and a staff as protection against wild animals or bandits. Here Matthew takes up the old meaning of the rules for equipping in Q. For him, proclaiming the gospel involves being unarmed and being poor.

How is this to be incorporated in Matthew's overall understanding of community? Is he simply concerned with missionary technique, so that poverty and defenselessness and non-acquisition belong to preaching the gospel but it is irrelevant what property the itinerant preachers leave behind at home? Calvin was not the first to favor this interpretation decisively.[32] The pseudo-Clementine letter *ad Virgines* already assumed that the wandering ascetics have property at home.[33] But there are two other text complexes in Matthew's Gospel which speak against this division of property at home and

---

31. Cf. 2 Cor. 11:6-13; 12:13, 17; Didache 11:5f.; Hermas *Mandates* 11, 12; Lucian, *De morte Peregrini* 11-16; secular references in Luz, *Matthew 8–20* (see note 5), p. 78 note 60.

32. Cf. note 9.

33. Pseudo-Clement, *Epistula ad Virgines* 2.2.1, speaks of their own houses.

poverty on the road. Immediately after the central section on prayer in the Sermon on the Mount comes the section on not storing up possessions and on generosity (6:19-34), newly composed by Matthew. At its center are the words about serving wealth (6:24), preceded by two warnings about storing up treasure and avarice (6:19-23) and followed by the famous text on the Father's care for his itinerant radicals (6:25-34). The command not to store up earthly treasures applies to the whole community.

The other passage important for this theme is Matt. 19:16-30. The command to the rich young man to give away his possessions is directly connected with the key word "perfect" and immediately follows the command to love one's neighbor, which Matthew has supplemented. We can hardly assume that Matthew thinks love of neighbor must be *supplemented* by renunciation of possessions in order to attain perfection. In the light of Matt. 5:43-48 where perfection is associated with love, and Matt. 22:34-40 where loving one's neighbor is the greatest commandment, the call to renounce possessions and give to the poor must be understood as the concrete enactment of the command to love one's neighbor. This is supported by the key phrase "treasure in heaven," a direct allusion to 6:19-21, and by the fact that in 19:23ff. the commandment to renounce possessions refers directly to all disciples.

It is not a special instruction for a select few but a command to everyone. In 19:29 it is linked with the break with the family. It seems clear to me, then, that for Matthew going without possessions is an essential mark of all disciples. His tendency in ch. 10, therefore, is not to allow the disciples everything at home and expect poverty of them only when they are missionizing on the road. Rather, life at home should resemble life on the road as closely as possible. Jesus' command to poverty applies to both. Matthew did not prescribe a minimum legal poverty or renunciation level, but under the heading "greater righteousness" he gives very clear directions on renunciation of possessions on the path to perfection.

It is unsurprising to find that this mark of the church in particular has been problematic in the history of interpretation. Matt. 10:9-10 was taken seriously in its literal sense when the text could be used to denounce opponents within the church who lived in luxury.[34] It was also taken literally and seriously of course by Francis of Assisi, for whom it became the crucial text of his life,[35]

---

34. E.g. Eusebius, *Historia Ecclesiastica* 5.18.7 (against Montanists); Heinrich Bullinger, *In Sacrosanctum . . . Evangelium secundum Matthaeum Commentariorum Libri XII* (Zürich: Froschoverum, 1546), 99B (against papal delegates).

35. Werner Goez, "Franciscus von Assisi," in: *TRE* XI, p. 300; cf. the *Regula non bullata* No. 8.14 in Hans Urs von Balthasar, *Die grossen Ordensregeln* (Einsiedeln: Johannes, 1974), pp. 295f., 300.

and by the Waldenses as a special rule for the *via apostolica*.[36] Otherwise, interpretation has been dominated by attempts to dilute the text. Its meaning was moralized, turning it into a warning against pride and meanness.[37] The text was allegorized and said to be concerned with putting one's cares aside or putting on the one true tunic, Christ himself.[38] Its impact could be weakened by pointing to the differences in the various versions of the text in the Gospels.[39] In the Reformation era it is at least still emphasized that although preachers should be able to live free of worldly cares they should only receive sufficient to feed and clothe themselves from preaching the gospel.[40] As far as the contemporary situation in our churches is concerned, I find it remarkable that in the current discussions on ministers' salaries occasioned by the large numbers of unemployed theologians[41] I have been unable to detect even a trace of Matt. 10 or Luke 10. The direction Matthew gives us is hardly taken seriously. Evidently Kierkegaard's experience is still valid. He was brought by our text to the conclusion that salaries paid to ministers as public servants were "directly contrary to Christ's instructions" and that there was quite literally not a single honest Christian around. He took this opinion to Bishop Mynster, who to his great surprise responded, "There is something in that." The answer, given in private, surprised Kierkegaard: "I had not really expected this, even though we spoke in private, for Bishop Mynster was otherwise a model of caution in this regard."[42] For Matthew the poverty of disciples is a decisive "nota" of the church. It means nothing less than adopting the poverty of Jesus himself.

36. Kurt-Victor Selge, *Die ersten Waldenser* I, AKG 37 (Berlin: de Gruyter, 1967), pp. 49f., 116f.

37. Cf., e.g., Martin Luther, "Annotationes in aliquot capita Matthaei," *WA* 38, 1912, p. 496. Similarly Huldrych Zwingli, "Annotationes in Evangelium Matthaei," in: Zwingli, *Opera* VI.1 (ed. M. Schuler, J. Schulthess) (Zürich: Schulthess, 1836), p. 265, which recommends moderation as a compromise between papal riches and the even more dangerous renunciation of wages by the Anabaptists.

38. Augustinus, *De Consensu Evangelistarum libri* IV, 1904 (CSEL 43), 2.30 (p. 75): going barefoot = without cares; Hilarius, *In Evangelium Matthaei Commentarius* 10:5 = SC 254, pp. 220f.: no second tunic = put on only Christ.

39. Cornelius a Lapide, *Argumentum in S. Matthaeum* (Antwerp: Meursius, 1670), p. 224, already distinguishes from the various litterae the "substantia" of the text, that is, keeping oneself from avarice.

40. Cf. Luz, *Matthew 8–20* (see note 5), p. 80 notes 83f.

41. This refers to the situation in Germany in the 1980s and 1990s.

42. *Der Augenblick* 7,8 = *Ges. Werke* 34 (Düsseldorf: Eugen Diederichs, 1959), pp. 253-255.

2.4. For Matthew, Suffering Is a
Constitutive Mark of Discipleship

In vv. 17ff. Matthew refers to community experiences in the mission to Israel such as legal proceedings, scourgings, and executions. The difficult verse 23 is probably included by the Evangelist because it speaks of the experience of fleeing from persecution from town to town. Vv. 28-29 and above all the saying about taking up the cross and losing one's life, in vv. 38-39, again focus on the sufferings of the disciples. V. 39 certainly has martyrdom in mind, and to those who lose their life for Jesus' sake there is the promise of eternal life.[43] We are concerned here with the constitutive character of suffering for discipleship. What does it consist of? V. 16 already emphatically formulates: ἐγὼ ἀποστέλλω ὑμᾶς (it is I who sends you). It is *Jesus*' commission which gives rise to suffering. Matthew's keyword in vv. 17-21, παραδίδωμι (hand over), is christologically loaded in the tradition. Readers of Matthew could scarcely read the passage vv. 17-21 without being constantly reminded of the one who was the first to be handed over, who stood before the Sanhedrin and the governor, who was scourged and finally killed. The suffering of the disciples as they proclaim corresponds to the suffering of Jesus. For this reason the experience of the disciples in the mission to Israel is paradigmatic and will be repeated in the mission to the gentiles: "And you will be hated by all," declares Matthew twice (10:22; 24:9). Luther translates this perceptively as "and (you) *must* be hated." The same thinking lies behind Matt. 10:38. The cross that every disciple must take up is the cross that Jesus took upon himself. We may assume that Matthew is not concerned, as the original Jesus saying probably was, with setting out on the way the condemned person must go, the end of which was execution on the very cross he had been carrying.[44] Mark had already understood the saying more broadly in the sense of self-denial and discipleship of suffering (8:34). Matthew too is likely to have clustered very varied experiences of suffering in his community under the keyword "cross."[45]

Most significantly, however, Matthew has reflected christologically on the necessity of suffering for disciples. Because the disciples took on Jesus' authority, his proclamation, his commission and his way of life, they were also confronted with his suffering. The gospel of the kingdom of heaven as Matthew interprets it evidently leads *eo ipso* to suffering.

---

43. Joachim Gnilka, *Das Matthäusevangelium* I, HThK I.1 (Freiburg: Herder, 1986), p. 397.

44. Rightly interpreted by Anton Fridrichsen, "Ordet om a baere sit kors," in: *Gamle Spor og nye Veier tydninger og tegninger* (FS L. Brun; Kristiania: Grøndahl, 1922), pp. 17-34.

45. Cf. Gnilka, *Matthäusevangelium* I (see note 4), p. 397.

Not until the time when suffering was no longer experienced did the history of interpretation misunderstand this saying. Carrying one's cross could then become a religious technique or an ascetic exercise, such as celibacy or an exercise in daily dying to oneself.[46] Alternatively, it became a code for withdrawal from the world, for despising the things of the flesh[47] and for putting aside cares displeasing to God.[48] Matthew on the other hand sees suffering as the inevitable consequence of taking on Jesus' commission, and thus it becomes a constitutive mark of discipleship.

We have identified some — though not all — of the important "notae ecclesiae" to be found in Matt. 10. We would have to deal, in particular, with defenselessness and the experience of breaking with one's own family. But we break off here to formulate one last consideration. Why are all these marks constitutive for Matthew's understanding of church? Why in particular is the experience of suffering, which *we* might expect to be present in some situations as a consequence of proclamation but not in others, fundamental to the church as Matthew sees it? Why did traveling, poverty, defenselessness and proclamation of the imminent kingdom of heaven lead *of necessity* to separation from the world and into suffering? At this point Matthew is reflecting christologically, and it is this christological dimension which makes all that has been said into "marks" of the church.

2.5. Discipleship as Christlike Life

It has been made very clear to us that the story of Jesus the Son of God is itself the key to understanding the disciple discourse. The disciples had taken on Jesus' preaching and authority. A life of poverty was in keeping with the way of life of the Son of Man, of whom Matthew says shortly before our chapter that he had no place to lay his head (8:20). Defenselessness and an itinerant life were marks of Jesus' existence. The suffering faced by the disciples is a reflection of Jesus' suffering and death. All this is brought together by Matthew in the verses he places at the center of the disciple discourse, vv. 24-25. Here it

---

46. Hieronymus, *Epistulae* 22.21; English translation: Jerome, *Letters,* NPNF II/6 (Peabody: Hendrickson, 1994), pp. 30f.; Thomas à Kempis, *The Imitation of Christ* 2.12.3f. (Macon: Mercer University, 1989), pp. 48f.

47. Clemens Alexandrinus, *Stromateis* 7.59.5 = ANF 2.546.

48. Cf. Johannes Tauler, "Sermon on Mt 6,33" after Reinhold Mokrosch and Herbert Walz (eds.), *Mittelalter,* KThQ 2 (Neukirchen: Neukirchener Verlag, 1980), p. 184. For the individualistic, ascetically oriented exegetical tradition in the church, the version of Mark 8:34 is crucial (ἀπαρνησάσθω ἑαυτόν! — deny yourself!).

is stated explicitly that the destiny of the disciple is that of the teacher, and that the slave can expect the same as the master. When read from this center, the disciple discourse reveals itself as a *discourse on the way of life of the disciples which corresponds to that of the master.*

This is in keeping with

1. Matthean *christology.* Matthew tells the story of Jesus as the story of the obedient Son of God who fulfils all righteousness, law and prophets (3:15; 5:17). This Son of God experiences hostility and suffering because he consistently follows the way of righteousness. For his disciples he is not so much an example as a basic model for life. They were formed by his authority, his mission and his suffering. In this sense the Matthean discourse on discipleship transfers the model of Jesus Son of God to the disciples. This makes it the pivotal text of Matthean ecclesiology. It shows how the story of Jesus is realized in the practice of mission. Matthew's narrative christology allows for the model of a concrete view of the church as we find it in Matt. 10.

2. The Matthean understanding of *proclamation.* The disciples are the light which they let shine in their works and for whose sake people will give glory to the Father in heaven (5:14-16). Proclamation of the εὐαγγέλιον τῆς βασιλείας (gospel of the kingdom) is unthinkable without Christian practice expressed in living and suffering. This is the reason why Matthew says so little in this chapter about what the disciples are to *say* in their proclamation, and so much about what they are to *do* and what they are to *be* in their suffering. The strongest expression of their lives is to be in the proclamation.

This corresponds in turn to

3. The Matthean understanding of *being a Christian.* For him it depends entirely on the fruits (Matt. 7:15-20), and on obeying the law of love (cf. Matt. 7:21-23) and the will of the Father (Matt. 12:49-50).

In *conclusion* we ask what characterizes the church according to Matt. 10. We have to say that it is lived and suffered devotion to Christ, and that for Matthew there is no church and no proclamation without it. Put conversely, it is because of their function as identifying marks of Christ in the church that "notae" such as itinerancy, poverty, defenselessness and above all suffering are of such fundamental significance. For this reason a discourse which seeks to deal with the commissioning of the disciples becomes of necessity one which speaks of their way of life, their obedience and their suffering.

3. The Ecclesiological Significance of the Matthean Disciple Discourse

I have deliberately spoken of the Matthean "notae" of the church, employing a concept from the dogmatic tradition of the Reformation to draw attention to the discrepancy between Matthew's approach and our own Reformation tradition. In conformity with chapter 7 of the Augsburg Confession we are accustomed to designating the gospel and the sacraments the only "notae" or marks which are constitutive for the visible church. Calvin expressed something similar in saying that the two *symbola* of the visible church are that God's word is purely preached and that the sacraments are administered according to Christ's institution (*Institutes* 4.1.8-9).

This Reformation thesis brings together a number of concerns. In the light of the doctrine of justification, something fundamentally important becomes visible. The true church cannot be recognized in this world by what people make out of her, do with her or do for her, but only by what God gives her. The visible church is always constituted by the gifts God has entrusted to her, that is, word and sacrament. This involves a distinction which Calvin expounds very clearly: the visible church is not recognized by her own holiness or righteousness. Rather, the "false conviction of . . . perfect sanctity" is destructive for the church, and "ill-advised zeal for righteousness" can become a grave sin if fellowship is denied to those whose fruit is not in keeping with the doctrine (*Institutes* 4.1.13). Here Calvin is turning against the Donatists and the Cathari, but also against the Anabaptists of his time. A second distinction is at once anti-Catholic and Catholic. The Reformation definition of "notae ecclesiae" means that other notae such as the papacy or certain ceremonies are not constitutive marks of the church. This avoids saying that the Catholic Church is not church, but at the same time denies the constitutive character of much that is basic to Catholicism. In particular, almost the entire legal structure of the church falls under this verdict.

In my opinion, however, the Reformation definition cannot produce a real distinction between true and false visible church. At best it can guard against premature distinctions. Calvin himself recognized this problem without being able to solve it. What if God's word is obscured (if not obliterated) in the church for centuries? Who is to decide which word is in keeping with the true doctrine of the gospel? Who decides on the content of proclamation?

Or does its mere existence suffice? The same applies to the sacraments. Errors may occur in their administration. Who is to say whether these errors are merely peripheral or whether they destroy the proper administration of the sacraments?[49] The mere existence of word and sacrament does not make them "notae ecclesiae." This makes it clear that in themselves these marks are not decisive. One could say that they are marks of the *concept* of the visible church, but whether the reality of the church corresponds to them is a difficult question.

Another open question is that of the holiness of the church. What is the *communio sanctorum* (community of saints) of which chapter 7 of the Augsburg Confession speaks? In Reformation tradition the *corpus permixtum* (mixed body) which is the visible church became, for a number of reasons, a central idea. But as a result the holiness of the church became an attribute that can only be believed and hoped. Is that sufficient? It is not entirely accidental that Luther increased the number of *notae* (marks) in various writings and that in "Von Conciliis und Kirchen" for example he also included suffering and persecution as a nota ecclesiae. In Reformation tradition after Calvin, *disciplina* (discipline) or *oboedientia* (obedience) was increasingly regarded as a third nota ecclesiae.[50] This was the first time in the Reformation tradition that Matthew's central idea of the practice and suffering of the church was taken up again, albeit in a particular refraction. Evidently the problem inherent in the legacy of the Reformation was recognized here. That is, if one understands the visible church as constituted entirely by God's gifts to her, regardless of the form of church in which these gifts exist, the threat of a kind of ecclesiological docetism looms. The *true* church to which word and sacrament have been given is completely separate from the *actual* form of this church. What this church is like and what it does become ultimately irrelevant so long as word and sacraments are there. But a word that is separated from the everyday reality of the church and from the practice of its preachers will be dangerously abstract and other-worldly and will bear little relation to what Matthew has to say about it. Rather, the understanding of the church in the Reformation tends towards idealism and is scarcely able still to define the real church.[51] The church is and remains above all a church of sinners.

49. *Institutes* 4.1.11f.

50. Cf. already Jean Calvin, "Letter to Sadolet," in: Calvin, *Opera Selecta* I (Peter Barth et al., eds., Munich: Kaiser, 1926), p. 467; on Reformed orthodoxy, cf. Heinrich Heppe and Ernst Bizer, *Reformed Dogmatics* (London: Allen and Unwin, 1950), Locus 27 note 19.

51. Here I allow myself to use an example from my own (Zwinglian!) church tradition: Because the visible church is born out of the word alone, her form and practice are external matters which can be ordered by the (Christian) magistrates.

The difference between Catholic and Reformation ecclesiology lies in the fact that the true church is visible not only in word and sacrament but also in the institutional church. The supernatural community is apparent in the visible office of teaching, a visible priesthood, a visible pastoral office, and in the whole visible body of the church.[52] The Second Vatican Council identifies the church acknowledged in the Creed with the Catholic church governed by the successors of Peter and the bishops.[53] The true church is Roman Catholic. While the Reformation understanding of church is in danger of excluding the real, visible church from the true church (docetism!), Catholic understanding of church corresponds more closely to an incarnational christology. The church bears the dual imprints of the incarnate and the resurrected Christ and is, like the Son of God himself, at once visible and invisible.[54] Analogous to the two natures of Christ, the visible and invisible church are mysteriously bound to one another. The difficulty of this bond is that the visible church, insofar as it is identified directly with the invisible church, is in danger of becoming invariable and irreformable.[55]

Matthew's reflections on the church appear to be in complete contrast with this. His starting point is discipleship, which in both Reformation and Catholic dogmatic tradition is not usually dealt with as part of the definition of church but mostly under ethics or the doctrine of sanctification, or not at all.[56] His decisive statement is that the proclamation of the word is inseparable from the life of the disciples, since the truth of the word proclaimed is always verified by their life. Indeed, their life itself becomes the word of proclamation for others. This is why for Matthew the deeds of obedience on the part of the disciples are marks of the church, for example, poverty, defenselessness and love. And this is why for him the consequences of these deeds are also marks of the church, that is, enmity, rejection, suffering and death.[57] In

---

52. Draft of the First Vatican Council for a constitution on the church 4 = Josef Neuner and Heinrich Roos, *Der Glaube der Kirche in den Urkunden der Lehrverkündigung* (Regensburg: Pustet, [11]1971), No. 389.

53. Constitution on the Church 1.8 = ibid. No. 411.

54. Cf. Karl Rahner, "Membership in the Church according to the teaching of Pius XII's Encyclical 'Mystici Corporis Christi'," in: Rahner, *Theological Investigations II* (Baltimore: Helicon, 1963), pp. 86f.

55. "According to this view, the Church believes in itself (Schmaus)"; cf. Alfred Adam, "Kirche III" in: *RGG*[3] III, p. 1311.

56. There are of course churches and communities which take discipleship as their base, among them de facto the medieval mendicant movements (Waldenses, Franciscans, Wyclifites), the Anabaptists and their successors (e.g., Disciples of Christ). If I see it correctly most of these groups did not develop a *doctrine* of the church but spoke almost exclusively of church *practice*.

57. Cf. Matt. 5:10: ἕνεκεν δικαιοσύνης (for the cause of justice) as a decisive criterion.

this way Matthew achieves something remarkable: he places his marks of the church right in the center of the concrete and at the same time ambiguous world.[58] Compared with Matthew, the problem of the Reformation "notae ecclesiae" seems to me to lie in their inability to place the church in the ambiguity of the world. Matthew's understanding of church begins at exactly the point which the Reformation tradition seems to relieve it of, namely its existence *in the world*. In speaking of the disciples' itinerancy, poverty, defenselessness and love, Matthew focuses on the holiness given to the church in the midst of the world. In this way Matthew helps us to speak of the church in worldly, concrete and thus real terms. His approach is at one with the Catholic understanding of church in that both speak of the real church existent in the world. But unlike the Catholic understanding, Matthew's view of church is dynamic. Church is never simply church as it is, but church in its obedience and its deeds. It does not own its existence, but owes it to what it has been given and must prove itself in obedience. So church does not *exist* apart from its obedience and its deeds but *becomes* church by proving in its deeds the commission and authority entrusted to it.

This gives rise to two problems, however. The first is that the Matthean marks of the church are not unambiguous. If they were, they would simply be ethical or even institutional laws. In our exposition we have seen again and again how Matthew gave a new accent or a new interpretation to Jesus' commands. Traveling, for example, was no longer a condition of discipleship in the different situation after Jesus' death and in different geographical surroundings; rather, it becomes the more radical form of that discipleship. Poverty in Matthew is not simply legally prescribed but required in response to a given situation. The Matthean concept of the *way* to perfection certainly sets the church the aim of Christ-likeness or godlikeness (Matt. 5:48) but does not say what is the minimum required in order still to be church. This minimum does indeed exist, but the Son of Man will not decide until the last judgment where his disciples' righteousness has been insufficient for them to enter the kingdom of heaven (cf. Matt. 5:20). So one could say that for Matthew the decisive mark of the church is *being on the way*, traveling on a road whose destination is righteousness and perfection. A church which is not *on the move* and which does not *strive* with all its might to be obedient to its Lord is not church for Matthew. This may well be what Matthew had in mind in speaking of the true family of those who do the will of the Father (12:50), a text justifiably read as Matthew's definition of church.

58. Jürgen Moltmann, *The Church in the Power of the Spirit: A Contribution to Messianic Ecclesiology* (New York: HarperCollins, 1991), p. 342.

The second problem is the question whether the decisive element in the Reformation approach, that is, the understanding of church as given and endowed by God and not a human creation, is obscured in Matthew. As I see it, the systematic force of the idea of discipleship should not be underestimated. Matthew makes it his central ecclesiological idea, and in doing so he gives human activity and human orientation a "vis à vis." What is far more decisive for the church than any human obedience is God's action through Jesus. According to Matthew, church does not simply *exist*. Rather, church *becomes* in that Jesus who heals among his people shares his authority with his disciples, and in that Jesus, who verifies his divine sonship through his obedience, gives his disciples a commission. Church does not simply exist. Rather, it *endures* in that this Jesus is with his church in various ways until the end of the age, strengthening it when its own faith is insufficient. Church does not simply exist. Rather, it *will become* at the time when Jesus the Son of Man separates the sheep from the goats in its midst, reminding it for the last time that it is not church by its own judgment. So we could say that where the Reformation speaks of word and sacrament given to the church as its constitutive gifts, Matthew *tells* of a living person in whose imitation the disciples live. It is because this partner is so concrete that Matthew is able to speak of the church in such dynamic terms.

It seems to me that Matthew's ecclesiological approach offers an opportunity for both Roman Catholics and Protestants to bring movement into the fixed basic concepts of church we have inherited.

9 The Primacy Saying of Matthew 16:17-19 from the Perspective of Its Effective History

1. The Problem

1.1. Introduction

The primacy saying of Matt. 16:17-19 is no longer a storm center of exegetical controversy. The "critical consensus" which now dominates is found in most Protestant and much Roman Catholic exegesis. In the United States it is represented by the ecumenical book on Peter by Brown, Donfried and Reumann,[1] and in Germany by the somewhat more critical book edited by the Ecumenical Institutes of the Universities, *Papacy as an Ecumenical Issue.*[2] There are three basic elements of consensus. First, that Peter did not receive primacy "directly and immediately" from Jesus. The saying about the rock is agreed to be post-Easter. Second, the saying is not concerned with an "actual juridical primacy" of the "visible head of the whole Church militant"[3] but with Peter's non-juristic precedence. Many scholars today see Peter as the "prime bearer of the Jesus tradition."[4] Third,

---

1. Raymond Brown, Karl P. Donfried and John Reumann, *Peter in the New Testament* (Minneapolis: Augsburg, 1973).
    2. Arbeitsgemeinschaft ökumenischer Universitätsinstitute (ed.), *Papsttum als ökumenische Frage* (Munich: Kaiser, 1979).
    3. *Pastor aeternus*, Cap. 1, Canon = DS^{36} 3055; cf. Cap. 3, Canon = DS^{36} 3064.
    4. Franz Mussner, *Petrus und Paulus — Pole der Einheit*, QD 76 (Freiburg: Herder, 1976), p. 123.

German original: "Das Primatwort Matthäus 16.17-19 aus wirkungsgeschichtlicher Sicht," *NTS* 37 (1991), pp. 415-433. Originally presented as the main paper at the 45th SNTS Conference in Milan, July 1990. The presentation style is retained.

Cullmann's book on Peter[5] in particular has made clear that the idea of apostolic succession is not to be connected with this text[6] but has been added to it in the history of its interpretation.[7] The controversial issues remaining are whether the post-Easter rock saying originated in the primitive Christian community or in the post-apostolic era, and whether verses 17-19 originated as a unit or came together from isolated traditions.

1.2. My Interest

It is a pleasant situation to be dealing with broad consensus here. I have no intention of shattering that consensus, so you may find what I have to say exegetically dull. My interest is a different one. You may well have noticed that my wording of the three elements of consensus was full of quotations from and allusions to the dogmatic constitution *Pastor aeternus* of the First Vatican Council. There they are derived from the canons, and each canon ends with a solemn anathema. As well as us Protestants, a large proportion of current Roman Catholic exegesis should strictly speaking be anathematized by these anathemas. But apart from a monition against Anton Vögtle in 1961 for his very cautious suggestion that Matt. 16:17 could be redactional[8] I know of no other recent cases. Evidently exegetes are so unimportant now that we have license to say and do almost what we like in our academic playground. Why do we have this license? As exegetes we deal with the historical original sense of our texts. But a text that is interpreted by historical-critical method *cannot* in its original sense determine the present of the church or society. This is why

5. Oscar Cullmann, *Peter. Disciple, Apostle, Martyr: A Historical Study* (trans. Floyd F. Filson, London: SCM, 1966). Cf. the clear conclusion drawn by Rudolf Pesch, *Simon-Petrus*, PuP 15 (Stuttgart: Hiersemann, 1981), pp. 162, 166: "It is clear from the beginning that in some of his roles and 'offices' Peter could not have a 'successor'.... As I see it, the idea of 'successors' to Peter could only develop when the monepiscopacy came to dominate in the Western church as well, after its beginnings in the East."

6. Cf. *Pastor aeternus*, Cap 2, Canon = DS[36] 3058.

7. Probably first in the *Epistula Clementis ad Jacobum* 2 (= GCS 42, 6f.), seen by Georg Strecker, *Das Judenchristentum in den Pseudoclementinen*, TU 70 (Berlin: Akademie, 1958), p. 90, as one of the foundational documents. In it Peter appoints Clement (!) as his successor in Rome.

8. Joseph A. Burgess, *A History of the Exegesis of Matthew 16,17-19 from 1781 to 1965* (Ann Arbor: Edwards, 1976), p. 163. The monition related to Anton Vögtle's 1957 essay "Messiasgeheimnis und Petrusverheissung. Zur Komposition von Mt 16,13-23," *BZ.NF* 1 (1957), pp. 252-272, and *BZ.NF* 2 (1958), pp. 85-103 = Vögtle, *Das Evangelium und die Evangelien*, KBANT (Düsseldorf: Patmos, 1971), pp. 137-170.

purely exegetical ascertainments of the original sense of our texts are always harmless.

This is more problematic for Protestants than for Roman Catholics. I should like to illustrate this from the history of reception *(Wirkungs-geschichte)* of the biblical texts. It is a history of application, repeatedly bringing new senses of the old texts to the fore. These new senses gave new answers to new needs in new situations. Roman Catholic exegesis can overcome this problem with the help of the classical idea of tradition. According to the Second Vatican Council, apostolic tradition "progresses in the church with the aid of the Holy Spirit; the understanding of traditional things and words grows."[9] Protestants find it more difficult to admit that the "sola scriptura" principle in its classical Reformation form has been dethroned by the Enlightenment, historicism and modern reception theory. This latter virtually identifies the meaning of the text with the development of that meaning in the text's reception history.[10] We learn from Hans-Georg Gadamer that understanding is always a productive activity, never simply reproductive, and that if we understand at all, we have to understand "in a *different* way." He does not see the temporal distance between text and interpreter as "a gulf to be bridged" but as the productive factor which makes different understanding and new understanding possible.[11] This raises the question of how the past literal sense e.g. of the original text in its original communication situation can determine the truth or untruth of later or current realizations. How can the past sense of a text determine its current meaning? Is not every new realization of a scriptural text permissible, including the Roman Catholic one in our case, since understanding a text is always production of meaning and not reproduction, renewal and not repetition?[12]

I should like to reflect on this question, a difficult one especially for Protestants, with reference to Matt. 16:17-19. I have chosen this text because its reception history has been both diverse and contradictory.

---

9. *De Revelatione* II 8 = LThK XIII 518f.

10. Hannelore Link, *Rezeptionsforschung,* UB 215 (Stuttgart: Kohlhammer, 1976), p. 125: "The truth of the text is its history"; Hans Robert Jauss, *Literaturgeschichte als Provokation* (Frankfurt: Suhrkamp, ⁴1974), p. 186: "The judgement of the centuries" concerning a text is the "successive unfolding of potential meaning, latent in the text and realized in its historical phases of reception."

11. Cf. Hans-Georg Gadamer, *Truth and Method* (New York: Seabury, 1975), pp. 264f.

12. Cf. Chlodovis Boff, *Theology and Praxis: Epistemological Foundations* (Maryknoll, NY: Orbis, 1987), pp. 138f.

2. Reception History

2.1. Papal Interpretation

Papal interpretation is characterized, first, by the link between the primacy of Peter and the idea of apostolic succession, and second, by the juristic interpretation of Peter's primacy, generally supported since the Counter-Reformation by v. 19.[13] Research in church history widely accepts the thesis that this is a later "re-reading of Scripture"[14] in the light of Roman Catholic church experience, or rather the experience of its leaders. The reading is clearly recorded by Bishop Stephen (254-57) in the middle of the third century,[15] and we should not exclude the possibility that it already existed in the first half of the third century, as Tertullian and Origen may have polemicized against it.[16] Occurrences in the 4th and 5th centuries are sparse. The major western Fathers, particularly Ambrose, Augustine, Jerome (mostly) and Hilary interpret differently.[17] Karlfried Fröhlich surmises that throughout the Middle Ages the interpretation of Matt. 16:17-19 in terms of the Pope was extremely rare and was almost exclusively found in legal texts whose sole purpose was to legitimate papal authority against the Eastern patriarchs or the Emperor.[18] It was thus an instrument used to legitimate power. My examination of numerous medieval commentaries confirms this. Thomas Aquinas is one of the very few who even mention this interpretation, as one possibility among others.[19] In

---

13. Cf., e.g., Cornelius a Lapide, *Commentarius in quatuor Evangelia. Argumentum in S. Matthaeum* (Antwerp: Jacobus Meursius, 1670), p. 319: Keys are the attribute of kings and rulers, not of teachers or preachers.

14. Walter Kasper, "Dienst an der Einheit und Freiheit der Kirche," in: Joseph Ratzinger (ed.), *Dienst an der Einheit* (Düsseldorf: Patmos, 1978), p. 85.

15. Cyprian, *Epistula* 75.17. Cyprian considers this interpretation an "aperta et manifesta . . . stultitia" (an obvious and manifest . . . stupidity).

16. Tertullian, *De pudicitia* 21. The interpretation as a polemic against Callistus of Rome now tends to be rejected by church historians. It could be supported however by a similar polemic of Origen, *In Matthaeum* 12.11 = GCS Orig X 86. Here too Rome is not named explicitly, though Origen is known to have been there once; cf. Eusebius, *Historia Ecclesiastica* 6.14.10.

17. Joseph Ludwig, *Die Primatworte Mt 16, 18.19 in der altkirchlichen Exegese*, NTA 19.4 (Münster: Aschendorff, 1952), pp. 61-70, names for the period before Leo the Great only Optatus of Mileve (who secures the authority of Rome in the struggle against the Donatists), the Council of Aquileia in 381 and Jerome (who gives this interpretation in a letter to the pope [*Epistula* 15.2] but not elsewhere).

18. Karlfried Fröhlich, *Formen der Auslegung von Mt 16, 13-18 im lateinischen Mittelalter* (Basel, Diss., 1963), p. 117.

19. Thomas Aquinas, *Super Evangelium S. Matthaei Lectura* (Turin: Marietti, ⁵1951), No. 1384.

Catholic exegesis it came to the fore in the 16th century, when Catholics had to resist Protestants laying claim to the traditional interpretations.[20] Indirectly, the triumph of the hitherto quite marginal "papal" interpretation of Matt. 16:18 is a product of the Reformation.

2.2. The Classical Patristic Interpretations

All other interpretations of Matt. 16:17-19, now largely submerged and unknown to the average Christian, derive from Origen and Tertullian. In agreement with Gnostic interpretations[21] and with Tertullian,[22] Origen interprets Peter *as a type.* He is the prototype of the pneumatic human being who "comprehended the building of the church in himself, effected by the Word, and thus gained strength" (*Contra Celsum* 6.77). Origen has accented this interpretation in various ways. In answer to the question of what the rock is on which the spiritual person is founded, he already points to *faith.*[23] Tertullian saw Peter as the guarantor of genuine and public apostolic tradition.[24] This reading was supported by the fact that the rock saying follows Peter's confession of Jesus as Son of God. In the Greek and Syrian churches[25] this became the sole interpretation, and for this reason we call it the "Eastern" one, even though it was widespread both in the Eastern and Western church throughout the Middle Ages. In the West, it was usually the second interpretation alongside the Augustinian one. It owes its popularity in the West to Ambrose, Hilary and Ambrosiaster.[26] This interpretation corresponded to the experience of the church, first in the dogmatic disputes of the fourth to sixth centuries and later in a world that had become Islamic. The church's sole basis was its creed, the faith on which it was founded and to which it unshakeably clung.

A different aspect of our passage came to the fore when it was combined

---

20. First recorded in Thomas Caietanus, *Commentarii in Evangelium* (Venice, 1530), p. 91; especially pointed in Roberto Bellarmino, *De Romano Pontifice* (Sedan, 1619), pp. 72-105. Cf. the text of Matt. 16:18 in the dome of St Peter's in Rome!

21. *Apocalypse of Peter,* NHC VII 71.14-72.4 (Peter as the typical bearer of revelation); Ulrich Luz, *Matthew 8–20,* Hermeneia (Minneapolis: Fortress, 2001), p. 368 note 117; Klaus Berger, "Unfehlbare Offenbarung," in: Paul G. Müller/Werner Stenger (eds.), *Kontinuität und Einheit* (FS Franz Mussner; Freiburg: Herder, 1981), pp. 261-326, here: pp. 279, 285.

22. *De Pudicitia* 21.

23. Fr 345 II = GCS Orig XII 149.

24. *De praescriptione haereticorum* 22.4f.

25. Wilhelm de Vries, *Der Kirchenbegriff der von Rom getrennten Syrer,* OchrA 145 (Rome: Pont. Inst. Orientalium Stud., 1955), pp. 24-33, 61-67.

26. Luz, *Matthew 8–20* (see note 21), p. 373 note 158.

with other references to rocks in the New Testament. Origen writes: "Every follower of Christ is a rock from which those drank who 'drank from the spiritual rock that followed them.'"[27] Tertullian (*Adversus Marcionem* 4.13.6) is familiar too with this interpretation that identifies the rock with Christ. It suggests itself as soon as the text is interpreted at the level of the canon and brought together with other references to rocks, such as 1 Cor. 10:4 and 1 Cor. 3:11. It is clear in Origen and Tertullian that the various interpretations, christological, typical and faith- or confession-related, are not mutually exclusive. Spiritually interpreted biblical texts are as it were polysemous, and various interpretations can be combined without contradicting each other. It was Augustine who later rediscovered the christological interpretation; he was the first to offer it as an alternative to the reading in terms of Peter.[28] In Augustine's version Peter is not the rock. *Christ* alone is the rock. Peter too stands on this rock, for no one can lay any foundation other than the one that has been laid, that is, Christ. One reason why this interpretation was important to Augustine was that weak, fickle Peter, who is founded on Christ the rock alone, offered a model for an imperfect office-bearer in the church. Augustine's interpretation was dominant throughout the Middle Ages, and known not only in the West. It was a truly popular reading. Ordinary believers could identify with Peter, the imperfect and weak Christian who was founded on the rock of Christ alone. There was of course no anti-papal edge to this interpretation, since Augustine was an adherent of Rome. The same is true of the large number of Augustinian interpretations in the Middle Ages. In almost every reading which identifies the rock with Christ, the identification with the Pope appears to be unknown.

2.3. Anti-Roman Emphases in Traditional Interpretations

There are only a few examples of how in the early church and in medieval times the Eastern or the Augustinian reading was given an antipapal emphasis. I would like to mention Ambrose, whose "Eastern" interpretation speaks symptomatically of a primacy "confessionis . . . , non honoris, . . . fidei, non ordinis" (of confession, . . . not of honor, . . . of faith, not of rank).[29] The antipapal slant is more frequent with the Humanists. Faber Stapulensis[30] supports the Eastern reading and says that Jesus added to this saying the Satan

27. Origen, *In Matthaeum* 12.10 = GCS Orig X 86. Origen alludes to 1 Cor. 10:4.
28. *In Johannem* 124.5; *Retractiones* 1.20.2; further references in Gert Haendler, "Zur Frage nach dem Petrusamt in der alten Kirche," *StTh* 30 (1976), pp. 114-117.
29. *De Incarnationis Dominicae Sacramento* 4.32 = CSEL 79 (1964), pp. 238f.
30. *Commentarii initiatorii in quatuor Evangelii* (Basel, 1523), 178 = 75.

saying of v. 23 to ensure that no one would assume Peter himself to be the rock. Erasmus is surprised at those who read the text in terms of the pope, and turns instead to Origen's "typical" interpretation.[31] Antipapal tones are even more rare in Augustinian readings.[32]

These rare examples of polemics are significant because the Reformation was able to make use of them. The Reformers did not develop their own interpretation of Matt. 16:18 but handed on the traditional Augustinian and Eastern readings, giving them an antipapal emphasis. Melanchthon for example sees an alternative between an interpretation in terms of Peter's person and one in terms of his "office and confession." He rightly refers to Origen, Ambrose, John Chrysostom, Cyprian, Hilary and Bede for his interpretation.[33] Luther takes up Augustine's interpretation and says: Christ wants to have one rock, but the papists have two.[34] Words of similar import can be found in other Reformation exegetes. The only really new element in Reformation exegesis was that it now usually excluded identification with the person of Peter even from the Eastern reading. Otherwise however the Reformers quite rightly referred to the consensus of the Church Fathers. Catholic exegesis on the other hand undertook a papal interpretation and thus initiated a far-reaching process of re-interpretation of the Fathers. It began with Salmeron, was evident in Bellarmine[35] and has had its consequences right up to the twentieth century. Hugo Koch is a case in point.[36]

2.4. Conclusion

It is important to me that the history of interpretation of Matt. 16:18 has shown a wide variety of readings. I have reduced them somewhat generously in this brief account to four basic types: the typical, the Eastern, the Augustinian and the papal interpretation. It is even more important that Matthew's text is one of the few that could be used for and against the same thing. It was

---

31. *Annotationes*, in: *Opera omnia* VI (Hildesheim: Georg Olms, 1962), p. 88.

32. Cf. Tostatus in Franz Gillmann, *Zur scholastischen Auslegung von Mt 16,18*, AkathKR 104 (Mainz: Kirchheim, 1924), p. 51.

33. *Tractatus de potestate Papae*, BSLK⁴ 480.

34. Erwin Mülhaupt, *Luthers Evangelienauslegung*, II (Göttingen: Vandenhoeck und Ruprecht, ⁴1973), p. 539 (Sermon of 1522) = M. Luther, "Sermon von Gewalt Sanct Peters (29. Juni 1522)," WA 10 III, 1211.

35. Alphonsus Salmeron, *Commentarii in Evangelicam Historiam* IV (Coloniae Agrippinae: Antonium Hierat, 1612), 3.2 = 387-400; Bellarmin (see note 20), 1.10-13.

36. Hugo Koch lost his position in Braunsberg because of his "episcopalistic" interpretation of Cyprian in 1910.

read as a mainstay of the papacy or as a crucial exegetical argument against it. In this case a text did not only provide the potential for a wide range of applications but was also the point of reference for opposing interpretations. There is a need for a decision from the point of view of the reception history itself. But how can a decision be made when developments and fresh realizations of potential meanings are part of the biblical texts themselves? A decision appears to be necessary yet impossible. The original sense of a text cannot regulate its later applications.

3. Exegesis

3.1. Two observations can be made at the *synchronic level*. On the one hand, our text comes at an important point in Matthew's Gospel, at the end of the main section 12:1–16:20 which deals with the separation between Jesus and Israel's leaders. The main section on discipleship and church (16:21–20:28) follows. It is here in our passage that the keyword ἐκκλησία (church) first occurs, in connection with the name of the first disciple to be called, Peter (4:18-20; 10:2). This is significant. In the composition of the Gospel, Peter is given prominence as the apostle for the church. Moreover, he is named very frequently in Matthew, whereas James and John are often omitted. On the other hand the text contains a large number of cross-references to other sections, which Matthew has probably introduced deliberately. There is for example the revelation of the Son to *all* disciples (11:25-27); the beatitude addressed to *all* disciples 13:16-17; the confession of the Son of God by *all* the disciples in 14:33; the instruction to *all* disciples to bind and to loose in 18:18; the contrast between Peter and the Pharisees who lock people out of the kingdom of heaven, 23:13. There seems to be nothing about Peter in our passage which is not true of all the disciples. This is supported by the fact that elsewhere Matthew replaces Markan disciples by Peter (15:15; 18:21) or, vice versa, replaces the Markan Peter by the disciples (21:20; 24:3; cf. 28:7). Thus Peter is the typical disciple, and when speaking of a typical disciple Matthew tends to choose Peter. So we can say that Origen's "typical" interpretation corresponds closely to what we find in the text. It is also significant that 16:21-28 takes up numerous topoi from 16:13-20. Σὺ εἶ Πέτρος (you are Peter) and σκάνδαλον εἶ (you are a scandal) are in pointed contrast. This contrast exemplifies the "ambivalence" in Peter's behavior[37]

---

37. Paul Hoffmann, "Der Petrus-Primat im Matthäusevangelium," in: Joachim Gnilka (ed.), *Neues Testament und Kirche* (FS Rudolf Schnackenburg; Freiburg: Herder, 1974), pp. 94-114, here: p. 100.

throughout the Gospel of Matthew. Peter is a realistic type, showing the disciples as they are.

3.2. In terms of *source criticism and history of tradition* I share with others[38] the opinion that v. 17 is a redactional transition from the Markan text to the traditional saying about the rock. I agree with Gnilka[39] that v. 19a, the saying about the keys, is also a redactional transition between the rock saying and the traditional saying on binding and loosing in v. 19bc. I do not find the theory of consistent Semitisms in the three verses convincing.[40] Vv. 17 and 19a are almost entirely in biblical language which is also a general characteristic of Matthew the Evangelist. Neither am I convinced by Kähler's thesis that vv. 17-19 correspond to a formal pattern of investiture of the bearer of revelation.[41] The evidence given is too varied and too sparse to constitute a genre. I concede that the marks of redactional language in vv. 17 and 19a are not unambiguous. Convincing reconstruction is apparent only within the coherence of the overall thesis. However, the cross references to the traditional verses 11:27; 13:16 cover most of the formulations of 16fin., 17ab. V. 19a has a transitional function, associating the idea of the church as a building with the contrast of earth and heaven. This is in keeping with the Matthean idea of the kingdom of heaven as a place one "goes into." As far as the individual saying about binding and loosing in v. 19bc is concerned, I consider the plural version of 18:18, which also occurs in John 20:23, to be earlier. The main argument against this, the fact that it is better anchored within the context of Matt. 16:17-19, can be discounted if Matthew himself has created the context.

If we are right, there are two consequences for the interpretation of Matthew's text. First, the cross references connecting Peter with the other disciples, which are especially frequent in the redactional verses 16 (end), 17 and 19a, are evidently of great importance to Matthew. Second, it is clearly Matthew himself who has emphasized the figure of Peter in his shaping of v. 17 and 19a and has placed the traditional logion 18:18 in the singular. In

---

38. Following Vögtle, "Messiasgeheimnis" (see note 8), pp. 166f., 169; Brown/Donfried/Reumann, *Peter* (see note 1), p. 89 (partly); Joachim Gnilka, *Das Matthäusevangelium* II, HThK I.2 (Herder: Freiburg, 1988), p. 54. Hans Klein, "Zur Traditionsgeschichte von Mt 16,16b.17," in: Karl Kartelge/Traugott Holtz/Claus-Peter März (eds.), *Christus bezeugen*, EThSt 59 (FS Wolfgang Trilling; Leipzig: St. Benno, 1989), pp. 124-135, here: pp. 124ff., suggests that Matt. 16:16b, 17 could be the confession of a person being baptized and the response of the baptizer. I can accept this inasfar as Matthew makes informal use of such formulations. This would further emphasise the typical character of Peter.

39. Gnilka, II (see note 38), p. 56.

40. Cf. Luz, *Matthew 8–20* (see note 21), p. 355 note 12.

41. See Christoph Kähler, "Zur Form- und Traditionsgeschichte von Mt 16,17-19," *NTS* 23 (1976/77), pp. 46-56.

diachronic terms he has not extended Peter's power to bind and to loose to the disciples in 18:18 but has concentrated the disciples' power to bind and loose in 18:18 in the person of Peter in 16:19.

3.3. *V. 18.* I would agree with most exegetes that the traditional v. 18 did not originate with Jesus.[42] The alternatives are, first, that the logion originated in the Aramaic-speaking earliest community, e.g. in a hypothetical account of the first appearance to Peter,[43] or second, that the logion came from a Greek-speaking community.[44] I favor the second alternative. In my judgment the language of v. 18 does not point unequivocally to a Semitic background. Πύλαι ᾅδου (the gates of Hades) in particular is clearly Greek.[45] I cannot see a direct relation between v. 18 and Gal. 1:16. Neither is polemically expressed, and it is symptomatic that researchers are completely divided on the question of which verse is dependent on the other.[46] I find Lampe's suggestion[47] that the word-play of v. 18 was originally Greek, since כיף in Aramaic largely means "stone" rather than "rock," still convincing in spite of Claudel's critical questions.[48] The theological interpretation of the traditional

42. Gérard Claudel, *La confession de Pierre. Trajectoire d'une péricope évangélique,* ÉtB 10 (Paris: Gabalda, 1988), p. 373, assumes for 16:18 authentic words of Jesus addressed to Peter, which however can no longer be reconstructed. I cannot say that I find reasons for this assumption. One has to concede however that the arguments against the authenticity of v. 18 are anything but strong either. Apart from the Greek character of the word play Πέτρος — πέτρα (see below) there is only the (correct!) observation that Jesus could not have spoken of the founding of his special community in Israel. But if we take the μου (my church!) to be Matthean redaction, which cannot be proved linguistically at all but would be formally in keeping with the Matthean βασιλεία of the Son of Man, we would be left only with the argument that ἐκκλησία does not correspond to Jesus' language.

43. See for example Brown/Donfried/Reumann, *Peter* (see note 1), p. 92, and all those who assume part of an ancient account of Easter to be behind vv. 17-19.

44. One does not necessarily have to assume a late origin. Rudolf Pesch, *Simon-Petrus* (see note 5), pp. 100f., suggests that 1 Cor. 3 refers polemically to Matt. 16:17-19. He assumes the Antiochian conflict to be its context. Kenneth Caroll, "Thou art Peter," *NT* 6 (1963), pp. 268-276, here: p. 275, suggests a declaration of independence from Jerusalem by the Antiochian church.

45. Luz, *Matthew 8–20* (see note 21), p. 358 note 35.

46. Cf. Luz, *Matthew 8–20* (see note 21), p. 360 note 46.

47. Peter Lampe, "Das Spiel mit dem Petrus-Namen," *NTS* 25 (1978/79), pp. 231-239.

48. Claudel (see note 42), pp. 338-343. Claudel's first argument is that a word play on the same word כיף is aesthetically more pleasing. Second, that the widespread familiarity of Cephas in early Christianity and his association with the Twelve (1 Cor. 15:5) suggest that this nickname was ecclesiologically significant from the beginning. The first argument is a matter of discretion. The second does not mean anything, as we do not know the original meaning of the nickname Cephas. Lampe's conjecture (pp. 238f.) that the nickname had a secular, humorous ring is supported by rabbinic and classical parallels (Aristokles = Plato is also widespread; cf. Luz, *Matthew 8–20* [see note 21], p. 359 note 42; classical parallel for metaphorical use of πέτρος — πέτρα

Aramaic name or nickname Cephas is then secondary, as in parallel cases.[49] The New Testament parallels support a late dating: On the one hand, the next Peter parallel is found in the late supplement to John's Gospel in 21:15-17. The Johannine figure of the disciple whom Jesus loved, usually occurring together with Peter, is both a bearer of tradition and a type, just as the Matthean Peter is. Parallels indicating the apostles to be the foundation of the building of the church, on the other hand, are found only in the post-apostolic era, namely in Eph. 2:20 and Rev. 21:14. In Paul's time the founding apostles did not call themselves the foundation but the "pillars" of the church (Gal. 2:9). Paul reserved the foundation image for Christ (1 Cor. 3:11). I take the saying about the rock to be post-apostolic, dating from the time when it was important for the church to look back on the foundational era of the apostles.

3.4. The post-apostolic retrospective on the foundational era of the apostles is closely associated with the idea of tradition. We need to keep this in mind when we now ask why it is *Peter* who becomes the key apostolic figure in the New Testament. As I see it, there are various reasons for this. It is certainly important to Matthew that there was a strong Petrine tradition in Syria, which also influenced the pseudo-Clementines for example. The Gospels of Matthew, John, and Luke and 1 Peter each make it clear in their own way that in the post-apostolic era Peter was the crucial apostolic figure, not for a particular group within the church or for a regional church but for the *whole* church. Attention has been drawn to the first appearance to Peter and to Peter's role in church history as the link between Jewish and Gentile Christianity. The texts however also point in a different direction. Matthew and Luke do not emphasize the first appearance to Peter as much as Jesus' calling of Peter as the first disciple. This is in keeping both with the reference in 2 Peter to Peter as eyewitness (1:16) and with the finding in many apostolic Fathers and in Justin that in the early 2nd century it was the κύριος (Lord), the living Jesus tradition, which constituted the decisive ecclesial authority. So I think that Peter's crucial role as the fundamental apostolic figure of the whole church, above Paul or even James the brother of the Lord, is connected with the fact that he more than all others represents tradition continuity with Je-

---

in Lampe, p. 241 note 9) but remains conjecture. The only substantive argument is the linguistic one. The question is this: Does the evidence of the Targums (not only Onqelos and Jonathan!), though only of the Targums, for כיף = סלע (rock) offer evidence of an older Palestinian-Aramaic use of language distinct from the later כיף = pebble, round stone, shoreline? Or are we dealing with a specifically biblical use of language resulting from the Targumists' desire to distinguish Hebrew צור from סלע? Only a precise analysis of the use of the words in the Targumim can provide an answer to this.

49. Lampe, p. 243; Luz, *Matthew 8–20* (see note 21), p. 358 note 38.

sus. Peter became the most important fundamental apostolic figure because *Jesus* was Lord of the church.

This is supported by findings in Matthew's Gospel. The disciples, represented time and again by Peter, are *pupils* of the earthly Jesus. They, and among them especially Peter as the typical disciple, ask Jesus questions, receive instruction from him and gain understanding through him. Peter's role as a pupil is a general one, not limited to specifically halachic questions.[50] For Matthew, "being church" means being and remaining pupils of the earthly Jesus.[51] The apostle-disciples are bearers of tradition and at the same time representatives of the community. On this basis it is part of the perspective of the text when contemporary Roman Catholic exegetes in particular see the "Petrine service" fundamental to the church as the constant and uncompromising accentuation of Jesus' teaching.[52]

4. Hermeneutical Considerations

4.1. How Do the Basic Types in the History of Reception Relate to the Matthean Text?

Superficially, the typical interpretation by Origen or Tertullian and the "papal" reading come close to the basic text. The papal interpretation has pursued most clearly the idea that *Peter* and nothing else is the rock of the church. The typical interpretation has pursued the idea that for Matthew Peter represents *all* true disciples. At a deeper level I regard the "Eastern" reading of the rock in terms of faith or confession of faith as particularly close to the idea of tradition in Matthew, especially because it makes concrete the *way in which* Peter became the rock of the church. The Reformation reading on the other hand places the rock function of Peter and the rock function of faith in opposition to each other. The Augustinian interpretation is more remote from the original text. At a deeper level the papal interpretation is also very remote from the original Matthean text for two reasons.

50. Critical of Reinhard Hummel, *Die Auseinandersetzung zwischen Kirche und Judentum im Matthäusevangelium,* BEvTh 33 (Munich: Kaiser, 1963), pp. 59ff.

51. See pp. 116-125 above. Hoffmann, *Petrus-Primat* (see note 37), p. 110, says that the historically unique bond between the disciples and Jesus, exemplified in Peter, is a "lasting characteristic" of the church.

52. Mussner (see note 4), p. 137; Pesch (see note 44), pp. 143f.; Gnilka, *Matt. II* (see note 38), p. 69; Rudolf Schnackenburg, "Petrus im Matthäusevangelium," in *Cause de l'évangile,* LD 123 (FS Jacques Dupont; Paris: du Cerf, 1985), pp. 108-125, here: pp. 124f.; Hoffmann (see note 37), p. 114.

(1) If Peter in Matthew's Gospel typifies *every* Christian, it is a huge step from there to an authority concentrated in *one* person *alone*. (2) If Peter became the "rock man" of the church because of his unique closeness to Jesus, this rock function can not be transferred to others by succession. This corresponds, by the way, to the image of v. 18. The church is built on the rock as its lasting foundation. But the church is not the rock, and the rock does not as it were develop into the church. In my opinion the distance between the papal interpretation and the Matthean text is greatest.

4.2. A Model for Understanding

The above does not yet answer the question of the truth of the various interpretations. I should like to explain briefly what I mean by "understanding the meaning of a text." Understanding means to me a *new* understanding of the text in a new situation. We cannot afford to ignore this insight of modern hermeneutics and literary criticism, prefigured to an extent in the Catholic idea of tradition. After all, it corresponds to the process of tradition in the Bible itself. Every text and every tradition in the Bible harbors a potential for freedom which becomes productive in a new situation. The Pentateuch narratives or the stories of Jesus for instance were always retold and not exegeted in biblical times. Up to the beginning of the Common Era the Torah was essentially rewritten time and again. Prophetic tradition and the sayings of Jesus[53] were not exegeted but constantly reformulated. It was the process of canonization of the biblical texts which gave rise to the phenomenon of both Jewish and Christian *textual* exegesis. This was something quite different however from the modern question of *the* unequivocal original sense of a text.[54] I should like to draw attention to what I see as three fundamental aspects of contemporary understanding of the meaning of a biblical text from a biblical perspective. These three points also indicate why I see the reception history of biblical texts, or — in the words of Hans Georg Gadamer — "effective history," as an important contribution to the understanding of their present meaning. Post-history means much more to me and is quite distinct from the accumulation of historical materials.

53. Migaku Sato, *Q und Prophetie*, WUNT II.29 (Tübingen: Mohr Siebeck, 1988), draws attention to the proximity between them.

54. I find important in this context what James A. Sanders, *From Sacred Story to Sacred Text* (Philadelphia: Fortress, 1987), partic. pp. 166f. terms "canonical process." This living process is not "frozen" by the completion of the canon but continues as a living process of interpretation.

a. For me, understanding a biblical text is a *holistic* process which involves human thought, feelings and action. This is why for me, as for pietist hermeneutics and for Gadamer, application is a significant aspect of understanding. Using water as an image, we can say that we fully "understand" a spring only when we drink from it or a river when we swim in it. So it is not only the history of *interpretation* of a text — in commentaries, for example — which reveals how it has been understood in concrete situations. Its whole reception history, for example in art, in prayers, in political activity or in church action, is important.[55]

b. For me, understanding a biblical text is a constantly *new* process in new contexts with different people involved. I agree with José M. Míguez-Bonino that there cannot be an abstract, ahistoric heaven of theological truth.[56] Biblical texts are not merely to be seen as vessels containing particular statements. They are also to be seen performatively, as a power giving rise to particular effects. Returning to the water image, we can say that biblical texts are like a spring whose water flows fresh into new parts. This is why for me the reception history of texts is part of the texts themselves, the expression of their power.[57]

c. Understanding biblical texts comes about only when we discover what we owe them and when we are moved by them to new action. Understanding comes about when the texts *connect with us.* So understanding means eliminating the distance from the text created by our historical-critical explication. Taking up the water image again, we can say that biblical texts are not a water sample we set about analyzing chemically as autonomous subjects, but a river which carries our own boat. Understanding a text means assessing the breadth, the source and the direction of this river that carries us, so that we can understand more fully to whom we owe our being. Understanding will also enable us if necessary to change direction if we carry off course. Effective history is fundamental because it teaches us what *we* have

---

55. Here the decisive impetus has come from Gerhard Ebeling, "Church History Is the History of the Exposition of Scripture," in: Ebeling, *The Word of God and Tradition* (London: Collins, 1968), pp. 11-31. In Ebeling too I find words crucial to my hermeneutic approach: "Church history is thus the history of the continued presence of that same Jesus Christ who was crucified under Pontius Pilate and rose again" (p. 30). This is precisely what I seek to develop in the following with my two criteria, the story of Jesus and love.

56. José Míguez-Bonino, *Theologie im Kontext der Befreiung,* ThÖ 15 (Göttingen: Vandenhoeck und Ruprecht, 1977), pp. 80f.

57. This is why Gadamer speaks of "effective history." Cf. also Alfred Schindler, "Vom Nutzen und Nachteil der Kirchengeschichte für das Verständnis der Bibel heute," *Reformatio* 30 (1981), pp. 261-277, partic. pp. 265f. Schindler likens the text and its history of interpretation and post-history to a root and a tree and says: "An element of the Bible itself is its many-voiced echo in the church down the ages" (p. 265).

become by means of the texts, and what our position on the river is. It also teaches us what others have become through the texts, and what our position on the river *could* be.

This model takes account of the fact that today "understanding" of our text may mean very different things, depending for example on whether I am Roman Catholic or Protestant, or whether I am in a situation of threatened Christian identity or one of fossilized Christian traditionalism. The mere proximity of a new realization to the original sense of a text does not in itself say anything about the truth of the realization. On the other hand, there must be a possibility of consensus on the texts among the Christian churches, for the sake of our common faith and our joint action on the basis of the common texts. Freedom of application must have its limits, or there can be neither church nor agreement within society. I should like to formulate two criteria to this end:

4.3. A Correspondence Criterion

I propose that in order to be true, an interpretation or a new meaning of a biblical text must correspond to the basic line of Jesus' story. So this criterion relates to the past. It does not apply to the original sense of an *individual* text but to correspondence with the New Testament testimony as a whole. Thus the Augustinian interpretation of the rock as Christ appears "true" to me in this sense. Although it does not correspond directly to the text of Matt. 16:18, it corresponds closely to the overall intention of the New Testament canon.

Of course, my formulation of this correspondence criterion has considerable systematic implications. I am well aware of the fact — indeed, I see it as fortuitous — that an uninterpreted "mere" story of Jesus does not exist. This means that my correspondence criterion is not simply "ready to use" but takes us straight into the interpretation dialogue. That is why I have used the narrative expression "story of Jesus" rather than a doctrinal one. This places me well away from Tertullian's anti-Gnostic approach in *De Praescriptione Haereticorum*,[58] in which the correspondence criterion is reduced to doctrinal agreement with the regula fidei. It follows that there can be no other truths but the "old" traditional doctrines, so that Tertullian rightly condemns the Gnostic quest for the new as the epitome of heresy.[59] In my opinion,

58. 13f.; the conclusion from this is to be expected: "One must not have recourse to Scripture" (19).

59. Ibid., 7-11.

Christian gnosis with its quest for *new* interpretations of the truth also relates positively to the biblical texts with their constant process of new realizations of old traditions. The narrative formulation of my correspondence criterion is intended to leave the door to such possibilities open. The criterion is not and should not be seen as a ready-to-use yardstick.

With respect to the papal interpretation of the text we are dealing with, the question that has to be asked is this: Has this interpretation, which can hardly be justified from the text itself, been in the service of truth, which is in the story of Jesus? Has it promoted Petrine *ministry,* which according to many Catholic exegetes should not consist in being an absolute authority itself but in recalling uncompromisingly the authority of Jesus the "one teacher" (Matt. 23:8)? There cannot be one final answer to this question. Clearly at this point the correspondence criterion turns into a question about the function of the institution of the papacy in past and present. For this reason a second, functional criterion must be added.

4.4. A Criterion of Effects

My second criterion relates to the present, or to church history. It does not look for correspondence but has in mind a more pragmatic understanding of truth. It is closer to the performative than the propositional nature of language. It seeks to take up what Dorothee Sölle once called "the hermeneutics of consequences."[60] A criterion of this kind, which seeks to establish the influence of the word, is exemplified by the Reformation distinction between law and gospel. Another possible one is the political or social liberation of the underprivileged, such as the poor or women. I shall not take up these examples but have recourse to Augustine's formulation in *De Doctrina Christiana.* His criterion for true interpretation of Scripture was love. Love as the effect of a text enabled him for example to accept an interpretation which did not correspond to the literal sense of the text, or on the other hand to keep to a literal interpretation in preference to an allegorical one.[61] I emphasize that I understand "love" not only (though partly) as what we humans do in response to God's love, but also (though not only) as what we experience in our encounter with the texts. It is also important to me that love as a criterion for truth is prefigured in many different ways in the New Testament, for instance in Paul,

---

60. *Phantasie und Gehorsam* (Stuttgart: Kreuz, 1968), p. 16. (English translation: *Creative Disobedience* [Cleveland: Pilgrim, 1995]).

61. *De Doctrina Christiana* 1.36 (40); 3.15 (23).

John, and Matthew.[62] Above all, it is important to me that in the New Testament the presence of the exalted Christ is most clearly and centrally expressed by love.

The question that must be put to the various interpretations and influences of Matt. 16:18 is, then, as follows: have they enabled love to be experienced, and have they fostered love? For me the Augustinian interpretation is the clearest expression of the reliability of Christ the rock, on whom all we unreliable people are built, Peter included. This reading enables God's love to be experienced and is no doubt the reason why it was so popular for over a thousand years. With the "Eastern" interpretation of the rock as the faith of the church, the answer to the love question may be negative if the faith of the church has become a fossilized traditional system to which believers can only — under different names — submit. With regard to the "papal" interpretation I would say that in principle a papacy could be *a* (not "the"!) legitimate means of making full use of the freedom the New Testament gives, for the purpose of building a church. So let us apply the love criterion to the papal interpretation of our text. I find it important that Matthew does not say anything about Peter which is not said of the other disciples. This is an implication of Matthean familial ecclesiology. On this basis I suggest that if a church has a monarchic head, this can only be in such a way that the head makes visible what *all* Christians are, and not as a "more than this." In other words, from the perspective of Matthean theology a pope can be the visible *representation* of the whole church but not its ruler. That would threaten to destroy love. Is such a headship possible, I wonder. Again I cannot answer with an unequivocal "yes" or "no." Remembering a unique pope such as John XXIII, who represented to a high degree the hopes of Roman Catholics and indeed of the *whole* church for unity, can make us hopeful. But history also shows that the papal interpretation of Matt. 16:18 has to a high degree been the interpretation and self-legitimation of church rulers so that it is not easy to give a hopeful answer.

4.5. Concluding Remarks

Studying the reception history of biblical texts makes us aware of their innate potential for freedom and of how this has unfolded in history. But it also draws our attention to how this potential for freedom was often destroyed when the texts were used as biblical legitimations of a doctrine or an institu-

---

62. Cf., e.g., 1 Cor. 1:10–3:23; 8:1-6; John 15:1-17; Matt. 7:15-23; 13:18-23; 1 John 4:16.

tion. In dialogue with the biblical texts, I have suggested two truth criteria for the meaning of the texts, namely correspondence with the story of Jesus and love as the presence of the exalted Christ. The distinctive feature of these criteria is that they cannot be used to declare applications of the Bible true or untrue for all time. I cannot even except the papacy from this. For me there is no theological truth in general, or truth in dealing with biblical texts in general. Truth is found in concrete history and in relation to concrete situations. And this in itself has to do with the fundamental truth of Jesus Christ, which in its two forms of past history and present love must be the mark of all new meanings of biblical texts. This brings us to an attempt at contemporary reformulation of the doctrine of the two natures of Christ — but at this point I have to end.

ETHICS

10 The Fulfillment of the Law in Matthew (Matt. 5:17-20)

Dedicated to Eduard Schweizer
in honor of his 65th birthday

1. Introduction

Matthew's understanding of the Law is a key theological question in the New Testament. There appears to be an unbridgeable chasm between Matt. 5:17: "Do not think that I have come to abolish the Law or the Prophets; I have come not to abolish but to fulfill," and Rom. 10:4: "For Christ is the end of the Law so that there may be righteousness for everyone who believes." Matthew is the clearest exponent of a Law-affirming Jewish Christianity. His entire theology is characterized by Old Testament Jewish piety toward the Law.[1] For Matthew, Jesus' commandments — and that includes Jesus' affirmation of the Law — are grace. Paul on the other hand is the exponent of a Hellenistic Jewish Christianity which tends to view the Law critically.[2] He reflects this criticism in a fundamental manner. Jesus' understanding of the Law with respect to these two exponents is unclear and can only be reconstructed with some caution in view of the difficult source situation.

The issue is further complicated by exegetical difficulties in Matthew's Gospel with regard to the understanding of the Law. Matthew has taken up

---

1. According to Hubert Frankemölle, *Jahwebund und Kirche Christi*, NTA.NF 10 (Münster: Aschendorff, 1974), the Matthean Gospel is a piece of writing drafted under the direct influence of the historical books of Deuteronomy and Chronicles.

2. On the frequently and rightly postulated theological relations between Paul and the Stephen circle see Peter Stuhlmacher, "Das Gesetz als Thema biblischer Theologie," in: *ZThK* 75 (1978), pp. 251-280, here: pp. 270f.

German original: "Die Erfüllung des Gesetzes bei Matthäus (Mt 5,17-20)," *ZThK* 75 (1978), pp. 398-435. Originally presented as a paper at a working conference of the EKK (Protestant-Catholic Commentary) in Zürich.

strongly contrasting traditions. A Jewish Christian wing of the community, represented by the Sayings Source (Q 11:42 = Matt. 23:23) and other sayings (Matt. 5:18, 19; 23:2-3), evidently saw Jesus as principally upholding the Law. His infringements of the Law are either treated lightly or suppressed.[3] In the Markan tradition on the other hand, where the controversy stories are crucial, considerable weight is given to criticism of the Law in Jesus' preaching and activity. Matthew is at the intersection of these two traditions. For him the various traditions were all Jesus traditions carrying the authority of the one who had promised to be with his community until the end of the age, and Matthew saw it as his theological task to integrate these traditions.[4]

There is disagreement as to whether Matthew has actually succeeded in combining the various conceptions he inherited to form a new model or is, to a greater extent, the loyal and conservative preserver of Jesus tradition. The problem is that almost every interpretation of Matthew proceeds from the assumption that there are traditions in his Gospel which can only partially and awkwardly be integrated in his overall concept. But which traditions are these?

If one were to assume that Matthew regards the ceremonial law as abrogated in principle, with ethical law now being positively summarized in the commandment to love,[5] then difficulties of course ensue with the elements of Jewish Christian tradition. Passages such as 5:18-19; 23:2-3 as well as 5:23-24; 17:24ff.; 23:16ff., 23, 26; 24:20 can then hardly be integrated. If, on the other hand, one assumes that according to Matthew Jesus observes the whole of Torah,[6] the difficulties are fewer. But with 15:11 as well as with some of the an-

---

3. There are hardly any controversy discourses about the Law in the Sayings Source!

4. It has to be kept in mind that Matthew's situation vis-à-vis Jesus was different from our own. *We* recognize that Jesus' relation to the Law was accentuated and interpreted in very varying ways in the different strands of primitive Christianity. Methodologically *we* are in a position to question the community tradition from the perspective of the historical Jesus. Matthew neither had this methodological option, nor would it have been theologically meaningful in view of his identification of Jesus as the present Son of God. Matthew has received the various interpretations of Jesus' understanding of the Law in the community as words of Jesus which, according to Matt. 28:20, are to be obeyed. This means that Matthew's own understanding of his situation and task makes it inadequate to suggest that he had to "mediate" between various traditions. Rather, for him the unity of authority of the whole Torah on the one hand and the commandment to love on the other hand was presupposed in Jesus the Son of God.

5. The best-known formulation is in Georg Strecker, *Der Weg der Gerechtigkeit,* FRLANT 82 (Göttingen: Vandenhoeck und Ruprecht, 1962), pp. 30ff.; followed by Siegfried Schulz, *Die Stunde der Botschaft* (Hamburg: Furche, 1967), pp. 174ff.

6. Günther Bornkamm, "End-Expectation and Church," in: Günther Bornkamm/ Gerhard Barth/Heinz Joachim Held, *Tradition and Interpretation in Matthew* (Philadelphia:

titheses which juxtapose Jesus and the Old Testament, in particular with 5:38, a fundamental abrogation of an Old Testament principle seems to be inevitable, albeit in favor of another Old Testament principle, that of love. Furthermore, the statement of 23:2-3 whereby the disciples are to observe the teaching of the scribes and Pharisees remains in tension with Matthew's overall aim. The interpretation of the Law by Jesus and by the Pharisees is at variance, even though the Law itself is the same. Hence Matthew invalidates his statement of 23:2-3 a priori by means of the redactional warning of 16:12 against the teaching of the Pharisees and Sadducees. Here too there is tension between Matthew and his tradition.

There is general agreement that for Matthew the commandment to love is the center of the Law. But how does this function? It cannot simply be a matter of reducing Torah to the commandment to love, since a number of ethical commandments remain which "cannot in every case be subsumed under the commandment to love."[7] Should Torah be valid as a whole, it is even more impossible to subsume the ceremonial laws such as the commandment concerning the Sabbath under the commandment to love. It is possible only to super- and subordinate commandments, a procedure familiar in Judaism.[8] On these grounds Hummel has consistently maintained that Matthean Judaism is distinguished from synagogue Judaism only by a partially different halakah.[9] But if that is so, can Jesus' words "But I say to you" in the antitheses be more than the introduction to a new interpretation of the old Sinai Torah, and can Christianity be more for Matthew than legitimate Judaism with Jesus the teacher as its restorer?

This is not the place for a systematic presentation of the whole of Matthew's understanding of the Law. Rather, two related questions are focused on. With regard to Judaism it is important, firstly, whether Matthew declares the whole or only part of Old Testament Torah to be valid. With regard to Je-

---

Westminster, 1963), pp. 15-51, partic. pp. 24ff.; Gerhard Barth, "Matthew's Understanding of the Law," in: Bornkamm/Barth/Held, pp. 58-164, partic. pp. 62ff.; Reinhard Hummel, *Die Auseinandersetzung zwischen Kirche und Judentum im Matthäusevangelium,* BEvTh 33 (Munich: Kaiser, 1963), pp. 66ff.; Eduard Schweizer, "Christus und die Gemeinde im Matthäusevangelium," in: Schweizer, *Matthäus und seine Gemeinde,* SBS 71 (Stuttgart: Katholisches Bibelwerk, 1974), pp. 9-68, here: pp. 44ff.

7. Strecker (see note 5), p. 136.

8. Cf. the material in Andreas Nissen, *Gott und der Nächste im antiken Judentum,* WUNT I.15 (Tübingen: Mohr Siebeck, 1974), pp. 372ff. Particularly relevant to the comparison with Christianity is the rabbinic tendency to give priority to duties towards God (e.g. cultic duties) over duties towards one's neighbor provided this did not result in completely unacceptable human and social hardship (pp. 373ff.).

9. Hummel (see note 6), pp. 57ff., partic. p. 74.

sus it is important, secondly, whether Torah has complete and absolute authority for Matthew or, as with Jesus himself, only mediated authority bounded by the kingdom of God. These questions will now be addressed in part at least by means of an exegesis of the key text Matt. 5:17-20.

2. Matt. 5:17-20: The Traditions

Do not think that I have come to dissolve the Law or the Prophets; I have come not[10] to dissolve but to fulfill. For amen I tell you, until heaven and earth pass away, not one iota or[11] one stroke of a letter will pass from the law, until all is accomplished. Therefore, whoever dissolves one of the least of these commandments, and teaches people accordingly, will be called least in the kingdom of heavens; but whoever[12] does them and teaches[13] will be called great in the kingdom of heavens. For I tell you, unless your righteousness surpasses by far that of the scribes and Pharisees, you will never enter the kingdom of heavens.

Most exegetes treat vv. 17-20 as one section, according it a key or titular function for the parts of the Sermon on the Mount that follow, in particular the antitheses.[14] The assignation of v. 20 is, however, uncertain, since in spite of the closely connecting γάρ (therefore) it does not fit well with the preceding

10. A dialectic semitising negation in the sense of "not so much as" (oral proposal by Rudolf Pesch following Heinz Kruse, "Die 'dialektische Negation' als semitisches Idiom" [*VT* 4 (1954), pp. 385-400]) is not appropriate here, since καταλύω and πληρόω are not complementary but mutually exclusive.

11. Ἤ with copulative sense; cf. Friedrich Blass and Robert W. Funk, *A Greek Grammar of the New Testament and Other Early Christian Literature* (Chicago: University of Chicago, 1961), p. 446.

12. V. 19b is lacking in some manuscripts (אDW). Antithetical juxtaposition of two general relative clauses occurs in a similar way in 12:32 and 16:25; cf. 10:32-33. Despite (or because of!) this formal pattern, the weak evidence for the short text suggests that the long text is the original, affected by mechanical loss of text (haplography).

13. The two halves of the sentence are not symmetrical, and without further differentiation διδάξῃ is very harsh. Thus it is tempting to follow the textual conjecture διδάξῃ οὕτως instead of διδάξῃ οὗτος (as in Klaus Beyer, *Semitische Syntax im Neuen Testament* I, StUNT 1 [Göttingen: Vandenhoeck und Ruprecht, ²1968], p. 172), although (and because!) it facilitates the text considerably.

14. Barth (see note 6), pp. 68, 87; and Joachim Jeremias, "Die Bergpredigt," in: Jeremias, *Abba* (Göttingen: Vandenhoeck und Ruprecht, 1966), pp. 171-189, see p. 182, consider only v. 20 the title to the antitheses and vv. 17-19 as a separate section; cf. also Wolfgang Trilling, *Das wahre Israel,* StANT 10 (Leipzig: St. Benno, ³1975), pp. 184ff.

verses. V. 20 does not substantiate vv. 18 and 19, only possibly v. 17.[15] The verse draws the line between the addressed community and the Pharisees and scribes, a line which is not so explicitly apparent in vv. 17-19 but is maintained from here onward at least as far as 6:18. The dominant keyword in vv. 17-19 is νόμος (Law), and from v. 20 onward δικαιοσύνη (righteousness, cf. 6:1, 33). The authoritative λέγω ὑμῖν (I say to you) on the other hand is retained throughout (vv. 18, 20 antitheses). Formal arguments thus speak for a certain distancing of vv. 17-19 from v. 20, even though a close association is undeniable.

The question of the boundaries is of some significance for the interpretation of both the programmatic verse 17 and the antitheses, and for Matthew's understanding of the Law overall. If one takes vv. 17-20 to be a coherent section, it introduces the antitheses. The keyword πληρόω (to fulfill) in v. 17 would then take its meaning from the antitheses. It would refer primarily to Jesus' teaching and mean something like: "complete, bring to an end, surpass, bring out the true meaning of." Verses 18-19 with their literal, "Jewish" understanding of the Law are then best interpreted as embedded units of Jewish Christian tradition. If on the other hand one takes vv. 17-19 to be a separate section, a kind of independent preamble to the great interpretation of the Law in the antitheses, with v. 20 alone forming the heading for the antitheses, πληρόω (to fulfill) in v. 17 will first have to be interpreted from vv. 18-19. The meaning of the word will then be more open and might include "set up," "do." Vv. 17-48 would then have two naturally related themes. First, the introduction would establish that Jesus fulfills the Law; then, second, the main section based on this would deal with greater righteousness. The case cannot be decided by formal structural arguments alone, but only in connection with the interpretation of the whole section. For this reason the decision will be deferred for the moment.

The first problem that needs to be solved for the interpretation of vv. 17-19 is that of the relation between redaction and tradition. The most difficult issue is deciding whether *v. 17* is an exclusively Matthean creation,[16] or whether Matthew has here reformulated a tradition.[17] In terms of language, the combi-

---

15. For this reason some earlier exegetes have taken v. 18 to be a subsequent interpolation; e.g., Emil Wendling, "Zu Mt 5:18.19," *ZNW* 5 (1904), pp. 253-256.

16. See, e.g., Barth (see note 6), p. 62; Hummel (see note 6), p. 66; Strecker (see note 5), p. 144.

17. The following, inter alia, reckon with tradition: Robert Banks, *Jesus and the Law in the Synoptic Tradition*, MSSNTS 28 (Cambridge: Cambridge University, 1975), pp. 204ff.; Rudolf Bultmann, *The History of the Synoptic Tradition* (Oxford: Blackwell, 1963), p. 138; Robert A. Guelich, *Not to Annul the Law* (Hamburg, Diss., 1967), pp. 216ff.; Hans Hübner, *Das Gesetz in der synoptischen Tradition* (Göttingen: Vandenhoeck und Ruprecht, 1973), p. 34.

nation of νόμος (Law) and προφῆται (Prophets), the verb πληρόω (to fulfill) and the close relation with 10:34,[18] and less clearly so ἔρχομαι (to come) with final infinitive[19] point to redaction.[20] It is not impossible that Matthew found in the tradition a saying with words such as "I have not come to abolish the Law but to fulfill it," perhaps connected with v. 18. This is supported by his predilection for using ἤ to connect single words or whole sentences when adding to his sources.[21] He has possibly supplemented the Law by the Prophets, analogous to 7:12 and 22:40. Only then could the quite strange ἤ (or) instead of καὶ (and) be understood.[22] However, it is scarcely possible to make any clear statements concerning the origin of a traditional saying.

A Jewish variant of our saying in the Talmud[23] shows that it was also known in Judaism. In a humorous anecdote intended to slander Christians, a Christian philosopher cites: "See the continuation in the 'Bad News' ('wn gljwn), which says: I have not come to take away from the Law of Moses but[24] to add to it ('wspj)" (b. Shabbat 116b).[25] The attempt to read this text as the Aramaic Urtext of our logion has failed, however.[26] The logion presupposes not only the Greek text of Matt. 5:17 (['wn] gljwn = [δύσ] αγγέλιον) but probably also an interpretation of the saying that was widespread in the early church.[27] The attempt to prove that the expression "fulfill the law" is character-

---

18. Μὴ νομίσητε ὅτι ἦλθον . . . οὐκ ἦλθον . . . ἀλλὰ. . . . In this verse it is almost impossible to distinguish redaction and tradition, making it difficult to use in solving our problem.

19. Cf. 2:2; 8:29; 10:34. Final infinitive is however also a formal characteristic of an ἦλθον saying.

20. Καταλύω, νομίζω and the form of the ἦλθον saying are traditional; cf. Mark 2:17; 10:45.

21. Additional words with ἤ: 6:25?; 10:11, 14; 12:25; 16:14; 17:25?; 18:8; new material with ἤ: 12:5, 29, 33; 26:53.

22. One frequently reads that ἤ is determined by the negative sentence, see Blass-Debrunner-Rehkopf (see note 11), p. 446 1b. But see Theodor Zahn, Das Evangelium des Matthäus, KNT 1 (Leipzig: Deichert, 1903), p. 207, note 69: The ὅτι sentence is not negative at all.

23. Šabbat 116a-b (text in Billerbeck I, pp. 241f.).

24. The tradition fluctuates between אלא (but) and ולא (and not).

25. The story is analyzed by Karl Georg Kuhn, "Giljonim und sifre minim," in: Walter Eltester et al. (eds.), Judentum-Urchristentum-Kirche, BZNW 26 (FS Joachim Jeremias; Berlin: de Gruyter, ²1964), pp. 50-58.

26. Against Joachim Jeremias, Neutestamentliche Theologie I (Gütersloh: Gütersloher, 1971), p. 87; Hans Joachim Schoeps, "Jesus und das jüdische Gesetz," in: Schoeps, Studien zur unbekannten Religions- und Geistesgeschichte (Göttingen: Musterschmidt, 1963), pp. 41-61, here: pp. 44f., also takes Šabbat 116b to be a Jesus logion. He reads "and not to add to," emphasizing Jesus' upholding of the Law.

27. Cf. Irenaeus, Haereses 4.16:4f.; Tertullian, Oratio 1.11; Ps.-Clem., Recognitions 1.39.1; source of Abd-al-Jabbar 70a (in Shlomo Pines, The Jewish Christians of the Early Centuries of Christianity. According to a New Source, Proceedings of the Israel Academy of Science and Humanities 5 [Jerusalem: Academy of Science and Humanities, 1966], p. 5); see also Adolf von

istic of Jesus' language cannot succeed:[28] both καταλύω (abolish) and πληρόω (fulfill) in Greek are used in connection with demands or laws.

The unfortunate conclusion to be drawn from these observations is that we have to give up the idea of interpreting our saying as part of pre-Matthean tradition. All attempts to interpret the meaning of the verb πληρόω (to fulfill) by recourse to an Aramaic equivalent are nothing but attempts to explain something relatively incomprehensible by means of something completely unknown.[29]

The problems of *v. 18* are also considerable but the case is less hopeless. The parallel with Luke 16:17 secures the logion in the tradition, though without determining anything about its original wording. The structure of Matt. 24:34[30] is closely related, as is the content of the following saying 24:35: "heaven and earth will pass away, but my words shall not pass away." The agreements cannot be coincidental, but they leave the most difficult question open: which of the two ἕως-ἄν (= until) clauses have been added by the Evangelist? Linguistic analysis does not help here, since Matthew has a preference for ἕως-ἄν[31] and post-positioned εἷς (one).[32]

Either the two ἕως-ἄν (= until) clauses both say the same for Matthew, in which case one of them is superfluous, or they are each to be interpreted differently, in which case the use of the same expression is very awkward. The explanation will need to take account, firstly, of the variant in Luke 16:17, and secondly of the similar sayings 24:34 and 35. Where our saying does not agree with the wording of Luke 16:17, it does agree essentially with Mark 13:30/Matt. 24:34.[33] The best-known hypothesis assumes that Matthew took v. 18 from Q. As the ἕως-ἄν clauses cannot both be from Matthew, the original wording of the first ἕως-ἄν clause must be preserved in Matthew and not in Luke;[34] the opening words ἀμὴν γὰρ λέγω (amen, I say to you) could be Matthean, as

---

Harnack, *Geschichte eines programmatischen Worts Jesu (Matt. 5:17) in der ältesten Kirche,* SPAW.PH (1912:1). pp. 184-207, here: 210f.

28. Contrary to Charles F. D. Moule, "Fulfilment-Words in the New Testament: Use and Abuse," *NTS* 14 (1967/68), pp. 293-320, see pp. 316-319.

29. This refutes all the frequent attempts since Gustav Dalman, *Jesus-Jeschua* (Leipzig: Hinrich, 1922), pp. 55-58, to explain πληρόω by recourse to Aram. *qjjm* (set up, confirm). This thesis is in any case supported by only a few references in the Targum, while in the LXX πληρόω is usually the translation for *ml'* and never for *qwm*. The Peshitta also reads *ml'* in 5:17.

30. Ἀμὴν γὰρ λέγω ὑμῖν ὅτι οὐ μὴ παρέλθῃ ἡ γενεὰ αὕτη, ἕως ἂν πάντα ταῦτα γένηται.

31. 10 occurrences in Matt., 3 in Mark, 3 in Luke. Matt. 2:13; 5:26; 10:11 could be redaction.

32. 9 occurrences in Matt., 1 in Mark, 1 in Luke. Matt. 6:27; 9:18; 19:6; 21:19, 24 are definitely redaction.

33. Cf. Trilling (see note 14), p. 168; παρελθεῖν is an exception.

34. Siegfried Schulz, *Q. Die Spruchquelle der Evangelisten* (Zürich: TVZ, 1972), p. 114;

well as the iota and the second ἕως-ἄν clause. But there are problems attached to this thesis. Εὔκοπος is not specifically Lukan, and a sentence opening with the preposition ἕως would be unique in the synoptic tradition. So it would have to be assumed that the introduction with ἀμὴν was part of the original saying.[35] But since Luke does not otherwise delete ἀμὴν γὰρ λέγω (amen, I say to you) without substitute,[36] it is unlikely that the Evangelists had common wording in their sources for Matt. 5:18 and Luke 16:17. Maybe the Q hypothesis for Matt. 5:18 will have to be abandoned[37] in favor of seeing Matt. 5:18 and Luke 16:17 as two tradition variants which are independent of each other in literary terms.[38] If this is so, Berger's observation must be taken seriously, namely that the sequence ἀμὴν λέγω ὑμῖν (amen, I say to you) — prophetic future with double negation — a temporal clause introduced by ἕως (or μέχρις) (until) is a form pattern occurring frequently in the Synoptic Gospels (Mark 9:1; 13:30; 14:25; Matt. 10:23; cf. Matt. 23:39; 5:26; Mark 14:30; John 13:38).[39] In these parallels the temporal clause introduced by ἕως is always in final position. This would suggest that in our logion it is not the first of the two ἕως ἄν clauses which was part of the original material but the second, often taken to be redaction. The wording also supports this idea: πάντα ταῦτα (all this) in Matt. 24:34 is typical of redaction;[40] but it is here in particular that the wording of 5:18d deviates from 24:34. So is the first of the two ἕως ἄν clauses Matthean redaction? This may be a surprising thesis in view of its consequences for interpretation of the content, but it is the most natural nonetheless. The form of the Amen saying ("truly I say to you") available to him reminded Matthew of Mark 13:30 and caused him to insert in the first part of the saying a passage from the following related saying Mark 13:31.[41] Linguistically too this is plausible: whereas Mat-

somewhat different in Anton Vögtle, *Das Neue Testament und die Zukunft des Kosmos,* KBANT (Düsseldorf: Patmos, 1970), pp. 101f.; not seen by Heinz Schürmann, "'Wer daher eines dieser geringsten Gebote auflöst . . .'" in: Schürmann, *Traditionsgeschichtliche Untersuchungen zu den synoptischen Evangelien* (Düsseldorf: Patmos, 1968), pp. 126-136; see p. 128.

35. Matthew inserts ἀμήν only twice in Markan texts (Matt. 19:23; 24:2) and deletes it once (Mark 8:12 par; cf. Matt. 12:43).

36. Cf. Schürmann, "Die Sprache des Christus," in Schürmann, *Untersuchungen* (see note 34), p. 97.

37. The assigning of Luke 16:13-18 to Q is difficult to prove, since a comparable order of the logia in Matt. and Luke cannot be ascertained. Schürmann (see note 34) assumes reminiscences from the Lukan context 16:14-15, 16 in Matt. 5:20, 17. Luke 16:14 is probably redaction, however.

38. Hübner (see note 17) assumes QMt; Ernst Lohmeyer, *Das Evangelium nach Matthäus,* KEK Sonderband (Göttingen: Vandenhoeck und Ruprecht, ²1958), p. 108, assumes two variants of the logion which Matthew collated, one of them approximating Luke 16:17.

39. Cf. Klaus Berger, *Die Amenworte Jesu,* BZNW 39 (Berlin: de Gruyter, 1970), p. 73.

40. Cf. 6:32; 8:33; found once in Mark and nowhere in Luke.

41. Cf. Schweizer, "Noch einmal Matt. 5,17-20," in: Schweizer, *Matthäus* (see note 6), pp. 78-85, here: pp. 82f. similarly takes up Berger's thesis and considers the logia, on the grounds of the relation between Luke 16:17 and Mark 13:31, to be variants connected in tradition history.

thew generally prefers the plural οὐρανοί (heavens), he mostly uses the singular οὐρανός in connection with γῆ (earth).[42]

The traditional Amen saying is then a prophetic word that speaks of the indissolubility of the whole Law. The final clause ἕως ἂν πάντα γένηται (until all is accomplished) may, like Mark 13:30, originally have been interpreted in the context of an eschatological discourse.[43] In Judaism this does not correspond primarily with the belief in the immutability of Torah,[44] although a number of rabbinic references express this belief in words very similar to Matt. 5:18.[45]

More significant are the few Jewish documents stating that in the age to come parts of Torah at least will no longer be valid.[46] Despite these parallels, the exact meaning of the traditional prophetic words is inaccessible to us. Why should nothing pass from the Law "until all is accomplished"? Did Jewish Christian groups react to mission to the Gentiles, who were not bound by the law, with the thesis that this mission and thus the end of the Law would be fulfilled by God only in the eschaton (cf. Matt. 10:23)? Or did πάντα (all) not refer to the events of the end of the age but to the fulfilling of the Law, so that complete fulfillment would be the precondition for the end of the Law? We do not know. Like other sayings with prepositioned ἀμήν (amen), this one is characteristic of Jesus' language. But attributing it to Jesus is problematic, since the

42. 8 occurrences (28:18 is redactional). The only exception is 16:19.

43. Cf. Schweizer (see note 41), pp. 83f.

44. Cf. Baruch 4:1; Wisdom 18:4; Tobit 1:6; *1 Enoch* 99:2, 14; 4 Ezra 9:37; *2 Baruch* 77:15; Philo, *Vita Mosis* 2:14-15; Josephus, *Contra Apionem* 2:227: Rabbinic parallels for the immutability of Torah (but not of the Prophets!) in Billerbeck, I, 246.

45. Cf. Exodus Rabbah 6.1: Solomon and a thousand like him will pass away, but the smallest stroke of you, sc. of the iota, will not pass away (Billerbeck, I, 249; further parallels p. 244); *Genesis Rabbah* 10.1: Everything has a measure. Heaven and earth have a measure, only one thing has no measure: Torah.

46. *Pesiqta Rabbati* 79a with par. and *Nidda* 61b state that sacrifice and other commandments will no longer be valid in the age to come (contrary to Billerbeck, I, 246, who points arbitrarily to the messianic age). On the other hand the periodisation of world history in three epochs, the age of Torah followed by the messianic age (cf. *Sanhedrin* 97 a-b and par.; Billerbeck, III, 826) need not assume that Torah is no longer valid in the messianic age (contrary to Leo Baeck, "Der Glaube des Paulus," in: Karl Heinrich Rengstorf (ed.), *Das Paulusbild in der neueren deutschen Forschung*, WdF 26 [Darmstadt: Wissenschaftliche Buchgesellschaft, 1964], pp. 565-590, here: p. 584). The facile construction of a general Jewish conviction that Torah will end in the messianic age, presented by Hans Joachim Schoeps, *Paulus* (Tübingen: J. C. B. Mohr, 1959), pp. 177-180, taking up Albert Schweitzer's basic theses, cannot be verified. So the fact remains that the conviction that the Law would be valid only until the end of the world, as presupposed in Matt. 5:18, has only peripheral parallels in Judaism whose material does not fully coincide.

evident contradiction between these sharp words and Jesus' own liberal practice cannot be overcome. Where the logion has recently been attributed to Jesus it has been softened and reinterpreted;[47] in older exegetical history the ritual law was either excluded or read in the figurative sense. The most probable explanation seems to be that a Jewish Christian prophet or teacher prophesied, perhaps in the context of an eschatological discourse, the indissolubility and immutability of Torah until the imminent end of the world.

V. 19 too can be assumed to be the product of intensive linguistic editing by Matthew.[48] As far as I know, no one has so far dared to suggest that the verse could originate with Matthew. Its strictly formal legalism and its idea of a hierarchy in the kingdom of God are hardly compatible with Matthean theology. In support of the traditional character of the verse one can point to λύω (to solve), which does not sit comfortably either with the antonym ποιεῖν (to do) or with καταλύω (to dissolve) in v. 17. There is also the non-Matthean καλέω (to call), and the traditional structure of the sentence. But one can scarcely avoid the assumption that Matthew has edited the sentence considerably. Possibly καὶ διδάξῃ οὕτως τοὺς ἀνθρώπους (and teaches people accordingly) and the whole verse 19b are his own work.[49] If so, he would have had as tradition a short legal saying: Whoever breaks one of the least commandments will be called least in the kingdom of heaven. But this is mere speculation. The important starting point for the interpretation is to note that a sentence so painstakingly edited by the Evangelist cannot have been simply irrelevant to him.

Probably this verse was originally an isolated logion from a similar environment to v. 18, but its perspective is different. Where v. 18 is concerned with the Law as a whole and speaks of the Law, v. 19 is concerned with single commandments and speaks of the disciples. But the possibility remains that both these logia were part of the tradition before Matthew. Plerophoric οὗτος may be an Aramaism,[50] not requiring explanation by means of a previous point of reference. In formal terms our saying is one of a large number in the New Testa-

47. Examples include: Banks (see note 17), pp. 218f., who does not take the verse literally but as a "rhetorical statement emphasising how difficult it was for the Law to perish." Thomas Walter Manson, *The Sayings of Jesus* (London: SCM, ²1949), p. 25, reads the verse as ironic ridiculing of the scribes.

48. Matthew has a preference for the general relative clause with ἐάν, οὖν, εἷς . . . τούτων, διδάσκω, ἄνθρωπος, οὕτως, βασιλεία τῶν οὐρανῶν, and anaphoric οὗτος ; the combination ποιεῖν/διδάσκειν (cf. 28:15) and the positive μέγας instead of the superlative is not uncharacteristic of Matthew (cf. 22:36).

49. There are however traditional sayings with a similar structure and antithetic parallelism: 10:32-33; Mark 8:35.

50. Cf. Dalman (see note 29), 58f.

ment consisting of a conditional relative clause with future apodosis, with subsidiary and main clause linked by a common keyword. Ernst Käsemann has termed them sentences of holy law, spoken by early Christian prophets.[51] Klaus Berger has disputed the legal character of these sayings and demonstrated their origin in wisdom parenesis.[52] If we take Käsemann's thesis to be concerned with the *Sitz im Leben* of the concrete New Testament sayings, and Berger's thesis to be concerned with the origin of a particular genre, the two need not be mutually exclusive. Certainly in our saying the sapiential background is clearly and doubly broken open. The apodosis is unambiguously eschatological, and the stated condition is not a generally recognized one. Rather, it comments on a question that was highly controversial in early Christianity: Is the breaking or abrogation of any Old Testament law at all permissible?

The answer is an almost categorical "no." Λύω[53] (to solve) can mean the abrogation and the breaking of a single commandment. The words about the "least commandments" can best be understood in the light of the rabbinic distinction between *mzwth qllwth* and *mzwth chmwrwth* (light and weighty commandments), although the term ἐλάχιστος (least) does not quite coincide with the Jewish designation. The rabbis distinguished between "light commandments" and "weighty commandments," determined on the one hand by the demand made on the person and on the other hand by the reward promised for observance of the Law. There was no complete systematization, however.[54] "Weighty commandments" generally included the forbidding of shedding blood, of idolatry, sanctification of the name of God and of the Sabbath; there was great reward for revering parents, peace-making, works of charity and Torah studies (*Pe'a* 1.1). "Light commandments" include for example those concerning the festival of booths, the mother bird and the eating of blood. Our logion agrees with the rabbinic parallels in insisting that the "light commandments" too must be observed, as according to the rabbis one cannot know what reward each commandment carries.[55] The observance of *all* laws, regardless of their content and their relation to the center of Torah, is explicitly demanded. Given this approach, any material criticism of the law is hardly to be expected.

Annulling one of the least of the commandments is declared to result in

---

51. Ernst Käsemann, "Sentences of Holy Law in the New Testament," in: Käsemann, *New Testament Questions of Today* (London: SCM, 1969), pp. 66-81; and "The Beginnings of Christian Theology," in *Questions*, pp. 82-107. On our verse see p. 86.

52. Klaus Berger, "Zu den sogenannten Sätzen heiligen Rechts," *NTS* 17 (1970/71), pp. 10-40.

53. Synonymous with καταλύειν; cf. notes 80-81.

54. Survey in Billerbeck, I, 901-5.

55. Cf. *'Abot* 2.1; cf. also 4.2; further references in Billerbeck, I, 249 and 903 sub d).

being called least in the kingdom of heaven. The idea of various heavens is familiar to Judaism;[56] with the growing interest in individual reward for individual fulfillment of the Law, the idea of a special placing or even of an individual paradise for every pious person gained increasing acceptance.[57] This speaks for a hierarchy of ranks in the kingdom of heaven in our verse, but the interpretation of the words remains uncertain. Käsemann, who derives the logion from early Christian prophecy, suggests that the Law-conforming Jewish Christians speaking here want to deny their Law-critical opponents church fellowship on earth without denying them the kingdom of heaven completely.[58] On the other hand, the final clause "will be called least in the kingdom of heaven" could have been formulated for reasons of rhetorical harmony, forming a parallel with the opening clause. This is a reasonable formal assumption on the basis of the sentences of holy law. In factual terms the final clause would then mean exclusion from the kingdom of heaven.[59] Overall, this second interpretation appears to be the more natural one.

Whichever is the case, the radical wording of our saying is unparalleled in rabbinic Judaism. Rabbinic Judaism distinguishes between the basic demand to turn back to God, which determines salvation, and the many single demands which can scarcely *all* be met by any individual.[60] By contrast, our saying is far more reminiscent of a perfectionist Judaism of the type found among the Essenes, or of the words from Deut. 27:26 which Paul presupposes in Gal. 3:10:[61] "Cursed is everyone who does not observe and obey all the things written in the book of the law." This is the voice of a Jewish Christianity which is extremely rigorist by Jewish standards.[62] It can again be concluded that the probability of this saying originating with Jesus is slight, given what

56. Cf. partic. Baruch passim and 2 *Enoch* 3-22, though not associated here with a hierarchy of "heavens." Rabbinic material in Billerbeck, III, pp. 531ff.

57. References in Billerbeck, I, pp. 249f.; IV, 1131f., 1138-1143 sub m-u.

58. Käsemann (see note 51), pp. 86f.

59. Eduard Schweizer, *The Good News According to Matthew* (London: SPCK, ²1978), pp. 108-109.

60. Cf. on the rabbinic "relative" concept of righteousness Nissen (see note 9), pp. 154ff., and on rabbinic repentance theology pp. 130ff.

61. The πᾶσιν that is decisive in Paul is found only in LXX and comparably in the Samaritan Targum. It also occurs however in a few rabbinic exegeses of these words; cf. Billerbeck, III, pp. 541f.

62. I cannot agree with Wolfgang Trilling, *Die Christusverkündigung in den synoptischen Evangelien* (Munich: Kösel, 1969), pp. 88ff., who speaks of a midway position of our text between the rabbinate and Gentile Christianity. Definitely not! It can be read as rabbinate-conforming only if we assume that it does not seek to deny the kingdom of heaven to anyone who has infringed a single commandment (cf. the interpretation in note 58).

we know about his attitude to Torah. There is a possibility that the saying originated with a Jewish Christian prophet or teacher making a pointed comment on the question of Torah in the debates taking place in the community.

Thus Matthew adopts traditions from strictly nomistic Christian circles. Evidently teachers or prophets had to define their viewpoint sharply against antinomian tendencies in Christianity. We do not know who these people were. It has always been tempting to see in the opponents of Matthew or of the Jewish Christian communities the figure of Paul.[63] Paul did indeed have to grapple with opponents who thought like those in the Matthean community (Gal. 2:12!) and often had to ward off antinomian consequences arising from his theology (Rom. 3:8; 6:1, 15). But we must keep in mind that Paul's mission to the Gentiles on the basis of freedom from the Law was not an isolated enterprise exclusive to him alone. He was part of a broad stream of earliest Christianity, the first of whose known precursors and representatives is Stephen, and to which the Markan communities probably also belonged. We cannot define the opposing position more precisely than this.

There is almost complete agreement that *v. 20* is redaction,[64] and there are good grounds for this. The combinations γραμματεῖς καὶ Φαρισαῖοι (scribes and Pharisees) and βασιλεία τῶν οὐρανῶν (kingdom of heaven) are unambiguously preferred by the Evangelist, and the prepositioned possessive genitive (cf. 5:16 and 19:21), περισσεύω (to exceed) and consecutive γάρ (for)[65] are also characteristic of Matthew's language. Redactional sayings on entering the kingdom of heaven are also found in 7:21 and 18:3; cf. 19:17. The structure of the verse with ἐὰν μή (unless) — οὐ μή (never) corresponds to 18:3. Λέγω γὰρ ὑμῖν (I say to you), of which there are only three occurrences elsewhere in the Matthean tradition,[66] remains conspicuous. Like 6:1, this verse functions as an editorial *kelal*, i.e. as a summary or title for the following antitheses.[67] In its present form the saying is an entry torah to the kingdom of heaven which has antecedents in the Deuteronomic discourses on entry into the land of Canaan (Deut. 4:1; 6:17-18; 16:20) and in the temple liturgies Psalm 15 and 24. Matthew took this form from Mark's Gospel (Mark 10:23-25; cf. 9:43, 45, 47)

---

63. Cf. Rudolf Bultmann, *Theology of the New Testament* (London: SCM, 1965), p. 54; Manson (see note 47), pp. 25-154. The argument: ἐλάχιστος (v. 19) = Π(φ)αῦλος, cf. 1 Cor. 15:9!

64. Seen differently e.g. by Banks (see note 17), pp. 224ff.; Sjef van Tilborg, *The Jewish Leaders in Matthew* (Leiden: Brill, 1972), pp. 126ff.; Hans-Theo Wrege, *Die Überlieferungsgeschichte der Bergpredigt*, WUNT I.9 (Tübingen: Mohr Siebeck, 1968), pp. 42ff.

65. Cf. 3:3; 9:5, 13; 16:27; 19:12; 25:14; 26:12.

66. Never in Mark; in Luke 5 times; cf. van Tilborg (see note 64), p. 127 note 1.

67. On the *kelal* cf. the rabbinic parallels in David Daube, *The New Testament and Rabbinic Judaism* (London: University, 1956), pp. 63ff.

and made frequent use of it. The fact that the verse is entirely redactional, to-gether with the above observations concerning its formal and linguistic inno-vations, suggests that in interpretation it should stand alone and not merely be read as an appendix to vv. 17-19.

3. Matt. 5:17-20: The Matthean Interpretation

Was Matthew, like the communities of 5:18-19, confronted with antinomians? 7:15-23 indicates this; however, our passage 5:17-20 addresses the whole com-munity in a fundamental thesis.[68] Μὴ νομίσητε (do not think) is not neces-sarily polemical.[69] In conjunction with the thesis of v. 17, the logia vv. 18-19 appear fundamental in character. Thus Matthew focuses on polemical sharp-ness at the end of the Sermon on the Mount but argues thetically in its open-ing passage.

In *v. 17* the exegetical difficulties accumulate around the word πληρόω (to fulfill). The term is so general that it is almost inevitably interpreted from the perspective of Matthean theology as a whole, in other words depending on each exegete's understanding of Matthew's doctrine of the Law. Two ques-tions are determinative for the interpretation: (1) Is the fulfillment of the Law found in Jesus' teaching or in Jesus' activity? (2) Are "Law or Prophets" to be interpreted from their first part (as normative) or from their second part (as prophecy)? These alternatives give rise to various types of interpretation:

1. If one takes πληρόω to refer to Jesus' teaching, several nuances in inter-pretation are possible:
   a. the interpretation "confirm, make valid." This interpretation has re-course to a — non-existent — Aramaic original. On the basis of the Greek meaning of the word πληρόω, it is not possible.
   b. a frequent translation is: "bring (the Law) to full expression, bring out the full meaning of (the Law)."[70] This interpretation is not sup-ported by the meaning of πληρόω, but is the result of reading a par-ticular understanding of the antitheses into v. 17.

68. Note should be taken of the dominant 3rd person plural for the opponents in 7:15-23, corresponding to the 3rd person of the Jewish groups in 5:20.

69. Cf. 10:34 and Alexander Sand, *Das Gesetz und die Propheten*, BU 11 (Regensburg: Pustet, 1974), p. 104; Strecker (see note 5), p. 137 note 4; Trilling (see note 14), p. 171.

70. Klostermann; cf. Werner Georg Kümmel, "Jesus und der jüdische Traditions-gedanke," in: Kümmel, *Heilsgeschehen und Geschichte*, MThSt. NF 3 (Marburg: Elwert, 1965), pp. 15-35, here: p. 34.

c. a large number of interpretations assume that πληρόω means "to fill (something not yet full)" or "to make perfect (something not yet perfect)." They are supported by Matt. 13:48 (tradition) and 23:32 (redaction), (although these are the least theologically significant occurrences of πληρόω in Matthew). Thus Jesus transcends Old Testament law.[71] It is no coincidence that this interpretation was popular in liberal theology.

d. differentiations of this interpretation are: Jesus "fills up the Law by adding to it what is lacking,"[72] thus supplementing the Law, and:

e. by "making the Law perfect," he brings it to its destination and end.[73] This interpretation, closely related to Rom. 10:4, is possible on the basis of the meaning of πληρόω.[74] However, it reverses what is meant by the juxtaposition with καταλύω (destroy, dissolve).

2. If one takes πληρόω to refer to Jesus' activity and life, two interpretations come to the fore, depending on whether one reads "law and prophets" as normative or as prophetic.

a. If one understands the Old Testament primarily as prophecy, πληρόω expresses the fulfilling of the prophecy. This corresponds to a use of language adequately verified in the Septuagint[75] and in the opening formulae of the fulfillment quotations.[76] There are of

71. E.g. Martin Dibelius, "Die Bergpredigt," in: Dibelius, *Botschaft und Geschichte* I (Tübingen: Mohr, 1953), pp. 79-174, here: p. 125; Harnack (see note 27), pp. 184f.

72. Cf. *Šabbat* 116b and note 23 above.

73. Cf. Schoeps (see note 26), 44, note 9: "Double meaning of perficere and ad finem perducere"; André Feuillet, "Morale Ancienne et Morale Chrétienne d'après Mt 5,17-20," *NTS* 17 (1970/71), pp. 123-137, here: p. 124: "conserver en perfectionnant et en dépassant." William D. Davies, "Matthew 5,17-18," in: *Mélanges Bibliques* (FS André Robert, Paris: Bloud et Gay, 1957), pp. 428-456, interprets on the basis of v. 18: By his death and resurrection Jesus has fulfilled the Law and thus brought it to an end in view of the future mission to the Gentiles.

74. Cf. references in (Walter Bauer) William F. Arndt/F. Wilbur Gingrich, *A Greek-English Lexicon of the New Testament and Early Christian Literature* (Chicago: University of Chicago, 1957), s.v. πληρόω No. 2.5.

75. References from LXX and from the Hellenistic area in Moule (see note 28), pp. 308-313.

76. For example, Guelich (see note 17), pp. 227f.; Moule (see note 28) pp. 317-319; Sand (see note 69), p. 186; Eduard Schweizer, "Matth 5,17-20. Anmerkungen zum Gesetzesverständnis des Matthäus," in: Schweizer, *Neotestamentica* (Zürich: Zwingli, 1963), pp. 399-406, here: p. 400; Wrege (see note 64), p. 37. Similarly Henrik Ljungman, *Das Gesetz erfüllen* (Lund: Gleerup, 1954), pp. 60-65, and Günther Harder, "Jesus und das Gesetz (Matthäus 5,17-20)," in: Willehad Paul Eckert et al. (eds.), *Antijudaismus im Neuen Testament?* (Munich: Kaiser, 1967), pp. 105-118, here: pp. 111f., interpret on the basis of the measure of God's plan or the filling up of the apocalyptic measure.

course difficulties with the immediate context (vv. 18-19) and the wider (vv. 20-48), and the opposing καταλύω (dissolve) does not seem to fit this interpretation either.

b. If one reads the Old Testament primarily as normative, πληρόω means fulfill in the sense of "do." This usage also occurs in Matthew, in an exposed position in 3:15. Jesus would then be presented as the (exemplary) fulfiller of the Law. This is indeed a Matthean idea, but one that does not otherwise occur in the whole context of 5:17-48.[77]

It can be assumed a priori that, since they have been intensively edited by Matthew, vv. 18-19 will have some significance for the interpretation of v. 17. We cannot trivialize them by declaring them to be simply part of embedded Jewish Christian tradition. These verses speak against an interpretation that focuses exclusively on Jesus' teaching, and especially against interpretations that reckon with a change or even an ending of the Law (1c-1e). They also speak against all interpretations of v. 17 as the fulfillment of prophecy (2a), because "Law or Prophets" is taken up as "Law" or "commandments" in vv. 18-19. This does not contradict the fact that Matthew probably added "or the Prophets" to the Law of v. 17. In the comparable verses 7:12 and 22:40 the expression also means the Old Testament as the demanding will of God. Verses like 9:13 and 12:7 indicate that Matthew sees the Prophets in connection with the commandment to love and thus reads the Law from the prophetic perspective.[78] The only point at which Matthew takes the expression "Law and Prophets" from the tradition and at the same time clearly understands it as prophecy, in 11:13, also supports this thesis. Here the Evangelist has changed the order of the tradition and formulated quite differently: "the Prophets and the Law prophesied." The thesis is substantiated by Berger's evidence that in the Jewish references to "Law and Prophets" it is mostly "the will of God committing to action" that is emphasized, and not the Old Testament as a book.[79] Καταλύω (to dissolve) in combination with νόμος (law) or similar expressions is frequent in Greek and Jewish Greek, almost to the extent of being a set phrase. Its meaning vacillates between "dissolve" in the sense of "abrogate"[80] and "dissolve" in the

---

77. This is the interpretation of Albert Descamps, *Les justes et la justice dans les évangiles et le christianisme primitif* (Louvain: Publications Universitaires de Louvain, 1950), p. 131 ("observer entièrement").

78. Contrary to Sand (see note 69), p. 186.

79. Klaus Berger, *Die Gesetzesauslegung Jesu* I, WMANT 40 (Neukirchen-Vluyn: Neukirchener, 1972), pp. 209-227, here: p. 219.

80. E.g. Xenophon, *Memorabilia* 4.4.14; Thucydides 8.76; Polybius 3.8.2; Philo, *On*

sense of "not keep" i.e. "break,"[81] though it is often impossible to distinguish precisely. The meaning of καταλύω makes an interpretation in terms of prophecy almost impossible, while vice versa an interpretation in terms either of Jesus' teaching or his activity is possible.

We now turn to πληρόω (to fulfill) itself. The combination of πληρόω with νόμος (law) is rarer than with καταλύω (to dissolve), but at least frequent enough to permit us to say that the Greek-speaking reader would relate it first to Jesus' deeds: Jesus fulfills the Law through his activity.[82] Two components reinforce this relationship: the immediately preceding verse 16 speaks of the good works of Christians, and the hitherto only verse in which Matthew's Gospel used πληρόω actively and unambiguously in the sense of "do," 3:15, is relatively close. Thus one can first assume πληρόω = "to do," as in interpretation 2b above.

A number of modifications to this result will be required, however. First, it is certainly no coincidence that the text speaks of πληρόω (to fulfill) the Law and not of ποιεῖν (to do) or τηρεῖν (to keep). Πληροῦν τὸν νόμον (fulfill the law), a distinctly un-Jewish expression, contains the element of wholeness and completeness which is also contained in 3:15 in the word πᾶσα (δικαιοσυνή, all righteousness). A further modification is required on the basis of ἦλθον (I have come): the form of the ἦλθον saying makes a christological statement. Jesus does not only declare his upholding of the Law. He declares this upholding to be the content and aim of his mission from God. The form of the ἦλθον saying makes it clear that Jesus does not simply submit to the authority of the Law and the Prophets but at the same time legitimates them through his own mission.[83] The text anticipates what will later be enlarged on in the ἐγὼ δὲ λέγω

Dreams 2:123; 2 Macc 2:2. Synonym λύω: Plutarch, *Solon* 82D; SIG³ 355, 21; Diodorus Siculus 1.27, 4; Dio Chrysostom, *Oratio* 58 (75), 10; Herodotus 1.29, etc.

81. 4 Macc. 5:33; Philo, *De specialibus legibus* 3.182; Josephus, *Antiquities* 16:35; 20:81. Synonym λύω: Herodotus 6.106; Lucian, *Abdicatus* 10; Demosthenes, *Timocrates* 700; Achilles Tatius 3.3, 5; Josephus, *Antiquities* 11:140; John 5:18 (imperfect!).

82. References for νόμος: Herodotus 1.199 (ἐκπλῆσαι); 4.117 (ἐκπλῆσαι); *Sibylline Oracles* 3.246 (πληροῦντες . . . ἔννομον ὕμνον); Rom. 13:8 (through love of neighbor; cf. Gal. 5:14, which may however refer to the summary of the Law in the commandment to love); Gal. 6:2 (ἀναπληροῦν); Rom. 8:4 (δικαίωμα τοῦ νόμου); *Testament of Naphtali* 8.7 (ἐντολαὶ τοῦ νόμου); from ἐντολή: 1 Macc. 2:55; *Polycarp* 3:3; *Barnabas* 21:8; Herodian 3:11, 4; fulfilment of words in deeds: Josephus, *Antiquities* 5.145; 14.486; 3 Kgdms. 8, 15; LXX Jer. 51:25; Philo, *De praemiis et poenis* 83; of God's will: Justin, *Dialogue* 12.3; further on εὐσέβεια, δικαιοσύνη, εὐχή, τὸ κεκελευσμένον: Bauer, (see note 74), s.v. πληρόω no. 4.

83. Cf. Günther Bornkamm, "Wandlungen im alt- und neutestamentlichen Gesetzesverständnis," in: Bornkamm, *Geschichte und Glaube,* II (Munich: Kaiser, 1971), pp. 73-119, here: p. 78; Lohmeyer (see note 38), pp. 106f.: Jesus is "not the servant of both [i.e., Law and Prophets] but their lord and 'fulfiller'" (p. 107).

ὑμῖν (I say to you) of the antitheses. From this christological basis one might ask whether it is coincidental that only Jesus is said to fulfill the Law, while the disciples are said to "do," and "works" is used. The limited number of references does not permit an answer, but this does not detract from the christological dimension of Matt. 5:17.

Finally, one can ask whether πληρόω is not so comprehensive a verb that the above rejected interpretations of the verse in terms of salvation-history fulfillment of prophecy and in terms of Jesus' teaching may at least be present as secondary connotations. The first is supported by the opening words of the fulfillment quotations, familiar to the reader. The second is supported by the more open negative concept καταλύω and by the fact that in Matthean christology Jesus as teacher and Jesus as model are closely associated, and that for the disciples also teaching and doing belong together (v. 19!). Of course, such considerations reinvoke the danger of making πληρόω a comprehensive commonplace, so that in v. 17 Matthew says all he could possibly have said! We cannot exclude such connotations, although in my opinion we must treat them with caution, at least with regard to the idea of Jesus' teaching because of the meaning of πληρόω, and with regard to the reader of Matthew's Gospel who is not yet aware that the antitheses follow in vv. 21ff.

On completion of the exegesis of v. 17 we summarize the main Matthean ideas:

1. Conceptual analysis has shown that the focus is on the doing of the Law. This corresponds to the decisive weight Matthew gives to the action of the Christian as the sole criterion for being a Christian (cf. 12:50).
2. The field of the Law and the Prophets is nowhere perforated, surpassed or relativized. Matt. 5:17 and Matt. 5:18-19 are not in tension but tend toward agreement. In the "confessional controversy"[84] between Jewish Christians and antinomians Matthew does not take a mediating position here but is on the side of the Jewish Christians.
3. It is implicit, though not made explicit, that the fulfillment of the Law comes about not merely through the Law's authority but in agreement with Jesus' divine mission.

In v. 18 Matthew is undoubtedly taking up a traditional Jewish Christian saying. "Iota" refers to the smallest letter in the quadratic Aramaic script common at the time, as we know partly from the Qumran documents. In rabbinic literature it can also be an expression for the very small.[85] Κεραία

84. Käsemann, "Beginnings" (see note 51), p. 86.
85. Cf. Billerbeck, I, pp. 244, 247f.

(stroke) presumably means the decorative strokes of the letters;[86] Greek readers will have associated accents and aspiration signs.[87] Matthew has probably inserted in this traditional saying the first ἕως ἄν phrase (until heaven and earth pass away). Two contrasting interpretations of this little phrase are possible: (a) Is it a popular paraphrase for "never"?[88] Or (b) does it mean, in terms of time, the limitation of the law's validity by the expected apocalyptic end of the world?[89] As we assume that this phrase originated with the Evangelist himself, its meaning can be determined by reference to the Matthean parallels, particularly the verse Mark 13:31 (= Matt. 24:35) which serves as a model. Then we can say two things: on the one hand, the comparison with 24:35 shows a clear contrast between Torah and the words of Jesus which will never pass away. The idea of a temporal limiting of Torah by the apocalyptic end of the world, which may have already been present in the traditional saying, is further accentuated by Matthew. This corresponds to the Matthean tendency expressed implicitly in the ἦλθον of v. 17 and explicitly in the antithesis formula: Christ is more than Torah and it is he who actually establishes its authority. Jesus' words are *eternal;* under the Torah the community is *in this world.* But Matthew is not concerned to fix a time for the end of the Law in the near future. Rather, his reference to the validity of Torah as long as the world exists is intended to emphasize how important it is for the Christian community to observe even the iota and stroke of the Law in this world.

There are four possible Matthean interpretations of the second temporal clause "until all is accomplished": (a) a temporal meaning and thus a tautological repetition of the first temporal clause has been suggested;[90] (b) a now widespread interpretation reads the phrase in terms of fulfillment of the Law in the community,[91] recalling that ἕως (ἄν) can also have a final nuance.[92] Less convincing is (c) the salvation history interpretation in terms of Old Testament promise[93] on the basis of v. 17. A special interpretation (d) considers the fulfillment of the promises and commandments in Christ's

86. Cf. Billerbeck, I, pp. 248f.

87. Cf. Bauer (see note 74), s.v. κεραία.

88. See e.g. Banks (see note 17), 215; Jacques Dupont, *Les Béatitudes* I, ÉtB (Louvain: Nauwelaerts, ²1958), p. 116 note 2; Klostermann; Strecker (see note 5), p. 144; Vögtle (see note 34), pp. 105ff. This is supported by texts such as Psalm 102:26-27; Job 14:12.

89. This is the majority view among exegetes.

90. E.g. Hübner (see note 17), 19.

91. E.g. Barth (see note 6), 65; Grundmann; Wrege (see note 64), pp. 38f.

92. Particularly Eduard Schweizer, "Gesetz und Enthusiasmus bei Matthäus," in: Schweizer, *Beiträge zur Theologie des Neuen Testaments* (Zürich: Zwingli, 1970), pp. 49-70, here: p. 51, with many references in note 7. These are fewer for ἕως ἄν than for mere ἕως (only *Testament of Job* 21:2; 22:3), which may have motivated deletion of ἄν in the Codex Vaticanus.

93. E.g. Guelich (see note 17), pp. 242ff.; cf. Schweizer (see note 76), pp. 404f.

death and resurrection, so that the new age and the end of the Law already begin at Easter.[94] The fact that v. 18c is tradition makes the decision easier. We are not obliged to attribute either an unappealing or an imprecise formulation to Matthew, but can restrict ourselves to asking how Matthew understood wording that he received. As I see it, the second interpretation above then suggests itself, particularly if one recalls that γίνομαι certainly can mean "be done."[95]

This brings us to the question of how Matthew sees the Law remaining valid to the last letter and the last stroke. It is clear that the individual commandments of Torah remain valid. The verse does not appear compatible with an abrogation of the ceremonial law or with a reduction of Torah to the commandment to love. Seeing it simply as a piece of embedded tradition is an awkward thesis, both in principle and for a number of specific reasons. V. 18 follows without discontinuity as an explanation of v. 17. Matthew does not simply include it as embedded tradition but edits it. With regard to this world in which the community lives, his editing is not critical of Torah. The position of this whole passage 5:17-20, immediately preceding the crucial antitheses of the Sermon on the Mount, makes it difficult in any case to postulate mere "embedded tradition" here. If this thesis holds, we shall have to see Matthew's understanding of the Law in great proximity to Judaism. And in Judaism the situational subordination of one Torah commandment when it is in conflict with another is possible, but the fundamental abrogation of a commandment is exceptional and possible only under certain circumstances.

The traditional saying of v. 19 also fits well in the context. Jesus' statement of principle on the Law is followed by the consequence for the disciples. If our analysis is correct, Matthew has reworked the text extensively here too, giving the logion additional weight by means of the wording of 19b. Λύω (to solve) refers both to the abrogation and to the breaking of a law, as the juxtaposition of "do" and "teach" in 19b indicates. The "least of these commandments" points back in today's context to the iota and strokes of v. 18, so that the saying still means that the breaking or abrogating of any Torah commandment is unthinkable.[96] As in the tradition, the

94. Above all in Davies (see note 73), pp. 440ff., on the basis of a Servant of God christology. Davies is then obliged to interpret the passing away of heaven and earth in v. 18a metaphorically in terms of Jesus' death and resurrection — a risky undertaking!

95. Cf. Bauer (see note 74), s.v. γίνομαι, no. 2a; the references are rendered unambiguous by the prepositions ὑπὸ or διὰ indicating the agent. In Matthew cf. 6:10; 26:42.

96. It was popular, particularly in rationalism, to restrict v. 19 to the moral law. Rationalism considers the keeping of ritual laws to be time-bound. In exegesis there was the option

interpretation of the final clause remains open. Matthew is familiar with the idea of various places in heaven (11:11; 18:1, 4; 20:21), so we can expect this interpretation from him too.

Regardless of how we see the details of Matthew's understanding of the Law, by the time we reach this verse we are faced with difficulties of interpretation. An interpretation which claims for Matthew the abrogation of the ceremonial law or the reduction of the Old Testament commandments to the one commandment to love will have to take v. 19 as completely outdated tradition.[97] It is difficult to understand why Matthew should have included this embedded tradition if it is so alien to him. An interpretation which takes the verse more seriously assumes that Matthew does not intend to abolish parts of Torah but only to defer them from case to case, should they be in conflict with the central commandment to love. Even then it is difficult to say that a Christian must never break one of the least of these commandments, only that the non-observance of such a commandment is authorized by Torah itself. For Matthew, Jesus' authoritative interpretation of the Law is decisive, making the commandment to love the greatest commandment under all circumstances and the one on which the rest depends (22:40). This does not remove the tensions between Matthew and his tradition but does at least lessen them.

Evidently the Evangelist found positive significance in this verse in the emphasis on the unity of teaching and doing, an emphasis that is constitutive for his whole Gospel. Moreover, in drawing attention to the disciples the verse creates a formally appropriate transition from the christological and toralogical vv. 18-19 to v. 20 which finally focuses on the doers of the Law, that is, the disciples.

The most striking feature of our exegesis so far is the considerable internal cohesion of verses 17 to 19. We have not been much aware of the "undeniable lack of clarity" in the three verses or of the "destructive influence" of vv.

---

of taking the least commandments to refer to the short commandments of the second decalogue, which also recur in the antitheses. Cf. Franz Dibelius, "Zwei Worte Jesu," *ZNW* 11 (1910), pp. 188-192, followed by Frankemölle (see note 1), pp. 300f. But who would have understood that these decalogue commandments are termed ἐντολαὶ ἐλάχισται (not βραχύταται)? Even more problematic is a proposal by Charles E. Carlston, "The Things That Defile (Mark 7,14 [!] and the Law in Matthew and Mark)," *NTS* 15 (1968/69), pp. 75-96, here: p. 79, which refers to the antitheses without mentioning the decalogue. Why are the antitheses ἐντολαὶ ἐλάχισται?

97. E.g. Rolf Walker, *Die Heilsgeschichte im ersten Evangelium*, FRLANT 91 (Göttingen: Vandenhoeck und Ruprecht, 1967), p. 135. Strecker (see note 5), p. 146, tacitly restricts vv. 17-19 to "Jesus' ethical teaching."

18-19 "for the developed meaning of the whole"[98] identified by Holtzmann on the basis of v. 17. If verses 17-19 are taken as a unit, vv. 18-19 appear fully integrated. Matthew presents himself as the opposite of a "'radical antinomian', who does not take 5:18f. literally at all."[99] Rather, he himself represents a "Jewish Christian" position. We are aware however that there is a price to be paid for the unity of these three verses. The problems are shifted, not solved. What is the relation between the righteousness of verses 17-19 and the greater righteousness of v. 20? And especially, how does this relate to the possible Torah abrogation of the antitheses? How do the Markan controversy discourses with their antinomian tendency relate to this? Evidently there is "without Torah no righteousness, and certainly not a better one than that of the scribes and Pharisees."[100] Our exegesis has proved this statement of verses 17-19 to be an independent Matthean statement which should not be understood only in the light of the antitheses. At the same time, Matthew has made it clear in v. 17 that his affirmation of Torah is not simply "still Jewish" but rests on the authority of Jesus' mission.[101] Our exegesis does not make the interpretation of v. 20 and of the antitheses any easier, however.

The opening of *v. 20* with γάρ (for) is remarkable in that γάρ stands at the beginning of a section (as in 20:1 and 25:14). It closely follows vv. 17-19, since the Law is part of the greater righteousness (cf. 7:12), but it also goes beyond 17-19. Δικαιοσύνη is, as in 3:15, righteousness that people do. The main problem with the verse has to do with the stressed comparative περισσεύσῃ . . . πλεῖον (surpasses by far). Is this to be understood exclusively or comparatively, and if so, how? An exclusive interpretation would point to a Semitic background.[102] But there is no reason at all why this text should not be interpreted just as the Greek wording suggests. The pleonastic formulation of the comparative (περισσεύσῃ . . . πλεῖον) is not

---

98. Heinrich Julius Holtzmann, *Lehrbuch der neutestamentlichen Theologie*, I (Tübingen: J. C. B. Mohr, 1896), pp. 506, 504.

99. Walker (see note 97), p. 135.

100. Hummel (see note 6), p. 69.

101. This is the crucial distinction between our interpretation and that of Hummel, which are otherwise closely related. The claim (Hummel [see note 6], p. 75) that Jesus restores the identity of Jewish-corrupted Torah with the original will of God is misleading in view of Matthew's claim for the Son of God, and the claim that "the revelation on Sinai . . . is the common point of departure for Jewish and Christian Law tradition" (loc. cit.) is, expressed in this way, actually false.

102. The most distinctive exposition of this thesis is by Wrege (see note 64), pp. 43f., who uses it to explain the traditional character of v. 20. He points to the so-called ṣdq-mn constructions such as Gen. 38:26; Jer. 3:11; Ezek. 16:51-52; Luke 18:14. These are only marginally comparable with our verse, however.

remarkable as such.[103] One wonders only why it is not formulated as elsewhere with μᾶλλον. In contrast to μᾶλλον, πλεῖον is closer to the idea of number and measure.[104] So in pointed paraphrase our sentence would read: "if your righteousness is not measurably more plentiful than that of the Pharisees. . . ." This paraphrase may be exaggerated, but the idea of a quantitative comparison between the righteousness of the Pharisees and that of the disciples is certainly present in the text. The preceding context indicates that the wording here is not coincidental. It corresponds to the insistence on fulfillment not only of the basic intention but also of the individual commandments of the Old Testament. The greater righteousness of the disciples is primarily a quantitatively greater fulfilling of Torah.[105]

We might well ask whether it would not be sufficient to interpret the verse in this way and thus separate it, together with vv. 17-19, from the antitheses, especially as no direct logical link between vv. 20 and 21 is suggested. There is much that speaks against this. The explicit separation from the Jewish leaders begins at this point. Δικαιοσύνη (righteousness) as a comprehensive term for the behavior of Jesus and the community can hardly be completely separated from what follows in 5:21ff. Matthew has a predilection for titular headings.[106] V. 20 appears to be both transitional and *also* intended to be read in the light of the antitheses that follow. It is from this perspective that the righteousness demanded of Christians is related to the commandment to love, underlined in the antitheses as the center of God's will. The righteousness demanded of the disciples is identical with the "perfection" (5:48) whose content is described in the commandment to love. This points however to a certain tension with the "quantitative" formulation of v. 20. In Jesus' interpretation the commandment to love, as the center and critical norm of God's will in the Bible (7:12; 22:34ff.), does not simply effect a quantitatively measurable increase. It effects a qualitative change in the righteousness of the disciples vis-à-vis that of the Pharisees. According to Matthew, Jesus' commandments are not merely

---

103. Περισσεύειν with μᾶλλον is frequent in the NT: 2 Cor. 3:9; Phil. 1:9; 1 Thess. 4:1, 10; cf. Mark 7:36; 2 Cor. 7:13 and Blass-Funk (see note 11), p. 246. For numerous classical references for μᾶλλον et al. with comparative see Raphael Kühner and Bernhard Gerth, *Ausführliche Grammatik der griechischen Sprache,* I (Hannover: Hahnsche Buchhandlung, 1890), p. 26.

104. Cf. in Latin *plus* and *magis.* On this see Eduard Schwyzer, *Griechische Grammatik,* II (Munich: C. H. Beck, 1950), p. 184 note 3.

105. There is a certain link with 23:2-3 in that in both instances the main distinction between disciples and Pharisees is in the doing. In 23:2-3 it is absolute, however, whereas here it is seen more relatively. Our verse shows how the tradition of 23:2-3 was probably adopted because of a specific intention expressed in it.

106. Cf. 6:1; 7:15; 24:3. 18:10 has a hinging function, and 18:35 is subscript.

demands to be added to the Law and the Prophets, making Christian righteousness quantitatively "greater" than that of the Pharisees. Rather, Matthew is concerned to place the complete will of the Father in the light of the Old Testament commandment to love which Jesus has made central. One of his most significant editorial decisions in shaping the antitheses has been to take as their frame the first and the sixth antithesis, each of which deals with love. In this way Matthew establishes the center from which he wants the greater righteousness to be understood. It is known that he wants Jesus' "new" demands too, such as renunciation of possessions (cf. 19:21 with 19!) or the putting aside of old commandments (cf. 12:7), to be understood in the light of the commandment to love, on which "hang" all the Law and the Prophets (22:40). Matthew draws Jesus' teaching to a close with an impressive reference to the practice of love within a presentation of the Last Judgment (25:31-46). True, Matthew does not go so far as to see the commandment to love as the founding commandment of the Old Testament in the sense that *everything* can be deduced from it. There are further founding commandments from God in the second table of the Decalogue (19:18-19; cf. 15:4, 19) and there is the original creative will of God (19:4-5). But it is evident that the commandment to love gives rise to a fundamental revaluation of the Old Testament Jewish torot.

Hence v. 20 seems to mark a transition not only from one literary complex (the thesis of Jesus' fulfillment of the Law in 5:17ff.) to another (the antitheses), but also materially from one understanding of the Law to another. That is, from a Jewish understanding of righteousness, oriented towards the fulfillment of single commandments and therefore to a certain extent quantifiable, to a qualitatively new understanding defined by the antitheses and filled by the commandment to love. The theological question is whether Matthew has coherently combined the two strands in his thinking. The exegetical question is whether v. 20 is more than a somewhat helpless, difference-blurring transition from one understanding to another.

This ambivalence in the understanding of the Law is paralleled by a similar ambivalence in Matthew's presentation of Jesus' relation to Torah. Jesus *affirms* its fulfillment. For Matthew as a Jewish Christian, this authority encompasses in principle the authority of each individual sentence and permits the option of deferring or even abrogating Torah only in the name of Torah. At the same time, in 5:17 and even more clearly in 5:21ff. Matthew establishes the authority of Torah *through Jesus,* who as God's Son is above Torah. So is Matthew a theologian who is both Jew and Christian?[107] Is he a traditionalist who cannot cope with the tension between the two?

---

107. The thesis by Kenzo Tagawa, "People and Community in the Gospel of Matthew,"

The following theses are helpful, in my opinion, for an understanding of the first Evangelist's position:

1. From the perspective of Jewish understanding of the Law there need be no contradiction between the formal authority of all the Torah commandments and the commandment to love. Rabbinic Judaism allowed for juridically regulated super- and subordination, deferral or even abrogation of individual commandments without calling the validity of Torah or its parts into question. Matthew made use of this option by interpreting the commandment to love one's neighbor in terms of Jesus' teaching as the highest commandment, taking precedence over every other commandment in every concrete conflicting case. However, Matthew is cautious with regard to a casuistic approach to conflict as practiced in the rabbinate.[108] For the Matthean community the iotas and strokes of Torah are valid so long as they are not deferred in a concrete case of conflict in favor of the "greater commandments" (cf. 23:23).

This presupposes that for Matthew there is in principle no abrogation of the validity of the Law. Only Jesus' words on what is pure and impure (15:11) are problematic for this interpretation but do not in principle present an obstacle. In 15:11 Matthew restricts what is a general formulation in Mark (οὐδὲν ἐστίν) to the case in point, that of food being defiled by unwashed hands (οὐ τό).[109] The commandments referring to the cult are of course no longer relevant for Matthew or for contemporary Judaism since the loss of the Temple, but this does not mean they are abrogated. 24:20 could suggest that the Matthean communities observed the Sabbath. Thus in formal terms Mat-

---

NTS 16 (1969/70), pp. 149-162, on the double (religious) sociological rootedness of Matthew in Judaism and in the community is valuable. However, in my opinion it does not adequately describe how Matthew himself understood this tension.

108. The beginnings of a Christian halacha, placed by Hummel (see note 6), partic. pp. 57ff., in the center of his thesis, do not seem to me to be crucial for the Evangelist himself. See Matt. 5:32; in 19:9 the permission for divorce on the grounds of unchastity probably originated in the community. Matt. 18:15ff. is important to the Evangelist as an example for the Christian code of forgiveness which perforates what can be legally fixed (cf. v. 21!). In my opinion he does not see 5:37 as an oath substitute formula. As I see it, 15:20 is not so much a halacha on handwashing as a relativizing of 15:11. 12:7, 12 are general principles and not halachot. To speak of a Matthean interest in "halakha" is not possible at least, in my opinion, when halakha means a binding legal clause.

109. Matt. 23:26 remains difficult and the Q text cannot be clearly reconstructed. Unlike Luke, Matthew always distinguishes between internal and external purity, and the purity Torah is not simply fulfilled by moral purity. Πρῶτον is closest to the distinction between weighty and light matters of the Law in 23:23. The difficult ἵνα would then mean that after fulfilment of the moral law the lighter ritual law can also be fulfilled.

thew's procedure corresponds to that of the synagogue, distinguishing between conflicting commandments by super- and subordinating them. The difference in Matthew is that he postulates *one* highest commandment which
supersedes all the others (7:12; 22:40), though without replacing them all to become the only commandment. This indicates a further Matthean departure
from mainstream Judaism, which (without any general decision on which was
to be regarded as the highest commandment in cases of conflict) does appear
to have tended, to some extent at least, to give the duties towards God, that is,
the cultic laws, precedence over the laws relating to others.[110] Here Matthew is
in line with Hellenistic Judaism which focused on the commandment to love
and the Decalogue, subordinating the others. I see a connection between the
commandment to love, whose observance cannot be casuistically planned,
and the fact that Matthew, unlike pharisaic Judaism, does not develop casu-
istry and halakah. The main difference between Matthew and rabbinic Judaism is that his interpretation of the Law rests on the absolute authority of one
teacher, Jesus. The Teacher of righteousness and his significance for the interpretation of the Law in the Qumran community[111] shows that this too is not
without analogy in Judaism.

2. Matthew must seek above all to establish the commandment to love,
whose practice is central to the community, as the *biblical* will of God. Only if
he defers single sentences of Torah in the name of Torah is he grounded in Torah, upholding its validity *as a whole.* This is why he is concerned to prove
that Jesus' ethics are *biblical,* the proof being offered in his redaction of the
Markan controversy discourses (e.g. 12:5, 7; 15:3-6, 19), his interpreting of the
commandment to love in 7:12 and his arguing of it in 22:34ff., and in his programmatic verses 5:17-19 preceding the antitheses. This proof is just as important to Matthew as the references to the fulfillment of the words of the
Prophets in the life of Jesus (formula quotations) are. The two are parallel
and go together. Verses 5:18-19 make clear that Matthew seeks to fulfill the
whole Torah and not just its core.

In order to understand this in perspective, we need to consider the historical situation of the Matthean community. The break between the community and unbelieving Israel is already in the past, but as I see it in the recent past. In Matthew's Gospel this break is reflected in a highly concentrated
manner. The destruction of Jerusalem in the Jewish War (22:7) is apparently
seen as the consequence of Israel's self-cursing after Jesus' condemnation
(27:25). This historical situation gives the question of continuity between

110. Nissen (see note 8), pp. 373ff.
111. Cf. the Temple Scroll.

Christ's activity and message and the Old Testament considerable urgency. In a situation in which the ties between church and synagogue have been cut, it is essential to be able to say, for the sake of the unity of God, that the Bible belongs to the Christians. Matthew does this by demonstrating that Old Testament prophecies have been fulfilled in Jesus. At the level of Torah, the formula quotations correspond to the thesis: I have not come to abolish the Law and the Prophets but to fulfill (5:17). This fundamental thesis is made necessary by the separation from the synagogue. It is much more fundamental than would be necessary to counteract Christian antinomians. What Matthew does here is to take the Bible away from Judaism.[112]

3. The foregoing thesis leads on to the question of Jesus' relation to Torah. Does Matthew's orientation of Jesus' ethical preaching towards Torah mean that Jesus is subordinated to the law? The question is all the more urgent because the kingdom of God is far more closely linked in Matthew with the expectation of the final judgment than in the tradition before him. Yet our text shows that this is not how Matthew is to be read. The preface 5:17ff. and the antitheses interpret each other, after all. While 5:17-19 is concerned to protect the antitheses from antinomian interpretation by emphasizing the validity of the *whole* Torah, the antitheses themselves have the opposite function. They make clear that the authority of Torah is not self-establishing but rests on the authority of Jesus Son of God. Thus the antitheses interpret the ἦλθον (I have come) of v. 17. The relation between the two passages is dialectic. They refer to each other and can be understood only in relation to each other. Given this relationship, even the statement that no iota and stroke will pass from the Law is not an expression of the authority of Torah but of Jesus' authority and his sovereign "Amen, I tell you." A similar finding can be established for Matthew's Gospel as a whole. From the beginning, Jesus is presented as accompanying the community (1:23), as the obedient and sovereign victorious Son of God (3:13–4:11). It is not irrelevant that the Sermon on the Mount and Jesus' interpretation of the Law are within the same narrative context, reminding us that Jesus' affirmation of the Law is part of a story of

---

112. Cf. the succinct words of Frankemölle (see note 1), pp. 305f: "Matthew has . . . severed the tie with Israel; the fight over the heritage has begun." A comparison with Paul suggests itself. Paul neither denied Israel its status as the chosen people, nor did he limit the reality of God's grace toward Israel (Rom. 9-11!). He can thus be said to do greater justice to the Old Testament heritage to which he too lays claim. It is easy to disqualify Matthew for this reason, and it is certainly necessary to criticize him. But we should not forget that in Paul's time the tie was not yet severed, the doors of the synagogues and the temple were not yet closed, and preaching to Israel was still taking place. Matthew's situation is different and in this matter it is far more difficult for him to be a "good" theologian than for Paul.

Jesus the Son of God.[113] Matthew's understanding of the Law is part of the basic theme of his christology.

4. We face far greater difficulties in trying to verify Matthew's concept on the practical church level rather than the conceptual theological level. The Matthean community undertook mission to the Gentiles (28:16-20). Did they require the Gentiles to observe the Sabbath, the purity laws and even circumcision, which after all was central to Jewish gentile mission?[114] The example of later Jewish Christians shows that circumcision and baptism could indeed go together.[115] This would place Matthew on the side of the Galatian heretics and the radical Jewish Christians of Acts 15:1, and render his influence on the main church in the course of church history somewhat surprising. It is difficult to find an answer to this in Matthew's Gospel. His theology, which seeks to orient the present community towards the preaching of the earthly Jesus as its Lord, is hardly compatible with the idea of a new and additional salvation-history event such as the Lukan apostolic council or the Pauline gospel revelation at Damascus. We could ask whether the validity of the law is outdated for Mat-

---

113. M. Jack Suggs, *Wisdom, Christology and Law in Matthew's Gospel* (Cambridge, MA: Harvard University, 1970), pp. 99ff. — later followed by Schweizer (see note 59), p. 109; cf. Ulrich Luck, "Weisheit und Christologie in Mt 11,25-30," *WuD* 13 (1975), pp. 35-51, who sees in Matthew's identification of Jesus with Wisdom the key to his understanding of the Law which both affirms and supersedes. Without disputing this idea altogether, I offer some critical comments: The total number of references is small. Readers of the Gospel are unlikely, on reaching the Sermon on the Mount, to have had this idea, whereas they have already been exposed in 3:13–4:11 to a compact piece of Matthean christology, to say nothing of the dense christological material of the prologue. Points at which Matthew *replaces* wisdom by Christ (23:34) need not indicate an identification of the two. Apart from 11:19, which does not yield a definite direct identification of Jesus with wisdom, there is above all the wisdom saying 11:28-30.

114. I consider Neil J. McEleney's thesis in "Conversion, Circumcision and the Law," *NTS* 20 (1973/74), pp. 319-341, here: pp. 328ff., of a possible status of "uncircumcised Israelite" in the early days problematic. Most rabbinic references given are concerned with permission to go without circumcision in borderline cases in which it would clearly endanger life. This is not a matter of the *general* possibility of being Jewish and uncircumcised. Jeb 46a indicates the position of Rabbi Jehoshua ben Chananja, who was Matthew's contemporary, that the problem was indeed discussed and that theoretically the position that circumcision need not be part of the status of a proselyte probably was expressed. This makes Jehoshua ben Chananja's position important as a parallel for Gentile mission by the Matthean community. It was however a minority opinion even at that time. The practice was different, as shown in different ways by Philo's defense of circumcision, by the consistent distinction, found also in the diaspora, between God-fearers and proselytes, by the conversion of Izates (Josephus, *Antiquities* 20:34ff.) and the famous Juvenal reference *Satire* 14:96ff.

115. References in Hans Joachim Schoeps, *Theologie und Geschichte des Judenchristentums* (Tübingen: J. C. B. Mohr, 1949), pp. 137-139. One of the reasons given is specifically Christian: imitation of the circumcised Christ.

thew within the history of salvation, as with the mission to Jews in 10:5-6, 23. But in the latter case Matthew has the post-Easter Jesus himself declare this explicitly in 28:16-20. An additional problem is that if the law is no longer valid, a large part of Jesus' preaching would become obsolete. Is this part intended only for the Jewish Christians in Matthew's communities? A limitation like this and the suggestion of a divided community are not even hinted at anywhere else. What I find most likely is the thesis that Matthew belongs to a community which, under the impression of being rejected by Israel (already in Q!),[116] of God's judgment in the destruction of the temple, and of Mark's Gospel, has started comparatively late to undertake mission to the Gentiles. This is why in the climax and culmination of the Gospel the exalted Jesus expressly authorizes this change (28:16-20). This corresponds to the fact that in the question of mission to Jews and Gentiles, and only here in Matthew's Gospel, the "time difference" is explicitly reflected. It corresponds also to the fact that under Matthean redaction the Gentiles topic is alluded to throughout the Gospel but reaches its actual climax for salvation history only at the end (21:43; 22:8ff.; 24:14; 25:31ff.; 28:16ff.). A purpose of Matthew's Gospel would then be to justify to the Matthean community the new initiative of mission to the Gentiles. The ensuing consequences for the understanding of the Law are hardly yet reflected in Matthew. This is of course only a hypothesis and cannot lay claim to certainty. Should it hold, it would allow us to redefine in many respects the relation between Paul and Matthew, making Matthew a belated adherent of a principal decision already taken exemplarily by Paul.[117]

After this excursion into principles, we return to the interpretation of v. 20, which we have defined as forming a transition from vv. 17-19 to vv. 21ff. We now need to elaborate its function for the antitheses that follow. The function is a double one:

1. In v. 20 the scribes and Pharisees are the negative counterparts to the disciples. Matthew makes them a group of two, as is his usual practice

116. I cannot give here my reasons for not adopting the thesis by Dieter Lührmann, *Die Redaktion der Logienquelle,* WMANT 33 (Neukirchen-Vluyn: Neukirchener, 1969), pp. 86ff., on the Gentile mission of the Q community.

117. It is interesting to compare with the Letter of Barnabas, whose writer (in my opinion a Jewish Christian) in 9:1ff. brings together various already traditional arguments relating to circumcision. The opening argument (9:1-5) runs: circumcision was always meant as a spiritual act; the physical act is the commandment of an evil angel to disobedient Israel (9:4). This presupposes the rejection of circumcision in the history of the church. Together with the affirmation of the Law, this developed to become a specific ecclesiastical interpretation of the law. The idea of Israel's disobedience is retained, as in Matthew.

when he speaks of Jesus' Jewish opponents.[118] In the antitheses themselves Jesus counterpoints the Old Testament in his preaching. The preface of v. 20 could suggest why Matthew does not simply adopt the form of the antitheses but even increases their number. He is concerned with the anti-Jewish direction of Jesus' interpretation of the Law.[119]

2. Matthew's preface makes clear that the existence of greater righteousness, including obedience to God's will as expressed in the antitheses, is the *condition* for entering the kingdom of heaven. This is not simply promised by grace, as in the original version of the Beatitudes, but is linked, as in the Matthean Beatitudes, with the requirement of obedience. V. 20 contains the most definitive connection between deeds and promise of salvation to be found in the chapter, namely that of the condition. The text is a classic expression of what Reformation theology terms justification by works. But Matthew's overall theology shows that the matter is not so simple. The preaching of the will of God by Jesus is preceded by the narrative of Jesus Son of God; the preacher of the will of God is the same Son of God whose power is in the community, helping it "always, to the end of the age" (28:20).

4. Matthew and Paul[120]

1. Both Matthew and Paul show in their doctrine of the law that all theology is a contextual way of dealing with certain experiences and situations. Decisive for *Matthew's* Gospel is on the one hand the conflict with an antinomian position which does not see Christian faith essentially as praxis, and on the other hand the experience of constantly falling short of what God requires ("little faith"!). But the most fundamental aspect for the formation of Matthew's doctrine of the Law is the conflict with the synagogue, which claims the Bible for itself but has rejected the Christian faith. *Paul's* theology of the Law is fundamentally determined by his own experience of failure under the

---

118. 11 occurrences of γραμματεῖς καὶ Φαρισαῖοι, 10 of them redaction; other frequent pairs are ἀρχιερεῖς/γραμματεῖς; ἀρχιερεῖς/πρεσβύτεροι; Φαρισαῖοι/Σαδδουκαῖοι. Walker (see note 97), pp. 11-38; similarly Van Tilborg (see note 64), pp. 8-38, 99-108, and passim.

119. Aptly formulated by Hans Windisch, *Der Sinn der Bergpredigt* (Leipzig: Hinrich, ²1937), p. 123: The Sermon on the Mount is "a manifesto of the Christian Messiah, in which the rift between the Christian community and the orthodox Jewish synagogue is being torn open."

120. The following theses are experimental. I include them here nonetheless, as they may provoke discussion and be a help to others.

Law in the Damascus encounter with Christ. His theology is, overall, an attempt to deal with this failure in the light of faith in the one, biblical God newly revealed in Christ. This experience permeates Pauline theology and was indeed a fundamental experience to which Paul referred time and again. It was at the same time a specific experience peculiar to Paul the Jew and persecutor of Christians.

On this basis we can define the relation between Paul and Matthew in various ways which are not mutually exclusive: (a) Paul and Matthew are, each in his own way, context-determined theologians whose theology cannot be arbitrarily generalized without reference to their own situation and experience. (b) Paul is in a sense a theologian of the beginning, Matthew a theologian of the continuation. Paul focuses more strongly on *becoming* a Christian, Matthew on *remaining* a Christian. In this sense Matthew is basically post-Pauline without directly being in a Pauline tradition. (c) Matthew is more strongly influenced by community experience and situations, Paul by individual experience.

2. Their contrasting situations help to explain why the concept of νόμος, which refers to the Old Testament law in both Matthew and Paul, develops a somewhat different profile in each. Paul does not only use the term "law" when considering the continuity of the word of God and the claims of God under the old and new covenant or the content of the will of God. Paul the converted Jew also uses it as a code for the way of salvation oriented towards human selfhood which Christ has overcome. This dimension of Pauline thought is completely lacking in Matthew. Instead, he focuses strongly on the element of continuity of the will of God and the word of God in Christian faith and the Old Testament. This element has taken on fresh relevance vis-à-vis Paul because of the separation of church and synagogue.

3. At the center of their faith, Matthew and Paul are in agreement that the key to every interpretation of the Law is christology. For each of them, (a) Christ is the place where the continuity between the Old Testament and New Testament will of God is revealed; (b) Christ is the instance that reveals and vouches for the continuing sacredness and validity of the Old Testament Torah, concentrating — in different ways — on the commandment to love; (c) obedience to God's law is made possible in Christ; (d) the idea of reward and judgment is hedged round with christology, albeit with differing accentuation.

4. Matthew does not differentiate between the Law and grace but follows the basic structure of Old Testament thought by understanding the will of God as grace. He drastically radicalizes by making "greater righteousness" the condition for entering the kingdom of God. Nonetheless, he cannot be called a

theologian of justification by works. Rather, for Matthew the will of God revealed in Jesus Christ as "will of the Father" is already grace in itself, a grace revealed in Jesus Son of God who is Lord and helper of the community, sustaining it with his power and helping it in its weakness until the end of the age. Matthew embeds the proclamation of the binding will of God in the narrative of the mission, work, obedience, powerful deeds and victory of the Son of God. This embedding of the proclamation of God's will within a basic narrative structure in the whole of Matthew's Gospel replaces the Pauline conceptual distinction between law and grace. Conversely, the function of the distinction in Paul between indicative (foundation) and imperative (consequence) is not to postulate that real grace in Christ can be effective apart from human action. Rather, the meaning of Paul's dialectic of indicative and imperative is that the human being is constituted by God *in* deeds. While Matthew describes being a Christian as doing the will of the Father, Paul describes faith as becoming effective through love (Gal. 5:6).

5. Matthew has nothing which corresponds to the radical nature of the Pauline understanding of sin and grace developed with the concepts of "Law," "works," "own righteousness," "flesh," etc. True, both Pauline and Matthean theology are based on a radicalized Jewish understanding of the Law and sin that is in a certain sense analogous.[121] Each of them offers, in his own way, a deepening and radicalization of the will of God on a christological level.[122] Matthew's understanding of sin is accentuated differently from Paul's, and its corresponding anthropology is comparatively undeveloped. Sin in its deeper dimension does not mean one's own righteousness and "works" for Matthew but "little faith," cowardice, lack of courage, falling behind, and half-measures. For Matthew, grace does mean constant help from the Lord who goes ahead of the community on its way, who strengthens and accompanies it. The relation between the Matthean and the Pauline understanding of sin and grace is not a question of right and wrong theology but of the difference between a Jewish-influenced community theology of the second generation and the theological thinking of an individual distinguished by a particular biography and capable of exceptional theological abstraction. Paul deepened in exemplary manner the community theology he received.

6. Matthew claims the Law and promises of the Old Testament for the community in such a way that they are denied to Israel. Paul takes both Law

121. There is a strange correspondence between the thesis of Gal. 3:10 and that of Matt. 5:19. Each represents a radicalized Jewish understanding of the Law.

122. Matthew: abolition, on the basis of the commandment to love, of the distinction between juridically ascertainable fulfilment of the Law and works of mercy and love that exceed it. Paul: rejection of God's righteousness as enhancing one's "own."

and promises more seriously by retaining their association with the people of Israel (Rom. 9-11). Matthew, who is influenced by the experience of the separation of church and synagogue, must be critically questioned on whether he takes sufficiently seriously his own basic idea of the fulfillment of the Law and the promises when he detaches them from Israel, their original addressee. It does not seem possible to bridge the difference between Paul and Matthew in their assessment of Israel's present and future. But the question is whether this difference arises from contrasting basic approaches of the two theologians, or whether it is not rather the result of Matthew's lack of consistency in his own approach.

7. Matthew probably assumes the validity of the whole Law, which in principle includes the validity of all its commandments, for the community in this age.[123] This is incompatible with the Pauline freedom of the Gentile Christian from the requirement of circumcision and obedience to the Law.[124] The thesis proposed in this chapter postulates that in undertaking mission to the Gentiles the Matthean community took a step in the direction long since taken by Paul and others. This would make Matthew's Gospel a document of Jewish Christianity which overcomes Jewish Christian exclusiveness. In his understanding of the Law, however, Matthew has not yet taken account of the resulting theological problems and consequences. In this sense he is "pre-Pauline."

8. Assuming the correctness of the overall thesis that Matthew is not a theologian of justification by works and that the lasting differences between Matthew and Paul are not necessarily fundamental ones, it can be concluded that Paul and Matthew are not opposites but brothers. With respect to the central point they mean the same, though they say it in different ways in their contrasting situations. Paul's greater consistency and depth must be acknowledged, but Matthew's approach has a strength of its own which makes it an important corrective to Paul. For him, grace is given in the form of commandment, and the commandments in turn are the epitome of grace. This enables him in exemplary manner to see practice as the essence of the Chris-

---

123. It should be noted that from the perspective of Jesus' preaching in Matthew there can be a relative devaluation of Mosaic law, expressed not only in the antitheses but also, e.g., 19:4, 7; cf. 15:4, 6; 22:31. The differentiation between the will of God and the Mosaic commandment, as found or alluded to in these references, has no analogy in Judaism as far as I know. It does however have a material variant in the Pauline re-interpretation of the Jewish idea that the Law is ordained (only!) through angels (Gal. 3:19-20).

124. The conflict remains even if one interprets — as I do — 1 Cor. 7:17ff.; 9:19ff.; Rom. 14:1ff.; Gal. 2:12ff. to mean that Paul did indeed accept the idea of Torah obedience for Jewish Christians, provided it does not affect the gospel and its realization in the unity of the church.

tian faith, and the effect of grace evidenced in Christians being sustained in action and called on to act. Paul's weakness is Matthew's strength, in that Paul's *distinction* between indicative and imperative, gospel and law, faith and works has led repeatedly in the course of church history to the isolation of "mere" faith, the relative devaluing of practice, the isolation of an inner person and the reduction of Christianity to religion, personal consciousness, and private devotion. The history of interpretation of Paul, from his own anxieties (cf. Rom. 3:8; 6:1) till the Lutheran interpretation of Paul, shows that he is relatively susceptible to such misunderstanding.

9. A close proximity between Paul's justification not by works, but by grace alone, and Matthean teaching lies not in Matthew's theology of the Law, but in the so called "cultic didache" of 6:1-18: Not the righteousness to be seen on the streets and to be trumpeted in the synagogues is true righteousness, but the one to be seen only by the heavenly Father. It is of great importance that Matthew, driven by the quest for wholehearted, not only external, obedience towards the Father's will, reflects on the question of the right direction of the heart as a decisive problem of the "better" righteousness. And it is not by chance that exactly in connection with this the Lord's Prayer is inserted (6:9-13). It is alone prayer which — in the end — is able to direct the human being into the right, not self-centered, attitude toward God.

MIRACLES

11 The Miracle Stories
of Matthew 8–9

For E. Earle Ellis, on the occasion of his 60th birthday

The collection of miracle stories in Matthew 8–9 seems uncharacteristic of Matthean interpretation of tradition. Normally a conservative Evangelist,[1] Matthew has taken exceptional liberties here with his sources. Instead of following the Markan narrative sequence as usual, he has interwoven two different sections of his Markan source (Mark 1:29–2:22; 4:35–5:43). Their relative order has been only generally maintained, and there are at least two striking re-arrangements.[2] Matthew's doubling of two miracle stories (Matt. 9:27-31; 20:29-34 = Mark 10:46-52; Matt. 9:32-34; 12:22-24 = Q 11:41f.) is particularly remarkable. He narrates them as two separate episodes occurring at different times in the story of Jesus. As such doublings cannot be assumed to occur unconsciously, Matthew must have changed and re-created Jesus stories deliber-

---

1. I agree with Earle Ellis that transmission and development of the synoptic tradition was probably more conservative and more loyal to tradition than was assumed in classical German-speaking form and tradition history. For this very reason I am presenting him with reflections on texts which appear to run directly counter to such important opinions. In view of the current research situation, with some bizarre historical hypotheses making headlines in magazines and popular literature, the difficulties of our own theses should be carefully identified and kept open. On my general view of Matthew as a "conservative" evangelist see Ulrich Luz, *Matthew 1–7. A Commentary* (Minneapolis: Augsburg, 1989), pp. 73-82.

2. Mark 1:40-45 (= Matt. 8:1-4) and Mark 10:46-52 (= Matt. 9:27-31) are brought forward. Of course a biographer in antiquity may reorder episodes in the life of the hero, departing from their chronological order in the interests of the moral and literary purpose of the portrayal. But it is striking that Matthew intervenes in a source which seeks to portray a compact chronological and geographical course of events, and in doing so creates one himself, albeit different from the Markan one.

German original: "Die Wundergeschichten von Mt 8–9," in: Gerald F. Hawthorne/Otto Betz (eds.), *Tradition and Interpretation in the New Testament* (FS E. Earle Ellis; Grand Rapids/ Tübingen: W. B. Eerdmans/Mohr Siebeck, 1987), pp. 149-165.

ately. In addition, he inserts two miracle stories from Q into the narrative (Matt. 8:5-13; 9:32-34).[3] He draws all this material closely together and thus creates an entirely new chronological and geographical sequence for Jesus' story. This action sits uneasily with the overall picture of a conservative and loyal approach to tradition. It sits so uneasily with Matthew's minimal alterations to the Markan thread from ch. 12 onwards that it has been suggested he drew on a particular source for chs. 8–9.[4] Moreover, Matthew intervenes radically in the wording of the miracle stories, in particular by abbreviating.[5] The impression is of a writer making drastic alterations to the tradition. Only occasionally does he appear to remind himself of what he owes to the tradition. In places he adds material which he has previously omitted, or alludes to suppressed material in the form of reminiscences, like someone discovering all sorts of useful bits and pieces in the wastebasket.[6] What is behind the liberties Matthew takes with the tradition?

1

The miracle stories of Matthew's Gospel have been somewhat neglected by researchers in recent years. The main reason is probably the resounding success of Heinz Joachim Held's monograph on them, published over twenty-five years ago.[7] In terms of genre, Held defined the miracle stories as paradigms and sought to identify the themes illustrated or illuminated by them. In Matt. 8:1-17 he found the christological theme of the Servant of God em-

3. I differ from Earle Ellis in assuming the existence of a written Sayings Source Q. Within Matt. 8–9, Matthew "excerpts" Q consecutively, i.e. without changing its order. The only exception is Matt. 8:11-12 (= Q 13:28-29). However, this saying is in a Q sequence already used by Matthew in 7:13-14 and 7:22-23.

4. Eduard Schweizer, *The Good News According to Matthew* (London: SPCK, 1976), pp. 72-73, conjectures for this reason that for chs. 4–9 Matthew used a collection of Jesus' sayings and acts which concentrated on "the conflict with Israel."

5. Cf. partic. Heinz Joachim Held, "Matthew as Interpreter of the Miracle Stories," in: Günther Bornkamm, Gerhard Barth, Heinz Joachim Held, *Tradition and Interpretation in Matthew*, NTLi (London: SCM, 1963), pp. 168-192.

6. The passage Mark 1:44-45a omitted in Matt. 8:1-4 is added in Matt. 9:30-31. Matt. 9:28; 20:32 delete the Markan θάρσει (Mark 10:49). Is this why it is anticipated in Matt. 9:2, 22? Matt. 9:26 uses the omitted ending of Mark 1:21-28. Matt. 9:20, 35 use the later abbreviated verse Mark 6:56. See also note 33.

7. Held (see note 5). Karl Gatzweiler, "Les récits de miracle dans l'évangile selon saint Matthieu," in: Marcel Didier (ed.), *L'évangile selon Matthieu. Rédaction et Théologie*, BEThL 29 (Gembloux: Duculot, 1972), pp. 209-220, here: p. 220, writes 12 years later: "On ne peut que le féliciter."

phasized, in 9:18-34 the theme of faith, and in 8:18–9:17 a theme so general as to be less convincing, "Jesus as Lord of his congregation."[8]

Held based his analysis of Matthew's redactional work on the individual pericopes he received. For this reason his exegesis of the individual pericopes is the most convincing aspect of his analysis. He is hardly concerned at all with the totality of Matthew's Gospel as the narrative frame for the miracle stories and as the key to understanding them. The fundamental insight into the "supersummativity" of the macrotext, i.e. the Gospel, determining the meaning of individual texts within it, was still lacking at that time. The meaning of the miracle stories was not sought in their placement in the Gospel but in their "themes." Held scarcely reflected on how the miracle stories determine the Matthean narrative and move it forward. Instead, he was concerned with the theme to which Matthew subordinated the stories. Their placement in the Gospel was basically irrelevant. It may be helpful here to draw attention to the background of such interpretation of the miracles in the history of theology. I see it as a typical example of modern Protestant interpretation of miracles, which seeks their kerygmatic *significance* rather than, or less than, what is reported to have *happened*.[9] Apparently Matthew, who treats the miracle stories as paradigms and makes them examples of faith, christology, discipleship or salvation history, comes closest of all the Evangelists to such modern interpretation. The success of Held's book may be attributed partly to the fact that interpreting the Matthean miracles as paradigms facilitated their reception by modern Protestant readers.

Even today most exegetes examine the miracle stories of Matthew 8–9 for their "themes."[10] As I see it, research since Held's book has opened up new perspectives relating to three points:

8. Held (see note 5), p. 249.

9. I restrict myself to a few points: Martin Luther can say that the real significance of the miracle is the forgiveness of sins and faith itself (Disputation for the promotion of F. Bachofen, 1543 = WA 39/II, 236; Sermon of 1535 = WA 41, 19). On this fundamental Reformation premise, Rudolf Bultmann states that it is the ambiguous nature of miracles that makes them theologically important ("The Question of Wonder," in: Bultmann, *Faith and Understanding* [London: SCM, 1969], pp. 247-261, here: p. 260). The redaction-critical interpretation of miracles which has dominated research reflects a fundamental lack of interest in the historical question. The widespread terminological distinction between the "miracle" (claimed as a fact) and the (believed) "wonder" actually tends to separate the two. Acceptance of the facts of miracles is a matter of one's world view; understanding the meaning of wonders reveals faith. Thus the miracles only point to the actual wonder of faith bestowed by Jesus, "with limited power of persuasion" (Günter Klein, "Wunderglaube und Neues Testament," in: Klein, *Ärgernisse* [Munich: Kaiser, 1970], pp. 13-57, here: p. 53) then or now.

10. An example is Joachim Gnilka, *Das Matthäusevangelium*, I, HThK I.1 (Freiburg: Herder,

a. The division of Matthew 8–9 into three main sections was largely found unconvincing, particularly as no clear "theme" could be identified for the very long central section 8:18–9:17. Christoph Burger and Jack Kingsbury for instance have returned to a division into four sections.[11] In purely formal terms this is supported by the approximately equal length of each section: 8:1-17; 8:18–9:1; 9:2-17 and 9:18-35.[12] For 8:18–9:1 the theme of "discipleship" was identified,[13] for 9:2-17 the "releasing of the Christian congregation from the association with Judaism."[14] Burger has made the two central sections the starting point of his overall interpretation and in doing so he has taken seriously the parts of chs. 8–9 which do not contain miracle stories (8:18-22; 9:9-17). He sees the founding of the church as the real theme of chs. 8–9, where Matthew has "transported his understanding of the church back into his portrayal of the life of Jesus." "Somewhat oversubtly," Burger states: "Chapters 8 and 9 of his gospel present the ἱερὸς λόγος (sacred story), the foundation legend of the Christian church."[15] Presumably Burger calls his thesis "oversubtle" because he hardly substantiates it himself. One's impression is that once again *one* aspect of the miracle stories is declared dominant at the expense of others. I do think Burger's thesis can be substantiated, though not in the way he does it.

b. Alongside the "thematic" interpretation but separate from it there have always been observations on the course of Matthew's story. On the narrative level the miracle stories of Matt. 8–9 are an essential prerequisite for ch. 10 in which Jesus hands on to the disciples the authority to perform miracles (10:1). Matt. 10:8 points back to Matt. 8:1-4; 9:18-26, 32-34. In his answer to the question from John's disciples in Matt. 11:5-6, Jesus refers even more clearly to the miracles of chs. 8–9. There has also been speculation as to whether the lake crossing into heathen territory (Matt. 8:23-34) corresponds to the reflection quotation on the "Galilee of the

1986), p. 350. The Matthean miracle stories are used for various "concerns which must have been of topical interest to the readers of the gospel." Hence there is not "a single pervasive theme."

11. Christoph Burger, "Jesu Taten nach Mt 8 und 9," *ZThK* 70 (1973), pp. 272-287, here: pp. 284-287; Jack D. Kingsbury, "Observations on the 'Miracle Chapters' of Mt 8–9," *CBQ* 40 (1978), pp. 559-573, here: p. 562.

12. The border between the second and third sections is between 9:1 and 9:2 and not, as often assumed on the basis of the Markan source, between 8:34 and 9:1. ἐμβὰς εἰς πλοῖον in 9:1 refers back to 8:23, διεπέρασεν and ἦλθεν εἰς τὴν . . . to 8:18. This results in three main sections of 37 Nestle lines each and a final somewhat shorter section of 34 Nestle lines.

13. Cf. Burger (see note 11), p. 285.

14. Cf. Kingsbury (see note 11), p. 568.

15. Burger (see note 11), p. 287.

Gentiles" (4:15-16).[16] Certainly such observations remind us to take equal account of the didactic and the narrative level of the Matthean miracle stories. It seems to me that this is where the truth of the old phrase suggested by Schniewind lies, that of the "Messiah of action" in Matt. 8–9.[17] Despite the Evangelist's numerous abbreviations particularly in the non-dialogic parts of the miracle stories, the narrative level remains highly significant.

c. Finally, important observations can be made about the composition of the two chapters. I do not think it helpful to speculate about the number of miracle stories. This means neglecting the three apophthegms 8:18-22; 9:9-13, 14-17, and it has also become apparent that there is no agreement on the number of miracle stories.[18] To my mind the reflections compiled above all by William Thompson on the way in which the miracle stories of chs. 8–9 are connected are much more helpful. The most important aspect for him is not the redactional work in individual stories but their composition within the overall framework of the Gospel.[19] A survey reveals that the keyword connections in these chapters are extraordinarily close, not only within the individual stories but also between stories and groups of stories. The final section 9:18-34 in particular is remarkable for its many linguistic and thematic reminiscences of 8:1–9:17.[20] On the narrative level there is "continuous movement"[21] between the individual stories of the section. This is especially remarkable because in chs. 8–9 Matthew has combined stories from two separate sections of Mark's Gospel and supplemented them by miracle stories from the Sayings Source Q. Despite this linking of strands from various sources, Matthew narrates a unified course of events. It runs as follows: Jesus comes down from the mountain, encounters the leper on the way, goes into the city (8:5) and from there into the house (8:14).

---

16. Gerd Theissen, *Urchristliche Wundergeschichten*, SNT 8 (Gütersloh: Gütersloher, 1974), p. 210.

17. Julius Schniewind, *Das Evangelium nach Matthäus*, NTD 2 (Göttingen: Vandenhoeck und Ruprecht, [8]1956), pp. 36, 106.

18. Do we have 10 miracle stories, i.e., 2 × 5 (most exegetes, following Erich Klostermann, *Das Matthäusevangelium*, HNT 4 [Tübingen: Mohr Siebeck, 1927], p. 72), often associated with an exodus typology; cf. Av 5:4f.? Or are there 9, i.e., 3 × 3 (following Willoughby C. Allen, *A Critical and Exegetical Commentary to the Gospel according to St. Matthew* [Edinburgh: Clark, [3]1942], pp. 73, 80, 94; and Paul Gaechter, *Das Matthäusevangelium* [Innsbruck: Tyrolia, 1963], p. 259)?

19. William G. Thompson, "Reflections on the Composition of Mt 8:1-9, 34," *CBQ* 33 (1971), pp. 365-388, partic. p. 387.

20. Cf. p. 228 below.

21. Thompson (see note 19), p. 387.

Seeking to withdraw from the crowd that gathers around him in the evening (8:16, 18), Jesus crosses the lake to the Gentile region of Gadara on the other side. There he heals two demoniacs, is asked to leave the area and returns to his own town (9:1). The stories of ch. 9 also directly succeed each other chronologically and geographically. In the town, Jesus heals the paralytic immediately after his arrival (and not, as in Mark 2:1-12, in the house).[22] He passes the tax booth and goes to dinner in the (Matthew's?) house (9:9a, 10a). From there the leader of the synagogue calls him to his house (9:18a). On the way to the house (his own?) two blind men follow him (9:27-28) and immediately afterwards the mute demoniac is brought to him (9:32). Without a doubt, Matthew seeks to present a course of events in which one story follows on another. True, there is some clumsiness[23] in the narrative, but Matthew's intention is unmistakable. In negative correspondence to the connected Matthean narrative, Matt. 8–9 cannot, as I see it, be arranged in thematic blocks. Rather, the "themes" mostly persist through a number of sections, with earlier themes recurring, anticipated themes becoming dominant and previously dominant themes being recalled. I find that Matthew's narrative in chs. 8–9 most resembles a rope or a plait, with first one, then another thematic aspect coming to the fore.[24]

Conclusion: Matthew is certainly not concerned merely to collect miracle stories which exemplify the deeds of the Messiah or explain various aspects of his teaching and of the Christian faith. His aim is to narrate a connected *story.* This must be the premise of our interpretation of chs. 8 and 9.

2

The following considerations therefore draw informally on insights of modern narrative criticism. We first concern ourselves with the function of the

22. The omission of the removal of the roof (Mark 2:4) is not a lapse on Matthew's part. He deliberately chooses not to use the house setting in 9:2-8.

23. Examples of such clumsiness are the presence of the crowd (8:1) combined with the command to keep silent (8:4), the presence of amazed people in 8:27 although there are no "other boats" (Mark 4:36), and the swineherds telling "the whole story," including "what had happened to the demoniacs" (8:33), even though their herd was "at some distance" (8:30).

24. Burger (see note 11) likens Matthew 8–9 to a mosaic or collage. I prefer the image of the "plait" because it emphasizes the directedness of Matthean narration. His miracle stories are not to be understood as making up a picture but as parts of a course of events with a clear opening and a (different) ending.

Matthean miracle stories on the narrative level, the level of Matthean discourse.[25] In a narrative, "courses of events are presented in such a way that an initial situation gives way to a changed final situation."[26]

The Matthean miracle stories of chs. 8–9 are essentially the beginning of a narrative structure which progresses toward a goal and can only be understood in the light of that goal.[27] Taking a narrative to be a sequence of the three basic elements "orientation," "complication," and "resolution,"[28] we find ourselves in chs. 8–9 at the beginning of the "complication." The opening chapters, 1–7, provide "orientation," albeit of a very particular kind.[29]

So what is the narrative of chs. 8–9 leading up to? In my opinion, Matthew formulates in 9:33 the aim of the first section of his discourse. Before the framework summary of 9:35 (= 4:23) he tells of the mixed reaction of God's people Israel to the miracles performed by Jesus. The crowds are amazed and say: "Never has anything like this been seen in Israel." But the Pharisees reject Jesus and say: "By the ruler of the demons he casts out the demons" (9:34). There are various indications that this is a key passage. It reappears in altered form in 12:23-24 and is recalled in 21:10-11, 14-17. In it two main groups of people from the preceding stories reiterate their characteristic reactions to Jesus: the crowds who are impressed by him (cf. 8:1, 16, 18; 9:8; cf. 9, 26, 31) and the

---

25. I use "discourse" in the sense of Seymour Chatman, *Story and Discourse. Narrative Structure in Fiction and Film* (Ithaca: Cornell University, 1978), pp. 19-27, meaning the concrete manner in which a story of something that has actually happened is told. For me "discourse" is synonymous with "narrative." The content of the narrative is the "story."

26. Elisabeth Gülich, "Ansätze zu einer kommunikationsorientierten Erzählanalyse (am Beispiel mündlicher und schriftlicher Erzähltexte)," in: Wolfgang Haubrichs (ed.), *Erzählforschung* I, LiLi Beiheft 4 (Göttingen: Vandenhoeck und Ruprecht, 1976), pp. 224-256, here: p. 225.

27. The ending is reached with the "I am with you" assurance of the exalted Son of God who sends his disciples to the Gentiles (28:16-20). In the prologue (1:1–4:22) Matthew the omniscient narrator gives his readers "signals" which point to this ending, such as the Immanuel prophecy of 1:23 or the Gentile adoration of the child Jesus persecuted by the King of Israel (2:1-12). These signals can be fully understood only on a second reading of the Gospel. Their initial function is to point the reader to the depth dimension of the Matthean story. Cf. Section 3 below.

28. Gülich (see note 26), pp. 250-252.

29. The prologue 1:1–4:22 does not have orienting function in the usual sense of exposition. Rather, the orientation consists in describing to readers the story of the infant Jesus as the story of the journey of the infant Messiah, persecuted by the King of Israel, into the Galilee of the Gentiles. In this way Matthew opens up to his readers the depth dimension of the story. The orienting function of the Sermon on the Mount, coming immediately after the beginning of the story proper (4:23-25), is quite different. It contains the lasting commandments of the Lord (cf. Matt. 28:20).

Jewish leaders who oppose him (cf. 9:2-17). It is notable too that 9:18-34 takes up the whole of the preceding stories in its language and in its content. References to faith (9:22, 28-29) take up 8:10, 13.

The discipleship of the blind (9:27, cf. 19) recalls 8:18-27; 9:9. The scene in which blind men are healed (9:27-28) returns to 9:9-10.[30] The sleep and awakening of the girl (9:24-25) corresponds to Jesus' behavior in the boat (8:25-26). The christological title κύριος in 9:28 takes up the fivefold κύριος (Lord) of 8:2-25. The presence of the disciples in 9:19 recalls the fact that 8:19-27; 9:8-14 are concerned with discipleship. In summary, my impression is that 9:18-34 is not primarily a compilation of three miracle stories in the perspective of faith.[31] Rather, Matthew recalls and draws together almost all the themes of the preceding sections. A further observation can be made: in the healing of the blind men Matthew formulates the ending (vv. 30-31) with the help of the Markan ending of the cleansing of the leper (Mark 1:44-45) which he had earlier omitted. This story was the first in the Matthean cycle (Matt. 8:1-4). So we could say that Matthew needs the story in Mark 1:40-45 as the frame for his complete cycle of miracles in Matt. 8:1–9:34. This too is a pointer to Matthew's deliberate closure of the cycle.

We may then well be justified in reading 9:33-34 as the final reaction of the people and the Pharisees not only to the last episode, the exorcism, but to Jesus' miracles in Israel in general.[32] Matthew's desire to formulate this final reaction, as well as the intention of providing evidence for the κωφοὶ ἀκούουσιν (the deaf hear) of 11:5 appear to be the motivation for adding and doubling the brief exorcism from Q 11:14-15).[33]

We can say therefore that at the end of the miracle cycle of Matthew 8–9 a split within Israel has occurred. The negative reaction of the Pharisees, for Matthew the most important and representative of the Jewish leaders who reject Jesus,[34] stands in contrast to the neutral or positive reaction of the crowds to Jesus. Within the macrotext of the Gospel, the function of the miracles of chs. 8–9 is to bring about this split within Israel. They form the exposition of the ensuing conflict.[35] Given this, it is meaningful that the Evangelist more than once deliberately characterizes the

30. Παράγω, ἐκεῖθεν, ἀκολουθέω (aor.), entering the house.

31. As in Held (see note 5), pp. 180, 248.

32. 9:33; cf. 4:23: ἐν τῷ λαῷ; cf. 8:10.

33. In both cases, 9:33 and 12:23, Matthew has in my opinion formulated the "neutral" reaction of the people himself, using parts of Mark 2:12 which he had omitted in 9:8. Cf. note 6.

34. Luz (see note 1), p. 170.

35. I agree with Jack D. Kingsbury, *Matthew as Story* (Philadelphia: Fortress, 1986), p. 3, that "the element of conflict is central to the plot of Matthew."

miracles reported in chs. 8–9 as miracles performed in Israel by Israel's Messiah.[36] The three controversy discourses with the scribes, the Pharisees, and John's disciples now have their meaningful place in chs. 8–9 in that they anticipate the split within Israel. Not only use of the Markan source obliges Matthew to include them (he has, by the way, reordered them quite freely in this section). Here as in other sections of his Gospel he harmoniously combines a conservative treatment of tradition with his own literary and theological purposes. This is Matthew's supreme literary achievement as an author.

There is a further result of Matthew's discourse in chs. 8–9 which is important for the Gospel as a whole. In 9:36 Jesus sees the crowds and pities them as sheep without a shepherd. Matthew has taken this verse from Mark 6:34a, b and brought it forward. His reason for doing so becomes apparent in 9:37. As the Pharisees, unlike the crowds, have rejected Jesus, they are no longer the true shepherds of the people. The split that has taken place between the people and their leaders because of Jesus has left them without a shepherd. In this situation the disciples are given the task of being laborers in the harvest among the people without a shepherd. After chs. 8–9 they are distinct from the people as apostles of Jesus.

A new situation is arrived at vis-à-vis the opening of the miracle cycle. At the beginning of the Sermon on the Mount the disciples were present *together with* the people as hearers of the gospel of Jesus who proclaimed the kingdom of God. They formed as it were the inner circle of the crowds listening to Jesus (4:25–5:2; 7:28–8:1). They were absent from the first section of narrative on Jesus' miracles in Israel. The change comes in 8:18. Is it coincidence that in 8:18, unlike Mark 4:34-35, Jesus does not give *the disciples* orders to go over to the other side? Instead, Jesus in Matthew sees great crowds around him and gives orders to go over to the other side. Is the order intended for the people, i.e. for everyone around him? In that case the people would not be the reason for Jesus withdrawing to the other side,[37] but would be called to go with him. The narrative is not clear on this point. It can be said in support of this interpretation that the first to approach Jesus and seek to

---

36. On the Son of David title central to this section, cf. partic. Christoph Burger, *Jesus als Davidssohn*, FRLANT 98 (Göttingen: Vandenhoeck und Ruprecht, 1970), pp. 72-106; Dennis C. Duling, "The Therapeutic Son of David: An Element in Matthew's Christological Apologetic," *NTS* 24 (1977/78), pp. 392-410; Jack D. Kingsbury, "The Title 'Son of David' in Matthew's Gospel," *JBL* 95 (1976), pp. 591-602.

37. This is the interpretation, e.g., of Walter Grundmann, *Das Evangelium nach Matthäus*, ThHK I (Berlin: Evangelische Verlagsanstalt, 1968), pp. 257f.; Schweizer (see note 4), pp. 219f., thinks it a possibility.

follow him is a non-disciple, the scribe of 8:19.[38] In 8:23 the word μαθητής (disciple) occurs in association with ἀκολουθέω (to follow): discipleship means following, and that in turn means separation from Israel and getting into the boat. The destination of the crossing is important. It is the Gadarene, the Gentile land of the Hellenistic cultural metropolis of Gadara.[39] Jesus cannot be active there yet. He is expelled by the inhabitants and returns to the land of Israel. From now on the disciples are on Jesus' side and on the other side from the people. They are addressed by the hostile leaders of the people as Jesus' representatives (9:11, 14), and they are presented vis-à-vis the tax collectors and the leader of the synagogue seeking help for his daughter as *Jesus'* companions. We could say that from the moment when the disciples get into the boat with Jesus and cross to the other side away from the people they have their place, and in Matthew's Gospel this place is now unambiguous. They belong to Jesus and are "on the other side" from the people. This place is constitutive for what is called the mission discourse in ch. 10.

In 8:18 Matthew has the disciples consciously separate from the people and set out for the other side. This is reinforced in the main section of the Gospel which follows, that is 12:1–16:12.[40] The section portrays in several stages how Jesus and his disciples "withdraw" from Israel. Jesus' withdrawal is his response to the Pharisees' conspiracy to destroy him (12:14-15). Once again Matthew states that "many crowds" follow him and that Jesus cures them all. Once again, as in 9:1-17, Jesus' withdrawal from Israel results in conflict with the Pharisees (12:22-45), ending with harsh words of judgment by Jesus (12:39-45). The evil generation is contrasted with the true kindred of Jesus, to whom he gives his blessing (12:46-50). After the parable discourse this sequence of scenes is repeated. Jesus hears the news of John the Baptist's death, a preview of his own, and withdraws once again (14:13; ἀναχωρέω). Again he is followed by the crowds, again he cures their sick (14:14c). Then come community texts: the first feeding of the people, with clear reminiscences of the community's experience of the Last Supper, and the stilling of the storm, which Matthew shapes as a discipleship story. In 14:34 a new narrative sequence begins, opening once again with a conflict with the Pharisees and scribes (15:1-20) and continuing with another withdrawal by Jesus (15:21). This time he is not followed by crowds from Israel, presumably because he goes to the Gentile district of Tyre and Sidon. There is further conflict with

38. The second, in Matt. 8:21-22, is described as a disciple presumably because his request is not preceded by the "Follow me" (Luke 9:59, probably supplementing Q).

39. This city of the Decapolis was known as a great Hellenistic city. Matthew even knew that, unlike Gerasa's, its territory extended as far as the lake.

40. Cf. Luz (see note 1), p. 177.

the Pharisees and Sadducees, ending in further words of judgment, after which Jesus leaves them (καταλιπὼν . . . ἀπῆλθεν [having left them, he went away] 16:4) and goes away with the disciples to the other side once again (εἰς τὸ πέραν; cf. 8:18). And to crown it all, the parable discourse of this main section has the same basic narrative structure. It begins beside the sea, with Jesus teaching the huge crowds from a boat (13:1-2). In the middle Matthew interrupts the discourse with a narrative interjection:[41] Jesus leaves the people and goes into the house, followed by his disciples (13:36a). Here again is the basic motif of separation of the disciples from the rest of the people.[42]

Thus the motif of separation of the disciples from Israel, previewed in 8:18-27, is repeated so often in the main section that follows that it cannot escape the readers' attention. The repetition makes it clear that the community is coming into being. Those who follow Jesus away from the people become his disciples, separate from the people of Israel. They are with Jesus and protected by him; they are taught and healed by Jesus and commissioned by him. So the theme of "discipleship" is not just one among several in chs. 8–9. The entire narrative of these two chapters is concerned with how the healing and merciful acts of the one who is Israel's Messiah, Servant of God and the Son of David give rise to a split in Israel and the coming into being of the disciple's community. In response to Jesus' merciful deeds a community comes into being (cf. 9:27; 12:15; 14:13; 20:34) which continues to experience Jesus' acts of healing. But it is these very healings which provoke the conflicts resulting in division in Israel (9:1b-8; 12:9-14, 22-45; 14:34–15:1; 21:14-16). So the healing activity of Israel's Messiah among his people is the decisive factor which advances the conflict and with it the narrative as a whole.

We formulate a brief *conclusion* at this point. In chs. 8–9 Matthew narrates the coming into being of the disciple community from Israel and the split in Israel that this involved. Hence Burger's thesis that Matt. 8–9 is concerned with "the foundation legend of the Christian church" is not "somewhat oversubtle"[43] but, in my opinion, correct. I would state more clearly than Burger however that it is not a matter of a back-projection of the reality of the church into the life of Jesus, nor a matter of describing the church by means of the linguistic medium of an account of Jesus. Rather, we are dealing with a *narrative of how, through the miracles of the Messiah in Israel, community came into being.*

41. Similarly in 24:1-3a.
42. This is prepared in 13:10-17.
43. Burger (see note 11), p. 287.

3

In our study of these two chapters we now come to what literary criticism terms the "plot" of Matthew's Gospel.[44] Its surface structure is quite confusing. After delivering a lengthy discourse, Jesus begins to heal (8:1-3). He heals throughout chs. 8–9, continuously so to speak, in one scene after another. Even readers who stay on the surface of Matthew's story will not be surprised to find Jesus falling asleep in the boat (8:24) after such hard work! Why did Matthew create this compact block of miracle stories? Why did he have to link all these miracles stories so closely in time and place, impressing firmly on his readers that he is telling a story and not merely giving a list of various miracles performed at different times by Jesus, in the manner of an ancient biography?[45] Why is there the unmotivated and quickly abandoned excursion into the Gentile country of the Gadarenes? Why do we have the unmotivated presence of people who acclaim Jesus' stilling of the storm and are amazed at it, when Matthew has deleted the "other boats" (Mark 4:36b) they could have been in? And why do we have in 9:36 a saying by Jesus that is very perplexing on the surface: the crowds are like sheep without a shepherd?

The problems with the surface structure continue after ch. 10: Why does the mission discourse break off so abruptly, without any report of the disciples carrying out Jesus' instructions (11:1)? Why the harsh reproaches and judgment of 11:20-24? Why does Matthew the narrator interpret his story with a long fulfillment quotation in 12:18-21 which is relevant to the immediate context at only one point? Why is there a change of audience in 13:36 which does not correspond to the content of the parables? Why is Jesus' withdrawal repeated three times in 13:54–16:12?

The peculiarities of the narrative are compounded by its distance from the history of Jesus. Whatever Matthew knew or thought or did not think about the history of Jesus, he must have known that *his* Jesus narrative, i.e.,

44. On the various definitions of "plot" cf. R. Alan Culpepper, *The Anatomy of the Fourth Gospel. A Study in Literary Design* (Philadelphia: Fortress, 1983), pp. 79f.

45. On the selective character of ancient biographies cf. Charles H. Talbert, *What Is a Gospel?* (Philadelphia: Fortress, 1977), p. 17; Philip L. Schuler, *A Genre for the Gospels* (Philadelphia: Fortress, 1982), partic. pp. 98f. Schuler points to Tacitus, *Agricola*, a biography which follows the historic course of events. However, this "biography" by Tacitus the Roman historian is hardly a typical example of the genre. According to Klaus Berger, "Hellenistische Gattungen und Neues Testament," *ANRW* 25.II.2 (Berlin: de Gruyter, 1984), pp. 1031-1432, here: pp. 1239f., only the opening and ending of biographies are chronological, and the other parts do not even claim to be.

his discourse, told as a connected and uninterrupted story, was fictitious. Matthew has taken a given story, the chronological outline of Jesus' activity, demolished it and put it together again, supplementing it with further traditions and creating a new and compact course of events in time and place. This could not have been undertaken naively and innocently, that is, without realizing that this new course of events *could not* correspond to the real history of Jesus. Quite possibly Matthew was not at all interested in the "real history" of the earthly Jesus, having an understanding of history which was very different from our modern concept. But in any case he *knew* his history of Jesus was a *new* narrative. He knew it to be fictitious, he knew its plot was *his own*. We cannot for example assume that Matthew doubles a Jesus story he has received, telling it as two stories that occurred at different times and in different places, without being aware that his narrative is historically fictitious. What then is the meaning of this undertaking?

As I see it, the Matthean narrative is meaningful and the Matthean plot comprehensible as discourse only if we recognize that they have a *depth structure* which enables the author to communicate with his readers.[46] Matthew's narrative is in my opinion so illocutionary, i.e. directed towards addressing the readers, that it can be adequately grasped only with the help of a text model from communication theory.[47] Below the surface of Matthew's story there are one or more depth structure(s) whose existence is apparent in the tensions of the surface structure.[48] At this level the Matthean story "says" something to its readers and has its influence on them. It consoles and confirms them, it encourages, warns and challenges them.

Let us recapitulate the Matthean narrative. The Evangelist tells of the activity of Israel's Messiah among his people. He tells how the disciple community comes into being through this activity (chs. 8–9). He then tells how the division in Israel becomes acute (ch. 11) and how Jesus and the disciple community following him withdraw repeatedly from Israel (12:1–16:12). He

---

46. I am not referring here to "depth structure" as in generative grammar, but to a "second level" of meaning in the Jesus narrative in which it surpasses its own past in approaching the reader.

47. Siegfried Joseph Schmidt, *Texttheorie. Probleme einer Linguistik der sprachlichen Kommunikation*, UTB 202 (Munich: Fink, 1973), p. 77, sees "reference" as "instructions of text constituents to communication partners" and pragmatics not as a subdivision of textual theory but as textual theory proper. On pragmatic narrative analysis cf. also Gülich (see note 26).

48. Further indicators of this depth structure are the "signals" particularly in the prologue (cf. Luz [see note 1], p. 41), the perforation of the past level by prophecies, the overlaying of the past level by the updating of traditional logia, the language of Jesus being identical with that of the readers, and above all the "God-with-us" christology which comprehends the various temporal levels.

then tells of the life and order of the community that has developed from within Israel (16:13–20:34). Finally he tells of the sharpening of the conflict in Israel, of how Jesus condemns hostile Israel in his parables, of his controversy discourses and his pronouncement of judgment, culminating in his final departure from the temple (24:1-3) and his execution (chs. 26–27). At this final point in the story the whole people reject Jesus (27:24-25). This is why after his resurrection Israel's Messiah sends his disciples to the Gentiles (28:16-20).

That is the plot of Matthew's story.[49] It becomes apparent that *Matthew is telling the founding story of his church.* As well as being the story of Jesus, it is at the same time the story of the Matthean community that follows him. They come from Israel themselves, they have had to leave Israel, they have been persecuted by Israel, they have fully separated from Israel and are now setting out on their mission to the Gentiles. The readers of Matthew's Gospel find the foundations of their own history in the history of Jesus. It begins with the healing activity of Israel's Messiah among his people (4:23; 9:35), which gives rise to all else. The community recognizes that it owes its own existence to the merciful activity of the Messiah in Israel (8:1-4, 14-17). The community learns how discipleship can develop from this activity (8:18-22 after 8:1-17; 9:9-13 after 9:2-8; 9:27-31). In the disciples' dangerous excursion to Gentile shores the community sees itself journeying from Israel to the Gentiles (8:23-34). In the story of Jesus it finds exemplified how God's saving activity reaches beyond Israel (8:5-13, 28-34). The community sees how because of Jesus the split in Israel begins, gradually becomes acute and will eventually determine their own historical experience (cf. 9:2-17, 32-34). It learns the story of Jesus as its own founding story, becoming aware at the same time of the continuity of God's activity before and after Easter. If we accept this basic thesis, some peculiarities of the Matthean narrative in chs. 8–9 which are difficult to interpret in the surface structure become more transparent.

1. Matthew begins his story of Jesus' activity in Israel with a block of miracle stories. This compact opening of the Jesus story is not simply to be read didactically, as if Matthew is seeking to document the "Messiah of action"[50] in ten examples. Even if on the surface this block seems strange as a description of one or two days in Jesus' life, the connected story of Jesus healing in Israel has its meaningful place in Matthew's plot. He uses it to suggest

49. This outline presupposes numerous exegetical decisions of course which cannot be substantiated here but are to be found in my commentary (see note 1).

50. Cf. Schniewind (note 17), p. 36. Schniewind provides a remarkable outline of a Messiah of action *narrative* (p. 17).

that the story of the community began with the connected and continuous activity of God through Jesus. The story of the community begins with the Messiah's acts of mercy.[51] Everything else, that is, the call to discipleship, the faith of those who are healed, and the conflicts surrounding Jesus, is reaction to this opening story of the Messiah's acts of mercy. Thus the miracle stories of chs. 8–9, forming the beginning of the story of the community coming into being in Israel, have a similar function to the placing of 4:23-25 before the Sermon on the Mount. Matthew wants to make clear in his narrative how the deeds of the Messiah, that is, the deeds of God through the Messiah, gave rise to everything else.

2. Matthew frequently perforates the chronological retrospective.[52] 8:11-12 and 9:15b are prophecies by Jesus as "omniscient" protagonist, related to the era of the church or to the last judgment. The generalization of Jesus' ἐξουσία (authority) in 9:8 (the authority of the Son of Man in 9:6 passes to all human beings) presupposes the experience of forgiveness of sin in the community. Jesus' crossing with the disciples to the Gentile country in 8:23-27 and his healing of the Gadarene demoniacs there is proleptic in character. In the light of Matthew's narrative as a whole one would seek to relate the πρὸ καιροῦ (before the time) of 8:29 to the time of mission to the Gentiles which has not yet come, but unfortunately the text gives no clues to such an interpretation.[53] Then there is the use of the historic present. As in the rest of Matthew's Gospel, it focuses here in our chapters too on Jesus' λέγει (he says; 8:4, 7, 20, 22, 26; 9:6, 9, 28). Although Matthew is not fully consistent here in his use of language, we can suggest that the frequent use of the present (i.e., λέγει, he says) when Jesus speaks is associated with the significance of his words for the present.[54] So our chapters are permeated by direct and indirect references to the coming era of the community whose founding is in the Jesus story.[55]

This structure of the basic story of the Gospel correlates with what Matthew anticipates already in his prologue (1:1–4:22). There he is concerned not

51. The quotation from Hos. 6:6 in Matt. 9:13 is in my opinion christological and only indirectly parenetic. It interprets Jesus' behavior towards the tax collectors and — as 9:27 makes clear — his healings in general. Gnilka accentuates differently (see note 10), p. 333.

52. Cf. Culpepper (see note 44), pp. 30f.

53. Cf. 8:29. Πρὸ καιροῦ cannot be thus interpreted with certainty, however. The expression can also be a colloquial phrase meaning "early, premature"; cf. Liddell-Scott s.v. καιρός III 1 b.

54. Cf. Luz (see note 1), p. 52.

55. This peculiarity of Matthew's narration continues in the following chapters. There are, for example, the interweaving of the past commissioning with present community reality in Matt. 10, the ending of the fulfilment quotation of 12:20c, 21 which can be read as a prophecy both of the resurrection and of mission to the Gentiles, the prophecies 12:40-42, etc.

only with the anticipation of the essential "evaluative point of view concerning Jesus' identity," namely the message of Jesus' divine sonship,[56] but with
more besides. He is concerned with a proleptic pre-*narrative* of the *story* of
God's Son "Immanuel." His story begins with the birth of the Davidic Messiah in Israel (1:18-25). After the crisis with the king of Israel (2:1-12), he
reaches the heathen land of Egypt (2:13-18) and finally Galilee of the Gentiles
(2:19-23; 4:12-17), where Jesus the Nazorean[57] will call his community (4:18-
22). The prologue already tells the founding story of the community, which
from 4:23 onward will be set out in detail before its readers in the story of Jesus' activity.

4

Our interpretation of the miracle stories in Matthew 8–9 is not yet complete.
*As well as their indirect present meaning as the beginning of the community's
history, Jesus' miracles also have a direct meaning for the present.* Since this level
of meaning does not refer to the miracle stories of Matt. 8–9 as part of the
Matthean macrotext but almost exclusively to the individual stories, I shall
deal with them only in outline. Unlike Held, who spoke of the paradigmatic
nature of the Matthean miracle stories, I prefer to speak of their transparency
for the present.[58] The word "transparency" emphasizes more strongly the ir-
replaceable nature of the past Jesus stories. The past deeds of Jesus make their
transparency for the community in the present possible. The transparency
functions in different ways. Jesus' miracles may report experiences which can
be identical in the community: Matt. 10:1, 8 shows that for Matthew healings
are constitutive for the disciples' mission and thus for the nature of the community. Matt. 17:19 evidences the same *e negativo:* the absence of experience
of miracles in the community is disastrous because miracles are the expres-

56. Kingsbury (see note 35), p. 55. Kingsbury is interested in the significance and hierarchy of christological titles. In my opinion this interest should be consistently subordinated to
interest in the flow and aim of the narrative.

57. Matt. 2:23. Ναζωραῖος is also the self-designation of Matthew's Syrian community; cf.
Luz (see note 1), p. 150. In this way 2:23 connects the Son of God with the readers of Matthew,
and the next fulfilment quotation Matt. 4:15-16 connects Jesus' destination in the prologue with
the future task of the community, the mission to the Gentiles.

58. Karl Barth, *Kirchliche Dogmatik*, IV.2 (Zollikon: Evangelischer Verlag Zollikon, 1955),
p. 234, speaks of "the transparent" following Heitmüller. He formulates very fittingly on p. 242:
The miracle stories are, "in that Jesus makes *history* in the actions they give account of, at the
same time actually *parables* of them."

sion of faith. The identity of experience is also given, e.g., by the word stem πιστ- (faith). Speaking of the faith of those healed or the little faith of the disciples makes clear that the faith experience of the community is directly included, encouraged or challenged. The same is true of the experience of forgiveness of sins (9:6, 8). Elsewhere Matthew makes use of metaphorical interpretations of individual expressions and motifs as received in the tradition. "Blind" and "seeing" for instance can be read metaphorically.[59] The physical healing of the blind is as it were only the core or physical expression of what happens to each person who encounters Jesus: that person becomes seeing. The word ἀκολουθέω ("follow") is also used figuratively by Matthew, becoming a code for traveling with Christ on the path of obedience and suffering, but also for being carried and receiving help. The stilling of the storm in Matt. 8:23-27 harbors a whole set of traditional metaphors, allowing the story to be understood as a symbolic representation of the community's experience of being guided and protected in the storms of life.[60] The transparency of the miracle stories is further enhanced by elements of liturgical language such as the prayer address κύριε (Lord).[61] In the story of the restoration to life of Jairus's daughter, Matthew's abbreviations of his Markan source emphasize associations with the coming resurrection from the dead.[62]

Three further remarks on this level of interpretation are necessary. First, we must emphasize that all this is not new in Matthew. He is only developing what is present in the tradition. In Mark for instance there is already metaphorical interpretation especially of the healing of the blind,[63] and Mark's stilling of the storm is also a symbolic encoding of the community's experience.[64] What Matthew does is to enhance the transparency of the miracle stories in particular cases, by means of abbreviations, by omitting names which indicate the singularity of a story,[65] and perhaps also by doubling the story of blind Bartimaeus. Second, most of the miracle stories in Matthew 8–9 are mul-

59. Cf. Wolfgang Schrage, "τυφλός κτλ.," *TDNT* VIII 276–278, 281–282.

60. Cf. most recently Gnilka (see note 10), pp. 317-319.

61. This is psalm language. Cf. Luz (see note 1), p. 77.

62. In 9:18 it is a question of restoring to life a girl who is already dead (different in Mark). In 9:25 Matthew deletes all Markan details pointing to this restoration being a return to the previous life (walking about, eating).

63. Cf. Eduard Schweizer, *The Good News according to Mark* (Richmond: J. Knox, 1970), pp. 103f., 224f.

64. Joachim Gnilka, *Das Evangelium nach Markus,* EKK II.1 (Neukirchen-Zürich: Neukirchener/Benziger, 1978), p. 197.

65. For example, the Matthean community which has experienced the separation from the synagogue would not identify easily with Jairus the leader of the synagogue, hence Matthew's unspecific ἄρχων in 9:18.

tilayered in their meaning. They have both "indirect transparency" for the story of the community within the overall Matthean plot, and they have direct transparency for the present. This is evidenced for example in the healing of the centurion's servant at Capernaum, which on the one hand points to the coming judgment of Israel and the salvation of the Gentiles, but is on the other hand directly transparent for the faith of the community. Another example is the healing of the paralytic in Matt. 9:2-8, where the portrayal of the conflict with the scribes is part of Matthean history and the assurance of forgiveness of sins in the community is transparent for the present. Third, the transparency of Matthew's miracle stories should not be confused with an allegorical interpretation in the sense that the stories mean something different from what they say. Rather, the real event of the Jesus story which they report opens up an area of experience greater than the event itself.[66] So the decisive element for understanding the Matthean miracle stories is the linking of the two constitutive levels of interpretation, on the one hand the traditional transparency of the (individual) story for the present experience of the community, on the other hand the placing of the individual stories (already evident in Mark but undertaken differently) within the overall design of the Jesus story. *Matthew's miracle stories are part of the history of Jesus which is the founding story of the community, and as such they have transparent meaning.*

5

The reality of Jesus' miracles is formed not only by their past history but also by what they gave rise to, namely the history of the church's coming into being. It is formed too by the present experiences of the community, to which the miracles gave rise and which they reflect. For this reason I propose that Matthew's Gospel, of which the miracle stories of chs. 8–9 are part, should be called an *"inclusive narrative."*[67] The diagram on page 239 illustrates this. The miracle stories achieve their full reality in the experience of their efficacy in history and in the present life of the community. Their reality is part

66. This does however essentially bring Matthew's miracle stories close to allegorical interpretation as it was practiced later in the church. Such interpretation does not seek to replace the literal meaning of Scripture by a spiritual meaning. Rather, the spiritual meaning is an attempt to grasp various aspects of the meaning of texts (for example, moral or salvific) for the present. It is the unconnected coexistence of several dimensions of interpretation which closely corresponds to Matthew's understanding of miracles.

67. In my article "Geschichte/Geschichtsschreibung/Geschichtsphilosophie, IV. Neues Testament," *TRE* 12 (1984), pp. 595-604, I wrote of "inclusive story" (pp. 597f.).

Inclusive narrative of Matthew

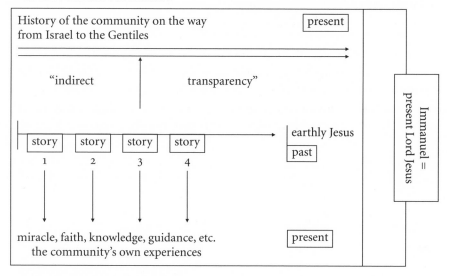

of past history but at the same time surpasses it to determine the present. This corresponds to Matthean christology. Jesus who performed miracles "at that time" is from the very beginning of Matthew's Gospel the "Immanuel" (1:23) who is with his community to the end of the age (28:20). The experience of Jesus' miracles effecting a history that surpasses them, and proving powerful in the experience of members of the community corresponds to Matthean christology.

In terms of literary criticism further thought is needed on the narrative type which Matthew's Gospel represents. I do not find it adequate to assign it simply to a theory of "the" narrative in general.[68] The characteristic of an "inclusive" narrative is that by means of direct or indirect transparency it *communicates* with readers in the present, even drawing readers into the narrative. So the decisive textual dimension for an understanding of the Gospels is in my opinion the pragmatic dimension, and the decisive semiotic question is that of the relation between sign and sign function. Narrative types related to the Gospels are for example myths, fairy tales and above all the founding stories of Israel in the Old Testament.[69] Attempts by Felix Martinez-Bonati to

68. This is my most important question to Kingsbury (see note 35). His model largely excludes the particular reader-response pattern of Matthew's Gospel and in doing so remains on the surface of Matthean discourse.

69. The Old Testament models of history, assuming in various ways an identification of readers with their founding story on Mount Sinai, come particularly close to the Gospels.

identify multilayering in a work of art[70] could be helpful for a literary critical description. Siegfried J. Schmidt's question on the "illocutionary potential of texts"[71] also seems useful.

It has been shown, then, that the meaning of miracle stories in the basic Matthean story can never be defined only statically. It must always be newly discovered by readers in their own concrete historical situation and by means of their own analogous experience. There is much work still to be done here in the fields of literary criticism, hermeneutics, and theology.

70. Félix Martinez-Bonati, "Erzählungsstruktur und ontologische Schichtenlehre," in: Haubrichs (see note 26), pp. 175-183.

71. Schmidt (see note 47), p. 150. "A text is every uttered linguistic part of a communicative act in a communicative performance which is thematically oriented and fulfils a recognisable communicative function, i.e., realises a recognisable illocutionary potential."

MATTHEW AND ISRAEL

12 Anti-Judaism in the Gospel of Matthew as a Historical and Theological Problem: An Outline

For Eduard Schweizer
on the occasion of his 80th birthday[1]

The last chapters of Matthew's Gospel make painful reading. I have found it much more difficult to identify with the discourse of the woes (ch. 23), Matthew's parables on salvation history (21:33–22:14), or with some texts of the Passion and Easter narratives than with earlier chapters such as the Sermon on the Mount. I approach these difficult chapters in an interdisciplinary attempt at understanding, and in the theological dialogue I develop on this final section of the Gospel I hope to maintain my own honesty.

1. A Survey of Matthew's Gospel

I read Matthew's Gospel as a Jesus story on two levels.[2] The surface level of the narrative tells the past story of Jesus in Israel, his activity and his rejection,

---

1. Of the shorter Matthew commentaries, Eduard Schweizer's is the best and richest in material. I have learned a great deal from it. On the problem of Matthew's anti-Judaism I have come to differently accented and saddening conclusions. Nonetheless, this outline is a birthday present for my teacher, one of whose great gifts is to be glad when his pupils disagree with him! — The term "anti-Judaism" used in this outline is not fully adequate. I take it to mean a religiously motivated rejection of Judaism. It is inadequate in relation to Matthew's Gospel insofar as Matthew himself is a Jew and sees the core of Israel in his Jesus communities. Only in relation to non-Jews should one speak of "anti-Judaism," i.e., when considering the post-history of Matthew's Gospel. On the other hand, Matthew himself has anticipated the term "anti-Judaism" with his pointed use of Ἰουδαῖοι in 28:15. I know of no other less inappropriate term!

2. For further detail see in this volume, "The Miracle Stories of Matthew 8–9," pp. 221-240 and "Matthew the Evangelist: A Jewish Christian at the Crossroads," pp. 3-17.

German original: "Der Antijudaismus des Matthäusevangeliums als historisches und theologisches Problem," *EvTh* 53 (1993), pp. 310-328.

his execution and his commission to his disciples to preach to the Gentiles. But at the same time this story of Jesus includes that of the Matthean community. I see the Matthean community as Jewish Christian, originating in Palestine. There the community's mission to Israel failed, and eventually, probably in the period preceding the Jewish War of 66-70, they were forced to leave the land of Israel. They found a new home in Syria and began to missionize among the Gentiles. It is because the Matthean Jesus story includes that of the community that I refer to it as an "inclusive" story.[3] For readers in the Matthean communities the story was never simply about the past. It was always at the same time their own story, the story of what they themselves had experienced. The story of Jesus was their own foundational story, and as readers they were part of it.

Matthew's story consists of the prologue and five main sections. Only at the surface level is the prologue (1:1–4:22) concerned with the beginning of the Jesus story, his childhood and the beginning of his ministry with John the Baptist in the wilderness. It anticipates at the same time the whole story of Jesus the Son of God and his journey from the royal city of Bethlehem to the Galilee of the Gentiles (4:14-16). In this way the prologue forms the prelude to the whole of the Jesus story that Matthew is to tell.

The main narrative thread of the Gospel of Matthew, beginning in 4:23, tells in several sections a story of Jesus' increasing conflict in Israel. The first section, 4:23–11:30, narrates the first stages of proclamation and healing by Israel's Messiah among his people, culminating in the split between Israel's unrepentant cities on the one hand and the "infants" on the other to whom the Son reveals the Father (11:20-24, 25-30). The following section, 12:1–16:20, describes in a series of episodes how Jesus and his disciples withdraw (ἀναχωρέω) from the increasing hostility of Israel's leaders (12:15; 14:13; 15:21; cf. 16:4). In the middle of an increasingly hostile Israel, the community of disciples emerges. The section ends with Peter's declaration, a text that speaks for the first time of the building of the church (16:13-20). It is logical, then, that the following main section, 16:21–20:34, a peaceful interlude in the life of Jesus, as it were, before the onset of the storm, outlines the life of the community as found among the disciples. Then come the final sections of chapters 21–25 and 26–28. The first of these can be described as "the final reckoning with Israel." After an introit, Jesus confronts Israel and its leaders in three sizeable text blocks. These are the three salvation history parables of 21:28–22:14, the disputes with Jewish groups in 22:15-46 and the great woes discourse of chapter 23. Jesus then leaves Israel's temple (24:1-2) and from now

3. Cf. in this volume, pp. 14-17, 238-240.

on he prepares the community for the day of judgment (24:3–25:46). The Passion and Easter narratives bring the Gospel to a close (chs. 26–28). Like earlier sections, they too have a double ending.[4] The story of Jesus' resurrection (28:1-10) is a story of death for Israel and its leaders. They fail to recognize "to this day" (28:15) the truth of Jesus' resurrection. This negative ending is concomitant with a positive development. In his last appearance on the mountain in Galilee, the Lord commands his disciples to make disciples of πάντα τὰ ἔθνη (all the nations) and promises to be with them to the end of the world (28:19-20). The two pericopes 28:11-15 and 16-20 mark the double ending of Matthew's story, leading to a hopeless situation for Jews and a new mission within salvation history for the community.

This brings Matthew to where his own community stands in his present time. They are separated from Israel and seeking new orientation outside the synagogue. Matthew endeavors to give them this orientation by showing them that in future their mission to the Gentiles will be central. The mission to Israel is complete. Overall it has been a failure, since it has not resulted in the people of Israel being led by Jesus to the kingdom of God. Rather, they have reconstituted themselves without Jesus under the leadership of the Pharisees. Instead of sitting on the twelve thrones of Israel, the disciples (with whom the readers of Matthew's Gospel identify) find themselves a minority outside "their synagogues" (4:23; 9:35; 10:17 etc.). Undoubtedly this was a traumatic experience for the community, and Matthew's version of the Jesus story seeks to help them in working through the trauma. That is why Matthew tells the story of Jesus as that of Jesus and Israel, a story of increasing hostility, of separation, of the apparent victory of Jesus' opponents, but also as the story of the reckoning with Israel and the hidden triumph of the coming judge of the world over his enemies.

2. A Look at Matthew 21–28

Chs. 21–28 portray the climax of Jesus' conflict with Israel. I shall formulate some provisional exegetical suppositions on a number of key passages in these chapters.[5]

---

4. Cf. partic. 11:20-30; 12:38-50; 16:1-20.

5. The scope of this article does not permit more precise exegetical explication of my assumptions. I refer readers to the third volume of my commentary, Ulrich Luz, *Das Evangelium nach Matthäus (Matt 18–25)*, EKK I.3 (Neukirchen/Düsseldorf: Neukirchener/Benziger, 1997). This article was written as a first test for my basic hypotheses to be developed in this volume.

2.1. Chapters 21–23

The ending of the allegory of the wicked vineyard tenants (21:43) is significant for Matthew's Israel theology: "The kingdom of God will be taken away from you and given to a 'people' (ἔθνος) that produces the fruits of the kingdom." From *whom* will the kingdom of God be taken away? In the context, ἀφ᾿ ὑμῶν (away from you) refers to Israel's leaders.[6] However, it seems incongruous that they are not to be replaced by other leaders but by a "people." So do the words mean that Israel, the old chosen people, is to be replaced by a new chosen *people* that produces fruit? Given Matthew's use of language up to this point, the association of ἔθνος (people) with the Gentiles certainly suggests itself. This is supported by the saying in Matt. 13:12 (= Mark 4:25) which is taken up here. In Matt. 13:12, even the understanding that they had was to be taken away from the people of Israel. As I see it, the saying of 21:43 has surplus meaning that goes beyond its placement in words by Jesus addressed to the Jewish leaders.[7] Matthew's Gospel as a whole will show that for the Evangelist the behavior of Israel's leaders has dramatic consequences for the whole people under their charge.

In the parable of the wedding banquet which follows, Matthew alludes to the destruction of Jerusalem as God's judgment on the wicked guests who refused the king's invitation (22:7). This takes up a familiar interpretation, found in the Old Testament prophets as well as in Josephus and rabbinic literature, of the destruction of Jerusalem as God's judgment.[8] The distinctive feature in Matthew is that the destruction of the city is followed by mission to the Gentiles. The original guests are no longer invited. Matthew does not see the destruction of Jerusalem as the Last Judgment, but he does treat it as a historically momentous event within the story of God with his people.

For the interpretation of the woes discourse of ch. 23, it is important to note the shift that takes place in the threats of vv. 34-36. Up to v. 33, the pro-

---

6. Cf. vv. 23, 45. The ὄχλοι who according to 21:11, 46 regard Jesus as a prophet are explicitly distinguished from them.

7. Moreover, readers will be familiar with the deuteronomic tradition of killing a prophet, taken up in 23:34. It forms an accusation against Israel.

8. Not because of their rejection of Jesus' messengers, however, but because of the evil deeds of the zealots (Josephus, *Jewish War* 6:109f.; cf. 124ff.). Important too are *Sibylline Oracles* 4.115-118 (noted by Wolfgang Schrage) and *b. Šabbat* 119b, a passage containing a number of rabbinic testimonies about which sins of Israel led to the destruction of Jerusalem (noted by Mrs. O. Franz, Lucerne). Matt. 22:7, whose wording is in the prophetic tradition, has had considerable influence. Many ecclesiastical authors following Origen, *Contra Celsum* 1:47; 4:22; and Tertullian, *Adversus Judaeos* 13 = PL 2:678 have seen the destruction of Jerusalem and the expulsion of the Jews from the land as divine punishment for the crucifixion of Jesus.

nouncement of judgment has been addressed only to the Pharisees and scribes. This changes in vv. 34-36. The Christian prophets, sages and scribes of v. 34 have not been sent only to the Jewish leaders.[9] So at this point, when judgment is pronounced on "this generation" (vv. 35-36),[10] Matthew's readers will broaden their perspective and read these words as a judgment on all Israel. That is the aim pursued in this chapter. Matthew states that the whole people, led astray by their leaders, will be subjected to judgment. The boundary between the leaders and the people is fluid. Matthew has positioned the lament over Jerusalem (vv. 37-39) here at the end of the woes discourse, confirming that he does indeed have the whole people in mind. Once again the destruction of Jerusalem is interpreted as divine punishment. Problematic though it is, I prefer to interpret v. 39 ("you will not see me again until you say, 'Blessed is the one who comes in the name of the Lord'") in terms of the Lord's *parousia* rather than the conversion of Israel.[11] Immediately after these words, Jesus and his disciples leave the temple which is to be destroyed. Never again does he speak to the crowds.

All this is in keeping with the bleak perspective presented here.

2.2. The Passion Narrative

The Passion narrative is notable for the frequency and character of the Evangelist's fictions, many of which occur at points relevant to our topic. I take the following to be pure fiction on Matthew's part, unsupported by the tradition: the episode concerning the second witness to Jesus' innocence, Pilate's wife (27:19), and Pilate washing his hands (27:24).[12] The fictional nature of the lat-

---

9. Here readers will be reminded once again of the deuteronomic tradition of killing a prophet.

10. Cf. 11:16; 12:39-45. Ἡ γενεὰ αὕτη is best translated as "this generation"; cf. Ulrich Luz, *Matthew 8–20*, Hermeneia (Minneapolis: Fortress, 2001), pp. 148f. Matt. 23:36 indicates however that Matthew, given the tradition of killing prophets, regards the killing of Jesus as the final link in an endless chain of evil deeds perpetrated by Israel against its prophets. For this reason he takes up 23:36 in 27:25 with πᾶς ὁ λαός.

11. Eduard Schweizer, *The Good News According to Matthew* (London: SPCK, ²1975), p. 445. Like many others, Schweizer considers the possibility of Israel's eschatological conversion as suggested by Rom. 11:25-26. The bleak context of Matt. 23:38; 24:1-2 speaks against this. Dale C. Allison, "Matt. 23:29 = Luke 13:35b as a Conditional Prophecy," *JSNT* 18 (1983), pp. 75-84, reads v. 39 as a precondition of salvation. Israel will see Jesus again only when it greets him with the words of Ps. 118. Attractive though it is, this interpretation of ἕως is countered by Matt. 5:18, 26; 16:28; 24:34.

12. Cf. Ulrich Luz, "Fictionality and Loyalty to Tradition in Matthew's Gospel, in the Light of Greek Literature," in this volume, pp. 54-79.

ter episode is particularly grotesque. The idea of the Gentile Pilate observing a Jewish-Biblical expiation ritual — the washing of hands — must have struck Matthew's Jewish Christian readers. Whether or not Matthew expected them to take it literally, this grotesque episode certainly signals what he wants to say. Together with the Jewish leaders who are plotting Jesus' death, the whole of God's holy people (λαός) is guilty of the death of the one who is attested innocent by three witnesses, Judas, Pilate's wife and Pilate himself. The verse 27:25 also refers back to 23:34-36, emphasizing that God will indeed judge Israel for this deed. Trilling speaks aptly of this passage as a narrated "dogmatic theologoumenon."[13] It is crucial to the course of Matthew's story.

The signs occurring after Jesus' death and the appearance of the risen saints in Jerusalem (27:51-53) are highly problematic. I read this passage similarly to *Testament of Levi* 4:1, which is influenced by it: "When the rocks are split and the sun is darkened . . . , Hades will be robbed." It will be the time of judgment for all sons of men. There is more to this than the portent accompanying the death of a religious hero. The resurrected are a sign of the judgment.[14] Following the high priest's judgment on Jesus the Son of Man who is the judge of the world (26:64-65), the tables are turned, and the coming judgment on the holy city and its temple becomes the writing on the wall.

The two sections on the guards at the tomb (27:62-66 and 28:11-15) are closely interwoven with the overall context of Matthew's Gospel. Now Jesus' saying about the sign of Jonah (12:38-40) comes to fatal fruition. The chief priests — and the Pharisees, inserted by Matthew — protest in vain that "that imposter" has said he will rise again after three days. Jesus' resurrection cannot be prevented by guards on the tomb or the sealing of the grave. It is, as Paul Hoffmann has put it, a fatal "sign for Israel."[15] The story of Judas' reward repeats itself. Faced with the fact of Jesus' resurrection, the chief priests can only resort to the false power of money by bribing the guard. The Jewish leaders act and take all the responsibility, while Pilate ceases to play an active part in directing events. The episode ends with the Evangelist's first outlook on the present. The rumor that the disciples stole the body is still told "to this day" among those who are "Jews" (28:15).

The second outlook on the present is found in the other final pericope

---

13. Wolfgang Trilling, *Das wahre Israel*, EthSt 7 (Leipzig: St. Benno, ³1975), p. 72.

14. Μετὰ τὴν ἔγερσιν αὐτοῦ is meaningful neither for this interpretation nor for a reading of the words as a mere portent. I consider Schweizer (see note 11), p. 516, correct in assuming a gloss inserted later (cf. 1 Cor. 15:20-28; Col. 1:18, etc.).

15. Paul Hoffmann, "Das Zeichen für Israel. Zu einem vernachlässigten Aspekt der matthäischen Ostergeschichte," in: Hoffmann (ed.), *Zur neutestamentlichen Überlieferung von der Auferstehung Jesu*, WdF 522 (Darmstadt: Wissenschaftliche Buchgesellschaft, 1988), pp. 416-452.

formulated independently by Matthew, that is: 28:16-20. The risen Lord remains with his community, who are now being sent to the Gentiles, to the end of the age (28:20). It is much debated whether πάντα τὰ ἔθνη is translated here as "all nations" or "all Gentiles." The second possibility corresponds, firstly, to the Jewish use of the Greek word ἔθνη and secondly to the meaning of the word in most instances in Matthew. Thirdly, it fits the context. The totality of the Gentiles, to whom the disciples are now sent in mission, is in opposition to "Jews"[16] (28:15) who have remained unbelievers "to this day." Fourthly, the opposition is further emphasized by a back-reference in the mission command to Jesus' earlier command to the disciples that they should go only to the lost sheep of the house of Israel (10:5-6). This is now superseded.[17] Ἔθνη (Gentiles) must have the same meaning in 10:5 and 28:19.[18] On the other side, the expression πάντα τὰ ἔθνη must be distinguished from mere ἔθνη and includes Israel. This argument carries weight, since in 25:32 a reading of the phrase "all nations" which excludes Israel is highly improbable, and also in Matt. 24:9, 14 "all nations" is a good possibility. But even if the translation "all nations" might be preferable, it is clear that there is an opposition between 10:5-6 and 28:19: The time of exclusive mission to Israel is definitively over. In the light of the parable of the wedding banquet (22:8-9) and of the logion 21:43 it is clear that for Matthew's church the orientation toward the mission of Israel has been replaced by the world-mission.

My exegetical *conclusions* are as follows:

1. Matthew's story ends with Jesus being rejected not only by the Jewish leaders but also by the chosen people with them (23:34-39; 27:24-25). This rejection puts Israel in a position of contradiction of its own scriptures, and causes its leaders to lie and deceive.
2. The *implication* is that for Matthew Israel ceases to be the people of promise (21:43). The church succeeds Israel as God's chosen people, provided it keeps Jesus' commandments.

---

16. At least the Evangelist does not say "the Jews," let alone "all Jews." This is emphasized by Hildegard Gollinger, "'. . . und diese Lehre verbreitete sich bei den Juden bis heute'. Mt 28:11-15 als Beitrag zum Verständnis von Israel und Kirche," in: Lorenz Oberlinner/Peter Fiedler (eds.), *Salz der Erde — Licht der Welt* (FS Anton Vögtle; Stuttgart: Katholisches Bibelwerk, 1991), pp. 357-373, here: p. 370.

17. On the interpretation of 10:5-6 cf. Luz (see note 10), 73f. I do not assume the whole of the Mission Discourse of Matt. 10 to be only a "retrospective" on the time of Jesus. This is true only of vv. 5-6 and v. 23, which situate the discourse in Jesus' story, following Jesus' own programmatic activity "among the (holy) people" (4:23).

18. The two alternatives might not be fully exclusive, because the two meanings of ἔθνη do not function as mutually exclusive homonyms.

3. From Matthew's perspective the mission to Israel is over. Given the brief period remaining before the last judgment, he sees the rejection of Jesus by the majority of Israel as definitive and final. Jesus himself has left the holy place (23:37-39; 24:1-2), followed by his disciples.

4. Matthew sees Israel as guilty of rejecting Jesus and his messengers (11:20-24; 12:22ff.; 21:33–22:7; 23:34-39) and of killing Jesus (27:24-25). They are also guilty in a wider sense in that their representatives do not do the will of God (cf. Matt. 23 passim).

5. Jesus pronounces judgment on Israel in both word and gesture (Matt. 24:1-2). "This generation" becomes a doomed collective which will not escape God's imminent judgment.

3. Considerations from the Perspective of History and Social Sciences

What has happened here? Let us attempt to gain an understanding of these terrible developments in terms of history and social sciences.

3.1. The "Family Conflict"

Drawing on a conflict theory as used in the social sciences, I see Matthew's anti-Judaism as arising from a situation of "family conflict."[19] One of the basic problems with Matthew's Gospel is that it contains a large number of contradictory traditions on the relation of Jesus and the community to Israel. On the one hand there are Jewish Christian traditions such as 5:17-20; 10:5-6; 23:2-3, on the other hand there are starkly anti-Jewish texts such as 8:11-12; 23:29-36; 27:24-25. This juxtaposition of seemingly conflicting elements can be explained in social science by theories of integration or conflict. Integration explanations are suggested by Gerd Theissen and his student Kun Chun Wong. They assume the Matthean community to consist of both Jewish and Gentile Christians, with the Evangelist attempting to stabilize the multicultural identity of the community by including various traditions in his Gospel.[20] Anto-

19. Rosemary Radford Ruether, *Faith and Fratricide. The Theological Roots of Anti-Semitism* (New York: Seabury, 1974), p. 30, rightly distinguishes between general ancient anti-Semitism and specifically Christian anti-Judaism. She describes the latter as "family hatred" associated with "rival claims to exclusive truth within the same religious symbol system."

20. Gerd Theissen, "Aporien im Umgang mit den Antijudaismen des Neuen Testaments," in: E. Blum et al. (eds.), *Die Hebräische Bibel und ihre zweifache Nachgeschichte* (FS

nio Saldarini sees the Matthean community as a "deviant" minority community within a functioning Jewish society,[21] with Matthew's Gospel attempting to stabilize their "deviant identity" between Judaism and a Christian self-understanding completely separate from Judaism.[22] My own preference is for an explanation in terms of conflict theory. Exegetically my reason is that the Gospel of Matthew tells the story of a conflict, that of Jesus with his people Israel and its leaders, and that the conflict ends in disaster.[23] As I see it, the "Jewish" and anti-Jewish elements of Matthew's Gospel cannot simply be juxtaposed. Rather, we must examine their function within Matthew's narrative. With the end of the narrative in mind, it seems to me that the anti-Jewish elements and the break with Judaism are dominant and integration is no longer possible. I see the Gospel of Matthew as representing a Jewish Christian community in conflict with the Jewish mainstream. They have been expelled from the synagogues and are now looking at "their" or "your" synagogues and scribes (i.e., those of the others!).[24] The harsh conflict between the commu-

---

R. Rendtorff; Neukirchen: Neukirchener, 1990), pp. 535-553, here: p. 538 note 10. Kun Chun Wong, *Interkulturelle Theologie und multikulturelle Gemeinde im Matthäusevangelium*, NTOA 22 (Freiburg/Göttingen: Universitätsverlag/Vandenhoeck und Ruprecht, 1992). A similar approach was taken by Kenzo Tagawa, "People and Community in the Gospel of Matthew," *NTS* 16, 1969/70, pp. 149-162.

21. Antonio J. Saldarini, "The Gospel of Matthew and Jewish-Christian Conflict," in: David Balch (ed.), *Social History of the Matthean Community. Cross-Disciplinary Approaches* (Minneapolis: Fortress, 1991), pp. 38-61, is based on a functionalist deviance theory (see partic. pp. 45f.). This results from his hypothesis that the Matthean communities are still part of the Jewish synagogue. "Deviance processes, far from driving a group out of society, often keep it in. Social theory has established that nonconformity, resistance to social structures, and deviance are always part of any functioning society" (pp. 38f). Although he rejects the question of whether Matthew remained Jewish, Saldarini concludes that the Matthean community had "many symbolic elements" in common with the Jewish community, as well as "numerous negative and positive relations" (p. 40). Saldarini's hypothesis accords well with the function of minorities in the open, pluralist society of the U.S. today!

22. Saldarini, p. 57.

23. Cf. Section 1.

24. Cf. Section 3.2. A review of research can be found in Graham Stanton, "The Origin and Purpose of Matthew's Gospel: Matthean Scholarship from 1945-1980," in: *ANRW* 25.3 (Berlin: de Gruyter, 1985), pp. 1910-1921. My position is similar to Stanton's; cf. Ulrich Luz, *Matthew 1–7* (Minneapolis: Fortress, 1989), pp. 79-89. A comparable view is taken by Wayne A. Meeks, "Breaking Away: Three New Testament Pictures of Christianity's Separation from the Jewish Communities," in: Jacob Neusner/Ernest S. Frerichs, *"To see ourselves as others see us." Christians, Jews, "Others" in Late Antiquity* (Chico: Scholars, 1985), pp. 108-114, and Benno Przybylski, "The Setting of Matthean Antijudaism," in: Peter Richardson et al. (eds.), *Antijudaism in Early Christianity* I (Waterloo: Wilfred Laurier University, 1986), pp. 181-200, 198f.

nity and Israel's leaders which Matthew's Gospel reflects is, then, a "family conflict."

The sociologist Lewis Coser has shown that the closer the relationships between groups, the more intense the conflicts between them.[25] This is even more markedly the case when the groups concerned are sectarian in character. Following Max Weber, I see "sects" as distinguished by being a voluntary and visible communion of saints,[26] whereas membership in a "church" is simply by birth. This explains why "family" conflicts among related sects are so intense. A sect requires self-definition as the basis of its existence, and such self-definitions compete with those of other related groups. The early Christian church was sectarian in character, defining itself by Jesus' preaching and refining this self-definition by means of its conflict with Judaism. So the idea that family rows are the fiercest rows does not apply only to families. It is generally true of the New Testament that the writers who judge the Jews most harshly, that is, Matthew, John, and the authors of the Epistle to the Hebrews and Revelation, are all Jewish Christians themselves.

3.2. Working through a Trauma

My second thesis is that Matthew and his Jewish Christian community are working through painful experiences. This may be interpreted in terms of individual psychology as grief externalized in the form of verbal aggression. In terms of social psychology it is frustration externalized in the form of verbal aggression.[27] The Gospel of Matthew gives a name to such frustrating experiences when it speaks of persecutions (5:11-12; 10:23; 23:34) against the missionaries on the part of the Jews. The Gospel also speaks of martyr deaths that have taken place (10:21, 28; 22:6; 23:34, 37), of floggings and being handed over to Gentile courts (10:17-18). The mission discourse speaks of divided families,

25. Lewis A. Coser, *The Functions of Social Conflict* (London: Routledge, 1998 = 1956), pp. 67-72 (after Georg Simmel); cf. also Graham Stanton, "Matthew in Sociological Perspective," in: Stanton, *A Gospel for a New People* (Edinburgh: Clark, 1992), pp. 98-104.

26. Max Weber, *Economy and Society: An Outline of Interpretative Sociology*, Vol. 2 (London: Berkeley, 1978), pp. 1203-1204. Thus the term "sect" is not constituted by being a minority vis-à-vis a "normative" majority.

27. The classic text is John Dollard, *Frustration and Aggression* (New Haven: Yale University, 1940). Cf. also Amélie Mummendey, "Aggressives Verhalten," in: Wolfgang Stroebe et al. (eds.), *Sozialpsychologie. Eine Einführung* (Berlin: Springer, 1990), pp. 275-304, here: pp. 280f.; Werner Bergmann, "Psychoanalysis and Personality Theory," in: Bergmann (ed.), *Error without Trial. Psychological Research on Antisemitism,* Current Research on Antisemitism 2 (Berlin: de Gruyter, 1988), pp. 20-25.

especially of division between generations (10:34-37). This is of course associated with vertical social mobility, probably often meaning social decline and insecurity for members of the family who have become Christians. According to sociologists, vertical mobility increases the tendency to develop prejudices towards "the others."[28] The texts I have mentioned come from the Sayings Source. My assumption is that the Matthean community emerged from the missionary activity of the Jesus messengers behind the Sayings Source, and that the source reflects the community's own story.

But caution is required. Douglas Hare has shown in a fine analysis that such highly dramatic experiences of persecution were probably relatively rare. Not until immediately before the outbreak of the Jewish War will there have been floggings or even executions.[29] Matthew's texts themselves suggest that it was primarily the preachers and missionaries who were subjected to negative experiences of this kind, and not necessarily ordinary men and women.[30] In the tense situation of the time the missionaries provoked such incidents with their strongly worded proclamation of Jesus. Why have these isolated negative experiences taken on such significance? I think it has to do with the separation of church and synagogue. Unlike John, Matthew does not refer directly to a formal exclusion from the synagogue.[31] On the other hand, the conflict with Israel's majority who do not believe in Jesus is so important to Matthew that he tells his Jesus story as the story of Jesus' conflict with Israel.[32] This perspective on the Jesus story lends greater weight to the confrontation with Israel both in history and in the present time of the Matthean community. Although Matthew would probably have defined his community as the core of the Israel God intended, in other words as the "true Israel," he is already using a new term for it: "my [that is, Jesus'] church" (16:18). He feels keenly the pain of the persecutions and discrimination of which he accuses the Jewish leaders, because they have resulted in separation from Judaism. His own community defines itself at least in part from the same traditions as

28. Cf. Werner Bergmann, "Group Theory and Ethnic Relations," in: Bergmann, *Error* op. cit. (see note 27), pp. 155f., with reference to Bruno Bettelheim, and Morris Janowitz, *Social Change and Prejudice* (New York: Macmillan, 1964), pp. 29-34.

29. Douglas Hare, *The Theme of Jewish Persecution of Christians in the Gospel according to St Matthew*, SNTSMon 6 (Cambridge: Cambridge University, 1967), pp. 19-79.

30. 5:11-12; prophets; 23:34: prophets, sages and scribes; 10:16-23: disciples who give the μαρτύριον; cf. 10:32-33.

31. Eduard Schweizer, "Christus und Gemeinde im Matthäusevangelium," in: Schweizer, *Matthäus und seine Gemeinde*, SBS 71 (Stuttgart: Katholisches Bibelwerk, 1974), pp. 9-68, here: p. 11.

32. My view of the relation between Matthew and Judaism is especially indebted to Schweizer, *Gemeinde* (see note 31), pp. 9-13; and Stanton, *Gospel* (see note 25), pp. 113-168.

other Jewish groups, that is, from the law and the prophets. It defines itself in part as identical with other Jewish groups in that it is the twelve-tribe people of Israel represented by the twelve disciples, as קהל (congregation), the assembled people of God. There was no contradiction for them between Jesus and the inheritance of Israel. And yet conflict *did* occur, forcing the community to define itself from Jesus, the law and the prophets, *against* others who disputed their right to do so.

3.3. *"Sibling Conflict"*

The conflict in the Matthean community is generally portrayed as conflict with Judaism as the mother religion. This makes the Matthean community the rebellious daughter and Pharisaic-Rabbinic Judaism the mother. Andrew Overman has suggested, I think more convincingly, an understanding of the Judaism of the time as transitional between "sectarian" and "normative" Judaism.[33] At the time of Jesus, Judaism is indeed largely "sectarian," characterized by rival sects isolating themselves from each other and defining themselves as the visible remnant or core of Israel. Among such sects were the Essenes, the Pharisees, the Sadducees as representatives of the priest class, the Zealots as a religious and political elite, and various quietist-pietist apocalyptic groups.[34] From Maccabean times at least, the religious history of Judaism was a history of competing sectarian self-definitions. It is a history replete with intra-Jewish polemics. Among these numerous sects, Jewish Christianity was one of those which attempted to represent the true Israel.[35]

According to Andrew Overman, strongly influenced here by Jacob Neusner, the development from the first to the second century is, approximately, one of sectarian to normative Judaism.[36] He sees normative Judaism in the second century and thereafter as determined chiefly by the rabbis and indirectly by the Pharisees. As I see it, there were in the period before A.D. 70 two groups — apart from the Zealots — among the Jewish sects which had

---

33. J. Andrew Overman, *Matthew's Gospel and Formative Judaism. The Social World of the Matthean Community* (Minneapolis: Fortress, 1990), partic. pp. 6-34.

34. Cf. the important essay by Joseph Blenkinsopp, "Interpretation and the Tendency to Sectarianism: An Aspect of the Second Temple History," in: E. P. Sanders (ed.), *Jewish and Christian Self-Definition*, Vol. 2 (London: SCM, 1981), pp. 1-27.

35. "Sect" is not defined as a minority distinguishing itself from a majority. At that time there was no "majority Judaism," apart from the ʿammê ha-ʾareṣ, which was defined but did not define itself.

36. Overman (see note 33), pp. 35-71.

the means and the will to form majorities: the Pharisees and the Jesus movement. The Pharisees did not isolate themselves from the people but attempted to adapt the Torah to life. This brought them close to the practical problems of everyday life. An important aspect of the Jesus movement is that Jesus himself is in a sense a religious spokesman for the *ʿammê ha-ʾareṣ*, the non-sectarian ordinary "people of the land." His preaching too was firmly anchored in everyday life, and his messengers sought to call the whole people of Israel to God. This proximity between Pharisees and Jesus adherents is the reason why the conflict between them was especially sharp. Both tried to define themselves as Israel, though in very different ways. The Pharisees won the fight in the end and the Jewish Christians lost.[37] The Pharisees — or their Rabbinic successors — did indeed succeed in defining Israel from themselves, while Jesus' followers could only define themselves as Israel.

So I submit that the conflict between Matthew and Judaism should not be defined only as a mother-daughter conflict but also as one between rival siblings. It is a harsh conflict. We are familiar with the judgment passed by New Testament writers such as Matthew and John on their fellow Jews who did not believe in Jesus. Corresponding Jewish judgments on Jewish Christians are virtually unknown. Since the end of the first century the synagogues had had the cursing of the "minim," i.e. the dissenters, in the *Shemoneh ʿEsreh*, their daily prayer. This meant that Jewish Christians could no longer participate in the synagogue service, whereas Gentile Christians were of course always able to go to the synagogue.[38] Only Jewish Christians were among the minim. But it is understandable that the subordinated minority, i.e. the Jewish Christians, now defined themselves as quite distinct from the majority.[39] They defined themselves in the name of Jesus as the true inheritors of the law and the prophets, which obliged them to state explicitly who were *not* the true inheritors. In this way anti-Judaism became part of Christian self-definition. Majority Judaism, developing sociologically into "church," did not require the defeated Jewish Christians for its self-definition.

---

37. On the basis of the New Testament I consider the part played by the Pharisees in normative Judaism much greater than Jacob Neusner suggests.

38. Laurence H. Shiffman, *Who Was a Jew?* (Hoboken: Ktav, 1985), pp. 64ff.; cf. partic. *Tosepta Ḥullin* 2. Important is Reuven Kimelman, "Birkat-Ha-Minim and the Lack of Evidence for an Anti-Christian Jewish Prayer in Late Antiquity," in: Sanders (see note 34), pp. 226-244, partic. pp. 228-232. It is clear that the expression "minim" cannot refer to Christians in general but only to heterodox Jews and thus to Jewish Christians (p. 244).

39. Cf. on this Henri Tajfel, *Human Groups and Social Categories. Studies in Social Psychology* (Cambridge: Cambridge University, 1981), pp. 309-312; Bergmann, "Group Theory" (see note 28), p. 144: self-definitions of majority and minority are interdependent.

As a rule, a majority does not define itself by demarcation vis-à-vis a minority. This is why the Rabbinic sources are so conspicuously silent on the subject of Jewish Christians.[40] The latter however needed "anti-Judaism" as part of their self-definition. When the risen Lord sent them to the Gentiles, they took with them this explicitly anti-Jewish identity. And when in turn Christianity became "church," a Gentile church in fact, anti-Judaism became part of its canonical tradition.

3.4. Prejudices

The Matthean judgments on scribes and Pharisees in ch. 23 bear little or no relation to reality. The judgments function in the community as ethical definitions of what, according to Jesus, one should not be.[41] They are prejudices against Jews, and as such they have an important function for the identity of the community. As a minority, the Jewish Christians had to set themselves off from the majority, and this in turn strengthened their own cohesion. Conflict always results in "increased internal cohesion."[42] As well as being a weapon,[43] prejudices protect the subordinated group "from fear and self-criticism, protect its sense of self-worth and make it possible to release aggression in a socially approved form."[44] If a group can demarcate itself vis-à-vis a different group, and knows that it is better than the other (Matt. 5:20!), its stability and self-worth are enhanced. Prejudices are negative patterns which provide simple cognitive orientation in a complex situation. This is exactly what the Matthean communities needed in a situation characterized by transition, reorientation and homelessness. They needed their anti-Jewish prejudices on their difficult journey to the Gentiles. And so it remained, *mutatis mutandis,* for a long period.

---

40. Turks do not define themselves as non-Kurds, Romanians not as non-Hungarians, etc. Rather, the majority tends to negate the existence of the minority by not mentioning it.

41. David E. Garland, *The Intention of Matthew 23*, NTSup 52 (Leiden: Brill, 1979), partic. pp. 117-124, 214f., has drawn attention to the parenetic function of Matt. 23.

42. Coser (see note 25), p. 95; cf. p. 87. Similarly, research into antisemitism has established a clear connection between ethnocentrism (i.e. a strong sense of cohesion among the majority) and antisemitism (Nancy C. Morse and Floyd H. Allport, "The Causation of Antisemitism: An Investigation of Seven Hypotheses," in: Bergmann, *Error* [see note 27], pp. 186-224, here: pp. 195f., 206f., 209-211).

43. Bergmann, "Group Theory" (see note 28), p. 143.

44. Ulrike Six, "Vorurteile," in: Dieter Frey/Siegfried Greif, *Sozialpsychologie. Ein Handbuch in Schlüsselbegriffen* (Munich/Weinheim: Psychologie Verlags Union, ²1987), p. 366.

3.5. A Post-Decision Conflict

The Matthean community left the synagogues. Its members had to decide between their Jewish brothers and sisters, fathers and mothers, their old fields and houses, and the Jesus community (19:29). They had to decide between their faith and loyalty to the new community and loyalty to the majority of their people. "After decisions there is dissonance."[45] Many will have found the decision a difficult one, and especially in the wake of a difficult and painful decision there will be a need to reduce dissonance. The alternative which has been rejected, i.e. Pharisee-dominated majority Judaism, is subsequently presented negatively. The Pharisees are portrayed as bad leaders of Israel who proclaim the will of God but do not do it (23:2-3). They are hypocrites who cannot be trusted. The killing of Jesus means the people have lost the βασιλεία (kingdom), which can now pass to the community (21:43).

4. Attempts to Exonerate Matthew

The debate on anti-Judaism in the New Testament in exegesis and theology has seen various attempts at exoneration of the Gospel of Matthew.

4.1. The sufferings of the Matthean community may serve to exonerate Matthew. He and his community have been ill-treated and need to work through a genuine trauma.

Comment: This can hardly be contradicted. It is always precarious to pass judgment on sufferers. But I would not want to overstate this point. In spite of Gal. 4:29 and 1 Thess. 2:14, persecution of Christians by Jews was not the normal situation. I think it plausible that the situation of the Jewish War increased the negative experiences in the communities, but even someone affected like Matthew must have recognized that the scribes and Pharisees were not responsible for this. *Part* of their function in Matt. 23 and other texts is that of the scapegoat.

4.2. Many exegetes point to the parenetic meaning of the anti-Jewish passages in Matthew. Israel is presented as the negative example for the Christian community that has to face God's judgment as well.

Comment: This is partly true for the discourse against the Pharisees in ch. 23. Not only does it serve, in terms of salvation history, to pronounce God's judgment on Israel and its leaders, the scribes and Pharisees, but at the

---

45. Werner Herkner, *Eine Einführung in die Sozialpsychologie* (Bern: Hans Huber, 1975), p. 91.

same time the community is warned by seeing them as a negative example.[46] In sociological terms, the Matthean community is not a "sect" in that it functions as a "selector" distinguishing between "the qualified and the unqualified."[47] Neither is it a pure community resulting from struggle and demarcation, practicing constant "self-purification" and thus constantly producing "heresy and schisms."[48] The community is *corpus permixtum*, a "mixed body" and in its *entirety* under the protection of Jesus as well as under the judgment parenesis. So far, so good. But I do not see how this exonerates Matthew from the accusation of lack of love and injustice, both of which run counter to the baseline of Jesus' preaching.

4.3. For Matthew the end of the world was near. This is especially important for the interpretation of Matt. 27:25 ("his blood be on us and on our children!"). Matthew did not envisage a historical "curse" being perpetuated down the centuries. Neither should the self-cursing of 27:25 be read as the condemnation of Israel at the Last Judgment. The verse points back to 23:36, where the words "all this will come upon this generation" most probably allude to the destruction of Jerusalem (cf. 23:38!).

Comment: Just as it is difficult to read into 23:39 the idea of Rom. 11:26 that all Israel will be saved, so it is impossible in my view to think in 27:25 of the blood of Jesus benefiting humankind in Holy Communion.[49] Matt. 27:25 confirms the hypothesis that Matthew sees disaster descending on Israel, namely the destruction of Jerusalem and the temple. Naturally, Matthew did not want to curse Israel for centuries. But he did interpret the destruction of Jerusalem as God's punishment for the rejection of Jesus. There is no hint at a positive future for Israel beyond this.

4.4. Matthew's confrontation with Judaism should be compared with contemporaneous conflicts within Jewish groups. Often these were anything but slight. Matthew's basic question is that of sectarian Judaism: What is the true Israel? Who represents it? Matthew is a Jew struggling with other Jews within the Jewish family.[50] He cannot be made responsible for the fact that over centuries his text was used by one religion to disqualify and reject another.

---

46. Cf. note 41.

47. Weber (see note 26), pp. 1204-1205.

48. Coser (see note 25), p. 101.

49. Schweizer, *Matthew* (see note 11), p. 509, considers whether in 27:25 Matthew has in mind the blood of Jesus which benefits humankind. However, in tradition history the association with biblical texts on bloodguilt is so strong that overtones of an entirely different idea like that of the Lord's Supper are unlikely.

50. Citing an oral comment by Rabbi Marcel Marcus (Bern): "In a family conflict, many things are permitted and possible which would be unacceptable in a conflict between strangers."

Comment: A differentiated view should be taken of this attempt at exoneration. There are indeed remarkable intra-Jewish parallels with Matthew's anti-Judaism. These are primarily Qumran texts (e.g., CDC 1:12-21; 1QH 4:5-22) but there are others too (e.g., *Assumption of Moses* 7–8; *Psalms of Solomon* 8).[51] What makes the Qumran texts especially interesting in this respect is that they too deal with experiences of suffering and persecution, the wrong inflicted on a founder figure and a perspective of eschatological judgment. But there are crucial differences between these texts and the Gospel of Matthew. In Matthew the exalted Lord commands his followers to go no longer to Israel but to the Gentiles. Above all, Matthew formulates his own anti-Jewish words in the name of the exalted Lord Jesus. Matthew sees Jesus, the Son of Man and Judge of the World, as an absolute authority. The fact that this Jesus has formulated them gives the harsh judgments against Israel more weight than parallel Jewish texts. Matthew works through his conflict with Israel in the name of Jesus the exalted Son of Man. This renders his anti-Judaism more fundamental and far-reaching than the sectarian Jewish polemics in which it is rooted. Matthew's christology actually heightens the impact of his anti-Judaisms.

4.5. Matthew is not responsible for the fact that his book has made anti-Judaism canonical.

Comment: Matthean anti-Judaism was important for the self-definition of a community in crisis and transition. When the church canonized his Gospel it made this self-definition, specific as it was to a particular situation, a permanent feature of Christianity. Anti-Judaism later became a basic feature of Christianity, quite independent of specific historical situations. The light of Christianity was contrasted time and again with the dark shadow of Judaism. As a result, Jewish people were time and again the victims of this shadow, powerless to act against it because it existed on the dogmatic level, independent of their own existence. Obviously Matthew is not responsible for this development.

5. Theological Considerations: Matthean Anti-Judaism and Jesus

Matthean anti-Judaism did not come out of nothing. Matthew's roots are in traditions and received patterns of thought which lead him to place strong emphasis on the rejection of Jesus by most Jews. There are the Sayings Source

---

51. Ingo Broer, "Antijudaismus im Neuen Testament?," in: Oberlinner/Fiedler (see note 16), pp. 347-349, points also to *Psalms of Solomon* 4; Sirach 50; *Epistle of Aristeas* 152.

and the Gospel of Mark, and there is Jesus himself. Matthew himself states which traditions he regards as crucial. The standard for the behavior of his community, including their attitude to Judaism, is what Jesus who accompanies the community has commanded (28:20). Thus most of Matthew's anti-Judaisms are part of his Jesus tradition. He sets a standard by which his theology is to be measured.

We are left with a strange contradiction. On the one hand it is undeniable that essential elements of Jesus' preaching are blurred in Matthew's Gospel, in particular the message of God's infinite love towards all who need it, especially those on Israel's religious and social margins. It is Israel to whom Jesus brings this message. Or there is Jesus' command to love one's enemies. Might this not be extended to the scribes and Pharisees? This command seems to have lost its force towards the end of Matthew's Gospel and with respect to Jews who did not believe in Jesus. On the other hand, Matthean anti-Judaism has its roots in Jesus' own proclamation. It is Jesus who knows from John the Baptist that God can raise up children for Abraham from stones (3:9). It is Jesus who warns unrepentant Israel that Gentiles will sit in their place and eat with Abraham (8:11-12). It is Jesus who in his antitheses (5:21-22, 27-28) goes far beyond Jewish claims to pitch his own authority against the word of God given in the Decalogue. He uses a familiar Jewish image but shocks most Jewish listeners when he says of himself what other Jews say of Torah: Everyone who hears *these words of mine* and does not act on them has built their house on sand (7:26-27).[52] Jesus says too that acknowledging him will be crucial for being acknowledged by the son of man in God's judgment (Luke 12:8-9). When Matthew says in his Gospel that Israel's rejection of Jesus *has* determined Israel's position in the coming judgment of the son of man, and when he seems to proclaim as definitive this judgment on Israel by Jesus, the coming eschatological judge, he is in fact close to Jesus himself. The only difference is that Jesus, however sharp his words concerning Israel, probably still offered the opportunity of repentance. It is only at this point that Matthew, after Jesus' Passion and the experiences of his own community in Israel which replicated the Passion, has taken a step beyond Jesus.

However, it is the Jesus tradition which has enabled Matthew to take this step. Critical assessment of theological anti-Judaism is actually concerned with the core of the Christian faith. Emphasizing the distance between the New Testament and its anti-Jewish impacts in later epochs is quite inadequate, since there are key anti-Judaisms in the New Testament itself. Equally,

---

52. It is no coincidence that in Jewish texts the image is used for study and practice of Torah and not to refer to an individual teacher; cf. Luz (see note 24), p. 452, note 6.

it will not do to put marginal passages of the New Testament aside and point to its christological center,[53] since christology itself has an anti-Jewish reverse side. When Jesus takes on absolute authority as Christ, the problem is apparent. Our questions take us to Jesus himself, from whom early Christian christology originates. What is the relation between his message of God's infinite love and his message of judgment? Is it acceptable that, as God's messenger who loves infinitely in God's name, Jesus should make such a huge claim for himself? Does not this claim violate people in the end, because if they refuse absolute love they are threatened with absolute judgment? Is the root of the problem to be found in the fact that Jesus made absolute claims for himself?

53. Lloyd Gaston, "The Messiah of Israel as Teacher of the Gentiles," *Interpretation* 29 (1975), pp. 24-40; here: p. 40.

HERMENEUTICS WITH
MATTHEW IN MIND

13 Reflections on the Appropriate Interpretation of New Testament Texts

Dedicated to Peter Stuhlmacher
on the occasion of his fiftieth birthday

Today we look back on a time when the necessity of exegesis has repeatedly been called into question. Some students have gone so far as to boycott exegesis, deeming it unimportant for the practice of ministry. It has also been questioned on a theoretical level. I have in front of me, for instance, a recent essay in which exegesis as an "informative discipline" is considered just good enough to assist in "dismantling authoritative Christian norms derived from biblical traditions and considered unquestionable."[1] On the other hand, the last few years have witnessed a revival of exegesis. This is not without its problems, especially since it is church leaders who tend to call up and advocate the revival. Exegesis shares its ups and downs with history as a discipline. After 1968, German education departments were seriously considering the removal of "history" from the secondary school curriculum. This had its impact. But in 1977 Hermann Lübbe declared the results of the discussions to be "a rehabilitation of scientific historicism."[2] Is the recent revival of historicism however only compensatory, running parallel to the rises and falls in the market for antiques, or does it represent real progress? All of this is reason enough for an exegete to reflect on the tasks of his discipline and the solutions he can offer.

1. Gerd Petzke, *Exegese und Praxis*, ThPr 10 (1975), pp. 2-19, here: p. 19.
2. Hermann Lübbe, *Geschichtsbegriff und Geschichtsinteresse* (Basel: Schwabe, 1977), p. 9.

German original: "Erwägungen zur sachgemässen Interpretation neutestamentlicher Texte," *EvTh* 42 (1982), pp. 493-517. The last section of this paper (pp. 286-289) contains a couple of theses that follow the outline of the paper and summarize its lines of thought.

1. The Problem

The basic problem seems to me to lie in the experience of many theologians that their intense preoccupation with the original sense of a text, deriving from historical-critical interpretation, actually makes it difficult or even impossible to answer the question of its present-day meaning. On the one hand, the historical-critical method, understood as an open scientific tool, has proved and established itself in scholarship. This is exemplified in the visible and widespread absorption and integration of a fundamentally ahistorical "structural exegesis" in the historical approach to the understanding and interpretation of texts.[3] On the other hand many people, including our students and a large number of clergy, find that historical-critical interpretation leaves them stranded in the past, with no methodological path into the present. Hence the widespread feeling (which in my opinion should be taken very seriously) that historical-critical exegesis has nothing to offer to church practice, ministry, or society.[4] The question of the truth of a text for the present and the question of the original sense of the text in the past appear to be completely distinct.

1.1. The basic problem is visible at various points. One example is the striking contrast today between scholarly exegesis with its high degree of specialization (already too demanding for many students of theology) and "lay exegesis" which is completely untouched by scholarship and for this very reason deeply fascinating to students of theology. This is illustrated by the impact of Ernesto Cardenal's *Gospel of Solentiname* among European students of theology.[5] This simple Bible study, almost untouched by scholarly exegesis,[6] holds an incredible fascination for many of our students, who in the face of today's advanced exegetical specialization are no longer able to develop

---

3. The problem of the relation between essentially ahistorical structuralism and the biblical texts which speak of a unique history was clearly recognized by Paul Ricoeur; cf., e.g., "Structure and Hermeneutics," in: Ricoeur, *The Conflict of Interpretations,* ed. Don Ihde (Evanston: Northwestern University, 1974), pp. 27-61, partic. pp. 44-54.

4. Jürgen Moltmann formulates succinctly the correspondence of the process of "objectification" of the historical "facts" and their evaluation, which is increasingly at the discretion of the subject. "To the extent to which it (that is, historical consciousness) establishes that Paul was a child of his time addressing his contemporaries, the present becomes free of what he has to say" ("Verkündigung als Problem der Exegese," in: *Perspektiven der Theologie* [Munich: Kaiser, 1968], pp. 113-127, here: p. 115).

5. Ernesto Cardenal, *El evangelio en Solentiname* (Salamanca: Sigueme, 1976-1978).

6. Typically, the theologian Cardenal does not attempt in the Solentiname Bible studies to bring the original sense of the texts critically into play with the "symbolic" interpretations of the peasants which relate the texts to their own life and situation.

genuine exegetical competence and who at the same time are stranded in historical criticism. The most striking element of such lay exegesis is its freedom toward the biblical text, allowing for direct confrontation between one's own experience and the text and for interpretation of the text symbolically in the light of one's experience.[7] I am not thinking here primarily of fundamentalist lay exegesis, which is not so much lay exegesis as a theological assault on lay exegesis. What I find fascinating and exciting about lay exegesis is its freedom from the meticulous adherence to the original sense of the text that characterizes scholarly exegesis.

1.2. Another point at which the basic problem becomes visible is the current contrast between exegetical and homiletic interpretation of the Bible.[8] Today's situation is apparent if we compare exegesis and sermon in the early church and up to the time of Reformation and Protestant orthodoxy. Before the Enlightenment, exegetical and homiletic interpretation were closely related. This is exemplified by the influence of John Chrysostom's homilies on the scholarly Bible commentaries of the Middle Ages, or the relation between Luther's lectures and sermons. Since the Enlightenment, however, scholarly and homiletic interpretations have gone separate ways, to the point that reference to the text is largely abandoned in preaching, both in homiletic theory[9] (at times) and in the practice of preaching (very frequently). Scholarly exegesis is concerned with the question of what people, whether authors or communities, considered true and life-determining at the time when the New Testament was emerging. Historical-critical exegesis is not competent to say whether this truth of a past age can claim to be truth today.

1.3. A further symptom of the great distance between the question of the past and the question of truth is, as I see it, the disparity between historical research, including historical-critical exegesis, and the philosophical concept of history and hermeneutical theory.[10] Today's hermeneutical theories, as exem-

---

7. Non-fundamentalist lay exegesis of this kind is well described by Carlos Mesters, "'Listening to What the Spirit Is Saying to the Churches.' Popular Interpretation of the Bible in Brazil," *Concilium* 1980:1, pp. 100-111.

8. Moltmann (see note 4), p. 113, speaks of "diametrically opposed tendencies."

9. An example can be found in considerations by Gert Otto which are neither naive nor unreflected (*Thesen zur Problematik der Predigt in der Gegenwart* [Hamburg: Furche, 1970], pp. 39f.): "The rule that a sermon is an address directly derived from the exegesis of a biblical passage must be recognized as being conditioned by the history of theology. It can no longer be declared original in an unreflected manner. Accountability of the sermon to the biblical text narrows the horizon."

10. History as an academic discipline is confronted with similar problems. Alfred Heuss, *Verlust der Geschichte* (Göttingen: Vandenhoeck und Ruprecht, 1959), distinguishes between "history as reminiscence" and "history as science," the latter constantly destroying the former.

plified by Gadamer, tend increasingly toward a holistic understanding of the past which takes in one's own present and one's own horizon. By contrast, historical-critical exegesis is becoming ever more obsessed with detail and, in our discipline particularly, takes such exaggerated interest in the original sense of letters and strokes of the text that there is little room for any unified understanding of the whole. Historical-critical research is largely uninfluenced by hermeneutical theory, and hermeneutics in turn no longer issues in a methodology for historical-critical work.[11]

The contrast between modern and classical hermeneutics — such as that of Matthias Flaccius Illyricus or Schleiermacher — is apparent. The tension between the concept of history which underlies our historical work and the much more thought-out concept in today's philosophical debate is similarly evident. Hans Weder has rightly pointed out that the "historicist" concept of history, although no longer fully subscribed to by the majority of historians or exegetes, continues de facto to inform historical-critical research.[12] This can be seen above all in the tendency of historical study to objectify facts in the past. The historical-critical understanding of a text isolates its original sense from the present-day exegete as well as from all exegetes of the past by attempting as far as possible to exclude from the process of interpretation the present situation of the exegete and all that has since occurred in history.[13] For this reason the historical-critical reconstruction of the text cannot speak

11. There are exceptions e.g. in the work of Frederik Torm, *Hermeneutik des Neuen Testaments* (Göttingen: Vandenhoeck und Ruprecht, 1930), and in Paul Ricoeur whose work consistently endeavors to bring together the question of truth and the question of method. A further exception is Peter Stuhlmacher's attempt (*Vom Verstehen des Neuen Testaments*, NTD Erg. 6 [Göttingen: Vandenhoeck und Ruprecht, 1979], p. 220) to concretize his hermeneutics of "assent" *(Einverständnis)* in the historical-critical field as a methodological "principle of apprehending" *(Prinzip des Vernehmens)*.

12. Hans Weder, "Zum Problem einer christlichen Exegese," *NTS* 27 (1980), pp. 64-82, here: pp. 66f.

13. At this point the insights offered by Arthur Danto's analytical philosophy of history are helpful, stating that only the future of past events enables them to be historically evaluated. One should also keep in mind however Rudolf Bultmann's recognition that historicism misunderstands present and past because it sees their relationship deterministically as a purely causal one. Rather, what the past *is* is decided in the present when we deal with the past. "Our past has by no means one meaning only. . . . Historicism also misunderstands the future as determined by the past through causality. . . . Historicism . . . overlooks the dangerous character of the present, its character of risk" (*History and Eschatology. The Gifford Lectures* [Edinburgh: University Press, 1957], p. 141). The crucial point as I see it is that the person considering the past "per se" and "objectively" has extracted him- or herself from the context of the influence of the past and dialogue with the past. The apparent objectivity of the past corresponds to apparent human autonomy towards it.

to the present, since today's reader cannot by definition be its addressee. As Gadamer rightly observes: "The text that is understood historically is forced to abandon its claim to be saying something true. We think we understand when we see the past from a historical standpoint — i.e., transpose ourselves into the historical situation and try to reconstruct the historical horizon. In fact, however, we have given up the claim to find in the past any truth that is valid and intelligible for ourselves."[14] For historical-critical exegesis of New Testament texts, for example, the fundamental question of the unity of New Testament testimony is strictly speaking unanswerable, since the canon is a later development than the individual texts and must therefore be excluded from the exegetical process.

1.4. It appears to me that the separation in modern thought between truth and history is one of the most far-reaching intellectual developments, a development whose roots are to be found in the emancipation of reason from history since the Enlightenment. Reason breaks through the shell of history and reaches towards eternal truth. Here I can only call to mind a few examples, starting with Rationalism. According to Spinoza, the divine law results from the observation of human nature by the human being itself; it consists in the idea of God as the supreme Good. Faith in history of whatever kind does not belong to the divine law, but rather has simply the pedagogical value of undergirding the teaching contained in the divine law.[15] As I see it, Lessing's thesis that contingent truths of history can never be proof of necessary truths of reason remains an unsolved problem in exegesis: "If no historical truth can be demonstrated, it follows that nothing can be demonstrated by means of historical truth."[16] Kant, for his part, makes the Bible, and with it exegesis, a crucial pillar in the structure of church dogma. He considers sacred writings to be works of authority for the spiritually immature and sees it as especially fortunate when the book of a religion holds "the purest moral doctrine of religion in its completeness."[17] The rationalistic devaluation of history, however, continues to be influential beyond the Age of Reason. I draw attention to Schleiermacher's words: "The true historical sense rises beyond history. All phenomena exist just as the sacred miracles for the purpose of di-

14. Hans-Georg Gadamer, *Truth and Method* (2nd rev. ed.; New York: Crossroad, 1989), p. 303.

15. Baruch Spinoza, "Theologico-Political Treatise," in: *The Chief Works of Benedict de Spinoza*, Vol. I (tr. by R. H. M. Elwes; New York: Dover, 1951), chs. 4 and 5.

16. Gotthold Ephraim Lessing, "Über den Beweis des Geistes und der Kraft. An den Herrn Director Schumann zu Hannover," in: *Werke* ,Vol. 8 (Munich: Hanser, 1979), pp. 11f.

17. Immanuel Kant, *Religion Within the Limits of Reason Alone* (trans. Theodore M. Greene/Hoyt H. Hudson, New York/London: Harper and Row, 1960), p. 98.

recting our attention to the Spirit which brought them forth with ease."[18] Finally, we hear the voice of the existential philosopher Karl Jaspers, who seeks to "arrive at a point before and above all history, a ground of being in the light of which the whole of history is phenomenon." He seeks the path toward this point in, inter alia, transcendence of the historicity of existence.[19] The same basic problem applies to an existential philosophy which understands existence in history ontologically as "the 'recurrence' of the possible" and in this way not only allows for possibilities within historical existence but also excludes impossibilities.[20]

2. Hermeneutical Goals

In this section I consider the basic elements necessary for understanding the "matter"[21] of biblical texts. To this end, I inquire of the biblical texts themselves what their understanding of understanding is and what kind of understanding their message requires. My basic presupposition is that a theological contribution to hermeneutical debate must begin with the basic biblical texts of theology and bring them into the debate. My approach, however, does not contain the hidden agenda of a special "sacred hermeneutic." Rather, I wish to draw, first, on the linguistic insight that different text types, that is, genres, communicate with the recipients in very different ways and need to be understood in different ways. The conditions for understanding vary greatly with the different literary documents, and are different again for nonliterary material.

Second, we have frequently found in the history of modern exegesis that no concept of a general hermeneutic applied to the biblical texts from outside

18. Wilhelm Dilthey, *Das Leben Schleiermachers* (Berlin: Reimer, 1870), Anhang, p. 117.

19. Karl Jaspers, *The Origin and Goal of History* (trans. Michael Bullock; London: Routledge, 1953), ch. III/5.

20. As I see it, Heidegger before the "shift" can be interpreted in this way, if he is not understood from the beginning in the light of his later philosophy. It is especially Bultmann's reception of Heidegger which seems to me to point in this direction. The citation is from *Being and Time* (trans. by John Macquarrie and Edward Robinson, Oxford: Basil Blackwell, 1962), p. 444.

21. Basic to what I have to say here is Karl Barth's distinction between "document" and "matter" in the preface to his *The Epistle to the Romans* (Oxford: Oxford University, 1933), p. 8: "Intelligent comment means that I am driven on till I stand with nothing before me but the enigma of the matter; till the document seems hardly to exist as a document; till I have almost forgotten that I am not its author; till I know the author so well that I allow him to speak in my name and am even able to speak in his name myself."

can ever fully do justice to them. This is exemplified by the criticism of Bultmann's "anthropocentric" existential interpretation. The theological questions asked of Bultmann's concept in countless variations all center on whether he succeeds in actually declaring the transcendental nature of his subject, namely *God's* action in history transcending the human being. A further example of the limitations of applying general hermeneutical concepts to biblical texts is the debate on the scope of structural approaches to the New Testament texts. It is increasingly doubted whether structural analysis, which treats the text as a semantic structure and examines the differentiations within this structure, can take seriously the reference beyond the text. The reference in biblical texts is primary: they signify something or someone; they proclaim something; they are not autonomous entities, but point to a history which lies beyond them and in which God acts.[22] Biblical texts speak of something very special, indeed unique. They speak of how God acts in the life and death of Jesus of Nazareth, and this makes them special texts in form and structure, calling for a particular and appropriate understanding.

Third, it must be kept in mind that no hermeneutical concept is completely neutral and not indebted to specific historical experience. We theologians do well to remember this, since we continue to appeal programmatically to our tradition. When considering the process of understanding, we shall need to take seriously and listen to our own specific form of tradition, i.e. the biblical texts.[23] Beginning the question of how to understand biblical texts by turning to the texts themselves is, then, not simply the product of current intellectual unease. Here I deliberately leave open the question of how far our reflections might be generalized beyond the understanding of biblical texts.

2.1. The first element which I consider basic to an understanding of biblical texts which speak of God is *the holistic nature of the process of understanding.* Biblical texts are "as it were, crystallized spiritual life" (and not

---

22. Ricoeur (see note 3), pp. 45-47.

23. My approach is related in its intention to Ernst Fuchs, who introduces into Bultmann's general concept of existential interpretation the idea of Jesus as "our help" in understanding the text. "If everything is not to go round in circles, the texts themselves will have to tell us who can help us" ("Was ist existentiale Interpretation B?" in: Fuchs, *Zum hermeneutischen Problem in der Theologie* (Tübingen: Mohr Siebeck, 1959), pp. 91-106, here: p. 97. I am also obliged to Peter Stuhlmacher, whose hermeneutics of assent seeks to take "the Bible as the book of education and the book of life for the Church" (see note 11, p. 206) seriously. I do believe however that it is not only the interpretation of individual texts but the overall horizon of understanding which must assent to the biblical texts. That is what I am endeavoring here.

only spiritual!).[24] Their message aims at an understanding which takes hold of the whole person and finds direct expression in that person's life.[25] Understanding is an event which involves the whole person.[26] This is why Jesus' parables, for instance, are not understood when only their teaching is understood. This may be sufficient for rabbinic parables, but not for the parables of Jesus. They are stories which seek to take hold of the listener's life and transform it. I have not understood the story of the laborers in the vineyard (Matt. 20:1-16) if I only *know* that God does not reward according to what is earned. Only when I am *glad* about that have I understood. Luke's composition of the parable of the great dinner makes abundantly clear that I have not understood if I can only formulate the point of the story correctly. Only when I put the story into practice in my own life have I understood it, for example when I am invited as a guest and have the choice between different places at the table (Luke 14:7-14). An especially emphatic example of what is meant by understanding in the New Testament can be found in the Gospel of Mark. Peter, who rebukes Jesus (Mark 8:32), knows perfectly well what Jesus means when he speaks of the Son of Man who must undergo great suffering, be rejected by the Jewish leaders and be killed. Nevertheless, he protests; and directly following this scene Mark condenses his theologoumenon of the disciples' lack of understanding very precisely. He makes it clear that one can "understand" Jesus only if one is ready to follow him on his road to the cross. One cannot understand Jesus in the way Peter did, but only in the way Simon of Cyrene did.[27] To give a further example: "Present your bodies as a living sacrifice, holy and acceptable to God, which is your spiritual worship. Do not be conformed to this world, but be transformed by the renewing of your minds, so that you may discern what is the will of God — what is

24. Alfred Schindler, "Vor- und Nachteil der Kirchengeschichte für das Verständnis der Bibel heute," *Reformatio* 30 (1981), pp. 261-277, here: p. 264.

25. It is thus correct, though too restrictive, to say of the hermeneutics of biblical texts: "In the field of theology, hermeneutics is the theological function which makes the texts . . . sermons" (Eberhard Jüngel, "Was hat der Text mit der Predigt zu tun?" in: *Predigten* [Munich: Kaiser, 1968], pp. 126-143, here: p. 140). This statement is too restrictive because in my opinion one could also say, instead of "sermon," "prayer" or "way of life" or "thanks," etc.

26. One can hardly emphasize enough the interpretation of understanding as "event," elaborated particularly by Ernst Fuchs, e.g., in the following succinct words: "Text and reader come together in understanding in such a way that the understanding itself becomes an event and participates in a history of which both text and reader are part" (see note 23, p. 93).

27. The associations between Mark 15:21 and Mark 8:34 were undoubtedly intended by the Evangelist, particularly as the sons of Simon will probably have been known to the Markan community as Christians. Cf. Joachim Gnilka, *Das Evangelium nach Markus* II, EKK II.2 (Neukirchen: Neukirchener, 1979), p. 315.

good and acceptable and perfect" (Rom. 12:1-2). The interrelation between knowledge and life could not be expressed more succinctly. Understanding the matter of the New Testament is thus tied in with life itself, and the understanding intended by the New Testament texts is ultimately inseparable from faith. This means that there is no such thing as a "sense" of the biblical texts in and of itself, separable from life.[28] This is in accordance with Hans-Georg Gadamer's recognition of application as "an integral element of all understanding" and not merely as an appendage to understanding. Gadamer draws consciously on the theological hermeneutics of the pietist Johann Jakob Rambach.[29] The various levels of textual interpretation can thus be terminologically distinguished as follows: (1) historical-critical exegesis of the original sense of the text; (2) interpretation of the matter of the text with reference to the present-day context of my thinking, my language and my situation; (3) realization of the matter of the text through suffering or through action. These levels of interpretation belong together, but it is clear that the understanding of biblical texts comes to completion and reaches its objective only on the third level.[30] If historical-critical exegesis is to contribute to understanding the matter of biblical texts, it is necessarily dependent

28. Here the term "sense" is used for the textual level of a text and the term "meaning" for the "matter" expressed in the text.

29. Gadamer (see note 14), p. 308. José Míguez-Bonino, *Doing Theology in a Revolutionary Situation* (Philadelphia: Fortress, 1975), p. 88, analyzes the prevalence of an abstract and supra-historical "truth" over against its secondary "application" in history in Western theology and exegesis as follows: "Truth is therefore pre-existent to and independent of its historical effectiveness. Its legitimacy has to be tested in relation to this abstract 'heaven of truth.' . . ."

30. The classical distinction by Wilhelm Dilthey between explaining and understanding remains noteworthy in my opinion. Ernst Fuchs' significant rendering of it is as follows: "Explaining is . . . different from understanding, although the two cannot easily be distinguished. Explaining chooses the object or the process that is to be explained. . . . Understanding on the other hand lives with the things themselves. . . . Explaining isolates, analyses and objectifies. This can have fatal consequences for the living object. Understanding relates from the outset to the situation in which something appears as it does." Thus understanding, unlike explaining, is based on the given relationship between the matter of the text and the listener. Fuchs terms this relationship "pre-understanding" (which is more than mere possibly erroneous or half-baked "foreknowledge" of something) and says: "Full understanding draws on and refines pre-understanding, thus making *us* move and perhaps even bringing us to rest." Explaining and understanding are however closely related, and the one does not exclude the other: "An explanation seeks to awaken appreciation and therefore presupposes possible understanding." Understanding can "more easily 'explain'" things because it is affected by them. Not only what is explicable can be understood. Rather, "all that is explicable (is) in the realm of understanding" (citations from *Marburger Hermeneutik* [Tübingen: Mohr-Siebeck, 1968], pp. 18f.).

on the other levels of interpretation and remains embedded as one element of the wider hermeneutical horizon.

2.1.1. This has consequences in the historical-critical quest for the original sense of the texts. As I see it, historical-critical interpretation of biblical texts must not remain on the textual level when enquiring into their sense. Rather, it must probe behind the texts to enquire into the history and life that is crystallized in them. Historical-critical exegesis must penetrate the structure of the texts to reach their historical life. Only then is it moving towards the matter of the texts. Historical-critical exegesis of a biblical text, then, means enquiry into the experiences which underlie the text. It means explaining how the text came about, what it intended and what it gave rise to.[31] Here I can refer to a well-worded formulation of Hans Weder, who sees narrative as the appropriate form of exegesis for most biblical texts: "The task of exegesis is to explain in narrative form the coming into being of a text" (and in my opinion its effects also), "taking account of its reference." Weder continues: "One could perhaps say that the truth of the text comes to light in such an explanation."[32]

2.2. The second basic element for the understanding of biblical texts is closely connected with the first. It is *the direct and necessary reference of the texts to the history* to which they bear witness and in which they originate. In the words of Christian Link: "Biblical texts are not such that they require an 'explanation.' In order to understand them, one has to enter their world, so to speak, and study the 'treatment' of the reality that has given rise to their statements."[33] It is events and experiences which have compelled the biblical authors to speak and write, and concerning these events and experiences the texts need to be interrogated and listened to. Attempting a more precise definition of the experiences, we can say that the New Testament deals with human experience with the history of Jesus Christ, a history which is not dead but living and active in experiences. In the New Testament texts, then, we encounter "history" in two ways. There is on the one hand the basic history of Jesus Christ, a unique event in the past. Because this history continues to "be effective" and attract people afresh, there are on the other hand the effects of

31. In this connection I find Wilhelm Dilthey's idea of understanding as "re-shaping, re-experiencing" (*Gesammelte Schriften VII* [Göttingen: Vandenhoeck und Ruprecht, 1958], pp. 213ff.) productive, although it must not be restricted to re-experiencing the genesis of the work in the author.

32. Hans Weder, *Das Kreuz Jesu bei Paulus*, FRLANT 125 (Göttingen: Vandenhoeck und Ruprecht, 1981), p. 250.

33. Christian Link, "In welchem Sinn sind theologische Aussagen wahr?" *EvTh* 42 (1982), pp. 518-540, here: p. 526.

Jesus Christ's history, which is history in its own right, for example Jesus' effect in the experience, thinking and mission of Paul. Thus the New Testament texts represent segments of the early "effective history" of Jesus. Understanding the texts means taking note of the experiences they originate in, comprehending the reality they reflect, and listening to the fundamental history to which they refer. One way or the other, understanding biblical texts means dealing with history. In contrast to the widespread current idea that the historical is, in the end, relative and therefore secondary, we must say that for biblical texts the history to which they refer and which they reflect is primary.[34]

2.2.1. This has a further consequence for historical-critical exegesis which I shall treat only briefly here. The now almost undisputed thesis that in exegesis synchronic analysis of the text must take precedence over diachronic analysis should, in my opinion, be critically reexamined. To the extent that we are dealing with *texts* which transmit history, this postulate is as correct as it is banal. The texts are to be analyzed, primarily, as they now stand. However, they result from a historical reality and seek to influence history. With this in mind one must say that synchronic analysis itself points to the diachronic dimension. Only then can one take seriously the fact that the texts see themselves as testimonies that owe their existence to an event and seek to re-create this event. With reference to the biblical texts we must, in my opinion, speak of the precedence of synchronic analysis in regard to method, and the precedence of diachronic analysis in regard to their matter.

2.3. The third basic element for the understanding of biblical texts *is freedom to change and renew.* Here too I can point to the Bible itself. Both Old and New Testament texts are intended to open up new meaning for new people in new situations. The interpretation of past history does not mean simply the exposition of the old stories, but retelling them in an entirely new way. The constant retelling of Israel's foundational story in different versions in the Old Testament and the retelling of Jesus' story in the different Gospels

---

34. Biblical texts are referential in that "historical grouping always takes precedence over intellectual and theological grouping" (Gerhard von Rad, *Old Testament Theology,* I [London: SCM, 1975], p. 116). For this reason, a theology of the Old or New Testament must have the character of a narrative and should not be structured according to systematic points of view which are external to the texts. Paul Ricoeur speaks with regard to history of "a surplus of what is signified, which opens towards new interpretations." He does not have in mind a text's hidden totality of meaning in history which the exegete may be able to ascertain. What he means is that the narrated history of biblical texts constantly produces new history and thus new texts. What the exegete does is "the repetition of the *Entfaltung* which presided over the elaboration of the traditions of the biblical base" (Ricoeur [see note 3], pp. 47f.).

bear witness to this. In the Old and New Testaments, then, it is primarily the narrated history which is interpreted and not (or not yet!) the texts which narrate that history. A similar thing holds true, mutatis mutandis, for non-narrative texts. Jewish tradition up to the time of *Jubilees* and the Temple Scroll is less an exegesis of the Torah than a reformulation of it. Jesus' use of the Old Testament tradition and the early Christians' use of the ethical sayings of Jesus reflect a similar, indeed even greater freedom. Only later did it come about, both in Judaism and in early Christianity, that the interpretation of the *text* replaced the actualization of the history and the reformulation of the Law. This happened around the same time for both groups and marked a decisive shift.[35]

This freedom in interpretation has to do above all with the fact that the purpose of the biblical message is to speak, time and again, to new people in new situations and to be interpreted in new ways in their lives. The proclamation and activity of Jesus establish the freedom which we see at work in the later actualizations.[36] This means that biblical texts are similar to many other texts in that they do not have a fixed, definable sense which can be established once and for all. Their meaning is not simply identical with their original sense.[37] Rather,

35. This shift is not fully identical with the canonization process of Old and New Testament. Josephus and Pseudo-Philo wrote their "new" original history of Israel, and the authors of the Temple Scroll and the Book of Jubilees wrote their "new law" at a time when the corresponding parts of the Old Testament had already taken on quasi-canonical status.

36. Weder, *Kreuz Jesu* (see note 32), pp. 56f., pp. 59f.; *Zum Problem* (see note 12), pp. 75f., draws a parallel between Arthur Danto's concept of history (the historian can speak properly of past events only when he incorporates their future: *Analytical Philosophy of History* [Cambridge: CUP, 1968], pp. 143-181) and the Gospels, which can speak appropriately of Jesus only in the light of his future, i.e., of the cross and resurrection. Although the comparison is useful, we should bear in mind the differences between the historian in Danto's sense and the Evangelists. The Evangelists do not simply harness *the* future for an understanding of Jesus, but *one* very specific and remarkable future (the resurrection of the one who was crucified). They make use of the freedom which Jesus himself gave. Quite deliberately, they want to claim (that is, proclaim!) Jesus in what they say, whereas Danto is concerned with the genuine "objectivity" of the historian. These are different emphases but are not in fact contradictory.

37. Gadamer's theses are decisive here: Understanding is "not merely a reproductive but always a productive activity as well." Understanding does not mean understanding a text better than its author did, but in order to understand at all "we understand in a *different* way." *Truth and Method* (see note 14), pp. 296-297. Hans Robert Jauss speaks of the "sense potential" of a work of literature. This seems a helpful expression to me, provided there is no suggestion that a work has a potential totality of sense but rather that it is the potentiality of the work itself which initiates actualizations in the course of its post-history. In: *Literaturgeschichte als Provokation* (Frankfurt: Suhrkamp, 1970), p. 186.

they can be said to have a firm basis[38] and a directionality[39] which continually open up new meanings. Thus biblical texts do not have a fixed sense which lies somewhere *behind* the text, not even on the level of ideas, which could then become *say*able in exegesis.[40] Rather, the biblical texts open up new meanings through encounter. This brings them close to poetic texts, which Emil Staiger says are, "like every genuine, living work of art, infinite within their finite boundaries."[41] They are texts whose understanding is, according to Gadamer, "historical," so that a text "is understood only if it is understood in a different way as the occasion requires."[42] As I see it, however, the understanding of biblical texts comes into this category not only because they are historical foundational texts of a specific type. In addition, this kind of understanding actually corresponds to the claim of the texts themselves to *urge* new attitudes in life and a new way of living, and to give the freedom to achieve this.

2.3.1. This conclusion gives rise to a further consequence for the historical-critical exegesis of New Testament texts. If the sense of a text is realized in a new way in each new historical situation by new listeners or readers, the text's recipients must, wherever possible, be accorded equal significance to the author.[43] This applies primarily to the original recipients, but also to later recipients of the text in the history of its reception, its actualization and its interpretation. As Schindler rightly says, "The polyphonic echo of the centuries belongs to the Bible as an element of itself."[44] The exegete must endeavor, in my opinion, to examine New Testament texts not only from the perspective of

38. Cf. Ricoeur (see note 34).

39. In using the idea of "direction" I am taking up what Paul Hoffmann/Volker Eid, *Jesus von Nazareth und eine christliche Moral*, QD 66 (Freiburg: Herder, ²1975), pp. 109ff. passim, have fortuitously termed "perspective." Míguez-Bonino (see note 29), p. 103, speaks of the "direction of the biblical texts."

40. Klaus Berger, *Exegese des Neuen Testaments* (Heidelberg: Quelle uns Meyer, 1977), whose approach is similar in many respects to what I present here, is concerned (p. 253) that Ricoeur's concept of "surplus of meaning" contains an unnecessary "metaphysical existence" of a sense lying behind the various historical receptions of a text. This is probably not what Ricoeur means (see note 34).

41. Emil Staiger, *Die Kunst der Interpretation* (Munich: dtv, 1971), p. 28.

42. Gadamer (see note 14), p. 309.

43. In exegesis it is Klaus Berger who has pointed most emphatically to the importance of reception theory questions (see note 40, pp. 92ff.). In literary history the following are important: Hannelore Link, *Rezeptionsforschung* (Stuttgart: Kohlhammer, 1976); Harald Weinrich, "Für eine Literaturgeschichte des Lesers," *Merkur* 21, 1967, pp. 1027ff.; Gunter Grimm, "Einführung in die Rezeptionsforschung," in: Grimm (ed.), *Literatur und Leser* (Stuttgart: Reclam, 1975), pp. 11-84; Hans Robert Jauss (see note 37); Wolfgang Iser, *The Act of Reading: A Theory of Aesthetic Response* (London: Routledge, 1978).

44. Schindler (see note 24), p. 265.

textual analysis but also — and more importantly — from the perspective of communication theory. The Word which has taken on written form in the New Testament texts is an event intended to be effective, or as Paul puts it, have a δύναμις (energy, force; cf. Rom. 1:16-17; 1 Cor. 1:18). In the New Testament texts, it is not only true that what is said or written contains what is meant. It is also true that through what is written, and even more through what is said, that which is meant comes into being.[45] If New Testament research takes seriously the fact that in general its texts do not provide information (or do so only superficially) on particular matters but witness to and transport events arising from the story of Jesus and seeking realization in history, then New Testament exegesis will have to take account of reception theory and reception history. By reception theory I mean the question of the intended effect of a text, and by reception history I mean the question of the actual effect of a text.[46] The interpretation of a text takes place largely in this area of conflict between the intended and actual effects of the text.[47] This provides, in my opinion, a starting point in exegesis for formulating questions on reception history.

3. The Question of Truth in the Interpretation of New Testament Texts

If the meaning of a New Testament text is more than the original sense of the text, and if understanding a text involves it changing in new situations, we are faced with a fundamental problem. What now constitutes the truth of an interpretation? If the "exposition" of Scripture also takes place in the life of the church and of Christians, "in doing and suffering, . . . in ritual and prayer, in theological work and in personal decisions, in church organization and ecclesiastical politics, . . . in wars of religion, and in works of compassionate love,"[48] the question concerning truth in the exposition of Scripture becomes

---

45. Iser (see note 43), p. 94.

46. On the terminology cf. H. Link (see note 43), pp. 43ff.

47. This does not provide us with criteria for assessing the claim of a text, but only touches on a very complex issue which is enlarged on further in the next section. On the one hand, we should be concerned if texts in their reception history continually give rise to effects that were not intended, or if their successful reception is based on elements that are in fact alien to them. On the other hand, it is self-evident that the successful reception of a text cannot be the basis for an assessment of its quality or its truth (as evidenced in literary history by trivial literature). The question of criteria for judging the effect of biblical texts is a theological question which has to be negotiated in dialogue with the texts themselves.

48. Gerhard Ebeling, "Church History Is the History of the Exposition of Scripture," in: Ebeling, *The Word of God and Tradition* (tr. by Samuel Henry Hooke; London: Collins, 1968), p. 28.

even more pressing, since the truth of exposition coincides with the truth of faith and of life. But if the sense of the text is not fixed and "the truth of the text . . . is its history," as the literary theorist Hannelore Link puts it, following Gadamer,[49] then there appears to be no answer to the question of truth. When the truth of biblical texts is indeed not a matter of certain predicates but a question of adequate treatment of the text in the context of life, the truth question becomes even more urgent. This is especially true for a church accustomed to saying "sola scriptura" and now being made aware, by means of hermeneutical reflections on Scripture, of the open market of possibilities.

The fundamental question is: Are there criteria for distinguishing between true and false interpretations? A hermeneutic of biblical texts which draws on Gadamer and affirms his opening of existential interpretation to the dimension of history is faced with the same question I would ask of Gadamer himself: How can one enter the open field of tradition history and at the same time retain one's critical faculties in the face of the superior force of history? How can one reject the claims of tradition when necessary?[50]

Jürgen Habermas criticized Gadamer's hermeneutical approach: "The right of reflection requires the self-limitation of the hermeneutical approach. It demands a system of reference that exceeds the context of tradition as such. Only then can tradition be criticized." At the same time, Habermas recognizes the danger that, with the help of such a system of reference, the human being might destroy the openness of history and the subject might once again overpower history. Hence he restricts his own postulate as follows: "But how shall such a system of reference be legitimized, if not by the appropriation of tradition?"[51] The relationship of the subject to tradition thus constitutes a circle whose parts are reciprocally determined. The person judges the tradition by means of evaluation and reflection, and the tradition in turn calls into ques-

---

49. H. Link (see note 43), p. 125.

50. Jauss (see note 37), p. 188, asks the same question: If understanding is nothing but entering into tradition, the "productive element in understanding" as described by Gadamer (*Truth and Method* [see note 14], p. 296) is in danger of being neglected. Jürgen Habermas, "Zu Gadamers 'Wahrheit und Methode'" in: Habermas (ed.), *Hermeneutik und Ideologiekritik* (Frankfurt: Suhrkamp, 1971), pp. 45-56, here: pp. 48f., suspects a "rehabilitation of prejudice" in Gadamer and points to the frequently disturbed communication processes in social reality which harden into the historical experience that "authority and knowledge (do not) converge" (p. 50). Habermas "denies" — and I can only emphasize this — Gadamer's concept "the power of reflection which . . . proves itself in being able to reject the claims of tradition" (p. 49). I also have the impression that Gadamer is in close proximity with questionable aspects of historicism. This problem was recognized by Bultmann and expressed concisely in his discussion of historicism: "Our past has by no means one meaning only" (see note 13, p. 141).

51. Habermas (see note 50), p. 50.

tion the person who judges. Habermas has described this circle as the inter-locking of knowledge and interest.[52] Human judgment of traditions is neces-sary, since it is only on the basis of such judgment that the human being reaches the point of action. At the same time, human ability to judge can be developed only in dialogue with the tradition.

In this analysis Habermas has, as I see it, brilliantly described the formal structure of the problem of truth and tradition. The question is, however, how we arrive at a system of reference which exceeds the realm of tradition. In contrast to Gadamer, Habermas postulates the "transition from the tran-scendental conditions of historicity to universal history" which constitutes the human person as a being of understanding.[53] Anticipating a philosophy of history is necessary, according to Habermas, for the extrapolation of a nor-mative system of reference with regard to action. Unlike Hegel and his follow-ers, Habermas is well aware of the danger of absolutizing the subject.[54] Hence his anticipation is "hypothetical"[55] and is only a postulate of the practical reason which necessitates it. Only in this way, concepts such as freedom and emancipation are to be understood as guidelines to action.

Theology cannot, in my opinion, follow Habermas in his attempt to ar-rive at criteria for truth by anticipating a universal historical system. Theol-ogy's search for truth criteria cannot hypothetically transcend history but must lead into it. The path theology must take involves asking its own special tradition, that is, the biblical texts, what criteria they offer for a critical evalu-ation of their tradition and of interpretations of that tradition. In this way the circle to which Habermas refers is present in a very specific manner. The tra-dition, which is to be critically interpreted, itself provides the criteria for that critique. In theology, the criticism of biblical tradition owes its own critical ability to that very tradition.[56] This circle in theology has a particular presup-

52. Jürgen Habermas, *Knowledge and Human Interest,* transl. by Jeremy J. Shapiro (Boston: Beacon, 1971).

53. Habermas (see note 50), p. 55.

54. In his reply in *Hermeneutik und Ideologiekritik* (see note 50), p. 307, Gadamer speaks of the danger of being in sole possession of the right conviction. This applies to orthodox Marx-ism but hardly to Habermas. Conversely, the same reply shows that one should exercise extreme caution in reproaching Gadamer with a critical deficit. In his struggle against a "depth herme-neutics" claiming to know better than tradition, he is concerned with the critical ability of the subject, not so much towards the tradition as towards the self.

55. Habermas (see note 50), p. 55, speaks about a "hypothetical anticipation of a philoso-phy of history in practical perspective." On the dominance of practice in Habermas — one of the main differences vis-à-vis Gadamer — see the differentiated considerations of Wolfhart Pannenberg, *Wissenschaftstheorie und Theologie* (Frankfurt: Suhrkamp, 1973), pp. 199ff.

56. Berger (see note 40), p. 255, expresses it admirably: "The norms (sc. of action, and

position, namely that the theologian, appealing to a special tradition, must in a fundamental sense already be in agreement with the tradition that is critically evaluated.[57]

Interpretations of New Testament texts are re-actualizations of the past history of Jesus Christ. Accordingly, the criteria for appropriate interpretations can be sought on two temporal levels, that of the past history of Jesus Christ and that of the later or present-day re-actualization of that history.

3.1. If we look for criteria in the past history of Jesus Christ, theology has the following formulations to offer: *The history of Jesus Christ is the truth criterion for the interpretation of biblical texts.* Or: The critical focus of exegesis can be none other than "the point of reference of the language of faith," namely the one who was crucified and raised from the dead.[58] Already in the New Testament this was formulated even more trenchantly by John: "I am the way, the truth and the life" (14:6). Such expressions are, as it were, historical variants on what Protestant theology has attempted to formulate as canon within the canon. Conceptual rather than historical formulations of this canon were for example "what promotes Christ," "justification by faith alone," "the kingdom of God," "the love of God."

The problems arising from such endeavors are the following:

3.1.1. These conceptual formulations have the advantage of determining, to a degree, the content of what took place in the history of Jesus Christ. On the other hand, they can give rise to misunderstandings in that they cause interpretations of New Testament texts to be judged primarily or exclusively on their doctrinal substance, e.g., questioning whether a particular interpretation of an individual text is in accordance with the basic doctrine of justification by faith. It is however extremely difficult on the basis of the New Testament itself to find an unambiguous and generally accepted conceptual expression for the "canon within the canon." For example, it is noteworthy that Paul formulates the principle of faith in a new way, namely as justifica-

---

thus also of the truth of biblical texts) are . . . not above history as such, since redemption itself was historical and can be historically experienced in history only through narrating and remembering."

57. I am here in agreement with Peter Stuhlmacher. Recognizing that understanding itself and the question of the truth of an interpretation must be determined by the texts themselves, he ends his book *Vom Verstehen des Neuen Testaments* (Understanding the New Testament) with a chapter that appears at first glance to be an appendix. It is entitled "Entwurf biblischer Versöhnungstheologie" (Outline of Biblical Theology of Reconciliation). In view of this, I consider it a weakness that he develops his (somewhat formal, in my opinion) hermeneutics of assent in the previous chapter quite independently of the final chapter.

58. Weder (see note 32), p. 248.

tion by faith alone, even though he certainly knew Jesus' principle of the coming kingdom of God. Overstating the argument, one could say that in the New Testament the history of Jesus is the constant basis, while its theological and conceptual explication is variable. This means searching for a criterion in the first-mentioned "historical" direction.

But here the difficulties loom even larger. What do we mean by saying that the history of Jesus Christ is the truth criterion for the interpretation of New Testament texts?

3.1.1.1. This cannot be taken exclusively to refer directly to the factuality of individual episodes or accounts. If that were the case, we would be obliged to remove from the New Testament canon faith legends that probably have no basis in the earthly life of Jesus, such as his walking on the water. Or, conversely, we would have to postulate the historicity of such legends for dogmatic reasons. It must be possible for a text to correspond in a "symbolic" sense to the history of Jesus in that it expresses appropriately what took place with Jesus for humankind and for the world. And there must be limits to a merely external application of this criterion. Those who adhere literally to genuine words or stories of Jesus do not necessarily correspond to his history. It is possible for a literal and correct interpretation of one of Jesus' commands, such as the prohibition of divorce, to run completely counter to what Jesus intended, i.e. to Jesus' history, in a different situation.

3.1.1.2. The story of Jesus itself requires interpretation, and it is we who have to interpret it. Yet when we consider how little consensus there is regarding the reconstruction of the real story of Jesus and his "genuine" proclamation, we may easily be discouraged. Moreover, we must always look to the center, that is, the main matter of the story of Jesus. Thus the criterion depends on our interpretation.

3.1.1.3. Furthermore, if we do not simply hold to the historically reconstructed account of the earthly Jesus but add to it the interpretations of post-Easter faith, the "truth criterion" slips completely from our grasp. If it is only the interpreted history of Jesus Christ (as interpreted by post-Easter faith) which is his true history — as in the New Testament — then the truth criterion is completely unusable. Whose interpretation is then the normative one? And how can I prevent or indeed deny *my* interpretation of the history of Jesus Christ becoming a criterion? If this is so, it is highly questionable what this criterion can in fact distinguish.

3.1.2. Nevertheless, the criterion does not seem to me to be simply an empty formula. It can be misunderstood if it is treated merely as the measure of a "correct" interpretation. Rather, as I see it the actual sense of pointing to the story of Jesus Christ as the truth criterion lies in the fact that it initiates a movement. The story of Jesus Christ, to which every interpretation has reference, is a truth criterion in a more fundamental sense than that it delimits and defines truth and distinguishes it from untruth. It is a truth criterion in the sense that it brings truth itself into being. Thus John interprets the truth that is Jesus by use of the words "way" and "life." Only to a small degree is Jesus truth in the sense of limitation and confinement. Primarily, he is truth in the sense of a way which he opens up and which we walk. If we understand truth not as a usable criterion but as a way we are to walk, then Jesus gives us direction and leads us into ever new environments. Jesus does not therefore make possible a conclusive definition of truth. Rather, his history is the constant point of reference to which the search for truth must time and again return.[59]

3.1.3. It is from this point that the fundamental significance of historical-critical exegesis for the Christian faith becomes apparent. Historical-critical exegesis asks after the original sense of texts, and the early history of faith is not "interpretation" in the holistic sense demanded by the texts. Historical-critical exegesis of a text cannot regulate in a direct and immediate sense the interpretation of that text in the present. Nonetheless, its significance for faith is lasting and fundamental in that it reminds us that faith derives irreversibly from a specific history. In its striving for the most objective reconstruction possible, historical-critical exegesis reminds us that this history is the given element of faith and thus cannot be arbitrarily changed or newly created.[60] By confronting us with biblical texts, biblical witnesses and biblical history in all their antiquity, it enables us to realize that the Christian faith owes its existence not to itself but to something alien which it has perhaps not yet understood.[61] By asking in a particular way after the early history of the faith and its early witnesses, historical-critical exegesis sets out the basic direction of the Christian way, with the history of Jesus as its point

59. Fuchs (see note 30), p. 38: "We ask after truth by asking where truth is apparent. We do not allow ourselves to be logically trapped in advance, but ask about the situation of truth. That is the special aspect of 'new' hermeneutics."

60. In this context the endeavor to achieve relative objectivity is an indispensable element of all academic history. For this reason historical-critical text exegesis will take the text first as a statement and not as a communication with us.

61. Gadamer too, in *Truth and Method* (see note 14), p. 306, speaks emphatically of projecting "a historical horizon that is different from the horizon of the present." This projecting is "only one phase" in the process of understanding, which "is overtaken by our own present horizon of understanding" (p. 306). It is no coincidence that the historian Karl-Georg Faber finds this formulation inadequate and suspects a premature bridging of the distance in Gadamer: "For the historian, the material truth established by historical methods takes priority over intelligibility, even when that truth resists understanding" (*Theorie der Geschichtswissenschaft* [Munich: C. H. Beck, ⁴1978], p. 120).

of departure. For these reasons, I do not believe that the historical-critical method can be replaced by "alternative" methods such as structural analysis or psychoanalytical interpretation. These can only supplement and develop it further in the direction of holistic understanding.

3.2. We can, however, also look for a truth criterion in the concrete realization of the story of Jesus in the present. My thesis is as follows: the texts of the New Testament are intended to instruct us in the love of God given to us in Jesus Christ.[62] This means that *New Testament texts and interpretations of them are true so long as they bring about love.* This formulation takes seriously the fact that understanding New Testament texts involves the whole person and that verbal interpretations of the texts cannot be detached from the situation in which they arose. All interpretations must be questioned as to whether the consequences they have correspond to the texts themselves. Here I draw attention to Matthew, who is the most consistent in the New Testament in using love as the criterion of truth and untruth in faith. At the end of his Sermon on the Mount, for example, he sets out how at the time of judgment Christ will say to many who knew him, prophesied in his name, did deeds of power in his name and even rightly confessed him to be the Lord, "I never knew you; go away from me, you evildoers" (Matt. 7:21-23). Here we find a distinctive feature of the whole New Testament. It is evident too in John 15:7ff., where abiding in Christ, abiding in his love, his words abiding in us and the keeping of his commandments are all closely linked. 1 Corinthians 13 is another profound text of similar import. Here love is contrasted with knowledge, and the chapter ends with the words, "And now faith, hope, and love abide, these three; and the greatest of these is love" (1 Cor. 13:13). Love is not a criterion which anticipates an eschatological totality of meaning in history. Given the spiritual phenomena in the Corinthian church, the statement that, in the eschaton, love remains, is a paradoxical one. It corresponds to the statement that the cross is the present-day form of eternal life. It may be said of knowledge, including the knowledge gained from interpretation of biblical texts, that — as in 1 Corinthians 13 — it "abides" so long as love is in it. The question of the truth of an interpretation of a biblical text or of a later interpretation of a biblical text is the question whether love comes about in it. This makes concrete the question of whether an interpretation "promotes Christ." It contains both an element of freedom and of commitment to tradition. The

62. The keyword "love" by which I attempt to "verify" truth here is inspired mainly by Augustine, *De doctrina Christiana* (transl. R. P. H. Green; Oxford: Oxford University, 1995), 36 (86), 40 (95). It is not contrary to the keyword "freedom" chosen by Ch. Link (see note 33), pp. 539f. I find it helpful because on the level of human action in Jesus or Paul it is love which determines the potentialities of freedom and thus makes it true freedom.

key word "love" takes up the direction of Jesus' history, and at the same time there is an element of freedom in that love cannot be defined in advance or in general.[63]

3.2.1. Love as a criterion of truth is not a theoretical or abstract criterion but historical and practical. Since love is not merely an idea, the question of love cannot be asked only in terms of reception theory. We cannot simply ask: Did or does this interpretation *intend* to bring about love? We must also ask, in terms of history of reception, whether the interpretation actually *did* bring love about, since it is characteristic of love to consider its own consequences. Love as a criterion takes seriously that the understanding of New Testament texts is a holistic understanding, of which application is an integral part.

3.2.2. Love as a criterion of truth has its limitations. As I see it, there are two in particular. Firstly, it is often difficult to establish definitively what love is or was, in relation both to the past and the present. Here theology needs a high degree of social studies reflection.

3.2.3. My second point is theologically even more important. The bringing about of love by human beings cannot be an exhaustive truth criterion for New Testament texts because human love is not the primary concern of the texts. They are concerned with the divine gift of love which brought about human activity. The lack of human love with which we are all too often confronted does not disprove the God who according to the texts is the originator of all love. This is why "love" cannot be an exhaustive criterion of truth. At this point the question of the significance of the Holy Spirit for the interpretation of Scripture should be taken seriously. Beside and above human theological truth criteria there is the power of the Spirit which makes up for the powerlessness of the human form of the Word of God.

3.2.4. In spite of the limitations of love as a truth criterion for interpretation of the gospel, the scope of this criterion is considerable. It can call into question attempts at "correct" interpretations of biblical sayings undertaken without reference to the concrete historical situation. It can call into question the separation of academic historical or dogmatic interpretation from practical living. The criterion of love is crucial in a situation where churches tend to locate the heart of the gospel outside the realm of their own behavior, for example when attempts are made to achieve agreement about the gospel without reference to politics, or when church budgets are hardly seen as a matter of the truth of the church's proclamation.

63. With this criterion too the concept of "direction," given by love and including commitment and freedom in new interpretations, is useful. Berger (see note 40) speaks in well-chosen words of a "tendency in action" which marks the "influence of the event of redemption."

3.3. The first of these two truth criteria, that is, orientation to the history of Jesus Christ, has certain affinity with philosophical attempts to understand truth as the correspondence between a statement and its object. The second criterion, love, which looks for truth in the interpretation itself, i.e. in the signifier and not in its reference, has a certain affinity with pragmatically oriented philosophical systems. The two criteria are valid only in conjunction with each other and even then they are neither exhaustive nor easily manageable. For this very reason it is essential that Christians should strive for this truth in dialogue with each other. The way of the truth of faith is in principle open-ended and can never be defined in a final sense by human beings. Nonetheless, every understanding aims at universal agreement for the sake of agreement concerning action.[64] Striving for consensus is part of the task of interpretation of biblical texts, for a twofold reason in particular. First, the *one* history of Jesus Christ sets the task of finding in the various interpretations the truth that all have in common. Second, since "the truth of faith is a way . . . of love," this truth offers "the possibility of a common path."[65] This is why the way of truth involves striving for agreement and consensus. Thus exegesis and interpretation of biblical texts for the present by means of teaching and everyday living are not the task of individuals but of the whole church. It need not be emphasized among Protestants that the criterion of consensus cannot be a final, absolute, and conclusive one. But it is a reminder to us Protestants which is perhaps not entirely superfluous. For the sake of its matter and of the truth of its claim, the interpretation of the New Testament is the task of the church and not only of individuals.

3.4. Theses

3.4.1. *The Problem* Historical-critical preoccupation with the original sense of a biblical text appears today to complicate rather than facilitate the answer to the question of its meaning and truth in the present. Historical-critical exegesis of a biblical text appears to silence it for the present time.

3.4.1.1. Symptoms: Today's academic exegesis, increasingly specialized

---

64. Both Jürgen Habermas, *Technik und Wissenschaft als Ideologie* (Frankfurt: Suhrkamp, 1968), p. 158, and Karl Otto Apel, "Szientismus oder transzendentale Hermeneutik?" in: Rüdiger Bubner et al. (eds.), *Hermeneutik und Dialektik,* I (FS Hans-Georg Gadamer; Tübingen: Mohr Siebeck, 1970), pp. 105-144, here: p. 105, strongly emphasize the significance of consensus as the precondition for action that is part of understanding.

65. Paul Ricoeur, "Skizze einer abschliessenden Zusammenfassung," in: Xavier Léon-Dufour (ed.), *Exegese im Methodenkonflikt* (Munich: Kösel, 1973), pp. 188-199, here: p. 198.

and too demanding even for many students of theology, is far removed from lay exegesis with its great freedom towards the texts.

3.4.1.2. Symptoms: Exegetical interpretation of the Bible and homiletic actualization of a text, which exegesis should in fact serve, are now hardly in touch with each other.

3.4.1.3. Symptoms: Many hermeneutical systems of today, aiming at holistic understanding, stand "beside" and are scarcely connected with the historical method which reconstructs and isolates events as past "facts" and texts in their "objective" original sense.

3.4.1.4. The background of the problem: Modern thought has been determined since the age of Enlightenment by the rationalist approach which sees in history only imperfect realizations of eternal truths of reason. Thus there is a qualitative leap between the question of the past and the question of truth.

3.4.2. Hermeneutical Goals In establishing a right understanding which corresponds to the biblical texts, theology can only listen to the texts themselves and should not rely on a general philosophical system of understanding. The reasons for this can be found in:

- linguistics: different models of understanding correspond to different text types;
- history of exegesis: the adoption of general, non-theological models of understanding has frequently resulted in the neglect of important concerns of biblical texts;
- hermeneutics: no concept of understanding is ahistorical and without a debt to particular traditions. This is especially important for theology, which owes itself in its very origins to a particular history.

3.4.2.1. Holism is the basic principle of an understanding of biblical texts. Biblical texts speak of God and aim at an understanding which is holistic and embraces the whole person. An understanding of biblical texts concerning God is bound up with faith, obedience, prayer and action.

3.4.2.1.1. Consequence for the historical-critical question of the original sense: Historical critical interpretation of biblical texts must not only enquire into the sense of a text on the textual level but reach back beyond the texts into the historical life which gave rise to them.

3.4.2.2. Historical reference is essential to the understanding of biblical texts. Gaining an understanding of biblical texts means becoming aware both of the history of Jesus Christ to which they point, and of the effects of that history to which they bear witness. Understanding biblical texts means becoming involved in a history.

3.4.2.2.1. Consequence for the historical-critical question of the original sense: In the exegesis of most biblical texts, the synchronic perspective takes precedence only methodologically, and intrinsic structural analyses have only propaedeutic significance. For the referential aspect of the texts, the history to which they refer and which they reflect, i.e. the diachronic dimension, is decisive.

3.4.2.3. Productivity and freedom are essential to the understanding of biblical texts. Biblical texts do not have a fixed, definable meaning which can be finally described. Rather, they have a firm core and a directionality which is realized in new interpretations in each new situation.

3.4.2.3.1. Consequence for the historical-critical question of the original sense: If the meaning of biblical texts is constantly realized afresh in the course of history, the question of the original sense of a text must be not only text- but also communication-oriented. It must enquire not only into the author but also into the recipients of the text.

3.4.3. Truth of Interpretation The criteria which help to distinguish between truth and untruth in the interpretation of biblical texts come from the biblical tradition itself. Theological criticism of biblical tradition owes its own critical faculty to the biblical tradition.

3.4.3.1. A truth criterion relating to the past history of Jesus Christ ("correspondence criterion"). As New Testament texts and their interpretations are testimony to historical effects of the history of Jesus Christ, their truth lies in the fact that they correspond to that past history.

3.4.3.1.1. Limitations of this criterion: the history of Jesus Christ is itself historically conditioned and in need of interpretation. This makes it only partially usable as a criterion.

3.4.3.1.2. The non-defining character of this criterion: the history of Jesus Christ is not a truth criterion in the sense that it defines and restricts the truth of its interpretations, but in the sense of a way that gives the direction in new contexts.

3.4.3.1.3. Historical-critical exegesis has lasting significance for the interpretation of biblical texts in that it reminds faith of its origins, which cannot be arbitrarily altered.

3.4.3.2. A truth criterion relating to the present-day actualizations of the history of Jesus Christ ("pragmatic" criterion). New Testament texts and their interpretations are true insofar as they bring about love.

3.4.3.2.1. As love does not operate only on the level of ideas, it is not sufficient to ask whether a text intended to bring about love, but also whether a text did bring about love.

3.4.3.2.2. Limitations of this criterion: It is often difficult to determine clearly what love is or was.

3.4.3.2.3. Limitations of this criterion: The lack of human love does not disprove God, with whom according to the texts all love originates.

3.4.3.2.4. The scope of the criterion: If love is the truth criterion for the interpretation of biblical texts, all reduction of the holistic nature of understanding to mere words, mere theology, mere dogmatics or mere exegesis is contrary to the gospel.

3.4.3.3. ("Consensus criterion") The reference of interpretations of the gospel to the *one* history of Jesus Christ (3.4.3.1) and the fact that the way of truth is a way of love and thus a way in common (3.4.3.2) enable us to recognize communication, dialogue and the search for consensus as essential elements in the interpretation of biblical texts. Interpretation is not a private task but a task for the church.

14 The Significance of the Church Fathers for Biblical Interpretation in Western Protestant Perspective

1. Introduction

Superficially at least, a ready answer can be given to the question suggested by my title. Nowadays the Church Fathers are, de facto, virtually without significance in Western exegesis. The difference between Roman Catholic and Protestant exegesis in this matter — as in others — is not a crucial one. Certainly this has not always been the case. On the contrary, in Catholic exegesis we need only go back to the Cursus Scripturae Sacrae series of commentaries published in the first half of the twentieth century. Joseph Knabenbauer's volume on Matthew, for example, dedicated to the memory of Pope Benedict XV,[1] is familiar and important to me. The commentary contains a highly traditional but very thorough exegesis in intense dialogue with the classical Greek Fathers and with a long series of Catholic exegetes from Jerome up to the nineteenth century. It was published only 75 years ago, yet how many Protestant or Catholic exegetes still know it? On the Protestant side we have to go back to the nineteenth century to find anything similar. I call to mind, for example, August Tholuck from Halle, one of the most prominent antipo-

---

1. Josephus Knabenbauer, *Commentarius in Evangelium secundum Matthäum*, CSS III 1.2 (Paris: Lethielleux, ³1922).

This paper was presented at the first all-European New Testament scholar's conference in Rila (Romania) in 1998. The main emphasis of this remarkable conference was on hermeneutics. The original German text of this paper has been published in the Rila congress-volume under the title: "Die Bedeutung der Kirchenväter für die Auslegung der Bibel. Eine westlich protestantische Sicht," in: James D. G. Dunn/Hans Klein/Ulrich Luz/Vasile Mihoc (eds.), *Auslegung der Bibel in orthodoxer und westlicher Perspektive*, WUNT I.130 (Tübingen: Mohr Siebeck, 2000), pp. 29-52.

des of Schleiermacher and teacher of Martin Kähler. Tholuck's *Ausführliche Auslegung der Bergpredigt*,[2] written in dialogue with the Church Fathers and the Reformers, remains one of the most fundamental and relevant commentaries on the Sermon on the Mount.

These exegetes found their most important dialogue partners in the Church Fathers and the classical exegetes of the church. Most volumes of the great commentaries of the era, such as those by Zahn, the early editions of the Meyer commentaries, the Études Bibliques or the older volumes of the International Critical Commentary also contain frequent references to specific interpretations by the Fathers. Such references have declined considerably in the historical-critical commentaries of today. They may occur as isolated materials, but they hardly place their stamp on the interpretations nowadays. There may be an exception in the Evangelisch-Katholischer Kommentar, which focuses on history of interpretation and history of reception. But its authors are not in agreement on why the Fathers are important and what their significance for interpretation might be.

The disappearance of the Church Fathers is of course even more obvious in synchronically oriented commentaries and interpretations. They have no place at all in a structuralist or reader-oriented commentary. On the whole, history of interpretation has become a special sub-discipline in patristics.[3] A profound knowledge of the history of interpretation has been accumulated, but scarcely any influence on exegesis is observable.

So is it possible for me, as a Western Protestant exegete, to give a meaningful paper on this topic? I am attempting to do so, but with two restrictions. Firstly, the topic of my paper is not Western exegesis today, but one of the great deficits of that exegesis. Thus I do not speak of the significance of the Church Fathers for Western exegesis, but only of their significance for me as — in this matter — a somewhat exceptional Protestant exegete. Secondly, I am not attempting to formulate this as a specialist, since I am not an expert in patristics. Moreover, much of what I have to say is influenced by exegesis of Matthew, which is my main area of research.

In the first section of this paper I shall discuss some ideas on the reasons why the Church Fathers have disappeared from Protestant exegesis in particular. In the second section I shall illustrate with a number of examples the exegetical significance of a preoccupation with the Fathers. The third, lengthy section focuses on the hermeneutical significance of the Church Fa-

---

2. August Tholuck, *Ausführliche Auslegung der Bergpredigt* (Hamburg: F. Perthes, [3]1845).

3. Cf., e.g., the series *Beiträge zur Geschichte der biblischen Exegese* (Tübingen: Mohr Siebeck, 1955ff.).

thers, and in the very brief final section I shall introduce some Protestant reservations.

2. The Decline of the Church Fathers in Western (Especially Protestant) Exegesis

The relative decline of the significance of the Church Fathers is a consequence of the Reformation scriptural principle. Not that the Reformers and their pupils did not value the Fathers and know them extremely well! But their principle that the church was to be founded on Scripture alone, and not on Scripture and tradition, implied a relative devaluation of patristic interpretations. Exegetical questions could no longer simply be decided on the basis of tradition, by referring to the authoritative testimony of the Fathers.

Decisions on the right interpretation of Scripture were now to be made on two different levels, which can be expressed with the help of Luther's distinction in *De Servo Arbitrio*[4] between the external clarity *(claritas externa)* and internal clarity *(claritas interna)* of Scripture. External lack of clarity in Scripture can be dealt with through careful exegesis, that is, by means of grammar, linguistics, and philology. This principle of the external clarity of Scripture is associated with the return of the Reformers to the literal interpretation of the Bible and its "natural sense," and their turning away from allegory.[5] "Internal clarity" in Scripture has its place in the human heart. Luther speaks in *De Servo Arbitrio* of the Spirit, Calvin speaks of the "internal testimony of the Holy Spirit." In terms of content this means the gospel rather than the law, and it means Christ, whom Luther wanted to promote against Scripture[6] if necessary.

These two kinds of clarity in Scripture are only indirectly connected with the Fathers' interpretations. The latter are part of tradition, which, honorable and important though it may be, is in the eyes of the Reformers secondary to Christ and Scripture. Thus the Church Fathers decline in importance for the Reformation exegetes. This is tellingly illustrated in the prefaces to Reformation Bible commentaries, most of which refer to Erasmus and his biblical text, his annotations and his paraphrases, but seldom mention the Church Fathers. Theologians adhering to the Reformation no longer write

---

4. Martin Luther, *De Servo Arbitrio*, BoA III, 103 = WA 18, 609.

5. Martin Luther, *Auf das überchristlich, übergeistlich und überkünstlich Buch Bock Emsers zu Leipzig Antwort*, WA 7, 650-652.

6. Martin Luther, *Propositiones . . . H. Weller* (1535) 49 = WA 39/1, 47.

commentaries in the form of glosses or catenae. This is partly true too of Catholic Bible commentators, but there are differences in content. The standard Catholic commentaries draw their lifeblood from the patristic interpretations. Examples are the commentaries by Juan Maldonado, a sixteenth-century Spaniard highly educated in humanism and rhetoric, and above all that of the Flemish Cornelius à Lapide in the seventeenth century.

I have spoken thus far of a relative decline in the significance of patristic exegesis as a consequence of Reformation understanding of Scripture. My second point has more to do with Humanism than with the Reformation. In the context of their rediscovery of antiquity, the Humanists paid close attention to the Church Fathers. Since the era of Humanism there has been a new type of commentary on biblical books, known as "adnotationes." The originator was probably Laurentius Valla, whose most famous successor was Erasmus of Rotterdam. The Geneva Reformer Theodore Beza also wrote a commentary of this type. "Annotations" contain philological and historical notes on the biblical texts. Those of Erasmus or Beza[7] for example have frequent references to the Church Fathers, but the Fathers are not treated as traditional authorities. Rather, they are a source of historical information or of certain philological interpretations. Thus in the wake of Humanism and the Reformation the Church Fathers became historical sources or partners in the exegetical dialogue. Calvin's preface to his commentary on the Gospels typically expresses this new function of the Church Fathers as historical sources.[8] Increasingly, the Church Fathers are evaluated by whether their historical judgments are reliable and whether their interpretations correspond to the exact natural sense of Scripture.

This leads us to the two reasons why the Church Fathers have lost more and more territory in the Reformation churches, especially since the Enlightenment. Their interpretations were often problematic in historical terms, their historical judgments often proved wrong. There was little understanding for or interest in what I regard as their most important legacy to us, that is, their hermeneutic achievement. On the contrary, Protestant liberal exegesis was concerned to go back beyond all the church interpretations to the true

---

7. Erasmus of Rotterdam, *Novum Testamentum, cui . . . subjectae sunt . . . Adnotationes,* in: *Opera Omnia* VI (reprint Hildesheim: Olms, 1962); Theodore of Beza, *Jesu Christi Novum Testamenticum* (Geneva: H. Stephanus, 1582).

8. Calvin here cites the Church Fathers Jerome and Eusebius as representing historical theses on the Gospels which he rejects. For him Mark is not — as for Jerome — a mere abstract of Matthew, and Paul is not — as for Eusebius — the true author of Luke's Gospel (John Calvin, *A Harmony of the Gospels Matthew, Mark and Luke* [tr. by A. W. Morrison; Edinburgh: St Andrew's Press, 1972]), pp. xiif.

sense of the original texts, to reach back beyond all dogmas to Jesus himself. In Protestantism, study of the Church Fathers was eclipsed by study of the Bible, which harnessed every exegetical, hermeneutic and historical endeavor.

I shall not treat this development in detail but focus on a Protestant exegete who, unlike others, did at least thoroughly study patristic exegesis. Adolf Jülicher and his book on the parables[9] were highly influential. I have chosen him as an example of how the historical-critical question of the original sense, together with the Protestant opposition between Scripture and tradition, of necessity devalues the study of the Church Fathers. With each individual parable, Jülicher guides the reader through the absurdities of interpretation that have accumulated over the centuries to the original, reasonable, obvious (if rather flat!) sense of the original parable. The Church Fathers are consigned, especially where they have offered allegorical readings of the parables, to the rubbish heap of the history of interpretation. Jülicher's judgments are harsh. He sees Origen's theory of the parables, for example, as — in Overbeck's words — no more than a "systematization of wrongness." He cites individually the very few cases in which Hilary got it right. He acknowledges Cyril of Alexandria to be a good exegete but claims he was too influenced by the culture of Alexandria.[10] Only John Chrysostom is treated more favorably. In other words, the original sense of a text is the measure of its correct interpretation. By this measure the patristic interpretations can only be secondary and of limited interest. This is compounded by Jülicher's basic exegetical thesis that Jesus' parables have nothing to do with allegory. The idea that the new and different patristic interpretations of Jesus' parables might make them significant and interesting was one that could not have come to Jülicher in his time.

The above can be summarized in two theses:

1. The decline of the Church Fathers in Protestant biblical exegesis is a result of the Reformation scriptural principle which focuses on the Bible in its literal sense and makes "Christ" rather than the tradition and doctrine of the church its interpretative canon.

2. The decline of the Church Fathers in modern Western biblical exegesis is a result of the academic search for the original sense of the biblical texts. This led to critical questions reaching back beyond the Church Fathers. In other words, it is a consequence of the scholarly thinking rooted in Humanism and the Reformation and reaching its breakthrough in the Enlightenment.

9. Adolf Jülicher, *Die Gleichnisreden Jesu,* I-II (Tübingen: Mohr-Siebeck, ²1910 [1899]).
10. Jülicher, pp. 224, 226, 238.

Today there is little difference between Catholic and Protestant exegesis as regards their relation to patristic interpretation. For Catholic exegetes too the Church Fathers have become marginal. Given the principle formulated in *sessio IV* of the Council of Trent (1546) that Scripture and tradition are to be accepted and revered "with an equal affection of piety and reverence,"[11] it is surprising to find Catholic exegesis so modern and Protestant in this respect. If "tradition" is not understood to be a particular source of revelation besides the Bible but, as stated by the Second Vatican Council, as the living and Spirit-led transmission of the one revelation testified in the Bible,[12] there is a close affinity to the Orthodox understanding of tradition and at the same time a difference from the Protestant emphasis on the precedence of the Bible as the given measure of all later processes of tradition.[13]

Be that as it may, the considerable loss of dialogue with the Church Fathers is a deficit common to both Catholic and Protestant exegesis. The awareness of this deficit among both Catholic and Protestant exegetes has given rise to the Evangelisch-Katholischer Kommentar. Something has been lost, on that there is agreement, but the significance of the loss is not so clear.

3. On the Exegetical Significance of the Church Fathers

My remarks on the exegetical significance of the Church Fathers will be very brief. Because they are quite close to the New Testament in time, place and language, the Fathers have transmitted numerous important exegetical and historical observations. These observations have in turn been handed down through Erasmus, Grotius, Wettstein,[14] and the older commentaries right

11. Henricus Denzinger/Alfonsus Schönmetzer (eds.), *Enchiridon Symbolorum* (Freiburg: Herder, [36]1976, No. 1501 = 783). English: *The Church Teaches: Documents of the Church in English Translation,* ed. John F. Clarkson et al. (St. Louis: B. Herder, 1955).

12. *De Revelatione* 2, 9: "Sacra Traditio . . . et Sacra Scriptura arcte inter se connectuntur atque communicant. Nam ambae, ex eadem divina scaturigine promanantes, in unum quodammodo coalescunt et in eundem finem tendunt." Here tradition is associated with the Holy Spirit, the apostles and their successors and the church, but not specifically with the magisterium. The Church Fathers are not given particular emphasis.

13. Cf. however Savas Agourides, "The Orthodox Church and Contemporary Biblical Research," in: Dunn et al., *Auslegung,* pp. 139-154. He emphasizes this Protestant concern because he sees here a great deficit in the Orthodox Church.

14. On Erasmus see note 7. Hugo Grotius, *Annotationes in Novum Testamentum* (reprint Groningen: W. Zuidema, I, 1826; II, 1827); Jacobus J. Wettstein, *Novum Testamentum Graecum,* I-II (Amsterdam: Dommeriana, 1751/52 [reprint Graz: Akademische Druck- und Verlagsanstalt,

into the modern ones. Their exegetical significance is undisputed. For this reason I restrict myself to three examples, all from the Gospel of Matthew.

It is generally known that in his *Homily* 16.7 on Matthew 5:22 John Chrysostom mentions that people in Syria say ῥακά to their servants, not as an actual term of abuse but as a very condescending form of address in the second person singular.[15] So there could well be an intensification from ῥακά to the very weak term of abuse μωρός.

But there are also less well known exegetical discoveries to be made in the Church Fathers. In Augustine for instance I found a note[16] that the rustics in Hippos, North Africa, call themselves "Chanani." Probably this expression is a self-designation on the part of the indigenous Phoenician population. Φοῖνιξ (Phoenician) is a Greek word, i.e., a foreign one. The Markan designation Συροφοινίκισσα (Syrophoenician) reveals a Western geographical location (in Phoenicia itself it would not be necessary to call the indigenous population "Syro"-Phoenicians). So I suggest that in Matt. 15:22 Matthew, who was Syrian and possibly bilingual, has replaced the unsuitable Markan designation "Syro-Phoenician woman" with the indigenous self-designation used by the Phoenicians. In my judgment this is not — or not primarily — a biblicism.[17]

My third example concerns a familiar exegetical puzzle, the interpretation of the double designation of time ὀψὲ δὲ σαββάτων, τῇ ἐπιφωσκούσῃ εἰς μίαν σαββάτων (late . . . on the Sabbath, with the daybreak of the first day after the Sabbath) in Matt. 28:1. The first temporal phrase refers to the early evening of the Sabbath, with ὀψὲ . . . σαββάτων usually understood to be a partitive genitive.[18] The second temporal phrase very probably refers to the early morning after the Sabbath. Both phrases must have meant the same to Matthew, however. There have been attempts to resolve the contradiction by declaring ὀψέ to be a preposition meaning "after" (for which there are very few isolated references!) or by taking the risk of interpreting the Greek verb ἐπιφώσκω from the Semitic.[19] However, Serverus of Antioch (which may have been Matthew's hometown!) informs us that in his time it was common to

---

1962]). The commendable new edition by Georg Strecker et al., whose second volume was published in 1996, concentrates on the ancient non-Christian parallels and includes only few patristic records.

15. *In Matthaeum* 1:7 = PG 57, 248; cf. Basilius, *Reg. brev.* 51 = PG 31, 1117.

16. *Exposition on Romans* 13 = CSEL 84, 162.

17. Ulrich Luz, *Matthew 8–20*, Hermeneia (Minneapolis: Fortress, 2001), p. 338.

18. Cf. Edwin Mayser, *Grammatik der griechischen Papyri aus der Ptolemäerzeit. II/2. Satzlehre* (Berlin 1934; reprint Berlin: de Gruyter, 1970), p. 127 d 2; p. 533 No. 13.

19. Cf. on this Ulrich Luz, *Das Evangelium nach Matthäus*, IV, EKK I.4 (Neukirchen-Düsseldorf: Neukirchener/Patmos, 2002), p. 401.

say ὀψὲ τοῦ καιροῦ παραγέγονεν (literally: he came late of time) or ὀψὲ τῆς ὥρας (late of the hour). This meant τὸ βράδιον καὶ κατόπιν τῆς ὥρας (later and behind the hour).[20] Probably ὀψέ was understood here as a comparative in the sense of "later" and the genitive understood as comparative. This may well be the clue to solving the puzzle. These are three examples of exegetical-historical-philological insights we owe to the Church Fathers.

I move on to two examples illustrating how close the exegesis of the Fathers was in many cases to the probable original sense of the texts. The first example concerns the history of interpretation of Matt. 5:3. It is notable that the vast majority of the Fathers interpret πτωχοὶ τῷ πνεύματι (the poor in spirit) in the sense of "humility," which does not really suggest itself in Greek semantics.[21] This suggests that the Fathers have preserved a fixed oral tradition of interpretation. My second example concerns patristic interpretation of the parables. We recall that Jülicher distinguished sharply between the original sense of Jesus' parables and allegorical interpretations of them by the Church. I believe he was only relatively right to do so. Matthew's interpretation of the parables, itself in part allegorical, already shows the two tendencies later designated as tropological interpretation (allegorization in the interest of parenesis) and mystical interpretation (allegorization in the perspective of salvation history). Today we have again become aware that allegories — by which I do not mean a consistent allegorical interpretation — are not alien to the original parables of Jesus. Almost all the parables contain metaphors with fixed meaning, such as "father," "harvest," "reckoning" etc., which were essential to their interpretation from the beginning and so of course influenced Early Church interpretation. Thus there is not only, as Jülicher claimed, discontinuity between Jesus' parables and the patristic interpretations of them. Matthew the Evangelist is relatively close to the Early Church interpretation of the parables, forming a bridge between Jesus and the Early Church.[22] These examples must suffice. I think it would be rewarding to discover anew the continuity between the biblical texts and the Early Church interpretations of them.

I close these brief remarks on the exegetical significance of studying the Church Fathers with a comment on the important role of the Alexandrian and Byzantine lexicographers. One of them, Photius of Constantinople, was a Church Father himself. Other lexicons such as the Suda make extensive use of

20. In Johann A. Cramer (ed.), *Catenae Graecorum Patrum in Novum Testamentum*, I. *Catenae in Ev. S. Matthaei et S. Marci* (reprint Hildesheim: Olms, 1967), p. 244.

21. Cf. Jacques Dupont, *Les Béatitudes III. Les Evangélistes*, EtB (Paris: Gabalda, 1973), pp. 399-411.

22. Cf. U. Luz, *Matthew 8–20* (see note 17), pp. 290-293.

church writers. For many New Testament scholars Bauer's dictionary and Liddell-Scott are the alpha and omega of lexicography, much to the detriment of exegesis.

4. The Hermeneutical Significance of the Church Fathers

Far more important than all these individual exegetical findings is the significance of the hermeneutics underlying patristic interpretations. As I see it, their methods of interpretation allow for some unexpected connections with more recent methods which now supplement historical-critical interpretation. This brings me to my *basic thesis. Patristic interpretation anticipates the unity of explaining and understanding through analogy of faith which has broken apart for us. Their interpretation reads the Bible as a unit and not as a fragmented collection of individual texts.* I have five points to make on this.

4.1. Allegorical Interpretation and the Meaning of the Texts for Us

It has become increasingly clear that scientific explication of texts is not identical with the establishing of their meaning for the present. Understanding a text takes place in two steps. We refer to them — indirectly after Wilhelm Dilthey and directly, e.g., after Ernst Fuchs[23] — as "explaining" and "understanding." "Explaining" is concerned firstly with the world of the text, i.e. its structure and its potential for readers (for example with the implied reader). It continues, secondly, with philological and grammatical explanation. Thirdly it is concerned, as historical explanation, with the actual author and the actual first readers of the text and their "encyclopedia," their situation in cultural and religious history, their social and historical environment and the communication situation which gave rise to the text. "Understanding" on the other hand means one's own engagement with the "concern" *(die Sache)* of the text. This corresponds to the French distinction between "sens" and "significance" and the English distinction between "sense" and "meaning." The German terms *Sinn* and *Bedeutung* are somewhat less precise. Thus "explana-

23. Ernst Fuchs, *Marburger Hermeneutik* (Tübingen: Mohr Siebeck, 1968), pp. 18f. This includes the notable passage: "Explaining isolates, analyzes, objectifies. That can have fatal consequences for the living object. Malicious farmers attribute to their vets the saying: 'You have to slaughter the animal to discover what was wrong with it.'"

tion" of a text is concerned with its sense, while "understanding" explores its meaning. This calls to mind the debate, basic to Western hermeneutics since Pietism, on the "application" of a text. Hans-Georg Gadamer has declared application to be an integral part of understanding.[24] Our students often experience what they learn in exegetical lectures and seminars as the mere "explanation" of texts. The sheer quantity of possible explanations of endless biblical texts by endless numbers of exegetes with all their different hypotheses often produces confusion. Students then turn for help to practical theologians, who have made a separate field of study out of what used to be called "application." In the end there is often not much left of what the exegetes "explained." Tradition-conscious Catholics turn to the teaching authority of the Church, the magisterium, which virtually ignores all the hypotheses ventured by exegetes in their historical, structural and linguistic playgrounds[25] and preserves the binding truth of faith largely without constitutive recourse to the biblical texts.[26]

In short, the "sense" and the "meaning" of texts, objective "explanation" and subjective "understanding," threaten to fall apart. The linguistically ascertained sense of the text is often a text-immanent world of its own, quite unconnected with the real reader. Historical explanation of the texts remains in the past, where it has to do with hypothetically reconstructed Romans and Corinthians in their time but nothing to do with us. The "ugly ditch," not between historical truth and the eternal truth of reason as Lessing once saw it,[27] but between truth then and truth now, can hardly be bridged. To put it differently, scientific explanation of texts distances them from our own reality and makes them objects of analysis, lifeless texts in other words. A new, second step is needed to bring the texts back to life in our own reality. Scientific explanation also distances the biblical texts from the church by taking them back into their own world in the past, when "churches" as we know them today did not exist. Hence Protestant exegetes frequently find that today's church structures and institutions influence the life of the church far more

24. Hans-Georg Gadamer, *Truth and Method* (2nd revised edition; New York: Crossroad, 1989), pp. 307-311.

25. One should bear in mind that all the historical worlds presupposed by exegetes and all their linguistic and reception theories are nothing but their own constructions!

26. Cf. Giuseppe Segalla, "Church Authority and Bible Interpretation," in: Dunn et al., *Auslegung*, pp. 54-72. My formulation indicates of course that I take a somewhat different view from his.

27. Gotthold Ephraim Lessing, *Über den Beweis des Geistes und der Kraft. An den Herrn Director Schumann zu Hannover,* in: *Lessings Werke in sechs Bänden,* Vol. VI (Leipzig: Reclam, n.d.), p. 223.

strongly than does the Bible, while Catholic exegetes find themselves relatively free to do as they like in the field of history and linguistics. The teaching office comes into play only when they touch on some of the very few sensitive points at which church dogma is directly affected by exegetical issues.[28]

My thesis is that the bringing together of literal and allegorical interpretation of Scripture in the exegesis of the Church Fathers provides the very link between "explaining" and "understanding" which we are in danger of losing as a consequence of scientific explanation of the Bible. As I see it, allegorical readings formulate the present meaning of a text. Concerned with the meaning of the text and not with its sense, such readings are applications in the broadest sense of that word.[29] This is immediately obvious in the case of moral allegories. When Matt. 5:29-30 is interpreted for example, which calls for the cutting off of parts of the body which cause a person to sin, the eye or the hand can be read in terms of evil thoughts, sexual temptation, false friends or money.[30] Such allegories open up the applications of the text. It would be naive to follow Jülicher's type of purism and declare that the biblical hyperboles are of course not "meant" in that way. This became clear to me in a very different way when I realized the proximity between some of Origen's spiritual interpretations and the depth-psychological reading of the Bible offered us today by Eugen Drewermann.[31] For Origen, spiritual understanding of the Bible means, in the end, that the divine logos with its δύναμις (power) touches the "eyes of the soul," so that "our eyes are opened" too.[32] Spiritual understanding means illumination of the individual by the divine logos, and thus in a deep and spiritual sense it means healing. The proximity to Eugen Drewermann's psychological interpretations, which I also read as applications of the biblical texts, is considerable. After all, Drewermann also does not seek to reduce the biblical message to inner, psychological human experience.

A connection of this kind between literal explanation and spiritual understanding can come about only if the literal explanation is not — as was of-

---

28. There is for example the historical question of whether Jesus had natural siblings. In historical terms this is highly probable!

29. With Franz Overbeck, *Christentum und Kultur. Gedanken und Anmerkungen zur modernen Theologie*, ed. C. A. Bernoulli (Basel: B. Schwabe, 1919), pp. 75, 89-91, and Ulrich H. J. Körtner, *Der inspirierte Leser* (Göttingen: Vandenhoeck und Ruprecht, 1994), pp. 80f.

30. Ulrich Luz, *Matthew 1-7. A Commentary* (Minneapolis: Augsburg, 1989), p. 298.

31. Eugen Drewermann, *Tiefenpsychologie und Exegese* I-II (Olten: Walter, 1984/85). Cf. also the discussion in Körtner (see note 29), pp. 76f., and in Henri de Lubac, *Geist aus der Geschichte. Das Schriftverständnis des Origines* (Einsiedeln: Johannes, 1968), pp. 442-459.

32. *In Matthaeum* 16.11 = GCS Origen X 508 on Matt. 20:29-34.

ten the case with Origen — a preliminary stage to be overcome, but an integral part of understanding itself. An example of the relation between literal and spiritual interpretation can be found in Thomas Aquinas' quaestio "utrum sacra Scriptura sub una littera habeat plures sensus" (if the holy Scripture has under one letter more than one meaning).[33] Thomas, in the tradition of Augustine, distinguishes two levels of meaning in God's word. The first level is the "significatio," which makes words signify things ("voces significant res"), i.e. the reference of the signifier to the signified. This corresponds to the "sensus historicus vel litteralis" (historical and verbal sense). On the second level the signified becomes the signifier again, i.e., the history, events, and persons designated by the "words" of the Bible have meaning themselves ("res significatae per voces iterum res alias significant"). This corresponds to the spiritual meaning of Scripture. Thus according to Thomas the historical meaning of Scripture is not eliminated or eclipsed by the spiritual meaning but is itself the bearer of that spiritual meaning. In all its dimensions the spiritual meaning is directed to us, the believers. As "sensus mysticus" it lifts the figures of the past into the faith of the present. As "sensus anagogicus" it speaks of our hope, as "sensus moralis" it speaks of our obligations today. For Thomas Aquinas the spiritual meaning of Scripture is the reading of faith, the application of the text in a comprehensive sense which far exceeds its mere use in Christian practice. Thomas no longer suggests, as Origen did, that the literal interpretation of Scripture is the perspective of ordinary Christians, while the allegorical perspective is for advanced and perfect readers. In this way Thomas avoids the danger of leaving the literal interpretation behind at some stage and drifting off into spiritual depths. The object of spiritual interpretation is after all not only the words of the Bible but the biblical text understood literally, the *history* that has been put into words and interpreted. The history itself becomes a symbol. It becomes transparent for the truths of faith.

4.2. Multiple Meanings of Scripture

Patristic interpretation corresponds to the new openness to multiple readings of a text, discovered by current readers response criticism. By contrast, historical-critical interpretation sees the biblical texts as closed texts. It attempts to reconstruct *the* original sense. Under the influence of Schleier-

---

33. Thomas Aquinas, *Summa Theologica* I art. 1 qu. 10 corpus; cf. also *On the Epistle to the Galatians*, Lectura No. 254 (on Gal. 4:21ff.) (Turin: Marietti, 1973).

macher, theological exegesis focused for a long period exclusively on the intention of the author. I see this as an attempt to establish an unambiguous instance for the sense of the text. The dominance of the author and the desire for an unambiguous sense of the text in modern Western exegesis have traditional theological roots. The biblical writings are apostolic writings, and the early church believed them to have become part of the canon because their authors were apostles. The authors of the biblical texts were thought to have been inspired. The belief that the *authors* of the texts, such as the apostles or the prophetic writer of the Johannine Revelation, were inspired by the Holy Spirit outlived the belief that the biblical *texts* themselves were inspired. Early Protestant orthodoxy was convinced that the biblical texts were clear and unambiguous in their literal sense.[34] Only then could they be the sole and sufficient foundation of a faith understood above all as doctrine. Modern readers response however has demonstrated the extent to which the meaning of a text is constituted by each reading of it, in other words by the reader in dialogue with the text.[35] Such ideas were alien to a theology which was convinced of the absolute precedence of the word over the readers, and which had suppressed any recollection that readers as well as texts and authors could be inspired. Ulrich Körtner has rightly reminded us of this in his book *Der inspirierte Leser* (The Inspired Reader) and has called for a reassessment of early church allegorical interpretation from this perspective.[36]

It is already apparent in Origen's interpretations that several spiritual readings of a text can coexist. The same is true of other Early Church commentaries such as those of Jerome or Ambrose, long before John Cassian systematized the spiritual reading of the text as its allegorical, tropological, and anagogic meaning. The medieval commentaries frequently speak of "a different interpretation," which may not mean a different sense of the text but an additional moral or mystical interpretation. Unfortunately, this phenomenon is now often regarded as "compilation" or mere handing on of tradi-

34. Cf. the traditional "proprietates" of Scripture in early Protestant orthodoxy: auctoritas, certitudo, sufficientia, perfectio, necessitas, perspicuitas (Heinrich Heppe, *Reformed Dogmatics* [revised and edited by Ernst Bizer, tr. by G. T. Thomson; London: Allen and Unwin, 1950], pp. 12, 21f.).

35. A useful survey is given by Moises Mayordomo-Marin, *Den Anfang hören,* FRLANT 180 (Göttingen: Vandenhoeck und Ruprecht, 1998), pp. 27-131. I personally am particularly attached to the moderate model of reader-oriented exegesis as found for example in Umberto Eco.

36. Körtner (see note 29), pp. 62ff. See partic. p. 86: The doctrine of the fourfold meaning of Scripture reminds us that the biblical texts have a poetic quality. "They are . . . many-voiced like polyphonous music, ambiguous, open to transference and association. Like sounding-boards, they make their readers and listeners vibrate and sound."

tions, and is no longer valued. As I see it, this is only a small part of the truth. Commentaries which bring together various interpretations, including the medieval catenae, see themselves expressing the measureless wealth of Scripture unfolding in a wide variety of coexistent interpretations. None of the interpretations excludes the others, none is the "correct" one. Rather, they are all possible and productive readings of the text. Origen consciously relates the various senses of the text to the different readings of different readers when he assigns the obvious literal sense of the text, the σάρξ (flesh) of Scripture, to the ἁπλούστεροι (simpler people), the moral reading of the ψυχή (soul) of Scripture to the ἀναβεβηκότες (those who have ascended) and the understanding of the πνευματικὸς νόμος (spiritual law) of Scripture to the τέλειοι (the perfected).[37]

4.3. Patristic Interpretation and the Hermeneutics of "Effective History"

Thirdly, the traditions collected in patristic interpretations document the reception history of biblical texts. From the perspective of reception history–oriented exegesis, the Bible contains "as part of itself its many-voiced echo in the Church through the centuries" as Alfred Schindler has aptly put it.[38] The Bible is like a piece of music, which does not consist merely of its score but has to be played time and again, and whose fullness can only be expressed in a collection of recordings. The Bible is like a collection of stories and themes which have to be painted and presented time and again. It is like a great river whose waters constantly reach new shores.[39] In the early years the biblical traditions were rewritten time and again, and later the biblical texts were constantly commented on and actualized anew. Their fullness of meaning unfolds in the course of history. This fullness is documented for instance in a catenae commentary containing centuries of interpretation of biblical texts, or in a church whose walls or iconostasis interprets biblical scenes and themes in paintings over the centuries. Such commentaries and paintings preserve something of the wealth of meaning of biblical texts as it has accumulated over time.

In "effective history" hermeneutics influenced by Gadamer, the past is not simply something historically previous to our own time. The past is the

---

37. Origen, *De Principiis* 4.3.2.
38. Alfred Schindler, "Vom Nutzen und Nachteil der Kirchengeschichte für das Verständnis der Bibel heute," *Reformatio* 30 (1981), pp. 261-277, here p. 265.
39. Cf. Ulrich Luz, *Matthew in History* (Minneapolis: Fortress, 1994), pp. 19-21.

horizon of our own situation; it is "a given" which shapes us.[40] Reception history cannot simply be put aside as a special concern of historical investigations.[41] What Gadamer means can be well illustrated by the image of a church building with its paintings. A church is not simply a large-scale history of art textbook. It is a space we enter, a space which receives us, attunes us and makes us welcome. The tradition of interpretation we have received from the Church Fathers, the Reformers and also from our immediate predecessors in the nineteenth and twentieth centuries has a similar role. What they thought and how they lived is not simply past. It is *our* past and as such a space that determines and shapes us. They are our "given," and we live on what we have received from them. "Effective history" hermeneutics can open our eyes afresh for the space of history that has shaped us, reminding us that as exegetes we are not simply autonomous subjects working in an ahistoric space. We owe ourselves to our history and it has made us what we are. That history especially includes the Bible, church history, and the Church Fathers. Attention to the history of their influence can open our eyes to who we are by telling us who we have become, and this is why the Eastern churches rightly attach great importance to the Church Fathers.

A further aspect of "effective history" hermeneutics is perhaps particularly significant for us as Western Protestants. It opens our eyes not only to our own history but also to that of others. It shows us who others have become, partly through the influence in their own history of the Bible we have in common. The "effective history" perspective shows us Protestants what we have become and who we are, but it also shows us what others have become under the influence of the Bible, be they Catholics, Orthodox, or, for instance, people of the Third World. Being open to others' history means widening our horizons and seeking dialogue. It offers the opportunity for self-correction and re-orientation. The patristic interpretations are our common historical heritage, yet they have become so strange to us Protestants that we may need the help of Orthodox eyes and their perspective on biblical reception history in the Fathers to rediscover them in a new and different way. "Effective history" hermeneutics widens our horizons to otherness, thus leading us into the ecumenical dialogue. The aim is not that Protestants should take on the Orthodox view of the Fathers, but that their view may enable us to develop a new perspective of our own.

40. Hans-Georg Gadamer (see note 24), pp. 300-307.

41. The challenge posed to us by the patristic interpretations is ignored if they are simply deposited in history-of-interpretation monographs as a collection of historical material. The challenge is fully accepted only when their interpretations play a part in determining ours.

4.4. Interpreting the Bible Is a Communicative Process within an Interpretative Community

Historical-critical biblical exegesis taught us to see the Bible as a large number of individual documents, created in a wide variety of times and situations and to be interpreted according to their situation of origin. It also raised the number of biblical documents and authors beyond those of the canon by drawing our attention to countless pre-forms of the texts (such as the Sayings Source), supplements, insertions and redactions, etc. To put it positively, it was through historical-critical exegesis that the Bible became a book of many voices. Seen negatively, historical criticism fragmented the Bible by dividing it into individual texts and declaring all attempts to define the norm of these individual texts (taking the canon or the "rule of faith" as the measure, for example) as well as all attempts to formulate the "center" of the Bible (as in the Reformation) to be post-biblical. Historical-critical exegesis and other scientific methods developed numerous hypotheses on all these individual texts, and these now coexist in confusing array. In short, the unity of the Bible seems to have been lost, and the attempts to recover it prove historically secondary to the Bible.

In this situation we are reminded by the patristic interpretations that behind the plurality of voices in the Bible itself and behind all the interpretations there is an interpretative community of which we ourselves are part, that is: the Church. For me the importance attached by the Eastern churches to patristic interpretation is a significant hermeneutic indicator of how fundamental the Church as interpretative community is for the reading of the Bible. I emphasize this as a Protestant, well aware that the Church as interpretative community carries little weight with us. Many of our clergy tend to preach their own Word of God; many of our theologians would like to see their own theology as the gospel. Many of our exegetes, glad not to have an ecclesial magisterium set over them, are content with their own authority. I insist however that interpreting and understanding the Bible is a community process, and that in the end the Church and not the individual is the interpreting subject. This does not mean I am seeking to restrict or standardize interpretation. As a Protestant, regarded by most Christian churches as being outside the "true" church right up to the twentieth century, it is not for me to say where the limits of what God will recognize as "church" are. I am also aware how important it is that many people read the Bible and regard it as *their* heritage without having any desire to belong to a church. For me any theological "canon within the canon" which narrows down and standardizes, no longer allowing itself to be questioned by the wealth of the Bible, and a magisterium which decrees what correct interpretation of the Bible is, without allowing itself to be qualified and corrected by the Bible, are not true to the gospel. As a Protestant exegete I want to give the biblical texts the opportunity to say all that they have to say, even if it goes against us and our churches.

However, I also know as a Protestant that the wealth of the biblical texts cannot unfold without an interpretative community, without exchange of interpretations and experiences with the Bible, and without a *common* piety and practice inspired by the Bible. Interpretation of the Bible is not borne by individuals but by the whole universal church. Only this can prevent individual hypotheses, exegetes, theologians and denominations becoming absolute. Only then can our dialogue about the Bible take place in a κοινωνία (community) that is not created by our dialogue but given to us. The Church Fathers belong in special measure to the κοινωνία we have been given. Their task is to remind us that the church is the bearer of interpretation, and to prevent us from becoming Fathers to ourselves. They point us to the communicative dimension of understanding the Bible, and to the church as interpretative space. Naturally, in my view the study of the Church Fathers does not restrict our reading of the Bible, but enriches it.

4.5. The Christological Center of Patristic Hermeneutics

Johannes Panagopoulos has sought in several publications[42] to interpret christologically the juxtaposition of literal and spiritual meaning of Scripture in the Greek Fathers. He finds neither the later developed fourfold meaning of Scripture nor Origen's threefold juxtaposition of corporeal, moral and spiritual perspectives on Scripture the most important. Rather, he sees the unity of literal and spiritual interpretation as corresponding to the doctrine of the two natures of Christ. "Holy Scripture is in perfect correspondence with the person and story of Jesus Christ,"[43] it is analogous with the incarnation. Panagopoulos takes Origen's doctrine of inspiration, which is christologically interpreted, as his starting point. The biblical texts are divinely inspired, and this inspiration is to be understood from Jesus' incarna-

---

42. Johannes Panagopoulos, Ἑρμηνεία τῆς Ἁγίας Γραφῆς στὴν Ἐκκλησία τῶν Πατέρων 1 (Athens: Akritas, 1991); "Christologie und Schriftauslegung bei den griechischen Kirchenvätern," *ZThK* 89 (1992), pp. 41-58; "Sache und Energie. Zur theologischen Grundlegung der biblischen Hermeneutik bei den griechischen Kirchenvätern," in: Hubert Cancik et al. (eds.), *Geschichte — Tradition — Reflexion* III (FS Martin Hengel; Tübingen: Mohr-Siebeck, 1996), pp. 567-584.

43. *ZThK* 89 (see note 42), p. 53.

tion: "Only with the coming of Jesus could the divine shine out in the words of the prophets and the spiritual in the law of Moses." For Origen there is an analogy between Christ and the Bible. Like Christ, Scripture is full of difficulties and stumbling-blocks as well as beauty and grace. In both the spiritual is clothed in the corporeal.[44] The analogy goes further. By means of the physical acts recorded in the Gospels, such as the driving out of the traders and money changers from the Temple, the incarnate Jesus creates σύμβολα τῶν ἰδίων πνευματικῶν πράξεων (symbols of his own spiritual deeds).[45] Thus for Origen understanding Scripture means that the eternal divine logos becomes, by means of the earthly stories recorded in the Bible, a spiritual event in those who understand. The logos both makes use of and breaks through the physical exterior. The historical material of the Bible becomes the vehicle of the spiritual, occurring in the understanding of the Word. Thus for example the many allegorical readings of parables in terms of Christ's activities[46] point directly to how Christ wants to become reality through the spiritual understanding of the believer.

I shall now exemplify this in Origen's interpretation of Matt. 26:17-19/ Mark 14:12-15. Origen is concerned here to go "beyond the letter of the law" but to stay within its spiritual power. Thus Christ's entry into the Upper Room to eat the Last Supper with his disciples represents the entry of the living Lord into the house of our own lives. The owner of the house is reason, preparing for the coming of the Son of God, cleaning and decorating the room. The house is in "the city of God, that is, in the Church." The water carrier "is Moses, the law-giver, bearing spiritual teaching in physical tales." After the disciples have given the house owner, i.e., reason, instruction in faith, the "divinity of the only Son will come and eat together with his disciples in the house."[47] Thus the entry of Christ into the Upper Room, announced by the disciples and prepared by the water carrier, becomes transparent for the entry of Christ the divine Logos into the human heart.

It is apparent from this interpretation that Origen is anything but an incarnational theologian. Jesus' earthly form is not so much the *place* and the *form* of God's reality as the exterior which has to be broken through. In concrete terms, the fact that Jesus does not want simply to have a spiritual last supper with his disciples but, first and foremost, to celebrate his last Passover, no longer

44. Cf. *De Principiis* 4.1.6 (quoted); 4.2.8f.

45. *In Matthaeum* 20 = GCS X 545, 11ff.

46. Cf. e.g. Origen's exegesis of Luke 10:30-37 = *Homily on Luke* 34 (GSC Origen IX 188-195) and its interpretation by Josef Pietron, *Geistliche Schriftauslegung und biblische Predigt* (Düsseldorf: Patmos, 1979), pp. 48-52.

47. *In Matthaeum* 79 = GCS Origen IX 189-191.

means much to Origen. In my opinion Origen must be corrected and deepened as far as literal interpretation is concerned. For him the story, including Jesus' story, is only the field in which the Holy Spirit has buried the treasure of the kingdom of God.[48] Using the image of his interpretation of Matt. 17:2ff., Origen notes that the disciples are not to stay with the earthly Jesus, who had neither form nor loveliness, but climb the high mountain with Jesus and there be moved by the transfigured and glorified Christ (*Contra Celsum* 6.77). In Origen we do not find literal and spiritual interpretation side by side or one inside the other as in Thomas Aquinas. Origen's literal interpretation is only the — albeit in most texts important — preliminary to spiritual interpretation.

Panagopoulos sees Athanasius, the Cappadocians, and above all Cyril of Alexandria and Didymus the Blind[49] as those who developed Origen's hermeneutics into a full incarnational hermeneutics doing justice to the paradox of the doctrine of two natures. I use his words to describe this: "The analogy between the divine Logos in its dual nature and the two-dimensional word of Scripture transfers to Holy Scripture the mystery of the person of Jesus Christ and leads to a corresponding biblical hermeneutic. . . . Biblical exegesis is concerned both with the scope of the incarnation and the pure, inseparable union of the dual nature in the person of Jesus Christ. As Jesus Christ is one and the same, so it is with Scripture. It contains his humanity, that is, its literary and historical sense, and his divinity, that is, its hidden spiritual sense. . . . Holy Scripture is in perfect correspondence with the person and history of Jesus Christ."[50]

I am not in a position to judge whether this really was the opinion of Cyril of Alexandria or whether these are the conclusions Panagopoulos draws from it. But the basic principle behind it is important. Origen's idea of inspiration expresses the fact that through the understanding of Scripture in those who are perfect the divine logos itself, the Spirit of God, becomes event. The Spirit does not cling to the text, as in a Protestant fundamentalist theory of inspiration, but passes in the form of divine energy to the believers in whom Christ becomes event in understanding. Christ the true human being, a figure of past history, is at the same time God, which also means divine Spirit and present reality. His past history can be understood only if it becomes spiritual reality today as divine event. A christological hermeneutics has its center in this union of past history and present revelation, a union brought about by

48. *De Principiis* 4.3.11 on Matt. 13:44.

49. Cf. on this Vasile Mihoc, "The Actuality of the Church Fathers' Biblical Exegesis," in: Dunn et al., *Auslegung*, pp. 3-28, partic. pp. 16ff.

50. Panagopoulos, *ZThK* 89 (see note 42), p. 53.

the interlocking of literal and spiritual interpretation of Scripture, corresponding to the human and divine nature of Christ.

The consequences of such an approach can be effective in two directions.

1. If Christ is the effective center of Scripture, and Scripture the vessel of the divine logos, then Scripture need not, for our understanding today, fall apart in countless individual texts and individual hypotheses. It has its unifying center and energy in the living Christ, the Spirit. It does not have this center however on the level of historical explanations, the earthen vessels of the logos, but on the level of today's understanding among believers.

2. If Christ is the center and energy of Scripture, explaining the past and understanding the present need not fall apart. They remain related to each other, as were the two natures of Christ in the understanding of the Church Fathers. In this way, understanding the Bible brings the Jesus of the past to life as the risen Lord in the present.

Like Panagopoulos, I have spoken of the doctrine of two natures as a hermeneutic key to a christological patristic hermeneutics. For me however, no human language can be the representation of reality in a direct sense, and even less so when we are dealing with divine reality and not human reality. For me the doctrine of two natures is a human linguistic construct, not a direct representation of the reality of God or Christ. Nonetheless, this doctrine and the christological hermeneutics based upon it is a theological construct with very great heuristic force.

Turning now to Reformation hermeneutics, I see a strong convergence between the Early Church's christological approach to understanding and that of Luther. There is evident affinity between the patristic christological hermeneutics and Luther's basic principle of the material canon, "what promotes Christ."[51] Luther's hermeneutics too is christological, or more precisely, it is incarnational. Gerhard Ebeling summarizes his analysis of Luther's hermeneutics with the words: "The logic of hermeneutics is none other than the logic of christology."[52] Allegorical interpretation, no longer appropriate in the age of Humanism, gave way to the existential reference of the story of Jesus "as sacrament for the individual."[53] The sense of the bibli-

---

51. Martin Luther, "Vorrede zum Jacobusbrief," *WA* Dt B 7, p. 384. "And the measure of all books, by which we may put them to the test, is whether they promote Christ or not. . . . Whatever does not teach Christ, is not apostolic, even if it were taught by Peter or Paul; and whatever preaches Christ is apostolic, even if it were taught by Judas, Annas, Pilate, or Herod."

52. Gerhard Ebeling, *Evangelische Evangelienauslegung. Eine Untersuchung zu Luthers Hermeneutik* (reprint Darmstadt: Wissenschaftliche Buchgesellschaft, 1962), p. 452.

53. Ebeling (see note 52), p. 424.

cal story is concentrated in the meaning of the story of the incarnate and crucified Lord Jesus "for us." A detachment of the past story of Jesus from its present meaning for us would have been unthinkable for Luther and the other Reformers. The story would then simply be dead past.[54] Thus Luther too assumes the indivisibility and unity of Christ's dual nature, and draws hermeneutical conclusions from it. Just as the divine Christ is unsurpassably incarnate and crucified, the literal sense of Scripture is for him the permanent vessel of its spiritual meaning.

In comparison with Luther and the Early Church, the situation in today's Protestant Bible interpretation is as follows: Christ's humanity has become independent of Christ's divinity, just as literal, i.e. historical-critical, interpretation has become separated from spiritual. As a result, the historical sense of the biblical texts and their meaning for us have fallen apart. The historical sense is in danger of becoming insignificant, of no longer speaking "for us," and the present meaning is in danger of losing touch with history. The christological hermeneutics of the Church Fathers point to the task of bringing the two together, and point the direction in which our contemporary New Testament hermeneutics should go.

It is quite possible that, in terms of the history of theology, the Reformation concentration on Christ's humanity and on the literal sense of Scripture has contributed to the autonomy of the historical and the detachment of historical sense from spiritual meaning. This is what we are struggling with today. Without formulating any thesis, I recall the fact that in the eighteenth and nineteenth centuries not only conservatives but also enlightened and liberal theologians referred to the Reformers. It might be worth considering whether, vice versa, the difficulties now experienced by many Orthodox Christians in integrating the historical-critical method and making it productive for spiritual interpretation today could be connected with their

54. Ebeling (see note 52), p. 422, gives impressive proof of this in citations which already hint at the "death" of living history, through its scientific explanation (cf. note 23 above). An example concerning Jesus' resurrection: ". . . maior pars audit resurrectionem Christi ut aliam historiam de Turca et sinunt eam esse ut pictam historiam in pariete. Es mus etwas bessers sein, ut canimus in cantico 'Des soln', ut inspiciatur, quod nostra sit, das sie mich an ghe et te, ut non solum videamus, quomodo resurrectio, sed ut agnoscas tibi fieri" (Sermon of 1529 on John 20:1-15, *WA* 29, 262, pp. 1-5). English translation of this wonderful German-Latin text: "Most people hear the resurrection of Christ like any other history about a Turk and tolerate it as painted history on the wall. But it must be something better, as we are singing in our hymn (there follows a part of the well-known Easter hymn: Christ ist erstanden . . . Des solln wir alle froh sein), so that it becomes visible that it is *ours*, that it concerns *me* and *you*, so that we do not only see how the resurrection (happened), but so that you acknowledge that it happened *for you*."

Origenist tradition in which the literal sense was less important. It might have been not so much the basis of spiritual meaning, but rather the starting point for an ascent, a transfiguration and a spiritual vision surpassing the literal and physical.

Many questions remain unanswered, such as the question of how Antiochian hermeneutics, with its theoretical focus on historical typology rather than allegory, relates to this model. Or there is the question of how the various forms of Catholic hermeneutics relate to it.

5. In Conclusion: Three Protestant Reservations

I believe the significance of the Church Fathers for today's interpretation of the Bible to be considerable, and I find them unjustifiably neglected in modern Western Protestant exegesis. The hermeneutical impetus they can give us seems much more important to me than the exegetical, however useful this may be.

But before I create a premature impression of consensus, allow me to emphasize that all I have said has been said by a Protestant. The study of the Church Fathers and their hermeneutics enables me to broaden my own permanently Protestant perspective, and probably to overcome specifically Protestant restrictions. From my fundamentally Protestant perspective I am convinced that the Bible takes precedence over all interpretations of it and all churches which interpret it. The Church Fathers are important for me for the sake of interpreting the *Bible.* They have become important to me because they help me to rediscover the present meaning of the Bible (§4.1), its wealth (§4.2), its ecumenical breadth (§4.3), the living Christ who speaks in it (§4.5)[55] and the church as the interpretative community shaped by its experiences with Christ (§4.4). I have been concerned here to rediscover the Bible as the book of life permeated by the living Christ, not misunderstanding it as, for instance, a devotional book for the individual, a historical or history of religion source book or a handbook of Christian doctrines. I have been concerned to understand *the Bible* better and more appropriately with the help of the Church Fathers, and not to merge biblical testimony with patristic or to standardize it on the basis of their work. I have rediscovered the Church Fathers *as a Protestant,* and to make this plain I shall end my presentation with three specifically Protestant reservations which are important to me:

5.1. I should like to define "Church Fathers" as broadly as possible, to in-

---

55. Which is not the same as a christological dogma that standardizes interpretation!

clude not only the Greek and Latin Fathers and of course the Reformers, but also those who have at some stage been characterized by one of the churches as heretics. We Protestants, so often treated as heretics ourselves, are alert to truths and concerns that the heretics among our Fathers in particular may have laid up for us. This was also the reason why I spoke so frequently of Origen in my presentation.

5.2. Related to this is the fact that I would not want to see patristic interpretation in any way as, in terms of content, a canon for "correct" interpretation of the Bible. The Fathers with their sheer wealth of thought would in any case not be appropriate for this purpose.[56] If it should be thought necessary to have a canon for correct biblical interpretation, the regula fidei recommended by Tertullian for this purpose would be far more practicable. But I have no need of such a canon, as "the unambiguity of Scripture is not the unambiguity of sentences, but that of the living, self-witnessing Lord in his church."[57]

5.3. Important though it is for me, patristic hermeneutics is not normative hermeneutics. It is an attempt to combine the scholarly thinking of the time, which included the allegorical method of interpretation and Platonic and Aristotelian theories of language, with the christology of the time. Patristic hermeneutics helped to understand how Christ the living Logos spoke through the biblical texts. We cannot repeat what the Fathers did. We can however attempt to combine our *contemporary* methods of interpretation and our *contemporary* linguistic theories with a *contemporary* christology, thereby learning from the Church Fathers that our attempt is analogous to theirs.

56. In agreement with Joannis Karavidopoulos, "Offenbarung und Inspiration der Schrift," in: Dunn et al., *Auslegung,* 157-168, here: pp. 158f.

57. Schindler (see note 38), p. 264.

15 Can the Bible Still Be the Foundation for a Church Today? The Task of Exegesis in a Society of Religious Pluralism

1. Preliminary Remarks

A presidential address provides the opportunity to define positions and to offer fundamental reflections on where exegesis now stands. As is to be expected in the era of postmodernism, my definition of position is fragmentary. The formulation of my title is a clear indication that I am speaking as a Protestant theologian. For Catholic theologians the Bible has never been *the* foundation of the church as it has in classical Protestantism. Unlike Protestant biblical scholars since Martin Luther, Catholic biblical scholars have never been *the* key figures in theology. I cannot speak here for Catholics, less still for historians of religion or philologists who study primitive Christian literature or take an interest in it from a Jewish or an atheist-humanist perspective.

A further restriction concerns my subtitle, "The task of exegesis in a society of religious pluralism." I am speaking as a Swiss and perhaps also as a Northern European, since the Swiss are — as they have still to learn — Europeans too. So I refer to *our* religiously pluralist society. I follow Eilert Herms in his definition of a religiously pluralist society: It is a society in which, for individuals, "religious-philosophical communication . . . no longer occurs within a unified context of communication and tradition, making use of a unified system of symbols and with the tendency toward a unified result," but "rather in a wide variety of different contexts of communication and tradi-

German original: "Kann die Bibel heute noch Grundlage für die Kirche sein? Über die Aufgabe der Exegese in einer religiös-pluralistischen Gesellschaft," *NTS* 44 (1998), pp. 317-339. Originally delivered as the Presidential address at the SNTS Annual Conference in Birmingham on August 5, 1997.

tion, making use of various systems of symbols; and in a competing variety of contexts of tradition."[1] This definition can be applied to Swiss, German, Dutch, Scandinavian, English, and perhaps French society. It is probably especially applicable to multicultural Birmingham, the city of John Hick and the Selly Oak College, a city in which more people can be found in Hindu temples and Muslim mosques than in Christian churches, but where more than 80% of the population have no part in institutionalized religion.[2] In Switzerland, a survey published in 1993 indicated that in terms of religion everyone is a "special case." Religion is a private matter in the strictest sense of the word. Its most significant supporters are individuals who choose what suits them from a wide range of religious offers of meaning, only some of which are to be found in churches. Religion is an individual "bricolage"[3] for which the churches are now responsible only to a limited extent.[4] The situation in Southern and Eastern Europe is different. The main difference in North America seems to be that commitment to and identification with the Christian churches are far more marked than in Europe. Here in Northern Europe, unlike North America, we do not have a developed "civil religion" which limits pluralism. For us, religious pluralism is probably limited by nothing more than the basic consensus that in a democratic society "claims to truth may not be asserted by violent means,"[5] since religion is a private matter and not the concern of public reason.[6] Probably Northern Europe is more strongly "post-Protestant" than North America in that we are united here by a strong experience of fundamental hiddenness of God. God now occurs for us *only* in the form of human texts, human theology, and human history, and in

1. Eilert Herms, "Pluralismus als Prinzip," in: Herms, *Kirche für die Welt* (Tübingen: Mohr Siebeck, 1995), pp. 467-485, see p. 471. Peter Berger speaks in *The Heretical Imperative: Contemporary Possibilities of Religious Affirmation* (London: Collins, 1980), pp. 26, 28 of a "pluralization of plausibility structures" resulting in a situation of modernity in which "picking and choosing becomes an imperative."

2. Werner Ustorf, "Von der Unheiligkeit heiliger Plätze. Theologische Arbeit in der multireligiösen Industriestadt Birmingham," in Joachim Mehlhausen (ed.), *Pluralismus und Identität*, VWGT 8 (Gütersloh: Kaiser, 1995), pp. 592-606, here: p. 601.

3. Alfred Dubach and Roland J. Campiche, *Jede(r) ein Sonderfall? Religion in der Schweiz* (Zürich/Basel: NZN/F. Reinhard, 1993), see book title and p. 304.

4. The sociologist Franz-Xaver Kaufmann states: "Even among Catholics, only a minority still see the Church as responsible for their 'personal salvation,'" in: *Religion und Modernität* (Tübingen: Mohr Siebeck, 1989), p. 200.

5. Wolfgang Huber in: Wolfgang Huber and Friedrich W. Graf, "Konfessorische Freiheit oder relativistische Offenheit. Ein theologisches Streitgespräch," EK 24 (1991), pp. 669-673, here p. 669.

6. Ingolf Dalferth, "'Was Gott ist, bestimme ich!' Theologie im Zeitalter der 'Cafeteria-Religion,'" *TLZ* 121 (1996), pp. 415-430; see pp. 415f.

the form of totally plural and ambiguous human religious experiences. All these human fragments can no longer be brought together to form a complete picture. I am reminded of Umberto Eco's famous image at the end of *The Name of the Rose*. When it comes to God, many of us Northern Europeans are like Adson, himself a Northern European, who finds among the ruins of the burned abbey only "disiecta membra" (dispersed members) of the former library. It is reduced to "a sort of gallery," "looking down into the void at every point."[7] To many of us contemporary Adsons, nominalist as we are, the attempt by the Birmingham theologian and religious studies scholar John Hick to see the range of forms of religious experiences as expressing the unique "Ultimate" and "Real"[8] is an impossible "realistic" presumption. In the end we can see it only as "a defensive argument against the self-radicalization of the pluralist paradigm."[9] That is my own Northern European and post-Protestant context of religious pluralism.

Colleagues from Eastern Europe will say, "That's exactly what we're afraid of!" I can assure you that we did not ask for or choose the situation we are in, neither do we bemoan it. We ask ourselves as theologians what our task is in the given situation. Colleagues from South America, Africa, or Southeast Asia will shake their heads and say, "If only we had *that* sort of problem!" I understand this reaction very well, but these are indeed the problems we *have*, and so these form the context of our theology.

It is in this context of ever increasing individualization of religion and ever more evident loss of significance of the major traditional churches for individuals' religion that we exegetes are at work. What role do we have in a society where 47% of the Protestants and 54% of the Catholics never read the Bible and some 30% just "a few times a year"?[10] In this society, what is the relevance of exegesis, disparagingly described by a systematic theologian as a "matter without consequences"?[11] What is the relevance of exegesis when one

---

7. Umberto Eco, *The Name of the Rose* (London: Pan Books [Picador], 1984), p. 500.

8. John Hick, *An Interpretation of Religion: Human Responses to the Transcendent* (New Haven: Yale University, 1989), pp. 246-249.

9. Jürgen Werbick, "Der Pluralismus der pluralistischen Religionstheologie. Eine Anfrage" in: Raymund Schwager, *Christus allein? Der Streit um die pluralistische Religionstheologie*, QD 160 (Freiburg: Herder, 1996), pp. 140-157; see p. 152.

10. Dubach and Campiche (see note 3), pp. 85, 339. The figures for young people are far worse, cf. Heiner Barz, *Religion ohne Institution? Jugend und Religion* 1 (Opladen: Leske und Budrich, 1992), p. 63.

11. Falk Wagner, *Zur gegenwärtigen Lage des Protestantismus* (Gütersloh: Kaiser, 1995), p. 85. Wagner characterizes what he calls the "amicable division of labour" among German exegetes as follows: "The specialists for matters of detail in half- and quarter-verses, whose work no one outside theology can still take note of, do not get in the way of those who are working on a

of the most frequent questions put to me is what other Gospels exist apart from the four in the Bible? This is *our* pluralist society.

At the Diet of Worms in 1521, Luther refused the Emperor's demand to retract his writings: "if I should not be overcome by written testimony or a clear reason, for I cannot believe the Pope or the Councils alone. . . . As long as my conscience is held captive by the Word of God, I cannot and will not retract."[12] His Reformation response is part of the Augustinian tradition of the inerrancy of canonical writings, which from 1508 formed part of the constitution of the faculty of theology in Wittenberg.[13] It is probably also in the tradition of William of Ockham and others who invoked the Bible against the Pope. Scripture is to take precedence in all decisions, "ut sit ipsa per sese certissima, facillima, apertissima, sui ipsius interpres, omnium omnia probans, iudicans et illuminans."[14] It was this understanding of Scripture which formed the basis of the Reformation and post-Reformation thesis that Scripture is clear in itself, accessible, unambiguous, and complete.[15] As such it is the sole foundation for the building of the church. Hence the task of exegetes is to clarify the foundations of the church through their interpretations of Scripture. The history of Protestantism in the modern age has shown that exegetes have not fulfilled this crucial task. The Augustinian and Reformation principle "sola scriptura" has not proved to be the foundation of the church but rather the *leitmotif* of its division. The Bible has not proved to be the foundation of the one church, but rather the basis of a wide variety of denominations.[16] Far from limiting denominational and theological pluralism, exegesis has tended to foster it. It is paradoxical that the Reformation understanding of Scripture seems to have launched its own deconstruction.

---

new biblical theology" (ibid.). These and other endeavors contribute, as Wagner sees it, to "the submerging of the once critical and enlightened profile of Protestant exegesis in a sea of new confusion" (p. 86).

12. *WA* 7 (Weimar: Hermann Böhlau, 1897), pp. 838,2ff.

13. Augustine, *Epistle* 82.3 (= CSEL 34, 354). Cf. Martin Tetz, "Mischmasch von Irrtum und Gewalt," *ZThK* 88 (1991), pp. 339-363, here: pp. 358f.

14. Martin Luther, *Assertio omnium articulorum . . . per bullam Leonis X, WA* 7 (Weimar: Hermann Böhlau, 1897), p. 97 (English translation: "so that it is by itself completely secure, completely easy, completely open, interpreting itself, proving, deciding and illuminating everything of everything").

15. Cf. Heinrich Heppe/Ernst Bizer, *Reformed Dogmatics* (tr. G. T. Thomson; London: Allen and Unwin, 1950), pp. 21f.

16. This conclusion is drawn by Ernst Käsemann, "The Canon and the Unity of the Church," in: Käsemann, *Essays on New Testament Themes* (trans. W. J. Montague; London: SCM, 1964), 95-177, here: p. 103.

I shall now examine with the help of three guidelines what exegesis has contributed to ecclesial and theological pluralism. The contribution is considerable. Modern exegesis, which set out to ascertain a stable and verifiable sense of its texts, has at the same time produced destabilizing and modifying factors. If one follows Jean François Lyotard in seeing "incredulity toward metanarratives"[17] as a characteristic of postmodernism, then exegesis as a precursor of pluralism was a driving force towards postmodernism. Personally I am not so keen on the term "postmodernism." Exegesis has helped to bring about a pluralism which I consider to be one of the good sides of modernism.[18] The three guidelines I shall reflect on in the sections below are as follows: history, language, and effective history. With the first guideline, the transformation of story into history and the historical-critical method, I shall review familiar material. With the second and third guidelines, both of which belong essentially to the twentieth century, I shall have more to say about my personal perspective. My thesis in these three sections is that our post-Protestant religious pluralism is in part the result of the effects of exegesis in history.[19] My final section will touch on what our task might be in this given situation of religious pluralism.

2. The Biblical Story as History and Historical Criticism

The transition from a Reformation understanding to a historical-critical understanding of the biblical story was associated with a shift in the understanding of truth and reality. As the Reformers saw it, the biblical story was both an external past reality *and* at the same time a present reality determining the life of the listener. Historical research meant the end of the "immediacy" of the biblical story for listeners.[20] It was replaced by historical distance. The truth of

17. Jean François Lyotard, *The Postmodern Condition. A Report on Knowledge* (Manchester: Manchester University, 1984), p. xxiv.

18. "Postmodernism" is particularly problematic when used to designate an era. If it is understood in a "tricky" way, not as an era, but "in its weaker version . . . as a theorem which does not seek abruptly to abandon modernism but to question it and to strengthen its good points" (Wolfgang Welsch, *Wege aus der Moderne* [Berlin: Akademie, ²1994], p. 2), one may wonder why the emphatic term "postmodernism" is necessary.

19. Of course, these considerations as applied to exegesis owe a great deal to the overall view of Protestantism as a shaping force of modernism in the work of Max Weber and Peter Berger.

20. It was replaced according to Hans W. Frei by "the reality of the author on one side and of the single, external reference of the words on the other" (*The Eclipse of Biblical Narrative* [New Haven/London: Yale University Press, 1974], p. 79).

the biblical story, determining the lives of listeners, was replaced by the probability of agreement between the sense of the text and the intention of the author, or the historical probability of a narrative. Neither was connected with the life of the listener. The truth that was binding on listeners was now visible only *behind* the texts. It could be understood in very different ways. For Spinoza the truth is the knowledge of the rational law of God and the love of God, accessible to all peoples. It is transmitted by means of the biblical narratives "to the masses whose intellect is not capable of perceiving things clearly and distinctly."[21] For Lessing it is the "new, eternal gospel" of reason,[22] the theological precursor of the "post-monotheistic monomyth . . . the story . . . of humankind's revolutionary emancipation."[23] For Odo Marquard this is "the only theology in regard to which secularization, so far, has failed."[24] For Schleiermacher it is the personal experience of revelation, of being driven by the divine spirit. It can never be merely repetition of those who "derive their religion entirely from another, or depend on dead writing, swearing by it and proving out of it." Hence for Schleiermacher "every sacred writing is . . . merely a mausoleum, a monument that a great spirit once was there, but is now no more."[25] In the liberal theology of the nineteenth century the binding truth is the historical Jesus, not existent anywhere *in* the Gospels but, as Martin Kähler perceptively noted, only "behind the Gospels."[26] For Bultmann the truth is the kerygma that occurs in the New Testament only "in words and sentences already interpreted in some particular way,"[27] i.e., as human theology, so that one can never state precisely in human theological terms what it is. The bind-

21. Baruch Spinoza, *Tractatus Theologico-politicus, Opera II* (ed. J. van Vloten/J. P. N. Land; Den Haag: M. Nijhoff, ³1914), p. 153. Quotation from: *The Chief Works of Benedict de Spinoza* (tr. by R. H. M. Elwes; Vol. 5; New York: Dover, 1951), p. 78.

22. *Die Erziehung des Menschengeschlechts, These 86* (= *Werke VIII*; Munich, 1979), p. 508. Lessing's dispute with Pastor Goeze of Hamburg was concerned with the significance of the Bible for the Christian religion. For Lessing, "religion . . . is not true because the evangelists and apostles taught it; rather, they taught it because it is true" (*Axiomata. Wider den Herrn Pastor Goeze in Hamburg,* IX = op. cit., p. 148). This is why Lessing attaches such importance to the (Catholic!) thesis that the Bible was not foundational for the doctrine of the earliest Church Fathers, and that the Bible itself is younger than Christianity.

23. Odo Marquard, "In Praise of Polytheism," in: Marquard, *Farewell to Matters of Principle: Philosophical Studies* (New York: Oxford University, 1989), p. 96.

24. Marquard, "The Question, To What Question Is Hermeneutics the Answer?" in *Farewell,* p. 125.

25. Friedrich Schleiermacher, *On Religion. Speeches to Its Cultural Despisers* (tr. by J. Oman; New York: Harper and Row, 1958), p. 91.

26. Martin Kähler, *Der sogenannte historische Jesus und der geschichtliche biblische Christus.* Theologische Bücherei 2 (ed. E. Wolf; Munich: Kaiser, ²1956), pp. 41, 29.

27. Rudolf Bultmann, *Theology of the New Testament,* Vol. II (London: SCM, 1955), p. 239.

ing truth can also be an archetypal basic truth, something "eternally valid" beyond all time-bound and external historical uniqueness, and into which all that is historically particular must be taken up.[28]

In summary, there is considerable plurality in the offers of truth released by the transformation of real history into "the history of then." My theses concerning this are as follows:

2.1. Historical criticism is a precursor of modern religious pluralism in that all its hypotheses operate without claiming existential binding truth for the present.[29] Thus in one crucial aspect modern historical criticism played into the hands of pluralism by abdicating the truth question.

2.2. This enables Bible readers to construct beyond the text what might be binding truth for them. The history of modern theology can be read as a history of competition and successive deconstruction of such assumptions of truth. Being human, they are necessarily pluralist.

Such assumptions of truth have proven to be foundational for theologies, but not for churches.

The basic claim of the Reformation that the Bible in its clarity and sufficiency was the foundation for the church failed not only because various competing confessions soon found themselves in a hermeneutical "civil war over the Absolute text."[30] It failed too because increasingly certain understandings of the Bible, rather than the Bible itself, proved to be the foundation of theologies rather than of churches. These theologies then became influential across confessional boundaries. In this way historical biblical criticism was the precursor of a pluralist theological post-confessionalism.

The following additional theses will not require further explication:

2.3. Historical criticism is a precursor of modern religious pluralism in that it replaced the existential binding truth of biblical texts by hypotheses on historical probabilities and hypotheses on the sense of texts. The diversity of methods developing in connection with historical criticism has further increased the plurality of hypotheses.

2.4. Historical criticism has atomized the Bible. The unity of the Bible as the logos-inspired word of God was replaced by a multitude of texts by a great variety of authors from very different situations. The living word of the incar-

28. Eugen Drewermann, *Tiefenpsychologie und Exegese,* II (Olten: Walter, 1985), p. 240.

29. As early as 1789, Johann Philipp Gabler made the basic distinction between historical and dogmatic theology in his essay "Von der richtigen Unterscheidung der biblischen und der dogmatischen Theologie und der echten Bestimmung ihrer beiden Ziele." The text is reprinted in Georg Strecker (ed.), *Das Problem der Theologie des Neuen Testaments,* WdF 367 (Darmstadt: Wissenschaftliche Buchgesellschaft, 1975), pp. 32-44.

30. Marquard (see note 23), p. 120.

nate Christ was replaced by a multitude of human testimonies witnessing to sometimes very different things.

Nowadays each and every person can select from within — or from outside — the historically analyzed Bible their own basic traditions, creating a "bricolage" made up of various blocks of biblical tradition. Exegetes and hermeneutics scholars paved the way in what has now become typical of many people with regard to religious traditions.

An indirect result of the historical understanding of the biblical texts was the separation of application from exegesis. August Hermann Francke distinguished in the Scriptures between Christ the kernel who satisfies the soul and the "husk of external history, of the letter and the words, reachable by external science."[31] He sees as the culmination of Bible reading the lectio practica whose beginning and end is prayer, whose basic attitude is humility. His successor Johann Jakob Rambach understood hermeneutics as the "habitus practicus." The application of the texts to one's own life becomes an integral part of the process of understanding.[32] In the hermeneutics of Halle pietism, the segregation of exegesis and application which later increasingly determined ecclesial reality is already apparent.

2.5. On the one hand there is an exegesis which attempts, with a claim to objectivity, to reconstruct the true intention of the author, the true and correct sense of the text or its real historical situation. On the other, there is an abundance of applications which assume virtually nothing more than the immediate experience of the text by recipients in the present. All scientific methods are, as Gerd Theissen points out, "remote from applications."[33] The more objective the former seem, the more subjective the latter become. Indirectly, an exegesis which is lodged in the past and cannot bridge the "ugly ditch" between past and present gives rise to countless arbitrary applications. God becomes entirely the object of personal, subjective faith.

My last point is perhaps the most important and the most difficult one. In modern times, God has as it were gradually withdrawn from history. Theology, previously a doctrine about God, became a doctrine about the word of God, then a presentation of human possibilities of speaking about God, then in the end a presentation of Christianity and thus a subdiscipline within religious studies. New Testament theology increasingly became a history of the theologies of primitive Christianity.

31. August H. Francke, "Christus der Kern Heiliger Schrift" (1702), in: Erhard Peschke (ed.), *Werke in Auswahl* (Berlin: Evangelische Verlagsanstalt, 1969), pp. 232-248; see pp. 232, 234.

32. Claus von Bormann, "Hermeneutik I," *TRE* 15 (1986), 108-137, here: p. 116.

33. Gerd Theissen, "Methodenkonkurrenz und hermeneutischer Konflikt. Pluralismus in Exegese und Lektüre der Bibel," in: Mehlhausen et al. (see note 2), pp. 127-140; see p. 129.

2.6. As a philological-historical discipline, exegesis can no longer under-stand its texts in the context of divine revelation, but only in the context of reli-gious and intellectual history of late antiquity. In its texts it no longer encounters God, only a wide variety of human verbal utterances about God. Where once God stood as revealer, his human substitutes now stand. Historical scholarship attempts to trace why they spoke of God in particular ways in particular situa-tions. God's own place remains empty, including the place of the God who ac-cording to orthodox Protestant belief was, ultimately, the one author of the Scriptures. Instead we have a multitude of human authors.

As I see it, God's disappearance from history is the ultimate reason for the inevitability of religious pluralism. History can then no longer be monopolized by a theological perspective[34] but has the opportunity to become an open field, accessible to various different interpretations, each of them incomplete.

3. The Biblical Texts as Linguistic Discourses

In his book *Plurality and Ambiguity,* an important one for me, David Tracy has given one of the main chapters the title "Radical Plurality: The Question of Language."[35] He describes there the "linguistic turn," the shift to new nominalism in European and North American thought under the influence of de Saussure's linguistics and of Wittgenstein. This posits that there is no di-rect link between signifiers and the sign system of a language on one side and a signified reality external to language on the other. In Tracy's words, "Reality is what we name our best interpretation."[36] Perhaps our German-language exegesis has not yet fully grasped the implications of this turn.[37] After all, vir-tually the whole of theological exegesis up to the Reformation was indirectly Platonic in its formation. Language was said to participate in the idea,[38] and the words and stories of Scripture were said to participate in the spiritual working of the divine logos. Hence biblical texts were the expression of a di-vine power, the ἐνέργεια (energy) of the logos.[39]

---

34. According to Marquard (see note 23), p. 96, "the Christian sole God brings salvation by monopolizing the story."

35. David Tracy, *Plurality and Ambiguity* (San Francisco: Harper and Row, 1987), p. 47.

36. Tracy, pp. 47, 48.

37. In Heidegger's ambiguous philosophical tradition it is possible, after all, to conceive of being as an event of truth which reveals itself in the λόγος.

38. In Plato's *Kratylos* however Socrates does not develop his thesis on the level of seman-tics but, to a certain extent at least, on the level of phonetics. I.e., it is the sound of the words which (sometimes!) corresponds to the idea they represent.

39. Johannes Panagopoulos, "Sache und Energie. Zur theologischen Grundlegung der

The linguistic turn has radically pluralized all theological and exegetical statements. They are linguistic constructions of reality which do not arise from correspondence with extra-linguistic reality. They could be constructed as they are, or differently. They are formed by the structure of our language, or rather by our constructions of this structure. They are formed by our own perception, our experience and our basic epistemological axioms. They are also formed by their possibilities of efficacy, e.g., by the way in which they enable us to cope with new experience of reality, or quite simply by the question of how well they will sell.[40] These examples indicate that there are many different ways of designing and ordering linguistic constructions of reality. What they have in common is that they are all human constructions and interpretations, not reality itself. This is true both of scientific and of theological propositions. Thus the object of theological propositions is always other theological propositions or, at best, experience expressed in language. Their object is never extra-linguistic history, and certainly not God.[41]

I cannot say yet whether this linguistic turn taken by our thinking in the twentieth century is as fundamental and irrevocable as the distancing of history that has taken place since the Enlightenment. But I suggest that theology should be content to live with this development. If the material, detectable reality of atoms, for example, is only accessible as linguistically constructed and interpreted world, how much more this is true of transcendental and contrafactual reality such as God, God's kingdom or the resurrection of Jesus!

---

biblischen Hermeneutik bei den griechischen Kirchenvätern," in Hubert Cancik et al. (eds.), *Geschichte — Tradition — Reflexion*, III (FS Martin Hengel; Tübingen: Mohr Siebeck, 1997), pp. 567-584, here: pp. 574-581.

40. The English Old Testament scholar David J. Clines presents this thesis under the innocuous title "Possibilities and Priorities of Biblical Interpretation in an International Perspective," *Biblical Interpretation* 1 (1993), pp. 67-87. Clines makes the assumption that it is the "interpretative communities" alone which produce the meaning of a text. There are echoes of Stanley Fish here! Clines states: "I will be giving my energies to producing attractive interpretations that represent good value for money" (p. 80). I shall not argue with Clines about whether this approach is "unethical" (ibid.) or not. In a pluralist society, he can have his opinion and I have mine. But it did surprise me to find that a quality journal such as *Biblical Interpretation* considers this "attractive."

41. Peter Lampe draws attention to this from the perspective of constructivism and sociology of knowledge in his lecture "Wissenssoziologische Annäherung an das Neue Testament," *NTS* 43 (1997), pp. 347-366. "Historians can consider themselves fortunate if they succeed, at best, in getting close to this world constructed by the early Christians. From a constructivist perspective we scholars and historians have no access *eo ipso* to the existential reality that paralleled the constructed reality of the early Christian Easter believers" (p. 360). What I wonder is how the various constructors of reality test the viability and falsification of their constructions when they are in dialogue with each other.

This was discovered in exegesis even before the linguistic turn. From the historical perspective, it was clear that the New Testament contained only interpreted reality.

3.1. The discovery of interpreted history made exegesis the precursor of religious pluralism. Jesus exists only as interpreted by Mark, Matthew, Paul, John, Origen, and others. The "real" Christ of the New Testament is none other than Christ interpreted in the language of Paul, Matthew, or others.

There are good reasons why New Testament exegesis has accepted the linguistic turn only hesitantly and selectively. There is hesitation because, firstly, most of us have resisted the demand that texts should be seen exclusively as structures, without consideration of the fact that in texts one person speaks to another or asks something of another. Partly under the influence of speech act theory, our discipline has maintained its approach to texts as "discourse" in Benvéniste's sense rather than as structures.[42] Texts are never simply systems *(langue)* but always *parole* as well. It follows that texts are events in time. They are read, and this takes time. They have effects. The second reason for our hesitation is that exegesis assumes a certain stability not only of the structures but also of the senses of texts. This is why there are reservations concerning reader-response theorists such as Stanley Fish, who expect nothing of the text and everything of the interpretative strategies adopted by the readers and interpretative communities.[43] Exegetes have preferred more moderate reader-response theorists such as Umberto Eco or Wolfgang Iser. Exegesis assumes that someone who invents a language game generally has something to say, and that the task of the exegete is to listen as closely as possible to the sense of the unfamiliar text.[44] Exegesis is certainly interested in inter-texts, and these are indeed especially important for the New Testament texts shaped by the language of the Bible. But this must be undertaken with restraint. Exegesis is aware of change and of newly consti-

---

42. Emile Benvéniste, *Problems in General Linguistics* (Coral Gables, Florida: University of Miami, 1971), pp. 208f., defines the (oral) discourse as "every utterance assuming a speaker and a hearer, and in the speaker, the intention of influencing the other in some way." As I see it, written language too has a communicative purpose in most texts and is thus "address" just as oral discourses are.

43. As far as I know, Stanley Fish's extreme position making meaning entirely dependent on the interpretative strategies of interpretative communities has hardly been received in theology, not even by Roman Catholics with integrationist tendencies to whom this might be expected to appeal.

44. Gerd Theissen (see note 33) has aptly formulated the ethical stance of exegesis by reference to the "hermeneutical superiority of love": "Every human utterance deserves to be understood for its own sake, since no human being is entirely means towards an end but always an end in itself" (p. 139).

tuted meanings in the course of history,[45] but if there were nothing but change and deconstruction this would be "the ruin of all reference, the cemetery of communication."[46]

I shall now formulate a second conclusion which assumes the basic legitimacy of a moderate reader-response approach and presents reader-oriented exegesis as the precursor of religious pluralism.

3.2. Exegesis which treats texts as discourses looks for the signals in the text which connect with the reader, i.e. the structured gaps of the implied reader, the anticipation of "the presence of a recipient without necessarily defining him," the prestructured "role"[47] which an actual reader can assume. This exegesis also looks for the guidance strategies in the text misleadingly referred to as the "implicit author." Texts contain guidance strategies and possibilities of freedom enabling open communication between text and readers. By shifting its interest from author to reader, exegesis becomes the agent of religious pluralism.

The biblical texts do not prevent this pluralism. Rather, their continual openness to new and different readings has given rise to pluralism. But "different readings" does not mean that *any* reading is possible. "Some interpretations are possible, but not all."[48]

I have a third point to add. It concerns the importance of the bridge between reader-response theory and history. The bridge is formed by the fact that the response-inviting texts are actually read. Acts of reading are acts in history. They take time, and they have their effects. The "gap" of the implied reader makes sense only if the space is filled by actual readers.

When actual readers fill the gap in the text, they bring into it their own personality, their biography, their religion, their experiences, their analysis of society. In filling the gap, they may well strain and distort it. Hence Severino Croatto refers to exegesis as "eisegesis," which means "entering into the biblical text with a cargo of meaning that recreates the first meaning."[49] Biblical texts claim repeatedly that they offer basic orientation for living. They want readers to enter them *with their whole lives,* bringing the cargo of their own situation and responding to what the texts offer. These texts need to be expe-

---

45. Paul Ricoeur in particular has drawn attention to this in his discussion of structuralism, in: *The Conflict of Interpretation: Essays in Hermeneutic* (Evanston: Northwestern University, 1974), pp. 44-47.

46. Terry Eagleton, *Literary Theory. An Introduction* (Oxford: Blackwell, ²1996), p. 126.

47. Wolfgang Iser, *The Act of Reading. A Theory of Aesthetic Response* (Baltimore: Johns Hopkins University, 1978), p. 34.

48. Gerd Theissen (see note 33), p. 131.

49. Severino Croatto, *Biblical Hermeneutics. Toward a Theory of Reading as the Production of Meaning* (Maryknoll: Orbis, 1987), p. 75.

rienced and lived afresh. Their deconstruction and re-interpretation take place in history. It is human search for identity, human life and practice and suffering. It is not mere intellectual patchwork but life as it is lived.[50] That is why I am far more interested in actual readings of the texts than in possible readings, and far more concerned with reception history than reception theory. Reception history does not merely document new interpretations and "deconstructions" of texts. It also teaches us to differentiate between seriously lived, suffered or practiced interpretations and intellectual games.

3.3. *The reception history of the biblical texts makes clear that believing the texts contain an "objective, permanent sense, directly accessible to the exegete at any time," is a Platonizing dogma of philological metaphysics.*[51] *Reception history draws attention to the contextuality of the biblical texts and thus to the wide variety of interpretations.*

I am concerned to emphasize that the linguistic turn is not a turning away from history. Those who withdraw from history into textual worlds or structured language systems may construct or deconstruct as they like, but they will no longer reach the world of history in which their readers are living. Odo Marquard has caricatured the semiotics and communications theorists as "code breakers." They themselves claim that the poor old hermeneutists never escape from history. To which Marquard replies, "But *must* one get beyond history? One who does not get out of history, does not arrive at an absolute position. But *must* one then arrive at an absolute position?"[52] Exegesis which combines the linguistic turn with the contextuality of interpreted history certainly does not have to do so.

4. Effective History *(Wirkungsgeschichte)*

The epistemological significance of Gadamer's concept of "effective history" lies for me in the fact that it gives the human being back to history. It transforms the perspective on history: History is no more an object of examination, but becomes a fundament sustaining human life. Gadamer's *Wirkungs-*

---

50. For this reason I find much of what is offered, e.g., in *Semeia* 54 (1991) under the title "Poststructuralism as Exegesis" rather irrelevant. It demonstrates the capacity of the authors for endless "layings on" which may well be aesthetically appealing (cf. Robert Detweiler, "Overliving," op. cit., p. 253), but fails to reveal what happens when people "lay on" the biblical texts their own lives, suffering and death and thus interpret *themselves* anew!

51. Hans Robert Jauss, *Literaturgeschichte als Provokation* (Frankfurt: Edition Suhrkamp, ⁴1974), p. 183.

52. Marquard (see note 24), p. 130.

geschichte, variously translated in English as the "history of effects" or "history of reception" of past historic events or texts, is more than this. It is "effective history" and thus a shaping power. Readers of a text, and of a biblical text in particular, are never autonomous subjects but owe themselves to the text they read. Gadamer is drawing attention here to the "living relationship to tradition" which scholars employing the historical-critical method have "reflected themselves out of."[53]

The study of the reception history of biblical texts has, first, revealed to me where I have come from and what history has made me. It has, second, broadened my horizons by making me aware of where others come from and who they have become. Our various readings of biblical texts reflect not only our present situation but also our history. What has this to do with plurality of perspectives? My first thesis is as follows:

4.1. The study of reception history makes readers of biblical texts aware of the specificity and particularity of their own readings. We owe our own existence to a specific and particular history, and the same is true of people in other cultures, other churches and other situations. In this sense every interpretation is a particular one. But its particularity cannot be selected at random, any more than we can select our place in history.

Thus the study of effective history requires us to accept our own particularity, not trying to interpret biblical texts neutrally but as who we are, be it Protestants or Catholics, South Americans or Europeans.

My second consideration stands in contrast to Gadamer's approach. He understands hermeneutics of "effective history" as "participating in an event of tradition, a process of transmission in which past and present are constantly mediated."[54] It has repeatedly been suggested, with some justification as I see it, that Gadamer subordinates the human being in the act of understanding to the power of tradition. However, those who study the reception history of biblical texts will know how ambivalent this can be. The reception history of Matthew's Gospel for example means Christianity of action, but it also means contempt for the Jews in the wake of Matthew 23, or even persecution of the Jews in the wake of Matthew's account of the Passion. All history is ambiguous, and "there is no innocent interpretation, no innocent interpreter, no innocent text."[55] This brings me to my second thesis:

4.2. "Effective history" is a precursor of pluralism because it can reveal the

---

53. Hans-Georg Gadamer, *Truth and Method* (2nd rev. ed.; New York: Crossroad, 1989), p. 360.

54. Gadamer, p. 290.

55. Tracy (see note 35), p. 79.

ambivalence of texts and their effects, and indeed the ambivalence of history it-self. Entering the horizon of history of tradition must not mean simply grateful acceptance of tradition. It must also mean, in the face of diverse traditions, making judgments, and that means saying yes or no. Entering the horizon of history of tradition requires decision-making on the part of the subject. Such decisions are a personal responsibility and therefore they will of necessity vary.

My third consideration is based on Gadamer's point that there can be no understanding of texts which is not an "understanding in a different way."[56] Those whose hermeneutics is grounded in liberation theology, feminism or psychodynamics will know what Gadamer means. This is exactly what the historical explanation of biblical texts is about. They have always been "texts in use, read and applied by people who made use of the messages of the texts in their concrete situation."[57] Thus the liveliness of biblical texts and traditions is shaped above all by their varied use by many different people in many different situations. The texts remain themselves by being changed. Like the intra-biblical history of biblical traditions, the reception history of biblical texts documents the living nature of traditions and texts and thus of plurality. Reception history documents what reader-oriented textual interpretation postulates.

Reception history is also concerned, however, with periods of stability in the senses of texts. It shows the interdependence of text-sense stability, world views, and the stability of institutions. The hermeneutics of effective history questions such periods of stability with a "hermeneutics of suspicion," asking whether the stability of sense in texts has not been associated time and again with the tendency of institutions, and of churches in particular, to monopolize the interpretation of biblical texts and attempt to establish "valid interpretations" for the purpose of self-legitimation. Reception history draws attention to the use and abuse of power that underlies such treatment of the texts.

4.3. Reception history is a precursor of pluralism in that it shows how the understanding of given biblical texts has always been a new and different understanding. In this way it draws attention to the association between living tradition, freedom and plurality. This association corresponds to the living tradition in the biblical texts themselves.

---

56. Gadamer (see note 54), p. 297.

57. Kirsten Nielsen, "Verantwortlicher Umgang mit Traditionen im religiösen Pluralismus," in: Mehlhausen (see note 2), pp. 37-53; see p. 39.

5. The Task of Exegesis in a Situation of Religious Pluralism

We have seen that our current situation of religious pluralism is in part a result of the history of biblical interpretation. Post-Reformation exegesis, whose mission was to clarify the foundations on which the church is built, has become a precursor of pluralism. In Protestant Northwest Europe at least, this pluralism is widely breaking up the churches and robbing them of their identifying force. Does this mean, then, that exegesis is destroying the church? This is the fundamentalist thesis. If the church is understood in the fundamentalist sense as the place where the *one* redemptive truth is taught, then the thesis is a valid one.

What then is the task of exegesis in this situation, which it has contributed to shaping?

An impressive lecture by Peter Berger likens the situation in today's church to its situation in late Roman society. At that time the church was no longer in a ghetto, but it did not yet constitute a social force which provided secular rulers with metaphysical myths to legitimate their rule. Rather, the church was at that time in the *agora,* in the open market of religions and philosophies.[58]

As I see it, Berger's image can be used to describe the task of exegesis in today's society. Three options are open to it. First, exegesis could provide legitimation for an exclusivist existence, at least in some cultures.[59] This has been seen in earlier absolutist Christian subcultures, some of them sects and others respected churches. Second, exegesis could contribute to the stabilizing of pluralism as "randomness."[60] It would then simply need to "lay on"

58. Peter Berger, "Wenn die Welt wankt. Pluralismus ist eine Chance für Christen," *LM* 32:12 (1993), pp. 12-16, here: p. 14.

59. Karl Dienst, "In Zukunft ganz pluralistisch?," in Richard Ziegert (ed.), *Die Zukunft des Schriftprinzips,* Bibel im Gespräch 2 (Stuttgart: Deutsche Bibelgesellschaft, 1994), pp. 207-221, here: p. 207, describes this with reference to a caricature he has in front of him: "Cannons are being loaded and the direction of fire is indicated by flags: against liberals, against charismatics, against fundamentalists, against feminists, against critics, etc. The caption reads: 'But we do have one thing in common: we are all using the same ammunition!' And that is the Bible!" (from *Idea Spectrum* 22 [1992] p. 19).

60. Herms (see note 1), p. 467, regards "pluralism on principle" as the opposite of "pluralism of randomness." He sees pluralism on principle endangered chiefly where "a uniform civil religion horizon" renders the competition between various philosophical and ethical convictions relative. What connects and is held in common is more important than what separates. I see it differently. To my mind this principle of pluralism is endangered where "randomness as principle" reduces competition between various convictions to absurdity and can only reject such competition as a return to a "modern" battle of totalitarian world views.

rather than interpret,[61] inventing postmodern stories and putting on the market whatever happens to appeal.[62] But there is a third option. Exegesis can take itself and what it has to say into the public domain of the marketplace. Contributing its knowledge of the linguistic structure of its texts, its knowledge of what the texts intended to say to their original readers and what they did say to the original and later readers, and indeed what they could say today, exegesis can take part in the academic dialogue in the *agora*.

What characterizes this dialogue? I shall summarize it in eight theses.

5.1. The nature of the dialogue is public. If religion has become merely a private affair, it is far removed from public reason. Academic exegesis can counteract this development, introducing biblical impulses into the public dialogue on the aims of society and the direction it is taking. The place of exegesis, like that of the prophets, is in the public domain. Its role model is the Lukan Paul: "he argued . . . in the marketplace every day with those who happened to be there" (Acts 17:17). The university is a good place to practice this.

5.2. The nature of the dialogue is rational. In the age of religious bricolage, when everyone puts together their own religious traditions and foundations without having to account for them, it is essential that exegesis should academically reflect the biblical foundations of Christian tradition and make this part of a rational dialogue. This will enable it to adopt a critical approach to the foundations of its own tradition and its uses to which it has been put. This is not a question of legitimizing other discourses by means of a metanarrative. Rather, the dialogue with other legitimation discourses will enable exegesis and exegetes to tell their own stories and to discover in dialogue the depths, opportunities and limits of the own and others' stories. Exegesis should ensure that life does not disintegrate into a rational public and political sphere and an irrational private and religious sphere. It should prevent rationality from becoming completely free of religion and religion from becoming completely free of reason.

5.3. The dialogue aims at consensus. Agreement is necessary for the sake of the κοινωνία (fellowship), and κοινωνία is necessary in the interests of common action. The biblical perspective is a universal one, and God's rule is all-embracing. It transcends every particular religion and all particular groups. For this reason we exegetes cannot be content to echo Lyotard's paralogic and say that "consensus is only a particular state of discussion, not its end."[63] We must aim for completer agreement in the sense of shalom. But Lyotard does remind us

---

61. See note 50.
62. See note 40.
63. Lyotard (see note 17), p. 65.

that no consensus is definitive and final in character, since no dialogue can realize a completely "ideal speech situation."[64]

A brief interjection is necessary here. Habermas's description of communicative competence and of the ideal dialogue has a utopian element. Among exegetes, his understanding of consensus calls to mind the kingdom of God. This is why, from a biblical perspective, I cannot give up hope at least of a partial and temporary presence of this utopian element. After all, the kingdom of God may already be "among you" (Luke 17:21). The churches in particular, seeking to be shaped by the Bible and even seeing themselves as "alternative societies," should be concerned to improve the speech situation in their midst. We exegetes should confront them with this in the texts we are dealing with. From the biblical perspective, plurality should be neither a dominant discourse that leaves a few insignificant spaces open, nor the expression of relativity and a companion of randomness.

The two fragmentary theses which follow are concerned with the significance of exegesis for the church.

5.4. The ecumenical dimension of the dialogue. Modern exegesis is not bound by the fetters of confessional interpretation of the Bible. In the modern pluralist society, confessional exegesis has repeatedly been revealed to be dominant discourse in partial kingdoms. But texts which are always contextualized and used, and statements of truth which are always linguistic constructions of truth, are unsuited to being metanarratives and dominant knowledge. By means of exegesis, confessional interpretation of the Bible has been replaced by plurality. The task is not to eliminate confessional interpretation by means of neutral historical exegesis. Rather, exegesis within the ecumenical dialogue involves people narrating to each other their own particular Bible-formed confessional part-interpretations and taking a critical approach to them. This will enable them, in the light of the Bible and of its reception history, to recognize each other and see where each has come from, what their limitations and biases are, and what they could become.

Can the Bible be foundational for the church in this ecumenical discourse? This depends how one defines "church." If the Bible is used in the manner outlined above, it cannot be the foundation of a church claiming exclusive redemptive knowledge based on biblical arguments. It can be foundational only for a church which is defined as a community in dialogue about the Bible, a community that crosses confessional boundaries, is found in all

---

64. Cf. Jürgen Habermas, "Vorbereitende Bemerkungen zu einer Theorie der kommunikativen Kompetenz," in Jürgen Habermas/Niklas Luhmann, *Theorie der Gesellschaft oder Sozialtechnologie: Was leistet die Systemforschung?* (Frankfurt: Suhrkamp, 1971) pp. 122, 136-140.

confessions and transcends them all. It seems to me that our confessional churches have work to do here, and that it needs to be done soon if their time is not to run out.

5.5. The strangeness of Jesus' story. Exegesis must point again and again to the antiquity and particularity of Jesus' story of which its texts speak. This story will always be strange and tend to resist our human and ecclesial expectations. It is not well suited to attempts to legitimize. The clearest expression of the church's dilemma with the Jesus story is perhaps the fact that all the Christian churches have reference to a Jew who had no intention of founding a Christian church. This Jesus is not an ideal central figure in a metanarrative, whether it be one of Christian churches or of Christian cultures or states.

5.6. The trans-ecclesial dimension of the dialogue. The methods of exegesis are those of philology, history, religious studies and linguistics. God encounters us in the biblical texts as human and contextual logos and as human and linguistic interpretation of reality. That is, God is encountered only indirectly. But this very indirectness makes God accessible to non-believers. God who is part of human language and human history is not the exclusive domain of believers. Thus exegesis makes dialogue with non-religious people on the texts of the Bible possible. In the future, biblical studies will become even more significant for interfaith dialogue.[65] *All this is not to be confused with proselytizing.*

5.7. The Bible as foundational for our culture. The reception history of biblical texts demonstrates the extent to which the Bible has been foundational for European culture, and not only for the culture of the continent's declining Christian churches. The Bible as effective and fundamental history continues to provide foundations in the lives of people who are no longer Christians. One of the tasks of exegesis in our society of religious pluralism is to call the Bible to mind as the common foundation of all Europeans and the shaping force of our common history.

As I noted above, we do not have the American model of civil religion in Europe. But we do have a common history, a history that is both ambivalent and multiform. The Bible is an important and at the same time ambivalent factor within it. Our lives are lived from within our history, and it is our task to work critically through it. Perhaps not having a civil religion is an advantage in that at least we do not need to demythologize this "myth."

5.8. Pointing to God. The most important task of exegesis as I see it is to point again and again to the one who is encountered only indirectly in the texts

---

65. As evidenced in exemplary manner in the Edward Cadbury Lectures delivered in Birmingham by Heikki Räisänen, *Marcion, Muhammad and the Mahatma. Exegetical Perspectives on the Encounter of Cultures and Faiths* (London: SCM, 1997).

as part of history and only in language as a lexical item in texts, i.e. God. Exegesis cannot demonstrate God. No exegete can prove that what Paul says of God is true, and that his discourse on God refers to an extra-language reality. Our biblical texts come to us from the past, and in them God is doubly mediated. In the Bible and other texts where the word "God" occurs, God is part of a human construction of reality. In texts from the past God is not part of our own construction of reality but comes to us in constructions by other people we know of only through texts. This doubly mediated God does not impose on others and is "resistable"[66] in that people of today are given the freedom to react to this word as they wish. God, accessible only in human language, can only be something quite different to this language, something inexpressible and unavailable in it if God is real. Vis-à-vis human — and theological — wisdom as it is articulated in metanarratives and foundational myths, God operates perhaps as a force for deconstruction. Paul had important things to say about this (1 Cor. 1:18-25).

This brings me to the end. The main task of exegetes in a society of religious pluralism is, then, to point to the God of whom their texts only *speak* and who is not in any way available to them. Unlike the early church, exegesis can no longer point to the ἐνέργεια (energy) of the divine logos and the divine spirit in the texts. Unlike classical dogmatics, it certainly cannot gather from the Bible the stones of a grand ecclesial metanarrative. It can perhaps, together with the Reformers, point out that God became human for all time, is incarnate for all time and, paradoxically, is among us for all time in the guise of one who was crucified. Above all, and in the face of the *conditio moderna*, exegesis must point out that it cannot go beyond the boundaries of human history and human language, and that possibly God is *the* great disturbance in human linguistic constructions of reality. But we cannot know for certain whether this is so.

---

66. Cf. Hans Weder, *Neutestamentliche Hermeneutik* (Zürich: TVZ, 1986), p. 393.

16 Canonical Exegesis and Hermeneutics of "Effective History"

For Urs von Arx, on the occasion of his 60th birthday

1. The Canonical Approach

The postulate of a "canonical approach"[1] has become increasingly significant in recent years. The canonical approach critically interrogates all tendencies to regard the Bible simply as a document of religious and cultural history in late antiquity or as a merely literary text. But what is meant by the "canonical approach"? The focus can vary considerably. Peter Stuhlmacher, one of the foremost representatives of German-language biblical theology, concentrates on the unity of the two Testaments within the one Christian canon. He is not only concerned however with the "assessment of the canonical process and the two-part Christian canon emerging from it,"[2] but with two further important questions. First, what is the κανὼν τῆς πίστεως (rule of faith)? The early church pointed to the regula fidei (rule of faith), the Reformation pointed to Christ as the center of the Scriptures. Second, Stuhlmacher inquires into the specific modes of interpretation which the Bible, as a canonical book, suggests to its interpreters. This is the question of a particular hermeneutic corresponding to the Bible as canon. Biblical hermeneutics must

---

1. Whereas German usage tends to speak of "canonical exegesis," I prefer the English expression "canonical approach." This indicates that we are not concerned simply with a particular mode of interpreting the Bible, as one among others, but with a basic attitude towards the Bible which may be expressed in very varied modes of interpretation.

2. Peter Stuhlmacher, *Biblische Theologie des Neuen Testaments*, II (Göttingen: Vandenhoeck und Ruprecht, 1999), p. 287.

German original in: Hans Gerny/Harald Rein/Maja Weyermann (eds.), "Kanonische Exegese und Hermeneutik der Wirkungsgeschichte," in: *Sentire cum Ecclesia* (FS Urs von Arx; Bern: Stämpfli, 2003), pp. 40-57.

absorb and reflect the very special claim of the biblical texts "to bear witness to a truth that is in advance of and superior to any human knowledge."[3]

Canonical criticism in the United States is chiefly represented by Brevard Childs.[4] For him "the term canon points to the received, collected, and interpreted material of the church and thus establishes the theological context in which the tradition continues to function authoritatively for today."[5] For Childs the relationship between the two Testaments is one of continuity and difference, each Testament having its own integrity.[6] He bases his work on a "realistic" understanding of language and history. The task of biblical theology is to investigate the historically multifarious relation between the divine reality and its historical representations in the Old and New Testament.[7]

If I see it correctly, these and other attempts at a canonical approach have a threefold concern:

1.1. They are concerned with a new perspective on the *unity* of the biblical testimonies. Academic exegesis, and historical-critical exegesis in particular, has tirelessly endeavored to understand the biblical testimonies from within their own specific situation, interpreting them as different and specific. The question of what connects the biblical testimonies with each other and what is their *common* concern and unifying center thus fell by the wayside. The findings of historical-critical exegesis present us with a plurality of faith testimonies from a variety of people, times, and places. Add to this the plurality of modern exegetical opinions concerning them, and the confusion is complete. For today's preachers and Bible readers as well as the various Christian denominations and churches, the findings of exegetical research are like a giant supermarket where everyone can choose whatever suits him or her. Alternatively, one need not shop there at all!

1.2. The canonical approach is concerned with renewing the challenge of the biblical texts' *claim to authority.* We cannot speak of the texts without reflecting on the fundamental claim they make on their readers. They speak of something, or rather someone, who is in advance of human life, who lays its foundation and lays claim to it, giving it meaning and future. The texts speak of God. This claim to authority on the part of the biblical texts is far

---

3. Stuhlmacher (see note 2), p. 323.

4. Brevard S. Childs, *The New Testament as Canon. An Introduction* (London: SCM, 1984); Childs, *Biblical Theology of the Old and New Testaments* (Minneapolis: Fortress, 1993).

5. Childs, *Theology* (see note 4), p. 71.

6. Childs, *Theology* (see note 4), partic. pp. 76ff. (in double confrontation with "biblical theologians" like Hartmut Gese and with Rudolf Bultmann) and pp. 78f.

7. Childs, *Theology,* pp. 85f.

more fundamental than any of its conceptual interpretations, such as "revelation" or "inspiration." It is more fundamental than any theological understanding of the canon. Over the centuries since the Enlightenment we have become so accustomed to emphasizing that the Bible is a book like any other human book, that we easily disregard its particular claim to authority. This particular claim to authority corresponds to a particular mode of understanding to which the Bible challenges us. Canonical criticism seeks to take the claim of the Bible to be the "guiding rule" seriously, reminding us that reading the Bible without reflecting on this does not do it justice and is in that respect not a scholarly approach. This is not to be confused with ecclesiastical claims to authority.

1.3. Finally, the canonical approach is concerned to remind us that the Bible is, primarily, a church book, indeed it is *the book of the church*. It was the church which created the canon and declared it to be the guiding rule. Today, "the" church no longer exists. It has dissolved into myriad churches, denominations, tendencies, congregations, communities, and groups which see themselves in many different ways as part of "the" church or as "the church" itself. This development has to do, *inter alia*, with very different readings of the Bible. The canonical approach reminds us that the Bible has been given to the churches and shapes them. It encourages reading of the Bible both in and for the churches. Among other things, this obliges us to take seriously the hermeneutical approaches to the Bible and the biblical interpretations which have shaped churches and denominations — others as well as our own — in past and present. At this point the affinity between the canonical approach and a hermeneutic of "effective history" in the sense of Gadamer becomes especially apparent.[8]

I should like to make clear at the outset that my own position as an exegete is an ecumenical one. After a period of confessional schism attributable in part to various "canonical" readings of the Bible, it is important to see the canon primarily as "commonwealth," as the *common* traditional deposit of the churches and as a *wealth* of different ways of interpreting faith. Today's canonical approach must take account of the experience that, in the face of the struggle for doctrinal unity and the apparent impossibility of ecclesiastical union, the canon as common wealth has proved itself an effective source of living unity in the churches. In the current ecumenical ice age, when churches can hardly agree on a common ecumenical agenda and when moves towards interdenominational worship services meet with disapproval in

---

8. Cf. my paper "Hermeneutics of 'Effective History' and the Church," in this volume, pp. 349-369.

some places,[9] I find the Bible to be the firm foundation supporting ecumenism. In this sense I see the ecclesiastical character of the canonical approach as ecumenical and not confessional.

I fully support these three basic concerns of canonical criticism. In this broad sense, the canonical approach is not a specific method or a specific hermeneutic but something much more fundamental. It is a perspective which must be adopted in the many different approaches and methods. In the following I shall adopt this perspective to reflect on my exegetical work, in particular that on Matthew, and on the hermeneutics of "effective history." I shall do this in three stages of reflection, the first on historical-critical exegesis and the canonical approach, the second on effective history and the canonical approach, and the third on some practical consequences for reading the Bible today. What I have to say is in the form of theses both comprehensive and fragmentary, and open to debate.

2. Historical-Critical Gospel Exegesis and the Canonical Approach

The two appear to be contradictory: the historical-critical exegesis of New Testament texts *cannot* in any direct sense be a "canonical approach," since the canon is chronologically secondary to the texts, i.e. part of their later reception history. It *cannot* in any direct sense be canonical exegesis, since it can only make *historical* statements about the claim to authority of the biblical texts. True, historical-critical exegesis, which is accustomed to differentiating in historical and literary terms, *can* inquire into what connects and binds together the various texts collected in the canon, but it cannot make canonical unity its principle. Being an academic discipline, it cannot read the Bible simply as "the book of the church." Its task is a broader one and has to take account for example of reception of the Bible outside the churches. For all these reasons, historical-critical exegesis cannot be canonical exegesis in any direct sense. A canonical approach to the Bible is a hermeneutical perspective which historical-critical exegesis with its questions can prepare for but not actually accomplish.

In the following I draw attention to three such "preparatory" questions which are significant for exegesis of the gospels.

2.1. Historical-critical exegesis which takes account of the canon question will pay close attention to "proto-canonical" tendencies in the Gospels and other biblical texts, i.e. tendencies in the texts themselves which make

9. What of the Lima Liturgy of 20 years ago — was it a stillbirth?

their later canonization comprehensible and logical. Such tendencies should not simply be dismissed as "early catholic."[10]

It is generally held that the writing down of the Jesus tradition was in itself a first step toward canonization. Mark wanted to preserve in his Gospel the ἀρχή (beginning, foundation) of the proclamation of his church (Mark 1:1). He is concerned with its beginning in time, but equally with its foundation.[11] Proto-canonical tendencies are apparent at the end of Matthew's Gospel. With the mission command διδάσκοντες αὐτοὺς τηρεῖν πάντα ὅσα ἐνετειλάμην ὑμῖν ("teach them to observe all that I have commanded to you," Matt. 28:20a), Matthew can actually be said to "canonize" his own book.[12] It contains — especially in the discourses of Jesus spoken into the present — everything the messengers of Jesus need for their missionary proclamation. It is thus logical that in the Matthean tradition the *Didache* already understands the εὐαγγέλιον (gospel) as a book.[13] A similar tendency is evident in the Lukan preface, which claims to be a complete and reliable account of the tradition fundamental to Christian catechesis (Luke 1:1-4). The next step towards the "canonization" of this tradition is the separation of the second volume of Luke's double book from the first and the placing of the latter among the "Gospels." This is likely to have occurred early, bearing in mind the probable antiquity of the Gospel titles.[14] In the Johannine tradition I draw attention to John 21:24, a verse which lends to the Gospel a virtually "supra-apostolic" dignity in that it declares the beloved disciple, who recognized Jesus more fully than did any other of the apostles, to be its author.[15]

10. I draw attention to the debate of the 60s and 70s in European Protestant theology on what was termed "Early Catholicism." Although he was not the first to use the concept publicly, Ernst Käsemann's (d)evaluation of Lukan theology (in "Paulus und der Frühkatholizismus," in: Käsemann, *Exegetische Versuche und Besinnungen*, II [Göttingen: Vandenhoeck und Ruprecht, 1964], pp. 239-252) contributed to initiating the debate. There is a prime example of unreflected devaluing use of the concept in Siegfried Schulz, *Die Mitte der Schrift. Der Frühkatholizismus im Neuen Testament als Herausforderung an den Protestantismus* (Stuttgart: Kreuz, 1976). On the conceptual problems cf. Christian Bartsch, *"Frühkatholizismus" als Kategorie historisch-kritischer Theologie* (Berlin: Institut für Kirche und Judentum, 1980); on the ecumenical debate cf. Joachim Rogge/Gottfried Schille (eds.), *Frühkatholizismus im ökumenischen Gespräch* (Berlin [DDR]: Evangelische Verlagsanstalt, 1983).

11. On this double meaning of ἀρχή cf. Rudolf Pesch, *Das Markusevangelium*, I, HThK II.I (Freiburg: Herder, 1976), pp. 75f.

12. Ulrich Luz, *Das Evangelium nach Matthäus (Matt. 26–28)*, EKK I.4 (Neukirchen/Düsseldorf: Neukirchener/Benziger, 2002), p. 455.

13. Probably the Gospel of Matthew; cf. Wolf Dietrich Köhler, *Die Rezeption des Matthäusevangeliums in der Zeit vor Irenäus*, WUNT II.24 (Tübingen: Mohr Siebeck, 1987), pp. 32-36.

14. Martin Hengel, *Die Evangelienüberschriften*, SHAW.PH (Heidelberg: Winter, 1984), pp. 14-23.

15. For further observations on John, I draw attention to the monography by Theo Heckel, *Vom Evangelium des Markus zum viergestaltigen Evangelium*, WUNT I.120 (Tübingen: Mohr Siebeck, 1999), pp. 158-218.

Overall I find that Brevard Childs's view of a "canonical process" does correspond to the New Testament texts. He uses the term "canonical" also to mean "the process by which the collection [of the canon] arose which led up to its final stage of literary and textual stabilization."[16] It has its basis in the "proto-canonical" character of the Gospels and other New Testament writings.

2.2. The "proto-canonical" character of the Gospels arises from the fact that they narrate the Jesus story as the new founding story of the communities. Israel's Bible is no longer the founding text for the Jesus communities, though it remains their most important, if not their only, reference text, which interprets their new founding story.

Like the biblical founding story of Israel, Mark's Gospel is an "inclusive" story which bridges the gap between past and present. With the disciples as identification figures, it brings its readers into direct contact with Jesus, or rather places Jesus the Son of God in the readers' present. As a founding story, Mark's Jesus story has a similar function as the biblical story about Adam as the "story of the beginnings of humankind." In Deuteronomy and elsewhere, these stories confront contemporaneous Israel directly with God's will as proclaimed through Moses at Horeb. They create a collective identity which links the Israel of the present with the Israel of the forefathers (cf. Deut. 26:5-9).

The Jewish Christian Gospel of Matthew is an actualizing retelling of this founding story. As such, it has a close affinity with the type of Jewish literature known as "rewritten Bible,"[17] "narrative midrash"[18] or "parabiblical literature."[19] The Gospel however retells a *different* story, namely the Markan story of Jesus. Unlike the writer of Mark's Gospel, the author of Matthew consciously places his work in relation to Israel's founding story. Indeed, a double relationship is created: on the one hand, the Gospel has literary features which will remind its readers of Israel's founding story and enable them to realize that a new story is now replacing it, the Gospel of Matthew forming a new "Book of Genesis."[20] The great discourses are reminiscent of the Pentateuch: the will of the Father is proclaimed — now by Jesus — from a mountain.

---

16. Childs, *Biblical Theology* (see note 4), p. 70.

17. Geza Vermes, *Scripture and Tradition in Judaism*, StPB 4 (Leiden: Brill, ²1983), pp. 67-126.

18. Addison G. Wright, "The Literary Genre Midrash," *CBQ* 28 (1966), pp. 105-138, here: p. 128.

19. Florentino García Martínez, *The Dead Sea Scrolls Translated* (Leiden: Brill, 1994), pp. 217-299.

20. By according it the book (!) title "genesis," the Evangelist has made the Markan story of Jesus a founding story with biblical dignity. On the title, see Ulrich Luz, *Das Evangelium nach Matthäus (Matt. 1–7)*, EKK I.1 (Neukirchen/Düsseldorf: Neukirchener/Benziger ⁵2002), pp. 117-119.

Thus the Gospel has the "look" of the biblical founding story, right down to wording that is shaped by the Septuagint. On the other hand, the Gospel relates consciously to this founding story as its primary reference text. The introductory words to the quotation formulas in particular, but also passages such as Matt. 5:17 and 22:40, indicate the unique character of the biblical reference text. The difference now is that Israel's Bible is no longer the founding story of the church. Rather, it is the "prehistory" to the new founding story, given condensed literary form in the genealogy of Matt. 1:2-17. Jesus' story and proclamation becomes the new center from which the biblical reference texts are selected and the whole Bible weighted anew.[21]

In a different but nonetheless comparable way, John's Gospel also claims to be a new founding story for the believers.[22] This is apparent at the beginning of the logos hymn, which opens up the perspective to include creation and makes Christ the mediator of that creation. The same claim is made very differently in Luke's bipartite work, where the divinely ordained "events that have been fulfilled among us" (Luke 1:1)[23] shape "us," that is, the communities of the third generation.

2.3. Historical-critical exegesis of New Testament texts which takes an interest in the canon will pay particular attention to the reception of the texts and text complexes which later came to be known as "Old Testament." Whereas Peter Stuhlmacher speaks of "just one, multilayered canonical process," "engendering the Hebrew Bible, the Septuagint and the New Testament,"[24] I prefer to see it as a process of selective reception of Israel's Bible in the New Testament, and a twofold canon formation.

The Gospels themselves support the thesis that in the first century the biblical canon was "still open or, at least, not completely closed."[25] I suggest that what Stuhlmacher sees as "just one" canonical process already consisted at an early stage of two separate processes of canonization of the First Testament, namely one Christian and one Jew-

21. This thesis is argued above, pp. 30-34.

22. J. Louis Martyn, *History and Theology in the Fourth Gospel* (Nashville: Abingdon, [2]1979), pp. 129-148, has shown the way to the "inclusive" character of John's Gospel.

23. The events referred to are those reported in the Gospel of Luke *and* the Acts of the Apostles.

24. Peter Stuhlmacher, *Wie treibt man Biblische Theologie?* BThSt 24 (Neukirchen: Neukirchener, 1995), p. 18, following Hartmut Gese. The danger of his formulation, it seems to me, is that a Christian perspective on this canonization process becomes the only perspective, losing sight of the quite different route to canonization undertaken by Israel from the same starting point, the emerging Tanach. As I see it, Childs more accurately emphasizes (in *Biblical Theology,* see note 4, p. 76) that the New Testament is not "a redactional layer above the Old Testament" and that the tradition process of the New Testament cannot simply be seen as analogous to the Old Testament and Jewish new versions of salvation history.

25. Julio Trebolle Barrera, *The Jewish Bible and the Christian Bible* (Leiden/Grand Rapids: Brill/Eerdmans, 1998), p. 12.

ish. The two different canonization processes had different starting points, the "proto-canonical" Hebrew Bible and what I term the "proto-Septuagint," that is, the Greek Bible used at that time in the Greek-speaking synagogues. The result was a two-part Christian canon consisting of the Greek Old and New Testament, and a two-part Jewish canon consisting of the Tanach and the Mishnah.

In the Christian congregations the biblical texts and text complexes were received highly selectively in the new tradition process of the new community. Some texts became key texts, some books such as Isaiah or Genesis were of central significance, while others were received hesitantly or not at all. In the early Jewish tradition process the phenomenon of "additions" and later the re-writing of fundamental traditions can be observed especially in the field of Torah. There is nothing comparable on the Christian side, with the exception of (in the broadest sense) some late prophetic texts, particularly in apocalypses and testaments.[26] But there is no Christian attempt to rewrite Israel's founding story, as drafted for instance by pseudo-Philo or Josephus. Rather, the genealogies in the Gospels of Matthew and Luke reduce and condense Israel's founding story, making it a "prehistory" to the Jesus story whose divinely ordained historical place in Israel is thus made apparent. The second strophe of John's logos hymn probably has a similar function.[27]

In regard to the Prophets and the Writings, the early church to a great extent created "its own" Septuagint canon. This may be said of the quantity of text, but also of the arrangement of texts. Placing the Prophets at the end became normative only in the Christian era and relatively late. It reflects a Christian understanding of the canon. The Prophets come at the end of the Septuagint canon because they are most closely associated with Jesus Christ.[28] Hence the often quoted thesis — a significant one indeed in today's theological situation — that Israel and the Christian church have a common canon in the Tanach/First Testament must be taken with a grain of

---

26. Most books of the Old Testament do not show Christian redaction (cf. Childs, *Biblical Theology* [see note 4], p. 75). Examples of Christian "continuation" can be found in the *Testaments of the Twelve Patriarchs* 5/6 Ezra, the *Sibylline Oracles, 2 Enoch;* cf. James H. Charlesworth, "Christian and Jewish Self-Definition in Light of the Christian Additions to the Apocryphal Writings" in: E. P. Sanders (ed.), *Jewish and Christian Self-Definition,* II (London: SCM, 1981), pp. 27-55.

27. John 1:5, 9-11. I interpret this verse of the pre-Johannine logos hymn as referring to the revelation of the logos in Israel's salvation history.

28. Martin Hengel, "Die Septuaginta als 'christliche Schriftensammlung', ihre Vorgeschichte und das Problem ihres Kanons," in: Martin Hengel/Anna Maria Schwemer (eds.), *Die Septuaginta zwischen Judentum und Christentum,* WUNT I.72 (Tübingen: Mohr Siebeck, 1994), pp. 182-284, here: pp. 219-228, 263-284; Hengel, "Die Septuaginta als 'christliche Schriftensammlung' und das Problem ihres Kanons," in: Wolfhart Pannenberg/Theodor Schneider, *Verbindliches Zeugnis I. Kanon — Schrift — Tradition,* DiKi 7 (Freiburg/Göttingen: Herder/ Vandenhoeck, 1992), pp. 107-127. Two New Testament examples of the "proto-Septuagint" used by New Testament authors are Matt. 23:35 and Luke 24:44. These assume a Greek Old Testament with the same structure as the Hebrew Bible!

salt. In fact, the form of the Christian canon of the Old Testament was to no small degree determined by the *new* perspective of the Christian church, i.e. its faith in Jesus
Christ. In both the churches of the Reformation and the Roman Catholic Church of
today in the West, the Hebrew text is recognized almost unquestioningly as the basic
text of the first part of the canonical Bible. The Orthodox churches of the East, in
contrast, have adhered to the Septuagint as the basic text of the Old Testament. It
would be naive to dismiss this as merely expressing a pre-academic biblical exegesis.[29]

The final "parting of the ways" and the accompanying "twofold" canonization
process became apparent in the second century A.D. when the New Testament joined
the Old as the second part of the canon. At the same time an analogous process took
place in Judaism. The Mishnah joined the Tanach as the "second canon." Just as the
New Testament became the fundamental and more important part of the canon in
the Christian church, determining the developments which followed, so the Mishnah
took on a similar function at least for rabbinic Judaism.[30] There are marked parallels
between the selective use of the Bible in the second canon of Judaism and in the second canon of Christianity. What this could mean for a biblical theology developed by
Jews and Christians working together has yet to be explored.[31]

3. Interpretation History, Reception History, and the Canon

Before the modern era, ecclesiastical reading of New Testament texts was always in some sense a canonical reading, i.e. a reading of individual texts
within the framework of the whole Bible. Canonical reading of the New Testament texts was shaped by faith, and prevented a fragmentation of the biblical message into various different individual messages. It was on this basis
that an individual New Testament text could be understood as "gospel."

3.1. On the level of literal interpretation of Gospel texts, it can be said
that they were read harmonistically, i.e. largely on the basis of a harmony of

---

29. I call to mind Hartmut Gese's programmatic words, "A Christian theologian must
never affirm the Masoretic Text, since it is highly detrimental to continuity with the New Testament" ("Erwägungen zur Einheit der biblischen Theologie," in: Gese, *Vom Sinai zum Zion*,
BEvTh 64 [Munich: Kaiser, ³1990], pp. 11-30, here: p. 16).

30. This is pointed out by Michael Mach, "Der Tanach in der Rezeption des nach-
biblischen Judentums," due to be published 2004 in the proceedings of the conference of Rila,
WUNT (Tübingen: Mohr Siebeck, 2004).

31. My remarks are not of course intended to express lack of interest in Jewish-Christian dialogue. On the contrary! The dialogue is by no means easy, however. Speaking of a "common Old
Testament" is facile and too one-dimensional. Rather, the two different versions, Jewish Tanach
and Christian Old Testament, reflect in their canonical form the very different reception processes
of two distinct faith communities. We cannot simply ignore this fact. A canonical approach which
takes this seriously can help to bring greater honesty into the Jewish-Christian dialogue.

the Gospels handed down through church tradition. The church saw this as corresponding to the life of Jesus Christ.

This "harmony" basically corresponded to the arrangement of the *Diatessaron,* which was not canonized in most churches but nonetheless determined their interpretation of the life of Jesus up to the modern era. Harmonies of the Gospels were written up to the seventeenth century, and there is also a notably large number of four-Gospel commentaries.[32] A good example can be found in the Passion story, which was harmonized essentially on the basis of John's account, with episodes found only in the Synoptics "inserted" into it.[33] A similar process is apparent in the nativity story, with a Gospel harmony determining the liturgical calendar and this in turn determining popular reading of the Gospels of Matthew and Luke up to the present.[34] Different traditions of the same story, which could not be harmonized — what we would now regard as variants — were taken to be accounts of separate incidents. This is especially apparent in the various episodes of feeding, or in the post-resurrection appearances.[35] The classical formative text for harmonizing the Gospel stories in western interpretation was Augustine's *De Consensu Evangelistarum.*[36]

3.2. In terms of its content, "canonical" exegesis in the pre-modern era might be of various types:

3.2.1. The interpretation could focus on the "regula fidei" as an abbreviated form of canon. This type goes back to Irenaeus and particularly Tertullian, for whom the rule of faith was a "gubernaculum interpretationis" (a helmsman of interpretation).[37] But in practice this became important only when certain interpretations of the Bible were to be excluded as heretical.

32. Cf. Dieter Wünsch, "Evangelienharmonie," in: *TRE* 10, pp. 626-636.

33. The sequence of texts in the Arabic Diatessaron 38-52 is as follows: the passion narrative begins with John 11:1–12:18 (with insertions from Mark 14:3-9; Matt. 26:9-12); this is followed by the entry into Jerusalem, the lament over Jerusalem, healings in the Temple, the discourses of John 12:20ff.; Luke 17; Matt. 23; John 12:36ff.; Matt. 24/Luke 21/Mark 13); Matt. 24:32–25:46; Matt. 26:1-15 (with parallels); John 13:1-22 (with Mark 14:18-21 par.); John 13:23-32; Matt. 26:26-29 (with par.); John 13:33-36 (+ insertions from Matt. 26:31-33 par.); John 14:1–17:26 (with insertion from Luke 22:35-39); John 18:1-2; Matt. 26:36-50 (with insertions); John 18:4-38 (with insertions); Luke 23:4-14; Matt. 27:12-28 (with insertions from the parallels); John 19:2-16 (Matt. 27:29-30, 24-26, 3-10). The crucifixion narrative is a blend from all the Gospels, ending with John 19:31-42 (with insertions). See Erwin Preuschen, *Tatians Diatessaron* (Heidelberg: C. Winter, 1926), pp. 181-231. This broadly corresponds to the sequence found in the big medieval cycles of paintings, e.g., by Duccio di Buoninsegna.

34. The order of the Nativity texts in the Diatessaron is as follows: John 1:1-5; Luke 1:5-80; Matt. 1:18-25; Luke 2:1-39; Matt. 2:1-23; Luke 2:40-52; Luke 3:1-3; Matt. 3:1-6; John 1:7-28.

35. Cf. on this Luz, *Matthew 26–28* (see note 12), pp. 406f.

36. Augustine, *De Consensu Evangelistarum libri 4* (CSEL 43, 1904).

37. *De praescriptione haereticorum* 9:1 (= CCSL 1, 1954), p. 195.

3.2.2. Much more frequent in both western and eastern interpretation is the referring of an individual text to Christ, with or without further biblical quotations.

Examples of christological interpretation of texts with the help of other New Testament texts include — since Augustine — reading the rock of Matt. 16:18 as Christ on the basis of 1 Cor. 10:4,[38] or — since Clement of Alexandria — reading the gate of Matt. 7:13 as Christ under the inspiration of John 10:9.[39]

3.2.3. "Canonical" interpretation equally often meant the extension of the meaning of an individual text within the horizon of salvation history.

Many allegories place the individual text in the horizon of the whole canon, without reference to other Bible passages. The individual texts speak of God's salvation history as witnessed by the biblical canon as a whole. Thus the working day described in the parable of the laborers in the vineyard (Matt. 20:1-16) became a metaphor for the history of the world. The morning is the equivalent of the time of Adam, the third hour that of Noah, the sixth hour that of Abraham, the ninth hour that of Moses, and the eleventh hour that of Christ.[40] The — usually literal — interpretation of an individual text in the horizon of apostolic tradition since Irenaeus very frequently meant an extension of the meaning of the text within the framework of the overall divine economy.[41] Already the design of a "Gospel" as such is an example of "extended" interpretation of an individual tradition: by placing individual traditions about Jesus within the horizon of the whole Jesus story — which opens with the nativity or with John the Baptist and ends with Jesus' passion and resurrection — something is done in a very similar way to the later canonical interpretations of an individual text within the horizon of the whole Bible.

3.2.4. The association of the interpretation of an individual biblical text with the Reformation "touchstone" that Scripture must "promote Christ"[42] is also a form of "canonical" exegesis. In this case the individual text is brought into contact — or in some cases confronted — with the center of the Bible as the Reformers understood it. The canonical principle "what promotes

38. Ulrich Luz, *Matthew 8–20*, Hermeneia (Minneapolis: Fortress, 2001), pp. 373f.
39. U. Luz, *Matthew 1–7. A Commentary* (Minneapolis: Augsburg, 1989), pp. 437f.
40. Origen, in Matt. 15:32 = GCS Origen X 446-448; Jerome, *In Matthaeum* ad loc. = CCSL 77:175; Cyril of Alexandria fr 226 = Joseph Reuss, *Matthäus-Kommentare aus der griechischen Kirche*, TU 61 (Berlin: Akademie, 1957), pp. 228-230 etc.
41. Cf. the fine study by Norbert Brox, *Die biblische Hermeneutik des Irenaeus*, ZAC 2 (1998), pp. 26-48.
42. Martin Luther, *Vorrede auf die Episteln Sankt Jakobi und Judas*, WA DB 7, p. 384.

Christ" means a centering of the text toward the center of the Bible. In a few cases, such as the Epistle of James, this "centering" takes the form of an explicit and distinct distancing from the text.

In various respects the christological interpretive approach of the Reformation prefigures modern exegesis and hermeneutics. More clearly than ever before in the history of exegesis, the Reformers recognize the varying theological profiles of biblical texts, and interpret them from the "center" in different ways. Reformation exegesis anticipates what we call today "content criticism" *(Sachkritik)* contrasted with the original sense of the text. However, this did not take the form of "criticism" coming from outside. Rather, it is a "centering" of the sense of individual texts based on their own "canonical" center, which is Christ. A fine example of this can be found in the interpretation of the talents parable in Matt. 25:14-30, which sounds to us suspiciously like "early capitalism" at work.[43] The "centering" of this parable means not only that the landowner was obviously interpreted as Christ, but also that the talents were understood as charisms or as the study of the Bible. In this way the Christian faith and its practice became the measure of the risk-filled activity demanded of the laborers.[44] Modern interpretation of this same parable provides a different kind of "centering": for most exegetes it is Jesus' understanding of the kingdom of God which governs the interpretation of this "risky" parable, and not vice versa, the parable governing Jesus' understanding of the kingdom.

3.3. In most cases the classical canonical exegesis of biblical texts has not served to restrict but to extend the sense of an individual text within the overall context of the Bible. It is the fullness of faith, witnessed to by the canon in its entirety, which enabled the reading of an individual text according to the fourfold sense of Scripture. This makes apparent that the canon, as understood by the early church in the second century, was only in rare cases a restricting rule of truth. Far more often, it formed the collection of the fullness of truth.[45] In contrast to the narrowing of Christian truth in the "regula fidei" or in dogma, canonical interpretation has actually preserved the fullness of its wealth.

43. There is a classic example of such criticism in Bertolt Brecht's "Dreigroschenroman" in: Brecht, *Gesammelte Werke. Prosa III* (Frankfurt: Suhrkamp, 1965).

44. Cf. the interpretations noted by Ulrich Luz in *Das Evangelium nach Matthäus (Matt. 18–25)*, EKK I.3 (Neukirchen/Düsseldorf: Neukirchener/Benziger 1997), pp. 510-512.

45. This corresponds with Hans Küng's view of "catholicity in the interpretation of the New Testament": see "Der Frühkatholizismus im Neuen Testament als kontroverstheologisches Problem," in: Ernst Käsemann (ed.), *Das Neue Testament als Kanon* (Göttingen: Vandenhoeck und Ruprecht, 1970), pp. 186-204.

This is evidenced by the unproblematic manner in which various "canonically" inferred senses of the text could coexist, without one excluding another. The rock in Matt. 16:18, for example, could be read as Christ *and* as Peter or, in the Middle Ages, the church.[46] In the older interpretations we always find the mystical/allegorical reading of a passage alongside its moral reading. The two complement each other, and both can be read in today's sense as "canonical" extensions of the original sense of a text. A very good example of this is the interpretation of the words "My God, my God, why have you forsaken me?" in Matt. 27:46 in various eras of church history. From today's perspective one can say that in the early church the words were read in a Johannine way,[47] and in the Reformation in a Pauline way.[48] Each time, a "canonical" extension was taking place.

In the history of interpretation, it was unusual for an earlier reading to be rejected. Rather, the later readings supplemented the earlier, the latter being preserved while the focus of the interpretation shifted. Between the anti-Gnostic struggle and the Reformation as a whole there is only rarely an internal Christian polemic concerning the *correct* interpretation of biblical texts.

3.4. The Reformation was the first schism in the church in which the Bible or rather particular interpretations of the Bible became a decisive factor, not for ecclesiastical but for *confessional* identity. It was at this point that, to some degree, different types of canonical exegesis became the "canon" for the *correct* interpretation of Scripture and the basis of an internal Christian dispute on the meaning of biblical texts.

The Reformation churches adhered to the sola scriptura principle. Since their identity was founded on the Bible alone, the conflict with the Catholics was necessarily concerned with the correct interpretation of the Bible. However, the conflict between Luther and Zwingli concerning the Lord's Supper made clear for the first time that the Bible itself could not be the basis of ecclesiastical identity, but that different interpretations of the Bible gave rise to different confessional identities. Both Luther and Zwingli interpreted the texts "canonically." Zwingli argued exegetically on the basis of many parallels in which ἐστίν (is) is the equivalent of "mean." As well as to the literal sense of ἐστίν, Luther pointed to the analogy with the doctrine of the dual nature. Calvin did something similar. Their Roman Catholic opponents "proved," also by means of biblical analogies, what they already knew as dogma. Such a biblical analogy was, for example, found in the water-to-wine miracle at Cana in which a "transubstantiation" of the elements was said to have taken place.[49]

In this way canonical exegesis became mired in confessional identity-forming and polemics. Particular readings of the Bible were understood more and more exclu-

46. U. Luz, *Matthew 8–20* (see note 38), pp. 374f.
47. U. Luz, *Das Evangelium nach Matthäus (Matt. 26–28)* (see note 12), pp. 335f.
48. Luz, *Matt. 26–28*, pp. 337-339.
49. Luz, *Matt. 26–28*, pp. 107-111.

sively, and used polemically against other denominations.[50] In the history of interpretation this marked a distinct shift, and the ascendancy of the "correct" interpretation in modern times began. It is scarcely possible to assign particular methods of canonical interpretation to the various denominational readings. It was above all the method of "proof" which became the hallmark of all exclusive denominational readings, biblical parallels being arbitrarily selected according to what was to be "proved." In all denominations, the biblical canon became the basis of secondary legitimation of dogmatic denominational convictions which it was said to "prove."

3.5. In the denominational era opened by the Reformation, "canonical" reading of the Bible meant, above all, that various different "centers" of the canon (especially of the New Testament) from varying contexts and times were confronted with each other and declared exclusive, for instance righteousness by faith alone, the historical Jesus in opposition to church doctrine, the "primacy words" as the legitimation of the Roman Catholic church, baptism in the spirit, the early Paul versus the Paul of the Pastoral epistles (and vice versa), etc. "Canonical reading" today has to be a matter of understanding such "centering" as "particularity" and pointing to the *whole* of the canon.

James D. G. Dunn formulates pointedly in his "Afterthoughts" on "Unity and Diversity in the New Testament": "The canon canonizes the diversity of Christianity. . . . To all who would say of only one kind of New Testament Christianity, 'This alone is Christianity," the New Testament replies, 'And that, and that too is Christianity.'[51] This thesis complements the one which states that the canon "canonizes the unity of Christianity."[52] Dunn understands unity as found in the person of Jesus Christ, which in turn makes the diversity of interpretations possible. One could also say that the New Testament canon forms a band uniting the churches, by preventing their standardization and uniformity.

4. The "Canonical Approach" Today

4.1. What "canonical exegesis" has to learn from the "canonical" hermeneutic of precritical ecclesiastical exegesis is this: that its most important task is to

---

50. A telling example can be found in the interpretation of Matt. 16:18. The reading of the rock as the pope, a marginal one in the Middle Ages, became the *only* correct interpretation in the age of denominational conflict. The old ecclesiastical readings, now supported by Protestants (cf. note 46 above), were rejected. Cf. Luz, *Matthew 8–20* (see note 38), p. 375.

51. James D. G. Dunn, *Unity and Diversity in the New Testament* (London: SCM, ²1992).

52. James D. G. Dunn, "Has the Canon a Continuing Function?," in: Lee M. McDonald/James A. Sanders, *The Canon Debate* (Peabody: Hendrickson, 2002), pp. 558-579, here: p. 578.

integrate and develop academic criticism — this is true in particular for historical-critical interpretation — which tends to isolate and atomize the individual texts and books of the Bible, into an understanding which reflects the whole fullness of faith in Christ.

4.2. The age of exclusive denominational readings of the Bible is over. These have lost their plausibility and their binding force. Following an age of denominational schism engendered in part by varying "canonical" readings of the Bible, the canon must now be seen primarily as a treasure of tradition which all Christian churches hold in *common* and which binds them together, and as the *wealth* of various different ways of interpretation of faith. A canonical approach today must take account of the fact that the biblical canon has proved itself an effective source of living unity among congregations and churches. It unites people and congregations of differing Christian denominations who find themselves still separated by dogmas, doctrines, legal structures, and Eucharists(!). Canonical reading of the Bible means an extension which overcomes the narrow denominational bounds set by emphasis on individual biblical texts and theologies and other "canons within the canon." By definition, therefore, canonical reading of the Bible today is ecumenical reading.

4.3. Academic exegesis has become more and more independent of the churches. Canonical reading of the Bible should serve as a reminder that the church is the primary place (though not the only place!) where the Bible is read and its testimony is to be lived. By establishing the canonicity of the biblical texts, the church has defined her own identity in such a way that "henceforth Scripture was to function as a mirror in which the church could continually rediscover her identity and assess, century after century, the way in which she constantly responds to the Gospel and equips herself to be an apt vehicle of its transmission."[53] This sets out precisely the task of canonical exegesis vis-à-vis the church.

4.4. Our thinking is determined by historical-critical exegesis. The various canonical readings of the Bible that have been undertaken throughout the history of the church can now be historically interpreted and differentiated. Historical-critical exegesis has not only fragmented the unity of the Bible into a multitude of individual texts from a wide variety of contexts. It has also led to the fragmenting of the unity of the Christian canon into a multitude of different denominational or individual understandings of the canon.

---

53. Pontifical Biblical Commission, *The Interpretation of the Bible in the Church*, in: *Origins*, January 6, 1994, III B1; cf. also: http://www.c-b-f.org/start.php under → Documents for the online text. The German translation is found in: Päpstliche Bibelkommission, *Interpretation der Bibel in der Kirche*, SBS 161 (Stuttgart: Katholisches Bibelwerk, 1995), p. 141.

For this reason, a canonical approach to the Bible is possible today only if exegetes lay open *their* view of the canon and make it part of the dialogue on the Bible. Thus canonical reading of the Bible today means facing the claims to authority expressed by the biblical texts and interpreted by the church's understandings of the canon, and responding to these claims in our own theological discourse.[54]

4.5. Through the "prism" of the individual text isolated and distanced by historical-critical exegesis, the preacher must express his or her *own* understanding of the *whole* Biblical faith of the church. The preacher cannot be "Jesusian" this week, then "Jamesian" or "Pauline" next Sunday! It is essential for the preacher to read each individual text "canonically" in the light of the *whole* biblical message. Commentaries on biblical books should provide help with this and not leave the preacher alone with this task.

Commentators should not only point to the claim to authority of a biblical text, but also indicate how they themselves treat it in terms of method and theology. They should inform on how their message of the individual texts relates to the whole of the biblical message, and what status they accord its message in their church, in relation to their tradition and in their current situation. Commentaries which fail to do this, subtly concealing the theological and ecclesiastical position of their authors beneath historical or synchronous analyses, are nothing but blunt swords for those in the church who need them.

54. Peter Stuhlmacher, *Biblische Theologie*, II (see note 2), p. 325, rightly formulates: "If exegesis is to do justice to the biblical texts, it must . . . take up the challenge of their claim to truth."

17 Hermeneutics of "Effective History" and the Church

1. Introduction

The framework of the Evangelisch-Katholischer Kommentar (EKK)[1] is the origin of my attempts at interpretation of Scripture oriented toward "effective history" *(Wirkungsgeschichte)*. I shall therefore begin by bringing into focus the two main hermeneutical interests of my work on the commentary. Each is related to the church, but each in its own way.

1.1. "History of interpretation and history of effects show what we have become on the basis of the texts."[2] We have to a considerable degree been shaped by them as they have contributed to our personal, theological, ecclesial, and cultural identity. Being conscious of the reception history of biblical texts means discovering our own involvement in them and thus illuminating our own hermeneutical situation vis-à-vis the texts. It means discovering what we owe the texts. It means discovering the past, not as an alien past but as our own, as a past that determines our thinking, our questions, our categories and our value judgments. The scholars involved in the EKK understood their work on the reception history of the text to be an essential dimension of understanding. This prevented the biblical texts being treated simply as objects of research, and helped to understand that interpreting the texts means also understanding who and what we are.

This hermeneutic interest means that the "Church" has to be present to a high degree, even from the outset. The church is present as the community

---

1. The *EKK*, founded by Eduard Schweizer and Rudolf Schnackenburg, is an interconfessional commentary series on the New Testament, which does not seek to neutralize, but to reflect the confessional perspectives of biblical interpretation. At present it is the most influential and most widely spread commentary series on the New Testament in German.

2. Cf. Ulrich Luz, *Matthew 1–7. A Commentary* (Minneapolis: Augsburg, 1989), p. 96.

which shaped and formed the biblical texts, and which made the Bible its book par excellence by creating and handing down the canon. The church is present as the "home" that enabled our predecessors to undertake their interpretations, actualizations, reshapings and after-experiences of biblical texts, and directed them in their task. The church is present as the area of society which was primarily formed by the biblical texts and as the place where they are effective. The church is present when the Bible is read, as a space open to the past, and the place where the biblical texts of the past are proclaimed, read, interpreted or celebrated. The church is the "mother" of such reading, guiding it or giving rise to protest to the biblical texts. The church may be the "midwife" of understanding, or quite simply a point of reference without which the biblical texts — which are after all the church's canonical texts — cannot come into view at all. Part of our gratitude for what we have become by means of the biblical texts, as well as, perhaps, part of our protest to what we have become, will for these reasons pass to the church.

1.2. The second hermeneutic interest is based on preoccupation with the reception history of biblical texts in churches and cultures other than one's own. This is a matter of showing what *others* have become by means of the biblical texts. It shows us what Roman Catholics or Orthodox, Pentecostals or secular people, African women, monks, or Anabaptist peasants owe the texts, and how they became what they are through the Bible. So here it is not a matter of opening up our own horizon, but of widening it by opening up others' horizons. In this way, reception history opens up the otherness of potential meanings of New Testament texts. So it is not primarily a matter of self-understanding but of understanding of others in the spectrum of the biblical texts. The texts are theirs as well as ours! Only indirectly is it also an exercise in self-understanding, in that we understand what we are not, but might become. In this way the history of interpretation and the reception history of the biblical texts provide correctives to our own readings.[3] It "shows in exemplary manner, what we could become by means of the texts," by showing what others have become by means of the texts.[4]

With this hermeneutical interest too, "church" is present to a high degree, in this case not as "mother" or "midwife" or as a space open to the past and the basis of our own life. Rather, the church is present as historically and culturally evolved diversity, as the church of the others, as a dialogue community or possibly a disputing community. Preoccupation with the reception

3. Luz (see note 2), pp. 97f.
4. It thus extends our own horizons by opening up those of others. Cf. Hans-Georg Gadamer, *Truth and Method* (New York: Continuum, ²2002), pp. 302f.

history of biblical texts opens an ecumenical dialogue in which both the living and those long dead relate how their identity was shaped through the scriptures. The scholarly community working on the EKK has always seen itself in this sense as an ecclesial dialogue community.

It is evident from all this that we do not understand "effective history" simply in Gadamer's sense of its being the foundation of "effective history consciousness" which makes the interpreting subject aware of his or her "relation to tradition." It is also a matter of "researching the effective history a work has,"[5] since we are exegetes and our exegetical work serves specific texts, namely those of the Bible. Hermeneutics of "effective history" is concerned with closeness to *and* distance from the texts, with fusion of horizons *and* widening of horizons. Gadamer's aversion to an "independent auxiliary discipline of the humanities"[6] must not influence the EKK, because the reception history of the Bible is that of the powerful impact of a very special work. A further reason is that, in an age whose sense of history is weak, such an auxiliary discipline may be the best means to draw attention both to how historical consciousness is woven into the effective power of history, and to the relationship between the biblical texts and their interpreters.

I understand "effective history" of the biblical texts as synonymous with their "reception history." "Reception history" I take in the broad sense given by my teacher Gerhard Ebeling to the term "history of interpretation." He took "church history as history of interpretation of holy scripture," and read "interpretation" explicitly as including "doing and suffering, . . . ritual and prayer, . . . theological work and . . . personal decisions, . . . wars of religion, and . . . works of compassionate love" and much more besides.[7] I prefer to speak of "effective history" rather than "history of reception" of the Bible, partly because the former focuses on the texts themselves and not on their human reception, reminding us of their "effectiveness."[8] A second reason is that the use of "effective history" enables me to connect with Gadamer, though my perspective is different from his. He is concerned with the place of the interpreting subject in the history which shapes that subject, while my primary concern is the

5. Gadamer (see note 4), pp. 343, 324.

6. Gadamer (see note 4), p. 285.

7. Gerhard Ebeling, *The Word of God and Tradition* (tr. by S. H. Hooke; London: Collins, 1968), p. 28: "Church history is the history of the exposition of scripture."

8. Cf. the term chosen by the English translator in Gadamer's *Truth and Method:* "effective history." For me this involves not only the "theological axiom of a power inherent in the biblical text" (Moisés Mayordomo-Marín, *Den Anfang hören. Leserorientierte Evangelienexegese am Beispiel von Matthäus 1–2*, FRLANT 180 [Göttingen: Vandenhoeck und Ruprecht, 1998], p. 350) but also the axiom that texts have a firm core of meaning which is not arbitrarily changed or deconstructed by readings of the text.

shaping force of particular texts, the texts of the Bible. I would restrict the term "history of interpretation" to areas of "effective history" in which the reception of the texts takes place through the medium of language, forming a direct interpretation. Thus "history of interpretation" is a narrower term for me than "effective history";[9] the two are related like concentric circles.[10]

I shall now develop three trains of thought on the relations between hermeneutics of "effective history" and ecclesial exegesis: in relation to the Protestant churches (2), in relation to the Roman Catholic Church (3), and in relation to the Orthodox churches (4). I emphasize at the outset that every textual interpretation and every hermeneutic is of course contextual, including my own. What I have to say here is thus not "objective" but formulated by a Protestant in relation to the Protestant churches. These are "my" churches, with which I am lovingly and self-critically engaged. In relation to the Catholic and Orthodox churches, which are not my own, I am also writing as a Protestant. With these churches too I am lovingly and critically engaged, though in a quite different way. So I formulate consciously from my own position. My main thesis is that, in contrast to the tradition-oriented hermeneutic axioms of all the denominational churches, hermeneutics oriented toward "effective history" has a "subversive" potential that is at the same time ecumenical.

2. "Effective History" and Protestant Ecclesial Interpretation

In Protestant theology, the Bible is foundational vis-à-vis of the church and takes precedence over it. The Bible is the fundamental instance of reference and legitimation for theology, so that according to Calvin "the church [does not make] any new dogma." Rather, church dogma is "as it were the grammar of the divine word."[11] The Reformation principle "sola scriptura" was di-

9. Thus I understand "effective history of the Bible" in a double sense. On the one hand it encompasses the whole of history of reception, i.e. *all* the effects of biblical texts; on the other hand it covers, in a narrower sense, the area of the history of effects that goes beyond "history of interpretation."

10. Heikki Räisänen, "The 'Effective History' of the Bible: A Challenge to Biblical Scholarship," in: Räisänen, *Challenges to Biblical Interpretation*, BIS 59 (Leiden: Brill, 2001), pp. 263-282, here: pp. 270ff., seeks to distinguish between "effects" and mere "use" or rather "misuse" of the biblical texts. In individual cases this distinction will always be controversial, and for this reason I would not want to make it the basis for conceptualization.

11. John Calvin, *Enarr. Symb. Nic.* 25/1V (see Emmanuel Hirsch, *Hilfsbuch zum Studium der Dogmatik* [Berlin: de Gruyter, ³1958], 104 = CR VII 576). This is not so far removed from some Vatican II statements. See for example *Dei Verbum* VI, 21 (= LThK² XIII 572): "Omnis ergo

rected against church tradition, particularly that of the Middle Ages, which was seen as having departed from the original truth. Following this principle, modern Protestant exegesis continues to act out this principle, although in a new way. It has always searched intensively for the original sense of the biblical texts; its approach has been decisively historical-critical (unlike that of French exegesis, for example). Even within the New Testament, liberal Protestant historical-critical exegesis has always tended to privilege the earliest sense of the text over all later traditions and interpretations (privileging Jesus, for example, over the post-Easter christologies, or Paul over his "early catholic" reception in the Pastoral Epistles). As I see it, all this is not only the legacy of historical thinking in the Enlightenment, but *also* an extension of that original Protestant approach. There is a deep-seated Protestant inclination to suspect later re-interpretations of the Bible and the faith as being aberrations, and to regard the temporal distance between the Bible and the present as a ditch which hinders understanding and needs to be jumped over. In my judgment, historical-critical exegesis of the Bible is the final phase in a long and specifically Western reception history of the Bible in which Protestantism has played an essential determining part.[12]

Preoccupation with the reception history of the Bible leads to self-critical questions regarding the Protestant way of understanding. I draw attention to four of such questions:

2.1. The Rediscovery of Tradition

Preoccupation with the post-history of the text has resulted in a different outlook at the historical distance between then and now. The ugly ditch between past and present was transformed into a highly diverse landscape with ups and downs, unexpected views and a wealth of wonderful and sometimes strange flowers. The interpreter of today is in one very specific place in this landscape, for example walking through a valley. In using this image I compare the start

---

praedicatio ecclesiastica sicut ipsa religio christiana Sacra Scriptura nutriatur et regatur oportet" ("Therefore, like the Christian religion itself, all the preaching of the Church must be nourished and regulated by Sacred Scripture"). *Dei Verbum* VI, 24 (= LThK² XIII 578): "Sacrae Paginae studium sit veluti anima Sacrae Theologiae" ("The study of the sacred page should be, as it were, the soul of sacred theology").

12. Orthodox theologians who are wondering whether they should admit historical-critical exegesis as a fundamental academic method in theology do well to bear in mind that each and every academic method has its particular contextuality, shaped by effective history. That contextuality may well be different from one's own.

of the walk with a mountain range to which the walker constantly looks back. Down in the valley, the walker has quite specific perspectives on the mountain range, while other perspectives are not visible. Sometimes the mountain hardly comes into view at all. There is no direct view of the starting point without taking in the landscape that is traversed and the quite specific positions and perspectives en route. The mountain at the starting point is the story of Jesus Christ to which the Bible testifies. There are only perspectives on the Bible which are determined by our own historical position and the landscape of history covered up to that point. This is not to be taken as a restriction, as if the mountain range were simply concealed by the landscape around it. Rather, the landscape traversed makes an *image* of the mountains possible which is not isolated but stands in a particular landscape.

In other words, preoccupation with the reception history of the Bible leads Protestant ecclesial exegesis to new insight into what the Catholic church has always termed "tradition." This also means a fresh appreciation of Protestantism's own tradition, including the confessional writings regarded by some in the Protestant churches as a kind of "regula fidei."[13] It also includes the Enlightenment and the "neo-Protestant" paths taken in the nineteenth century. Regardless of what can be learned from individual stages en route, or of whether some paths led astray, the paths have been taken and there is no going back. The paths taken give us *our* perspective on the mountains. For me this also includes the Middle Ages. We should not attempt to undo or forget tradition, but look with gratitude on the paths it has taken and learn from them. There cannot be a direct and unmediated faithfulness to the Bible or simultaneity with its texts. There can only be applications and reinterpretations directed by tradition.

2.2. Openness to Non-Verbal Interpretations

Looking at "effective history" of the Bible, and here I am thinking particularly of those areas of it which exceed history of interpretation in the narrow sense,

---

13. Walter von Loewenich, *Luther und der Neuprotestantismus* (Witten: Luther, 1963), pp. 321, 429, refers disparagingly to this as "small catholicism," which I find unhelpful. Luther did not simply advocate a formal "Sola Scriptura." Rather, this was always associated with Christ as the center or guideline for interpretation. Christ could even take precedence over Scripture. Cf. *Disputatio de fide* of 1539, partic. no. 40f., 49-53 = *WA* 39/I, pp. 47f. The development of the confessional documents in Old Protestant orthodoxy from being a guideline to becoming a traditional norm corresponds precisely to the development of the apostolic tradition we see in the early church after Irenaeus and Tertullian.

is a salutary reminder for us exegetes that it is not only we who interpret the Bible. In terms of devotional history, the Reformation was a radical concentration and at the same time a reduction of devotion to the hearing of the Word. It subordinated many areas of human reception of the Bible to listening, reading and learning — or led to their suppression. This meant a huge enhancement of theology. The famous painting of the crucifixion by Lucas Cranach in the city church of Wittenberg offers an example of how the Reformers subordinated image to word, even to the extent of largely displacing the image.[14] There was similar treatment of plays, processions, rites, and gestures and other forms of devotion which interpreted, represented, or recalled biblical texts. Even music was sometimes affected. Preoccupation with the reception history of the Bible brings all this back to us. It reminds Protestant ecclesial exegetes that words are not the only medium of interpretation for biblical texts. Images, plays, dances, processions, oratorios, etc. which responded to biblical texts, interpreting and transforming them, have mostly survived the Reformation. Some forms which were suppressed have been secularized,[15] others have become part of religious subcultures in Protestant areas, others returned sooner[16] or later to Protestantism in old and new guise. "Effective history" places exegetes and theologians in community with poets, painters, dancers and musicians, reminding them that there are areas of non-verbal textual interpretation which are essential to human wholeness and which cannot — or can only partially — be directed by verbal interpretation. In this way "effective history" helps to return interpretation of the Bible to human devotion as a whole, which is taken more seriously in most other Christian denominations than in our own.

2.3. The Complexity of the Truth Question

In *De servo arbitrio* Luther speaks of the inner and outer clarity of Scripture, assigning the inner clarity to the testimony of the Spirit in human hearts, the

---

14. Hans Belting, *Bild und Kult. Eine Geschichte des Bildes vor dem Zeitalter der Kunst* (Munich: C. H. Beck, 1990), pp. 510-523; a copy of Cranach's picture can be found on p. 521.

15. The development of a separate field of "art," initiated by the introduction of pictures (especially devotional pictures) into urban Renaissance homes and encouraged by the increasingly "secular" presentation of religious themes and above all by the discovery of "secular" themes, was much fostered by the Reformation.

16. In the case of Passion music this occurred — following initial reservations — very rapidly in the Reformation churches; cf. Kurt v. Fischer, *Die Passion. Musik zwischen Kunst und Kirche* (Kassel: Bärenreiter, 1997), pp. 56ff.

outer clarity to the "ministry of the word" whose task it is to illuminate all that appears dark and ambiguous.[17] The hermeneutics of "effective history" makes the question of the truth of an interpretation a complex one, drawing attention to the contextuality of every interpretation of the Bible. Every understanding of a text must, according to Gadamer, be an "understanding differently," since every understanding is a productive act, a new act of fusion of horizons.[18] How is the "truth" of this "differently" to be assessed? If today we seek to relate the outer clarity of Scripture to the clarity of its original historical sense, which can be illuminated only partially, it becomes apparent that this will not ensure clarity of proclamation of the gospel for today. A further complication for the question of truth lies in the fact that "effective history" includes interpretations in non-verbal media. Is it possible to speak of the "truth" of a painting, a piece of music, a ritual or a dance? Among the various dimensions of truth identified by contemporary philosophy, the most adequate category for artistic interpretations of the Bible is "truth in relation to the speaker," i.e. authenticity.[19] Such "truth in relation to the speaker" cannot be directed by a tradition of church doctrine.

I should like to illustrate this from the Western tradition of icon painting or biblical images. The difference between east and west is that our Western tradition of religious painting has seen many changes, so that biblical images today use contemporary art forms. The "authenticity" and in this sense the "truth" of Western religious art are especially enhanced for today's Western recipients by the fact that it is far less (or not at all) directed by tradition than is Eastern icon-painting. Yet still the words of the Ecumenical Council are true of Western biblical images too: "they raise those who contemplate them to be mindful of the original images (πρωτότοπα) and to yearn for them."[20] Even if western religious art shows these original images realistically or surrealistically, and certainly shows them in a wide variety of forms and highly individually, they remain effective interpretations of original biblical images and thus have the character of icons.

What does all this mean for the Protestant principle of the clarity of Scripture? All that is "clear," it seems, is that a huge wealth of potential meanings, illustrations, interpretations and creative forms has been released by the Scriptures. The hermeneutics of "effective history" directs us to accept this with gratitude.

17. Luther, "De servo arbitrio," *WA* 18 (1908), p. 609.

18. Gadamer (see note 4), p. 297. This is not to be understood, however, in the sense of radical randomness.

19. Jürgen Habermas, "Was heisst: Universalpragmatik?" in: Karl Otto Apel (ed.), *Sprachpragmatik und Philosophie* (Frankfurt: Suhrkamp, 1976), p. 176.

20. *Concilium*, Oecumenicum VII, DS[36] No. 601.

2.4. "Christ as the Center of Scripture"

Reformation hermeneutics takes the form of an ellipsis with two foci, the principle of "Scripture alone" at one end and the principle of "Christ alone" or "Christ as center" at the other.[21] "Christ as center" was the Christ interpreted by the Reformation, the Christ who died on our behalf, who works in us as "gospel" through the witness of the Spirit, the "Deus revelatus," the Christ of grace. Luther even subordinates to this interpretation of Christ the "commands and writings of the apostles."[22] This is nothing new. Preoccupation with the hermeneutic tradition of antiquity and the Middle Ages makes clear that the hermeneutic principle "Christ as center" in various interpretations has always been the hermeneutic principle of ecclesial interpretation of Scripture.

For the Greek Church Fathers the center of Scripture was Jesus Christ in his two natures. Sometimes they understood the literal and spiritual interpretation of Scripture by analogy with the two natures of Christ. The spiritual interpretation of the letter of Scripture reveals the effectiveness of the divine Logos, just as Christ's human nature is always allied with the divine nature.[23] In the Western church, Irenaeus and — even more decisively — Tertullian referred to the regula fidei handed down in the apostolic tradition of the church as the measure for interpretation of Scripture. The anti-Gnostic conflict, which included the experience of the ambiguity of Scripture, made it necessary for them to confront the ambiguity of Scripture with an unambiguous measure of interpretation.[24] Both approaches endeavor to formulate a christological criterion for ecclesial interpretation of Scripture.

21. Cf. Gerhard Ebeling, *Evangelische Evangelienauslegung* (reprint; Darmstadt: Wissenschaftliche Buchgesellschaft, 1962), partic. pp. 402-412. For Ebeling, "Luther's theological approach . . . in his understanding of Scripture is not the doctrine of inspiration but of incarnation" (p. 402).

22. Christ is above all laws. "Yet, since we are at the present time unalike in spirit, and the flesh is the enemy of the spirit, it is needful because of the enthusiasts to adhere to the various commandments and writings of the apostles, so that the church shall not be rent asunder" (*Disputatio de fide,* Thesis 58, WA 39/1 [1926], p. 47).

23. Henri de Lubac, *Geist aus der Geschichte* (Einsiedeln: Johannes, 1968), pp. 393-404; John Panagopoulos, "Christologie und Schriftauslegung bei den Kirchenvätern," *ZThK* 89 (1992), pp. 41-58; Panagopoulos, Ἡ Ἑρμενεία τῆς Ἁγίας Γραφῆς στὴν ἐκκλησία τῶν Πατέρων (Athens: Akritas, 1991), 260-281, 329-333, 398-406; Panagopoulos, Εἰσαγωγὴ Πραφῆς στὴν ἐκκλησία τῶν Πατέρων (Athens: Akritas, 1994), pp. 430-458.

24. On Irenaeus cf. Norbert Brox, "Die biblische Hermeneutik des Irenäus," *ZAC* 2 (1998), pp. 26-48.

A consideration from the perspective of the effective history of the text shows, then, that Reformation hermeneutics is certainly anchored in mainstream ecclesial hermeneutics. At the same time, the interpretative approach of the Reformation is called into question. "Christ" can never be a neutral instance but it is always the Christ interpreted by the church who becomes the guideline for interpreting Scripture. The study of the hermeneutic approaches in church interpretation of Scripture, which is one of the essential tasks for Bible interpretation reflecting on the text's effective history, draws attention to this important fact. Christ, common to all as the guideline for the interpretation of Scripture, is both a uniting and a distinguishing feature of the different exegetical traditions. It will be no help to others, who have their own traditions, simply to declare one's own hermeneutic and christological tradition to be *the* definitive one. In this respect, hermeneutics oriented toward "effective history" makes life and thought difficult for traditional Protestant ecclesial exegesis — but for others too!

3. "Effective History" and Catholic Ecclesial Exegesis

Joachim Gnilka once formulated the impression that stronger "orientation towards the Church distinguishes Protestant and Catholic theologians." "What I elaborate and communicate as an exegete must prove itself in the forum of the church, become part of its faith and take shape within its life." Just as New Testament writings gradually assumed canonical status by means of their reception in the church, Catholic exegesis is also subject to the "criterion of acceptance by the church."[25] Gnilka's impression, expressed politely and indirectly, that on the whole Protestant exegesis pays scant attention to its acceptance by the church, is correct.

The question is, however, how this acceptance takes place. In Protestantism, reception of exegesis means, by and large, reception in congregations. If we exegetes take reception seriously at all, then — unfortunately — we see it largely as a didactic issue and not a theological one. In the Roman Catholic Church, by contrast, the ecclesial magisterium plays a vital role in reception processes. The "Dei Verbum" constitution of the Second Vatican Council brought magisterium, Scripture and tradition inseparably together.

25. Joachim Gnilka, "Die Bedeutung der Wirkungsgeschichte für das Verständnis und die Vermittlung biblischer Texte," in: Katholisches Bibelwerk e.V. (ed.), *Dynamik im Wort. Lehre von der Bibel — Leben aus der Bibel* (FS 50 Jahre Katholisches Bibelwerk Deutschland; Stuttgart: Kath. Bibelwerk, 1983), pp. 329-343, here: p. 339.

> But the task of authentically interpreting the word of God, whether written or handed on, has been entrusted exclusively[26] to the living teaching office of the Church. . . . This teaching office is not above the word of God, but serves it, teaching only what has been handed on. . . . It is clear, therefore, that sacred tradition, Sacred Scripture and the teaching authority of the Church, in accord with God's most wise design, are so linked and joined together that one cannot stand without the others.[27]

If one takes the regula fidei to be the essence of tradition, then reception of the Bible means the combined work of Bible, faith tradition and church magisterium, directed by the Holy Spirit. This is an ideal that doesn't quite correspond to the reality of Catholic exegesis we experience today.

Our time is one of a plurality of biblical exegeses. A wide variety of exegetes, living in a wide variety of contexts, shaped by a wide variety of church and other traditions and employing a wide range of constantly evolving methods, produce an incalculable number of meanings of biblical texts. Some of us find that this expresses the immeasurable wealth of the Bible; others interpret it as expressing the inability of the texts to impose their original sense to their readers,[28] or as expressing the impossibility of texts being carriers of a logos that is stable over time. This pluralization is tragic for Protestantism, since Protestant churches take Scripture as their foundation. If Scripture is endlessly interpretable, it cannot be the foundation of churches but only of particular communities, groups or religious individuals — unless of course we declare diversity to be a founding principle of Protestantism.[29] The theological reactions to this vary. Protestants like me view the looming failure of a formal "sola scriptura" principle with

26. On the embedding of "exclusively" in the overall context of the decree cf. Heinrich Fries, "Kirche und Kanon. Perspektiven katholischer Theologie," in: Wolfhart Pannenberg/Theodor Schneider, *Verbindliches Zeugnis I. Kanon — Schrift — Tradition*, DiKi 7 (Freiburg/Göttingen: Herder/Vandenhoeck, 1992), pp. 291-293.

27. *Dei Verbum* II, 10 (LThK² XIII, 528).

28. Stanley Fish's thesis that the meaning of texts is determined by interpretative communities (*Is There a Text in This Class? The Authority of Interpretative Communities* [Cambridge, Mass.: Harvard UP, 1980]; Fish, *Doing What Comes Naturally: Change, Rhetoric and the Practice of Theory in Literary and Legal Studies* [Oxford: Clarendon, 1989]). He does not refer to the Roman Catholic church but his thesis could easily be verified there. Protestantism on the other hand tends to document the weakness and continuing disintegration of interpretative communities.

29. James D. G. Dunn in his important work *Unity and Diversity in the New Testament* (London: SCM, 1977), p. 376, says of the New Testament canon, drawing on Ernst Käsemann: "It canonizes the diversity of Christianity." He does however emphasize that this diversity is related to a "unifying centre."

disquiet;[30] Catholics like Joseph Ratzinger see it as the predictable self-disintegration of Protestantism in neo-Protestant subjectivity.[31] In the face of this dilemma, Marius Reiser has urged the necessity of a basic Catholic position. The regula fidei and the magisterium have an essential part to play, he writes, if theology is not to dissolve into religious studies, exegesis into literary studies and the church into a loose association of devout subjects. Only the "living tradition of the Rule of Faith" can be an "appropriate pre-understanding" leading properly into the "process of understanding" biblical texts;[32] only the church can be the experiential space in which the "living relationship of the interpreter to the matter"[33] finds its proper place.

The hermeneutics of "effective history" cannot resolve this dilemma, but asks questions about how it is resolved by the church.

3.1. *Can the truth of exegesis of biblical texts be defined by a rule of truth?* Interpretations of biblical texts are always interpretations of life in concrete situations by concrete and whole human beings, interpreting by means of verbal and non-verbal media. The hermeneutics of "effective history" asks the same question of Catholic church exegesis as of Protestant, only with a different interest. It does not only examine interpretations of biblical texts that are measurable by the "regulative norm" of the ecclesial rule of faith.[34] It also looks at interpretations to which this measure can be applied only in very limited degree or not at all, such as prayers, hymns, images or political decisions. The question of the truth of such interpretations cannot be decided by reference to a rule of truth comparable to the "rule of faith." Interpretations of the Bible are much richer than to be defined by a formulated conceptual truth.

3.2. *"Effective history" draws attention to the problem of the contextuality of every interpretation.* All interpretations and actualizations of biblical texts are contextual; their truth and power are valid only within those contexts. We often observe for example that biblical interpretations handed down to us

30. Ulrich Luz, "Was heisst 'Sola Scriptura' heute? Ein Hilferuf für das protestantische Schriftprinzip," *EvTh* 57 (1997), pp. 28-36.

31. Joseph Cardinal Ratzinger: "Es scheint mir absurd, was unsere lutherischen Freunde jetzt wollen" (What our Lutheran friends now want seems to me absurd), *Frankfurter Allgemeine Zeitung* 221 (September 22, 2000), pp. 51f.

32. Marius Reiser, "Bibel und Kirche. Eine Antwort an Ulrich Luz," *TTZ* 108 (1999), partic. pp. 64-71, 80f.

33. Rudolf Bultmann, "Das Problem der Hermeneutik," in: Bultmann, *Glauben und Verstehen II* (Tübingen: Mohr Siebeck, 1961), pp. 211-235, here: p. 217.

34. Reiser (see note 32), p. 68.

may be "true" in an exegetical or theological sense, i.e. they correspond to the original sense of the text or to the traditional rule of faith, and yet in a different sense they are not "true." They have become blunt swords, they no longer move or distinguish anything or have effect in the way biblical texts were originally intended to do. Preoccupation with history of interpretation in the narrower sense in particular shows that over the centuries exegetes have constantly repeated what their predecessors had to say. This may make them "true" as far as ecclesial norms are concerned, but it also makes them very dull.[35] Really effective interpretations of the Bible have often been innovative ones, suspected of heresy from the perspective of the traditional norm. A traditional norm tends to neglect the problem of contextuality and to be "abstract" and thus contextless. In terms of "effective history," I am not disputing that truth can be recognized,[36] but I do contest the reduction of truth to stated truths which can be established according to a correspondence criterion and regulated by means of a traditional norm.

More than once in history, the struggle against heresies gave rise to exegetical innovations whose validity was assured directly by the truth of faith and not by the exegetical tradition of the church. A good example can be found in the interpretation of Matt. 16:18. The interpretation of the rock as the papacy had been relatively insignificant in medieval times, but in the 16th century it suddenly became dominant in Catholic exegesis, taking precedence over the traditional reading of the rock as the faith of the church (the rule of faith!). This latter interpretation was now continued by the Protestants.[37]

3.3. *History of exegesis and "effective history" show that the harmonious cooperation of Bible, tradition and magisterium postulated by the Second Vatican Council has in practice been rather limited.* This is certainly the case if we take "magisterium" formally and understand "tradition" in the narrow sense as the rule of faith. Giuseppe Segalla has shown in an impressive apologetic that the magisterium has intervened in the process of biblical interpretation only rarely and in exceptional cases.[38] Historically, the rule of faith has rela-

---

35. This is true not only of many tradition-oriented exegetes who simply assembled patristic opinions, but also of a large number of modern commentaries especially in the twentieth century.

36. This is assumed by Reiser (see note 32), p. 76.

37. Ulrich Luz, *Matthew 8–20* (Hermeneia; Minneapolis: Fortress, 2001), pp. 374f. A further example is given by Frances Young, *Biblical Exegesis and the Formation of Christian Culture* (Cambridge: Cambridge University, 1993), pp. 37-40 (the anti-heretical interpretation of Proverbs 8:22 by Athanasius).

38. Giuseppe Segalla, "Church Authority and Bible Interpretation. A Roman Catholic

tively seldom functioned directly as an interpretative norm. This was usually the case only when scriptural interpretations had an anti-heretical scope and served directly to legitimate the doctrinal tradition.[39] For ecclesial interpretations of the Bible, the rule of faith and the magisterium acted as an "assistentia negativa" ("negative assistance")[40] for the purpose of excluding heretical readings at critical points. Apart from this, biblical interpretation developed its own dynamic. In the Catholic church as in the Protestant, the Bible largely interprets itself ("scriptura sui ipsius interpres"); in other words, the most effective and widespread "regulation" of ecclesial exegesis of the Bible took place through ecclesial church exegesis itself. Ecclesial interpretation lived on the traditions of ecclesial interpretations of the Bible, handing them down, continuing them and being inspired by them. One can see this negatively as traditionalism. But one can also interpret it positively and recognize the fundamental power of an interpretative community, which did not so much restrict as carry, enrich and inspire biblical interpretations. As the early interpreters of the Bible always saw themselves as *ecclesial* interpreters, they honored Scripture and tradition "pari pietatis affectu ac reverentia" ("with an equal affection of piety and reverence").[41] For these exegetes, "tradition" was primarily the fundamental interpretative tradition of the Bible itself, just as the Second Vatican Council meant it.

Endeavoring to define the relation between biblical exegesis of the church and the regula fidei and magisterium from the perspective of reception history, I do not see it as that of two concentric circles but again as an ellipsis with two foci which are relatively independent of each other. Ecclesial exegesis reflects the wealth, diversity, plurality, liveliness, openness, catholicity and non-normativity of the life of the church thanks to the wealth of Scripture. Its embeddedness in the tradition of ecclesial exegesis reflects the church's loyalty to this wealth and diversity. Ecclesial interpretation of Scripture points to the fact that the Christian faith is richer and greater than a magisterium can encompass. The regula fidei on the other hand, and the ecclesial magisterium which protects it, represent the focusing of the diversity to a — nicely Protestant! — center to which it relates but by which it is not absorbed. In the church, regula fidei and magisterium on the one hand, and wealth of ecclesial interpretations inspired by the wealth of Scripture on the

---

View," in: James D. G. Dunn et al. (eds.), *Auslegung der Bibel,* WUNT I.130 (Tübingen: Mohr Siebeck, 2000), pp. 55-72.

39. A classic example can be found in Tertullian: *De praescriptione haereticorum* 14, 3-5.

40. Reiser (see note 32), p. 66.

41. Conc. Trid. Sessio IV = Decretum de libris Sacris et de traditionibus recipiendis, DS[36], 1976, No. 1501 = *Concilium* Vat. II, *Dei Verbum* II, 9 (= LThK[2] XIII 524).

other hand stand side by side, interlinked or separate, providing a norm for each other or being in conflict. Modifying the text of the Second Vatican Council, it is not the case that "one cannot be without the other." Rather, it is the case that "each in its own way," as the two foci of an ellipsis, "under the action of the one Holy Spirit contribute[s] effectively to the salvation of souls."[42] I experience the wealth of Catholic ecclesial exegesis of the Bible as a significant and productive *counterweight* to the constraints of the regula fidei and the magisterium. At the same time I accept that this interpretation has to do with my own position,[43] and that some Catholics would, from their own position in their church, formulate it differently.

3.4. *The hermeneutics of "effective history" interrogates decisions by the magisterium,* concerning itself with "heretical" e.g. Protestant, or so-called "unbelieving" interpretations of the Bible. It is in principle open, its premise being that any and every person may understand something of the concern of a biblical text. A further premise is that every interpretation of a text as well as every decision of the magisterium concerning textual interpretations is itself contextual and in that sense historical. The hermeneutics of "effective history" endeavors to understand both textual interpretations and magisterium decisions in their context. Its approach is unblinkered, enabling it to reopen questions that are said to have been dealt with.

From the perspective of "effective history" it can be said that, overall, Catholic exegesis of the Bible shows close proximity to that of the Protestant or Orthodox churches. It is close to Protestant exegesis in that both live in creative tension between the canon-based wealth with its diversity of the faith and the concentration on a center, this being the magisterium in the case of the Catholic church. It is close to Orthodox biblical exegesis in seeing its "equal affection of piety and reverence" especially towards the patristic exegetical tradition as a basic feature. The Orthodox Church seeks to be directed by the wealth of that tradition, without standardizing it further by binding the tradition to an ecclesial magisterium.

---

42. Cf. *Dei Verbum* II, 10 (= LThK² XIII 529).

43. I particularly appreciate the interpretation by Karl H. Schelkle, *Die Petrusbriefe. Der Judasbrief*, HThK XIII.2 (Freiburg: Herder, 1961), p. 245: "Instead of measuring the New Testament by such a norm, should we not rather measure the critical norm by the wealth of the New Testament and then accord it at most a relative right?" Schelkle's proposition is formulated against Luther's principle of the canon within the canon, but I suggest it can also be used to criticize reductions of the wealth of the Bible by the regula fidei and the magisterium.

4. "Effective History" and Orthodox Ecclesial Exegesis

While Protestant understanding of the Bible can be summarized as "the Bible as vis-à-vis of the church" or "Bible *before* church," the Orthodox understanding of the Bible is "the Bible *in* the church."[44] The Bible is a liturgical text; the Word of God itself has sacramental effect. In John Breck's impressive formulation: "In authentic Orthodox experience, the Word comes to its fullest expression within a sacramental context. Whether proclaimed through Scripture reading and preaching, or sung in the form of antiphons . . . and dogmatic hymns . . . , the Word of God is primarily communicated — expressed and received — by the ecclesial act of celebration, and in particular, celebration of the eucharistic mystery."[45] According to the late John Panagopoulos, following Origen, the Word of the Bible must be understood in the sense of the "real presence of Christ in the Word."[46] According to Januari Ivliev, "Holy Scripture, the text of the Bible, is a verbally expressed image of the New Reality revealed to humankind in the incarnate Word of God."[47] For this reason the Divine Liturgy is the prime place in which and through which the "energy of the Gospel"[48] becomes effective. As Ivliev sees it, both the alienation of the historical-critical method from the concern of the gospel and the disciplining of that concern by a restrictive ecclesial magisterium result from "the loss of the eucharistic experience, the reduction of church life to ritual norms."[49]

What is the relation of "effective history"–oriented hermeneutics to this embedding of the Bible in the eucharistic and sacramental life of the church? One expects to find a deep affinity, since effective history has to do par excellence with the Bible *in* the church and not with the Bible *vis-à-vis* the church or even *before* the church. Can we conclude then that there is a predetermined harmony between "effective history"–oriented interpretation of the Bible and the orientation of Eastern Church hermeneutics and patristic exegesis? Both are concerned to embed interpretation in tradition and in the life of the

44. Cf. the programmatic title of the book by John Breck, *Scripture in Tradition* (Crestwood: St. Vladimir's Seminary Press, 2001).

45. John Breck, *The Power of the Word in the Worshipping Church* (Crestwood: St. Vladimir's Seminary Press, 1986), pp. 17f.

46. John Panagopoulos, *ZThK* 89 (see note 23), p. 47.

47. Jannuarij Ivliev, "Die Macht der Kirche und die Auslegung der Bibel. Eine orthodoxe Perspektive," in: Dunn et al., *Auslegung* (see note 38), p. 73.

48. This is the title of an essay by Hans Weder, "Die Energie des Evangeliums," *ZThK* Supplement 9 (1995), pp. 94-119.

49. Ivliev (see note 47), p. 77.

church; for both the basic position toward the life- and identity-giving legacy of tradition is one of gratitude.

There is more to be said on the matter, however. "Effective history" means *history*. Effective history is aware that the paths we have traveled determine our own position, but it is also aware that those paths lie irrevocably in the past. Effective history knows that some paths have led astray or have been diversions. It draws attention to the contextuality and ambivalence of the historical legacy that shapes us. Effective history invites us to learn from history but also, within our own new context, to learn *new* and *different* things. It reminds us, whenever we are confronted by church traditionalism, that the interpretation of biblical texts in each new situational context must be a *new* interpretation. I agree with Savas Agourides:

> The Fathers absorbed the material for their own time. . . . They could not do this chewing for us, as they could not know our exact situation. . . . There is the spiritual principle created by them that everybody must do his or her own chewing.[50]

Effective history leads us to our *own* inescapable position, calling on us to undertake a *new* interpretation of the biblical texts in and from this position. Effective history is not a "ready made banquet for us."[51] In this respect it is a challenge to purely tradition-oriented Orthodox exegesis.

5. "Effective History" and the Boundaries of the Church

Effective history–oriented exegesis exposes in a double sense the limits of ecclesial exegesis, drawing attention to the limits of the church.

5.1. An analysis in terms of effective history also means a wider ecumenical horizon. The Bible is not only the basic book of the church, but the basic book of *all* Christian communities which are not regarded as church by other churches. The Bible belongs to *all* those who read it and live by it. This defines the field of effective history studies. They are not governed by what one church or other defines as "ecclesial exegesis." I can personally attest to having learned a great deal from the interpretations and actualizations of those who have been consigned to the scrap heap of heresy. In the case of the Gospel of Matthew, for instance, I am thinking of the Arian *Opus*

---

50. Savas Agourides, "The Orthodox Church and Contemporary Biblical Research," in: J. Dunn et al., *Auslegung* (see note 38), p. 147.
51. Agourides, "Orthodox Church," p. 147.

Imperfectum[52] preserved under the protection of its being attributed to John Chrysostom, or the testimonies of persecuted Anabaptists in the Swiss Emmental, which hold a special interest for me as a Bernese citizen. Together with their Anabaptist contemporaries, they showed a better and deeper understanding of Matthew's Sermon on the Mount than did the Protestant preachers in Berne. Once again, the study of effective history reveals the limits of ecclesial exegesis. These limits are already apparent in the fact that agreement on what "ecclesial exegesis" is can be reached only at the level of sociology of religion, since the various denominations in various ways accord or deny each other recognition as "church."

5.2. An analysis in terms of effective history exceeds the field of ecclesial interpretations. Its academic approach requires analysis of biblical interpretation by people outside the church with the same interest and the same openness as ecclesial interpretation. Hermeneutically, these non-church interpretations deserve the same basic principle of sympathy. Quite possibly, they will reveal something of the truth of biblical texts just as well! In academic ethics, the basic principle is that of respect for all that is human, a principle that has a great deal to do with the effective history of the Bible. I can illustrate this by calling to mind interpreters of the Bible such as Mahatma Gandhi, Bertold Brecht,[53] Marc Chagall,[54] Nikos Katzantsakis,[55] or Jewish exegetes such as Claude Montefiore,[56] or Marxists such as Milan Machovec.[57] All of them confront us with the question of the limits of the church. References to "anonymous Christians" or a "latent church"[58] are in conflict with the basic principle of respect for all that is human. Those I have named above would certainly

---

52. Josef von Banning (ed.), *Opus Imperfectum in Matthaeum*, CCSL (Turholti: Brepols, 1988).

53. Cf. Hans Pabst, *Brecht und die Religion* (Vienna: Styria, 1977).

54. Roland Berthold (ed.), *Marc Chagall, Die Bibel. Gouachen, Aquarelle, Pastelle und Zeichnungen aus dem Nachlass des Künstlers* (Exhibition catalogue, Bonn/Mainz 1989/1990, Mainz: von Zabern, 1989); Pierre Provoyeur (ed.), *Marc Chagall. Die Bilder der Bibel* (Darmstadt: Wissenschaftliche Buchgesellschaft, 1996).

55. Cf. partic. his first novel of the passion Ὁ Χριστὸς ξανασταυρώνεται (Athens: Diphros, 1954), but also Ὁ τελευταίος πειρασμός (Athens: Diphros, 1955).

56. Claude G. Montefiore, *The Synoptic Gospels I-II* (London: Macmillan, 1927); Montefiore, *Rabbinic Literature and the Gospel Teachings* (1930 = reprint New York: Ktav, 1970).

57. Milan Machovec, *Jesus für Atheisten* (Stuttgart: Kreuz, 1972).

58. Karl Rahner, "Das Christentum und die nichtchristlichen Religionen," in: Rahner, *Gesammelte Schriften zur Theologie V* (Einsiedeln: Benziger, ²1964), see pp. 154-158; Rahner, "Die anonymen Christen," in: Rahner, *Gesammelte Schriften zur Theologie VI* (Einsiedeln: Benziger, 1965), pp. 545-554; Paul Tillich, *Systematic Theology III* (Chicago: University of Chicago, 1963), pp. 152-155.

have declined to be made part of some "latent church." Effective history-oriented biblical exegesis will need to remind ecclesial exegesis that the effect of the Bible reaches far beyond the church.

6. Hermeneutics of "Effective History" as Ecclesial Exegesis?

I have reached the end of my deliberations. Is what I understand by hermeneutics of effective history actually an ecclesial exegesis of Scripture? I hope I have made clear that it is an ecumenically open, ecclesially interested approach to the Bible which is at the same time critical and subversive of fundamental traditions of interpretation of Scripture in the churches. Does it deserve the title "ecclesial," i.e., "churchly" exegesis? The answer depends on what we mean by church.

For me, this exegesis is indeed ecclesial, since I understand "church" as a dialogue community of denominations and persons to whom the Bible has been given and among whom the Bible is at work. Similar to Origen and John Panagopoulos, it is my belief that in reading and hearing of the Bible there is something akin to the "real presence of Christ in the Word." In this reading the Holy Spirit is at work, not at the level of an inspired text claiming to be absolutely true in itself, but as the power of the texts in the hearts and minds of their readers.[59] Evidently, reading of the one Bible does not lead to the overcoming of divisions in the church, and hopefully it does not lead either to the cementing of the numerous different denominations, as Ernst Käsemann seemed to fear.[60] Rather, the reading of the biblical texts by members of different confessional churches should make the experience of κοινωνία (community) possible. This experience does not mean replacing the plurality of different contextual interpretations by one uniform interpretation. Rather, it means that people from different churches who have taken different paths in effective history and whose reading of the texts has led them to different positions come together to tell each other of their own contextual confessional and individual interpretations. The telling of their own stories involves self-

59. Cf. Ulrich Körtner, *Der inspirierte Leser. Zentrale Aspekte biblischer Hermeneutik* (Göttingen: Vandenhoeck und Ruprecht, 1994). Within the framework of reception aesthetics, Körtner finds an unexpected fresh approach to the allegorical Bible interpretation of the early church.

60. Ernst Käsemann, "The New Testament Canon and the Unity of the Church," in: Käsemann, *Essays on New Testament Themes* (London: SCM, 1964), pp. 95-107. "The New Testament canon . . . as such (that is, in its accessibility to the historian) . . . provides the basis for the multiplicity of confessions" (p. 103).

questioning and a widening of horizons. In the light of the Bible and its effective history, they realize who they are and whence they have come, as well as their own limitations and biases. They recognize what they could and should become. All this does not engender a uniform interpretation, but it awakens understanding for other interpretations and thus for difference encircled by the bonds of love.

In our dialogue on the Bible reflected by "effective history" we are of course also seeking theological agreement. Reversing the image of the path and the mountain range that I used earlier, and taking the mountain as the destination rather than the starting point of the journey through the valleys, we can try to construct a map of the mountains as they really are, on the basis of the various perspectives on them from the various different valleys. But it will remain a construct, a hypothetically constructed anticipation of the truth. Such constructs cannot replace the real views of the mountains from different paths, hills and valleys. They can at best offer help only in understanding these views, and perhaps indicate the direction that should be taken. What I have done here is to outline the best that theology, understood in Protestant terms as exegesis of Holy Scripture, can achieve.

Is this "ecclesial exegesis of Scripture"? Yes, it is, if we take church to be a community in dialogue over the Bible, making its way towards what God might have meant by "church." Is it possible to combine this understanding of church with an ecclesial magisterium? Yes, it is, if we see the function of the magisterium far more radically than Karl Lehmann as dialogic, indeed exclusively dialogic, in the sense that the dialogue is not the preliminary to "examination" and condemnation but their overcoming.[61] Naturally this is utopian, just as Habermas's "ideal dialogue situation" is, but must we put aside such a utopia as an "alarming irreality,"[62] or can it give us an aim and direction?

At this point my Roman Catholic and Orthodox friends will say: "An interdenominational dialogue community over the Bible is a good thing which we already enjoy, but this dialogue community is not and can never be the church."[63] True, it is only a dialogue about the Bible between members of churches and "church communities," "which are not churches in the proper sense." A dialogue concerning the Bible which seeks to include those "who are

61. Karl Lehmann, "Notwendigkeit und Grenzen des Dialogs zwischen Theologen und Lehramt," in: Wolfhart Pannenberg/Theodor Schneider, *Verbindliches Zeugnis II. Schriftauslegung — Lehramt — Rezeption*, DiKi 9 (Freiburg/Göttingen: Vandenhoeck, 1995), pp. 157-174.

62. Hans Georg Gadamer, "Replik," in: Karl O. Apel et al., *Hermeneutik und Ideologiekritik* (Frankfurt: Suhrkamp, 1971), p. 314.

63. Reiser (see note 32), p. 78.

not part of the Body of Christ by baptism" but who like to read the Bible, *cannot* by definition be ecclesial exegesis.[64] Marius Reiser then asks: "In a dialogue community, who administers the sacraments?"[65] For me, this is not the most important question. I find it more important to ask who may *receive* the sacraments administered. This question exposes the fact that, for example, the Orthodox understanding of the Bible, centering on the celebration of the Eucharist, cannot be the real form of ecclesial exegesis for me, since I am excluded from that center by a one-sided decision on the part of the Orthodox church. I find this painful, and I shall probably have to accept that many of my Orthodox or Catholic friends will not regard what I have attempted to present here as ecclesial exegesis.

Ecclesiologies, however, are always contextual and shaped by effective history. They are perspectives on the church from certain positions along a path, and as such they are neither freely chosen nor can they be made absolute. My own ecclesiology is neither simply right or wrong, but determined by its context. In terms of effective history, its basic experience has been anathematization. For that reason I cannot claim that the true church "is realized in this world"[66] in one of the Protestant churches consisting of the descendants of Luther, Calvin or Zwingli. I can only speak of the true church in the form of hope which we have been promised and towards which my own church too is journeying. I *cannot* have a better ecclesiology than this. As a member of a community which is for many not yet church in the proper sense, together with members of other communities, none of which is yet church in the proper sense, I am on my way to the promised church. Ecumenism means, for me, the field of experiments for the church which is hoped for. This is why for me, as a Protestant, the ecumenically orientated, subversive and self-critical hermeneutic of effective history which I have outlined is at the same time an attempt at ecclesial exegesis. The attempt is typically Protestant; it is not deficient, but it is certainly contextual.

64. Cited from: Congregation for the Doctrine of the Faith, *Dominus Iesus* (2000), No. 17.
65. Cf. Reiser (note 32), p. 78.
66. Cf. *Lumen Gentium* 8 = LThK² XII 173.

18 The Significance of Matthew's Jesus Story for Today

1. My Understanding of the Gospel of Matthew

1.1. I understand Matthew's story of Jesus as *a story*. The Evangelist *narrates* who Jesus is. For this reason we should not refer in an unreflected manner to a christo*logy* of the Gospel of Matthew.[1] Rather, Matthew's *story* of Jesus forms the framework for what the Evangelist conveys about Jesus by means of concepts and titles. Matthew does make use of christological honorific titles from the Christian and — indirectly — from the Jewish tradition, but as a rule he does not use them to explain Jesus' significance. The opposite seems to be the case, since Matthew's story of Jesus makes the significance of the traditional christological titles apparent. In using them, he draws on the Jewish or Jewish Christian messianic assumptions of his readers, deepening and modifying them by means of his Jesus story. This is visible, for example, in Matthew's use of the expression "Son of David." He employs it chiefly to connect the various miracle stories in which Israel's Messiah heals among his people (9:27; 12:23; 15:22; 20:30-31; 21:15). Matthew extends and transposes the traditional hopes associated with "Son of David" by narrating his healings.[2] He introduces the Suffering Servant passage from Isa. 42:1-4 in a key position as a formula quotation, but his purpose is not to develop a particular Suffering Servant christology. Rather, the quotation is used because it focuses the whole of the Jesus story, from his baptism to his final judgment of the peoples.[3] This is most clearly evident in the expression "Son of Man," a conceptual shorthand for the whole

---

1. Cf. in this volume "Matthean Christology Outlined in Theses," pp. 83-96.
2. Cf. in this volume "The Miracle Stories of Matthew 8–9," pp. 221-240.
3. Cf. Ulrich Luz, *Matthew 8–20*, Hermeneia (Philadelphia: Fortress, 2001), pp. 192-196.

370

of the Jesus story.[4] Matthew makes use of the christological titles to focus the story of Jesus. At the same time, his Jesus story is far richer and his Jesus figure far more colorful than revealed by the texts containing christological titles. Thus Matthew *narrates* a story which includes considerable detail about Jesus.

1.2. I understand Matthew's story of Jesus as a story which gives its readers *new access to God.* The story tells of Jesus as "Immanuel." Through him, God is present with his communities "to the end of the age" (Matt. 28:20). The miracle stories, transparent for the experience of members of the Christian communities, show how God helps and saves through him.[5] It is to him, the Lord, that they address their prayers (e.g. 8:25; 9:38; 14:30; 15:22, 25; 20:30-31). It is he whom they confess to be "Son of God" (14:33; 16:16; 27:54), and it is he who will sit on the throne of his glory and judge them as Son of Man (25:31-46). For the readers of the Gospel, it is Jesus who determines and shapes their "image" of God. The most important designation of God in the Gospel of Matthew is "Father." It is the term Jesus himself uses as the Son (11:25-27; 26:29, 42 etc.) and teaches his disciples to use (6:9). It is from Jesus that they learn of God as "Father." He gives them access to the "Father," and this determines their relationship with God. The Matthean story of Jesus corresponds to the core of early Christian resurrection faith in that it forms an indissoluble bond between Jesus and God.[6] In Matthew's story of Jesus, however, this bond does not come into being after the resurrection but exists from the beginning. From the time of his birth, the earthly Jesus is "Immanuel" (1:23).

1.3. I understand Matthew's story of Jesus as an *"inclusive" story.*[7] Matthew models his story on that of Mark, and like the Gospel of John it is a story which "includes" the experiences of the communities and of their individual members. The *christological* foundation for this type of narrative is the conviction that the Jesus of the past whose story is told by Matthew is the Christ who is present with his community.[8] The *hermeneutical* consequence of this

---

4. Cf. in this volume "The Son of Man in Matthew: Heavenly Judge or Human Christ?," pp. 97-112, following the significant study by Douglas R. Hare, *The Son of Man Tradition* (Minneapolis: Fortress Press, 1990), pp. 113-182.

5. Cf. pp. 236-238 in this volume.

6. Cf. Peter Stuhlmacher, *Biblische Theologie des Neuen Testaments,* I (Göttingen: Vandenhoeck und Ruprecht, 1992), partic. pp. 175, 178f.

7. Cf. in this volume pp. 84f. and 239.

8. The best text on this is still the classical essay by Günther Bornkamm, "The Risen Lord and the Earthly Jesus," in: James M. Robinson (ed.), *The Future of Our Religious Past* (FS Rudolf Bultmann, New York: Harper and Row, 1971), pp. 203-229.

is that Matthew's story of Jesus is not to be understood from outside as an alien story but as one in which readers and listeners connect their own experience with the story narrated by the Evangelist. They are to understand and interpret their own story and their own experience on the basis of Jesus' sto , or to be encouraged and inspired by the story to experience Jesus them .ves. So Matthew's story of Jesus is not intended as a "source" of inforr .ion on the life of Jesus, but as a "resource" for one's own life. Its readers ? to be participants rather than mere observers, and what they read w' oth inform and form them.

1.4. I understand Matthew's story of Jesus as a *st y of conflict with Israel*.[9] The conflicts begin at the very start of Jesus' a .vity among his people (9:2-8, 32-34) and reach a climax in Jerusalem, wh e Jesus confronts the hostile Jewish groups and their leaders (21:23–23: , and then leaves the temple and the city with his disciples (23:37–24:2). e conflicts do not end with the apparent victory of Israel's leaders over .sus when he is put to death, but with the uncovering of their deceitfv' .ctivities after Easter (27:62-66; 28:11-15) and with Jesus' command on th .nountain in Galilee to make disciples of all nations (28:16-20; cf. 22:8-10' .ike all stories of conflict, this one too must be understood from its endir , which focuses on the gospel being taken to all nations and Jesus being r cted by Israel's majority. In this story of conflict, Matthew works throug' .iis own distress at the separation of the Jesus communities from "mot' r Israel" and offers his community a new orientation and new stabilitv Ve find harsh, negative sweeping statements about the scribes and Ph sees which are neither historically nor theologically justifiable in the li . of Jesus' message of love for one's enemies. We also find craftily malic .s historical fictions (27:6-7, 24-25, 62-66; 28:11-15). Here we are confr .ed with the darkest and most problematic aspect of the Matthean Jesu .ory.[10]

The conflict was inevitable. For Matthew and his community, the authority of Jesus Son of Man is paramount, and his story in Israel is so essential that only the person and the message of Jesus can be Israel's foundation. For his opponents the scribes and Pharisees who, after the disaster of the Jewish War and the destruction of the Temple, were seeking to reconstitute Israel's identity on the basis of Torah, Jesus could not of course be the foundation of this identity.

1.5. I understand the five *great discourses of the Gospel of Matthew* as being spoken "out of the window," *directly addressed by Jesus to the communities*

9. Cf. in this volume pp. 243-250.
10. Cf. in this volume pp. 57-60.

in the present.[11] Matthew has distinguished these discourses from others in his Gospel (e.g., 11:7-30; 12:22-45; 21:23-44; 23:1-39) by the use of a particular closing formula. Unlike the other discourses, these five do not move forward the plot of the Jesus story, i.e. the conflict with Israel.[12] With the exception of a few points in the third discourse, the Parable Discourse, they scarcely interpret the conflict. They are the "gospel of the kingdom," that is, Jesus' own proclamation which is basic for the church.[13] The first, programmatic discourse, the Sermon on the Mount, is especially significant for the proclamation of the Matthean community. It is also addressed to the people (5:1; 7:28-29) and contains the substance of what is to be proclaimed: "all that I have commanded you" (28:19). The other discourses are addressed almost exclusively to the disciples.[14] The Mission Discourse (ch. 10) and the Disciple Discourse (ch. 18) are to be understood as "manifestos" on the church in its relations with the world and in its community life.[15]

2. On the Significance of Matthew's Gospel Today

In general, exegetes tend to speak marginally or not at all about the current significance of their texts. They leave this task to the practical theologians (as far as they are still concerned with the Bible!) or to individual clergy preaching sermons. Exegetes prefer to withdraw into the textual worlds or their reconstructions of the past — much to the detriment of the biblical texts! The texts are not intended merely to be historically reconstructed or treated as autonomous textual worlds which are only indirectly connected with our own reality, to be interpreted one way or another in books and commentaries. Rather, the texts want to engage their readers. Those who read them are to participate in them and be led from the texts into practice of what they read. The texts do not seek to be illuminated as objects of scientific analysis; rather,

11. Cf. in this volume pp. 22-24.

12. The narrative interjection 13:36 is an exception. Jesus leaving the people and continuing his instructions to the disciples alone in the house corresponds to Jesus' repeated withdrawals from the people as reported in the main section 12:1–16:20 (12:15; 14:13; 15:21; cf. 16:4-5). This corresponds, further, to the way in which the traditional preface to the explanation of the Parable of the Sower (13:10-17) comments directly on Israel's rejection as narrated in the story of Jesus.

13. This is not true however of 10:5-6 (cf. 23). The command of 10:5-6 — and this alone — is deliberately referred to and modified by the Risen Lord in 28:19.

14. 13:1-35 forms an exception.

15. On Matthew 10, cf. in this volume "Discipleship: A Matthean Manifesto for a Dynamic Ecclesiology," pp. 143-164; on Matthew 18, cf. Luz, *Matthew 8–20* (see note 3), pp. 478f.

they are lamps to their readers, enlightening their understanding of not only the texts but also their own lives.[16] They belong to the category of texts in which application is an integral part of understanding.[17]

What, then, could be the significance of the Matthean Jesus story for us today? I cannot give a general answer to this, of course, but only an answer shaped by the context in which I live. That context is Western Europe, and within it, Switzerland. The context is that of a largely secularized country in which the Christian faith has lost its function as a unifying and binding religion of the people. This is especially true of the traditional big churches, Roman Catholic and Reformed. For many of our people today, the Bible is a book they hardly know. Religiosity is now hardly found in the traditional churches but has shifted to New Age groups, charismatic Christian communities, discos, open air festivals, walks in the mountains, and the experience and management of individual crisis situations. There is religious experience in plenty, but most people do not seek or find it in the traditional church services. The churches continue to provide the rites and ceremonies that people expect, but they are hardly identity-forming. Our context is one of increasing ethical disorientation. For many individuals there are indeed binding values and standards, but if we look at society as a whole there is a great lack of orientation. The "anything goes" attitude of the postmodern society makes it difficult to assert the validity of supra-individual truths and standards. Our context is one of increasing uncertainty, of deep-rooted pessimism and latent fear of the future. There is a diffuse fear of economic decline, of increasing destruction of the natural world and natural resources, of wars rashly started whose consequences are incalculable, and of accelerating technological developments which scarcely allow time for heads and hearts to come to terms with them.

That is how I experience my own context. My own perception is subjective, of course. Undoubtedly the context within Europe varies considerably, in particular the religious and ecclesial context. My own basic experience in Switzerland is not applicable to the transforming countries of Eastern Europe, and not necessarily to Britain, Italy, or Spain either. This is even more true of North America. Between Europe and North America lies an ocean

16. Gerhard Ebeling, "Wort Gottes und Hermeneutik," in: Ebeling, *Wort und Glaube* (Tübingen: Mohr Siebeck, 1960), pp. 319-348, writes: "The primary phenomenon of understanding is not understanding *of* language but understanding *through* language" (p. 333). Language does not have to be understood; rather, language *creates* understanding. A biblical text is not, primarily, an object of understanding, but "a hermeneutic aid to understanding present experience" (p. 347).

17. Cf. Hans-Georg Gadamer, *Truth and Method* (New York: Seabury, 1975), pp. 274ff.

which many Europeans experience as increasingly wide and deep. And in Africa or India, how different again is people's experience of their world and ours! All this precludes my speaking of *the* significance of the Gospel of Matthew for today. I can speak only of its significance for me in my Western European, Swiss context. What I have to say is intended to inspire my readers to formulate the significance of Matthew's Jesus story *for themselves,* from the perspective of their own experience. I shall follow the five main points of my interpretation of Matthew, as outlined above.

2.1. The *story.* Matthew *tells* of Jesus. Stories are colorful and contain many potential meanings. Stories engage their listeners in many different ways, encountering them in their own experience and allowing them to respond. Stories defy definitions. They create many images in their listeners, and not just a *single* image. Stories are not the basis of orthodoxies. The christological content of Matthew's Jesus story can only be stated with reference to its various potential meanings. Stories are constantly open to new potential meanings. The meaning of stories is never closed.

In Christian tradition, Jesus was delivered into the hands of theologians and teaching authorities that *defined* who he is. Definitions are "closed" and oblige us to distinguish between what is right and wrong. Matthew's story of Jesus, on the other hand, does not give us a complete and closed picture of Jesus, and seldom distinguishes between right and wrong definitions of Jesus.[18] It does however distinguish between right and wrong practice. According to 7:21, what matters is not the — right — use of the words "Lord, Lord," but doing the will of the Father in heaven. The Matthean story tells of Jesus as an "example," a "model in life and action." Role models are not particularly valued in contemporary education,[19] and conservative theology in the twentieth century liked to emphasize polemically that Jesus, contrary to the liberal image of him in the nineteenth century, was certainly not a "mere role model." I find this unsatisfactory. "Role models" are not only people who teach us or whose deeds we imitate, but they are people who impress and inspire us. The courage and strength they give incite us to strive for that wholeness of life and that unity of word and deed which make people credible. According to Matthew, this is the identifying mark of the Christian life (cf. 5:19; 7:21-23, 24-27). With Jesus as their model, his disciples then and now have the courage to bear their own cross and hope for their own resurrection. Part of the strength of

---

18. Cf. 9:33 and 12:23-24. It is notable that the positive formulations concerning Jesus are certainly neither closed nor titular: "Never has anything like this been seen in Israel" (9:33) and "Can this be the Son of David?" (12:23).

19. Cf. Herman von Lips, "Der Gedanke des Vorbilds im Neuen Testament," *EvTh* 58 (1998), pp. 295-309, here: pp. 297ff.

Matthew's story of Jesus lies in Jesus' effectiveness as an example and a model. To me, this is a fundamental significance of his Jesus *story*.

2.2. *God*. To many Europeans today, the idea of a personal God or of God as part of metaphysics is no longer self-evident. If God should exist, this God cannot be experienced or explained. This God is diffuse and unpredictable and has become "faceless."[20] Many people who have not simply become atheists or agnostics now have nebulous and vague experiences of "transcendence." For many people who are moved and grieved by the injustice, wars, and misery in the world, the personal and almighty biblical creator and lord of the world has fallen victim to the theodicy question.[21] In this situation, it is of fundamental importance to me that Matthew speaks of God by speaking of a human being. "Jesus is Immanuel" (1:23-24) means that God does have a face. God can be experienced, and God has a will. God is concrete. God heals and helps, and God hears. God is weak and suffers. God is encountered as a human being, and his story can be told. By making Jesus the "face of God" in his story, Matthew makes God accessible to people of today for whom speaking of God is neither natural nor perhaps even possible. Of course, the question of whether Jesus really *is* the Immanuel is one which cannot be decided by means of a theory but only through existence.[22] But Matthew's Jesus story does liberate us from looking for a nebulous, phantom-like and obscured "Gott an sich" (God as such).[23]

2.3. The *inclusive Jesus story* enables us to have our own *experience* of Jesus the "Immanuel." "God is with us" means that something also *happens* in our life and in our churches. So often our churches now are fossilized in rituals and mere words. Matthew's story of Jesus can make clear that salvation and healing belong together, as do understanding and practice, confession and suffering, faith and prayer, sacrament and satisfaction. Grace is something concrete! Grace does not simply mean *knowing* that there is a gracious God, just as understanding is more than simply grasping who Jesus is and what he wants. *Experiencing* God's living presence is more than simply knowing that Jesus is the "Immanuel." Matthew's story of Jesus is concerned with

20. Cf. the reception of Matt. 26:36-46 and Matt. 27:45-46 in the 20th century in Ulrich Luz, *Das Evangelium nach Matthäus (Matt. 26–28)*, EKK I.4 (Neukirchen/Düsseldorf: Neukirchener/Benzinger, 2002), pp. 148-151, 340-342.

21. Here I quote a bright confirmation candidate whose words, related at the time to the Vietnam War, have stayed with me through the years: "If there really is a God in control of world history, he must be a complete idiot!"

22. In Kierkegaard's sense of the word!

23. I draw attention to Dorothee Sölle, *Stellvertretung. Ein Kapitel Theologie nach dem 'Tode Gottes'* (Stuttgart: Kreuz, 1965).

experience and not with mere propositions. When the Evangelist *tells* of confessions of Jesus by the disciples or by outsiders (as in 14:33; 16:16; 27:54), he associates them with the experience of Jesus these individuals have. When Matthew inserts the ethical "gospel of the kingdom" (4:23) into the Jesus story, he is at the same time inserting Jesus' demands into the story of what his listeners have experienced or might experience with Jesus the Immanuel. The "inclusive" Jesus story requires a holistic hermeneutics in which faith and life, theology and practice come together. "Ordinary" readers not schooled in theology often find easier access to Matthew's inclusive Jesus story than do theologians.[24] They quite naturally connect their own experience with the stories of Jesus, re-interpreting them and sharing their experience with others in Bible study sessions, for example. The inclusive Jesus story counsels sensitive theologians not to seek to define who "the Lord Jesus" is but to allow his story to work on them again and again. It counsels them not to separate their own theology from their experience of Jesus and their Christian lives.

2.4. Matthew's story of Jesus challenges us to rethink our *relationship with Judaism.* The Matthean Jesus community was a minority confronted with rejection and possibly even persecution at the hands of Israel's majority. During the difficult era of consolidation in Israel following the disaster of A.D. 70, the Christian community was pushed to the margins and perhaps forced out of Israel altogether. Our situation today is a completely different one. The vast majority of Christians who now read the Gospel of Matthew are not Jews but Gentiles. We now know that Jesus the Jew certainly was not aware of being sent to the Gentiles, and that he certainly had no intention of founding a new religion called Christianity. That we Gentile Christians may believe in the God of Israel with reference to Jesus the Jew is the consequence of a number of historical contingencies, such as the work of the apostle Paul. It was essentially Paul who opened up the way to Jesus Christ for Gentiles, and at the same time made it more difficult for Israel to affirm Jesus.[25] Gentiles have never had to face persecution from Judaism. The opposite is the case. Over many centuries the church was one of the chief persecutors of the Jews. Despite all the traumatic experience the Jews have had to face and deal with at the hands of the church, dialogue between Jews and Christians is now possible again. This dialogue is vital to our identity as Christians. In short, our experience with Israel is quite

---

24. It is no coincidence that the Gospels have always been — and still are — *Volksbücher.* In the past they have often fascinated and influenced lay people, uneducated people, children, poets and painters more than theologians.

25. The same is true of Matthew's Gospel. The commandment of the risen Christ to go to the nations (Matt. 28:19) is the consequence of the rejection which the earthly Jesus experienced in his proclamation to Israel.

different from that of the Jewish Christian communities. *In the light of our own experience with Israel, our own story of Jesus the Immanuel must be differently accented from Matthew's.* Like Matthew, we are called on to bring together our *own* experience with the basic story of Jesus. Matthew's experience differs from ours, and so the result will be different. However, the Matthean story of Jesus has become part of a canon and has discarded its historical contextuality in the process. For this reason we shall not be able to avoid an explicit contradiction of Matthew's Jesus story in this matter.[26]

2.5. The discourses inserted in Matthew's story of Jesus encourage us, on the basis of the experience with Jesus "the Immanuel" which the story offers us, to be confronted with the "will of the Father" that Jesus proclaims. That basis of "experience with Jesus the Immanuel" is a fundamental requirement. In the context of our increasingly secular and post-Christian western society it seems essential to me that we should be reminded that our life and its foundations are not of our own making. We owe them to God's fundamental and life-giving care for us, to the Christian experience of "Immanuel" in Jesus. Life and health, healing and salvation are not ours by possession but ours by grace. Foundations of life and the creation are not means of production or commodities but a gift that is not ours to dispose of. Readers of the Gospel of Matthew who, accepting this experience through the story of Jesus, are led to the inserted discourses will realize that at the center of the Sermon on the Mount is the Lord's Prayer (Matt. 6:9-14), at the center of the Mission Discourse is the reference to the Lord (10:24-25) and at the center of the Community Discourse (18:19-20) is the promise of Jesus' presence.

Only then — and all the more seriously — do we have to countenance the fact that the Matthean "Gospel of the Kingdom" consists almost exclusively of imperatives.[27] They make huge demands on humanity and on the

---

26. Cf. in this volume "Anti-Judaism in the Gospel of Matthew," pp. 243-261; see also Ulrich Luz, *Das Evangelium nach Matthäus (Matt. 18–25)*, EKK I.3 (Neukirchen/Düsseldorf: Neukirchener/Benziger, 1997), pp. 396-401 (on Matt. 23); Luz, *Das Evangelium nach Matthäus (Matt. 26–28)*, EKK I.4 (Neukirchen/Düsseldorf: Neukirchener/Patmos, 2002), pp. 288-291 (on Matt. 27:24-25). I do not support the reiterated calls to purge the New Testament canon of its anti-Judaisms, i.e., to revise the canon. In literary terms, deleting material from a text, particularly a narrative text, means destroying the whole. Moreover, we must bear in mind that the canon of the Christian churches comes to us from tradition. Eliminating individual sentences or texts will not prevent the eliminated parts from having their influence! We cannot retrospectively undo the influence of a text which has been effective in history. What we can do is to deal critically with the influence of the texts and with the texts themselves, and this must be done explicitly and publicly.

27. The Matthean editing of the Beatitudes makes the "imperative" character of his Gospel in contrast to the tradition in Luke 6:20-22 particularly clear.

church. The Sermon on the Mount with its central command to love one's enemies (framing the antitheses, 5:25-26, 43-48) is not simply addressed to a Christian elite but, by way of the disciples, to the whole world. Their proclamation is not least to be found in the "shining light" of their works (5:16). The central main section of the Sermon on the Mount ends with the Golden Rule (7:12) in a positive formulation. This needs to be read with the command to love at its center: "In everything, as you would have others do to you" — that is, justice, love and peace — "do also to them." This is not merely reactive but active. The positively formulated Golden Rule is an attempt radically to pervade, universalize and make plausible the command to love. Today it is a challenge not only to individuals but also to politics. Carl Friedrich von Weizsäcker used the expression "intelligent love of enemies" for political behavior inspired by the Sermon on the Mount.[28] Whatever reasons may be given for them, preventive wars are the opposite of such behavior.

The second and the fourth discourses in the Gospel of Matthew present similar challenges to the church. The discourses understand the church as a community of disciples whose distinguishing marks are authority, obedience, poverty, suffering, infinite readiness to forgive, and love.[29] Neither teaching nor sacraments nor legal structures are seen as decisive marks of the church. Those who were close to the kind of church Jesus had in mind in Matthew's Gospel are a number of monastic communities, radical movements of the late Middle Ages such as the Franciscans and the Waldensians, the Anabaptists of the Reformation era, and some base communities today. Those who are far removed from the kind of church Jesus had in mind are a hierarchically organized Roman Catholic Church, or Protestant churches claiming to be determined "by the Word alone." In my own ecclesial context in Switzerland, as well as in other European countries, the traditional churches are in danger of becoming empty institutional shells. Their rituals still function, their institutions may still be intact, but there are hardly any members left who commit their lives to the church, and hardly any communities which support this commitment. Reading the Matthean discourses in this situation is very rewarding!

---

28. Carl Friedrich von Weizsäcker, "Intelligente Feindesliebe," in: Weizsäcker, *Der bedrohte Friede. Politische Aufsätze 1945-1981* (Munich: Hanser [3]1982), pp. 533-538.

29. Cf. pp. 149ff.

Index of Names and Subjects

Selective Index of Biblical References